10/99

Frank O. Gehry

The Complete Works

Francesco Dal Co
Kurt W. Forster

Building descriptions by
Hadley Arnold

THE MONACELLI PRESS

First published in the United States of America in 1998 by
The Monacelli Press, Inc.
10 East 92nd Street, New York, New York 10128.

Copyright © 1998 by Electa, Milano
English edition copyright © 1998 by
The Monacelli Press, Inc.

Library of Congress Cataloging-in-Publication Data
Dal Co, Francesco, date.
[Frank O. Gehry. English]
Frank O. Gehry : the complete works / Francesco Dal Co,
Kurt W. Forster ; building descriptions by Hadley Arnold.
p.   cm.
Simultaneously published in Italian.
Includes bibliographical references.
ISBN 1-885254-63-6
1. Gehry, Frank O., 1929– —Criticism and interpretation.
2. Architecture, Postmodern—United States. I. Gehry,
Frank O., 1929– . II. Forster, Kurt Walter. III. Title.
NA737.G44D3513   1998
720'.92—dc21   98-42480

Printed and bound in Italy

Contents

Acknowledgments

This book would not have been possible without the ready and friendly help offered at every phase of the project by Joshua White and Keith Mendenhall of the Gehry office. We owe to them and to Randy Jefferson a debt of thanks.

We thank Salvatore Settis, who facilitated in every way our stay at the Getty Center for the History of Art and the Humanities in Los Angeles, where we accomplished a great deal of research necessary for this book.

For advice and help on the text, we thank Denise Bratton, Verena Schindler, Nanni Baltzer, Philip Ursprung, Lucas Steiner, Tim Kammasch, Elisabetta Terragni, and, in particular, Sergio Polano.

We are grateful to Elisa Seghezzi, Stefano Tosi, and Laura De Tomasi for their dedicated editorial work; Myriam Tosoni paid careful attention to the details, and we owe her special thanks.

Frank and Berta Gehry and Julia Bloomfield, in addition to the gratitude we owe them, may also depend upon our affection.

—F.D.C., K.W.F., H.A.

HOUSE STUDY - '88   F. Gehry

Architectural Choreography

Kurt W. Forster

Common Strangers

The architecture of Frank Gehry looms on the horizon like a huge boulder in an otherwise carefully cultivated landscape. One can simply disregard it and turn instead to more familiar buildings, or one might react passionately to its startling and unruly appearance, but one is not likely to overlook it. Gehry's buildings strike some as alien intruders into the landscape, and others as homegrown hybrids springing from the very seedbed of our culture. Either reaction touches on significant aspects of Gehry's work, for it is precisely the way in which he transforms the familiar that estranges it for the viewer.

Gehry's capacity for endless transformation of the commonplace leaves unaltered almost nothing that falls into his hands. His architecture does not bear the dubious imprint of the modern form-giver but seems instead to have been released from its imprisonment in convention. At his best, Gehry manages to free his projects from typological constraints, enabling his buildings to assume shapes of unprecedented kind and configuration. They are neither formally fixed and repetitive, like those of Michael Graves, nor hypothetical and largely self-generated, like those of Peter Eisenman. These comparisons are fair, and they work both ways: if the New York Five have pursued formal autonomy in their work across all personal differences and along a wide arc of time, Gehry has chosen an architecture he can make with his own hands. His buildings are able to stand on their own because they result from an inventive transformation of their circumstances rather than from an expostulation of their problems.

Gehry does not "sign" his projects with a personal touch but instead *transforms* whatever he takes up. These transformations eventuate in objects that have as definite a history (of *their* own) as they have a char-

acteristic shape (of *his* making). Not only have his buildings changed over time—so also has the architect. Today Gehry is less a lonely hero battling the status quo than he is an explorer of unanticipated possibilities. He has shifted ground only gradually and still starts mostly from what he finds, lifting some of the most ordinary things from their familiar places and urging new purposes on them. Where there is little to be found that would lend itself to his treatment, or where there are only obstacles to overcome, he likes to play hide-and-seek with contingencies, causing happenstance in the midst of hindrance.

The Knife and the Fish

On August 5, 1996, Francesco Dal Co and I walked into Frank Gehry's office to greet him and begin our work on this book. An atmosphere of simplicity reigns in the studio. There is nothing fancy or high-styled about it. With the familiar feel of a workshop, the crowded loft space shelters nooks and tables crammed with equipment. The walls are lined with models. They are displayed less as trophies of profes-

Frank Gehry, sketches of houses, 1988.

Office of Frank O. Gehry and Associates, Santa Monica, California.

sional success than as records of past projects and as quarries for new ones that are casually being assembled from old parts. The only area partitioned off from the open loft—even though wide windows and sliding doors hardly secrete it from the other workspaces—is the white cubicle of Gehry's study. It resembles captain's quarters brought down to a lower deck. Walls and tables carry images and objects that play catalyst for the works currently at hand, or recall impressions of other places and projects. Vaguely surreal still lifes seem to assemble themselves spontaneously from leftover pieces, photographs, and the latest lunch packages. Surrounded by a kind of impromptu *Kunstkammer*, everybody moves about in casual absorption. Questions are answered quietly and the tranquil hum is barely punctuated by the chirping of phones and the clanking footsteps of visitors ascending the metal stairs.

After handshakes had been exchanged all around, even before we sat down in the worn and comfortable cardboard chairs, Gehry remarked, apropos of nothing: "Palladio faced a fork in the road, and he took the wrong turn." "What did he do wrong?" I wondered to myself. As if to respond to my puzzlement, Frank added: "He should have recognized that there's chaos; he should have gone ahead and done

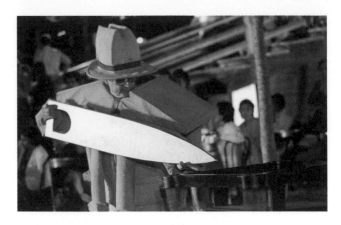

The *coltello* (knife) for *Il corso del coltello,* conceived by Frank Gehry with Claes Oldenburg and Coosje van Bruggen.

Frank Gehry costumed as Frankie P. Toronto for *Il Corso del coltello,* Venice Biennale, Italy, 1985.

what Borromini did. He would have been a pioneer."[1] There you have it. When pressed for an explanation, Frank dropped a rare avuncular hint, quoting himself: "I've said it all as *Frankie P. Toronto*." Frankie P. is the nom de plume Gehry chose for the character he played in the performance piece *Il corso del coltello* (*The Course of the Knife*), the spectacle he and his friends Claes Oldenburg and Coosje van Bruggen staged in Venice in 1985.[2]

This modern *commedia dell'architettura* dramatized the predicament of art in a city that seems to have congealed in the past. Where everybody is a tourist and the past is everybody's object of desire, nothing new can be created. Where canonical images of order stand in splendid isolation, the chaos surrounding them only undermines their purpose and drains them of their substance. Or, as Gehry put it succinctly at the time, "To be in the middle of Venice, so close to Palladio—and so much architecture today refers to Palladio . . . to be talking about disorder, another kind of order, is a bit irreverent . . . Western culture just thinks of one kind of order . . . of symmetry, classicism, and the idea of central focus. But the whole world can't be built on axes alone."[3]

With a touch of foolery, Gehry wore a costume reminiscent of one of those French figures done up in volutes, column shafts, and capitals, a sort of madcap mannequin of classical architecture. His shoulders gave substance to a pediment, and a row of columns dangled on his back, spoofing the vocabulary recently adopted by postmodernists with a comparable flair for styling. Sporting a hat with a wide brim and cleft crown, he seemed fit indeed for the Venetian carnival. He took his seat behind an overhead projector and let

Wright. These qualities of Gehry's architecture did not spring fully formed from his imagination but evolved gradually over time. Their origin lies in historical and subjective images whose familiar appearance explains nothing of their enigmatic nature. "Buildings become people. Before people, there were other creatures," Frankie P. Toronto explained, and, among the latter, it was the fish he liked best.[5]

The fish had never had a share in architectural imagery beyond inspiring topical ornament, such as that of the town hall of Zurich, where fish were carved on the facade in celebration of nature's abundance and the city's prosperous fortune. When the fish first appeared in Gehry's work, it seems to have been

his pen dance in its beam of light. As he sketched directly on the facades of nearby Venetian buildings, they began to quiver and mutate under a palimpsest of stenographic drawing.

Playing the joker in the stacked deck of 1980s architecture was Gehry's way of deprecating the pomposity of so much contemporary design. Up to that time, few of his buildings had taken shape in the way he imagined them, but they gave clear signs of the divergent direction he had chosen. When he assumed the guise of Frankie P. Toronto in Venice, Gehry enacted a parody of the architect as destructive genius. The knife was his weapon, destruction his purpose. Entering a small temple and slicing his way out of it, he brought about the collapse of architecture's sanctum sanctorum. Critics reacted strongly, many of them negatively, to Gehry's travesty of classical and modern vocabularies. He parodied the hodgepodge of columns, capitals, pediments, and ornaments of postmodernists, but went beyond merely ridiculing them when he proffered an altogether different idea of his own that proved equally alien to modern architecture and infinitely more startling: the fish.

Just what meaning the fish carries in his work not even Gehry himself may know for sure. Apart from its array of symbolic significances,[4] however, the fish has given shape to formal qualities entirely distinct from those embodied in the geometric abstractions of modernism or in the organic shapes of a Frank Lloyd

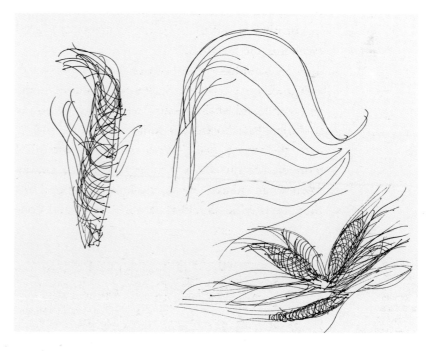

either as folly or as ornament, with one exception: Gehry's collaboration with the sculptor Richard Serra in 1981. For an exhibition at the Architectural League of New York, Gehry and Serra envisaged a link between the Chrysler Building and the twin towers of the World Trade Center. A giant fish-shaped pylon designed by Gehry and a tilted pylon by Serra anchored this aerial bridge in the Hudson and East Rivers. To be sure, the project never progressed beyond the photomontage, but it was neither the only nor the last time that fish have emerged from their natural habitat to assume a place among Gehry's

ture's symbolic origin, as in the famous frontispiece of Abbé Laugier's treatise, turning instead into the emblem of its own spectacular demise.

It may be an exaggeration to say that the fish replaced the temple as the symbolic focus of architecture in Gehry's mind, but it is not too much of an exaggeration, for his architecture evolved during the 1980s in ways no one could have foreseen. Just as the fish could be read either as a child's toy or as a mysterious creature rising from clouded depths, certain aspects of Gehry's personal history erupted spontaneously, and often contradictorily, in such projects as the collaboration with Richard Serra. These moments of tension set the stage for a confrontation with himself, and their obligatory histrionics enabled him to act out the competing meanings of his imagination.

buildings. In one of his sketchbooks dating from 1981,[6] Gehry placed the rough outlines of a house and a fish side by side, even adding a section of the fish to the plan of the house as if to confirm their equivalence as pure structure.

A Flick of the Tail Made the Temple Fail

In another instance, acting as his own client, Gehry toyed with the idea of appropriating the narrow space between two multistory buildings on New York City's Lafayette Street in order to create an atrium. Between two dissimilar elevations, a small pavilion in the form of a vaguely oriental temple and, farther back, a fish were placed on a steeply foreshortened gridded floor. The overtly theatrical nature of this idea is apparent when the juxtaposition becomes antagonistic: though the drawings for the Lafayette Street lofts render both pavilion and fish as inert props suspended above the ground, the study model introduces into the composition a bright red plastic fish, the kind children play with in the bathtub; this fish springs to life, displacing the flimsy pavilion with a flick of its tail. The temple-pavilion also served as Gehry's main prop in his *coup de théâtre* during the Venetian spectacle of 1985, when he emerged from just such a four-columned structure only to cause it to collapse behind him. The pavilion had become a house of cards. It ceased to be the icon of architec-

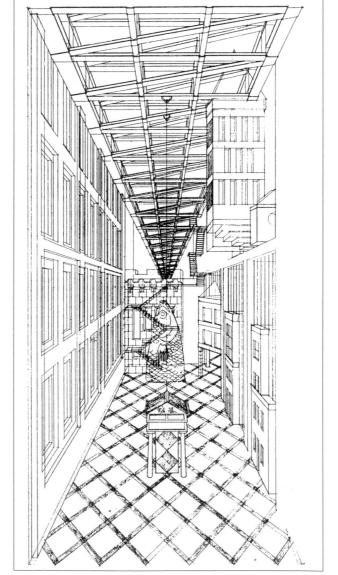

Such moments of personal self-confrontation are never very far, however, from the professional circumstances of the architect: either Gehry interacted with himself without a client entering the scenario, or he played along and against another artist. From this vantage point, his frequent collaboration with artists appears to be less a demonstration of happy-go-lucky bohemianism than an exercise of calculated risk. By putting his own ego at stake, Gehry has sought to explore regions of his being that have thus far been left undisturbed. The way we look at ourselves is not the way we are seen by others, just as our interactions with others are forever fraught with the asymmetries of experience between the protagonists and the differing perceptions of third parties. Seeking the trial of collaboration with artists, Gehry has engaged in more than a contest of will. He has put himself in the kind of circumstances that often prevail in architect-client relationships. What is even more troublesome in artist collaborations is envy and the risk to personal friendship. Allowing artists to enter the arena of his architecture and, conversely, extending himself into the realm artists jealously guard as their own, Gehry needed to assume another identity. Slipping into the guise of Frankie P. Toronto vis-à-vis Claes Oldenburg, or sparring with Richard Serra, Peter Eisenman, or Philip Johnson, Gehry casts himself as another, transforming his identity, not just his objects. Such trials have tended to stiffen his somewhat caustic estimate of values and ideas, but they have not stilled his appetite for such experiences.

Lifelines

When Gehry speaks of his youth in the United States, or when he fields questions about the peculiar shapes of his buildings, he tends to toe a certain line. His answers steer along the contours established by American autobiographies such as those of Louis Sullivan and Frank Lloyd Wright. Accidents of time and place account for a great deal in these personal stories, and the Goldberg family's immigration from Canada to Los Angeles (where they changed their name to Gehry) plunged Frank into the unknown and left him with a deep sense of hesitancy. The transplant had been sudden, and its complications tested

his bearings. School—even as late as college—drove home a painful recognition of uncertainty and left him with a residue of doubt in his own abilities. He was at once incredulous and keenly curious about the culture of his adopted country. To this day, Gehry feels easily perplexed by events he thinks he should have anticipated, but he is just as quick to recognize the powers and machinations behind them. A player whose desire for acceptance is forever in conflict with his drive for distinction, Gehry can famously disarm an opponent or put off a friend while reconciling his own feelings about them. At once a jovial interlocutor and an obsessive achiever, he has proven to be as persuasive with politicians and power brokers as he is chummy and loyal with artists.

It took many years to achieve a balance between these two Gehrys, a balance that can be maintained only through perpetual motion, for his youthful curiosity and openness play against his defensive reactions and professional savvy. He became a hockey player when he was reaching sixty, not only out of loyalty to a son with a knack for the sport but also because hockey proved the perfect metaphor-in-action for his personal disposition: encased in protective clothing, he rushes out onto the ice, where everything depends on swiftness and surprise. The turbulence and speed of the game are barely chastened by the risk of imminent disaster as the team negotiates artificially treacherous ground. Every move, even a fall, is followed by the next.

Time-Out

If it had not been for a little recognition from an art teacher or two, Gehry might not have mustered the courage to take up architecture, even after-hours, much less propelled himself into graduate school. At Harvard he reacted with indignation to the smug assurance of his professors. Doctrinaire judgments repelled him, and he resisted the pressure to conform by scouting Harvard Yard for exciting intellectual fare. The day of reckoning came early, when, after an angry row with Professor Reginald Isaacs,[7] he cut short his studies in the department of planning. In a huff, he returned with his wife and two small children to Los Angeles in 1957. Formal schooling had proved

sorely disappointing to him. His crack at advanced professional study left him disgusted, but it did not fail to open doors to other interests, chiefly artistic and historical ones. Gehry's subsequent work in the Los Angeles office of Victor Gruen brought more stimulation, but little recognition and reward.

In 1961, Gehry embarked on another of his forays, packing up and leaving for Paris, where he found work in the office of André Rémondet. It was a brief but truly eye-opening experience. Finally out of the corridors of advanced education and grinding practice, Gehry came face-to-face with European buildings he knew only slightly from textbook illustrations. Architecture in the flesh held more worthwhile secrets than his old teachers had ever revealed. In France, Romanesque churches vied for his attention with buildings by Le Corbusier; in Germany, it was the baroque churches of Franconia and Bavaria that captivated him. The contrast between French Romanesque and Bavarian rococo could hardly be more extreme. Tautly volumetric and dimly lit, French Romanesque chapels and churches envelop visitors in their massive masonry, whereas German baroque churches impress with exuberantly sculpted, perforated vaults and piercing illumination. It takes no more than a superficial knowledge of Gehry's buildings to recognize that this contrast between Romanesque and baroque continues to fuel his imagination.

Gehry's acquaintance with these, rather than with other, examples of architecture raises issues of acci-

dent and coincidence. It was largely chance that brought Romanesque and baroque churches to his attention, but they happened to coincide with his own vague notions of what buildings ought to be. Because his first claim on a space of action situated him between such contrasting fields as those of Romanesque and baroque churches, he operated in a state of tension so strong that it could at any moment snap into antagonism. Every move he made was as much directed against as it was addressed to the objects of his interest. He learned to resist while yielding. Before he dealt with real clients, he struggled with conflicting authorities. The play of forces within his range of interest moved him in a direction that had only begun to take shape in such unruly work as Le Corbusier's church at Ronchamp and Philips Pavilion for the 1958 World's Fair, in Brussels.[8] Considered eccentric—if not outright misguided—at the time of their construction, these buildings remained quasi-invisible behind far more prominent landmarks in Gehry's development. Over the years, however, and most definitely with the post-1990 stages of the Disney Concert Hall project, Ronchamp

has been restored from remote, if revered, background status to new prominence in Gehry's continuing negotiation between sheltering interiors and daringly fractured shells.

Gehry's stint in Paris was relatively brief. By 1962, he was back in Los Angeles, opening an office first in partnership with Greg Walsh and later on his own. Gehry's determination to stay on where his parents settled after leaving Toronto is a bit puzzling given his peripatetic nature and his professional success around the world. Major jobs in Los Angeles have been tantalizingly few, and the biggest plum that the city has dangled before him, the Disney Concert Hall, has turned into unrelieved, seemingly unstoppable frustration. Gehry's life in the alleged capital of fun, fitness, and limitless possibilities weaves darker

Le Corbusier (with Iannis Xenakis), Philips Pavilion, Brussels World's Fair, 1958.

shades into his dazzling fame of recent years. Ever wavering as to whether he should remain in the city yet always ready to plunge into its imbroglio, Gehry experiences his presence there as a constant struggle between tenacity and escape, stability and change. Far beyond his conflicted passage through the corridors of education, Gehry's experiences recall the biographical pattern Louis Sullivan traced in 1924 in his autobiography.[9]

Sullivan's parents immigrated to Boston from different countries, but even before they met, Sullivan later fantasized that "the finger of fate was tracing a line in the air that was to lead on and on until it reached a finger tracing a line now and here."[10] Not only did Sullivan feel that his lineage linked his existence back to his ancestors but he also viewed himself as metaphorically destined to spend his life tracing lines in an effort to recapture and recast his childhood in the abstract lineaments of his professional work. Gehry has never staked such a total claim to the workings of fate, but the idea of biographical continuity is ultimately no weaker in Gehry's mind, despite his perception of its many ruptures and endless tangles, than it was in Sullivan's. Sullivan stated that he was "to be and to remain life of [his mother's] life," not just in the obvious biological sense but additionally by bringing the maternal realm into the male world of his profession.[11] Gehry also recognizes the central role his mother played in establishing his sense of continuity. One is tempted to say that as long as Gehry sought to become an architect according to the terms of a powerfully paternal identity, he remained unable to construct his own identity as we know it today.

An Autobiographical House

Gehry broke the male identity of his earlier professional self with his famous house of 1977–78, in Santa Monica. He subverted the conventional division between the public appearance of the house as a four-square presence on the block in favor of a much more ambiguous stance. Conventionally, the domestic sphere is considered a female realm, receptive, cozy, and relaxed; the public appearance of the house is rather a tablet on which masculine notions of social standing and safety are inscribed. Gehry broke down this division, not only between inside and outside but within the house and on its exterior. An androgynous trait emerges from interior spaces clad in exterior siding and exteriors left in a state of undress. A wish to expose disguises itself in modesty, while run-of-the-mill materials turn up in unexpected places, adding a surprising touch of refinement. The Gehry house rehearses change, not only in the familiar cycle of its use but also in the state of its being. Gehry and his second family have lived there since 1978, and he has continued to transform the building, most recently (and quite thoroughly) in 1991–94. The house gained notoriety for reasons that appear oddly unprofessional—the building was routinely treated as a freak or a prank, the act of either an exhibitionist or a frustrated showman. Considered within the category of building to which it belongs, if such a house can be said to belong to any category at all, Gehry's residence is anything but quixotic. The idea was to start from a commonplace house and to arrive at a result that could be both personal and open-ended. In beginning with a commonly accepted type and ending up with a unique dwelling, the architect revisits the construction of identity in a manner no less powerful than when a pack of social clichés is disassembled.

Whether a building is truly complete as conceived and built, or whether it allows for further growth and alteration, is less a matter of circumstance than of approach. The classical definition of perfection precludes any changes lest the whole should be diminished, but a work of art, especially a work of architecture, can be differently constituted. It need not encapsulate a precise moment and a single possibility to the exclusion of all others. Instead, it can be so conceived as to remain susceptible to change—in a formulation analogous to the changes that occur over the lifespan of living subjects. Musical compositions are equally susceptible to deliberate as well as unintentional changes. There are different ways of keeping the door open: one can undertake periodic revisions and alterations, as the composer Pierre Boulez does time and again with some of his major works. There is also the possibility of opening the very order of a work to accidents and improvised parts. The latter was the theory and practice of John Cage, with whom

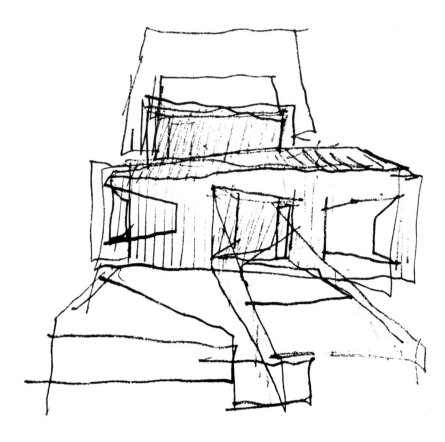

First sketch for the Gehry Residence, Santa Monica, California, 1977.

Boulez conducted a long epistolary exchange during the 1950s on the premises of composing.[12]

Gehry came to know Boulez during the composer's stays in Los Angeles and Ojai, where he performed contemporary music with his Parisian ensemble. Another friend of Gehry's, Ernest Fleischmann, the music director of the Los Angeles Symphony Orchestra, was instrumental in securing Boulez's expertise as Gehry developed his winning project for the Disney Concert Hall. For one of his decisive works of 1954–55, Boulez chose poems from René Char's *Marteau sans maître* (*Hammer without Master*), regrouping them as he set them to music. This work has received repeated and especially clamorous performances in Los Angeles.[13]

As a matter of fact (and incidence), the first line of part 5 of René Char's *Le Marteau sans maître* could stand as the signet of the very issue of time and change in buildings, a dimension contesting the permanence of tectonics; Char's poem begins "Bel édifice et les pressentiments . . ." ("Beautiful edifice and forebodings . . .") and juxtaposes boyhood and manhood as fatally separated from one another.[14]

"Edifice" stands against the "foreboding" of change, which, in turn, unavoidably alters the nature of the building. To permit time and its incalculable incidents to enter the very conception of an edifice converts it from a static object into a field of potentialities. The traditional claim that is made for modern works, namely that they are of their time as completely as possible, also implies its obverse—their cancellation by the very passage of time. The aspiration to represent the essence of a particular historical moment (to the exclusion of any historical dimension) is likely to produce a meager document of its time rather than a timeless example of the art of building. As illustrations of this contrast, two buildings of the eighteenth century, one of the swiftest to be built and one of the slowest to take shape, are particularly apt.

The Duc d'Artois had the Château de Bagatelle in the Bois de Boulogne built during the fall of 1777 to the designs of François-Joseph Bélanger. It took only sixty-four days.[15] By contrast, Thomas Jefferson spent his entire adulthood laboring on Monticello, only to leave it unfinished and his estate bankrupt.[16] If the Château de Bagatelle needed to be a model of typological clarity, Monticello mutated over time from a Palladian derivative to a highly personal habitat in which every link between architecture and custom, every aspect of convention and use, had been thought and rethought. Almost as soon as it was fin-

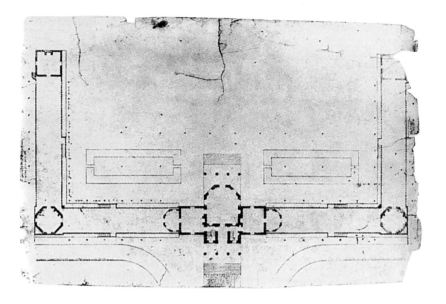

Thomas Jefferson, Monticello, Charlottesville, Virginia, 1772. Plan of executed project.

ished, Bagatelle became a showpiece, for it exhibited to perfection an entirely known idea of building. The sheer feat of producing it virtually overnight endowed it with qualities that only a *model* building could have, and it would play an ancestral role for the many instant buildings created for purposes of exhibition ever since. Jefferson, on the other hand, built Monticello very slowly, adding to it and altering it in spurts. He gradually extricated it from borrowed schemes and ceaselessly continued to incorporate features that were inspired by domestic life (and cultural interests) rather than by architectural example.

Many nineteenth-century examples could be mentioned as instances of an ever-expanding, self-propelling concept of building, but Karl Friedrich Schinkel's later work would surely claim a special place among them. The Court Gardener's House at Charlottenhof in Potsdam, which had been incompletely constructed in parts during the 1830s, implies an ever-changing sequence of possible extensions. The pinwheel plan of the house called for counterbalancing additions, progressively engaging more distant features of the surrounding park and joining them in a play of dynamic (im)balances. Step by step, an artificial lake, canals, and special plantings were brought within reach of the house, and the campaign found its provisional conclusion in the addition of the Roman Baths.[17] Commenting on the buildings, Schinkel stressed the fact that the "picturesque ensemble" could "in accordance with its nature, be

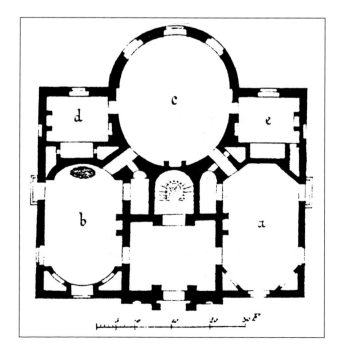

Friedrich Gilly, Château de Bagatelle (designed by François-Joseph Bélanger), Paris, 1777. Plan.

Karl Friedrich Schinkel, Court Gardener's House, Charlottenhof, Potsdam, Germany. West elevation and plan, 1834.

ever further expanded and enriched, assuring in this way the perpetual pleasure of production."[18]

The complex of Schinkel's buildings at Charlottenhof left a deep mark on Philip Johnson. His Glass House of 1949 at New Canaan, Connecticut, and numerous other structures he added in the course of half a century reciprocally accentuated the rapports among them and strengthened their connection with Schinkel's model. Johnson began to populate a sizable territory with distinctive new buildings and pavilions, deploying them on the land like signs on a map: in more ways than one, Johnson's estate forms an imaginary chart of the architect's life. This chart took shape in unforeseen ways, its features extended and transformed as the architect added new buildings in different styles and materials. Johnson transposed biographical events to the New Canaan landscape and thereby converted it into a lifescape.

Jefferson's evolving buildings at Monticello proved interminable because they were conterminous with their architect's biography. This autobiographical dimension of building is, I suggest, equally important for Johnson and Gehry. Whereas Johnson was able to occupy ever new places for the reformulation of his changing experiences, Gehry had only one small lot and one old house at his disposal. Moreover, the expansive topography of Johnson's life—which, as is well known, has moved through many and seemingly disjointed phases—allowed him to keep the different stages of his personal metamorphosis largely separate from one another.[19] If the Johnson estate could

cumulatively function as a table of contents for that architect's professional itinerary, Gehry's house required unavoidable destruction and construction in one and the same place and, in a manner of speaking, under the same roof.

It may be a coincidence that Peter Eisenman formulated his thoughts on Johnson's Glass House just when Gehry was completing the first version of his residence in Santa Monica, but the timely connection suggests a moment of extraordinary sensitivity to the biographical dimensions of architecture. Eisenman was certainly perspicacious when he wrote of Johnson's house, and Johnson's own publication of it, "text, building, and person fuse to shatter the paradox."[20] This paradox sprang from the degree of abstraction in the architecture of the house and certain painful realities of the architect's life.

Philip Johnson evolved a strategy of spatial separation between the buildings on his estate. As a way of keeping everything in its place, the promenade through the property assumes the form of a biographical narrative leading the visitor across the various stages of the architect's life, even on to posterity, for which a visitors center has already been built. Free to inspect the grounds, one is both baffled by what remains concealed in some of the most transparent

Philip Johnson, New Canaan compound, Connecticut. Site plan:
1. Glass House
2. Guest House
3. Pavilion
4. Painting Gallery
5. Sculpture Gallery
6. Study
7. Ghost House
8. Lincoln Kirstein Tower
9. Visitors Center

Gehry Residence, Santa Monica, California, 1977–78.

structures as well as virtually unable to discover their continuity:[21] time as the agent of change is no longer manifest in the buildings themselves but only in the visitor's experience. Gehry, on the other hand, compressed all distinctions, collapsing all changes in the house itself. First he exposed the conventional elements, and even the physical assembly of the existing structure, and then he injected ideas and forms of his own. What for Jefferson had proven a difficult process of gradual deviation from the printed plans of neo-Palladian models for Johnson assumed the form of disjointed chapters and episodes on the biographical (play)grounds of the New Canaan estate and finally led for Gehry to a deft disassembly of an unremarkable suburban house. The Gehry Residence becomes the site of almost chaotic intersections between "found" and "fancied" parts.

The scandal is not that the Gehry house appears willful or ugly but that it dismembers the very notion of the suburban dwelling by shattering the paternal imposition of protection over the maternal realm. Through its fractured exterior, we glimpse, in almost kibitzing fashion, interiors shot through with the rough materials of the outside. By this reversal alone, the house engages us in a game of hide-and-seek, entrapping us while exposing our refuge. It is a house

that denies itself the male ostentation of acting both as protective cover and showpiece, exposing instead its many small and diverse coves along with their linings. The game, however nifty, will not let one off the hook that easily: the *corpus* of this house became the site of a regeneration of Gehry's own *body of architecture*. With his residence, he began to make buildings in another image, one that did not hold still but that instead induced clashes with its surroundings and transformations within itself.

Gehry's sense of being "life of his mother's life"— as Sullivan had put it—trapped him in the dilemma of gender roles. This dilemma was heightened by Gehry's wavering relationship not just to his male identity but also to his identity as an immigrant to America and as a Jew, a Jew recently remarried to a Panamanian Catholic.[22] At times, Gehry puts on the classic emblems of aggressive male identity—as when he rushes out on the ice in hockey gear—but as soon as the game is over (and a game it is), he reassumes a much more complex identity. His way of working defies professional categories. To explain his ideas, Gehry tells stories, confessing antipathies and invoking powerful feelings, trailing with a bemused "I don't know." He does know, to be sure, but doesn't let on; instead of scoring points, he makes one linger over an admission, a rueful or ironic comment. In an essay on Jewish autobiography, the historian Alvin H. Rosenfeld stated: "Within traditional Judaism, to aspire to the condition of intellect . . . has been to aspire to the masculine condition."[23] Inasmuch as Gehry struggled to break free from this exclusively masculine condition, he was drawn to his mother's and grandfather's sphere of life. His grandmother's gefilte fish seemed to hold more secrets than his father's professional work. In order to lead a life that stemmed as much from his mother's lineage as from the Goldbergs', Gehry was attracted to a woman who was struggling to emerge from a colonial condition. The simultaneity of their efforts to decolonize themselves—to break through their respective shells of Judaic masculinity and the double indemnity of colonial and Catholic femininity—and to create a house that would be both actually and metaphorically autobiographical must be reckoned a singularly felicitous event.

by the masculine condition, only to be infiltrated by women. In place of the traditional split between the formalities of appearance and the practicalities of use, between an exterior entirely for show and an interior exclusively for privacy, Gehry articulated another experience, that of a life lived in *breakthroughs* from one segregated sphere to another.

Unlike Michael Graves, who has indulged in elegantly confected houses ready for upscale construction, Gehry picked up the identical parts—clusters of boxlike rooms with roof terraces, decks, and pergolas—and broke them apart before exercising his imagination on their surprising reassembly. These exercises were extended into the Benson House (1979–84) and soon spilled over into such new projects as the (later aborted) Whitney House, the Indiana Avenue houses (1979–81), and the Smith Residence (project, 1981). With the latter, Gehry returned to what may rank as his very first independent moment as a designer, the Steeves Residence (1958–59). To this day, Gehry keeps a rough model of it close at hand, like a talisman he rarely neglects to reference. Built of cardboard and sticks, it is composed of ten elementary volumes, the first glimpse of the house as a hamlet or, conversely, as a congregation of rooms.

Gehry transformed the existing house as thoroughly as anyone could ever hope to edit the past. His sketches for the house render the intended acts of dissection and displacement. In the finished house, startling juxtapositions between old and new parts throw different textures—found and new—into relief. Only a few years earlier, the artist Gordon Matta-Clark, who died while Gehry was finishing his house, had exhibited wall segments he had cut from a condemned house in a New York City gallery.[24] Notwithstanding the violence that had brought them into being, Matta-Clark's segments made for unwittingly pretty parts. Gehry's action upon the house he purchased as well as the anarchic resistance of old and new to the traditional ideal of integration suggest something other than a splitting of, and from, architecture.[25] It suggests condemning the house as defined

However idiosyncratic or—as local slang would have it—"off the wall" Gehry's own house may have appeared for years after its construction, and however deeply it was motivated by his own experiences at the time, the design also reestablished connections with

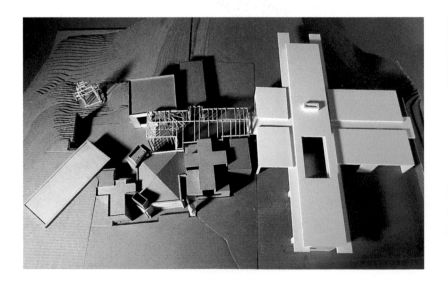

Gehry Residence (second remodeling), Santa Monica, California, 1991–94. Kitchen.

building department, the closed concrete box."[27] Schindler's irreverent handling of convention reacted against another kind of (historical) confinement than did Gehry's, but they both opened up the traditional concept of the house as a refuge from the hardships of life—the small, private dwelling—to encompass a reckoning with father and mother. Formally, Schindler's jaunty accents on 30- and 60-degree angles, his employment of open latticework, his rotation of volumes within one another, and his use of light materials are similar to those Gehry used for his own residence, and subsequently for his Familian Residence (project, 1978) and Spiller Residence (1978–79).

Gone Fishing

Gehry dedicated the first book on his work to "Mother, Milton and Berta."[28] Milton Wexler is Gehry's psychiatrist and friend; one is inclined to think of him as a father freely chosen. Through Milton and Berta, Gehry made himself into another person, a maker of buildings that aim at the perfection of a fish. For this is what the fish represents in Gehry's mind: a more perfect creature than he had been able to create so far. Its shape had escaped the architect's imaginative powers, but he said: "I kept

important local precedents: Rudolf Schindler's work had been a distant model for Gehry, both in its informing ideas and its uninhibited execution.[26] In the words of Esther McCoy, who worked in Schindler's studio in the 1940s and became the doyenne historian of the period, Schindler's extraordinary, fragile buildings captured "the fleeting, the impermanent. This was a kind of protest against The Establishment, the finely built eclectic house, the nest culture, the

Frank Gehry, fish and bird sketches.

drawing it and sketching it and it started to become for me like a symbol for a certain kind of perfection that I couldn't achieve with my buildings."[29] The superior qualities of the fish also suggest a triple filiation of meaning: it represents a legacy of nature, a personal childhood experience, and an abstract ideal that required him to exercise his talent over many years before attaining his goal. For Gehry, the antiquity of the fish also evokes the beginnings of architecture, the "zoomorphic yearnings" of architects.[30]

Over the course of modern history, the shapes of animals and allusions to plant forms have periodically

Michelangelo, Porta al Prato d'Ognissanti, Florence, Italy, 1528–29. Studies for the bulwarks.

Michelangelo, Sforza Chapel, Santa Maria Maggiore, Rome, Italy, c.1560. Plan.

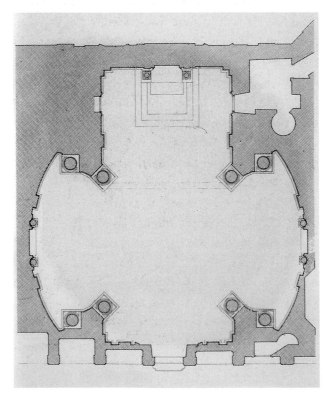

infiltrated architectural imagination, perhaps most explicitly in works that carried powerful associations with natural forces. Renaissance fortifications needed to be designed so as to counterbalance the impact of offensive artillery. The problems of building effective bastions—to shield the defenders passively from the aggressors while allowing for retaliatory fire—were highly technical, and yet the forms they took were almost completely metaphorical. Bastions were seemingly configured as a result of calculated impact and offense, but they assumed the biomorphic shapes of crustaceans, claws, spurs, pincers, and fins, among other things. Michelangelo virtually invented the formal components of bastions and applied them in astonishingly novel ways during his only foray into military engineering, on the eve of the Florentine Republic's collapse. His later work deployed into civil architecture the shapes he had first explored for the design of modern bastions, precedents clearly echoed in his Roman studies for the Porta Pia and the Sforza Chapel.

It has long been recognized that these works helped set the course for Borromini's pursuit of an architecture of his own. He took up shapes derived from plants and animals, some of them already filtered and translated into solid form by Michelangelo. At times, these forms attained no more than a latent presence, but in some instances they assumed meanings that can be confirmed by Borromini's own comments. For the Oratorian Order of the Filippini in Rome, Borromini developed a vast rebuilding scheme that accommodated a new oratory within a grand monastic palazzo. He lavished inventive imagination on every detail. In the vestibule of the refectory, he erected two fantastic lavabos on socles patterned after gothic fountains.[31] Their tall, tulip-shaped tanks feed water through four spigots into a four-lobed basin. With these fountains Borromini allowed himself to fantasize, claiming the inventive liberties that made him "appear to move far away from customary design." Such works entitled him to protest that "he would never have taken up his profession in order to be a copyist, even if the invention of new things is slow in bringing recognition."[32] Describing the lavabos in loving detail, Borromini not only suggested their origin in nature but he also rationalized

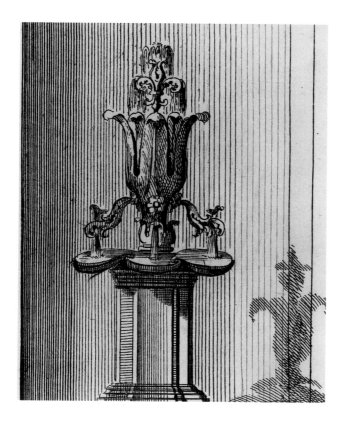

Francesco Borromini, lavabo in the vestibule of the Palazzo dei Filippini, Rome, Italy.

their appearance as truly fabulous objects and hybrids in the realm of forms, for they mutate before our eyes from historically determined geometries back to natural shapes. Only the imagination of a sculptor could produce such infinitely complicated contours and insinuate a continuity between Euclidean geometries and natural algorithms.

The desire for imaginative leaps from one kind of geometry to another arises frequently in moments of hesitancy or creative impasse. When human-made forms inhibit the mind, nature's infinite capacity to produce new ones beckons for fresh attention. No doubt out of a certain frustration with his solitary stance, Le Corbusier confided in 1952 that he found

Le Corbusier, "figures toward animal shapes," 1952 (Fondation Le Corbusier, Paris).

himself developing "figures toward animal shapes which are carriers of character." Beyond their metamorphic capabilities, these shapes also possessed "an algebraic ability to enter into connection with each other and thus release a poetic phenomenon."[33] It is precisely this poetic capacity of metamorphosis that endows animals with meaning and allows them to escape the confines of rational analysis. When Le Corbusier chose the vaguely scientific term "algebraic" he must not have thought in Cartesian, but rather in alchemical terms. It is their metamorphic quality that destines the shapes of animals to represent the poetic manifestation of things that have no inherent shape or manifest character of their own. That animal shapes returned to architecture—not simply as images, but as the agents of something other than themselves—can now be recognized as an early sign of architecture's discontent (with itself) in the early years after World War II.

As images of origin and metamorphosis, plant patterns and the shapes of animals have the capacity to fuse, rather than divide, the essence of a thing to its bodily manifestations. Thus the fish appears to hold the secret of life that gave it its shape and tenders the promise of discoveries to be made about its existence. To recognize the fish's functional perfection makes us wonder how it came about. For Frank Gehry, the mystery of the fish resided in the harmless guise of a childhood memory that brought with it a less-than-harmless conclusion. Whether Gehry merely embroidered the story about the carp his grandmother bought every Thursday and kept in the bathtub until she prepared her gefilte fish on the eve of the Sabbath, or whether he invented the tale from whole cloth need not concern us. That he *did* tell the story, and has repeated it many times since, hints at the personal significance the fish has come to assume in his mind. There is a shocking conclusion to the homely tale: Gehry "would play with the goddam fish for a day until the next day [when] she'd kill it and make gefilte fish."[34] The killing of the fish is precisely the event that changes the story from a charming tale to a cryptic drama, when the fish as a marvelous incarnation of life is suddenly killed, only to be consumed as an image of revival.[35]

torted and accentuated by grossly textured materials, these ensembles convert Oldenburg's happenings into mute scenography. They have the appearance of empty stage sets whose haunted and scaleless objects exhibit latent tensions even in the absence of any action. We are familiar with the cinematic use of fragmented interiors that have been constructed only to the extent that they will actually appear on the screen: a segment of a vanity, mirroring the man standing behind a woman, a sofa or overstuffed chair haunting a scene of repressed anger, and the like. Enigmatic episodes of domestic disaster seem nowhere so quietly threatening and so ludicrously overstaged as in Oldenburg's interiors. The furniture has suffered not just perspectival but psychic distortion. With their glitzy surrogate materials they announce the blatant power of domestic events.

A decade after Oldenburg built his ensembles, Gehry began to conceive of buildings in terms of a

Marco Antonio de Valdivia, portrait of Frank Gehry with fish lamps.

Congeries in a Menagerie

In the early 1960s, Claes Oldenburg often fashioned the same objects in hard and soft versions, in sketchy collages and solid finishes. The *Light Switches* of 1964 exist in three versions of virtually identical size but completely different shapes and surfaces.[36] At the same time, he began to make models of miniature pieces of furniture, and in 1963 exhibited the first full-scale *Bedroom Ensemble*, which was followed in 1965 by *Bathroom Group in a Garden*. These projects consist of geometrically and materially independent objects framed within a single field. Perspectively dis-

Claes Oldenburg, *Bedroom Ensemble, Replica I*, 1969 (Museum für Moderne Kunst, Frankfurt am Main; photograph by Rudolf Nagel).

Egyptian oxyrhynchus with disk and horns of the sun god; the fish symbolizes the bond between darkness and light. Bronze votive figure, late Ptolemaic period.

number of individual objects that float apart like boats on a pond. His studies for the Jung Institute (project, 1976) in Los Angeles envisioned a compound of distinctive buildings, loosely framed within a common field, in this case an expanse of water. Gehry was obviously discovering something important at this stage, when he relaxed, and even severed, the links that had hitherto locked the various parts of a building into a single whole. The unexecuted Gunther Residence (project, 1978) and Familian Residence (project, 1978) fractured the very notion of the house

Jung Institute
(project),
Los Angeles,
California,
1976. Sketch.

Jung Institute
(project),
Los Angeles,
California,
1976. Sketch.

as a unifying shell, instead arising as a collection of seemingly free-floating rooms. These houses took the shape of loosely assembled and barely concatenated volumes, each resting on its own footing and tending in a different direction. It comes as no surprise that these projects were not built, and that it fell to Gehry himself to realize the first example of his new line of thinking. Like a surgeon who cannot find volunteers for a novel procedure, he was forced to operate on himself, as it were. The outcome secured landmark standing among the many thousands of architect-designed dwellings of recent decades. Whereas the assembly of component parts is entirely internal to the logic of a traditional house, the unity of the Gehry Residence has been suspended in the

"encounter" of its freely congregating parts. Its identity results from the simultaneous aggregation and segregation of an array of components, not from an externally coerced cohesion.

From his own to much grander houses—such as the Sirmai-Peterson House (1983–88) and the Schnabel Residence (1986–89), not to mention the somewhat excessive and belabored Lewis Residence (project, 1989–95)—Gehry profoundly transformed the very idea of the single-family house, but these experiments have also been a wellspring for other strategies. In the first place, he has enormously expanded his capacity for mapping complex situations in architectural terms. It may come as a surprise that his experiments with the breakup and disassembly of the house should lend themselves to a varied set of other design tasks, such as creating buildings for college campuses, business complexes, and cultural institutions. Yet Gehry has been informed by precisely these experiences, starting from when he first laid out the plans for the Loyola University Law School (1978–), in downtown Los Angeles. Laboratory and museum buildings and, finally, the Disney Concert Hall (1989–)[37] and the grand Bilbao Guggenheim (1991–97) demonstrate how virtually inexhaustible this well of architectural invention has turned out to be. What he started to tap with his own residence has

Familian
Residence
(project),
Santa Monica,
California,
1978. Model.

marks a return to integration: composed in the manner of a habitable still life, Edgemar strikes a balance between its individual components and their multiple roles within an ensemble. If one can indeed compare it to a still life—for example, Le Corbusier's 1929 painting *Sculpture and Nude (Sculpture et nu)*—it would be in the dual sense of a pictorial assembly of familiar parts and an inanimate moment framed off from life.

Gehry reached the most decisive stage in the evolution of new urban strategies with his winning entry in the competition for the Disney Concert Hall in Los Angeles. It is perhaps ironic that a project still unbuilt a decade after it was first formulated, in 1989, served as a sort of rocket, which, after lifting Gehry into his own highest orbit, crashed back to Earth, empty and spent. To be sure, the metaphor is more apt than the image, for the Disney Concert Hall project itself has undergone profound transformation. Unable to realize the concert hall, on which he had expended such efforts, Gehry expanded his new liberty of imagination on the next major project. On the scale of his earlier commissions, the Disney Concert Hall was a grand project; by almost any standard, the Guggenheim Museum in Bilbao is a building of superlatives: beginning with its scale and intricately ramified setting, and ending with one of the most complex spatial experiences to be had anywhere, its architectural qualities are virtually unique in our time.

Edgemar Development, Santa Monica, California, 1984–88.

Loyola University Law School, Los Angeles, California, 1982– . Model and view.

continued to flow beyond the narrow confines of the house and inundate the city. The strategies he originally developed to transform the confining nature of the house find new application within the segmented order of the city. Gehry's projects cluster disjointed buildings and propose self-sustaining expansions.

The Loyola University Law School was envisioned as a public sphere with a model-like array of different institutional buildings and sites that have proven their potential for expansion and modification over the years. As an overtly stagy setting in which the buildings, like the particulars of personal behavior, are left blank, the campus virtually solicits personal reaction. The Edgemar Development (1984–88) perhaps

Le Corbusier, *Sculpture et nu*, 1929 (Fondation Le Corbusier, Paris).

Both the Disney Concert Hall and the Bilbao Guggenheim are located in what have become derelict urban areas, scored by traffic arteries and crisscrossed by major sight lines. In Los Angeles, the concert hall was expected to serve as the centerpiece in a scheme to rebuild a grand municipal complex of museums and hotels in the midst of future corporate and private establishments. In Bilbao, a swath of raw embankment along the Nervion River where heavy industry and fluvial warehouses had been abandoned was chosen for redevelopment. The site is not only cramped by rail and street corridors alongside the river but also by its fringe location and an inclined suspension bridge plunging from the east over steep riverbanks right into the new town (*ensanche*). Between the bifurcating ramps of the bridge, the slope, and the river, a large irregular area was set aside

for Gehry's project. The compromised conditions of the site make an apt metaphor for the complex circumstances under which the commission was precipitated by Spanish regional and municipal governments in negotiation with the Guggenheim Museum in New York City.

Architectural Pantomime

If the Disney Concert Hall set the tone for the expansive thinking that led to the Bilbao museum, Gehry's interminable work on the Lewis Residence (begun in 1989 and abandoned by the client in

1995)[38] played out one of those middle voices that, gradually expanding into the upper registers, ascend to prominence in the finale. It is noteworthy that the old theme of the private residence, treated to Gehry's favorite tune of increasing autonomy among its component parts, was kept going while grander public buildings began to claim his attention. It is fair to say that the headquarters of the Swiss company Vitra International (1988–94) in Biersfelden, the Center for the Visual Arts at the University of Toledo (1989), the Frederick R. Weisman Art and Teaching Museum at the University of Minnesota (1990–93), and the EMR Communication and Technology Center (1991–95), at Bad Öynhausen, further expand the themes that had been announced in the competition model for the Disney Concert Hall. Loosening the

Guggenheim Museum, Bilbao, Spain, 1991–97.

Walt Disney Concert Hall, Los Angeles, California, 1989– . Model.

Lewis
Residence
(project),
Lyndhurst,
Ohio, 1989–95.
Model detail.

expanding from one wing to another, gathering force in a crescendo of heights, or ebbing away into the surroundings. Perhaps the most striking example of this kind of bodily innervation among stereometric parts is the Nationale-Nederlanden Building (1992–95), in Prague. Its nickname—Ginger and Fred—alludes to a marvelous kind of highly choreographed but improvisational performance, a testimony to Gehry's now virtually unmatched handling of impossibly tight situations. As if Astaire's arm were slung around Rogers's twirling figure in order to arrest her motion and immediately propel her away again while he brings himself momentarily into a tight embrace, the two bodies of this building seem forever frozen in a movement of their dance. This may be the secret desire that Gehry seeks to fulfill when he pursues, day after day, the problem of setting rigid shapes into motion and choreographing their animation among the flow of rooflines and the flutter of sheet metal.

joints among ever more imaginatively sculpted volumes allowed for a new kind of flexing of the building's body, tensing one part while relaxing another and thereby compressing volumes and extending passages according to the functions of its various parts. A sense of corporeal action sprang from this tension,

Choreographer of Chance

Pieces and parts of architecture have been compared to the human body and its limbs at least since classical antiquity. When we speak of a lintel supported by

Nationale-
Nederlanden
Building, Prague,
Czech Republic,
1992–96.

Ginger Rogers
and Fred Astaire
in E. H. Griffith's
Top Hat, 1943.

posts or herms, when we think of a beam lifted high and braced by arms, we enliven a static order by analogy to the bodily effort and work required to erect it and hold it aloft. This analogy does more than perpetuate a primitive way of imagining the interplay of invisible forces—it also registers the spacing of solids and voids and even engenders a sense of symmetry, balance, and tension.[39] We have become so conversant with these notions that a special effort is required to restore them to their bodily reality in our experience of buildings. Our ability to sense inanimate objects in their relationships with animate bodies depends, almost by way of contradiction, on our capacity to outwit the power of language: language always renders experience in symbolic rather than physical terms. The mere sight of a juggler or a trapeze artist induces a spontaneous bodily reaction in the spectator. Our bodies react mimetically—without mediation of language—to the antics of a balancing act, just

Jacques-Henri Lartigue, *Biarritz, Cerf-volant*, 1905.

Merce Cunningham, *Events,* performed at the Lyon Dance Biennial, 1989.

as our kinetic sense works infinitely more subtly and quickly than do our words.

We imagine objects in motion with ease: a row of falling dominoes rushing toward collapse, a house of cards tumbling to the ground, a flimsy crate crushed beneath one's foot. If we play out in our minds the dynamic rapports among the elements of a building and conceive of its volumes as having been arrested in a moment of motion, we come close to imagining the state into which Frank Gehry has propelled his architecture. Were we asked to think of analogous images, surely those of Jacques-Henri Lartigue would spring to mind. His photographs capture improbable moments of objects in motion, as when kites are hanging in the breeze,[40] a person is leaning steeply forward into the wind created by the propeller of an airplane, or friends and family members are "flying" into a garden down a flight of stairs. These photographic moments possess a virtually surreal quality,

because insofar as they arrest motion and freeze it in an image, they suspend the very sensation of time that alone brought them into being.[41]

Gehry's delight in massing volumes or suspending them (permanently) in a (fleeting) moment endows his buildings with a sense of vitality that seems beyond the realm of architecture. Among American artists working prominently in the decade of Gehry's professional formation, the sculptor David Smith anticipated the architect's desires with his series *Cubi,*[42] rising and falling stacks of volumes that tumble and turn through implied motion. A similar sense of arrested movement informs Gehry's later projects, which seek to fix en passant what cannot stay in place. Over the years, Gehry has cultivated a highly personal studio practice of working with models, because it permits impossibly cantilevered parts and vertiginous piles of volumes in fluid transformation. As he began to shape buildings from mobile parts, his sense of space transcended Cartesian notions. This special sense defies verbal definition, but it might be compared with the sensation of moving bodies in a medium akin to water. To the extent that his buildings arrest volumes in continuous motion (and transformation), time becomes their formative dimension. Correspondingly, they de-form the neutral concept of Euclidean space and enter into a conterminous function with the fields within which they occur.

In his late works, Alvar Aalto molded spatial relationships into a constantly varying continuum, as if space were able to break free of Cartesian abstraction

David Smith,
Cubi XVII,
stainless steel,
1963.

and assume a viscous state. After World War II, Le Corbusier increasingly confronted the abstraction of space with the volumetric presence of bodily shapes, curving ramps, and shell-like alcoves. But this antinomy of body and cage, which he had put to analytic purpose in his paintings since the late 1920s, was progressively resolved, or rather suppressed, with the unchecked ascendancy of the cage over the body. As an abstraction reinforced by economic imperatives, the skeletal structure of building became so pervasive after the war as to make a virtual prisoner of the body. In the 1980s, Frank Gehry returned to an architecture of bodies and volumes. At first these bodies still displayed the traces of their previous incarceration. Peeled, tattered, bruised, and scarred, they appeared on the witness stand to testify against the brutality of bureaucratic design and to protest a general lack of imagination.

Gehry does not envision the volumes of his buildings within the confines of abstract space (which is also the space of economics); rather, he engages these volumes in intimate relationships with one another. In short, he sets the bodies of his buildings in motion as a choreographer does his or her dancers. One need only observe Gehry's manner of drawing to gain an immediate impression of his way of thinking: the pen does not so much glide across the page as it dances effortlessly through a continuum of space. Gehry's studio practice recalls nothing so much as performance rehearsals: days and weeks of choreographic invention and refinement, at which all dancers must be present all the time. The architect's affinity for the transitory and his conjurer's grasp of minute displacements are fueled by his knowledge of performance art and enriched by his collaborations with artists. At Bilbao he planned with and for artists, providing spaces for specially commissioned installations as well as flexible galleries for a great variety of displays.

The building complex includes generously proportioned areas for public events and unforeseen opportunities, vastly expanding the breadth of the contemporary museum.[43] It is entirely purposeful that the museum has been anchored in the cityscape of Bilbao like a vast circus tent surrounded by a congerie of caravans, for the variety of anticipated events requires large and ever-varying venues. Subsidiary spaces are clustered together, squeezed through the bottleneck between river and embankment, made to duck under bridges, and finally allowed to soar over the building's core in a spectacular canopy. All this implies motion, induced by internal tension and external compression, which gives rise to the towering, and seemingly revolving, space of the central hall. If it is possible to speak of a spatial realm without figural contours yet possessing powerful bodily qualities, if ambulation can unlock the complexities of a building's order beyond the outlines of the plan, then the museum in Bilbao reawakens an architecture that has lain dormant for centuries. The suggestion may sound extravagant, but the reality of this building, which has been fashioned from segmented shells, will surely bear it out.

If one were to seek an index for the historical standing of this building, one need only consider the novel applications of computer technology in its making. For the Bilbao museum, Gehry tapped the full capacity of computer-assisted design. Leaving its auxiliary role far behind, he and his collaborators made use of programs originally developed for the design of airplane fuselages but that in this case provided the matrix for the shaping of every part and the refinement of every element in the museum's design and construction. The age-old split between the hands that design and the instruments that execute has been overcome: the separate phases and techniques of conceiving and executing a building were woven into an unbroken loop. Every volume has been shaped in three dimensions, tested and modified by computer plotting, just as every part of its physical assembly—steel frame, cladding, and all—was fabricated on the basis of computer-generated construction documents.[44] Only in this way can the inaccurate fit among the conventionally separate phases of invention, transcription, and execution be perfected, and the exponential degree of geometric complexity of such a structure be realized without costly trial and error.

The Bilbao museum will not only go down as one of the most complex formal inventions of our time but it will also stand as a monument to the productive capacities that are now at our disposal if an architect such as Gehry puts them to imaginative use. Hackneyed applications of computing do no more for architecture than pencil sharpeners used to do. When complexities of an order that is commensurate with our understanding of the world can be restored to architecture, we shall no longer have to be content with the subsistence diet dictated by the economics of our own time and the impoverished aesthetics of an earlier era.

Borromini and Gehry: "Shame of Their Centuries"

The way in which Gehry's work has been characterized and criticized is hardly new to our times.[45] Both in terms and in tone, these criticisms recall the controversies surrounding the architecture of Francesco Borromini in the seventeenth century. Borromini was as deeply appreciated by some of his patrons as he was despised by some of his critics. The theoretician Giovanni Pietro Bellori decried the baroque architect as

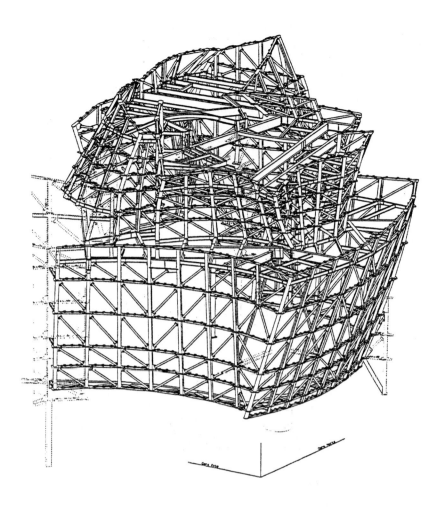

Three-dimensional rendering of steel structure for the Bilbao Guggenheim.

"a complete ignoramus, the corrupter of architecture, the shame of our century."[46] The procurator of the Trinitarian Brothers, however, considered their church of San Carlo alle Quattro Fontane to be so unique as to have no equivalent: "This building is not simply the first of Borromini's [independently executed] works, but it is also first in concept and artistic execution, so excellent in fact that there is nothing as fantastic, rare, and exceptional . . . anywhere in the world."[47] It is significant that the procurator praised Borromini's architecture not only for its general excellence but also for qualities that are intimately associated with the personal capacities of its designer, with the inventive power of his "fantasy" as the originating (and authenticating) will to singular results.

By its very nature, fantasy has no categorical or lexical limit, and neither is it confined or externally attached to anything in particular; it is instead the compass of purely individual inventiveness. Borro-

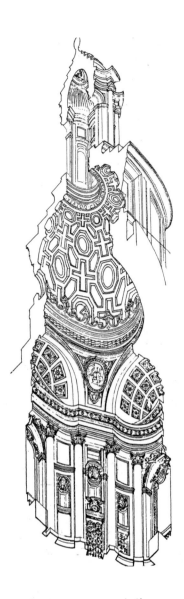

Francesco
Borromini,
San Carlo alle
Quattro Fontane,
Rome, Italy.
Axonometric
of interior.

profound difference in the way forms are brought forth and consequently made to project elusive images into the solid fabric of a building.

There is something explosive in the inventive power of fantasy. Ideas can burst unbidden onto the page or glimmer through chimerical transformations of the familiar. Manifestations of fire and bursts of light abound in Borromini's work. The fiery temperament of the architect, whose pace of work tended at times to be as spasmodic as at other moments his thinking was languid, left its most complete imprint on shapes that had undergone *de*formation and *trans*formation at his hands. Beginning with his method of drawing and culminating in the free transformation of any of the architectural members he employed, Borromini assumed the materials of his building to be plastic and malleable. His biographer Filippo Baldinucci recorded the architect's restless elaboration of ideas in the form of models, not the customary kind constructed in wood but what we would call working models. He is said to have fashioned them from the materials sculptors used in their studios: wax and clay.[50] Borromini must have preferred these soft substances to the brittleness of wood, because he wished to overcome the rigidity of conventional walls and to replace them with a ductile medium. Clay and wax could as easily be stiffened into crisp ridges as melded into the smoothest transitions between one shape and another. In Borromini's buildings, neither the mass of walls nor the weight of vaults lose any of their definition, but they assume the appearance of a different material state. This state implies another aggregate of matter, as if the walls and vaults were made of stuff that had been cooked up for these new purposes. Segmented views and perspectival distortions abound; lopped shapes reveal sliding transitions and induce a sensation of ever-shifting relationships among the architectural members. In the reactions of Borromini's contemporaries, laypeople and learned alike, we can glimpse their struggle to express their experience, describing it as something akin to that of a floating eye.[51]

Added to this new material state and its visual sensations was the fact that an entirely new rapport was beginning to establish itself among the different members and segmented spaces of Borromini's archi-

mini's groundless fantasy manifests itself less in particular features of a building than in its all-pervasive claim over his entire work. The novelty of his solutions challenged the implicit limits of his commissions, and, where he was successful, produced unique results. This novelty is not superficial but rather transforms the work entirely. It did not sit well with the defenders of artistic orthodoxy, such as Bellori, who, a few years after Borromini's death, still could throw a verbal tantrum denouncing those barbarians "who frenetically invented the most varied fantastic fantasies until they finally had architecture turned into the ugliest monstrosities."[48] "Fantasy" was precisely the word Borromini chose too, when he spoke of his formal invention in solving a problem, whether accommodating stairs or connecting rooms of different height and use. The distinction he drew between a "mere caprice" and his own *"fantasticare"*[49] marks a tecture. His forms are not only conspicuous for their novelty but also for the juxtaposition of shapes that vary grossly in size and kind. In a frequent reversal of dominant and subsidiary forms, Borromini challenged the hierarchy of structure over ornament. Frames of doors and windows inside and out no longer define themselves in size and treatment relative to their positioning but instead grow voluminous volutes, open their pediments to embrace floating cartouches, and spawn other sculptural excrescences. Fireplaces acquire gigantic mantelpieces that dwarf their practical purpose, and a lantern assumes the shape of a tumulus.

"The Oval Saved My Life" ("La forma ovata mi diede la vita")[52]

Some architectural set pieces, such as fireplaces, had long been a staple of inventive exercises, insofar as they posed intriguing problems of scale and signification. Because it is their role to mediate between the reach of the body on the one hand, and the more abstract notion of the whole room (and, by extension, the building) on the other, mantelpieces frequently

acquired a full tectonic apparatus. For centuries, they formed the subject of elaborate designs such as those published by Serlio, du Cerceau, Dietterlin, and Piranesi. Fire was the true subject of these design inventions. Although ostensibly constrained to benevolent domestic purpose, fire always remains a menace to architecture. While it is indispensable to construction—it is needed to fire brick and burn lime, to smelt ore and forge iron—it is also a constant threat to a building's survival. Fireplaces forever recall the origins of manufacturing skills and the society able to sustain them. They lend a ceremonial presence to the fulcrum of civilization and as such assume highly charged meanings.

Borromini had seized an opportunity to articulate the design of a large mantel in the guise of such a metaphorical montage when he projected a capacious fireplace for the Palazzo dei Filippini in Rome. Overreaching its practical purpose and decorous limit, he admitted to designing "a fireplace, which . . . oversteps the bounds set by the friars."[53] Its ambivalent (but large) scale invades the "lounge" for which it was built.[54] And it assumes added significance as soon as

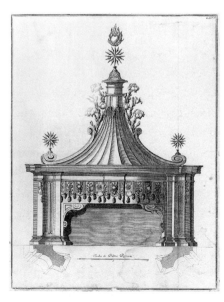

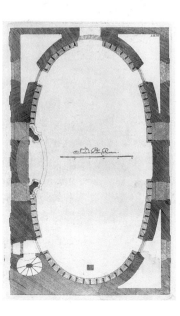

one recognizes that the fireplace is nothing other than a miniature version of the entire ovoid room—or, put another way, that the symbolic locus of the community is formally homologous with the locale it symbolizes. One would seriously underestimate Borromini if such effects were put down to happy

Francesco Borromini, door details, fireplace, and plan of the *sala della ricreazione* of the Palazzo dei Filippini, Rome, Italy. (*Opera del Cav. Francesco Boromino.*)

coincidence rather than recognized as the result of his "ceaseless speculation about matters of his art."[55]

More than once Borromini touched on the nature of his manifold shapes. For example, when to his great relief he hit upon an oval plan for the refectory and lounge of the Filippine friars, he wrote: "That oval saved me, for it not only achieved the desired effect, but also brought with it a thousand other benefits."[56] Borromini emphasized the significance of this fireplace by calling it a "pavilion," or an ample cope, that protected the life of the monastic community.[57] Intended as a symbolic structure, the mantelpiece was replete with images of remote origin (the tent, cope, and heavenly protection) and chiefly ceremonial use. As the source of warmth and communal well-being, it was intended to be richly adorned, according to Borromini's design, with the symbols of the confraternity in an ornamental crescendo that the architect reserved for places of the highest significance.[58]

From the Horse's Mouth

Gehry is at his most inventive when he seeks to reintegrate distinct and tendentially autonomous parts, be they the separate rooms of a house, the different functions of a building, or spatial and material characteristics. During his work on the Lewis Residence (project, 1989–95), Gehry sought seemingly in vain to contain the numerous, and constantly multiplying, pavilions and rooms within the compass of a single dwelling. Over the years, he had refined his strategy of breaking down complex tasks and synthesizing their constitutive elements into a collectivity of functions. Typically, his single-family houses now took the form of hamlets of rooms, and even small buildings, such as the Winton Guest House (1982–87), were composed of materially distinct components. Gehry had long extended his approach to individual houses into the wider context of the city, and now his experiences with urban complexes began to affect his ideas about single-family houses. At the height of the process of expanding the Lewis Residence, he toyed with connecting corridors, canopies, and pergolas, but it was only by applying textile material that he was able to fashion a kind of atrium. With the gravitational center of the house thus reestablished, he

began to search for a shape equal to the singular role this space would perform. Gradually, with the kind of luck that made Borromini exclaim "the oval saved my life," Gehry tried his hand at a shape he later called "the horse's head." While clearly zoomorphic in appearance and vaguely similar to a horse's skull, its formal properties recall infinitely slow processes in nature, such as glacial carving of the bedrock or the growth of bones. As this shape emerged from Gehry's hands, it assumed the qualities of a *trouvaille*. "Found" it was in the sense that Gehry knew instinctively where he was headed with it, but a "find" it became when he sensed that metamorphosis had been accomplished. Such finds belong to the very rare shapes that can be transferred from the site of their gestation to a place in other projects. When the commission for the Lewis Residence collapsed, Gehry took up the horse's head, teased a few more

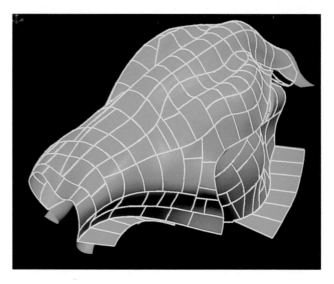

Three-dimensional rendering of "horse's head."

refinements from its form, and suspended it in the atrium of Pariser Platz 3 (1994–), a bank building in Berlin.

The transfer of this shape does not negate the logic of its original purpose, for it had been evolved to gather together the centrifugal components of the Lewis Residence under a complex canopy. First draped like a billowing mantle over a flock of objects, the canopy will shelter a conference room at the bank, where it gives body to an institutional space inside a huge atrium. The roof of the atrium appears

to float on an airframe in allusion to a zeppelin, while the compressed curves of the conference room seem to hover in midair beneath it. Gehry is usually averse to transferring forms from one project to another, but in this case he thought of the shape less as an object than as an instrument for bringing objects into the fold of an ensemble: the horse's head thus represents Gehry's way of thinking through a task in terms of generalized formal characteristics.

If the standard manual of the history of architecture in the English language characterizes Gehry's work as "relaxed, inclusive and opportunistic," it no doubt wishes to distinguish Gehry's from standard American practice while conversely inscribing it precisely, and completely, within it.[59] The paradox—that an architect's work can be so highly individualistic as to stand out from everything else, and yet so deeply rooted in its culture as to wind up its very incarnation—only goes to show that Gehry has successfully made his problems universal within the realm of American building, or, put in more personal terms, that his ideas tap deeply into the forces at work within his culture. Both are undoubtedly true, as is the surprising relevance of Gehry's thinking to other lands and continents. It is no exaggeration to say that his architecture is rich in timbres, free of the tinny sound of high-tech, and a far cry from the puritanical strains of the New Simplicity. His ideas are always polyphonic, moving among widely diverse registers

and adding shading and character to his voices. His architecture has expanded from a painful reckoning with its most constraining practices to a freedom of invention that finds its match only in some of the greatest works of baroque architecture.

The sculptors and architects of the Bavarian baroque managed to make any part of a building appear to float on clouds. A year ago, Gehry was well on his way to conceiving the Samsung Museum of Art (1995–), in Seoul, in the shape of a mountain divided by horizontal banks of clouds. A Korean scroll hung in his studio for months, spurring him on to match the appearance of an enchanted mountainscape in the hard and solid materials of a building. Before the project was put on hold, he had reached his goal of representing the character of his building in the intransitive terms of natural processes. In this case, "character" is not meant to express the physiognomic or typological cast of the building; rather it

Photographs
of models for
Samsung
Museum of
Modern Art,
Seoul, Korea,
next to a Korean
painting on silk
representing a
rocky countryside,
a gift from the
client to Gehry.

adumbrates different states of being within the contours of a single edifice. Karl Friedrich Schinkel had glimpsed such a potential for architecture when he challenged design to represent poetically such actions as "pressing, bending, sustaining, oscillating, linking, fastening, reclining, and resting" and to make them manifest—experientially tangible—in the material fabric of a building.[60] Material qualities are forever bound up with reality, but making them speak of processes and ideas, as Gehry does with bold eloquence, answers our secret desire for the siren song of fantasy.

1. Quite unwittingly, I'm sure, Gehry's words echo those of Sir Reginald Blomfield: "Borromini's extravagance was perhaps the inevitable reaction to the dogmatism of Palladio." Blomfield, *Six Architects* (London, 1935), 36.

2. Gehry takes no responsibility for the story, but he did choose his stage name and character, and he invented his costume along with some of the props, such as the snake and the temple.

3. Germano Celant, *Il Corso del Coltello/The Course of the Knife* (New York, 1987), 67. These are Gehry's own words, slightly reedited. The *coltello*/knife serves as both an instrument and a symbol for Gehry's action of cutting through thick layers of the past.

4. The symbolism of the fish is not only extremely wide and varied, it also needs to be assessed within the figural range of modern art, an aspect Peter Arnell pressed in his interview of Gehry in 1984, insisting inconclusively on the significance of paintings by Magritte. Peter Arnell and Ted Bickford, eds., *Frank Gehry: Buildings and Projects* (New York, 1985), xvii.

5. Arnell and Bickford, *Frank Gehry*, 213.

6. Numerous sketchbooks and spiral-bound sketchpads are held in Gehry's office archive without numbering or other identification. For this reason, only circumstantial evidence or personal recollections allow the individual sketches to be dated.

7. Isaacs is, among other things, the hagiographer of Walter Gropius. See Reginald Isaacs, *Walter Gropius: Der Mensch und sein Werk,* 2 vols. (Berlin, 1983–84).

8. Karen Michels, "Le Corbusier, poème electronic: Die Synthese der Künste im Philips Pavillon, Weltausstellung, Brüssel," in *Idea: Jahrbuch der Hamburger Kunsthalle* 4 (1985): 147–63.

9. Louis Sullivan, *The Autobiography of an Idea* (1924; reprint, New York, 1957).

10. Sullivan, *Autobiography of an Idea,* 15.

11. Sullivan, *Autobiography of an Idea,* 183.

12. See Jean-Jacques Nattiez et al., eds., *The Boulez-Cage Correspondence* (Cambridge, 1993), and Clytus Gottwald, "Boulez, Nono und die Idee der Perfektion," *Musik-Konzepte* 89–90 (1995): 132–53. While the issues of perfection in musical composition debated by Pierre Boulez and John Cage did not concern Gehry at that time, he became deeply familiar with their music and is a personal friend of Boulez. If one compares Gehry's way of conceiving of his architectural work with the ideas on musical composition discussed by Boulez and Cage, one will discover deep affinities between Gehry's and Cage's ideas.

13. See *From Pierrot to Marteau: An International Conference and Concert Celebrating the Tenth Anniversary of the Arnold Schoenberg Institute* (Los Angeles, 1987), and Dominique Jameux, *Pierre Boulez* (Paris, 1984).

14. In this regard, the decisive lines are: "Enfant la jetée—promenade sauvage / Homme l'illusion imitée" ("Child the sea-side pier—a wild stroll / Man imitated illusion").

15. See Allan Braham, *The Architecture of the French Enlightenment* (Berkeley and Los Angeles, 1980), 223–26. To gauge the significance of the Château de Bagatelle for German architects of the early nineteenth century, particularly for Karl Friedrich Schinkel, see Friedrich Gilly, "Das Schlösschen Bagatelle von Bellanger, bei Paris," in *Sammlung nützlicher Aufsätze und Nachrichten, die Baukunst betreffend* 3 (1799): 106–15, recently translated by David Britt and commented by Fritz Neumeyer, *Friedrich Gilly: Essays on Architecture, 1796–1799* (Santa Monica, 1994).

16. Jack McLaughlin, *Jefferson and Monticello: The Biography of a Builder* (New York, 1988) gives a usefully updated account of Jefferson's interminable campaign. For recent illustrations see William Howard Adams, *Jefferson's Monticello* (New York, 1983). For biographical resonances in Jefferson's architecture, see George Green Shackelford, *Thomas Jefferson's Travels in Europe, 1784–1789* (Baltimore and London, 1995).

17. There is no comprehensive study of the entire ensemble of Schinkel's buildings at Charlottenhof and its open-ended concept, but see Heinz Schönemann, *Karl Friedrich Schinkel: Charlottenhof, Potsdam-Sanssouci* (Stuttgart and London, 1997).

18. Carl Friedrich Schinkel, *Sammlung architektonischer Entwürfe, enthaltend theils Werke welche ausgeführt sinc theils Gegenstände deren Ausführung beabsichtigt wurde: Neue Vollständige Ausgabe* (Berlin, 1866), 11 (my translation).

19. Jeffrey Kipnis rightly insists that "in truth, though the Glass House has never been complete, neither has it ever been incomplete," and he goes on to say that the estate grew "by annexation and diverse development," resulting "in an amalgam of disjointed components . . . endlessly capable of growth." David Whitney and Jeffrey Kipnis, eds., *Philip Johnson: The Glass House* (New York, 1993), xxxi. Peter Eisenman's 1979 article on the Glass House, reprinted in *Philip Johnson: The Glass House* as "From the Introduction to *Philip Johnson Writings,*" 77–79, takes a more compelling view of the project's underlying personal dilemmas.

20. Eisenman, "From the Introduction," 78. Eisenman further observes that the Glass House "is at once a ruin and also an ideal model of a more perfect society" (79). One might add that Gehry's house, too, is also a ruin—according to a superficial view that had much currency at the time—and a model, though less a model of a historical dilemma than of an existential experience.

21. Francesco Dal Co has expressed a similar reading of the entire estate. He found its order to be in the nature of a labyrinth and its ultimate effect that of a museum—a museum, moreover, of the architect's life. Wrote Dal Co, "'Reality' is in fact excluded from the labyrinth, whose center remains the enigma." Francesco Dal Co, "The House of Dreams and Memories: Philip Johnson at New Canaan," in Whitney and Kipnis, *Philip Johnson: The Glass House,* 118.

22. It is significant to add that it was Berta Gehry who found the original house on Washington Street in Santa Monica that her husband was to transform into their new residence.

23. Alvin H. Rosenfeld, "Inventing the Jew: Notes on Jewish Autobiography," in *The American Autobiography,* ed. Albert E. Stone (Englewood Cliffs, N.J., 1981), 155.

24. *Gordon Matta-Clark* (West Broadway Gallery, New York, 1974). Cf. *Gordon Matta-Clark* (exh. cat., Valencia, Marseille, London, 1993), 224–25. See also Herbert Muschamp, "Proliferations," in *Thinking the Present,* ed. K. Michael Hays and Carol Burns (New York, 1990), 90.

25. This is Herbert Muschamp's reading of Matta-Clark's work in his essay "Proliferations," 90.

26. I first argued this point in my essay "California Architecture: Now You See It, Now You Don't," in *Edge Condition: UCLA Architecture Journal* (1986): 5–22.

27. Esther McCoy, *The Architecture of R. M. Schindler (1887–1953)* (University of California, Santa Barbara, and Los Angeles County Museum of Art, 1967), 8.

28. Arnell and Bickford, *Frank Gehry.*

29. Arnell and Bickford, *Frank Gehry,* xvi.

30. Gehry stated in 1984 that "the fish preceded man on this earth," suggesting thereby a link between times immemorial and his own most pressing desires. Arnell and Bickford, *Frank Gehry,* xvi.

31. Joseph Connors, *Borromini and the Roman Oratory: Style and Society* (Cambridge, Mass., 1980).

32. "Quando tal volta gli paja, che io m'allontani da i communi disegni . . . ed io al certo non mi sarei posto a questa professione, col fine d'esser solo copista, benche sappia, che nell'inventare cose nuove, non si puo ricevere il frutto della fatica se non tardi." Connors, *Borromini and the Roman Oratory,* 5.

33. *Le Corbusier Sketchbooks,* ed. Françoise de Franclieu, 2 vols. (New York and Cambridge, Mass., 1950–54), 2:700.

34. Gehry has been fond of telling this story in one version or another for many years. The version quoted here is taken from Arnell and Bickford, *Frank Gehry.*

35. Before the Christian symbolism of the fish, the fish figured prominently in the Egyptian myth about the dismemberment and resurrection of Osiris. His sister/wife Isis searched for the scattered parts of Osiris until she recovered his penis, which had survived in the form of the fish oxyrhynchus. Once the last (missing) link had been restored, the cult of Osiris found a center between lower and upper Egypt at a place named for the fish. Small bronze votive offerings of oxyrhynchi have been found in great numbers. See Günther Roeder, *Ägyptische Bronzefiguren: Staatliche Museen zu Berlin, Mitteilungen aus der ägyptischen Sammlung* (Berlin, 1956), 410–12. In most cases, the disk and horns of the sun god are affixed to its head. The oxyrhynchus, an inhabitant, like the carp, of murky waters, carries the emblem of the sun on its back. One is made to think of Gehry's fish lamps of the 1980s, which similarly raise the creature from dark waters and install it, aglow with electric light, on a pedestal.

36. See *Claes Oldenburg: An Anthology* (New York, 1995), 201–3.

37. I have written a detailed analysis of the competition project: "Il pesce e il serpente al vertice," *Zodiac* 2 (1989): 182–93; and in Spanish translation as "La serpiente y el pez en la colina," *Arquitectura Viva* 10 (1990): 27–31. As director of the Getty Center for the History of Art and the Humanities (1984–92), I commissioned a comprehensive documentation of the project's evolution. Based on this chronology, Carol McMichael Reese wrote "Eine verblüffende Inszenierung: Die Geschichte des Entwurfs für die Walt Disney Concert Hall in Los Angeles," in *Archithese* 1 (1991): 40–60. The project has evolved further and is, almost a decade after the competition, fully detailed and ready for construction.

38. In May 1997, a two-day symposium was held at the Guggenheim Museum in New York with the participation of the client and the architect, in an effort to examine the wider implications of current architectural patronage and its particular nature in the case of the Lewis Residence.

39. Though it mainly pursues other issues, see Joseph Rykwert, *The Dancing Column* (Cambridge, Mass., 1997).

40. A particularly striking photograph of Lartigue's is *Cerf-volant*, shot on the beach at Biarritz in 1905, because it captures a kite with a cubic central part, in the manner of certain Chinese aerostats, to which two soft wings of complex curvilinear shape have been affixed. This conjunction of cubic and curvilinear forms can be matched precisely in several of Gehry's projects of recent years, such as the Vitra International headquarters (1988–94), in Biersfelden, and the Children's Museum (1992–96), in Boston.

41. The uneven flow of time—in contrast to the mortal ticking of the clock—is perhaps one of the fundamental Surrealist experiences, from Man Ray's eye affixed to the pendulum of the metronome to Salvador Dalí's soft watches, from Marcel Carné's film *Paris qui dort* (in which time itself is controlled by bandits) to the cinematic ploys and the significance of dreams in Surrealist works of art. Chance and automatism, so indispensable to Surrealist thinking, may be considered punctuations in the passage of clock-time, irruptions that fracture the continuum of time and drain it of its categorical significance.

42. See *David Smith, 1906–1965: A Retrospective Exhibition* (Cambridge, Mass., 1966). I have discussed affinities between the works of Smith and Gehry in my article "Choreographie des Zufalls," *Archithese* 11(1991): 16–29.

43. For a discussion of some of the key characteristics of the modern museum, see my "Shrine? Emporium? Theater? Two Decades of American Museum Building," *Zodiac Architectural Review* 6 (1991): 30–75.

44. See Hal Iyengar et al., "The Guggenheim Museum, Bilbao, Spain," *Structural Engineering International* 4 (1996): 227–29. The authors observe that the "capability of directly and instantaneously converting geometric information into finite elements was a crucial step in the structural analysis of the complex framework," and they explain that the "finite element model involved approximately 6000 joints and 3200 beam members arranged in the complete, undeformed, theoretical position of the members based on the computer-generated wire models . . . The fabrication/erection concept for the complex three-dimensional frames was formulated based on 3 m tall 'bands' of framework, shop-connected in horizontal lengths that could be shipped to the site and then 'stacked' vertically and spliced horizontally to create the complete assembly."

45. Criticism of Gehry's work tends to fall into two categories. He has frequently been treated as a symptom of this age and hence made to suffer the brunt of objection to its corrupting influences; more recently, critique has been directed at particular buildings and their alleged shortcomings. For an example of both, see Diana Ketcham, "Frank Gehry in Vogue," *New Criterion,* March 1988, 50–57, in which the following observations are made: "Certain drastic limitations are inherent in Gehry's approach. These derive from his dubious—though highly fashionable—assumption that the ends of art and architecture are the same . . . Gehry differs most radically from mainstream postmodernism in the way he has ignored architecture itself as a source of imagery, preferring the contents of his own psyche and the events of his own biography." Both points were made with regard to Borromini in his own day and in later times. The accusation of nihilism and artistic hubris has been leveled at both with conspicuous frequency and mostly in the name of normative aesthetics and conservative values, as when Ketcham concludes her high-handed piece with the following condemnation: "Under the spell of the architect's persona, with its appealingly democratic association, his fans do not realize what they are getting in Gehry—a nihilist under the jeans."

46. Giovanni Pietro Bellori, *Le vite de' pittori scultori et architetti moderni* (Rome, 1672), I:12 (reprint, ed. Eveline Borea, Turin, 1976).

47. Quoted in Leo Steinberg, *Borromini's San Carlo alle Quattro Fontane: A Study in Multiple Form and Architectural Symbolism* (New York and London, 1977), 328.

48. Bellori, *Le vite de' pittori,* I:12: "perche quei barbari edificatori, dispregiando i modelli e l'Idee Greche, e Romane, e li più belli monumenti dell'antichità, per molti secoli freneticarono tante, e si varie fantasie fantastiche d'or-

dini, che con bruttissimo disordine mostruosa la [l'architettura] resero."

49. Francesco Borromini, *Opera del Cav. Francesco Boromino cavata da suoi originali, cioè l'Oratorio, e fabrica per l'abitazione dei PP. dell'Oratorio di S. Filippo Neri di Roma* (Rome, 1725; reprint, Francesco Borromini, *Opus Architectonicum,* ed. Maurizio de Benedictis, Anzio, 1993), 37. Borromini distinguished "mere caprice" from genuine architectural invention using such phrases as the virtually untranslatable "fantasticando pensai" ("my imaginings").

50. Francesco Baldinucci, *Notizie dei professori del disegno da Cimabue in qua,* ed. F. Ranalli (Florence, 1948), V:139, VII:120.

51. This sensation of "transport" is exactly what Juan de San Bonaventura tried to capture in his *Relatione del Convento,* when he described the characteristic reaction of visitors to San Carlino. Overwhelmed and awed, they perceived that "all parts of this church are so disposed that each calls to the other." Quoted in Steinberg, *Borromini's San Carlo,* 328.

52. Borromini, *Opus Architectonicum,* 77.

53. Cf. Annamaria Pandolfi, "Appunti sulla struttura morfologica e sull'iter di formazione del progetto Borrominiano," *Bollettino d'Arte* 84–85 (1994): 105–20. Virgilio Spada characterized the "camino . . . fatto dal Borromini tanto superbo e ricco di intagli e lavori di marmo" as to have prompted the friars to wish it removed. See Incisa della Rocchetta, "Un dialogo del P. Virgilio Spada sulla fabbrica dei Filippini," *Archivio della Società Romana di Storia Patria* 90 (1967): 199. Borromini himself acknowledged that he may have surpassed the limits of what the padres found permissible: Francesco Borromini, *Opera del Cav. Francesco Boromino,* 72.

54. Designated as the *sala della ricreazione,* the ovoid space served the padres as a place of relaxed conviviality after observing the discipline of the refectory and before engaging in individual and solitary activities.

55. Baldinucci, *Notizie dei professori,* 68.

56. Borromini, *Opus Architectonicum,* 77.

57. Borromini, *Opera del Cav. Francesco Boromino,* chap. 19.

58. See Pandolfi, "Appunti sulla struttura," 108. Among the numerous designs for mantles, cartouches, and aediculas, compare, for example, Albertina, 912a. Here the canopy over the mantle dwarfs the fireplace itself and assumes a shape that compares closely with Gehry's Lewis Residence pavilions.

59. *Sir Bannister Fletcher's A History of Architecture,* ed. Richard Longstreth (London, 1996), 1529.

60. See *Karl Friedrich Schinkel, Lebenswerk: Das Architektonische Lehrbuch,* ed. Goerd Peschken (Munich and Berlin, 1979), 33.

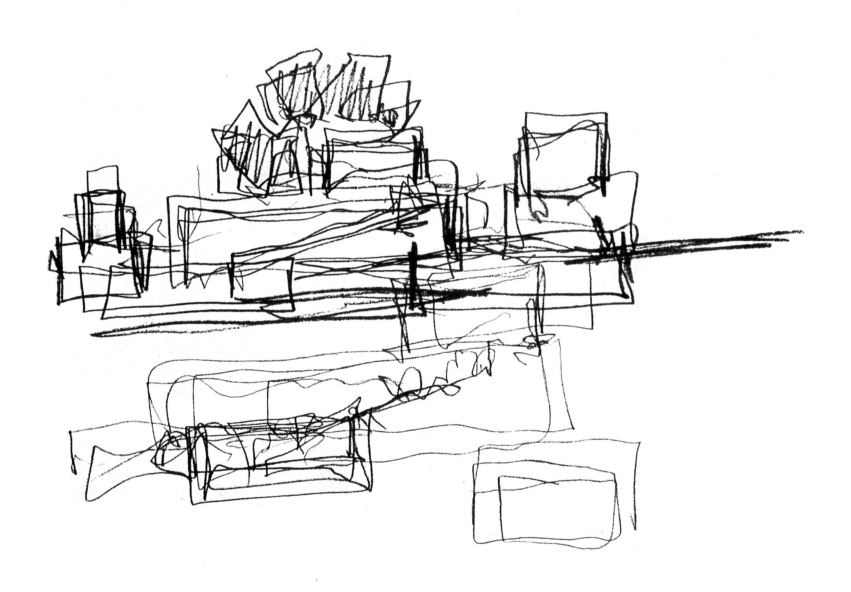

The World Turned Upside-Down:
The Tortoise Flies and the
Hare Threatens the Lion

Francesco Dal Co

In final eras, when the historical substance is exhausted and incapable of even guaranteeing the geological order of the species, there has always been a return to mythology, based on a gloomy, inexpressive sort of expectation. Theology runs aground, and theognosis takes its place; men no longer want to know anything about the gods: they want to see them.

—Ernst Jünger[1]

Kurt Schwitters,
Merzbau,
Hannover.

In a letter written in 1977 to Ernst Nündel, the Hungarian painter Lajos d'Ebneth recalls strolling on the beaches of Holland in the summer of 1926 in the company of Kurt Schwitters. D'Ebneth remembers that Schwitters carried a sack over his shoulder, stopping now and then to poke about in the sand, gathering objects left on the shore by the sea during the night. When the sack was full, they headed home. Back at the house, Schwitters deposited the booty from this "treasure hunt" in the studio, materials that could be used for the construction of a new *Merzbau*.[2]

Apart from offering some useful indications with which to put the subject of this essay into the proper perspective, this episode clarifies the sense of the *Merzbau* that Schwitters began to build from the *Merz-Säulen* in his home-studio at 15b Waldhausenstrasse in Hannover after 1919. Not only is the *Merzbau* the result of a work that is open to the unexpected, based as it is on a strict discipline that cancels the distance between intuition, construction, and representation, with a radical overlapping of casualness and rigor, but it is also a formidable metaphor for the state of contemporary art. The *Merzbau* is an endless *opera*, susceptible to repetition, determined by chance, everywhere and anywhere. The fundamental mechanism expressed lies in the declaration and display of

the infinite number of interpretations that can be extracted by the composition from the accidental quality of objects, with all the provocations this implies. The *Merzbau* is a "total" *opera*, as Hans Richter has pointed out, explaining it in the context of the progressive reduction of the meaning of art to pure representation of artistic action. At the same time, the *Merzbau* technique is part of the process that leads to the fulfillment of "art for art's sake" in the direct display of the subjectivity of the artifice, as Georg Simmel has noted.[3] Moreover, the *Merzbau* construction expresses an aspiration for a creative experience that goes beyond the diversity of genres, that applies the same technique of mixture used in the composition of Schwitters to select the challenges of the randomness of things to the various arts in order to "pass over the corpse of the object," as he asserted, but also over the boundaries of the different artistic experiences. Finally—and this is the point of greatest relevance—the way Schwitters chooses his materials, as glimpsed in the recollections of d'Eb-neth, reveals unexpected analogies with the very nature of the institution the contemporary era has selected for the celebration of the secularization of the artwork: the museum.

In fact, in the museum, the "relics" of time land casually as the objects washed up on the beach by the sea. Each of these objects challenges and nourishes the metamorphosis of art, which "derogated from eternity declines in the quotidian."[4] For this reason, and because the shipwrecks produced by time are incalculable in number and unpredictable in effect, "the museum gains ground in the same way the desert expands: it advances there where life retreats and, a pirate armed with good intentions, loots the wreckage life has left behind."[5]

The *Merzbau* of Hannover spreads, occupying the entire place where it takes form. It replaces the spatial configuration of the place with its own growth dynamic; the finiteness of the environment is replaced by the representation of incompleteness; utility is replaced by rejection of use. Moreover, it aims at reducing the distance between the material-ization of artistic conception and the intuition to zero; and it foreshortens the timing of perception: it displays the fact that giving form is an essential oper-ation—so essential that it makes the materials it uses superfluous or, more precisely, interchangeable. The technique of *enfouissement* further confuses things, confirming the analogy between the simultaneously ironic and melancholic narration interpreted by the *Merzbau* and the museum. *Wunderkammer* where the figures conserve themselves as shadows and traces, relics that the growth of their growth tends to pre-serve by concealing, the *Merzbau* makes its con-stituent elements imperceptible: the only presence it permits is the continuously evoked presence of its artifice. The work represents the modes of its making, an archive of the unmerciful murders perpetrated in its name, while the figure of its creator, Schwitters

himself, occupies the center of the labyrinth to which the construction alludes.[6]

Because this is its nature (a theme to which we will have to return), the *Merzbau* interjects, even before any critical assessment, as Schwitters claimed, the modes of development of the contemporary city and the rhythms of the life that takes place there. In the perspective of an overall evaluation of the meanings of avant-garde art, Walter Benjamin identified the relation that lies at the origin of this phenomenon, observing: "All things, in a relentless process of min-gling and contamination, lose their natural physiog-nomy, and the ambiguous takes the place of the authentic; the same is true of the city."[7] Because in the city the modes of perception follow a syncopated rhythm and are stimulated by increasingly partial, fragmentary perspectives, it becomes all the more dif-ficult to trace our way back from constantly contam-inated simulacra to authentic representations. One perceives a chaotic absence of form that nevertheless puts the observer in direct contact with the seething aspects of frenetic productivity, the only real image offered by the contemporary city. Cities, Ernst Jünger believes, "with their tangle of architectures and their innovations that completely transform their visage every ten years, are gigantic workshops of form; but precisely because they are cities, they have no form themselves. They have no style, unless we can define anarchy as a particular type of style. Today there are two criteria of judgment, regarding cities: we can assess either their quality as a museum, or their qual-ity as a hotbed of new ideas."[8]

It is no coincidence that since the period of the historical avant-gardes an essential component of contemporary art has been surrealistically operating in two different directions. On the one hand, it sal-vages (from the wreckage) what has been repressed, worn out, utilized, random elements to be reinserted in the cyclical pattern of novelty, material for lan-guages that embrace their own parodies. On the other, it claims that action, once things have been reduced "to image, stripped of all symbolism, mere facts stripped of any justification," is the sole realm of artistic value and judgment. Creation is expressed as desire for form (once again, both ironic and melan-cholic, simultaneously) and renunciation of content; it works to extract the fantastic from the banal, because, to paraphrase the way Roy Lichtenstein put it decades after the first experiments of Schwitters, "Pop Art is based, first of all, on the use of things that are usually scorned."[9]

In performance art the mixture of artistic genres completes this process. The compassionate archaeology applied to everyday life by dada evolves into the "gag art" described by Harold Rosenberg. In performance art the presence of the artist cancels out the difference between the temporal and visual components of the work while the pace of judgment is accelerated, and every reflection on meaning is transformed into a pure instant of reaction. This is another way for art to adapt to, and participate in, the modes of production of the "immense hotbed of forms" the contemporary city has become.

Just as in the factory or the workshop one must wear the proper apparel for the job to be done, so it is in performance art. The mask, explicit or allusive, is used to underline the factual character of the experience and the symbolic-captional presence of the artist in the scenario. When Frank Gehry played the part of Frankie P. Toronto in the performance *Il Corso del Coltello* (*The Course of the Knife*) in Venice in 1985, he designed his own costume, a curious unconscious revisitation of the engravings by Benigno Bossi of the *Mascarade à la Grècque* of Ennemond-Alexandre Petitot (1771).[10]

This coincidence has certain telling overtones. The knife that Frankie P. Toronto "maneuvers" amid the Venetian canals has a clear meaning: it refers to the way the architect, like the artist, must operate by cutting the ties to tradition, the ties that prevent architecture from working in the area of pure expression rather than awareness of the past (or, in other words, as in the epigraph above, that prevent it from adapting to the needs of a world that wants only to see, not to know). But can this claim—we may logically ask, since this is an instructive paradox—be possible without the many precedents that support it, including the *Mascarade* of Petitot, which records the corrosive insinuation of parody in an analogous, enlightened program of renewal of architectural language?

The features of the mask do not express only irony regarding history. The action of Frankie P. Toronto also has a programmatic meaning. Not by chance, Gehry takes advantage of another aspect of performance art, emphasizing the fact that his participation in the "recital" of *Il Corso del Coltello* corresponds to the composition of a sort of manifesto. Because in performance art every situation tends to assign a leading role to the body, the movements of Frankie P. Toronto allude to the need to recognize the freedom of expression the erotic-sensual component must be granted when the architect lets himself be taken up in the flow of things, rejecting distrustfully the crutches history may provide (and here it is interesting to recall that among the works of Schwitters before the *Merzbau* there is one entitled *Kathedrale des erotischen Elends* [*KdeE*]). The sensual, tactile pleasure Gehry seems to experience as he meets the challenges of "the demon of unexpected combinations," in fact, reveals the distance between his works (especially the more recent ones) and the facile, frigid regressions cultivated by contemporary architecture, sheltering him against the temptation to exploit "the past as a storeroom of props with which to decorate our cell."[11]

To renew the sense of the mutable after immersion in its flux (*le voluptuosisme*, to use an expression of Baudelaire, is, however, a danger that hovers over the most recent results of Gehry's research), to challenge the brazen exhibitionism of nostalgia, practicing a sort of surreal archaeology of the "too well-known": this is the program Gehry presents by participating in

La Mariée à la Grecque

Frank Gehry, sketch of costume for Frankie P. Toronto for *Il Corso del Coltello*, Venice Biennale, 1985; Ennemond-Alexandre Petitot, la Madame à la Grècque, for *Mascarade à la Grècque*, 1771.

Il Corso del Coltello.[12] He reaches this conclusion as a result of a dual experience.

Those who have discussed Gehry's work, and Gehry himself, have paid so much attention to the theme of his relationships with artists, from the late 1960s to the present, that it would be superfluous to examine this theme in any detail today. Donald Judd, Ron Davis, Larry Bell, Ed Moses, Gordon Matta-Clark, Robert Rauschenberg, Carl Andre, and, above all, Claes Oldenburg and Richard Serra are the names that most frequently appear in the writings and interviews. As has been demonstrated, there is little doubt that these relationships have had an important influence on his work.[13] Even this sketchy list of names demonstrates the diversity of the experiences with which Gehry has come into contact; and it says something about the way he looks at the different projects in contemporary art, observing them with the same disenchanted gaze with which he selects the "materials" that, for one reason or another, he uses for his works of architecture.

Taking Gehry's explanations, which are not always very thorough, at face value, we must admit that when he says he has learned, from Picasso, that "any idea can be good and can be utilized," he is providing us with a convincing elucidation of the way he has assimilated contemporary experiences in American art. Naturally such a purely utilitarian attitude must also be sustained by more precise considerations. And it should not be difficult, for those who wish to venture into this field of study, to identify which aspects of the work of the artists listed above have been selected, utilized, or reworked by Gehry. There are obvious parallels, for example, between the experimentation of Larry Bell on the chromatic cohesion of surfaces and the research conducted by Gehry for the facing and cladding of his architecture: how can we avoid thinking of the sculptures of Bell and Judd, for example, when we look at the facade on the freeway of the Team Disneyland Administration Building (1987–95) in Anaheim? In like manner, since the end of the 1970s, there have been moments of dialogue between the works of the architect and those of Oldenburg so dense as to appear to be, if not true citations, at least evident transmigrations of images.[14] Oldenburg's nonchalant metaphors suggest, for

Gehry, a compositional strategy that he refines, definitively, beginning in the mid-1980s. This strategy translates into architectural "forgeries" that make use of gratuitous, interchangeable forms, unstable and continuously revolutionized, that aim to astonish and, in so doing, to prolong the effect by means of the display of unexpected combinations.

To better understand this aspect of Gehry's work (the consequence, as we have said, of the first of the two premises behind his program), we must first clarify what might be called its "operative" implications.

Regarding the experiences of the artists close to him, Gehry's curiosity is not ingenuous, and in some ways it is even aggressive. The fact that he is "influenced" is not a sign of a passive, receptive character. His use of the suggestions provided by contemporary art is a necessary part of his program of the redefinition of the nature and utilization of the language of architecture, a program described by Kurt Forster in his analysis of the behavior of Frankie P. Toronto in *Il Corso del Coltello*. Observing the activities of his favorite artists (and assimilating their procedures), Gehry understands that it is possible to "occupy," with architecture, the spaces that art is no longer able to dominate, assigning to architectural design the task of taking the experiments of the historical avant-gardes to their extreme consequences. His aim, in fact, is to establish a new way of using architecture, in a certain sense updating the techniques developed by the dada movement. This leads to significant innovations in professional and design practice, because this program can be realized only when the constructed work is assigned the task of establishing a relationship not with a public of users, but with an audience of spectators. In this way architecture tends to mutate, to change its nature, eschewing usage and becoming entertainment.

Although it has never been formulated in an explicit manner, this program is anything but ambiguous or undeclared. This can be seen, interestingly enough, in the more or less consequential reactions of the artists thought by many to have inspired the program. Consider, for example, the words of Richard Serra, one of the artists closest to Gehry, in defense of the traditional differences between art forms in an explicit reference to the work of architects: "I don't think there is any possibility for architecture to be a work of art," says Serra. "I've always thought that art was non-functional and useless. Architecture serves needs which are specifically functional and useful. Therefore architecture as a work of art is a contradiction in terms . . . I would hope that architects could accept the fact that they are architects and *useful* as architects, and could stop flirting with the notion of being both artist *and* architect."[15]

The evolution of Gehry's architecture over the last twenty-five years has gone well beyond the sort of flirtation described by Serra; when Gehry has directly or indirectly been urged to move in the direction of moderation, he has always replied in polemical tones. And his replies hinge precisely on the intrinsic contradiction revealed in the work of artists like Serra. The mutations undergone by the "symbolic values," Serra asserts, have obliged sculpture to "come out of the galleries and down from its pedestal" in pursuit of a new audience, of new forms of communication and expression.[16] But the fact that "the world is full of advertising posters, and we get bored if they are not changed on a weekly basis"[17] is not "only a tragedy for modern architecture." When art abandons its sheltered enclaves and enters *this* world, as John Cage puts it, its aim coinciding with the production of "objects that are facts and not symbols," whose appearance contains the legacy of chaos, all distinctions among artistic genres fall by the wayside. And classifications based on the utility of "objects" also become useless at the point when the objects, as Schwitters had envisioned, proclaim that their only justification "is to give form."[18]

If this is the motivation that pushes the work of Gehry to still loftier heights, it is curious to note just how pragmatic and apparently reductive are the justifications he tends to offer. But once again, and to get to the second of the above-mentioned premises behind his architectural program, Gehry's explanations, apart from their anecdotal style, shed real light on an eloquent, paradoxical aspect of his work.

The project that first attracted the attention of the California art scene and brought Gehry international fame was the Danziger Studio and Residence in Hollywood (1964–65). Seen in relation to the design for an office complex that was to have been built on North Rodeo Drive in Beverly Hills (1964), the work for Louis Danziger reveals a design approach and intentions that, at first glance, seem to have little in common with the artistic experiences and techniques discussed above.

The small house/studio is an assemblage of simple geometric forms, an elementary game of interlocking parallelepipeds, "fairly tidy-minded mainstream modern."[19] Introverted, closed, the house seems to reject programmatically any contamination with the (truly chaotic) activities of the important Los Angeles artery where it is located. Nevertheless, in spite of its apparent rigor, underlined by the anonymous color of the exterior (in contrast with the rainbow of other facades along Melrose Boulevard), Gehry's construction is not extraneous to the characteristics of its environment, in spite of the fact that Reyner Banham went so far as to perceive a vague Parisian atmosphere in its interiors. The Danziger Studio and Residence is actually the result of a hermetic attempt at stylization of the commonplace (that is, a revisitation of the typical). The design attempts to abolish, using the language described by Banham, all that noisily disguises the banal functional conformism of the nearby constructions (the vulgar ingenuousness of the billboards and the shop windows, the anarchy of the facades at the mercy of the confusion of consumption, and so forth, are ephemeral masks for uniformly utilitarian buildings). Observing the house in this light, we can see that it is the result of an operation of selection based on a reductionist mental attitude—which has nothing to do with any minimalistic inclinations. On close examination, this is a negative collage, still concerned with the transparency of the form with respect to the content, but the material utilized is that of the impoverished scenario it reflects. The Danziger design attributes a style to the material it uses, similar (if not identical) to the paltry things in which the misery of the surrounding situation is reflected. The procedure thus set in motion by Gehry is the direct predecessor of the experiments that were to lead to his most prestigious works of the 1980s. Building for Louis Danziger, he had the possibility of making use of the "modernist" language in a free manner, coherent and apparently without compromises. But having reached this point, he understood intuitively that that language (that style) was the product of the same necessities and the same state of affairs he wanted to challenge, giving form to an elite space for a sheltered life far from the aggressive surroudings of a world without quality. In this way, he found himself in the position to grasp fully one of the most disturbing (and productive) paradoxes expressed by contemporary architecture: language, when its aim is that of abolishing appearances, must renounce expression.

The small construction on Melrose Boulevard represents the first significant chapter in Gehry's career. When he began the project, his office had been operating for just two years. His training, after difficult formative years clearly described by Thomas Hines,[20] followed a pattern of tried and true phases. He attended the University of Southern California; he came into contact with important personalities, like Raphael Soriano and Garrett Eckbo, with the scene that revolved around Schindler and Neutra, John Entenza, Charles Eames, Julius Shulman. After earning his degree in 1954, he worked for Victor Gruen, during the years in which the office was working on the design of a series of innovative shopping centers. This experience was beneficial for his future, similar assignments, such as those of one of his most assiduous clients, the Rouse Corporation (Santa Monica Place, 1972–80, for instance). In 1956 he studied urban planning at Harvard, a must for any serious architect. But the period in Cambridge was disappointing, and by 1957 Gehry was already back in Los Angeles, where he continued working with Gruen. After a trip to Europe, he opened his own office.

The first works built by the firm bear the mark of eclectic indecision: Frank Lloyd Wright and Raphael Soriano, Gregory Ain, and, above all, Harwell Hamilton Harris are the influences evident in the Steeves Residence (1958–59), the most important work designed and built before 1964. But the Danziger Studio and Residence is already removed from the refined experimentation of Soriano, Ain, and Harris, and, in particular, from Eames's abstract, elegant, overstated pursuit of constructive perfection. Starting with the lessons learned from these architects, Gehry matured in his professional practice, acquiring that solid experiential base that was to prompt Banham to describe him as "just like an old Jewish poppa who builds things as best he can . . . as to building things, he certainly knows all that stuff."[21] Moreover, there are valid reasons to conclude that one of the themes on which Gehry began to work with increased continuity, from the late 1960s on, was based precisely on a critical reevaluation of the experiences of the most radical Californian architects of the preceding generation.

With the Merriweather-Post Pavilion in Columbia, Maryland (1966–67), the O'Neill Hay Barn at San Juan Capistrano (1968), and, above all, the Davis Studio and Residence in Malibu (1968–72), Gehry came to grips with a problem he had not considered in the Danziger design. The different typologies and locations of these four projects certainly played a role, but it is evident that these factors cannot suffice to explain the new design strategy Gehry was developing. The houses, in particular, of Soriano, Ellwood, Eames, Harris, and Neutra, beginning in the prewar era, were lucid manifestations of a concept of construction based on a rigorous taxonomy of parts. The structures designed by these architects are the result of a rational logic that finds its highest expression in the virtuoso display of the lightness, the essentialness, and the adaptability of the frames. The coverings become transparent panels or mere screens. The lightness of the structural grilles and facings ensures permeability (even if only in visual terms) between the indoors and the outdoors. This lightness represents the dialectical mediation, so to speak, that in spite of the diversity of the performance and the nature of the construction elements employed reunites in immateriality *Kernform* (formal structure) and *Kunstform* (artistic structure), as Carl Bötticher taught.[22] As a result, these works seem to bypass the distinction made by Gottfried Semper between *Bekleidung* (covering) and *Verkleidung* (disguise).[23] The dialectic among the materials such architects used and the expression of the functions leads to the gradual elimination of the formal specificity of the covering or the facing, whose role becomes subordinate to that of the structure. Because the facing components are selected and used, above all, in order to make function evident, "utility and functional aims become the fundamental concepts of architectonic creation."[24]

Gehry pays a sort of retroactive homage to these

experiences in his facade for the "Strada Novissima" exhibition at the 1980 Venice Biennale. The Davis project, in fact, had already marked a new phase in his research. The exterior, as is evident in the preliminary sketches for the project, which also reveal a new approach to drawing, is seen as a continuous skin. On the non-orthogonal planes of this surface, the openings delineate a curious, amused mixture of traditional and non-traditional profiles, while the inclined roof is treated as if it were an elevation. The cryptic character of the facings is contrasted—as a result of a compositional technique that from this point on becomes a part of Gehry's repertoire—by a series of internal elevations that gives rise to a surprising play of transferences and slippages; the configuration of these nervous (neurotic?) concatenations liquidates the pursuit of spatial fluidity theorized by Rudolf Schindler. And the volumes interlock with one another vertically, while horizontally they aggregate freely, following the rotational movement the architect seems to have imposed on the entire composition. It is evident that here we are beyond any concerns of an organic-functionalist nature; this detachment is accompanied by a gesture-based compositional approach made possible by the recognition/acceptance of the independent expressive value of the facings.

The conception of the interior of the Davis Studio and Residence, where any impression of continuity is thwarted by the throng of sculptural intrusions, foreshadows the solution Gehry uses for the layout of a building on a very different scale, in a very different situation: Santa Monica Place. And there is a coincidence here that is worth mentioning: the project was begun the same year—1972—as the publication, in New York, of the work of the Five Architects (Peter Eisenman, Michael Graves, Charles Gwathmey, John Hejduk, Richard Meier), discussed during a seminar held at the Museum of Modern Art in 1969.

The similarities between the works of the New York Five and the work by Gehry (and others of the period) are just as evident as the differences. The language employed (simplifying as far as is permissible the analysis of the works of the Five) comes from similar matrices, and the design techniques tend to resemble one another. The similarities are even more evident if we compare, in particular, the designs of Eisenman and Hejduk with those of Gehry, because all three make use of the rotation of the axes in order to emphasize the formal independence of the structural cage—a procedure particularly evident in both House III by Eisenman and Santa Monica Place. But these affinities vanish when we look beneath the surface of the experiences. There is no trace, for example, in Gehry's work of the rarefied, selective, formalistic use of linguistic instruments that is a common platform of research for the New York architects, whose "objects" display a poetics of nostalgia not immune to evocative excess.[25]

Nor can we observe, in Gehry's work, the radical pursuit of an elegance free of contaminations, such as that which distinguishes the projects presented in the catalog-volume *Five Architects*. Instead, linguistic contamination and studied disdain are devices the Californian architect was already employing, with nonchalance.

The shopping center in Santa Monica, in fact, is a sort of theoretical presentation of how to represent the independence of the structure from the skin and a demonstration (in two versions) of the potential of this division. Gehry designs the entrance in correspondence to the main axis of the building (shifted with respect to the "natural" axis of the lot), excavating it, making it emerge "in negative" from the volume. The resulting facade is composed of a fragmented collage, using different bits and pieces left over from the underlying spatial grid, which is thus subjected to an arbitrary metamorphosis that changes its meaning, while openly declaring the freedom of the design choices thus displayed.

In contrast with the procedure used for the Danziger house, here the language is "dirtied" and displayed in all its impurity, even with a will to achieve cacophony. This experiment, significantly enough, formed the basis for a compositional technique that Gehry has continued to refine over the years, with the aim of making his works spectacular and surprising. Many of his designs are based on effects of alienation or awe created at the entrances or in nearby portions of the facades, those places where it is most natural, and easiest, to establish a dialogue between the architecture and its users. For this reason,

Gehry often inserts, excavates, or extracts, even from the most banal elevations, veritable "machines" that astonish and disorient the visitor. The lobbies of his buildings, explosions of arbitrary gestures and fantasy, full of improbable, unexpected, gratuitous material elements, are designed to shock and entice, transforming users or visitors into spectators.

Gehry resorts to this device no matter what constructive materials or language he is using, as can be seen even in a rapid overview of his works, with all their differences. The gigantic portico at the entrance to the Herman Miller Western Regional Facility in Rocklin, California (1985–89), the binoculars designed by Claes Oldenburg and Coosje van Bruggen as the portal for the Chiat/Day Building in Venice (1985–91), the "awnings" designed for the Children's Museum in Boston (1992–96) or for the Disney Community Ice Center in Anaheim (1993), the "floral" outcroppings invented for the first versions of the project for the museum grouping in Berlin (1994–97), and the cafeteria in the Condé Nast tower in New York (1997–) are but a few examples of the different effects Gehry has managed to achieve using the same strategy. To grasp the origin and explain the overall significance of this approach, we can turn to the considerations made by Mikhail Bachtin on the relationship between play and art, concluding with the observation "The aesthetic moment is not necessarily a prelude to play; it is brought there only by a spectator who actively contemplates."[26]

To return to Santa Monica Place, we should note the different treatment Gehry applies to the parking-garage volume beside the shopping mall. Here the facing is a mere veil wrapping an anonymous prestressed-concrete spatial grid. Attached to a secondary structure in iron, the metal screen wrapper resembles a transparent fabric upon which full-height letters display the message "Santa Monica." Even in such a particular context, this solution (which recurs in many of his subsequent works, on different scales and with different functions) demonstrates how Gehry's way of working leads him unconsciously to come to grips with one of the fundamental principles of modern architecture. It is easy to see that the way the garage has been covered offers a natural reinterpreta-

Disney Community Ice Center, Anaheim, California, 1993. Model of first scheme.

tion of the precept Gottfried Semper deduces from his considerations on the nature of facings, beginning with an analysis of the most ancient examples of the art of building. "The wall (*Wand*)," Semper writes, "should never be permitted to lose its original meaning as a spatial enclosure by what is represented on it; it is always advisable when painting walls to remain mindful of the carpet as the earliest spatial enclosure. Exceptions can be made in such cases where the spatial enclosure exists materially but not in the idea."[27] As Harry F. Mallgrave asserts: "For Semper the wall and (by spatial extension) architecture gain their essential artistic meaning through the denial of their material basis"—a denial that, in the case of Santa Monica Place, involves both linguistic and constructive elements.[28]

This experience opened up new perspectives for Gehry's work, but the issues addressed confirm the basic hypothesis on which the observations in this essay are centered: the admission (in borrowed words) that "art does not undergo linear progress, but only, always new vertical leaps. Only artistic techniques and media give the impression of progress. Actually, what is possible is only mutation. And the changes that result from new works instruct us for new perceptions, new emotions, a new awareness."[29]

In Gehry's "reformulation," Semper's principle implies the presentation of the mutable as something permanent, although the textile metaphor expressed by the wall makes use of the humble, mechanical, homogeneous consistency of a metal screen. The architecture, in any case, takes on a strong character as an object: it offers images without communicating values, it celebrates (as we said when speaking of the *Merzbau* of Schwitters) the supremacy of making over the importance and the specificity of material.

Gehry's intense professional activity in the mid-1970s enabled him to understand that this is an obligatory path. The work gave him the opportunity to realize that the decadence of contemporary building practice does not allow the architect to express himself with refined, elegant construction solutions, as was still possible for the architects of the previous generation. Given this state of things, he reacts by calling on the contributions of artists, involving them in the work in order to compensate for the mediocrity of the constructive solutions he is forced to employ: one good example of this is the Lewis Residence in Lyndhurst (1989–95), which also demonstrates the sort of excesses to which this practice can lead. At the same time, Gehry continued with his critique of the apparatus of values that prevents comprehension of just how radical the changes are that have transformed the meaning of works of architecture in an era in which "the historical substance appears to be exhausted," a state of affairs Gehry sees reflected in the impoverished quality of everyday life, caused by the regression of constructive skills and expertise.

From this point of view, the furniture in corrugated cardboard he designed toward the end of the 1960s, Easy Edges, still contains the signs of an unresolved ambiguity. In choosing his material, Gehry wants to astonish, and to point an accusing finger at the obtuse clichés that limit the use of things. But at the same time, in contrast with what happened with the cardboard furniture of the second generation, Experimental Edges, which depicts utilization and consumption, he sets a serious limit on freedom of experimentation, giving the first family of chairs forms that evoke the recognized values of continuity and tradition.[30] What counts is the way he makes sarcastic use of the material, because the irony of the photograph that illustrates the surprising strength of the cardboard chairs—immortalizing them as they bear the weight of an automobile—demonstrates how even the most banal things can become a part of the domain from which architecture can select its raw materials.

The game begins with the acceptance of the given possibilities; it is up to the architect to assign them an aesthetic role, gathering them into the *body* that is the materialization of his efforts. At the level of design, this principle is applied and developed in the works that precede the start of the construction in 1977 of Gehry's own house in Santa Monica, both a "manifesto" and an ingenious operation of self-promotion, summing up the research conducted and setting the stage for the work of the decade to come (at least up until the monumental works at its conclusion).

Among the many critics who have discussed the Gehry house, Rosemarie Haag Bletter has underlined the fact that the construction responds to a "need for continually changing expression," as occurs in the *Merzbau* of Hannover by Kurt Schwitters.[31] The process of growth represented by both the *Merzbau* and the Gehry house takes place in opposing spatial conditions, but beginning with a similar situation. The *Merzbau* occupies, overflows, and overwhelms an entire interior; the additions Gehry designs for his house enclose a volume (*wrapping* it, to go back to one of Semper's concepts). But both the dwelling Schwitters overwhelms with his construction and the house Gehry transforms, adapting it to his needs, are similar expressions of anonymous middle class housing, of an everyday life filled with empty values, tied to the most banal clichés. Both are "proper" houses.[32]

Easy Edges Cardboard Furniture, 1969–73.

To unmask the cliché of the typical middle-class house by disguising it: this is Gehry's objective, as he operates, according to his claim, in order to "erase its iconic significance." There is a resemblance to all the other houses containing the DNA of the American suburb, where a Pavlovian process of imitation runs amok leading to grotesque embodiments of frustrated ambitions, in which each detail is a pseudo-detail, the materials pseudo-materials, each form a pseudo-form. Gehry's program is neither one of exhibition

Gehry Residence, Santa Monica, California, 1977–78.

nor one of moralizing education of the neighbors. Anything but: "the neighbors," as such, are a necessary component for the success of Gehry's operation. They are the first portion of the audience he addresses; they represent the *other* required for a display of diversity.

No less than in the *Merzbau*, the Gehry house is the result of an operation of autobiographical spectacularization. It is no coincidence that the construction continues for years, without any sign of reaching a conclusion. It is a performance, intended to continue for a lifetime, because this work of architecture materializes the aesthetic identity between the architect and its existence.[33] Moreover, as the expression of autobiographical overlapping, the house represents the sublimation of the mechanism that leads to the process of transformation of the user into an audience, a mechanism that, to use an expression borrowed from literary criticism, is presented here in the "personal identification between the hero (the protagonist of the story) and the author,"[34] or between

the architect and the client. The client, according to the many statements made by Gehry on this subject, is the main interlocutor of the architect, because the client is the preferred spectator, the "nucleus" around which the mass of the audience at which the architecture aims takes form. In this sense the client is the "father" of the work, as is claimed by a long tradition that, already in the mid-1400s, was codified in the treatise of Filarete (in which the architect, however, is spoken of as a "mother").[35] The two figures tend to coincide in the autobiographical narrative of the Gehry house. This identity leads to the hermaphroditic nature that the house shares with the *Merzbau*, and to the syncretism that characterized both constructions, although Gehry's work reveals a clearer propensity for heterogeneity.

The materials Gehry uses are the most various, traditional, banal, modest, and facile, those most widely used in the anonymous, miserable constructions that clutter American cities. But in the house at Santa Monica wood and corrugated sheet metal, metal screening and glass give life to a series of figures whose real nature is indistinguishable from their functional nature, while the openings are a game of incisions of different depths shaped without any apparent justification. The multimaterial volumes follow an arhythmic movement of contraction and dilation; the whole appears fragile, temporary, thanks to a compositional technique that alternates the use of the scalpel with that of glue for the creation of a sarcastic "monument to Americanism." Each and every representation of qualities of stability, completeness, and decorum traditionally flaunted in American housing is excluded: the *other*, which without differentiation is utilized in the anonymous utilitarian constructions of the city, becomes part of the panorama of a subverted domesticity. Inside this oxymoron-filled construction, the spaces are not organized according to a functional hierarchy; the interlocking rooms and interruptions are designed to stun, while encouraging a sense of voyeuristic pleasure.

Were this autobiographical construction not so refined, we would be tempted to imagine that it is the product of the activity of a mentality (but not a mind) that is prelogical, primitive, infantile, but not disorderly, capable of grasping reality only as "thing" or "material" (or, better, as a "property of things") The precise object-oriented character of the forms Gehry employs for his house and for other residential projects in the late 1970s and early 1980s is clear evidence of the distance that separates these works, at the level of program and ideology, from the research conducted by the German expressionist architects, to which they are often compared. Although the drawings of Hans Scharoun, Hermann Finsterlin, Wenzel Hablik, and, above all, Carl Krayl often display surprising resemblances to those of Gehry, the similarities are limited to the area of graphic expression.[36]

Making use of the formal repertoire developed in the Santa Monica house, with respect to the vernacular, the spontaneous, or the picturesque, Gehry also carries out an operation that is the opposite (and implicitly critical) of the one effected a few years earlier by Robert Venturi. Whereas Venturi, in his writings and designs, proclaimed a sort of sanctification of the ambiguity and contradictions of the trivial, raising these values to the level of poetic principles, Gehry identifies the ordinary with everyday life, from which he gathers, "at random," the materials of his constructions.[37] This is an operation very similar to Oldenburg's, attempting to give architectonic meaning to the banal. But as such, the operation runs the risk of redundancy; the architectural works that are its expression face the danger of a short-circuit effect, which threatens not only the Gehry house but also all of his other, more extreme experiments. As Walter Benjamin has pointed out, *redundancy* is the "foundation," the "value" of the petit bourgeois conception of the *intérieur* and of furnishings. When disdain is so openly flaunted, as in the case of the Gehry house, it runs the risk of becoming a parody of itself, of becoming, in the sense of the term used by Benjamin, redundant, bringing architecture back to the starting point, coming full circle. The line of demarcation between expression and redundancy, in this circle, is the fine line between the work that is a mere production of form and the work that contains something more, communicating, admonishing, educating. This fine line can be compared to the borderline of the territory of kitsch, where the decisive factor is the desire to "illustrate the world not 'as it is' but 'as we wish it were or fear it to be.' "[38] After all, isn't kitsch

"the ultimate mask of the banal," the "sublime of the obvious"? And doesn't novelty hide in the nooks and crannies that are formed when the circles of the return to the past, rather than overlapping precisely, slip apart and intersect? And to come "face to face" with the new, don't we need to decide to try to represent what is hidden between the lines?

Gehry's little stories occupy spaces of this type, and it is here that his work takes form. The gaps and intervals attract him, irresistibly: just observe the house in Santa Monica. Discontinuities make it possible to trace back to the phenomenology of the void, and the possibilities the void offers to architecture define the theme he repeatedly investigates, after the mid-1970s, in the pavilions for Shoreline Aquatic Park in Long Beach, California (1975), and, even more clearly, in the Cabrillo Marine Museum in San Pedro, California (1977–79).[39] To give form to the pauses, to ransom formally the functional voids contained in every object, Gehry makes use, above all, of iron screen. Attached to slender metal structures, this material allows him to create virtual, imaginative spaces that contain nothing and protect nothing. They are metaphors—in three dimensions—for those formless, residual lots of land protected by flimsy chain link fences, which can still be seen everywhere in American cities, an image of the squalor of the void. This urban metaphor, in turn, is incorporated into the dwellings Gehry builds or designs at the end of the 1970s, occupying skimpy, anonymous lots. The houses built in Venice, the Spiller Residence (1978–79) and the Norton Residence (1982–84), and the Indiana Avenue Houses in Oakwood (1979–81), inhabited by three artists, are good examples, demonstrating how the work of transformation of his own house takes on the character of a sort of laboratory. And so it is no coincidence that these works are positioned along that fine line of demarcation described above.

The three house-studios on Indiana Avenue, in fact, are three refined, controlled, elegant *boîtes à miracles*. They are modeled in keeping with minimal decisions, of incisions and intelligent subtractions, a free play of deformations that permits the internal spaces to display a complexity that would appear unthinkable given the modest size of the volumes.

Like vessels full of water over which we can bend to watch the goldfish inside, they seem to have been drawn by a hand that wants to imitate a child's imagination, on paper. In comparison, the Norton Residence, whose oceanfront facade seems to be winking at some very improbable "local genius," is a stylistic exercise.

The Norton project, like the Gehry Residence, is a story. It has two contrasting elevations, one redundant (facing the beach), the other obvious (facing the street)—once again, therefore, a montage of opposites, curiously involving, as in the case of the restructuring of the Wosk Residence in Beverly Hills (1981–84), "homages" to Luis Barragán. Architecture as a form of narration implies going beyond typological conventions and, at the same time, abandoning the pursuit of a style.[40] Gehry's way of narrating often (as is vividly demonstrated in the sketches for the Tract House of 1982) takes on "a childlike bearing: in the manner in which men observe the child, and imitate him" we might say, borrowing a phrase from Hofmannsthal.

The monumental cadences of the Schnabel Residence in Brentwood (1986–89) and the Sirmai-Peterson House in Thousand Oaks (1983–88) allow us only partially to appreciate this characteristic of Gehry's work. The grand Brentwood villa is too busy trying to achieve an effect; the facing of the house at Thousand Oaks tends, excessively, to identify with a refined, homogeneous patina. Neither of these two renowned works can provide us with meaningful data with which to comprehend the formal implications of the narrative vein that appears with increasing clarity in Gehry's works beginning in the 1980s.

For this purpose, it is more productive to focus on the first designs for the house for a film director in Santa Monica (1980–81), the Lewis Residence, and, above all, the Winton Guest House in Wayzata, Minnesota (1982–87). In the latter example, the premises developed in the Gehry Residence in Santa Monica are taken to their logical conclusion. Naturally, as in the other examples cited, the house is based on a plan composed of irregular geometric figures grouped around a slightly deformed central nucleus. The entire composition revolves around this theme: the deformation is reworked in a surprising number of varia-

tions, involving the corners, the axes of communication, the openings, and the enclosures of the rooms. The same approach is applied vertically; in spite of the small size of the five volumes, placed one against the others, they offer a tangible demonstration of the instability of geometry as a basis for compositional logic. Furthermore, the volumes, scattered in space and shifted with respect to the axes of the layout, are grouped around a precariously symbolic form: a truncated pyramid with a vaguely square base, an out-of-scale skylight space. Each of the volumes has a specific role to play in the montage: a parallelepiped with

F. Gehry, sketch of Luis Barragán's Purísimo Corazón de María Convent in Mexico City, 1981 (?); Frank and Alejo Gehry, drawings, 1981 (?).

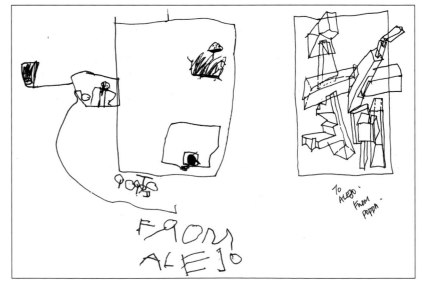

an enclosure featuring abstract geometric decoration; a chopped pyramid that brashly declares its function; a metal cube resting on a column; a "cabin" that seems to come straight out of a drawing by Oldenburg; a room with a pitched roof that looks like something from a photographic plate from the 1800s. Each object has its own covering; the enclosures are formed by a series of "different carpets." One has the impression of watching a *ballet mécanique* with a strenuous rhythm in which five actors seem to be concentrating on ignoring the language of the others. Actually, they are merely instruments utilized to produce a coordinated effect; they are players, assigned the task of making perceptible the dualism of an aesthetic experience, an experience that attracts and repels, involves and alienates, an experience that sub-

Winton Guest House, Wayzata, Minnesota, 1982–87.

jects the audience to the sensations caused by a rapid leap from the impressions produced by abstraction to those produced by empathy, as occurs, although in different ways, in all of Gehry's constructions,[41] including the Guggenheim Museum in Bilbao (1991–97), which is the most explicit demonstration of this dynamic.

It is clear that these works are a representation of the outcome of the conflict between (rhythmical) forms of cyclical symmetry and (centripetal) forms of axial symmetry that Gehry subjects to preliminary variations in his very personal un-isotropic sketches. The houses we have discussed, seen as "groupings of pavilions," make no use of any one of these forms of symmetry: they are examples of the dynamic of the

clash between the forms of symmetry. If we look at the idea of style in the most reductive sense,[42] it becomes clear that the continuous breaking of the rules of symmetry is a part of Gehry's critique of the conventional view that style should be one of the institutional objectives of architecture.

On the other hand, recognition of the connection between style and equilibrium leads to the attribution of decisive values for the expression of characteristics of unity and completeness in architecture, of which there is no trace in the compositions of Gehry. We have seen, in fact, how his narratives tend to extend outward in time and space, employing strategems whose premises are now clear to us. These *coups de main*, at the expense of the values of style, make nonchalant use of the ancient principle *ludica seriis miscere* and take on the form of veritable episodes of "kitchen humor," for which literature offers an abundance of examples. The *Küchenhumor* genre, in which Oldenburg excels, is evident in many of the works of Gehry. The Lewis Residence is a good example, as are the designs for a skyscraper "that holds a newspaper" (the project developed for the Progressive Corporation Headquarters in Cleveland, 1986–91), a fish used as a "prison" ("Folly: The Prison Project" of 1983), and a tower at One Times Square in New York (1997) shaped by using the technologies of pop concerts, giant screens, and advertising supergraphics, an enclosure that wraps the structure in the way Christo does (although Gehry avoids a "composed" quality). Like a *Merz-Säule*, the famous triangular skyscraper in Times Square, remodeled by Gehry, has the appearance of a totem pole on which any type of information or message may be broadcast. Here the architecture coincides with the narrative modes that define its form, a form that is necessarily unstable given the mutable nature of the technological effects that permit infinite variations. Returning, on a conceptual plane, to the experience of the design of the Guggenheim Museum in Bilbao, the wrapper Gehry creates for the tower in Times Square makes the only permissible use of spectacle. The architecture coincides with the flow of formal metamorphoses that follow the very rapid rhythms of the sequence of information projected on the cloud of opaque material that enfolds the building.

The Schnabel, Norton, Spiller, and Familian houses also appear to have been designed by a spinner of yarns. They are "incomplete enumerations," endlessly extensible lists of objects and figures. These houses, like the project for Times Square, are "overturned architectures," contemporary versions of the Latin *adynata* (*similitudo impossibilium*), which were the beginning, in the Middle Ages, of the configuration of the topos of the "world turned upside-down": "What must the swans do, when the crows sing such a song, and the parrots imitate the Muses?"[43]

The upside-down world takes form, in these yarns, through concatenations of metamorphoses that cancel out the identities usually attributed to architectonic configurations and are free of the limitations of typological categories. There is a definitive blurring of the borders and margins of the usual concepts of type and genre, truth and illusion, real and unreal, meaning and value, dream and life experience. The images in the compositions are employed as interrupted metaphors. It is no coincidence that the project for Camp Good Times in the Santa Monica Mountains (1984–85), again the result of a collaboration of Gehry, Oldenburg, and van Bruggen, seems to imitate the way in which all kinds of different things are grouped in the display cases of the artist's studio in New York; greatly enlarged, these concrete objects give form, in keeping with the dictates of the metaphor, to the abstract notion of heterogeneity.[44]

The complex of buildings for the small campus of the Loyola University Law School in Los Angeles (1978–), in this sense, is a demonstration full of interesting implications. If the Telluride house, the Schnabel Residence, and the Winton Guest House are miniature villages, the Loyola complex is a city segment (a "forum," as some have asserted, but devasted by an earthquake) that confronts the undifferentiated, confused character of the urban area in which it is built with its own "designed disorder." Built in phases, the complex is composed of different episodes that coexist in an eccentric manner. Each is characterized by the use of design artifices with an evolution and meaning known to us (for example, the "dramatic" way in which the entrances of the single buildings are devised), and the urban layout is modeled by means of the overlaying of different symme-

tries. In this way Gehry manages to isolate, from the rest, the most representative building, Merrifield Hall, making it into a "miniature tribunal" whose axis is shifted seven degrees from the main axis, along which the larger construction, the Burns Building, is aligned. Four columns are freely positioned in front of Merrifield Hall; detached from the wall surface behind them, they appear as traces of an abolished pronaos. In spite of their perfect cylindrical form, they are true relics; but their diameter is too large for their height, and they do not comply with any of the rules of classical proportion. They enact a metaphor for the *columnatio*, which in the campus itself (as in the Schnabel Residence, for that matter) is evoked, instead, with trilithic configurations.[45] The dual nature Leon Battista Alberti attributes to the column, —as support and ornament—is negated here. These columns are mere ornaments; undergoing this metamorphosis, they extend, in Gehry's work, the process that began with the recognition of the otherness of the facing with respect to the structure. At the same time, by reducing the column to the status of a pure object, Gehry transmits the principle that informs his compositions, in this case and nearly all those discussed above, to the construction detail. Constructed as simple cylinders, mere hollow symbols, the columns used in the Loyola campus eloquently confirm the way Gehry's architecture identifies with a series of various demonstrations of the ineffectuality of the imposed norms and moral values implied in the concept of *order*, of *Ordnung*.[46] Like his tall tales, in other words, these elements are not intended to reassure but to narrate the story of an irremediable loss, because the focus of their digression is the fact that "we live"—as Cyril Connolly has written, in a fine passage—"in such a desperate era that any happiness we possess must be kept hidden, like a deformity, because we know—rebel as we might, with all our nature—that we can only create thanks to what we have suffered"[47] (in our case, the losses we regretfully acknowledge).

To underline fully the meaning of this intentionally careless way of building (heedful of the fact that studied nonchalance becomes evident precisely in the design of the columns, in defiance of the precepts defined in *De re aedificatoria*: "In all of architecture there is no part that requires greater care or attention, and is of greater gracefulness than the column"[48]), alongside the cylinders in front of Merrifield Hall we find the sculpture *Toppling Ladder with Spilling Paint* (1986) by Oldenburg. Ironically, the structure is sustained by only one of its four upright elements. This puts it in a condition of instability that is the exact opposite of that of the columns. Moreover, the sculpture is covered in the same pattern, greatly enlarged, of the metal screen Gehry uses so often; this clarifies the way in which the ornaments, in this complex, are the result of a unified design that aims at draining them of meaning, presenting them in a state of alienated objectness.

This contrast between stability and equilibrium appears quite regularly in Gehry's works. Not only does he often juxtapose images derived from opposite static conditions, but he also extends the implications of the materials he uses, as a connotation of the parts of his nondialectic architectonic tales. The California Aerospace Museum and Theater in Los Angeles (1982–84) is one example; others include the Iowa Laser Laboratory in Iowa City (1987–92), the University of Toledo Center for Visual Arts (1989), and, above all, the Nationale-Nederlanden Building in Prague (1992–96), where the opposition between dynamically aggregated volumes and statically configured ones also very obviously involves the facings. The result of this approach is groupings of free forms (more and more compact as the years go by) that, having gone beyond the narrative stance found in the different episodes of the campus of Loyola University, tend to become veritable outdoor sculptures openly expressing their indifference to their surroundings. Collages made with gigantic forms (in conceptual terms, once again, similar to the procedure used by Oldenburg to create sculptures like *Spitzhacke* of 1982 or *Extinguished Match* of 1987), these works make use of architectonic material after having reduced it to a mercurial state. As in the *Merzbau*, many drops of metal coagulate in expressive-dynamic forms that combine in landscapes where "the last traces of comfortable familiarity vanish."[49]

Thus the architecture can take on any form, and demonstrate that an antimetaphysical vision of the world implies a rejection of the conviction that

Fritz B. Burns Building, Loyola University Law School, Los Angeles, California, 1978–82. *Toppling Ladder with Spilling Paint* by Claes Oldenburg is in the foreground.

"everything finds its form beginning with that hieroglyphic that is the body, the ultimate constriction and the depth of necessity."[50]

The compositional procedures Gehry has developed foreshadow the exit from the convolutions of the "hieroglyphic" spoken of by Gottfried Benn. If, as Erwin Panofsky sustains, "the Renaissance fused the cosmological interpretation of the theory of proportions with the classical vision of 'symmetry' as the fundamental principle of aesthetic proportion,"[51] what Gehry puts into crisis is the anthropocentric correlate of this vision, attacking the foundations of architectural values and the combinations of values on which it is based.

In the introduction to the third volume of Vitruvius's *Ten Books on Architecture*, in the translation by Daniele Barbaro, we find the following passage: "The more ingenious the proportions, the more beautiful will be the inventions of man," because "divine is the force of numbers related to one another with care"— intertwining beauty and goodness—in the very knot that is undone by the pursuit of novelty, since "a monumental thought and a monumental perception

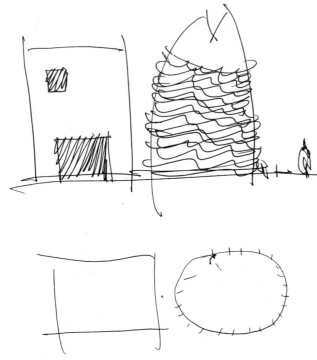

Frank Gehry,
sketch, 1984 (?).

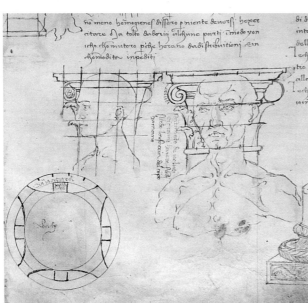

Francesco di
Giorgio Martini,
*Trattato di
architettura civile
e militare*, Turin,
Biblioteca Reale,
Codice Saluzziano
148, f. 15.r.

of the world are no longer accessible for depleted contemporary consciousness."[52]

"Nature, our teacher," in Barbaro's translation of the third volume of Vitruvius, "instructs us regarding the organization and divisions of the spaces of our buildings: she wants us to learn the reasoning behind the symmetries we should apply to buildings and temples, to learn from the sacred temples built in the image and likeness of God, and of man, in whose composition all the marvels of nature are included. Yet with wisdom the ancients derived all their measures from the human body, where Vitruvius so aptly declares that no composition can be justified if it is not, first of all, based on the symmetry of human limbs."[53]

Is it possible, in the contemporary world, even to perceive the immanence of these connections, which in 1775 Goethe could still observe in the cathedral of Strasbourg, where "the creative force lies in the plentiful sense of the relations and the proportions"? We can agree that "an ancient lansquenet who had taken part in the sack of Rome would be amazed by just how little there is to plunder in our big cities"[54]—here, the only materials that offer themselves for use are the humble things Gehry gathers, as Schwitters gathered on the Dutch beaches; in human beings there is no longer any reflection that ennobles them with respect to the measure of creation, and nature is nothing more than *generationis uterus*. Architecture, which is simply something *done*, can make much better use of technical potential, to the extent that the designer frees himself from its archetype, challenging fate by reversing the order of means and ends. Architecture without symmetries, incapable of using measure (if not in a purely technical sense), hostile to style—Gehry's architecture uses technique and observes nature with maximum liberty, treating them as tools and materials.

Given this state of things, it should come as no surprise that since the beginning of the 1980s, Gehry's image bank includes, as a stable element, the profile of a fish (occasionally combined with that of a serpent). This figure lends itself to any purpose and any manipulation. A lamp or a skyscraper can take the form of a fish, and in this way the architect asserts that "giving form" is separate from any practical-functional consideration that might induce architecture to acknowledge the constriction of a necessary reference to the human figure, seen as the reflection of divine perfection, which the architect can only imitate. The functional metamorphoses to which the figure of the fish lends itself help us to understand that Gehry does not view nature and the animal world as a source of norms, as a standard from which to derive measurements, proportions, and rules; he sees them as a source of suggestions and behaviors that can be incorporated in the spectacles he constructs. We cannot, therefore, imagine that the many variations of the figure of the fish that provide the stimuli for so many of Gehry's designs are a mere indication of the fact that he too has become involved in the metamorphoses he designs, transforming himself from *simia dei* into *simia naturae*.[55] The fish is not just a "symbol" employed to announce the idea that the human being is no longer the measure of the form, it is also a way of evoking everything that architecture cannot be: darting, in constant movement, with an iridescent "skin"—like the mutable reflections of the "scales" with which Gehry covers his constructions, alluding to a veritable whirling in dance of embraced figures that couple (once again in a hermaphroditic configuration), as in the volumes of the Nationale-Nederlanden Building in Prague.

While the structural calculation Gehry employs in finite elements is indifferent with respect to "static-structural truth as a way of revealing beauty"[56] and permits him to challenge the very notion that a structure can present itself as *truth*, it is still the collage technique of composition that permits him to overturn even this ultimate consequence of the anthropocentric conception of architecture. Having transformed his office into a workshop of forms, Gehry's way of designing is no different from the manner in which Schwitters constructed the *Merz-Säulen*. If we observe, in succession, the great number of models he builds for his projects, we can clearly perceive the way they take form through the gradual layering and sedimentation of visual decisions and tactile manipulations. From an unlimited quantity of forms, Gehry visually and manually selects those that are to be removed from their random state, correlating them, superimposing them, cementing them together, until

the range of possibilities assumes a homogeneous configuration on the plane of his personal aesthetic perception, independent of the multiplicity of the materials used. These multimaterial, precarious, unstable objects, where construction and composition coincide, are then processed by the sophisticated electronic apparatus of Gehry's studio-workshop to produce the drawings required to transform these models into spectacular sculptural events.

The constructions conserve the multimaterial character of the models. The structures are ramified and diversified, in keeping with the requirements of the facings, and can assume all kinds of configurations, because they have been freed of any responsibility regarding the "truth" of the work. Thus, as in the Nationale-Nederlanden Building, or in several versions of the design for the Samsung Museum of Modern Art in Seoul (1995–), the structural elements may appear to be derived from the sculpture *Clothespin* (1976) by Oldenburg; or as in the American Center in Paris (1988–94) or the project for the Walt Disney Concert Hall in Los Angeles (1989–), they may look like the experiments conducted by Serra, beginning with *House of Cards* (1969).

The apparently random quality of the materials used in the models remains in the built works; it is sufficient to look at the projects for One Times Square in New York and for the Experience Music Project in Seattle (1996–) to comprehend the extreme design sophistication required for such representation. This affectation is also reflected in the spatial organization of the buildings, which tend to take on labyrinthine layout configurations rendered more or less perceptible in keeping with their image expectations. The enticing shock value of the incoherent concretions placed at the entrances to Gehry's constructions is quickly replaced, for the visitor, by sensations of disorientation caused by vast, directionless spaces, like three-dimensional expansions of his sketches, lines entangled like balls of yarn (and this is why we cannot help but view Gehry's sketches as the expressions of a sort of "automatic writing").

The sequences of diastoles and systoles, contractions and dilations that set the rhythm for the enclosures Gehry has been designing since the mid-1970s, invading the entire space and every element of the

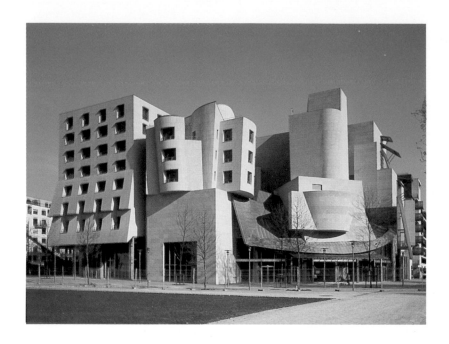

deviating movement, guided by the architecture, becomes similar to that of a dance, marked by a rhythm that is transmitted to the body without the aid of the senses. Inside one of the greatest architectural masterpieces of the twentieth century, we are faced with a condition well known to historians. Those who have studied the medieval liturgy, in fact, are well aware of the many versions of correspondence between the maze and the spiral, but they also know that the (not merely literary) association between labyrinth and dance represents an invocation of order and salvation.[57] In spite of the temporal distance, this precedent explains the symbolic character of Wright's Guggenheim: an allegory, such as took place in the Middle Ages, for the "triumph of order, whether in the aesthetic or the moral sphere" and thus evidence of the greatness of the architect.[58]

While Wright's spiral encourages the natural movement that enables us easily to identify the way out of the labyrinth, inside the Vitra Museum one has the impression that Ariadne's thread not only fails to indi-

composition, become independent in their configuration: freely dancing in the void, as occurs in the hall of the American Center in Paris and in the large domed space of the Guggenheim Museum in Bilbao. The Vitra International Design Museum in Weil am Rhein (1987–89) is a good example of the composition of the rhythm of the kaleidoscopic surprises Gehry offers his audience. The highly sculptural wrapper of the construction foreshadows the labyrinthine organization of the interior. As can be intuitively understood by observing the figures into which the volume is broken down, the leading role here has been assigned to the spiral. This image is associated with the idea of the labyrinth in an age-old tradition. The Guggenheim Museum by Frank Lloyd Wright in New York is the extreme manifestation of this association; for this reason, it is also a useful term of comparison for the analysis of the building at Weil am Rhein.

In spite of what one might normally expect, the effects of disorientation produced upon visitors by the Guggenheim in New York are not due to the unnatural movement of walking down a spiral ramp while observing paintings on the walls. Visitors find themselves in an utterly natural condition, in which their bodies respond to the force of gravity; it is this natural condition that makes it difficult for them to use the museum space in a conventional way. This

cate the path to freedom but also contributes to confuse visitors, leading them deeper and deeper into the maze. This museum is composed of a system of discontinuous groupings, seemingly without end. Gehry opposes the determinate spatial quality of Wright's Guggenheim with the indeterminacy of a swarm of spaces, with an effect that does not correspond to the arithmetical sum of the surprises they offer.

This same spatial characteristic is accentuated in the Guggenheim Museum in Bilbao. One enters this imposing building, upon whose metal surfaces are reflected the last rays of sun of our century, by descending a wide staircase, a sloping plaza. Before entering, the visitor experiences a strong compression, which only serves to augment the sense of awe once the threshold has been crossed. In the large entrance hall, dominated by a totemic *Merz-Säule*, one can observe the flow of the facings and the contortions of the structure. Offered multiple options, each human movement appears to be absorbed by the spatial tumult, a confirmation of the space's labyrinthine nature. To an even greater extent than at the Vitra Museum, the audience is captured by the spectacle offered by the architect, who can now make use of a truly monumental set.

As in the American Center in Paris, the main space of the Bilbao Guggenheim is arhythmically marked, crossed by aerial passages, while the wrapper is interrupted to allow light to fall on its curves, or to provide views of openings made toward other rooms. The cavernous hall frays, giving form to a succession of empirical intuitions, and nothing here can be traced back to a Cartesian conception of space, seen as the materialization of calculations, measurements, mathematical operations. The architecture declares its powerful identity while, simultaneously, renouncing it, given the fact that in the *interiors* of the museum the architecture appears in profoundly varied configurations, almost a narration of the conflict that dominates the scene. The protagonists of this clash are the same we have seen at work (although neutralized) in the models Gehry builds for the different phases of development of his projects: the composition and the construction, the acts and the decisions that nourish the operation the work exhibits. "The composition," Pavel Florenskij taught the students of the VChUTEMAS, "is what the artist brings to the work, the construction is that with which he must come to terms. The construction is what the world requires be recognized of itself. These two principles, from the moment in which they coexist in a single work, influence and oppose each other. Each of them tries to force the other into submission, meaning that the moment of construction of the work deforms the composition, not allowing it to be realized in the purest form in which it would prefer to appear."[59]

At Bilbao, all the effects produced by the efforts made by the composition are grouped in the central volume of the museum. At the same time, the construction reveals all the blows it has taken, displaying deformations, ruptures, and tensions that must be supported by the structure as a part of the overall spectacle.

This state of tension is transmitted to the visitors, modern-day Jonahs, who are forced to experience the dismay of moving about in a space of enormous proportions, configured like the inside of a whale (the outside, obviously, has the form of a fish); but it is also reproduced without solutions of continuity, in spite of the fact that the configurations of the different spaces of the museum vary enormously. This variety reinforces the disturbing impressions communicated by the central space, because it confirms the suspicion of a kaleidoscopic, unlimited spatiality of the construction. As in the autobiographical narrative set in motion by Gehry in the construction of his own house in Santa Monica, the Bilbao Guggenheim is a space without end, the result of a conception of design that seems to abhor the moment in which the hand of the architect must cease to assemble the things with which he has decided to compose the work, leaving it to live its own life, to be used as the world sees fit. For this reason, the arbitrary approach that reigns in the space of the museum, whose form coincides with intuition, contains an explicit evocation of the presence of its creator. As in the *Merzbau*, the only true "inhabitant" of the Guggenheim is the architect himself, he who wishes to see himself reflected in an endless work and offer his operation as the only spectacle. Visitors are granted no alternative. From this point of view, the analogy with the other Guggenheim, in New York, is evident: what they both display is only architecture; they exhibit themselves.

Inside both of these works it is possible to feel a sense of vertigo, although the sensation is caused by two opposing situations. Nothing in the work of Gehry, in fact, alludes to stability, and there is nothing useful for those who believe that order is the objective human being pursue with their constructions. The disconcerting sensation provoked by Gehry is comparable, on the other hand, to the vertigo one feels "when looking at the irrational world of the

Walt Disney
Concert Hall,
Los Angeles,
California,
1989– .

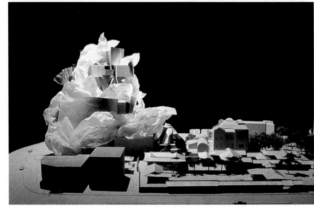

Samsung
Museum of
Modern Art,
Seoul, Korea,
1995– .

Guggenheim
Museum, Bilbao,
Spain, 1991–97.

Carceri, provoked not by the lack of measure (because Piranesi was never a more accurate surveyor than in these works), but by the multiplicity of the calculations, which must be accurate, but which lead to proportions that must be erroneous."[60]

In this sense, recalling the suggestions of Florenskij, the interpretation (albeit very important) of Ernst Cassirer regarding the nature of "intuitive space" is only partially adequate to explain the phenomena we must examine at this point. When Cassirer states that "in the intuitive space the two moments of dividing and putting together, of complete separation and complete connection, are in a certain sense equivalent: they are in a sort of ideal equilibrium,"[61] he offers us an explanation that is useful to understand just who the "protagonists" of Gehry's spatial constructions are, but this does not suffice to explain their strident coexistence.

The exteriors of the Bilbao museum take the liberty of manipulation of the facings, which we have seen in so many of Gehry's works, to its extreme consequences. Once again, we are faced with a montage of heterogeneous forms gathered around a central volume, that of the grand hall. The volumes are based on different formal definitions: some are squarely hewn, others bent with curves of different orders; in their midst, reclining along the bank of the river, there is the chopped-off body of an enormous fish. Like a monstrous flower or a fairy-tale castle, the construction is reflected in a large pool, and in the river itself. It stands in a decayed urban area, and the limitations of the location require it to nestle down beneath the structures of a large viaduct. From the center of the city, it is possible now and then to glimpse the museum, and to feel the disturbing sensation of a presence that is utterly alien to all its surroundings.

Different types of facings or claddings are used for the different volumes, from titanium sheets to the most ordinary stucco. In each situation, the materials are used to produce the effect that is appropriate for particular surfaces. For this reason, the joints are subjected to torsions and slippages, while the contours of the cladding vary in a declaration of the atectonic character of the materials used, the evocation of an albeit distant kinship between the way they have been applied and weaving or braiding. The titanium-panel cladding grants homogeneity to even the most irregular forms, reminding the observer of a sort of continuous elastic sheath[62] composed of a material that permits the hand of the architect to model the forms. The action of the designer would seem to be deposited directly on each of the volumes; the centrality of his figure, constantly evoked in the succession of spatial interventions in the interiors, is thus also displayed on the exterior. The entire construction offers itself to view, from the city, as a gigantic sculpture, also definitively inclusive of the dimension of time due to its multiple appearances from the different possible urban vantage points.

Inside this "unheard-of" world cavities and eddies open and gape, as in the *Merzbau*, which contained caves for Mondrian, Arp, Gabo, van Doesburg, Mies van der Rohe, and so on,[63] a "museum" of memories and mysteries at the center of which stood the figure of he who could continuously update it, constructing it. But the Bilbao Guggenheim is not a construction with anything secret about it: it is an open celebration of the supremacy of sight, containing one cave only, set aside for its designer. The museum visually occupies the heart of the city, and its mass has become the city's center; all that can be admired and viewed inside the museum is of no importance. Built on an abandoned portion of industrial land, Gehry's edifice has grafted a genetic mutation so spectacular that not even the most reckless of scientists could ever have imagined it: the city of Bilbao, once the "forge" of Spain, has become a single, great museum. As in a gigantic game of Chinese boxes within boxes, this museum contains the Guggenheim Museum, or the museum of architecture, where the latest metamorphoses of the many things that in an apparently random manner are thrown up on the beach by the sea of architecture take form, that beach where the designer has set up his drawing board and his computer.

This is a mutation that would certainly have attracted the attention of Jünger; here, in fact, the contemporary bulimia of vision has led to the erection, atop the ruins of a factory-city, of a new museum-city, which now hosts a gigantic, friendly metal monster, beached on the banks of the river that crosses Bilbao, transforming the city into the last "oasis where bourgeois security" finds refuge.[64]

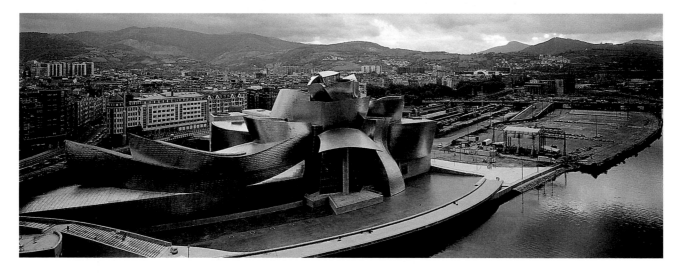

Guggenheim Museum, Bilbao.

1. E. Jünger, *Eusmenswil* (Stuttgart, 1977).

2. Cited in E. Nündel, *Kurt Schwitters* (Reinbeck bei Hamburg, 1981), 59.

3. G. Simmel, "L'art pour l'art," *Zur Philosophie der Kunst* (Potsdam, 1922).

4. J. Clair, *Considérations sur l'état des beaux-arts: Critique de la modernité* (Paris, 1983). The observations on the theme of the museum are partially inspired by the writings of J. Clair on this subject, which seem to have made adequate consideration of the many occasions on which E. Jünger focused on the symbolic significance of this institution, a demonstration, in his opinion, of the fact that our era has "achieved a sort of historical fetishism that is directly proportional to a lack of productive energies." E. Jünger, *Der Arbeiter: Herrschaft und Gestalt* (Stuttgart, 1981).

5. Clair, *Considérations sur l'état des beaux-arts.*

6. See P. Falguières, "Décœuvrement de Kurt Schwitters," in *Kurt Schwitters* (exh. cat., Paris: Centre Georges Pompidou, 1994), 152–57.

7. W. Benjamin, *Gesammelte Schriften*, ed. R. Tiedemann and H. Schweppenhäuser (Frankfurt, 1982).

8. Jünger, *Der Arbeiter.*

9. The essay by R. Barthes, "Art, This Old Thing . . . ," which contains these quotations, is an important reference for these passages. See R. Barthes, *L'obvie et l'obtus: Essais critiques III* (Paris, 1982).

10. Where this performance is concerned, see the essay by K. Forster in this volume, and G. Celant, *Il Corso del Coltello/The Course of the Knife* (Milan and New York, 1987). For the observations that follow on the relationships between Gehry and many important exponents of the American art avant-garde, among other things, see G. Celant, "Reflections on Frank Gehry," in *Frank Gehry: Buildings and Projects*, ed. P. Arnell and T. Bickford (New York, 1985); *The Architecture of Frank Gehry* (New York, 1986) with essays by T. S. Hines, R. Haag Bletter, J. Giovannini, M. Friedman, C. van Bruggen and P. Viladas; S. Lavin, "Auf unkonventionellem Wege," *Archithese*, January–February 1991; K. W. Forster, "Choreographie des Zufalls," *Archithese*, January–February 1991; K. W. Forster, "Lungo i sentieri dell'immaginario," in *Frank O. Gehry: America come contesto*, ed. M. Zardini (Milan, 1994).

11. M. Fumaroli, *L'Etat culturel* (Paris, 1991). "The demon of unexpected combinations, that derives and deduces from what exists the most astonishing consequences with which to compose what will be" is a passage from P. Valéry, *Regards sur le monde actuel et autres essais* (Paris, 1945).

12. See Celant, "Reflections on Frank Gehry," 11.

13. In general, on this theme see Celant, "Reflections on Frank Gehry," and the considerations (especially those regarding the comparison between the works of Gehry and Gordon Matta-Clark) made by S. Lavin in "A proposito di Gehry," in *Zodiac*, 15 (1996).

14. We will return to this subject, examining certain characteristic structural configurations employed by Gehry from the early 1980s on. C. van Bruggen tells of the work experiences of Oldenburg at Gehry's studio in Santa Monica in the catalog *Claes Oldenburg: An Anthology* (New York, 1995), 454 ff. The same author, in *The Architecture of Frank Gehry*, makes an apt comparison between Gehry's late entry to the Chicago Tribune Tower Competition (1980) and Oldenburg's collage *Proposed Colossal Monument for a Skyscraper for Michigan Avenue, Chicago, in the Form of Lorado Taft's Sculpture "Death"* (1968). There are also other similarities between drawings by Oldenburg and Gehry that deserve closer analysis, while the figures that appear in the drawings of the artist, such as, for example, in *Colossal Floating Three-Way Plug* (1965) and *Building in the Form of an English Extension Plug* (1967), regularly reappear in the designs of the architect. Finally, if we observe the sculpture (just one of many possible examples) *Feasible Monument for a City Square: Hats Blowing in the Wind* (1969), we can clearly see the influence of Oldenburg on the evolution of Gehry's formal research.

15. R. Serra, *Writings Interviews* (Chicago, 1994), 104, 109.

16. The interview-discussion between P. Eisenman and R. Serra in *Skyline*, April 1983 (reprinted in Serra, *Writings Interviews*, 141–54) is a document that fully reveals the contradiction we are examining. It contains a series of observations that help us to understand that the "interaction" between artists and architects that has developed in the United States over the last two decades is very competitive in nature. In the interview, Eisenman (as Gehry would have done) insists upon the notion that the analogy between the work of the sculptor and that of the architect cannot be rejected out of hand due to the fact that in the work of the architect considerations of "usage value" prevail. Moreover, the remark made by Serra during the course of the interview: "I know, there is absolutely no audience for sculpture" (143) is of great importance in understanding the way the "project" of Eisenman and Gehry aims at reattracting, through architecture, an audience for experimentation in contemporary art. On this subject, we can also refer to G. Celant, "The Sculptor versus the Architect," in *Claes Oldenburg: An Anthology*, 364.

17. J. Frank, *Architektur als Symbol* (Vienna, 1931).

18. W. Benjamin in *Gesammelte Schriften* has left this illuminating note *on appearances*: "No artwork can appear absolutely alive without becoming mere appearance, and without ceasing to be an artwork. The life that trembles inside it must appear to be frozen, fixed in an instant. The life that trembles in the work is beauty, the harmony (*Harmonia*) that pervades the given case, and only appears to tremble."

19. The complete phase of R. Banham is as follows: "His earliest independent work was fairly tidy-minded mainstream modern—tidy-minded enough for the professionalism and natural design talent to be immediately comprehensible and an award-winning studio for the graphic designer Lou Danziger of 1964 established him as a coming man." R. Banham, "Building Inside Out," in *New Society*, July 24, 1987 (reprinted in *A Critic Writes: Essays by Reyner Banham*, ed. M. Banham, P. Barker, S. Lyall, C. Price, Berkeley, Los Angeles, London, 1996, 266–67).

20. See T. S. Hines, "Heavy Metal: The Education of F.O.G.," in *The Architecture of Frank Gehry*, 11 ff.

21. Banham, "Building Inside Out," 266.

22. C. Bötticher, *Die Tektonik der Hellenen* (Berlin, 1869), 20 ff.

23. See H. F. Mallgrave, introduction to G. Semper, *The Four Elements of Architecture and Other Writings* (Cambridge, New York, 1989).

24. H. Quitzsch, *Die ästhetischen Anschauungen Gottfried Sempers* (Berlin, 1962).

25. See M. Tafuri, "Les bijoux indiscrets," in *Five Architects NY*, ed. C. Gubitosi and A. Izzo (Rome, 1976), 7 ff; and M. Tafuri, "American Graffiti: Five x Five = Twenty-Five," in *Oppositions* 5 (1976). Naturally all that is said here refers to the work of the Five Architects before 1972.

26. M. Bachtin, *Estetika slovesnogo tvor čestva* (Moscow, 1979).

27. G. Semper, *Die Vier Elemente der Baukunst* (Brunswick, 1851). On the ways in which this theme has been addressed in the history of contemporary architecture, see G. Fanelli, R. Gargiani, *Il principio del rivestimento* (Rome, Bari, 1994).

28. Mallgrave, introduction to Semper, *Four Elements*, 40.

29. I. Bachmann, *Frankfurter Vorlesungen: Probleme zeitgenössischer Dichtung* (Munich, 1980).

30. The Easy Edges furniture clearly reveals the influence of Aalto, confirming Gehry's interest in the work of the Finnish master. This topic deserves greater study, beginning with a conference held by Aalto, of which Gehry speaks in B. Lacy, "Interview with FOG," in *Innovative Architecture from Los Angeles and San Francisco*, ed. B. Lacy and S. de Menil (New York, 1992). In particular, a stimulus for the reconstruction of the extent to which Gehry is indebted to Aalto can be found in the way Gehry reuses (in the Norton Simon Gallery in Malibu, 1974–76, and thereafter) the motif of screening openings and elevations with wood planking, similar to the work of Aalto in the Finnish Pavilion for the New York World's Fair in 1938.

31. R. Haag Bletter, "Frank Gehry's Spatial Reconstructions," in *The Architecture of Frank Gehry*, 47. Although Haag Bletter's essay is one of the most intelligent among the vast quantity of writings on Gehry, I cannot always agree with what she writes. First of all, the statement "[Gehry's] interest [is] in assigning symbolic and mnemonic values to elements of design" is the result of an interpretation that differs greatly from the viewpoint I am expressing here. Second, I do not agree with the comparison Haag Bletter makes between the way Gaudí uses residual materials in his works and the procedures of Gehry. The fine book by J. J. Lahuerta, *Antoni Gaudí, 1852–1926* (Milan, 1992), enables us to understand how the manipulation of materials, seen as a metaphor for the temptations of the flesh, has religious sig-

nificance for Gaudí, expressing a profound sense of sin, which cannot be reconciled with the sensuality of the "architectonic gestures" of Gehry. Given these references, it is worth suggesting that an analysis of the work of Gehry in comparison to the "architectural designs" and constructions of Salvador Dalí might lead to some interesting surprises; see *Dalí arquitectura*, ed. J. J. Lahuerta (Barcelona, 1996).

32. "To be as one should be. Someone who is as one should be must be, first of all, one like the others. The more one is equal to the others, the more one is as one should be. It is the sacred nature of the Multitude . . . [this] Commonplace expresses, with unique energy, the evangelical commandment of absolute Unity: *Sint unum sicut et nos*. Because the Divine Word is true in every sense, it is certain that the Bourgeois will fulfill, in his own way, the Will of which he knows nothing, when he insists that the human cattle should form an immense herd of imbeciles." This might also serve as an appropriate "explanation" for the Gehry Residence, offered to us (though written about eighty years ago) by L. Bloy, *Exégèse des lieux communs* (Paris, 1983).

33. Important here are the beautiful passages by M. Bachtin on the genre of autobiography in the essay "The Author and the Hero in Aesthetic Activity," in *Estetika slovesnogo*: "By biography and autobiography we mean the immediate transgressive form in which I can objectify myself and my artistic life . . . Biographical values are values shared by life and art, they can determine practical acts as their end; they are the form and the values of the *aesthetic of life*." We should also recall the fact that Kurt Schwitters speaks of the *Merzbau*, which was destroyed in 1943, as "the work of life" in a letter to Christof Spengemann in January 1946, cited in W. Schmalenbach, *Kurt Schwitters* (New York, 1967), 129.

34. Bachtin, *Estetika slovesnogo*.

35. A. Averlino [Filarete], *Trattato di architettura*, ed. M. Finoli and L. Grassi (Milan, 1972), 40.

36. On this topic it is not, however, superfluous to underline the way these analogies become much more significant when we consider the more recent works by Gehry (from the Vitra Design Museum to the Bilbao Guggenheim) in the light of the "projects" developed in the context of the *Gläserne Kette* by Finsterlin, Scharoun, Hans Luckhardt, and Max Taut.

37. For these considerations on the positions of Venturi, see M. Tafuri, *Teorie e storia dell'architettura* (Rome, Bari, 1968), 257–58 (English edition, *Theory and History of Architecture*, New York, 1979); M. Tafuri, *La sfera e il labirinto* (Turin, 1980), 358–59 (English edition, *The Sphere and the Labyrinth*, Cambridge, 1987); V. De Feo, "Robert Venturi e il mito dell'ironia," *Rassegna dell'Istituto di Architettura e Urbanistica* 17 (1970).

38. H. Broch "Das Böse im Wertsystem der Kunst" (1933), in *Philosophische Schriften*, ed. P. M. Lützeler, vol. 9, no. 2 (Frankfurt, 1977), 119–56.

39. On the void as "structure" in architectural figuration, see the interesting exchange of opinions between P. Eisenman and R. Serra in the interview in *Skyline*.

40. Concerning the analysis of the "role" assigned to typology in the work of Gehry, see K. W. Forster's essay in this volume. An in-depth analysis of the initial design (1993) for the house in Telluride, Colorado, could permit meaningful development of the observations suggested by the sketches for the Tract House.

41. The fundamental dualism of the modern aesthetic experience has been defined by W. Worringer in *Abstraktion und Einfühlung: Ein Beitrag zur Stilpsychologie* (Munich, 1908; English edition, *Abstraction and Empathy*, New York, 1953): "Whereas the precondition for the urge to empathy is a happy patheistic relationship of confidence between man and the phenomena of the external world, the urge to abstraction is the outcome of a great inner unrest inspired in man by the phenomena of the outside world: in a religious respect it corresponds to a strongly transcendental tinge to all notions. We can describe this state as an immense spiritual dread of space" (15). The interaction of these two processes leads to the possibility, for man, of a radical "self-alienation" in the artwork, of "'losing oneself' in the contemplation of a work of art" (24). I have commented on these aspects of the work of Worringer in *Figures of Architecture and Thought* (New York, 1990), 139.

42. Broch, *Das Böse*, 25.

43. Teodulfo as cited in the extraordinary pages of E. R. Curtius, *Europäische Literatur und lateinisches Mittelalter* (Bern, 1948). Here, to furnish an example of the medieval topos of the world turned upside-down, Curtius writes: "In the *Architrenius* of Jean de Hanville the Hill of Arrogance is the place of the 'overturned world': the tortoise flies, the hare threatens the lion."

44. See the photographs of the "collections of objects" in Oldenburg's studio on Broome Street in New York in *Claes Oldenburg: An Anthology*, 358–59.

45. See L. B. Alberti, *L'architettura [De re aedificatoria]*, ed. P. Portoghesi (Milan, 1966), vol. 2, book 7, 562–64.

46. On this theme, see the essays of C. Thoenes, "'Sostegno e adornamento': Gli ordini architettonici come simbolo sociale," "Gli ordini architettonici: rinascita o invenzione?," in *Sostegno e adornamento: Saggi sull'architettura del Rinascimento: Disegni, ordini, magnificenza* (Milan, 1998).

47. Palinuro [Cyril Connolly], *The Unquiet Grave: A Word Cycle* (London, 1944).

48. Alberti, *L'architettura*, vol. 1, book 1, 70.

49. Jünger, *Der Arbeiter*.

50. G. Benn, *Sämtliche Werke: Prosa 1, Prosa 2; Gesammelte Werke: Essays, Reden, Vorträge* (Stuttgart, 1959; Italian edition, Milan, 1992). In Italian, the text reads: "Il corpo è l'ultima costrizione e il profondo della necessità, è il portatore del presentimento, sogna il sogno . . . tutto trova la sua forma a partire da quel geroglifico che è il corpo: stile e conoscenza; tutto dà il corpo: morte e piacere" (43).

51. E. Panofsky, *Meaning in the Visual Arts: Papers in and on Art History* (Garden City, N.Y., 1955).

52. The original text by Daniele Barbaro reads as follows: "Le belle inventioni degli homini tanto hanno del buono, quanto più ingegnosamente sono proportionate . . . Divina è la forza de i numeri tra se con ragione comparati." *Vitruvio: I dieci libri dell'architettura, tradotti e commentati da Daniele Barbaro* (1567; new edition, with commentary by M. Tafuri and M. Morresi, Milan, 1987), 97. The second quotation comes from P. Florenskij, *Lo spazio e il tempo nell'arte* (Milan, 1995), 101.

53. The original text reads: "La natura maestra ci insegna come havemo a reggerci col compartimento delle fabbriche: imperoche non da altro ella vuole che impariamo le ragioni delle simmetrie che nelle fabbriche che de i tempij usar dovemo, che dal sacro tempio fatto a imagine, et simiglianza di Dio, che l'huomo, nella cui compositione tutte le altre meraviglie di natura sono comprese. Et però con saggio avvertimento tolsero gli antichi ogni ragione del misurare dalle parti del corpo humano, dove molto a proposito Vitruvio dice che opera niuna può havere ragione di componimento, se prima non haverà riguardo alla simmetria delle membre humane." Barbaro, *Vitruvio*, 110.

54. Jünger, *Der Arbeiter*.

55. See H. W. Janson, *Apes and Ape Lore in the Middle Ages and Renaissance* (London, 1952), especially the chapter "Ars Simia Naturae."

56. E. Benvenuto, "Un libro che fece epoca," in E. Torroja, *La concezione strutturale* (Milan, 1995).

57. See P. Reed Doob, *The Idea of the Labyrinth from Classical Antiquity through the Middle Ages* (Ithaca, London, 1990), 125. Also see the chapter "Mazes in Medieval Art and Architecture."

58. Reed Doob, *Idea of the Labyrinth*, 144.

59. Florenskij, *Lo spazio*, 309.

60. M. Yourcenar, *Sous bénefice d'inventaire* (Paris, 1962).

61. E. Cassirer, *Philosophie der symbolischen Formen*, vol. 3: *Phänomenologie der Erkenntnis* (Berlin, 1923).

62. See R. Gargiani, "Il rivestimento di Frank Gehry, o della lamina elastica," *Casabella* 632 (1996).

63. See H. Richter, *Dada Profile* (Zurich, 1961).

64. Jünger, *Der Arbeiter*, 184.

**Senior Thesis
University of Southern California
May 1954**

Program: Affordable housing
Materials: Wood frame, concrete block
Project Team: Frank O. Gehry,
C. Gregory Walsh Jr.

Perspective of
a house from
the rear courtyard.

**Romm Residence
Los Angeles, California
1954 (not built)**

Client: Julius Romm
Program: Single-family residence
Area: 2,200 square feet
Materials: Wood frame, stucco
Project Team: Frank O. Gehry

Model views with
and without roof.

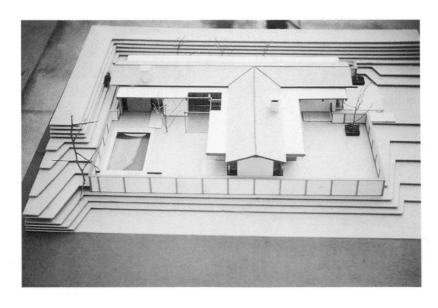

**Third Army Day Room
Improvements
Fort Bragg, North Carolina
1956**

Client: Special Services Division,
United States Army
Program: Remodel of nine existing
recreational facilities
Budget: $3,000,000
Materials: Wood frame, drywall
Project Team: SP3 Frank O. Gehry,
SP3 Dominick Loscalzo,
PFC Orman Kimbrough

View of entrance from
Veterans Circle.

**David Cabin
Idyllwild, California
1958**

Client: Melvin David
Program: Single-family vacation home
Area: 2,000 square feet
Materials: Wood frame, concrete block,
redwood siding
Project Team: Frank O. Gehry,
C. Gregory Walsh Jr.

Steeves Residence
Brentwood, California
1958–59

Client: Edgar C. and Mary Lou Steeves
Program: Three-bedroom single-family residence
Budget: $60,000
Area: 2,800 square feet
Materials: Wood frame, stucco
Project Team: Frank O. Gehry,
C. Gregory Walsh Jr.

The Steeves Residence, Gehry's first substantial commission, served as an exploration of Frank Lloyd Wright's formal vocabulary and as a testing ground for applying Japanese design principles to Southern California residential construction. Later, in the remodeling scheme proposed for the Smith family, in 1981, the original house served as an orderly backdrop for the disparate colors and forms of the new addition.

Perched on a hillside in Brentwood, the house is approached through a narrow right-of-way. While most houses in the neighborhood adjoin the street, Gehry's original site strategy exaggerated the setback, maximizing privacy, exploiting a dramatic view, and securing a large, level area for an expansive yard. A trellis-covered entryway joins the garage to the house and initiates a long, narrow axis extending through the living room and ending in a second, balancing trellis. Bougainvillea-laden and west-facing, this slightly elevated trellis acts as a sun shade while framing a reflecting pool below. The cross axis—a lower, wider volume—contains bedrooms overlooking the San Fernando Valley. The kitchen, dining room, and service rooms open onto the front yard.

Despite Gehry's claim that he was offended by Wright's perceived architectural and social pretensions, the building's cruciform plan, elongated and low-slung profile, and continuous clerestory reflect the young architect's need to come to terms with the master's legacy. Whatever his reservations about Wright, Gehry was nonetheless working within the framework of Wright's formal and spatial innovations. Wright's impact can be seen in the flat, extended relationship between the house and the ground plane, which brings outdoors in; the flexible open plan; and the Japanese-inspired construction methods.

Steeped in the teachings of instructors returned from the war, Gehry and his schoolmate, close friend, and longtime collaborator, Greg Walsh, were avid students of Japanese construction methods and detailing when the original house was designed for the Steeves family. Interior finishes, cabinetry, and exterior details were to be of select-grade unfinished wood with exposed joints. During construction, however, ordinary workmanship and budget constraints compromised their intentions.

Gehry describes his early interest in Japanese design—seen most obviously in the Romm Residence (1954), the Marais & Miranda Residence (1960–61), the Kay Jewelers Office and Warehouse (1962–63), and the Gehry-designed

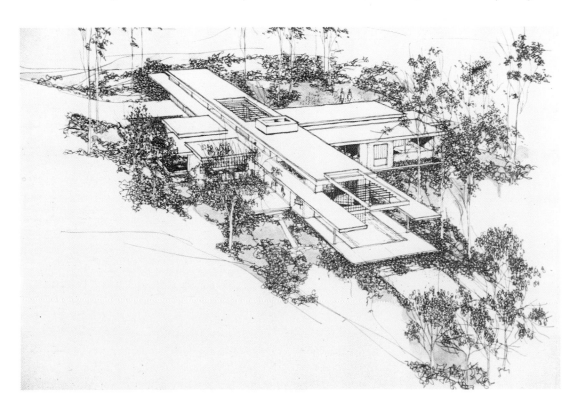

museum exhibition "Art Treasures of Japan" (1965)—as "episodic," and cites the Steeves Residence as the first proof that it was inappropriately applied within the context of the Southern California building industry. Gehry felt instinctively that Japanese post-and-beam construction was affordable, easy, and "democratic," an approach that "fit with my politics." He carefully studied—even revered—the work of such architects as Rafael Soriano, Craig Ellwood, Gordon Drake, Harwell Harris, and Gregory Ain, all of whom adapted various principles of Japanese design to the idiom of California modernism. The Steeves Residence was nonetheless an early lesson, a cautionary tale, in the potential disjunction between a designer's aspirations and the realities of building within the limits of the local vernacular.

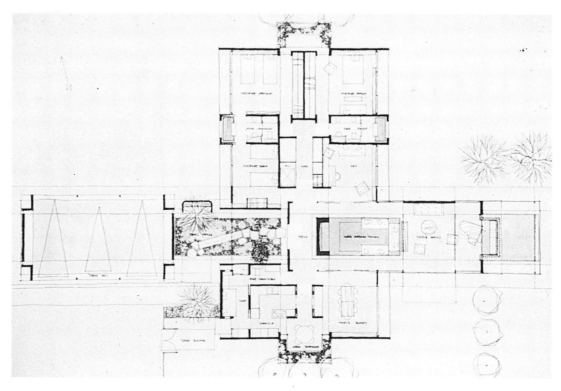

**Clifton Springs Resort
Port Phillip Bay,
Clifton Springs, Australia
1960**

Client: Willmore and Randall Real Estate Developers
Program: Resort master plan, including residential complex, retail center, golf course, tennis club, and marina
Materials: Wood frame, stucco

Project Team: Victor Gruen & Associates; Frank O. Gehry; Carlos Diniz

Perspective views of motel cottages from the golf course and from the beach.

**Marais & Miranda Residence
Los Angeles, California
1960–61**

Client: Josef Marais
Program: Residential remodel, including new kitchen, dining room, bedroom, and garage
Area: 2,500 square feet
Materials: Wood frame, stucco
Project Team: Frank O. Gehry; Kurily & Szymanski, structural engineer

Hillcrest Apartments
Santa Monica, California
1961–62

Client: Development project
Program: Six-unit apartment building
Budget: $85,000
Area: 7,200 square feet
Materials: Concrete block, wood frame, stucco, redwood trim, cedar shingle
Project Team: Frank O. Gehry, C. Gregory Walsh Jr.; Fereydoon Ghaffari, architect and planner; Joseph Kurily and Moshe Rubinstein, structural engineer; Wesley Bilson, developer

Views from
Highland Avenue.

Kay Jewelers Office and Warehouse
Los Angeles, California
1962–63

Client: Kay Jewelers Company
Budget: $42,000
Area: 5,000 square feet
Materials: Concrete block, wood frame, redwood trim, clay-tile roof
Project Team: Frank O. Gehry, C. Gregory Walsh Jr.

After one year of living and working in Paris, Gehry returned to Los Angeles in the fall of 1962 and opened his own office. Among his first clients was the owner of the western franchises of Kay Jewelers, who admired Japanese art and architecture. The client commissioned designs for a five-thousand-square-foot office-and-warehouse building, to be located at the heavily trafficked intersection of Pico and Fairfax Boulevards, and four stores to be located in suburban malls throughout Southern California.

The composition and scale of the office and warehouse are minimalist. A low wall, capped in redwood, surrounds a Japanese garden that buffers the building from the street. Cast concrete slabs form a walkway across the gravel-covered ground and past a small pool surrounded by rocks, low bushes, and bamboo thickets. The building itself, at the rear of the lot, sits on a Miesian plinth, hovering several inches above grade. Narrow concrete columns with square capitals form a shallow, two-story portico, contrasting with a carefully detailed wall of glass and dark redwood bands. Inside, sliding *shoji*-like panels and screens divide the open plan into flexible office spaces, and wood banding extends the Japanese aesthetic.

If in composition the Kay office shows a preoccupation with minimalism, Gehry's choice of materials reveals another emerging, and distinctly antimodernist, interest in cheap, popular materials and raw finishes. The garden perimeter wall is exposed concrete block; the columns were formed of cardboard sonotubes; the gabled roof is Spanish red clay tile; and, while Gehry composed a carefully detailed front facade, the building's side and rear walls are unadorned concrete block.

Sketch and view of entrance garden and facade.

Kay Jewelers Stores
South Bay Shopping Center, Redondo Beach, California
Buena Park Shopping Center, Buena Park, California
1962–64

Client: Kay Jewelers Company
Program: Retail facades and interiors
Area: 1,400 square feet each
Materials: Wood, plaster, terrazzo, ceramic tile, glass
Project Team: Frank O. Gehry, C. Gregory Walsh Jr.

Gehry was commissioned to design stores for the Kay Jewelers Company as well as the office-and-warehouse building. In plan, the layouts of the stores in the South Bay Shopping Center and the Buena Park Shopping Center were dictated by the long, narrow shape of the leased spaces and the client's requirements for display cases of predetermined sizes and relationships. In materials and detail, however, both stores glittered with jewel-like finishes—tile, glass, polished walnut, and terrazzo—careful spotlighting to showcase goods, and overscaled proscenium-like entries. Eventually, both were remodeled beyond recognition.

Together, the Kay Jewelers projects constitute Gehry's first commercial commission. Commercial projects of increasingly larger scale were to sustain his practice until approximately 1980. As such, commercial venues provided Gehry with an ongoing context for distancing himself from modernism and shaping his own architectural vocabulary. The marketplace became an arena for exploring, through form, materials, and light, a self-conscious stagecraft: an urge toward theatricality and an equal and simultaneous need to reveal the workings back-of-house.

Elevations, sections, and views of the Buena Park store.

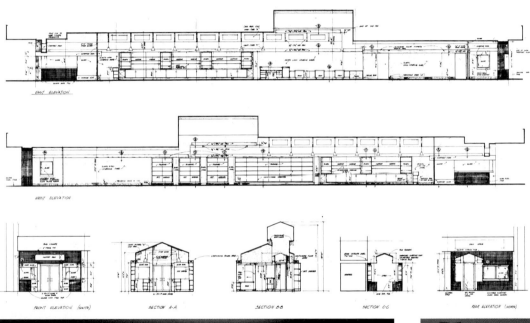

Sixth and Hill Apartments
Santa Monica, California
1963 (project)

Client: Development project
Program: Fourteen–unit apartment building
Materials: Concrete block, wood frame, stucco

Project Team: Frank O. Gehry, C. Gregory Walsh Jr., Fereydoon Ghaffari; Joseph Kurily and Moshe Rubinstein, structural engineer; Wesley Bilson, developer

Street elevation.

SMIV Apartments
Santa Monica, California
1963 (project)

Client: Development project
Program: Thirty-three–unit apartment building
Materials: Wood frame, stucco

Project Team: Frank O. Gehry; C. Gregory Walsh Jr., Fereydoon Ghaffari; Joseph Kurily and Moshe Rubinstein, structural engineer; Wesley Bilson, developer

View of the corner.

**Steeves Office Building
Santa Monica, California
1963 (project)**

Client: Edgar C. Steeves
Program: Six-story office building and
parking structure
Budget: $370,000
Area: 19,500 square feet
Materials: Poured concrete, steel, glass
Project Team: Frank O. Gehry, C. Gregory
Walsh Jr., Frederick A. Usher, Carlos Diniz

Typical plan; section;
rendering of entrance
facade.

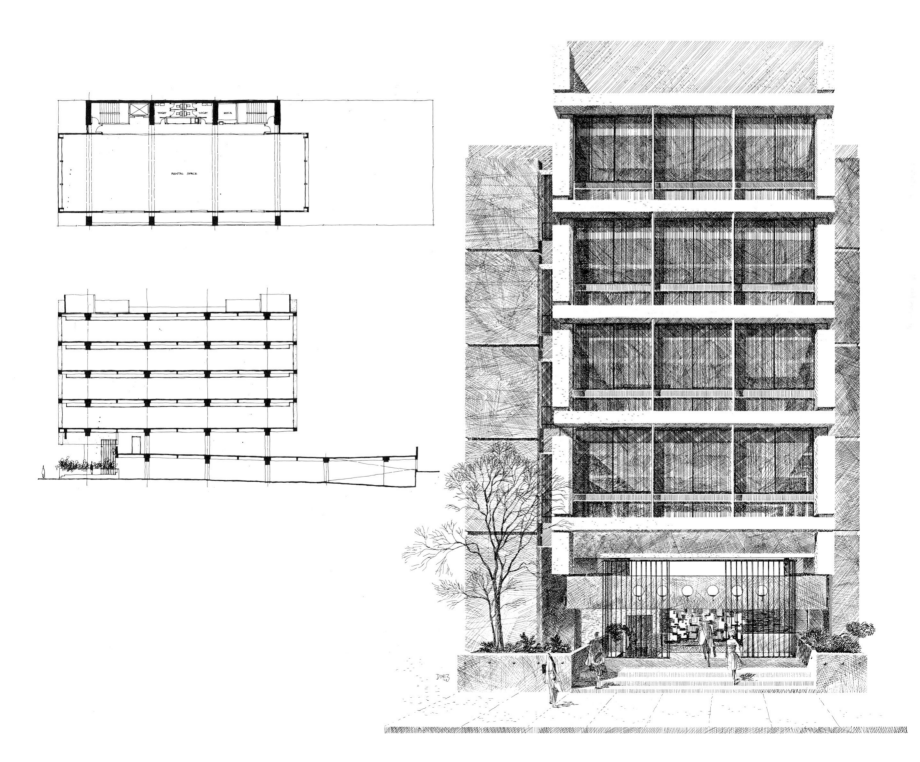

Kenmore Apartments
Los Angeles, California
1963–64

View from South Kenmore Avenue.

Client: Schottland & Miller Company
Program: Fifty-four-unit, three-story apartment building with below-grade parking
Budget: $650,000
Area: 48,000 square feet
Materials: Wood frame, stucco, redwood trim, concrete (parking garage)
Project Team: Frank O. Gehry, C. Gregory Walsh Jr.

Faith Plating Company
Hollywood, California
1963–64

Plan of existing building with outline of new structures; facade along office-zone street.

Client: William Kermin, Faith Plating Company
Program: Industrial remodel, including manufacturing and office space
Budget: $90,000
Area: 5,200 square feet
Materials: Steel frame, stucco
Project Team: Frank O. Gehry

The addition of manufacturing and office spaces to a metal-plating facility on a gritty stretch of Santa Monica Boulevard presented Gehry with a particular logistical challenge: designs for the renovation and expansion of the existing brick building, as well as for the shop and yard areas around it, were restricted not only by the narrow parameters of the budget, site, and schedule but also by the need to keep the facility fully operational throughout construction. Gehry studied the existing operations of the plant and designed new systems for assembly production that allowed the plant to remain in operation while a second-story office area was added. Later, Faith Plating was to adopt a similar organizational strategy for its sixty-thousand-square-foot automobile-bumper factory in Compton.

The design of the second-story addition was a direct response to the light-industrial urban setting. Separated from the brick street-level facade by a deep reveal, the second-story volume is coated in a rough, textured stucco. Two starkly minimal windows set deep into the stucco face the street. To screen the parking, loading, and yard areas from the street, a new stucco wall was added along the sidewalk, balancing and extending the proportions of the new facade.

The building, frank and spare in detailing, has an increased street presence due to the austerity of its materials and the unity of its scale, a presence that borrows identity from the surrounding context while asserting a unique identity through a kind of stalwart introversion.

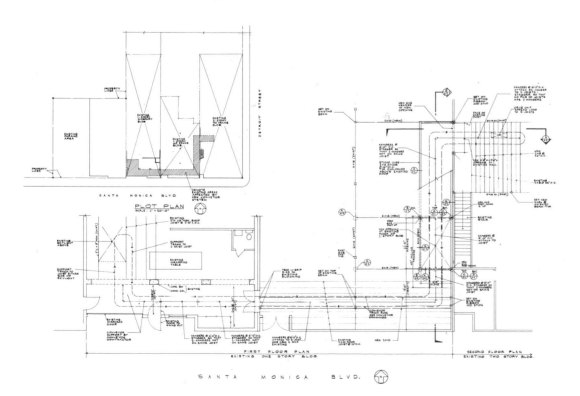

**Atkinson Park Recreation Center
Santa Maria, California
1963–64**

City of Santa Maria, Department of Recreation and Parks
Program: Multipurpose public recreation building
Budget: $93,000

Area: 3,500 square feet
Materials: Concrete block, wood trim
Project Team: Frank O. Gehry, C. Gregory Walsh Jr.; Eckbo, Dean, Austin, and Williams, landscape architect

Views of the facades.

**Hauser–Benson Health Resort
Yucca Valley, California
1964 (project)**

Client: Gaylord Hauser and Dr. C. S. Benson
Program: Health resort master plan, including mineral baths, spas, apartments, recreational areas, and art galleries
Materials: Concrete, wood, glass

Project Team: Frank O. Gehry, C. Gregory Walsh Jr.

Perspective view.

**Kline Residence
Bel Air, California
1964**

Client: Mr. and Mrs. Melvin Kline
Program: Single-family residence
Area: 2,500 square feet

Materials: Wood frame, stucco
Project Team: Frank O. Gehry,
C. Gregory Walsh Jr.

Views of exterior;
details of interior.

**Kay Jewelers Stores
San Fernando, California
Alameda, California
1964 (project)**

Client: Kay Jewelers Company
Program: Retail interiors
Area: 1,400 square feet
Materials: Wood, plaster, terrazzo, tile, glass

Project Team: Frank O. Gehry,
C. Gregory Walsh Jr.

Sketch.

**Los Angeles County Museum
of Science and History Planning
Study
Los Angeles, California
1964 (project)**

Client: City of Los Angeles
Program: Museum remodel

Project Team: Frank O. Gehry, C. Gregory
Walsh Jr., Frederick A. Usher, Carlos Diniz

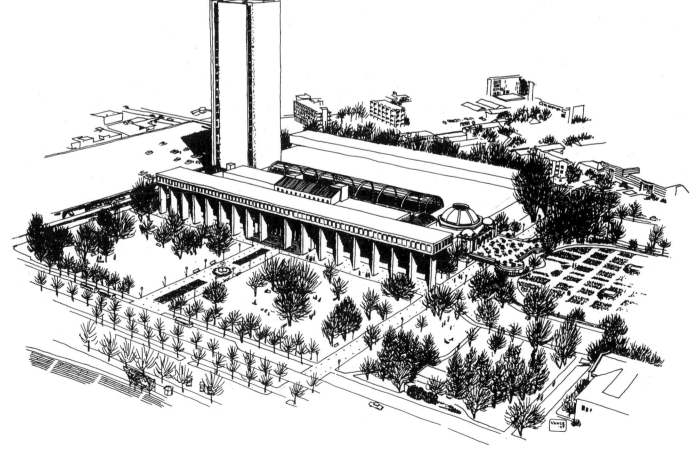

Perspective of
reconstruction plan.

77

Newburgh Feasibility Study
Newburgh, New York
1964 (project)

Client: City of Newburgh
Program: Urban renewal master plan, including residential, commercial, civic, and industrial zones, park system, and parking
Budget: $13,400,000
Area: 65 acres

Materials: Steel frame, concrete
Project Team: David Rosen Associates, planners; Frank O. Gehry, C. Gregory Walsh Jr., Richard Berry; Eckbo, Dean, Austin, and Williams, landscape architect; Nicholas Cirino, structural and civil engineer

Site plan of new construction; perspective view of Community Plaza.

Office Building
Beverly Hills, California
1964 (project)

Client: Schottland & Miller Company
Program: Eight-story office building and parking structure
Budget: $800,000
Area: 26,000 square feet
Materials: Steel frame, reinforced concrete, glass
Project Team: Frank O. Gehry, C.Gregory Walsh Jr., Carlos Diniz

North Rodeo Drive facade.

Danziger Studio and Residence
Hollywood, California
1964–65

Client: Louis and Dorothy Danziger
Program: Graphic-design studio and
one-bedroom single-family residence
Budget: $50,000
Area: Studio: 1,000 square feet;
residence: 1,600 square feet
Materials: Wood frame, stucco
Project Team: Frank O. Gehry, C. Gregory
Walsh Jr., Frederick Usher

Like the Faith Plating Company building
(1963–64), the Danziger Studio and Residence
represents an early attempt to define an urban
language, to articulate a position to the street,
and to find ways to both contribute to and
come to terms with the urban context at the
scale of a small project. As a studio and residence for a noted graphic designer and his wife,
the building required privacy, quiet, and security. As a place of business at the busy commercial junction of Melrose and Sycamore Avenues,
it called for a visible connection to the surrounding context.

Gehry's designs for the Danziger Studio and
Residence were attempts to articulate the two
distinct elements of the program while achiev-
ing an overall formal coherence from the street.
In early schemes a small parking courtyard separated the residential from the commercial portion. A more integrated and affordable solution
was to create an enclosed compound of two
two-story volumes pulled apart, turned inward,
and recessed from the street, with the residence

sequestered behind a high garden wall.

While the industrial and commercial nature
of the neighborhood guided Gehry's choice of
materials and composition for the smooth container of the complex's exterior, spatial flexibility and material unpretentiousness, as with the
Davis Studio and Residence (1968–72), steered
his design of the interiors. The one-thousand-
square-foot workshop, partially convertible to
living quarters, was left as an open space with
no permanent partitions except a darkroom
enclosure. A clerestory skylight admits north
light and a large corner window is set in industrial metal frames. Plaster was considered too
cold for the interior finish, so, for the first time
in Gehry's career, wood framing and ventilation
ducts were left exposed.

The sixteen-hundred-square-foot townhouse, connected to the studio by a soundproof
door, has its own entrance through the front
garden. The glass wall of the two-story living
room faces the enclosed garden, buffered from
the street by the outside wall. Except for a deep
slot in the kitchen wall, no windows face the
street at eye level; all are screened or placed high
in the wall. The double thickness of the wood
and stucco walls—originally planned as concrete—reduces street noise, as do the soundproof doors.

Gehry had full-scale mock-ups of the exterior wall constructed in order to experiment
with finishes, one example of a step that
remains integral to the office's design process.

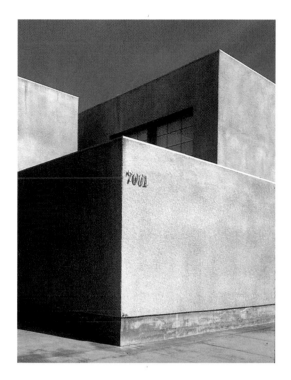

Views of the exterior with
garden wall in foreground.

The goal was to approximate the finish used on the California highway system's tunnels; in the end, heavily textured blue-gray stucco was applied by machine and left unsanded. Gehry said of the project in 1984: "I was interested in the texture of plaster, in getting a texture and a color that never had to be painted. I was also interested in the idea of connection, of putting pieces together, in a way very similar to what I am still doing, twenty years later. I suppose we only have one idea in our lives."

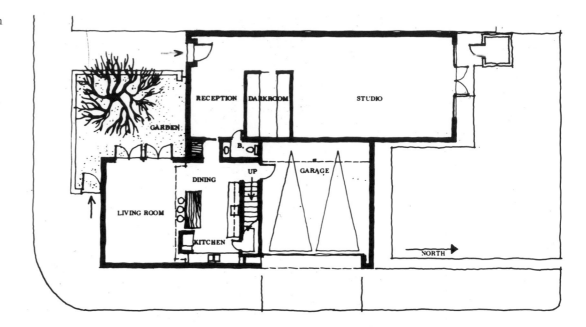

Plans of the two levels
of the final design; section
from first proposal.

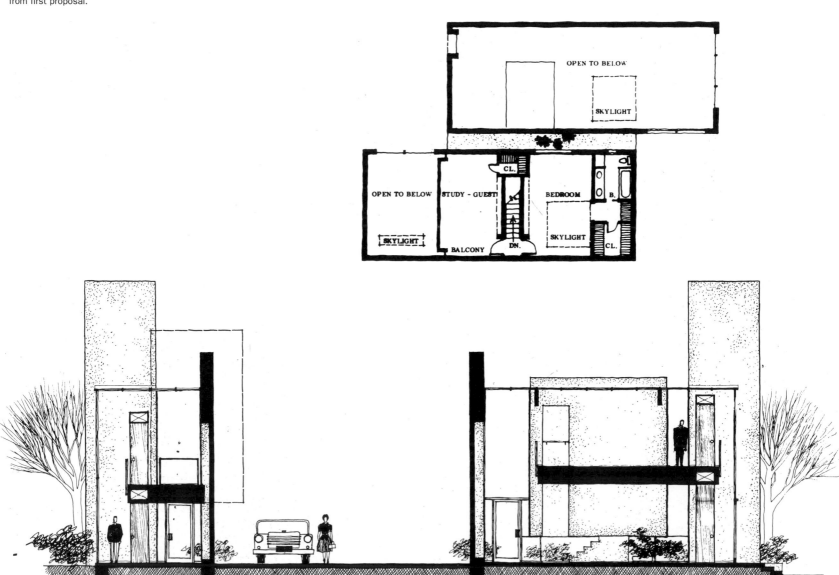

View of the exterior with the living zone in the foreground and the studio in the rear; interior of the studio.

Art Treasures of Japan
Los Angeles County Museum
of Art, Los Angeles, California
1965

Client: Los Angeles County Museum of Art
Program: Exhibition design and installation
Materials: Painted plywood, redwood, fabric,
sand, stone
Project Team: Frank O. Gehry,
C. Gregory Walsh Jr.

Details of installation.

**Clinton Laboratories
Torrance, California
1965 (project)**

Client: Schottland & Miller Company
Program: Four-story medical research
and office building
Area: 16,000 square feet

Materials: Steel frame, stucco, metal roof
Project Team: Frank O. Gehry,
C. Gregory Walsh Jr.

Perspective from Sepulveda
Boulevard.

**Reception Center
Columbia, Maryland
1965–67**

Client: Rouse Company, represented
by Morton Hoppenfeld
Program: Exhibition gallery and
information and sales offices
Budget: $450,000

Area: 20,000 square feet
Materials: Steel frame, concrete block, plaster,
glass, clay tile
Project Team: Frank O. Gehry,
C. Gregory Walsh Jr., David O'Malley

Exterior view.

Merriweather-Post Pavilion
Columbia, Maryland
1966–67

Client: Rouse Company, represented
by Morton Hoppenfeld
Program: Three-thousand-seat outdoor music
pavilion
Budget: $449,000
Area: 35,000 square feet
Materials: Steel frame, concrete, wood siding
Project Team: Frank O. Gehry, C. Gregory
Walsh Jr., David O'Malley, Alfredo Javier;
Christopher Jaffe and Associates, acoustical
engineers

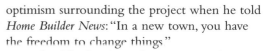

Perspective and view of
insertion into the
countryside.

The new town of Columbia, Maryland—on a
parcel of land slightly larger than the island of
Manhattan, fifteen miles from Baltimore and
twenty miles from Washington, D.C.—was one
developer's response to the fragmented and
piecemeal growth that had marked America's
postwar lateral sprawl. Decrying the oppressive
scale of the metropolis and the dreary homogeneity of the suburbs, James Rouse enlisted the
aid of planners, sociologists, educators, environ-
mentalists, and religious, cultural, business, and
medical leaders to create a community that
would be, he hoped, a "comprehensive response
to the aspirations of a free society" and, at the
same time, profitable. When Gehry accepted the
first of his four Columbia commissions, the
Reception Center (1965–67), he echoed the

optimism surrounding the project when he told
Home Builder News: "In a new town, you have
the freedom to change things."

In the fall of 1966, Gehry was invited to
work on the Merriweather-Post Pavilion, the
first of several important music hall commissions that would come over the course of his
career. Structural and acoustical engineers had
already begun work on the pavilion's design.
The site, a natural bowl in the woods of a
thirty-five-acre downtown park, had been chosen, as had the steel-joist roofing system. Gehry
was offered the commission with the stipulation
that he work within the existing designs, a
modest budget, and a tight schedule: the open-
air amphitheater, intended as the summer home
of Washington's National Symphony Orchestra,
was scheduled to open eight months later.

In site strategy, the design explores the building's presence as an object in the landscape, pre-
figuring such later works as the O'Neill Hay
Barn (1968), the Davis Studio and Residence
(1968–72), and the Concord Performing Arts
Center (1973–76). Concealed from view by the
surrounding hills, the pavilion cannot be seen
even from the parking lot; it appears only as it is
approached on foot. Oriented along a northeast
axis in order to shield audiences from the setting sun and prevailing winds, it seats three
thousand people in amphitheater style under an
overhanging fan-shaped roof, with seating for
an additional four thousand under the trees
beyond. The thirty-five-thousand-square-foot
roof structure is supported on six columns, four
at the rear of the building and two in front of
the stage housing. Exposed steel joists spanning
150 feet with fifteen-foot cantilevers support
the entire roof. The trapezoidal structure is
sheathed in unstained Douglas fir, with a ring
of inexpensive theatrical lights around its
perimeter. The stage, measuring forty by sixty
feet, overlooks an eighty-musician orchestra pit
and faces a continental seating arrangement,
with two aisles dividing the audience into
thirds. Gehry's office was also responsible for
the signage, symbols, lighting, and landscaping
for the ten-acre site.

Acoustical devices, developed with Christopher Jaffe and Associates, include two canopies:
the acoustical canopy hangs over the orchestra,
and the forestage canopy extends thirty feet
over the audience and distributes the sound.
Made from fiberglass-reinforced polyester, each
canopy consists of a series of interconnected
structural baffles eight feet long and three feet
wide. The movable baffles, which have humped
reflective surfaces, make it possible to tune the

Concert pavilion during a performance; structural design; side view.

house for each performance. No amplification is used within the pavilion itself. For those seated on the grass, sound is reinforced by five high-fidelity speakers mounted in the rear fascia. A tape-delay system records stage sound, delays it, and then plays it over the loudspeakers, allowing natural sound (which must travel 150 feet to the grounds) and reinforced sound to arrive at the same instant.

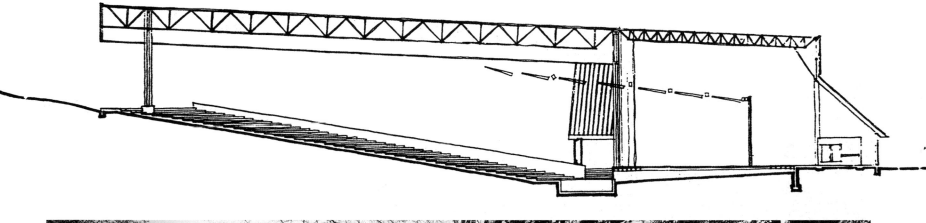

Assyrian Reliefs
Los Angeles County Museum
of Art, Los Angeles, California
1966

Client: Los Angeles County Museum of Art
Program: Exhibition design and installation
Materials: Steel frame walls on Teflon glides
Project Team: Frank O. Gehry,
C. Gregory Walsh Jr.

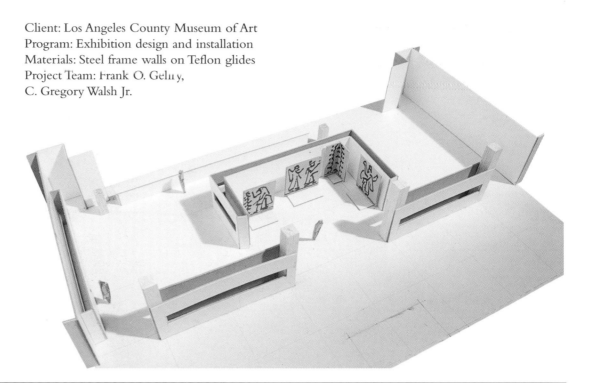

Model view.

Hotchkiss Residence
Santa Monica, California
1966

Client: Frank Hotchkiss
Program: Exterior residential remodel
Area: 350 square feet

Materials: Concrete block, brick
Project Team: Frank O. Gehry,
C. Gregory Walsh Jr.

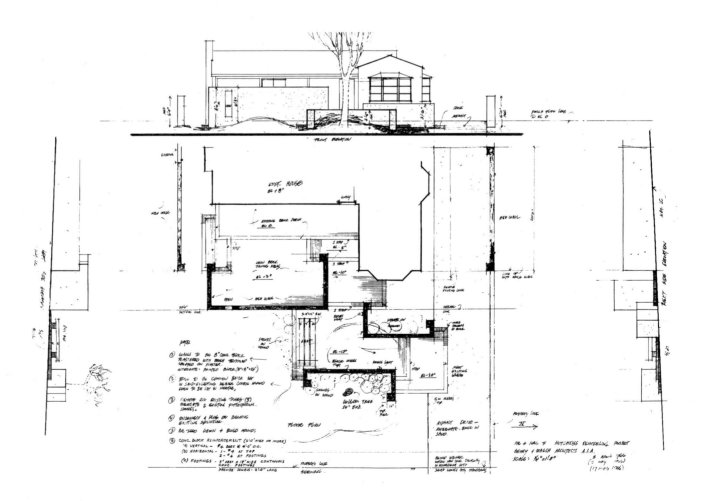

Plan and details
of exterior.

**Ahmanson Gallery Planning
Study
Los Angeles County Museum
of Art, Los Angeles, California
1967 (project)**

Client: Los Angeles County Museum of Art
Program: Museum remodel
Area: 75,000 square feet

Project Team: Frank O. Gehry,
C. Gregory Walsh Jr.

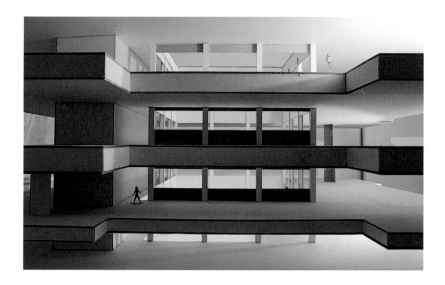

Model view.

**Marr Ranch Land Use Study
Simi Valley, California
1967 (project)**

Client: Milan Roven
Program: Master plan for residential
development, including 5,733 medium-density
single-family residences; 2,601 townhouses and
garden apartments; 350 low-density single-
family residences; mixed-use community center;
elementary school; park; lake; and recreational
amenities
Area: 2,700 acres
Project Team: Frank O. Gehry, C. Gregory
Walsh Jr.; Jerry Pollock, planner

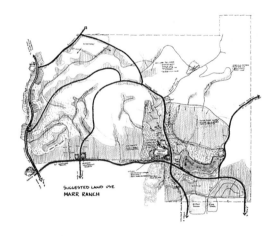

Land-use plan.

**Central Business District
Planning Study
Hermosa Beach, California
1967 (project)**

Client: Godkin Group
Program: Urban renewal proposal, including
retail, office space, two-hundred-room hotel,
and parking
Budget: $20,000,000
Area: 20.6 acres
Project Team: Frank O. Gehry, C. Gregory
Walsh Jr.; Radoslav Sutnar, planner

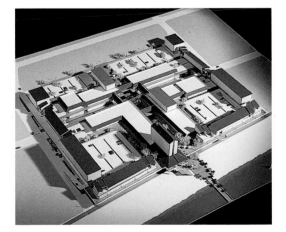

Model view.

**Vernon–Central Redevelopment Project
Los Angeles, California
1967 (project)**

Client: Los Angeles Community Redevelopment Agency, represented by David Crompton
Program: Urban renewal feasibility study, including housing, hospitals, school, retail, and rapid transit.
Project Team: Frank O. Gehry, C. Gregory Walsh Jr.

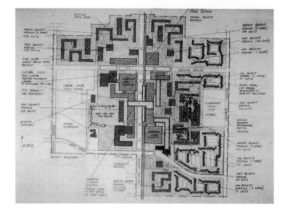

Site plan.

**Greber Studio
Beverly Glen, Los Angeles, California
1967 (project)**

Client: Jacqueline Greber
Program: One-bedroom residence and artist's studio
Area: 1,200 square feet
Material: Wood frame
Project Team: Frank O. Gehry, C. Gregory Walsh Jr.

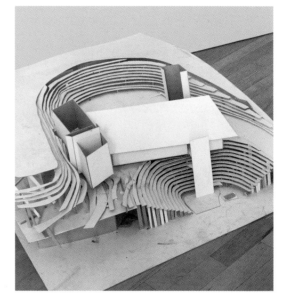

Model showing project in site.

**Watts Automotive Park
Los Angeles, California
1967 (project)**

Program: Roller coaster and amusement park
Area: 250,000 square feet
Project Team: Frank O. Gehry, C. Gregory Walsh Jr.

Site plan.

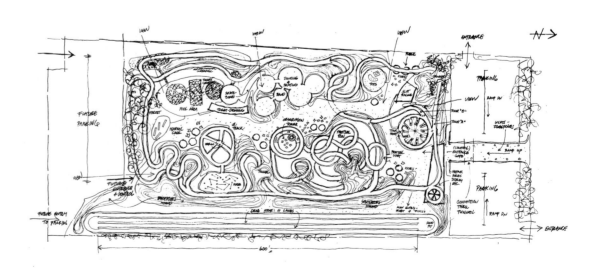

Public Safety Building
Columbia, Maryland
1967–68

Client: Rouse Company
Program: Fire, police, and emergency services
Budget: $60,000
Area: 4,000 square feet
Materials: Steel frame, concrete
Project Team: Frank O. Gehry, C. Gregory Walsh Jr., David O'Malley

This inexpensive concrete structure was built to house Columbia's volunteer fire, police, and emergency services. The open-plan shell contains two fire-fighting equipment storage bays, a hose-drying tower, and sleeping quarters for the firefighters. The final scheme, designed primarily by Gehry's associate David O'Malley, was intended to accommodate later expansion with minimal interference in operations.

The building's significance in Gehry's development is perhaps most apparent in the separation of the roof structure as a distinct mass with its own scale and importance, placed on the pedestal of bearing walls. This preoccupation with the articulation of the roof as a discrete volume is seen first in the Hillcrest Apartments (1961–62) and the Atkinson Park Recreation Center (1963–64) and in Gehry's apartment-building and single-family-residence designs through 1970.

Gehry's Columbia commissions initiated a long and fruitful client-architect relationship. Between 1965 and 1976, Rouse commissioned ten designs by Gehry, or approximately 20 percent of the office's work in that period. Gehry had been philosophically drawn to urban-planning projects since his days as a graduate student at Harvard and as a young architect in Victor Gruen's office. In his own practice, Gehry has designed proposals for seventeen urban-renewal and public-housing projects. Only two of these projects—the University Park Apartments (1970) in Irvine, and the Goldstein Housing Project (1991–96) in Frankfurt—have been built. The self-proclaimed radicalism of Gehry's youth has been tempered, even thwarted, by the economic realities of realizing public-sector projects and replaced by a kind of optimistic realism. Rouse's vision for Columbia, combined with Gehry's professional experience in Gruen's office, introduced the architect to the power of private investment as a vehicle for urban renewal and social change in the United States. Future Rouse commissions were less overtly social in intent—in fact, they were large urban and suburban shopping malls—but they allowed Gehry to design at the scale of the city block, and in so doing to revise his vision of the role of the architect and the nature of architecture's political and social possibilities. Rouse's capital provided Gehry the opportunity to use spatially innovative and contextually complex design strategies to create aesthetically and economically vital spaces.

Model view; built project.

Norton Simon Sculpture Courtyard
Los Angeles County Museum of Art, Los Angeles, California
1968

Client: Los Angeles County Museum of Art
Program: Design and installation of fourteen large-scale sculptures in existing courtyard
Material: Precast concrete
Project Team: Frank O. Gehry, C. Gregory Walsh Jr.

Rockdale Urban Renewal Study
Rockdale, Georgia
1968 (project)

Client: City of Rockdale
Program: Suburban land-use study, including 1,500 units of affordable housing, commercial and recreational amenities, church, schools, and health facilities
Area: 250 acres

Project Team: David Rosen and Associates; Frank O. Gehry, C. Gregory Walsh Jr., David O'Malley

Site plan.

Billy Al Bengston
Los Angeles County Museum of Art, Los Angeles, California
1968

Client: Los Angeles County Museum of Art
Program: Exhibition design and installation
Materials: Wood frame, galvanized corrugated steel, plywood
Project Team: Frank O. Gehry

Details of installation.

O'Neill Hay Barn
San Juan Capistrano, California
1968

Client: Donna and Richard O'Neill
Program: Ranch outbuilding
Budget: $2,500
Area: 1,200 square feet
Materials: Wood, galvanized corrugated steel
Project Team: Frank O. Gehry

Built as one increment in an unrealized master plan—which was to have included the redesign of the main house, guest house, caretaker's house, stable, tack room, dressage ring, and pool—for the ranch of longtime friends Dick and Donna O'Neill, the hay barn represents an attempt at strongly sculptural architecture that serves an unpretentious, utilitarian purpose. The given program of storing hay and farm vehicles did not present inherent problem-solving challenges except the necessity of using simple, inexpensive means. The project could be seen as an almost archetypal challenge: the one-room building, the proverbial blank canvas.

The resulting structure consists of a simple rectangular frame with a trapezoidal roof, tilted between diagonal corners, that creates the perspectival illusion of upward thrust. The roof and walls are sheets of corrugated galvanized steel supported by evenly spaced telephone poles. The modest materials and form were a response not only to the small budget and simple program but also to the surrounding landscape: the metal reflects the shapes and colors of the sky and hills while the corrugations exaggerate the play of light and shadow moving across the barn's surfaces.

The hay barn was the first built work in which Gehry explored a strong non-orthogonal geometry and played with the illusionistic and expressive possibilities of distorted perspectives. These incipient ideas became part of a developing dialogue between Gehry and the artist Ron Davis, who commissioned Gehry to design his residence and studio in 1968. Permutations and transformations of these early explorations in geometry shaped much of Gehry's work through the 1970s.

Views and study designs for the profile of the roof.

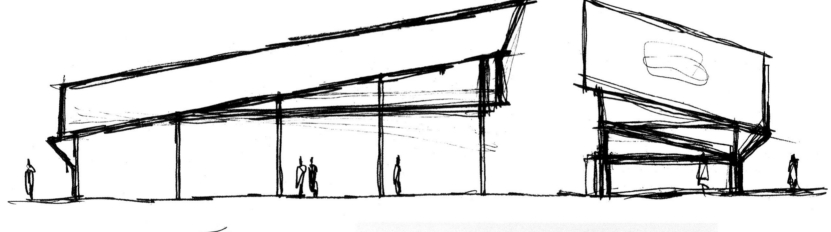

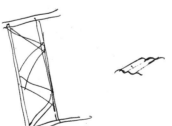

**Clark County Family Housing
Henderson, Nevada
1968 (project)**

Client: Joseph Sanson Investment Company
and Las Vegas Urban Renewal Agency
Program. Affordable housing, including one
hundred apartments and townhouses and
recreation and administration buildings

Materials: Wood frame, stucco
Project Team: Frank O. Gehry,
C. Gregory Walsh Jr.

Perspective of the houses.

**Rose Gardens
North Las Vegas, Nevada
1968 (project)**

Client: Joseph Sanson Investment Company
and Las Vegas Urban Renewal Agency
Program: Affordable housing, including 216
studio and one-bedroom apartments, 120
garden apartments and townhouses for the
elderly, and maintenance, recreation, and
administrative buildings
Materials: Wood frame, stucco

Project Team: Frank O. Gehry,
C. Gregory Walsh Jr.

Perspectives of various
buildings; site plan of
housing for the elderly.

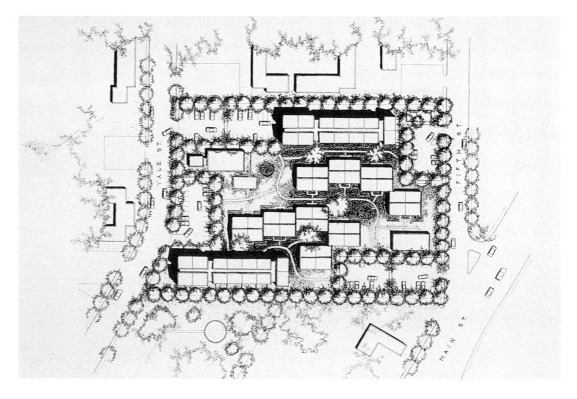

Joseph Magnin Stores
Costa Mesa, California
San Jose, California
1968–69

Client: Joseph Magnin Department Stores
Program: Retail space, salon, and restaurant
Budget: Costa Mesa: $900,000;
San Jose: $700,000
Area: Costa Mesa: 41,000 square feet;
San Jose: 32,000 square feet
Materials: Exterior: stucco, glass;
interior: steel, gypsum drywall, paint
Project Team: Frank O. Gehry, C. Gregory
Walsh Jr., Robert Beauchamp; Geré Kavanaugh,

colors and graphics, Costa Mesa; Deborah
Sussman, colors and graphics, San Jose

Functionally, design objectives for the Joseph
Magnin stores evolved from an analysis of one
typical department-store problem: a profusion of
colors, textures, and objects that compete with
merchandise for the shopper's gaze. In the existing layout, fixed interior walls and decor elements obstructed shoppers' movement and visibility and prevented the stores' management
from responding to rapid changes in fashion.
Exposed mechanical systems and lighting fixtures distracted from merchandise already inade-
quately displayed in tight clusters of racks and
haphazard stacks.

The proposed solution was to create neutral
floor areas demarcated by movable architectonic
elements as well as a central spatial climax that
heightened the spectacle of shopping. Gehry
approached the design of these retail spaces in a
manner similar to the way he had designed
exhibition galleries, installing "tree towers" in
which flexible display systems and hidden,
upward-turned lighting fixtures were housed.
"Supergraphics" labeling departments were
placed above the shoppers' heads. All other
visual distractions, such as air-conditioning dif-
fusers, ceiling tiles, and extraneous lighting fixtures, were either concealed or eliminated.

At the Costa Mesa location, the store was
organized around a central skylight-atrium surrounded by glass-fronted departments. A small
restaurant occupies the atrium's ground level at
the foot of a baroque stairway designed as a theatrical platform for the parade of shoppers. The
San Jose store is only one story but is also organized around a high-ceilinged central open
space, lit by glass-enclosed fixtures. Both stores
were extensively altered in the 1980s.

Plan of San Jose
store; interior views
of San Jose and
Costa Mesa stores.

Bixby Green
Garden Grove, California
1968–69

Client: Bixby Ranch Company, represented by Neil Crawford
Program: Eighty-four townhouses, 1,300–1,500 square feet each
Budget: $5,000,000
Area: Five acres
Materials: Wood frame, stucco, concrete (garage)
Project Team: Frank O. Gehry, C. Gregory Walsh Jr.; Ken Oliphant, acoustical engineer

When representatives of the Bixby Ranch Company, owners of a vast tract of Spanish land-grant property in Orange County, approached Gehry for the design of eighty-four luxury townhouses on a five-acre site, Gehry questioned whether the market existed for such a community. After considerable discussion with the developers, however, he accepted the project as an opportunity to identify and define a set of properties that could constitute quality multi-family housing without relying on status features or fashionable architectural cosmetics.

To transform a flat, treeless site surrounded by undistinguished housing tracts and commercial developments, townhouses were grouped to face inward toward a parklike setting, with parking concealed below grade. Two subterranean garages with generous light wells house fifty-eight cars each. The townhouses, ranging from 1,310 to 1,516 square feet, are grouped around landscaped courts or face garden areas within the park. All have family or dining rooms on the first floor, two and a half baths,

and large, private patios shielded from above by trellises. Staggered to face opposite directions and separated by wing walls, the townhouses were designed to provide complete visual and acoustical privacy. Insulated air space between party walls provides soundproofing up to fifty-five decibels; a mariachi band played at the opening party to demonstrate that it worked. Recreation facilities, including a putting green and pool, are located at the perimeter of the park.

The architectural language of this project is situated somewhere between the "dumb stucco box" and an evolving sculptural vocabulary. The roofs, for example, can be seen from some angles as traditional peaks covered with inexpensive asphalt shingles; from other angles, the roofs become the sloping walls of angular objects sitting atop rectangular pedestals. The asphalt shingles, chosen for their economy, would appear again many years later as wall materials in the Benson Residence (1979–84) and the Indiana Avenue Houses (1979–81). Chimneys and garden walls are combined as additional freestanding sculptural elements.

In site strategy, this project and other master plans—for example, the Newburgh Feasibility Study (1964), Marr Ranch (1967), Clark County Family Housing (1968), University Park Apartments (1970), and even the Goldstein Housing Project (1996)—reflect Gehry's disenchantment, shared by many of his contemporaries, with the rational grid of modernist city

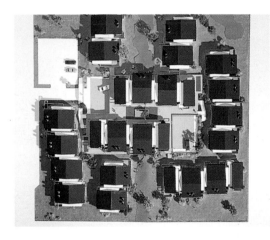

Model views.

planning. Drawing instead on the humanism of the nineteenth-century planners Camillo Sitte and Ebenezer Howard, and inspired by the passionate anti-modernism of Jane Jacobs's urbanistic models, Gehry's master plans repeatedly emphasize privacy and individuality, intimacy of scale, low-rise elevations and irregular plans, and careful consideration of pedestrian circulation, as well as extensive landscaping heavily influenced by Gehry's University of Southern California professor Garrett Eckbo.

Typical apartment plans; views of various buildings.

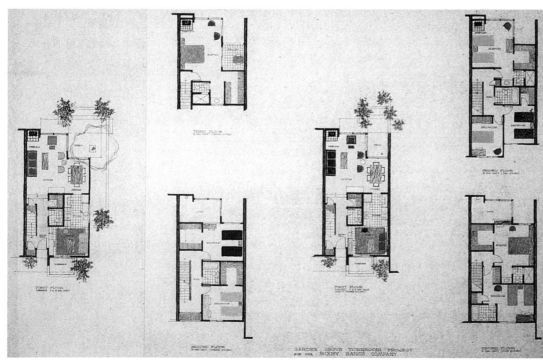

Davis Studio and Residence
Malibu, California
1968–72

Client: Mr. and Mrs. Ronald Davis
Program: Two-bedroom residence and painter's studio
Area: 4,000 square feet
Materials: Wood frame, galvanized corrugated steel, plywood
Project Team: Frank O. Gehry, C. Gregory Walsh Jr., Stephen Dane

After the artist Ron Davis asked Gehry to build two separate buildings for his home and studio on three and one-half pastoral acres in Malibu, a dialogue developed between the two men on perspective, geometry, and perceptual illusion, issues increasingly central to the work of each. The collaboration between the painter creating the illusion of three-dimensional space and the architect reducing space to the virtual perspective of the picture plane grew convoluted and eventually was simplified. The building was ultimately conceived simply as a container for movable things, a singular, barnlike structure that would sit on the landscape and confront the terrain in an uncompromising way. Inside, the space would be adaptable to the artist's life and work. In the end, a trapezoidal shell with a strong sculptural relationship to the earth and flexible spatial organization inside incorporated both studio and living quarters.

The building was framed in Douglas fir and clad in sheets of corrugated galvanized steel and exposed plywood. The steel roof, following the slope of the hillside, tilts steeply from a thirty-foot height at one corner to ten feet at the diagonal corner. A twenty-by-twenty-foot central skylight and carefully positioned windows frame views of the sky, ocean, and surrounding hillsides. Two poured-concrete terraces bracket the house on opposite sides. The siting is such that the building is always approached obliquely.

Inside, an enclosed spine containing the kitchen and bathroom separates sleeping lofts from work spaces at the ground level, while a stairway-bridge reconnects them overhead. The open interior accommodates not only a garage but also the production and exhibition of over-sized artwork, a continuation of the dialogue between artist and architect. As Gehry explains, "I built the most beautiful shell I could do, and then let him bring his stuff to it, and convert it to his use. In its optimum, it's a kind of confrontation between the client's aesthetic and values and my own." The building was designed to allow phased additions of different levels to increase the usable floor space, and the crawl space beneath the building (except under the garage area, which sat on an on-grade slab) was designed to permit changes in the mechanical and electrical systems.

Sketches; views toward hill and toward ocean.

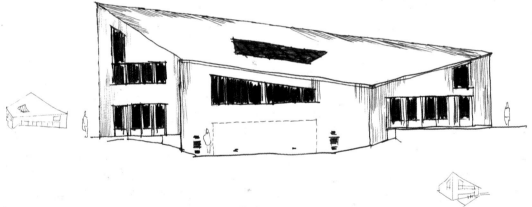

Construction phases
of the interior; view
of studio area.

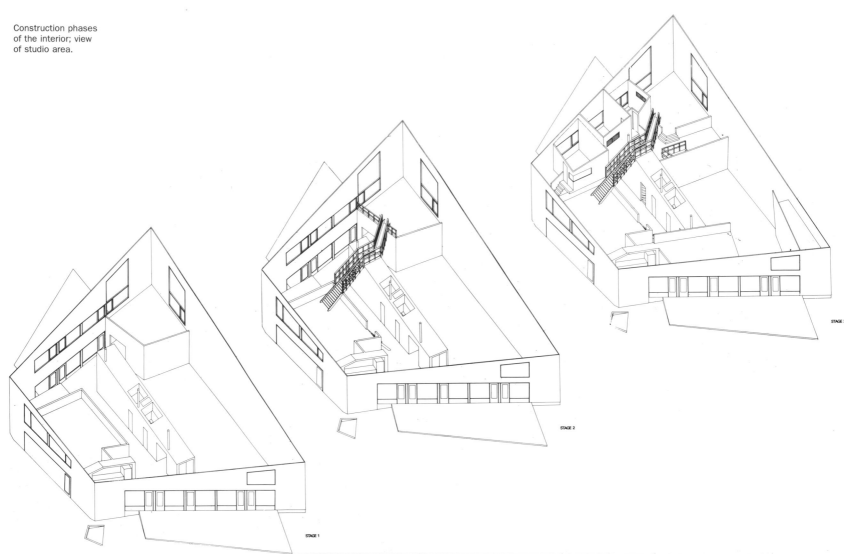

STAGE 1

STAGE 2

STAGE 3

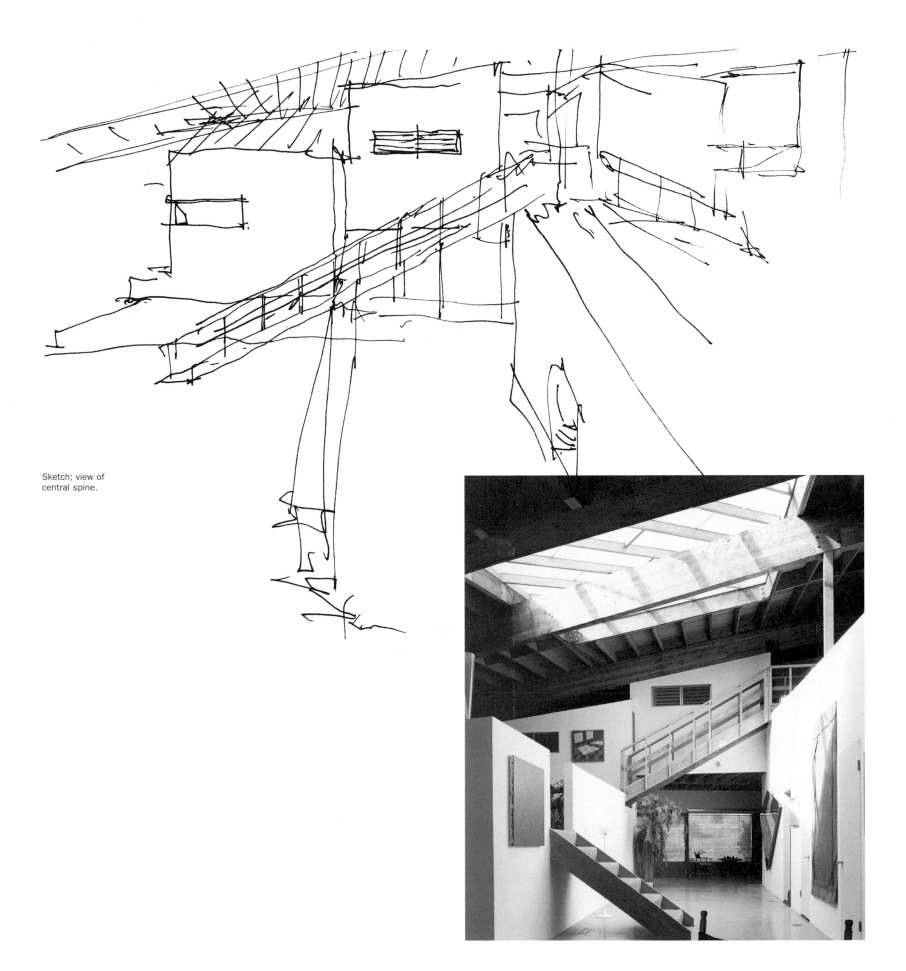

Sketch; view of
central spine.

99

Easy Edges
Cardboard Furniture
1969–73

Retail Prices: $15–$115
Materials: Glued and laminated corrugated cardboard with masonite edge banding
Project Team: Frank O. Gehry, C. Gregory Walsh Jr., Robert Irwin; Jack Brogan, prototypes; Stephen Dane

The exposed cut-and-layered edges of a cardboard site model inspired Gehry to investigate cardboard's potential as an inexpensive and versatile alternative to traditional furniture materials. The initial result of this investigation was the development of Edgeboard Sections, a lightweight, durable, and structurally sound material formed by cross-laminating individual sheets of ordinary corrugated fiberboard into stacks that could then be inexpensively die-cut into any prescribed profile. The color, warmth, and strength of Edgeboard were found to be comparable to that of wood. Edgeboard also had the advantage of being both structural and finished: its suedelike texture required no paint or varnish, and its structure lent itself to a variety of sculptural shapes, elastic enough to bend and spring back. The material was found to be flexible and affordable enough to produce for its potential applications to range from buildings to furniture to floor tiles.

Easy Edges, a line of commercial and residential furniture, was developed directly from Edgeboard, taking full advantage of the functional and aesthetic appeal of its combed surfaces. Hardboard facing was required to protect the relatively fragile smooth surfaces on the sides of the furniture; the exposed corrugated surfaces, however, were found to be highly durable. In one of many research tests, three small Easy Edges bar stools supported a two-thousand-pound Volkswagen. After extensive market research, a collection of seventeen patented pieces was introduced at major department stores in New York and Los Angeles. The collection, priced between $15 and $115, included body-contoured chairs, bar stools, rockers, dining room and conference tables, side chairs, lamp tables, desks, nesting cubes and chairs, chaise longues, and bed frames.

The collection received extensive critical acclaim within both the trade and the popular press. Financing and production complications, however, convinced Gehry that in order to sustain his success in furniture manufacturing he would have to sacrifice his architectural practice, a step he was unwilling to take. After the initial output, production was stopped, resulting in the transformation of the pieces from inexpensive household furniture into high-priced collector's items.

Chair and stages of
its assembly.

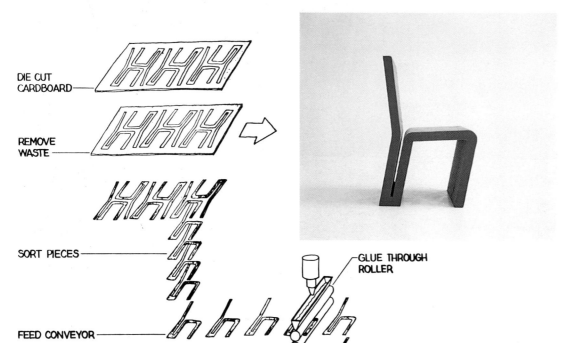

DIE CUT CARDBOARD

REMOVE WASTE

SORT PIECES

FEED CONVEYOR

GLUE THROUGH ROLLER

ALIGN IN JIG

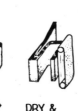

COMRESS SLIGHTLY

LAMINATE MASONITE EDGES

DRY & SAND

ADD DOWELS FOR GLIDES & STIFFENERS

PACK & SHIP

Various pieces from series.

Rouse Company Headquarters
Columbia, Maryland
1969–74

Client: Rouse Company
Program: Four-story corporate headquarters office building
Budget: $7,300,000
Area: 150,000 square feet
Materials: Steel frame, stucco
Project Team: Frank O. Gehry, C. Gregory Walsh Jr., Donald Carlson, Ronald Altoon, Marc Appleton, Rene Ilustre, Alfredo Javier, Adolfo Ortega, Barton Phelps, Hak Sik Son; Robert Doyle, associated architect

The Rouse Company Headquarters occupies a lakefront site in the town of James Rouse's creation. Designed for interior flexibility and future expansion, the plan is organized along a naturally lit pedestrian "street," while a grid of thirty-by-thirty-foot structural bays allows for growth on both the north and south sides of the building. The raised flooring system accommodates telephone and electrical lines, and enclosures house structural columns and HVAC ducts and registers, leaving the ceiling free of ductwork. A combination of fluorescent and custom-designed quartz-iodide lighting fixtures (part of ongoing lighting research that started with the Joseph Magnin Stores in 1968) provides an efficient blend of ambient and direct light easily integrated with individual workstations. Glazed and acoustical panels and fabric-covered partitions erected directly on the raised floor allow for different configurations of the interior layout, from low, open stations to completely enclosed offices and conference rooms. The skylit central atrium provides a zone of vertical circulation. Major stairways and plantings are surrounded on each level by the internal street, which links a variety of "event spaces" and connects open offices to the atrium, creating a central meeting space. Stepped open-air terraces similar to those of the Cochiti Lake Recreation Center (1972–73) break down the scale of the building and imply its open-ended program while providing views over the lake and surrounding countryside. Even the exterior wood trellises are designed to be unbolted and readapted for use in other locations.

SITE PLAN

0 20 40 60 80 100 feet

Site plan; view from the lake.

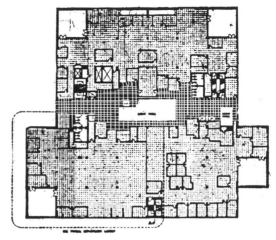

Typical plan showing permanent and temporary subdivisions; typical distribution of office sector.

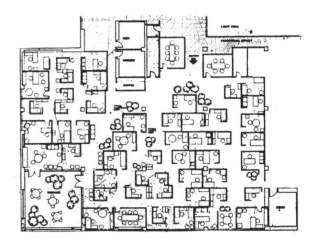

View along a pergola; facade facing lake.

View of spine, lit from
above, that defines
various sectors.

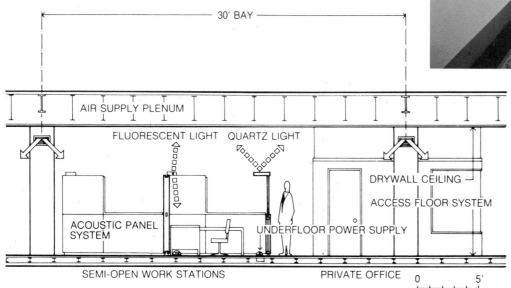

30' BAY

AIR SUPPLY PLENUM

FLUORESCENT LIGHT QUARTZ LIGHT

DRYWALL CEILING

ACCESS FLOOR SYSTEM

ACOUSTIC PANEL
SYSTEM

UNDERFLOOR POWER SUPPLY

SEMI-OPEN WORK STATIONS

PRIVATE OFFICE

0   5'

Schematic structural
section; work areas.

**American School of Dance
Los Angeles, California
1969 (project)**

Client: Schottland & Miller
Program: Eight dance studios, classrooms,
library, and administrative offices
Area: 40,000 square feet
Materials: Steel, stucco
Project Team: Frank O. Gehry,
C. Gregory Walsh Jr.

**University Park Apartments
Irvine, California
1970**

Client: Irvine Company
Program: Affordable housing, including 256 one-, two-, and three-bedroom apartments, and recreation building
Budget: $2,315,000

Area: 260,000 square feet
Materials: Prefabricated stud frame, stucco
Project Team: Frank O. Gehry, C. Gregory Walsh Jr.; P.O.D., landscape architect

Views of buildings and exterior spaces.

Hollywood Bowl Renovation
Hollywood, California
1970–82

Existing amphitheater.

Client: Los Angeles Philharmonic Association and Department of Parks and Recreation, City of Los Angeles

Temporary Renovation, 1970
Program: Temporary modification of existing orchestra shell
Budget: $149,000
Materials: Cardboard sonotubes

Master Plan, 1971–73
Program: Six-phase master plan for renovations

to existing outdoor amphitheater
Budget: $2,688,991 for all phases

Phase I, 1976
Program: Renovation of backstage areas, administrative offices, and control booths
Budget: $1,293,000

Phase II, 1978 (project)
Program: Flexible above-stage equipment storage and demountable orchestra shell
Materials: Steel frame with acoustical panels

Day and night views
of temporary orchestra
shell system.

Cardboard sonotubes;
administrative offices.

Phase III, 1980
Program: Permanent acoustical modification of existing orchestra shell
Budget: $133,000
Material: Fiberglass spheres

Phase IV, 1981
Program: Two-level parking deck
Budget: $568,491
Materials: Steel frame, concrete

Phase V, 1982
Program: Renovations to existing toilet facilities
Budget: $150,000

Phase VI, 1982
Program: Open-air restaurant
Budget: $544,500
Area: 10,000 square feet

Project Team: Frank O. Gehry, C. Gregory Walsh Jr., Barton Phelps, Hak Sik Son, Ken Francis, Rene Ilustre, Adolfo Ortega, Sharon Williams, Ed Woll, Steven F. Tomko; Jaffe Acoustics, acoustical engineer

Temporary modifications of the Hollywood Bowl were undertaken during a four-month period in 1970 and 1971 as a response to problematic acoustics that prevented musicians from hearing each other on stage. The design changes, however, were also part of a changing identity for the bowl, described by the executive director at the time, Ernest Fleishmann, as "dynamic new directions in programming, [reflecting] profound changes in the contemporary presentation of the performing arts." Specifically, the phased renovations would parallel the Los Angeles Philharmonic Association's

efforts to increase the Hollywood Bowl's intimacy, informality, and flexibility in mixing a broader range of media and appealing to a wider range of ages.

Although Gehry admits that his formal study of music went no further than "the Hawaiian guitar, by the number method" and acoustical engineer Christopher Jaffe had only "seven traumatic years on the fiddle," this was the second of three award-winning collaborations between the two. An arrangement of sixty cardboard sonotubes, three feet in diameter and twenty feet tall, was installed within the existing shell in time for the season opening on July 7, 1971. Architecturally, the inexpensive tubes, replaced annually until a permanent solution was installed in 1980, could refer equally to classical columns and disposable pop art; acoustically, they improved diffusion at the

Views of second-phase model with proposal for removable roofing for orchestra shell.

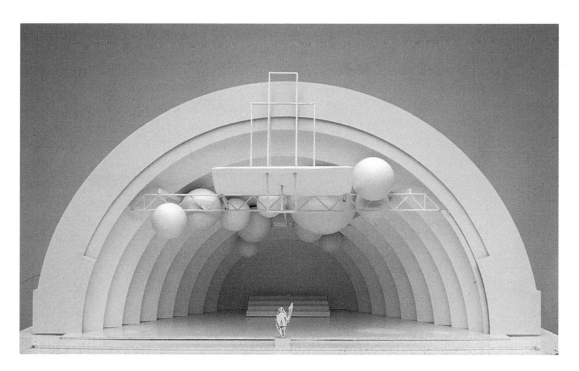

Model and detail of permanent acoustical system in roofing over orchestra.

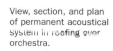

View, section, and plan
of permanent acoustical
system in roofing over
orchestra.

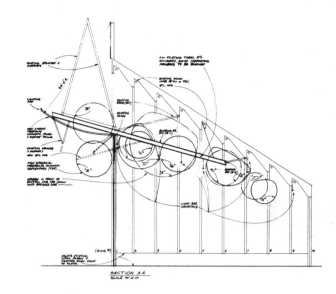

SECTION A-A
SCALE ¾" = 1'-0"

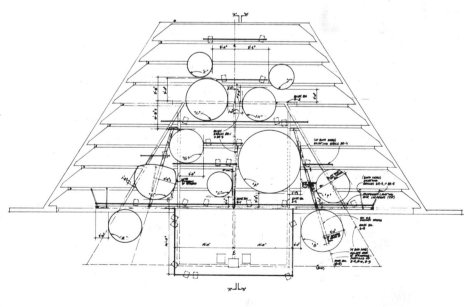

source, allowing the musicians to hear one another properly while projecting balanced orchestral sound to the eighteen thousand seats in the amphitheater. Sound was further enhanced by a new electronic amplification and time-delay system.

A master plan was developed in 1971 and approved in 1973 for the eventual upgrading of the entire facility. Phasing and scheduling were critical factors, since the bowl's summer season had to continue uninterrupted each year. The first phase entailed the renovation of backstage areas, administrative offices, utility tunnels, and control booths; new warehouse and maintenance crew quarters; renovation and addition of toilet facilities; and various circulation improvements.

The second phase, which was unrealized, called for a new, flexible above-stage structure capable of supporting various pieces of stage equipment, including a demountable orchestra shell. In successive years, additions and renovations were made on tight schedules during the five-month off-season. In 1980, a permanent acoustical modification of the existing shell was designed. Fiberglass spheres of varying sizes were suspended inside the shell to reflect and distribute the sound to the orchestra. In 1981, a two-level concrete parking deck was designed and installed north of the understage building, and in 1982, a new ten-thousand-square-foot open-air dining pavilion was designed and built.

New service area and pavilion for open-air restaurant.

Handler Residence
Santa Monica, California
1971–73 (project)

Client: Mr. and Mrs. Kenneth R. Handler
Program: Four bedroom single-family residence
Area: 5,000 square feet

Materials: Wood frame, stucco
Project Team: Frank O. Gehry, C. Gregory
Walsh Jr., Donald Carlson, Hak Sik Son

Plan; south elevation.

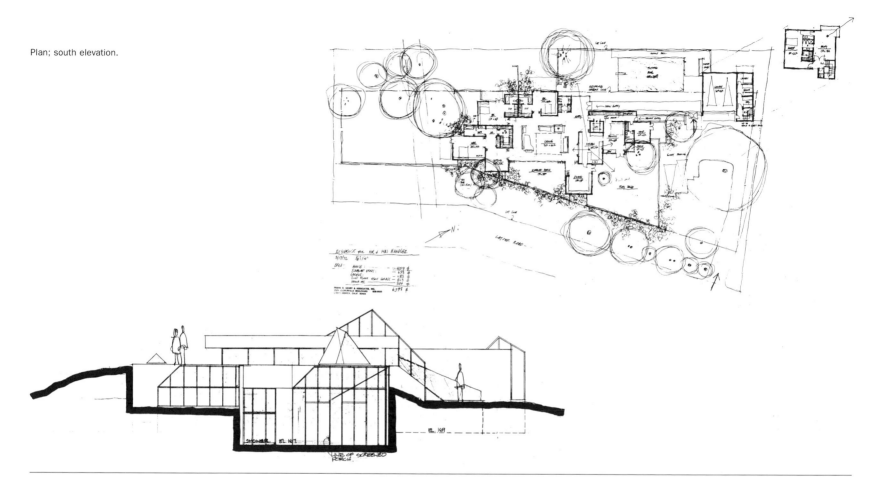

Hollydot Park Townhouses
Hollydot Park, Colorado
1971–73

Client: Mr. Holland Duell, A. B. Duell Realty
Program: Master plan for 200 luxury
townhouses; four showcase houses built
Budget: $566,000

Area: 28,000 square feet
Material: Wood frame
Project Team: Frank O. Gehry,
C. Gregory Walsh Jr.

Model view.

Recreation Center
Cochiti Lake, New Mexico
1972–73

Client: Great Western Cities, Inc.
Program: Community recreation facility, including multipurpose indoor recreational area, outdoor swimming pool, kitchen/snack bar, locker rooms, tennis courts, playground
Budget: $380,000
Area: 20,000 square feet
Materials: Wood frame, stucco
Project Team: Frank O. Gehry, C. Gregory Walsh Jr.; Sasaki Walker Associates, Inc., landscape architect

The Cochiti Pueblo—a one-thousand-person Native American tribe living on thirty thousand acres midway between Santa Fe and Albuquerque—consented in 1965 to the development of 7,500 acres of tribal lands. Great Western Cities, a developer, intended to convert the tribe's alfalfa fields and grazing lands into a leisure and resort area, by 1980 a city of fifty thousand. The elaborate program for the town center called for housing, retail, services, restaurants, hotels, a museum, and a twelve-thousand-square-foot recreation center with two tennis courts, a playground, and a swimming pool. Gehry designed the master plan, but ultimately only the Recreation Center was built.

By using materials and design to control desert heat, sun, and wind, Gehry created a building that tempers the harsher aspects of the climate while exploiting the desert's scenic assets. The building's stepped terraces, echoing the pueblo architecture indigenous to the southwest, open toward the north and east, away from the hot sun and prevailing winds. The clerestory windows provide air circulation and daytime lighting for the multipurpose space within, where ventilation ducts and mechanical systems were left exposed. The complex includes a kitchen and snack bar as well as showers and lockers adjoining an enclosed swimming pool area. Two tennis courts complete the facility. Wooden trellises, like the shade poles found in pueblo dwellings, shade the entrances to shops run by Native Americans. Long stucco walls painted a light sky blue surround the open central plaza, intended as a focal point for residents and tourists alike, and visually tie the building form into the surrounding landscape, mediating the horizon between earth and sky.

The building, a strongly defined horizontal shape in a landscape of flat mesas and rolling hills, was not only a response to the high-desert climate and terrain but also a formal continuation of the minimalism first seen in the Faith Plating Company (1963–64) and the Danziger Studio and Residence (1964–65). The building can be viewed as the beginning of the end of Gehry's emphasis on the rectangular stucco box. It additionally marks a development in Gehry's exploration of the open courtyard as a container for other objects and a device for affecting the perception of horizon and sky, inspired in part by significant work in the 1970s by such Southern California artists devoted to issues of light, space, and the earth-sky relationship as Larry Bell, James Turrell, and Robert Irwin.

Recreation center inserted into site; site plan.

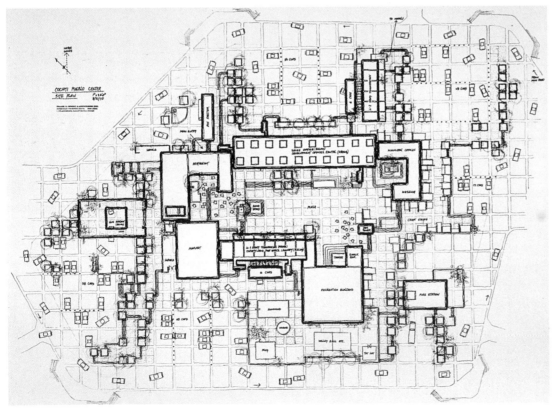

Aerial perspective; views
of recreation center and
surrounding spaces.

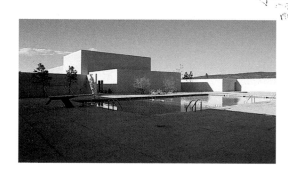

Janss Residence
West Los Angeles, California
1972–74

Client: Mr. and Mrs. Edwin Janss Jr.
Program: Single-family residence
Area: 4,200 square feet
Material: Wood frame
Project Team: Frank O. Gehry,
C. Gregory Walsh Jr.

This house for a modern art collector was initially designed as a simple shoe box, with a bedroom extending to a second floor at one end. The designs call for the bedroom, slightly cantilevered over a carport, to open onto a greenhouse and outdoor sitting area cut into the roof. A clerestory lights the main central room from above. Gehry intended the house to have cement-asbestos siding and corrugated transite panels, along with an unpeeled redwood tree-trunk portal above the driveway's entrance, a treatment that would reappear in the Norton Residence (1982–84). When built, the house's plan and massing were kept largely intact but the material articulation of the exterior was not. Only one large room, with exposed joists and a bottleneck skylight, was built according to Gehry's specifications.

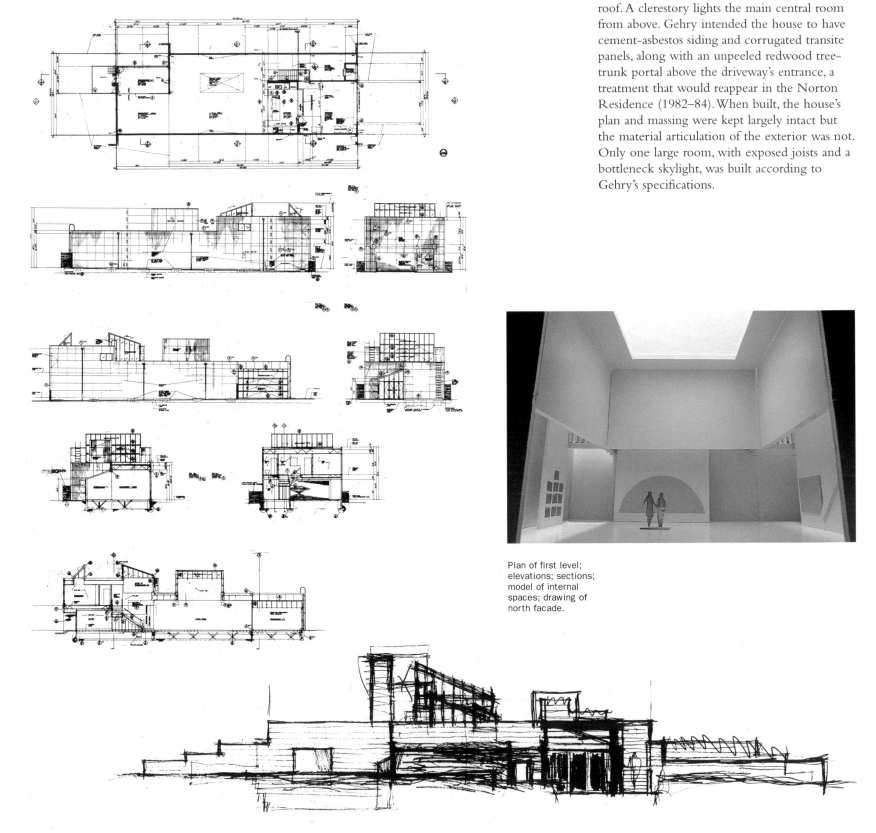

Plan of first level;
elevations; sections;
model of internal
spaces; drawing of
north facade.

Santa Monica Place
Santa Monica, California
1972–80

Plan of shopping-center
level; view of complex.

Overleaf:
Entrance facade; facade
of south parking garage.

Client: Rouse Company and Santa Monica
Redevelopment Agency
Program: Shopping center and two six-story,
one-thousand-car parking structures
Budget: Shopping center: $30,000,000;
parking structures: $12,000,000
Area: 585,000 square feet
Materials: Steel frame, concrete, stucco,
chain link

Project Team: Frank O. Gehry, C. Gregory
Walsh Jr., Hak Sik Son, Steven F. Tomko,
John Clagett, Ronald Altoon, Donald Carlson,
Frederick Fisher, Rene Ilustre, Ed Woll; Craig
Hodgetts, associated architect; Victor Gruen
and Associates, associated architect; Johnson
& Neilson, structural engineer; Donald
Dickerson & Associates, electrical engineer

Santa Monica Place, developed by the Rouse
Company and the city of Santa Monica as an
urban-renewal project, is a 585,000-square-foot
complex consisting of two department stores,
163 shops and restaurants, landscaped courts,
outdoor observation decks, and two six-level
parking structures. While the Rouse Company
invested $50 million for the acquisition of the
site and the construction and stocking of the
retail space, the voters of Santa Monica
approved a $14.5-million bond issue to pay for
the complex's two parking garages—land pur-
chase, relocation, site preparation, and construction—to be leased from the city by Santa Monica Place.

The ten-acre site is one block from the Pacific Ocean and the Santa Monica Pier, and on axis with Santa Monica's Civic Center to the south and downtown pedestrian shopping area to the north. Designed by Gehry's firm as part of a revitalization program for Santa Monica's ailing central business district, the original plans for the ten-acre site proposed a mixed-use development with low buildings at street level, binding the development to the existing urban context. When the program was simplified to the scale of a shopping mall, design goals remained the same: to break down the scale of such an enormous project into architectonic pieces suitable to the scale of the surroundings, and to develop a framework in which each individual store could determine its own identity without introverting the project and excluding its environs.

Two large department stores, each designed by the stores' own architects, are located diagonally across from one another, and the two parking structures, with one thousand spaces each, anchor the remaining corners of the site. The name of the mall is affixed in large white chain-link letters to the south parking structure's blue chain-link wall facade. The internal circulation of the mall is tied to existing city streets and the older pedestrian mall. Four generous midblock courtyard entrances draw people into the central atrium, and walkways and escalators link the three floors of retail spaces. A clerestory allows the mall to be lit almost entirely by daylight; even at the lowest level, artificial light is required only at night, when indirect fluorescent light is bounced off the clerestory ceiling. Large outdoor terraces, mandated as public open spaces by the Coastal Commission, frame views of the ocean from the building's west side.

For tenant improvements to Bubar's Jewelers, the only store he designed in the mall, Gehry arranged various types of jewelry merchandise into separate, freestanding pavilions organized along a central "street" running the length of the eighteen-by-one-hundred-foot space. The typical dropped ceiling was eliminated, leaving the full height of the space open. The assemblage of simple forms differentiated by material and color was extended to the facade facing the mall.

If measured by gross sales, lease and property-tax revenues to the city, the creation of jobs, and the burst of office and commercial building construction in and around downtown that followed its construction, Santa Monica Place can be said to have played a significant role in the economic revival of downtown Santa Monica during the 1980s. In 1990, as part of its turnaround on ten-year leases, the shopping center underwent extensive restyling by another design firm.

**Woodlands Metro Center
Woodlands, Texas
1972–77 (project)**

Client: Woodlands Development Corporation
Program: Shopping center, including
department stores, offices, hotel, restaurants,
and cincmas
Area: 800,000 square feet
Project Team: Frank O. Gehry, C. Gregory
Walsh Jr., Donald Carlson, Morton Hoppenfeld

**Larkspur-Greenbrae Mall
Marin County, California
1973 (project)**

Client: Rouse Company
Program: Shopping center, including three
department stores, two hundred shops and
restaurants
Area: 65 acres
Materials: Steel frame, concrete
Project Team: Frank O. Gehry,
C. Gregory Walsh Jr.

Model view.

**Illinois Center
Chicago, Illinois
1973 (project)**

Client: Rouse Company
Program: Shopping center, including two department stores, hotel, shops, and parking
Area: 750,000 square feet
Project Team: Frank O. Gehry, C. Gregory Walsh Jr., Donald Carlson, Eugene Kupper, Ron Altoon

Model views.

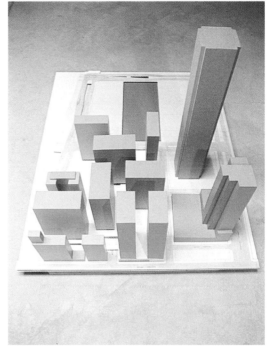

**Golden Cove Shopping Center
Palos Verdes Estates, California
1973**

Program: Shopping center renovation, including facades, interiors, entry, kiosks, and signage
Material: Wood frame
Project Team: Frank O. Gehry, C. Gregory Walsh Jr., Don Swiers

Site plan.

Concord Performing Arts Center
Concord, California
1973–76

Client: Concord Performing Arts Center Authority and Department of Leisure Services, City of Concord
Program: Outdoor performing-arts pavilion
Budget: $3,600,000
Area: 35,000 square feet
Materials: Steel, concrete, concrete block, chain link
Project Team: Frank O. Gehry, C. Gregory Walsh Jr., James Porter, Rene Ilustre, Eugene Kupper, Hak Sik Son; Jaffe Acoustics, Inc., acoustical engineer; Kurily & Szymanski, structural engineer; Aaron Garfinkel, structural engineer; Irving Schwartz, electrical engineer; John Kerr and Associates, mechanical engineer; Sasaki Walker Associates, landscape architect

Thirty miles from Berkeley, on the eastern edge of the San Francisco Bay Area's sprawl, lies the town of Concord, a town of one hundred thousand. When 122 acres of open land with views of Mount Diablo and the Lafayette-Orinda Hills to the Carquinez Strait were donated to the city by a developer in exchange for a variance elsewhere, the city commissioned a new home for its Summer Music Festival. The program required not only the flexibility to stage musical, theatrical, and dance performances but also a variety of other public functions, including graduation ceremonies, concerts, performances, and special events for ten regional high schools.

In essence, the building is a concrete slab slung by a steel-truss roof over a thirty-five-acre crater. Twelve trusses, each twelve feet deep, support four hundred thousand square feet of steel decking and lightweight concrete two inches thick; the trusses cantilever forty feet past the four columns supporting the roof. Because of the site's proximity to an active seismic fault, the columns are four and one-half feet in diameter with fourteen-inch-wide flange steel reinforcements and fireproof concrete bases.

The stage, two hundred feet in diameter, has a three-level, concrete-block backstage structure containing offices and dressing rooms. The stage can be converted among four formats: a traditional proscenium, an arena theater, a thrust stage projected into the audience, and an intimate theater for six hundred. Of the 3,500 fixed seats, none is more than ninety feet from the stage, and of the 4,500 outdoor seats, none is more than 180 feet away. The front portion of the stage can be hydraulically lowered for increased performance flexibility. An entire seating bay at the rear can be removed to allow trucks to drive onto the stage to load props and equipment. Lighting catwalks and control booths are suspended from the truss structure. An orchestra pit, located directly understage, is surrounded by an open acoustical moat to aid in sound amplification. A concrete-block wall encloses the rear of the amphitheater, separating it from the backstage support facilities. Assisted Resonance, an electronic sound-reinforcement system developed by the project's acoustician, Christopher Jaffe, enables the amount of reflected sound in the lower and middle frequencies to be changed in order to provide optimum reverberation-time relationships.

On the approach from the grass-covered parking area, the view of the pavilion is obscured by an enclosing berm, an earthwork inspired by the work of artist Robert Smithson. A chain-link ticket booth is Gehry's first built use of the material.

Study drawing.

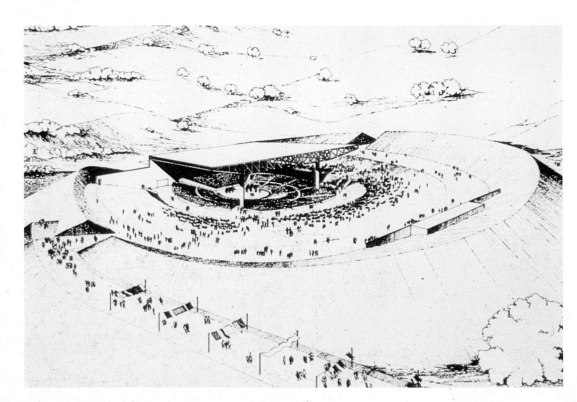

Site model with first
roofing proposal: earthwork
hiding the pavilion from
the parking.

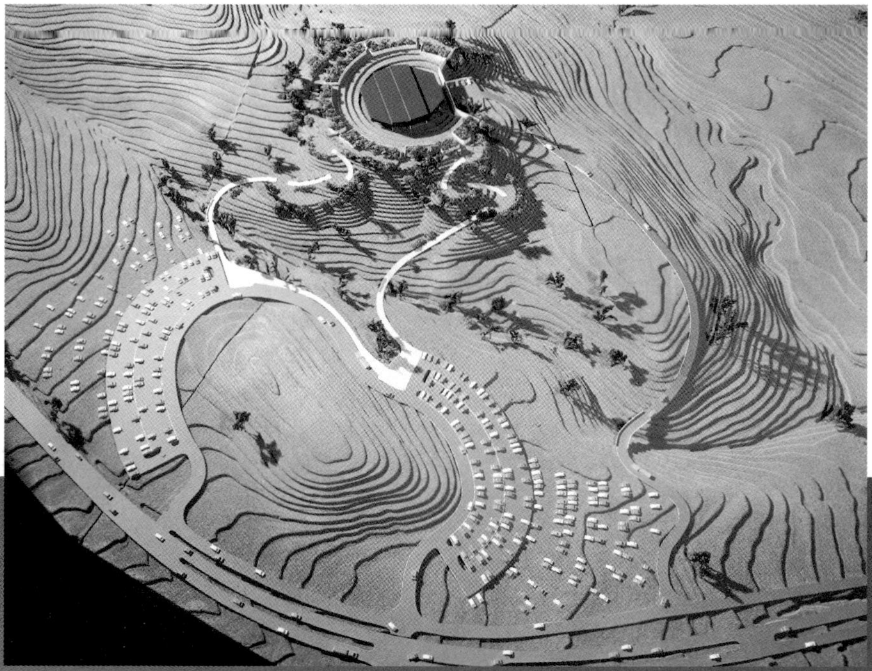

Section and views with
stage and variable seating.

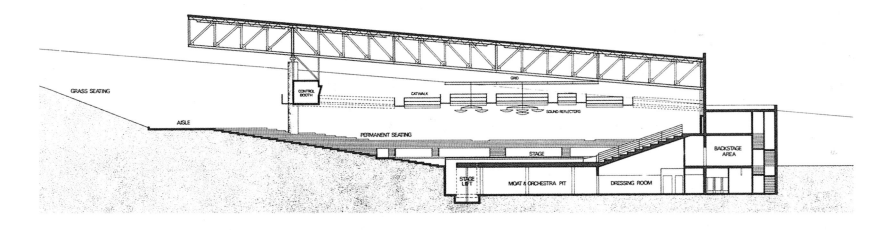

GRASS SEATING
CONTROL BOOTH
AISLE
CATWALK
GRID
SOUND REFLECTORS
PERMANENT SEATING
STAGE
BACKSTAGE AREA
STAGE LIFT
MOAT & ORCHESTRA PIT
DRESSING ROOM

Model views; night view of
stage; support equipment.

Placement and Career Planning Center
University of California, Los Angeles
1973–75

Model; view
of building.

Client: University of California, Los Angeles
Program: One-story office building
Budget: $673,000
Area: 16,000 square feet
Materials: Wood frame, stucco, brick

Project Team: Frank O. Gehry, C. Gregory
Walsh Jr., Eugene Kupper, Rene Ilustre,
Hak Sik Son, Marc Appleton

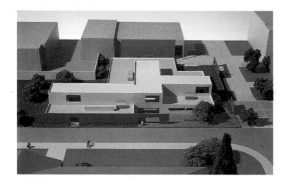

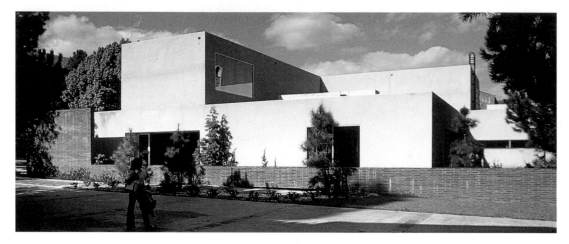

Westinghouse Distribution Services Office Building
Flair Industrial Park, El Monte, California
1974

Views of complex
and of one building.

Client: Westinghouse Distribution Services
Program: Warehouse and offices
Budget: Exterior: $564,000; interior: $175,000
Area: 25,000 square feet

Materials: Steel frame, concrete block
Project Team: Frank O. Gehry, C. Gregory
Walsh Jr., Ron Altoon, Eugene Kupper

Horton Plaza
San Diego, California
1974 (project)

Client: Rouse Company
Program: Shopping center master plan, including three department stores, shops, offices, restaurants, and one-thousand-room hotel
Area: 2,050,000 square feet
Project Team: Frank O. Gehry, C. Gregory Walsh Jr., Hak Sik Son

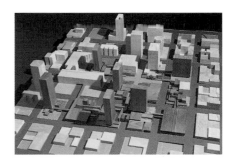

Model view.

The Atrium
Rudge and Guenzel Building,
Lincoln, Nebraska
1974–76

Client: Hawthorn Realty Group
Program: Shopping center within existing landmark building, including retail, restaurants, entertainment, offices, and health club
Budget: $1,825,000

Area: 250,000 square feet
Materials: Steel frame, galvanized corrugated steel
Project Team: Frank O. Gehry, C. Gregory Walsh Jr., Hak Sik Son, Ronald Altoon, Rene Ilustre, Vaughn Babcock

Exterior;
interiors.

133

Shoreline Aquatic Park Pavilions
Long Beach, California
1975

Client: City of Long Beach
Program: Boathouse and conservatory
Area: Boathouse: 1,500 square feet;
conservatory: 2,600 square feet
Materials: Boathouse: wood frame, stucco;
conservatory: concrete block, steel posts,
chain link

Project Team: Frank O. Gehry, C. Gregory
Walsh Jr., Donald Carlson; SWA Group
(formerly Sasaki Walker Associates), landscape
architect

Sketches; models of
pavilion and conservatory
in chain link.

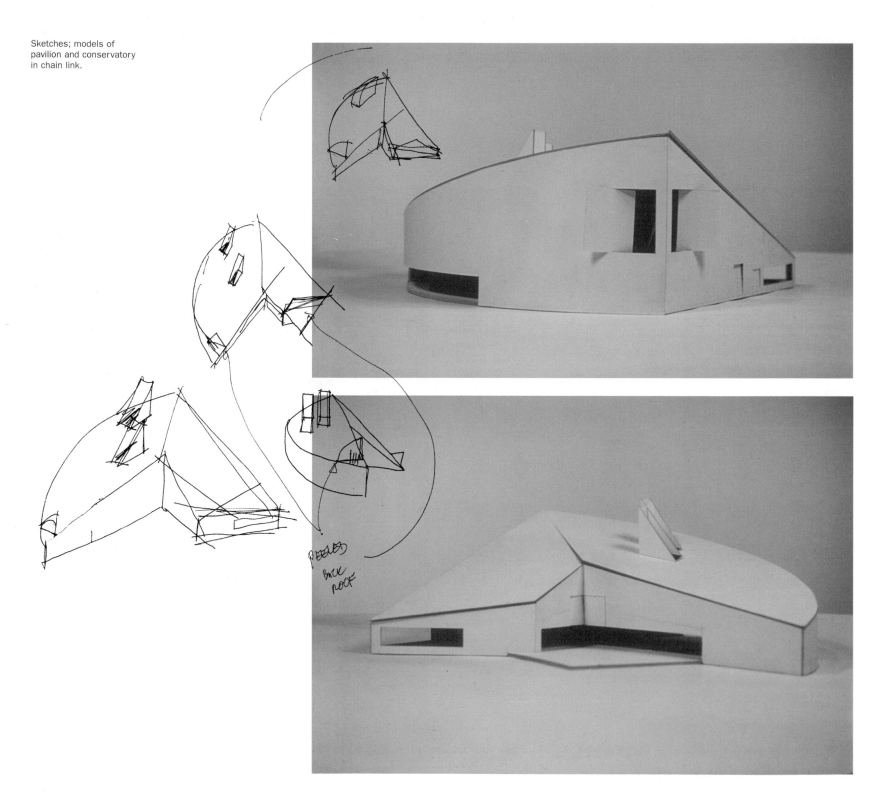

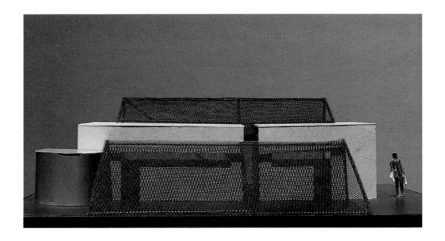
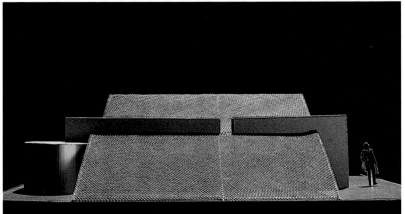
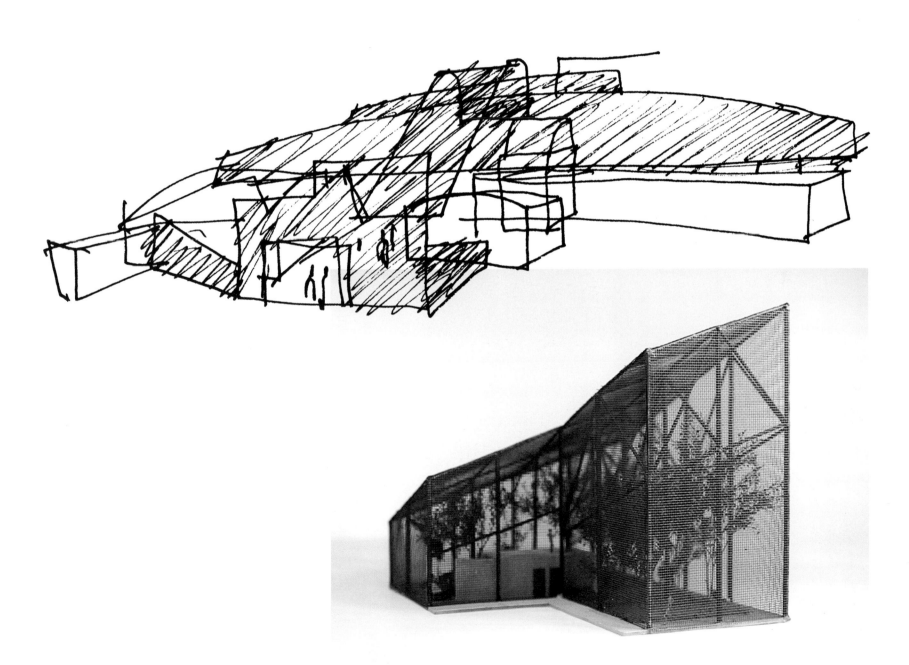

Norton Simon Gallery and Guest House
Malibu, California
1974–76

Client: Norton Simon
Program: Residential remodel
Materials: Wood frame, exposed wood lathe, glass, unmilled timber, plaster, brick
Project Team: Frank O. Gehry, C. Gregory Walsh Jr., Rene Ilustre, Hak Sik Son, Marc Appleton; Michael Taylor, interiors

An eight-thousand-square-foot Spanish-style beach house was extensively remodeled to provide a gallery for the clients' Asian art collection as well as add a suite of guest quarters to supplement the main residence on the adjoining lot. The idea of joining the two residences was initially explored but discarded in favor of preserving the clients' privacy. The guest house was left detached, with the gallery on the first floor and the guest rooms on the second and third.

On the ground floor, most existing partitions were removed to create one open space with a continuous glass wall facing the beach. A large skylight was cut into the roof; plaster ceilings were taken out and the structural framing left exposed, recalling high-ceilinged temples, appropriate for the collection of large-scale Asian sculptures. Two of the original structural columns were replaced with unpeeled logs. Lath-and-plaster walls were replaced with new wood lath, left exposed as in the Nelson (1978) and Gehry (1977–78) Residences. Theatrical track lighting and ambient indirect lighting concealed in recesses in the framing bounce warm light off the sandblasted-wood ceiling. The floors are brick, set without mortar on a bed of sand in which the electrical power supply is run, allowing flexibility for the location of floor outlets. Besides the gallery and entertainment area, the ground floor, furnished by interior designer Michael Taylor, also houses an office and curatorial room.

Outside, a wooden trellis necessary as a sunscreen on the southwest facade was transformed into a sculptural element—a pile of lumber appears to slide from the roof at one end—and extends the exposed wood framing from inside to out. The second and third floors contain guest quarters opening onto a large roof terrace.

Stairs leading to guest rooms; open gallery space facing exterior.

Sketch; pergola.

Harper House
Village of Cross Keys, Maryland
1976

Client: Rouse Company
Program: Fifteen-story condominium tower and parking garage
Budget: $8,390,000
Area: 220,000 square feet

Materials: Steel frame, concrete, brick
Project Team: Frank O. Gehry, C. Gregory Walsh Jr., Hak Sik Son, Rene Ilustre, Alfred Javier, Adolfo Ortega; Robert Doyle, associated architect

Views of front facade.

**Thornwood Mall
Park Forest South, Illinois
1976 (project)**

Client: New Community Enterprises
Program: Shopping-center master plan
Budget: $2,862,000
Area: 110,000 square feet
Materials: Concrete block, galvanized
corrugated steel

Project Team: Frank O. Gehry, C. Gregory
Walsh Jr., Hak Sik Son, Ronald Altoon, Vaughn
Babcock, Rene Ilustre, Eugene Kupper

Model view.

**Santa Monica Pier Renovation
Santa Monica, California
1976 (project)**

Client: Department of Recreation and Parks,
Santa Monica
Program: Exterior remodel of commercial
and recreational pier

Budget: $215,000
Project Team: Frank O. Gehry, C. Gregory
Walsh Jr., Barton Phelps, Hak Sik Son

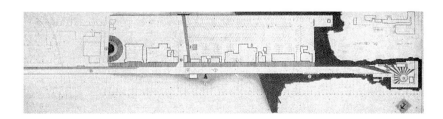

Site plan.

**Manhattan Tower
Los Angeles, California
1976 (project)**

Client: Los Angeles–Wilshire Partnership
Program: 14-story affordable housing tower,
including 212 apartments, street-level retail,
and recreational facilities

Materials: Prefabricated steel frame modular
units, concrete bearing walls
Project Team: Frank O. Gehry,
C. Gregory Walsh Jr.

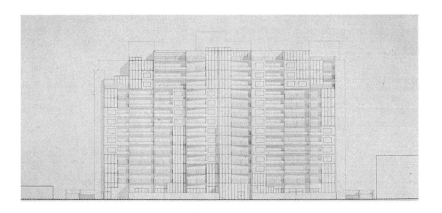

West elevation.

**Jung Institute
Los Angeles
1976 (project)**

Client: Jung Institute, represented by
Sam Francis
Program: Offices and research facility
Area: 10,000 square feet
Material: Wood frame
Project Team: Frank O. Gehry, C. Gregory
Walsh Jr., Don Carlson

Sketch; model views.

The Vineyard
Escondido, California
1976 (project)

Program: Shopping-center renovation
Area: 250,000 square feet
Project Team: Frank O. Gehry, C. Gregory
Walsh Jr., Hak Sik Son

First- and second-floor
plans; elevations,

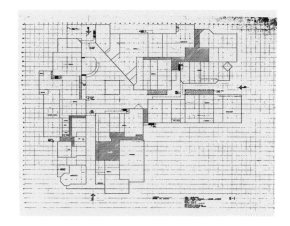

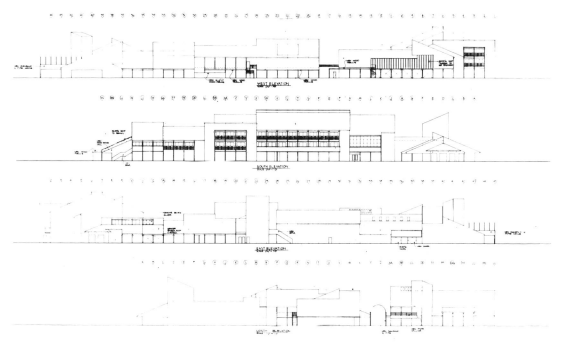

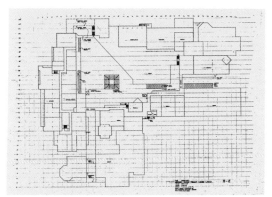

St. Ives Residence
Santa Monica, California
1976–78

Client: Development project
Program: Residential remodel
Area: 2,300 square feet
Materials: Wood frame and stucco
Project Team: Frank O. Gehry, C. Gregory
Walsh Jr., Hak Sik Son, Rene Ilustre

Existing house;
remodeled exterior.

Mid-Atlantic Toyota
Glen Burnie, Maryland
1976–78

Client: Mid-Atlantic Toyota Distributors, represented by Frederick R. Weisman
Program: Two-story office building
Budget: $2,165,000
Area: 25,000 square feet
Materials: Steel frame, concrete block, galvanized corrugated steel
Project Team: Frank O. Gehry, C. Gregory Walsh Jr., Frederick Fisher

Gehry was asked to transform a concrete-block warehouse into a corporate headquarters that would both replicate the experimental open offices associated with the increased productivity of Japanese companies and inspire an understanding and pride in Japanese culture itself. On the exterior, the building's shell is punctured by strip windows for the offices, three projecting bays of corrugated metal that hold executive offices, and the company's sign. Inside, the basic structure of the warehouse was retained. Reception and service areas sit on the ground floor at the base of the main stairway, lit by a skylight thirty feet above. Rather than translate the client's wishes for a Japanese-inspired aesthetic literally, Gehry proposed a scenographic interpretation: the new second floor was conceived as a spatial evocation of Japan's Inland Sea. Its angular partitions, narrowing passageways, and suspended trapezoidal chain-link panels imply mountains, inlets, and clouds. Open office areas lie on either side of a funnel-shaped hall painted in progressively deepening wall colors to increase the perspective illusion of length. Long lighting troughs containing continuous fluorescent fixtures run obliquely through the space.

Views of facade with projecting bays.

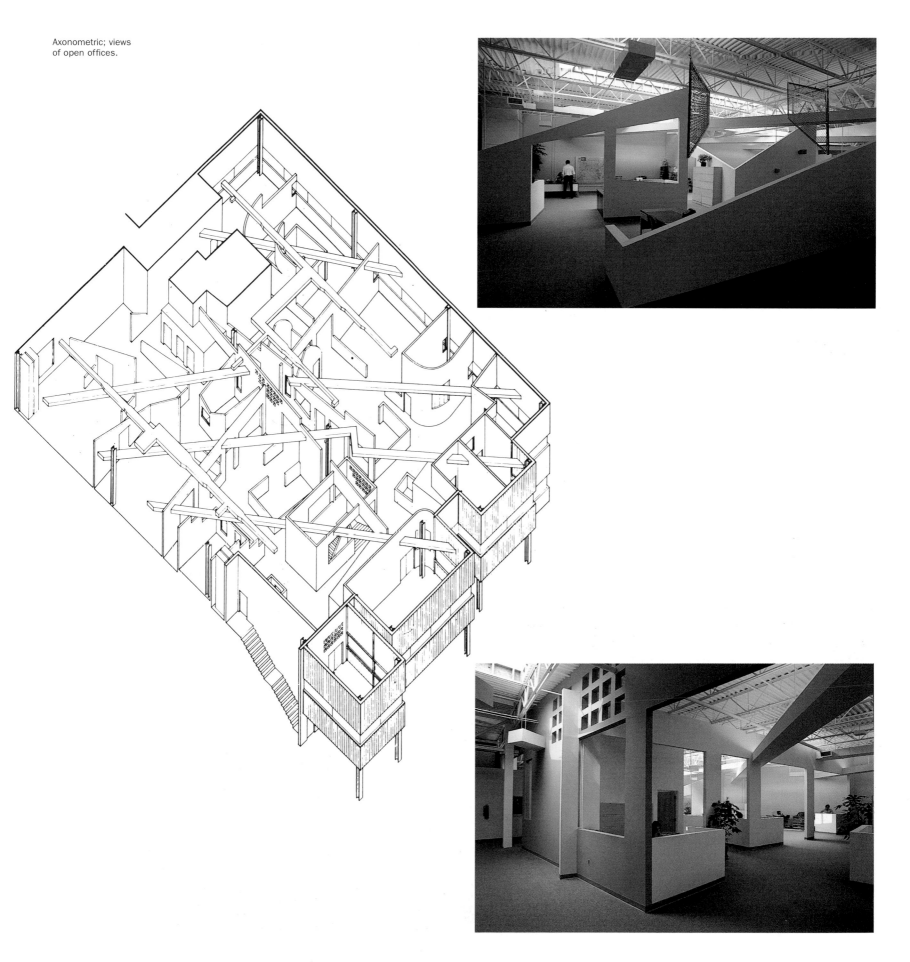

Axonometric; views
of open offices.

Gemini G.E.L.
Los Angeles, California
1976–79

Client: Gemini G.E.L. Fine Art Lithographers, represented by Sidney Felsen and Stanley and Elyse Grinstein
Program: Remodel of art-lithography company
Budget: $200,000
Area: 6,000 square feet
Materials: Wood frame, stucco
Project Team: Frank O. Gehry, C. Gregory Walsh Jr., Hak Sik Son; Kurily & Szymanski, structural engineer

This complex of studio, storage, and gallery spaces for one of the most important fine-arts graphics studios in the United States was designed in two phases. In 1976 Gehry began the renovations to the existing building on Melrose Avenue by addressing the building's relationship to the street. Exploring the possibilities of a thin, paperlike stucco skin, Gehry wrapped the existing building in a new facade of dark gray stucco, leaving remnant details of

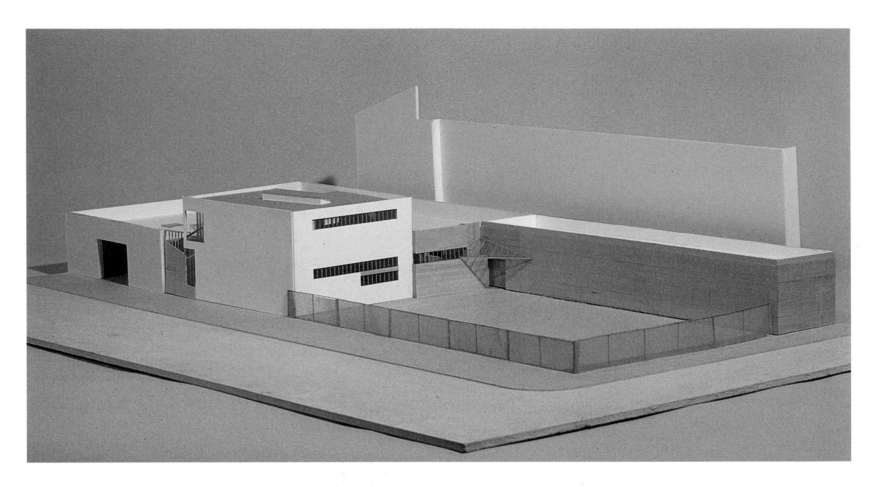

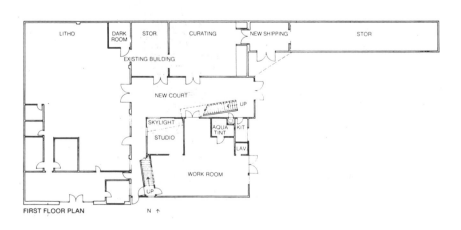

FIRST FLOOR PLAN   N ↑

Model of complex; plan of
ground floor; model of new
building; plan of upper floor
and roof of new building.

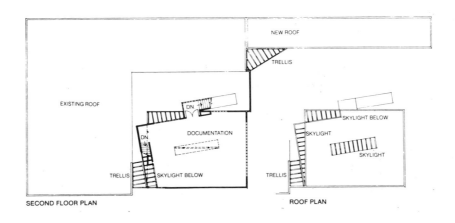

SECOND FLOOR PLAN

ROOF PLAN

Principal entrance between new and old buildings; skylight over stairs; street facade of existing building.

the old building's stud construction exposed behind windows as though the stucco could be peeled from the framing. The southwest corner of the facade was angled upward in acknowledgment of a large billboard overhead.

For the second phase, a new two-story, five-thousand-square-foot building was added to the east of the old building, creating an L-shaped court between the two. Here the skin is again a thin veneer, with windows tacked onto stud framing visible behind the glass. The new structure contains a silk-screen and intaglio workshop, artist's studio, gallery, and documentation room.

In a twisting circulation pattern also seen in designs for the Familian Residence proposal (1978), a stairway is skewed ten degrees off the structure's grid, wrapping and piercing two sides while connecting the open loft spaces within. The rear stair, on the outside, is exposed; the angularity of the front stair, the main entrance to the building, distorts perspectival perception. The simple form is further fragmented by two skylights; two frames that shade the court visually complete the form of the stucco box as well as activate the shipping and receiving space left over between the old building and the new.

A plywood wall, extending along the northern edge of the property and implying a third object-building, sits between the new studio and a one-thousand-square-foot storage vault.

Views of new building from
courtyard and street.

**Weisman Beach House
Trancas, California
1977**

Client: Frederick R. Weisman
Program: Residential remodel
Area: 3,300 square feet

Material: Wood frame
Project Team: Frank O. Gehry, C. Gregory
Walsh Jr., Hak Sik Son

View along beach facade.

**Trancas Beach House
Trancas, California
1977**

Client: Frederick R. Weisman
Program: Interior residential remodel
Materials: Wood frame, drywall

Project Team: Frank O. Gehry,
C. Gregory Walsh Jr.

Detail of stair handrail.

Berger, Berger, Kahn, Shafton & Moss Law Offices
Los Angeles, California
1977–78

Client: Berger, Berger, Kahn, Shafton & Moss
Program: Interior office remodel
Budget: $426,500
Area: 15,600 square feet
Materials: Steel frame, gypsum board
Project Team: Frank O. Gehry, C. Gregory Walsh Jr., Ken Francis, John Clagett, Frederick Fisher

For a fifteen-thousand-square-foot floor of law offices in a new office building, Gehry subverted the usual hierarchies of office layout. In plan, the traditional organization of private offices lining exterior walls is partially reversed so that open workstations and glazed passages are located along the perimeter walls, allowing daylight to penetrate to corridors and inner offices. The formal variation of the individual offices was intended to indicate the individualism of their occupants. The gleam of customary finishes was omitted in favor of exposed wood-frame-and-drywall construction, with each office treated as a sculptural composition of colliding geometries. The scattered array of distorted platonic solids is pierced by the unifying elements of exposed duct, structure, and light troughs slung from the white-painted slab above.

Compositionally, the project represents a first attempt at blending two previous organizational strategies: first, the linear spine or pedestrian "street" seen in the Los Angeles Museum of Science and History proposal (1964) and Rouse Company Headquarters (1969–74), and second, the arrangement of discrete object-forms to create a whole, beginning in 1976 with Gemini G.E.L. and the Jung Institute project. In these law offices, the strategies of the internal street and the arrangement of objects are employed simultaneously, resulting in the winding circulation and compressed spaces of an interior village.

Offices; open workstations; plan.

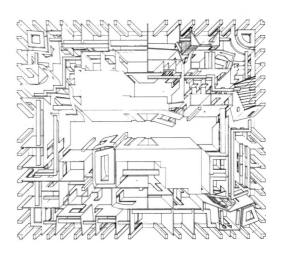

Gehry Residence
Santa Monica, California
1977–78; 1991–94

Client: Frank and Berta Gehry
Program: Residential remodel
Area: 3,100 square feet
Materials: Wood frame, galvanized corrugated steel, chain link, plywood
Project Team: Frank O. Gehry, Paul Lubowicki, Jon Drezner

Detail of skylight over kitchen; existing house; view of reconstruction from northeast.

In 1977, Frank and Berta Gehry bought a pink, two-story, gambrel-roofed bungalow on a corner lot in Santa Monica, built around 1920. A radical remodel within a limited budget ensued.

Working closely with his associate Paul Lubowicki, Gehry's intention was to explore ideas about materials he was already using—corrugated metal, plywood, chain link—and further explore the expressive possibilities of raw wood-frame construction. By developing ideas in models, he drew on the Wagner, Familian, and Gunther "sketches in wood," all proposals of 1978, and committed himself to expressing the same vitality in a finished product that he had in his sketches. Still playing with issues of perspective and movement, as well as

drawing axonometrically in three dimensions, the result is an assemblage and collage of familiar materials with new connotations.

Gehry wrapped the house in a new exterior envelope, with the old house still visible within, each enriching and commenting on the other. Leaving the rear and south facades of the house virtually untouched, corrugated sheet metal wraps the most public facades, to the north and east. A tilted glass cube, wedged between the new exterior and the old, was positioned above the north-facing kitchen; a second distorted cube forms a window for the dining room in the northeast corner. Along the north edge, shaded by a row of preexisting cedars of Lebanon, the corrugated wall extends to enclose the backyard, making it a private courtyard. A giant cactus in the courtyard is framed by a trapezoidal opening in the metal wall. At the east end of the house, a terraced garden leads to the front door, chain-link screens above revealing the rooflines of the old house. Inside, walls and ceilings were stripped down to the underlying wood lath and left exposed.

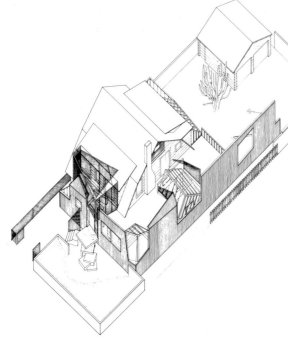

In the fall of 1991, construction began on a remodel of the remodel. Programmatically, the family's needs had changed—two little boys were now teenagers. Structurally, the old house's foundations, framing, siding, and electrical and plumbing systems needed shoring up, as did some of the leaky work of the 1977–78 remodel. Again working closely with only one associate, this time Jon Drezner, Gehry designed some parts prior to construction and other portions simultaneous with construction.

Using the house as a full-scale model, Gehry responded to conditions revealed by the contractors. Work started in the back and moved forward. The existing garage was converted into an outpost for the boys that could also double as a guest room. Leaving the monumental cactus intact, a lap pool clad in luminous green four-by-four-inch Japanese tiles was added. The pool's fish belly derived less from formal than practical consideration: it was easier for the backhoe to dig a rounded hole than a rectilinear one on such a tight site. A temporary footbridge made of Douglas fir two-by-fours connects the driveway (eventually to be covered by a carport) to the terrace at the rear of the house. The terrace, shaded by retractable awnings, is clasped in the arms of two two-story metal-clad storage and mechanical enclosures.

The indoors meets the outside at the western edge of the house, where floor-to-ceiling sliding glass doors separate the kitchen and living room from the terrace. The old house, formerly exposed, is now refinished in parts: pink exterior shingles still appear but less lath is visible. The kitchen was enlarged and the palette simplified to white. The dining room is now distinct from the kitchen, separated by glass doors. Two new bedrooms and bathrooms for Gehry's sons occupy the southern edge of the house: one room, lined in dark Finnish plywood, was promptly coopted as an exercise room upon the elder son's departure for college, and one was lined with built-in cabinetry of Douglas fir. Independent circulation for a blind and aging dog leads down a new ramp from the front vestibule to an enclosed yard on the south side of the house.

Upstairs, the new master bedroom's partially glass floor and glass table-box allow natural light to leak into the living room below. A second bath, with the same tiles as the pool, was added,

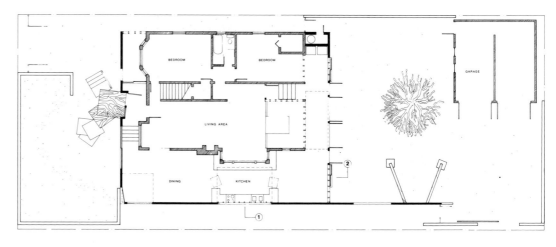

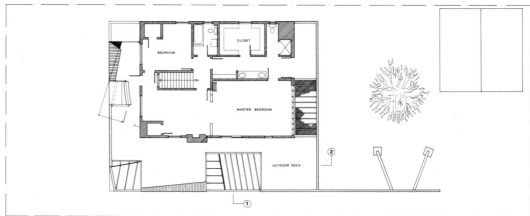

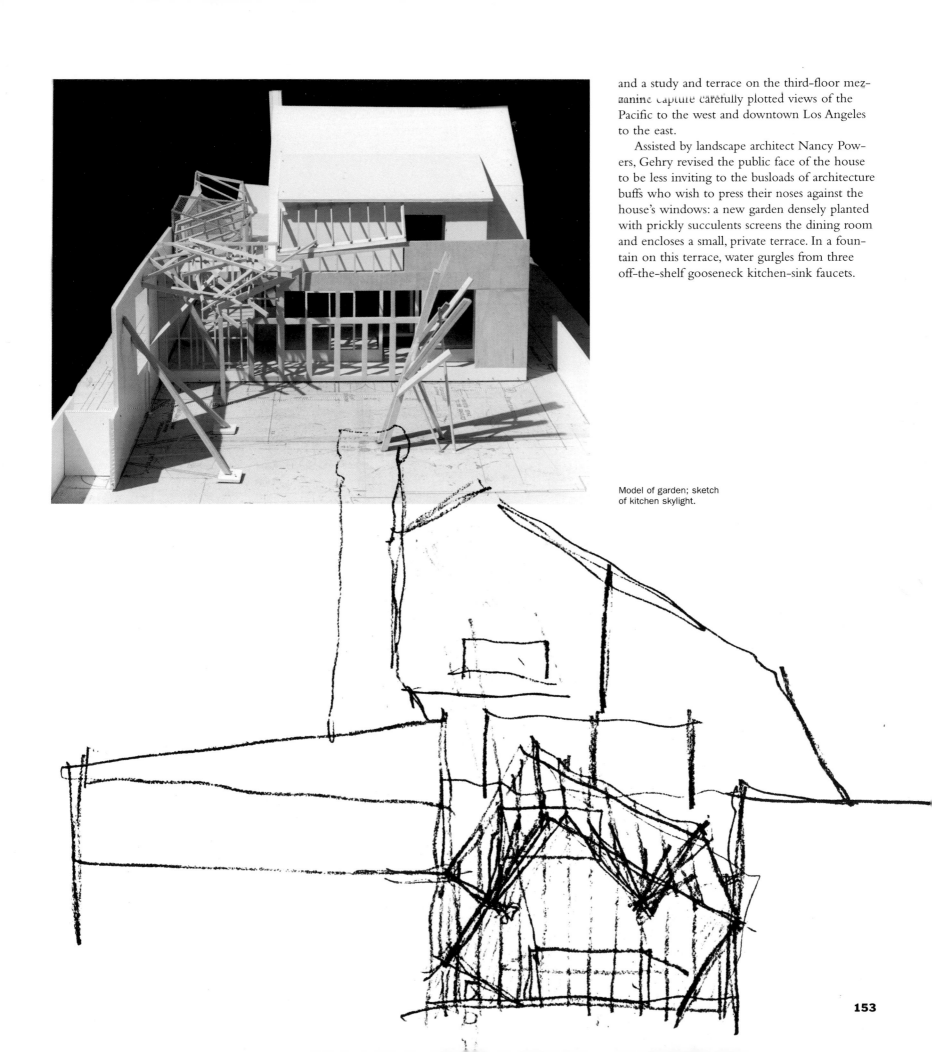

and a study and terrace on the third-floor mezzanine capture carefully plotted views of the Pacific to the west and downtown Los Angeles to the east.

Assisted by landscape architect Nancy Powers, Gehry revised the public face of the house to be less inviting to the busloads of architecture buffs who wish to press their noses against the house's windows: a new garden densely planted with prickly succulents screens the dining room and encloses a small, private terrace. In a fountain on this terrace, water gurgles from three off-the-shelf gooseneck kitchen-sink faucets.

Model of garden; sketch of kitchen skylight.

Kitchen with skylight;
detail of east facade
with skylight glazing.

154

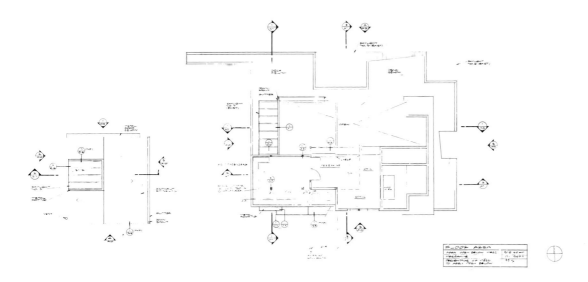

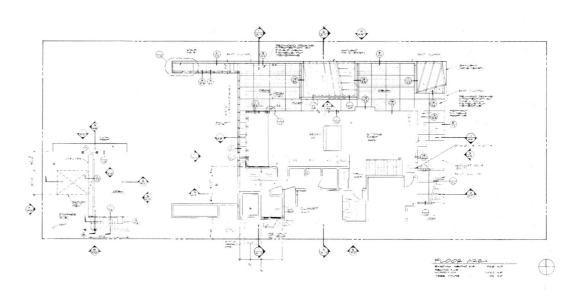

Ground- and second-floor
and attic plans of the
second remodeling.

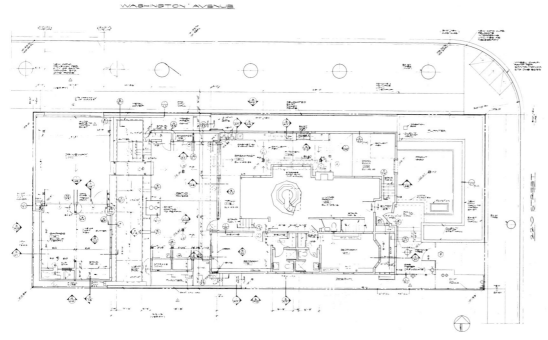

Sections and details of
the second remodeling.

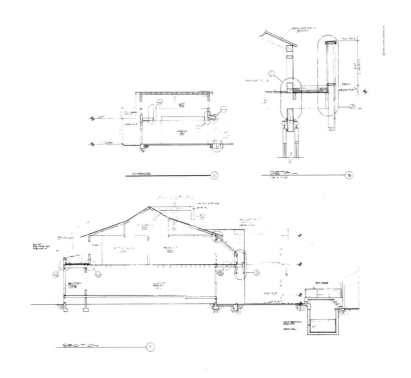

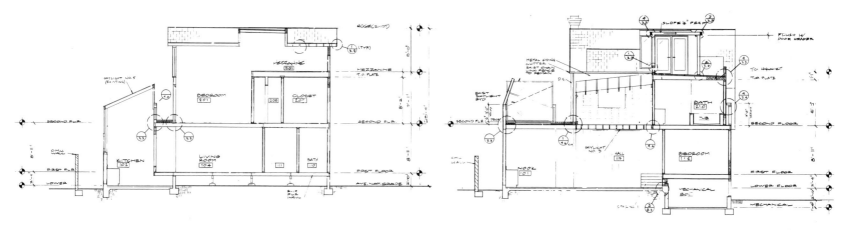

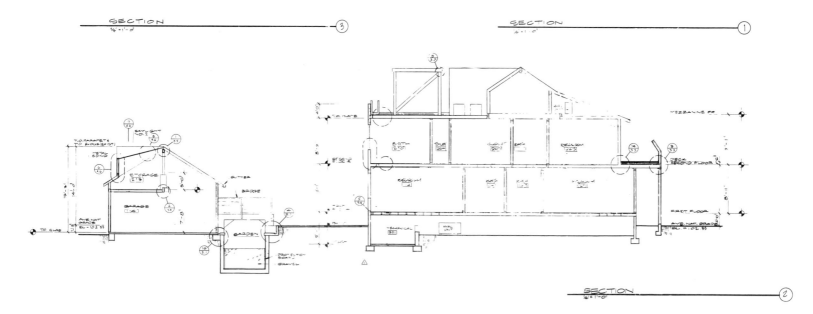

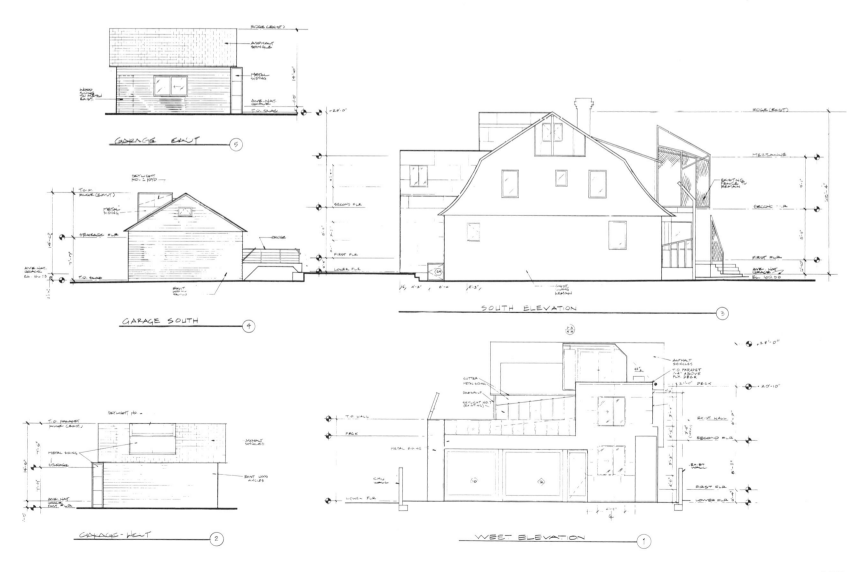

Garden with pool in foreground; elevations for the second remodeling.

GARAGE EAST   5

GARAGE SOUTH   4

GARAGE - WEST   2

SOUTH ELEVATION   3

WEST ELEVATION   1

Main entrance; auto court transformed into living space; model with new volumes in garden.

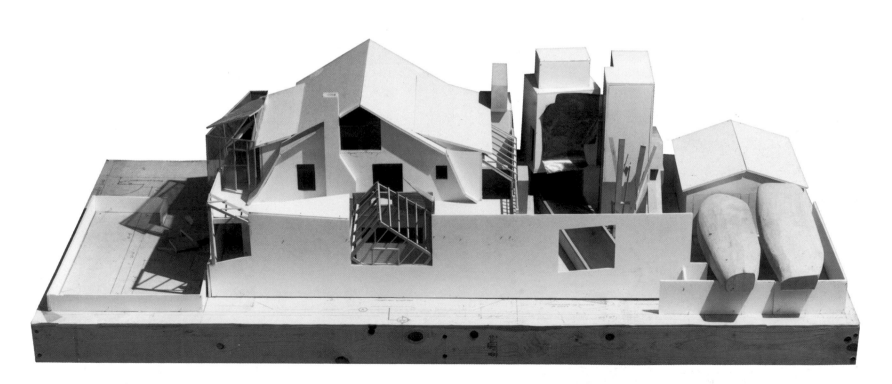

Window looking
onto garden; details
of bedrooms.

Skylight over living spaces;
living area; new kitchen.

Cabrillo Marine Museum
San Pedro, California
1977–79

Client: City of Los Angeles Department of Recreation and Parks
Program: Aquarium, laboratory, and exhibition hall
Budget: $2,600,000
Area: 20,000 square feet
Materials: Wood frame, galvanized-corrugated-metal and stucco siding, steel posts, chain link
Project Team: Frank O. Gehry, C. Gregory Walsh Jr., Rene Ilustre, John Clagett, Steven F. Tomko, Ken Francis, Hak Sik Son; Kurily & Szymanski, structural engineer

Occupying the site of a former parking lot near an industrial harbor, this twenty-thousand-square-foot facility is devoted to research and education about California's coastal marine life. The site's existing asphalt surface, chain-link fencing, and industrial shipping context informed the design of simple boxes connected by an ephemeral gauze of chain link.

Specifically designed to take advantage of the temperate climate, all major circulation areas are outdoors, linked to the separate museum building by an overhead chain-link "shadow" structure. Simple concrete-and-stucco pavilions house the exhibit hall, a 287-seat auditorium, the research laboratories, and a classroom, while an office and control area clad in corrugated metal projects from the roof of the exhibit hall. These buildings surround the central courtyard and administration building. From the courtyard, which functions as a gathering space and outdoor exhibition area, the interiors of the research laboratories are visible; from a dimly lit tunnel winding through the aquariums, viewers can look face-to-face with fish; along the peripheral route, lit by a combination of daylight and indirect artificial light, visitors peer into the maintenance and mechanical systems of the aquariums.

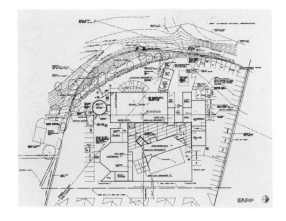

Site plan; exterior;
view into courtyard.

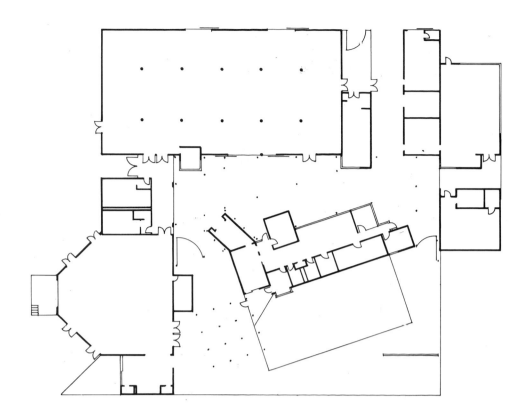

Plan; model inserted
into site

North elevation/section;
south elevation; east
elevation; view from north.

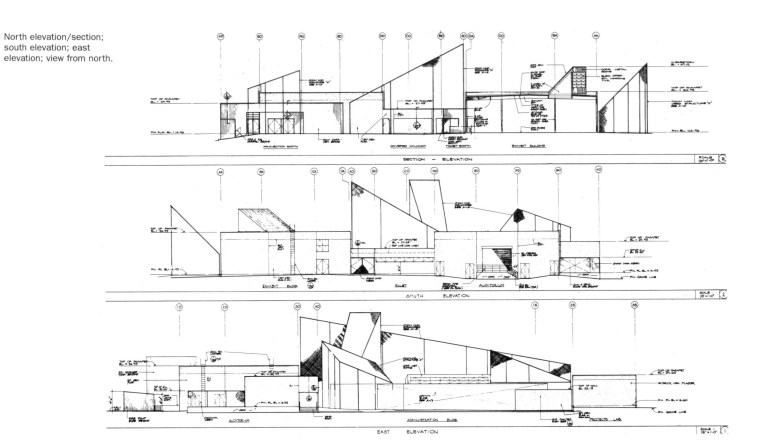

Chain-link-covered
walkways.

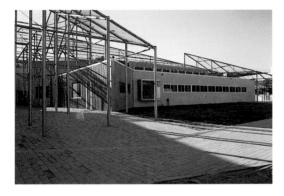

Wagner Residence
Malibu, California
1978 (project)

Client: Georgie Fink Wagner
Program: Single-family residence
Area: 3,200 square feet
Materials: Wood frame, galvanized-corrugated-metal roofing and siding, plywood; carport: concrete block, stucco; chain link
Project Team: Frank O. Gehry, C. Gregory Walsh Jr., John Claggett, Ken Francis

This project, along with the 1978 proposals for the Gunther and Familian Residences, was undertaken as an exercise in exploiting, and exploding, the possibilities of typical American balloon-frame construction. The single-family house with a psychiatrist's office on its lower level was designed on a strict budget for a sloping site in an environmentally sensitive area.

Aerial view of model; plan of living level.

West view of model.

North elevation; west
elevation; northwest
view of model.

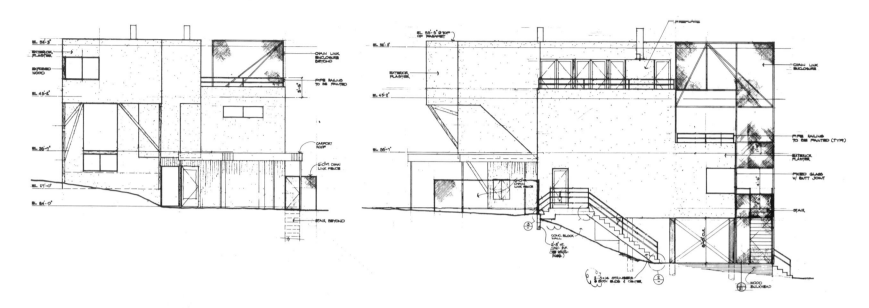

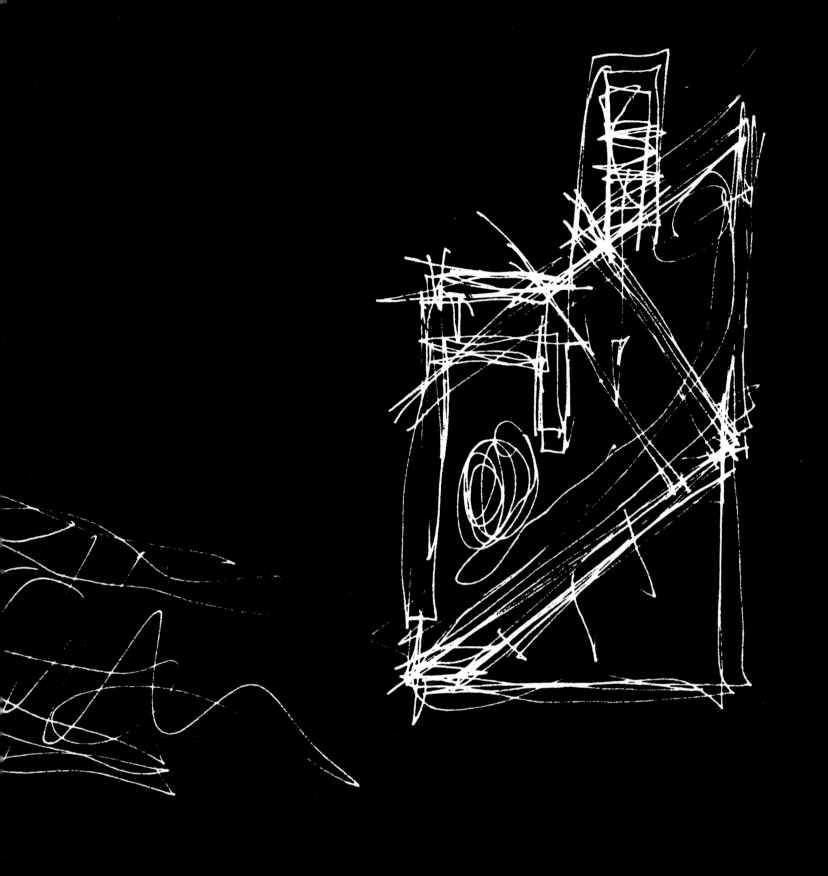

Familian Residence
Santa Monica, California
1978 (project)

Client: Gary and Elizabeth Familian
Program: Single-family residence
Area: 3,600 square feet
Materials: Wood frame, stucco
Project Team: Frank O. Gehry, C. Gregory
Walsh Jr., John Clagett, Ken Francis

The Familian Residence was designed for a residential neighborhood, to be located on a narrow lot that drops off sharply in the rear to unobstructed views of the Santa Monica Mountains. The project represents a response to the complex programmatic requirements of a family whose lifestyle is divided between highly public and intensely private. The resulting architectural composition questions the distinction between the complete and the unfinished, the stationary and the static, and the idea of the house as both refuge from and confrontation with its surroundings. The project also explores the use of rough wood tract-house technology (normally covered up) as a tool for sketching with wood.

The house is composed of two separate pieces, a 20-by-110-foot flat bar-shaped object oriented to the street at the front of the house and a 40-by-40-foot cube-shaped object set at an angle to the bar. The two buildings almost touch, creating a crevice or "cleavage" between them. Wood-stud bridges, pavilions, and lattices tie the structures to each other and to the landscape, which also incorporates a tennis court, swimming pool, permanent staff quarters, and on-site parking for thirty vehicles.

Public and private functions are divided between the two main buildings. The cube is a single volume reserved for public gatherings, although it does contain some living spaces. A skylight monitor tilts backward as it perforates the roof of the cube, flooding the area below with natural light. The end wall of the adjacent building is pushed out to form a balcony but the internal volume of the bar remains undisturbed. The relatively narrow width of this building transfers the load entirely onto the exterior walls, allowing all interior surfaces to be placed according to functional and aesthetic considerations. A flexible interior system and a high degree of exclusion from the public spaces were required for this second structure, which houses the family's bedrooms and private quarters.

Both main buildings are primarily stucco-sheathed. Window openings are placed independently of the structure, revealing the wood framing as it continues unobstructed and uninterrupted behind the glazing. Elsewhere, exposed structural wood serves to heighten the sense of the sketch. The model is in the collection of the Museum of Modern Art.

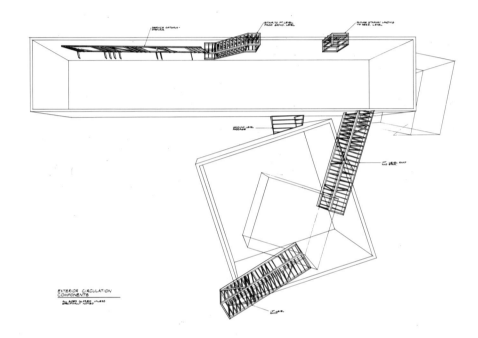

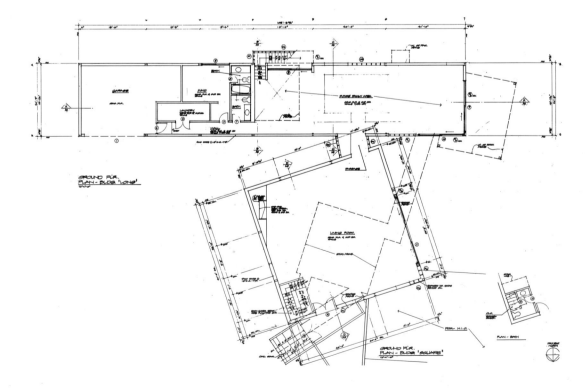

Elements of exterior
sequence; ground-floor
plan of the two buildings.

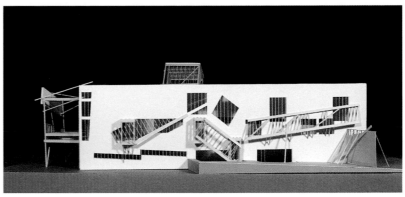

Sketch of intersection
between the two
structures; model views.

Carriage House
New York, New York
1978 (project)

Client: Christophe de Menil
Program: Residential remodel
Area: 6,500 square feet
Materials: Concrete, steel
Project Team: Frank O. Gehry,
C. Gregory Walsh Jr.

Designs for this home consist of remodeling almost to the point of rebuilding a turn-of-the-century carriage house. The client, an active patron of the arts, asked for a sculpture in which she and her seventeen-year-old daughter could live independently when required and communally when desired. The renovation was not executed as planned.

In the designs, the existing exterior facades remain with only slight modifications, wrapping the first two floors. At the third floor, the new building emerges from the existing facade to become the exterior wall. The first floor contains the existing garage, a kitchen, a sixty-by-eight-foot swimming pool, and a multiuse space for guest quarters, studio space, and dining. The second floor consists of

several levels: a lower level on the front street side, rising with banks of stairs to a middle level, then to a higher level at the rear. This space includes the main living, dining, and entertaining area.

Upon this irregular podium sit two architectonic towers: a two-level apartment for the daughter and a two-level apartment for the mother. These objects, twisted slightly in the rectangular envelope, create eccentricities within the vertical and horizontal spatial organization of the building. The two new towers were to be built of poured-in-place concrete with simple rectangular openings. Between them is a large, vertical skylit space, onto which the front apartment opens. The rear apartment faces a specimen tree and receives ample natural light. Each of the apartments has private access from the street. Staff quarters, sandwiched between the first and second floors at the rear, have direct access from the garage and kitchen. A basement with natural light from the sidewalk level serves as office space.

Street facade of existing building; model views; plans.

Opposite:
Section.

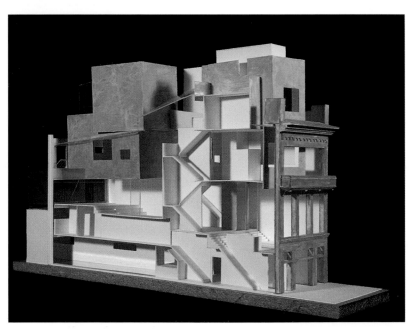

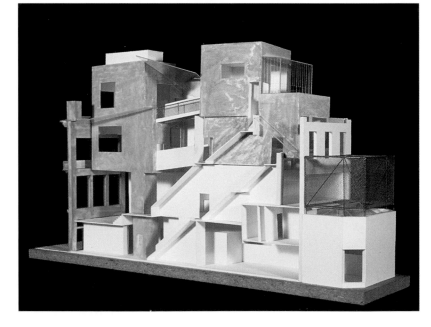

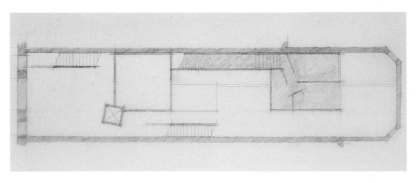

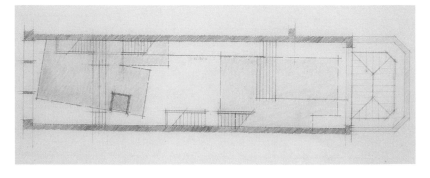

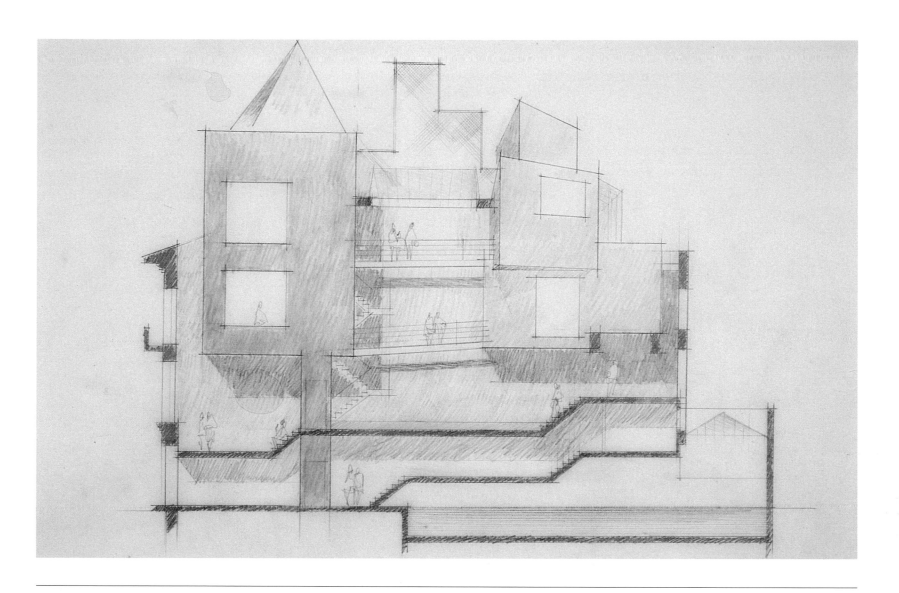

**Valley Cultural Center
Warner Ranch Park,
Woodland Hills, California
1978 (project)**

Client: Department of Recreation and Parks,
City of Woodland Hills
Program: Phased master plan for performing-
arts center, including 3,000-seat outdoor
amphitheater, 500-seat multipurpose meeting
room, classrooms, kitchen, library-bookstore,

gallery, 300-seat experimental theater, and
2,000-seat enclosed theater
Budget: $2,000,000
Area: 21 acres
Project Team: Frank O. Gehry,
C. Gregory Walsh Jr.

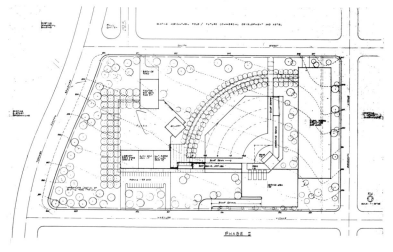

Plan for second phase.

Arts Park
Van Nuys, California
1978 (project)

Client: San Fernando Valley Arts Council and
City of Los Angeles
Program: Outdoor center for the performing
and visual arts, including 2,500-seat theater,
studios, classrooms, and multiple exhibition areas
Budget: $10,000,000
Area: 80 acres
Project Team: Frank O. Gehry, C. Gregory
Walsh Jr., Frederick Fisher; Lawrence Halprin,
landscape architect

Views and details of model.

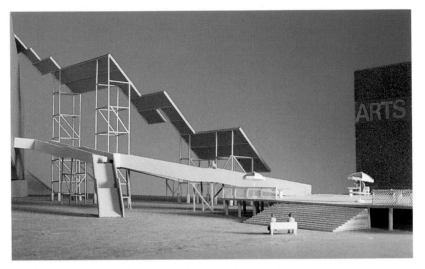

Spiller Residence
Venice, California
1978–79

Client: Jane Spiller
Program: Single-family residence with detached
rental apartment and garage
Area: 2,900 square feet
Materials: Wood frame, corrugated galvanized
steel
Project Team: Frank O. Gehry, C. Gregory
Walsh Jr., Hak Sik Son, Rene Ilustre,
James Gibb

Bounded by a three-story brick apartment
building on one side and one-story courtyard
residences on the other, the Spiller Residence
was designed to be self-contained and private.
The program called for a residence and rental
unit on a narrow lot one block from the Pacific
Ocean, and the Coastal Commission dictated

that the complex be a two-unit project with
off-street parking for four cars. The two units
are compact boxes, one behind the other, separated by an open court in the center of the lot.
All roof areas have been turned into outdoor
living terraces accessible by stairs from the units
below. A gate and walled passage on one side
leads from the street to the front rental unit and
opens onto a walled garden. A passage on the
opposite side of the lot extends to the private
central court, where a stairway and bridge lead
up to the main entrance of the owner's unit.
This three-story, fifty-foot tower in the rear,
designed to relate in scale to the neighboring
apartment building, is capped by a roof
deck with a view of the coastline. Stacked
one above the other are a studio and garage,

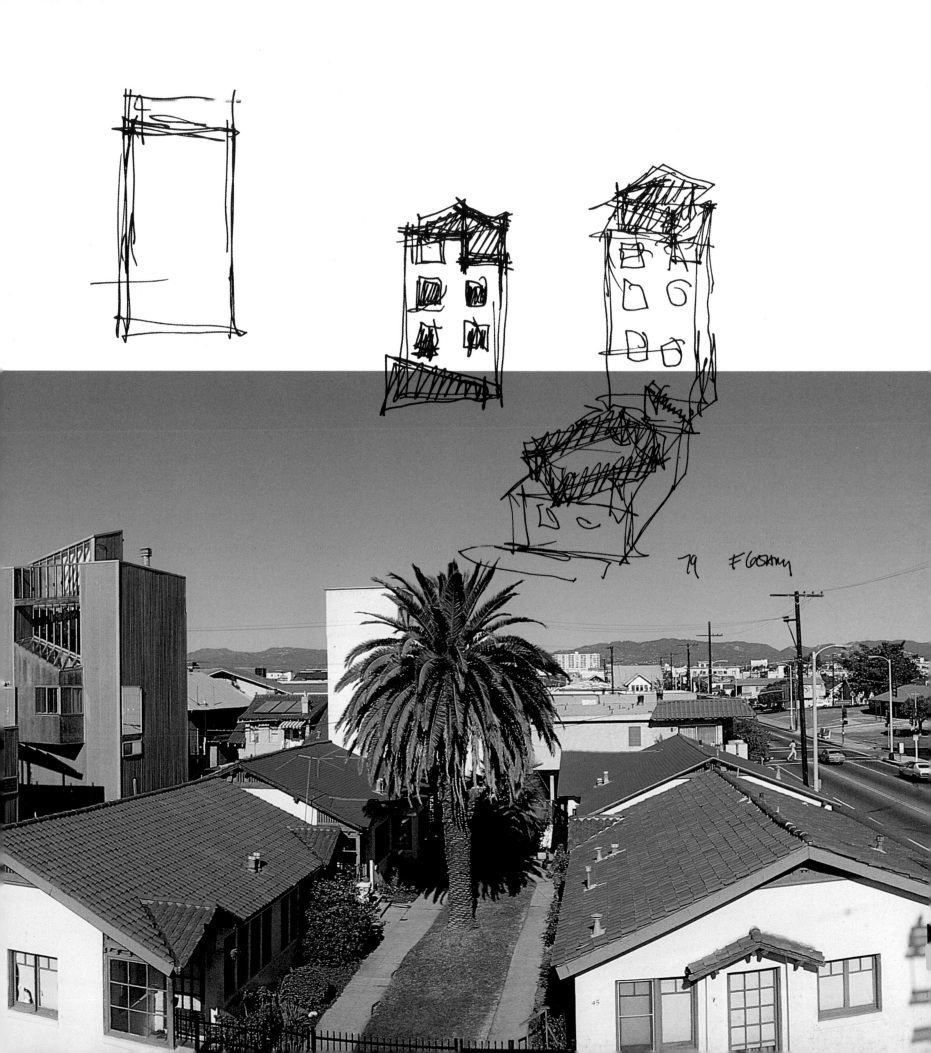

79 F Gehry

Owner's unit from rear;
skylighted stairway joining
upper levels.

First- and second-floor
plans of two buildings;
views toward courtyard
of owner's building.

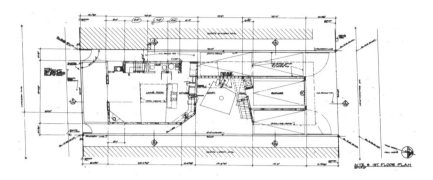

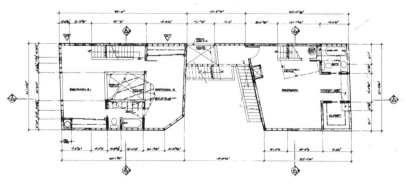

Plans and sections
of owner's house.

Overleaf:
Views of kitchen
and living area.

living and dining area, sleeping spaces, and the roof deck. A skylight extends vertically over the second-level kitchen window and terminates in another skylight above the level of the roof. An open stairway rises up into this second skylight to connect with the roof deck and a future sleeping loft. The rental unit's ground-floor living and dining area opens near the center to the second-story bedrooms, both spaces pierced by a large, angled skylight. A roof terrace is shielded from the rear by an angled wall.

Construction is concrete slab on grade and wood frame above. The exterior wall material is primarily unpainted galvanized corrugated-metal siding. Unpainted plywood is used on the bay that projects from the rear unit into the court. Stud wall and roof framing is exposed behind window glazing and used for guard rails. Interior finishes are painted drywall, unpainted exposed wood ceilings, and plywood, carpeted or tiled floors. Solar panels on the roof of each unit provide hot water, and forced-air gas-fired units provide heating. The owner, a former employee of Charles Eames, was as fastidious as the Eames office about detail: she insisted on selecting all the lumber and carefully supervising the carpenters. The result is a hybrid of finished rough framing and impeccable lumber selection.

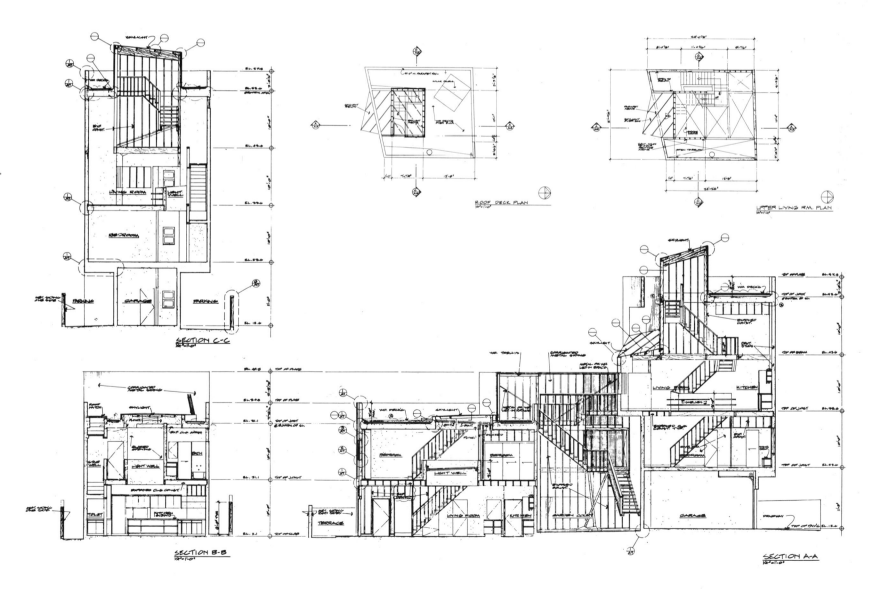

Loyal Heights Manor
Seattle, Washington
1978–80

Program: Three-story, fifty-four-unit apartment building for the elderly with below-grade parking
Budget: $1,007,000
Area: 37,500 square feet
Materials: Concrete, wood frame, stucco

Project Team: Frank O. Gehry, C. Gregory Walsh Jr., Robert Cloud, Steven F. Tomko, Rene Ilustre, Hak Sik Son

Perspective of main facade.

Centerpoint Mall
Oxnard, California
1978–80

Client: Oxnard Center Company
Program: Commercial remodel
Budget: $1,300,000
Area: 25,000 square feet
Materials: Wood frame, drywall, exposed redwood lathe

Project Team: Frank O. Gehry, C. Gregory Walsh Jr., Steven F. Tomko

Interior.

Loyola University Law School
Los Angeles, California
1978–

Early sketch.

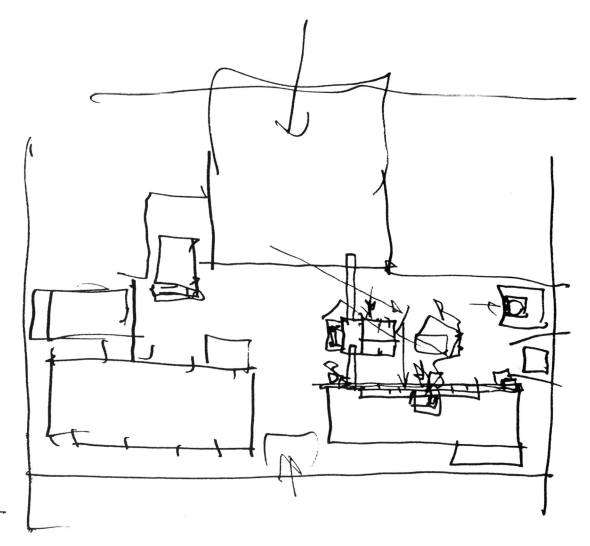

Client: Loyola Marymount University

Phase I, Fritz B. Burns Student Center, 1978–82
Program: Master plan and four-story student center with student and faculty offices, meeting rooms, seminar rooms, cafeteria, bookstore
Budget: $3,646,000
Area: 45,250 square feet
Materials: Steel frame, concrete, stucco

Phase II, Merrifield Hall, Donovan Hall, Hall of the 70s, and Chapel, 1978–84
Program: Three 80–120-seat classroom buildings and a non-denominational chapel
Budget: $957,000
Area: 8,800 square feet
Materials: Merrifield: wood frame, brick, sheet metal; Donovan: wood frame, stucco; Hall of the 70s: wood frame, stucco; Chapel: wood frame, Finnish plywood (late copper sheet metal)

Phase III, Rains Library Renovation, 1983–85
Program: Renovation of existing building, including law library, moot court, and classrooms
Budget: $2,400,000
Area: 55,000 square feet
Materials: Wood frame, plaster

Phase IV, Casassa Building, 1989–91
Program: Library annex, classrooms, and student and administrative offices
Budget: $6,000,000
Area: 34,600 square feet
Materials: Steel frame, stucco

Phase V, Parking Garage, 1992–94
Program: 7-level, 850-automobile parking garage; acoustical renovation of Merrifield Hall
Budget: $8,800,000
Area: Garage: 325,000 square feet
Materials: Concrete, stainless-steel sheet metal

Phase VI, 1995–
Program: Library addition, new classroom buildings
Materials: Wood frame, stucco

Project Team: Frank O. Gehry, Robert G. Hale, Rene Ilustre, Hak Sik Son, C. Gregory Walsh Jr., Josh Schweitzer, James M. Glymph, Carroll Stockard, Edwin Chan, Randy Jefferson, Jon Drezner, Sharon Williams, David Kellen, Dane Twichell, Ed Woll, Bob Cloud; Brooks/Collier, associate architect; Johnson & Neilsen, structural engineer; Kurily & Szymanski, structural engineer; Don Dickerson, mechanical engineer; Ove Arup & Partners, structural, mechanical, and electrical engineers; SYART, mechanical engineer

In 1978, Gehry was invited to develop a master plan for the Loyola University Law School. At the time, the school consisted of a parking garage and a single building on an undistinguished urban site. The goal of the original five-phase plan (a sixth phase was recently added) was to create an identity of place for an urban sanctuary that would dignify and enrich the study of law without drawing much attention to the school. The result is a small village of buildings encircling and scattered across a plaza.

Given the extremely tight budget of the project, the initial design strategy was guided by pragmatic concerns: by separating the large classrooms from the administration building, expensive long-span construction was avoided. With the budget requiring economical construction of the individual buildings, the spatial relationships between them became the principal design opportunity.

General plan of project;
model of first phase.

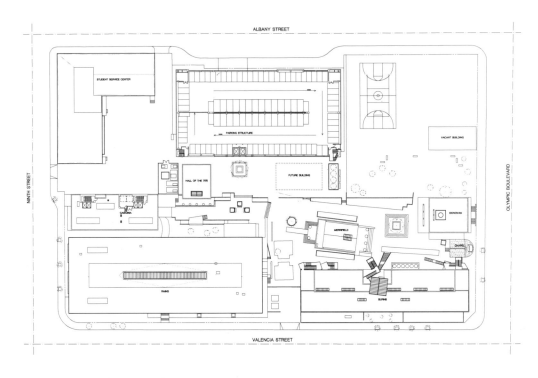

Axonometric; model
of first phase.

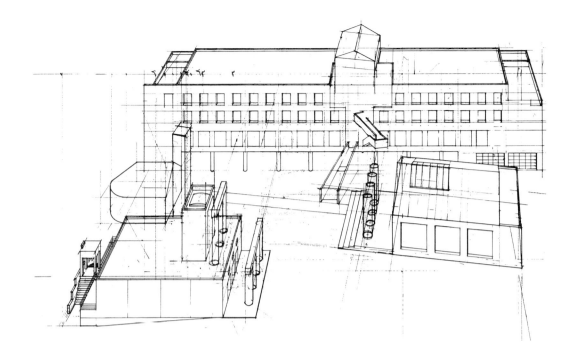

Courtyard elevation
of Fritz B. Burns Student
Center; views of
Merrifield Hall and Burns
Student Center; sketch.

Burns Student Center.

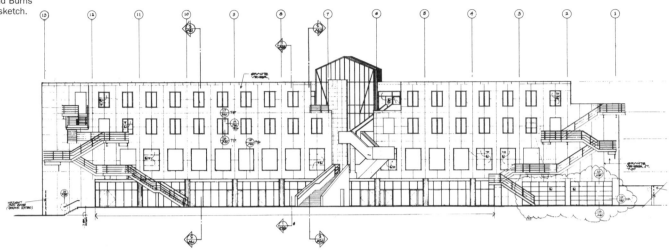

The first phase of the project was the Fritz B. Burns Student Center, a long, simple, four-story block. Its back is turned to the street while its bright yellow stucco front splits open and spills a greenhouse-covered baroque stairway onto the plaza. The Burns building acts as a backdrop for the composition of three free-standing buildings at its feet, forming an ell, that encloses the southern end of the site and screens it from Olympic Boulevard.

Merrifield Hall was designed as a reductive, stripped-brick courthouse complete with oversized columns across its facade. In this case however, the unadorned columns are detached from the building, standing as a row of minimalist sculptures. Donovan Hall is a wood-frame-and-gray-stucco box with a two-story column-and-lintel facade. A third, wood-frame-and-stucco classroom building, Hall of the 70s, was later added to the north. The chapel's wood frame was sheathed in glass and Finnish plywood, later replaced by copper sheet metal; its glazed north-facing surfaces glow by night.

The renovation of the original 1963 law-school building was completed in 1985. Claes Oldenburg's *Toppling Ladder with Spilling Paint* was installed in 1986. The Casassa Building, completed in 1991, houses the library annex, classrooms, and student and administrative offices. The fifth phase, completed in 1994, included a seven-level parking garage and the interior renovation of Merrifield Hall.

The playfulness of the archetypal buildings, rotated axes, surreal scale jumps, and sculptural fragments creates the sense of a city in miniature. More importantly, a campus was created out of a commuter school, a stimulating, debated, and provocative environment for law students and professors. The Loyola project still occupies a special status in Gehry's own opinion, perhaps because it was in this project more visibly than in any other that form gave birth to collective identity—a distinct sense of place and an intensified sense of community—and where architecture succeeded in revitalizing not only space but the psychic life of its inhabitants.

Donovan Hall next to chapel; model of last phase.

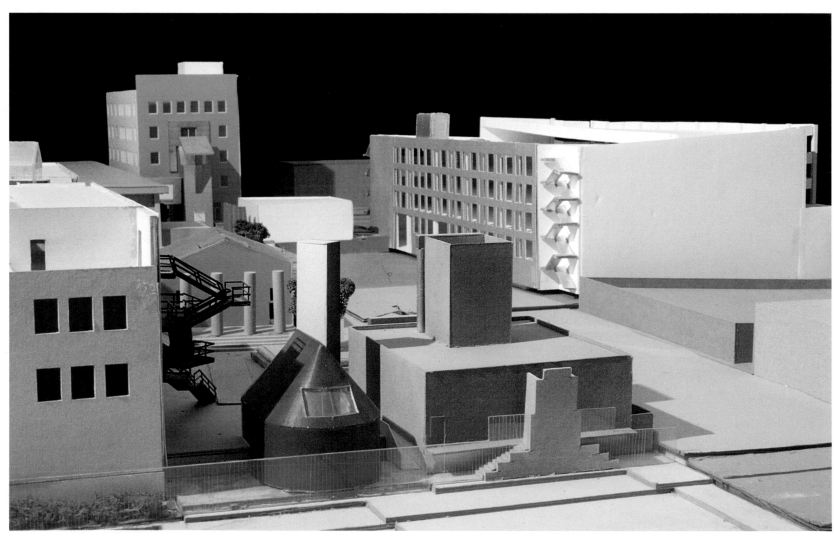

199

Interiors of chapel;
elevations of chapel
and campanile.

Opposite:
Principal view of chapel
from campus; sketches;
model views.

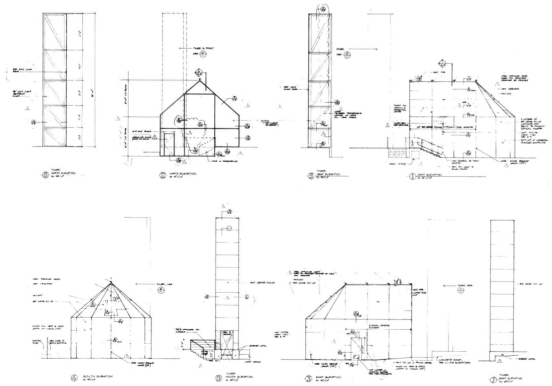

Exterior and interior views
of Casassa Building.

Parking garage; model
showing sixth phase.

203

Model views; south
elevations; east
elevations; roof plans;
north elevations.

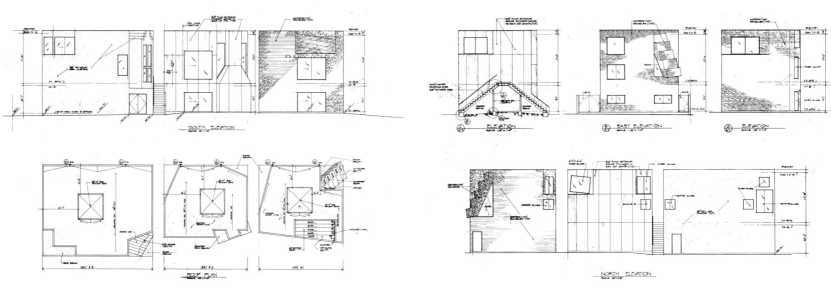

East end of complex;
detail of west building;
view of north facade.

Experimental Edges Cardboard Furniture 1979–82

Materials: Glued and laminated corrugated cardboard furniture
Project Team: Frank O. Gehry, Paul Lubowicki

The first phase of in-house design for Experimental Edges, between 1979 and 1982, produced three designs. In contrast to the sculpted forms and strong linear profile of the Easy Edges cardboard furniture (1969–73), Experimental Edges furniture has a solid, shaggy profile. The irregular, corrugated surfaces result from the use of a structural cardboard commonly utilized in the production of hollow-core doors. This commercial cardboard product is available in four "flute" sizes in precut sections ranging in thickness from three-quarters of an inch to six inches. A wide range of chairs designed in a variety of shapes and corrugations takes advantage of the material's rich texture and varied thicknesses. In some cases, sections are laminated to each other slightly out of alignment, pushing individual stacks of corrugation into relief. These pieces appear to fulfill more accurately the expectations for paper furniture: their solidity is unexpected. Like Easy Edges, the Experimental Edges furniture pieces possess high sound absorbency and require little maintenance, withstanding rough treatment without marring. The Experimental Edges furniture was not developed commercially. Later, in association with Fred Hoffman and Joel Stearns, Gehry would form New City Editions, developing and marketing twelve designs between 1986 and 1988.

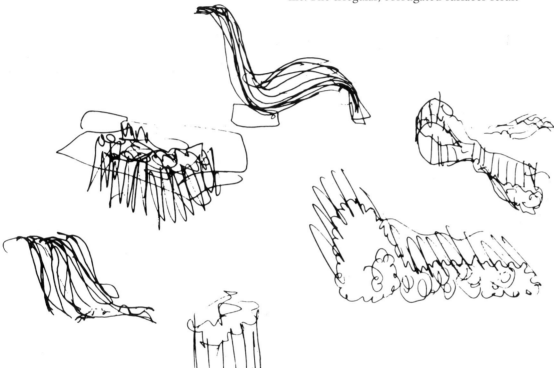

Sketches; prototypes.

210

Benson Residence
Calabassas, California
1979–84

Client: Robert and Lesley Benson
Program: Single-family residence
Budget: $120,000
Area: 1,500 square feet
Materials: Wood frame, asphalt shingles
Project Team: Frank O. Gehry, C. Gregory
Walsh Jr., Paul Lubowicki, Rene Ilustre,
Sharon Williams, Steve Tomko

Designed for a Loyola University Law School
professor and his family, this house was to be
built for less than eighty dollars per square foot.
Situated on a small hillside site in the San Fernando Valley, the house is made up of two separate building elements joined by second-story
bridges. Breaking down the scale of the building
to make very simple pieces with very short
spans fulfilled the difficult requirement for privacy within such a limited space and budget.

Both buildings are cut into the existing
slope. The deep spaces between the building
parts and the retaining walls are suggestive of a

moat; wood bridges and connecting stairways
lace the two buildings together above the
ground level. The brown-shingled tower houses
the bedrooms while the lower structure, clad in
gray asphalt shingles, contains living, dining, and
kitchen areas. Two tablelike carports and a redwood rooftop deck on the smaller box were
added during a second building phase. A rough
wood railing extends from an exterior stairway
to enclose the deck and its roofscape of pro-
truding skylight and chimney volumes. As-yet-
unbuilt roof elements include a small log-cabin
structure atop the tall building and a steel draw-
bridge-stairway that would link the cabin to the
carport roof.

Instilled in this project is an element of fantasy that resulted in part from consultations
with the clients' children, who suggested the
log-cabin tree fort and for whom a secret pas-
sageway-closet-stairway was designed to allow
access to the roof from their ground-floor bedroom. The parents' bedroom occupies the double-height area upstairs and contains a mezzanine study. The bedroom tower is visible from
an enormous light monitor in the kitchen of
the adjacent building. Windows are placed
throughout both structures in such a way as to
offer views of adjoining building parts and the
trees and sky beyond.

Aerial view of
model; sketch.

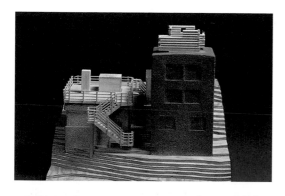

Model views; exterior.

**Late Entry to the Chicago
Tribune Tower Competition
1980 (project)**

Client: Chicago Tribune
Project Team: Frank O. Gehry

Sketch.

**Stolte Office Building
Portland, Oregon
1980 (project)**

Model view.

Client: City of Portland, Oregon, Office of
General Services
Program: 360,000-square-foot office building;
80-car parking garage
Budget: $22.2 million
Area: 360,000 square feet
Materials: Steel, concrete, glass
Project Team: Frank O. Gehry, C. Gregory
Walsh Jr., Hak Sik Son, Robert Cloud

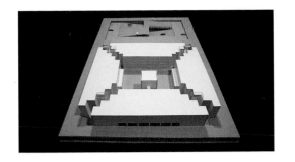

**In the Presence of the Past:
Strada Novissima
Corderia of the Arsenale,
Venice, Italy
1980**

Client: First International Exhibition of
Architecture, Architectural Commission,
Venice Biennale
Program: Exhibition design and installation

Materials: Exposed wood frame, drywall,
plywood
Project Team: Frank O. Gehry,
C. Gregory Walsh Jr.

Installation.

The Avant-Garde in Russia, 1910–1930
Los Angeles County Museum of Art, Los Angeles, California
1980

Client: Los Angeles County Museum of Art
Program: Exhibition design and installation
Materials: Exposed wood frame, drywall
Project Team: Frank O. Gehry,
C. Gregory Walsh Jr.

The long association between Gehry's office and the Los Angeles County Museum of Art began in 1965, when Lou Danziger was designing the catalog for *Art Treasures of Japan*. Knowing of Gehry's interest in Japanese architecture and Gehry's associate Greg Walsh's study of Japanese art and architecture during his service in the navy, Danziger recommended them for the job of designing the exhibit's installation. It was to be the first of ten designed by Gehry's office for the museum. The objective common to each of the exhibition designs was to modify a portion of the museum's uniform galleries to suit the particular character of an artist or culture's body of work. Working closely with the museum's curatorial staff—and within budgets ranging from twenty to fifty thousand dollars—the goal was always to create environments compatible with the works displayed without competing for the visitor's gaze. In most cases, this was achieved by two means: reducing the imposing scale of the galleries, and enhancing or masking the ubiquitous track lighting.

This exhibition, the most comprehensive showing of the Russian avant-garde in the United States to date, was also one of the most complex the Los Angeles County Museum of Art had ever presented. The show included 450 paintings, sculptures, constructions, architectural models, books and periodicals, and costumes, as well as stage furniture reconstructed from photographs and built by the museum's staff. Gehry's installation recalled constructivist stage techniques by exposing studs spaced at varied intervals; colors dominant in the paintings and graphics of the period—reds, blacks, whites, and grays—were used on the partitions to define display groupings. The show, organized primarily by theme and style rather than chronology, included a re-creation of a 1915 installation by the painter Kazimir Malevich and a full-scale replica of El Lissitzky's *Proun* room.

Details of installation.

216

Angel's Place
Los Angeles, California
1980 (project)

Client: Maguire Partners
Program: Four-story mixed-use complex, including artists' studios, and retail
Area: 25,000 square feet
Materials: Steel frame, stucco
Project Team: Frank O. Gehry, C. Gregory Walsh Jr., Paul H. Krueger, Jeff Daniels, Ed Woll, Sharon Williams

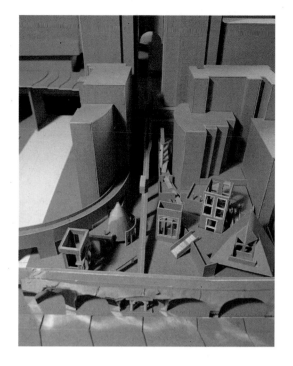

Model view.

United States Embassy & School
Damascus, Syria
1980 (project)

Client: U.S. State Department
Program: Office building, chancery, and school
Budget: $4,800,000
Area: 73,000 square feet

Materials: Steel frame, concrete, wood
Project Team: Frank O. Gehry, C. Gregory Walsh Jr., Paul Krueger, Hak Sik Son

Model view.

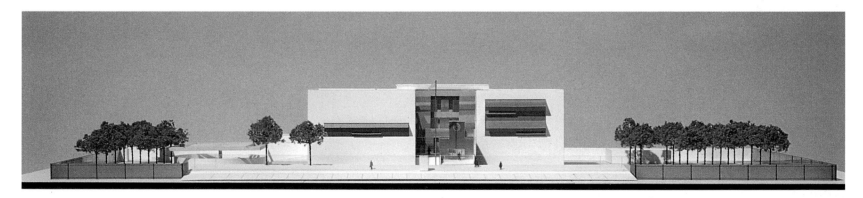

Bubar's Jewelers
Santa Monica Place,
Santa Monica, California
1980

Client: Bubar's Jewelers
Program: Retail shop
Area: 1,800 square feet
Project Team: Frank O. Gehry, C. Gregory Walsh Jr., Steven F. Tomko

Store entrance.

World Savings and Loan Association
North Hollywood, California
1980

Client: World Savings and Loan Association
Program: Vault, tellers, seating area, offices, meeting room
Budget: $275,000
Area: 2,400 square feet
Materials: Wood frame, stucco
Project Team: Frank O. Gehry, C. Gregory Walsh Jr., Hak Sik Son, Steven F. Tomko

The North Hollywood branch of World Savings and Loan sits as a freestanding structure on the rectangular island of land formed between two intersecting streets and an L-shaped parking lot. The north facade, facing the street, is a thirty-foot wall of glass fixed within an aluminum frame. Parking, and therefore the main access for most patrons, is at the rear of the building, so another tall, imposing entrance faces that direction: like a false front on a stage set for a western, a stucco wall six inches thick looms twenty-eight feet above the rear entrance. Sandwiched between the two tall entrance pieces, the building itself is a modest one-story wood-frame structure with white plaster walls and exposed joists. The teller stations and open office areas are grouped around a central bottleneck, pitched-roof skylight. Small offices, the vault, and mechanical systems are enclosed along one side.

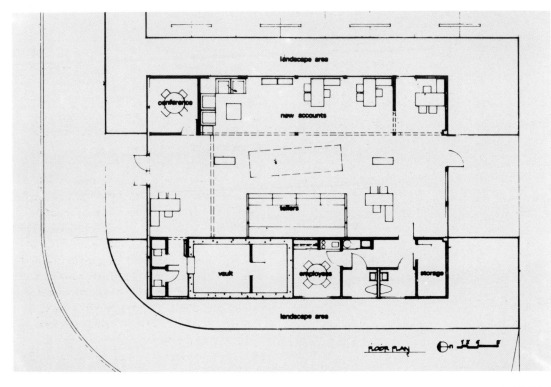

Plan; exterior; model views.

House for a Filmmaker
Santa Monica Canyon, California
1980–81

Client: John Whitney
Program: Single-family residence with guest house and greenhouse
Budget: $100,000
Area: 2,500 square feet
Materials: Wood frame, plywood cladding, stucco, concrete block, glass, stone

Project Team: Frank O. Gehry, Steve Tomko, Heather Kurze, John Clagett

This home, for a bachelor, is located on a rural site, bounded on the west by a stream with a view to a lush ridge and on the east by a steep hill. The program elements are loosely distributed throughout separate and distinct volumes, each treated as an independent unit, placed across the entire site.

The master-bedroom suite is a two-story exposed-plywood box at the western edge of the site; a private roof deck offers views across the canyon and upstream. The entire box can be closed off with plywood shutters or opened up to the courtyard and the stream through the large sliding wall panels. It is the most finished and comfortable of the rooms.

The living room and kitchen are in a long, low concrete-block volume, the south wall opening into the courtyard with views of the canyon ridges through the skylight. The guest bathroom is in a tower across the courtyard. The interior is roughly finished with stone floors and simple functional details. A greenhouse and sitting area are enclosed in a glass-and-stud-wall volume. The three-car garage includes one bay to be used as an office and studio space and opens onto the yard as well as onto the driveway. A pink stucco box functions as a guest house with a private roof deck and view of the hill. The west wall of the guest house serves as an outdoor movie screen. The halls of the house are disconnected from the rooms and placed in the yard.

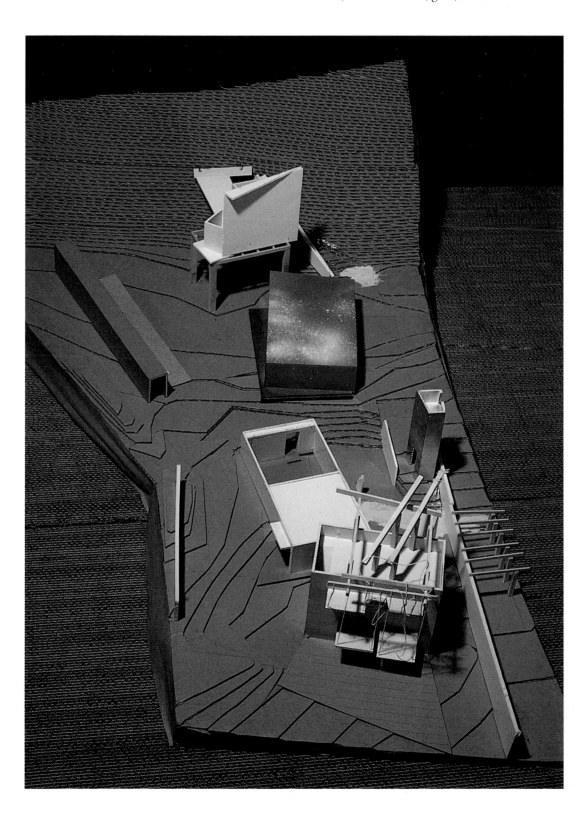

Model of buildings forming house.

Model view;
building details.

Lafayette Square
New Orleans, Louisiana
1980–84 (project)

Client: Downtown Development District, Arts Council of Greater New Orleans, and City of New Orleans
Program: Park renovation, including outdoor performing-arts stage with 2,500–5,000-person capacity grass seating area and backstage facilities, children's arts and crafts studio, exhibition space, kiosks for food and dining
Budget: $250,000
Materials: Steel frame, wood

Project Team: Frank O. Gehry, C. Gregory Walsh Jr., Hak Sik Son, John Clagett, Ed Woll, Robert G. Hale

Model of auditorium.

Smith Residence
Brentwood, California
1981 (project)

Client: Robert and Joanne Smith
Program: Renovation of and addition to existing single-family residence (Steeves Residence, 1958–59)
Area: 2,500 square feet
Materials: Wood frame, glass, tile, stucco
Project Team: Frank O. Gehry, Paul Lubowicki, C. Gregory Walsh Jr., Pam Donnely, David Kellen, Sharon Williams, Antonio Romano

was broken down into its constituent parts, each articulated as a small, separate building-object. Gehry left the original house virtually intact and placed the dense new scheme in juxtaposition with the controlled uniformity of the old. The Bel Air Fine Arts Commission failed to approve the design for the addition on the grounds that it did not look like a house, and the project was ultimately abandoned in favor of another architect's more conventional design.

In the unbuilt proposal, an eagle and "jumping fish" colonnade along the driveway side of the new house introduce, upon arrival, a first line of objects, smaller in scale than the house itself. A light-filled lanai connects the new addition to the truncated south wing of the existing house at an angle slightly skewed from the original axis. Clustered along the lanai, which was to contain an entry as well as gallery and living and dining areas, is the series of building-objects. To the east, the kitchen and family-room buildings are edged by a gravel-filled, moatlike ditch. The kitchen is in a green-tiled cruciform structure with clerestory windows and skylights; an adjoining pedimented service shed is sheathed in sheet metal. A white stucco box with a gable roof encloses the family room and opens onto an elevated fiberglass-screened cube overlooking the swimming pool. One wall of the family room's adjacent brick bathhouse extends south to become part of the pergola. To the west of the lanai, the master bedroom suite is housed within two plywood boxes built into the existing slope. Exterior stairs lead to the stepped roof decks of these structures. The south facade of the suite is fronted by three freestanding columns and detailed to suggest, through perspective, a deeper volume.

Plan; model views.

Gehry's Steeves House as well as an undeveloped adjacent lot was sold to Robert and Joanne Smith, who in 1981 commissioned Gehry to design an addition. "Obsessed with the idea of breaking the coherent order of my early work," and responding to the increased density of the surrounding neighborhood, Gehry proposed a small village of disparate forms and disjointed connections. The program

222

Collaborations: Artists and Architects
Architectural League of New York, New York, New York
1981 (project)

Client: Architectural League of New York
Program: Bridge and tower design
Material: Steel
Project Team: Frank O. Gehry, Richard Serra

View of installation;
drawing.

Westlake–Thousand Oaks Industrial Park
Thousand Oaks, California
1981

Client: Binder Development Corporation
Program: Mixed-use development, including light manufacturing, office, and research and development spaces
Budget: $25,000,000

Area: 345,000 square feet
Material: Tilt-up concrete
Project Team: Frank O. Gehry, Hak Sik Son, Bob Cloud

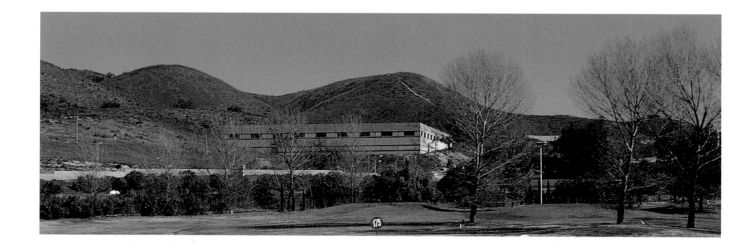

Exterior view.

14th Street Housing
Atlanta, Georgia
1981

Client: Considine Company, Inc.
Program: 490-unit housing development
Budget: $24.5 million
Area: Seven acres
Materials: Steel, concrete, wood

Project Team: Frank O. Gehry, Paul Krueger, C. Gregory Walsh Jr., Robert G. Hale, Hak Sik Son, Ed Woll

Fish Sculpture
New York, New York
1981 (project)

Program: Monumental outdoor sculpture
Project Team: Frank O. Gehry

An existing six-story building and an adjoining two-story building with an open courtyard were to be renovated for use as studio-loft spaces. Three freestanding small loft buildings are placed on the raised terrace of the courtyard. The lowest level of the existing building is cut open to reveal three similar forms projecting out of it and relating sculpturally to the buildings in the court. A monumental fish sculpture sits in the courtyard.

Model views;
study drawings.

Seventeen Artists in the Sixties
Los Angeles County Museum of
Art, Los Angeles, California
1981

Views of installation.

Client: Los Angeles County Museum of Art
Program: Exhibition design and installation
Materials: Wood frame, drywall
Project Team: Frank O. Gehry,
C. Gregory Walsh Jr.

In the Billy Al Bengston retrospective designed by Gehry in 1968, Gehry appropriated the artist's pop sensibility, employing industrial-grade materials, garish textures and colors, and street symbolism to re-create Bengston's métier. For "Seventeen Artists in the Sixties," however, Gehry's intention was to create an environment that was relatively neutral in relation to seven-teen disparate sensibilities but that at the same time explored or amplified some of the perceptual and minimalist strains running through the artists' work. Many of the seventeen artists were collaborators and friends whose work had informed Gehry's architecture for almost two decades. Each artist's work was shown in a separate room of standard wood-frame-and-drywall construction, organized along a central spine and painted either white or subtle shades of primary colors. The interrelatedness of the works was conveyed with sight lines that punctured the partition walls, and perceptual subtleties were highlighted by careful lighting.

Paramount Theater Shell
Oakland, California
1981 (project)

Client: Oakland Symphony Orchestra
Program: Demountable orchestra shell
for existing theater
Materials: Wood frame and cladding, cardboard
Project Team: Frank O. Gehry, C. Gregory
Walsh Jr., Ed Woll

Model view.

Screen Actors Guild
Studio City, California
1981

Client: Keith Kennedy in joint venture with
the Screen Actors Guild
Program: Speculative office building
Budget: $15,000,000
Area: 140,000 square feet
Project team: Frank O. Gehry, C. Gregory
Walsh Jr., Ed Woll

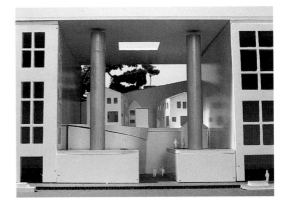

Model views.

Binder House
Los Angeles, California
1981

Client: Ronald and Sharon Binder
Program: Residential remodel
Budget: $150,000
Area: 4,000 square feet
Materials: Wood frame, stucco

Project Team: Frank O. Gehry, C. Gregory
Walsh Jr., Steve Tomko, Frederick Fisher

Sketches.

**Central Business District
Kalamazoo, Michigan
1981**

Client: City of Kalamazoo
Program: Mixed-use urban redevelopment proposal
Project Team: Frank O. Gehry, Ed Woll, Antonio Romano

Drawing; model views.

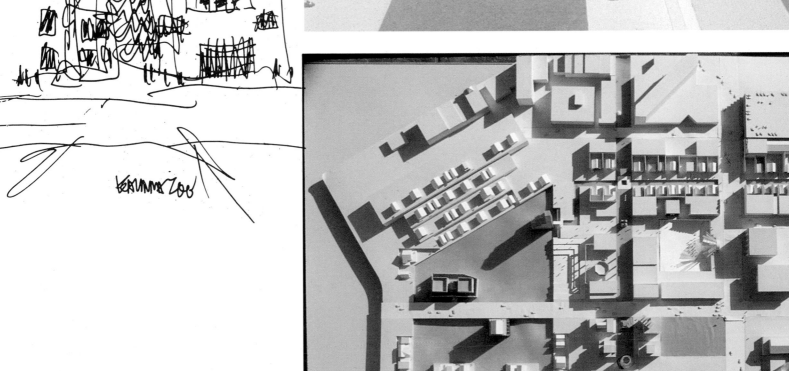

**Galleria Shopping Mall
Oklahoma City, Oklahoma
1981**

Client: Carrozza Properties
Program: Shopping center master plan,
including nine-level parking garage

Budget: $10,800,000
Area: 650,000 square feet
Project Team: Frank O. Gehry, Ed Woll,
Antonio Romano

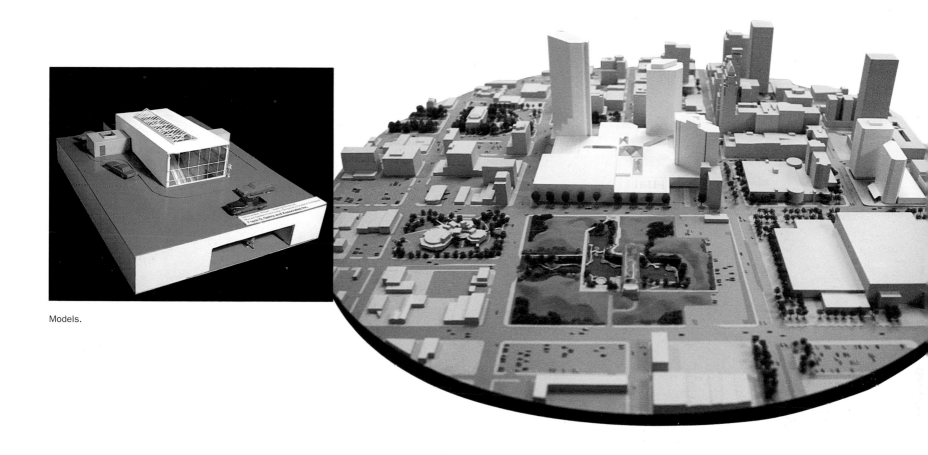

Models.

**Brooks Avenue Development
Project
Venice, California
1981**

Client: Development project
Program: Mixed-use beachfront development
proposal

Area: 20,000 square feet
Project Team: Frank O. Gehry, C. Gregory
Walsh Jr., Steven F. Tomko

Sketch.

**Frank O. Gehry and Associates
Office
Venice, California
1981**

Client: Frank O. Gehry and Associates
Program: Interior office renovations
Area: 8,200 square feet
Materials: Wood frame, drywall, plywood

Project Team: Frank O. Gehry, C. Gregory
Walsh Jr., Steven F. Tomko

Office after renovation with model of Wosk Residence in foreground.

**Wosk Residence
Beverly Hills, California
1981–84**

Client: Miriam Wosk
Program: Renovation of existing four-story
apartment building, to include one large single-
family residence with rental apartments
Materials: Wood frame, stucco, stained glass, tiles,
corrugated aluminum, black granite

Project Team: Frank O. Gehry, C. Gregory
Walsh Jr., Paul Lubowicki, Sharon Williams,
Rene Ilustre, Antonio Romano, David Kellen

New single-family house
on roof.

Fleck Residence
**Los Angeles, California
1982 (project)**

Client: Glen and Beverly Fleck
Program: Single-family residence and studio
Materials: Wood frame, stucco
Project Team: Frank O. Gehry, John Clagett,
Rene Ilustre

Model of two volumes.

Fleck Office Building
**Los Angeles, California
1982**

Client: Glen Fleck, Inc.
Program: Two-story office building and
residential rental apartments
Budget: $270,000
Area: 4,500 square feet
Materials: Wood frame, stucco
Project Team: Frank O. Gehry, John Clagett,
Robert G. Hale, Rene Ilustre

Front and aerial views
of model.

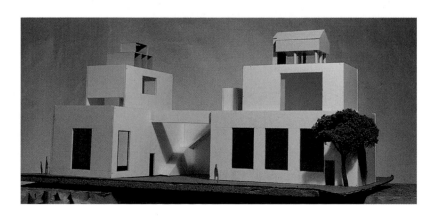

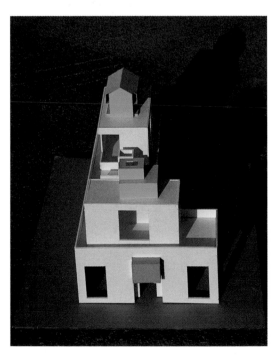

**Tract House
1982 (project)**

Program: Single-family residence
Area: 2,500 square feet
Materials: Wood frame, stucco, asphalt shingles,
wood siding
Project Team: Frank O. Gehry

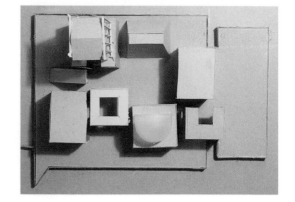

Model; sketch.

**World Savings Bank
Denver, Colorado
1982 (project)**

Client: World Savings Bank
Program: Two-story office building
Materials: Wood frame, stucco
Project Team: Frank O. Gehry

Model view.

**Century View Office Building
Los Angeles, California
1982**

Client: Samuel Goldwyn Corporation
Program: Office remodel
Budget: $650,000
Area: 10,000 square feet
Project Team: Frank O. Gehry, C. Gregory
Walsh Jr., Robert G. Hale, Rene Ilustre,
Sharon Williams

Exterior; detail.

**Civic Center Competition
Beverly Hills, California
1982**

Client: City of Beverly Hills
Program: Civic center master plan
Materials: Steel, concrete, wood frame, stucco
Project Team: Frank O. Gehry, Robert G. Hale

Model view.

**The Temporary Contemporary
Los Angeles, California
1982–83**

Client: Museum of Contemporary Art,
Los Angeles
Program: Renovation of two existing warehouses
to include exhibition space, public programs,
and support space for museum of contemporary
painting, sculpture, and performance art
Budget: $1,000,000
Area: 62,000 square feet
Materials: Steel frame, masonry wall, plaster,
plywood
Project Team: Frank O. Gehry, Robert G. Hale,
C. Gregory Walsh Jr., Rene Ilustre, David
Kellen, Michael Moran, Tomas Osinski,
Sharon Williams

The Temporary Contemporary was initially
intended to provide a temporary home for the
Museum of Contemporary Art's public programs, including exhibitions of contemporary
painting, sculpture, and performance art. Work
on the original facility involved the rehabilitation and transformation of two warehouse

buildings, including seismic upgrading, the
installation of new mechanical and electrical
systems, the design and installation of flexible
exhibition lighting, and the construction of
public restrooms and ramps that made the entire
facility accessible to the handicapped.

Working within a budget of $1.2 million,
seven-eighths of which was consumed by electrical and seismic upgrading, Gehry had little
choice but to allow the character of the two old
adjoining warehouses to persist, permitting the
same industrial spaces long favored by contemporary artists to be seen as a welcoming and
flexible space for exhibiting their work. The
renovation began by simply steam-cleaning and
sandblasting the existing floors, ceilings, and
skylights. Gehry's principal architectural gesture
was to knit the existing column grids together
in the steel-frame-and-chain-link canopy outside, giving the building not only some additional outdoor space but also a substantive
exterior presence.

New exterior space.

234

**World Expo Amphitheater
New Orleans, Louisiana
1982–84**

Client: Louisiana World Exposition, Inc.
Program: Temporary five-thousand-seat outdoor amphitheater
Budget: $2,900,000
Area: 55,000 square feet
Materials: Steel frame, metal deck
Project Team: Frank O. Gehry;
Perez Associates, associate architects

Exposition site;
study model.

Exterior view.

Steel structure; roof.

California Aerospace Museum and Theater
Los Angeles, California
1982–84

Client: California Office of the State Architect, Museum of Science and Industry
Program: Museum, including exhibition areas, 430-seat theater, terraces, and gardens
Budget: $5,000,000
Area: 28,000 square feet
Materials: Steel frame, concrete, stucco, sheet metal
Project Team: Frank O. Gehry, Rene Ilustre, John Clagett, Ron Johnson, Patricia Owen, C. Gregory Walsh Jr., Yuk Chan, Dean Perton; Kurily & Szymanski, structural engineer; Store, Matakovich & Wolfberg, mechanical/electrical engineer

In 1982, Gehry was invited to participate in the master planning of five new museum projects, all to be built in Exposition Park, near downtown Los Angeles, in time for the 1984 Summer Olympics. The Aerospace Museum and Theater was the only one of the originally planned projects to be completed before the Olympics.

The original Aerospace Museum was housed in a massive brick armory building, constructed in 1913. Since the cost of renovating the armory was well beyond the available budget, it was decided that a new exhibit building would be placed in front of the older one, with outdoor terraces and gardens connecting the two. A 430-seat Imax theater was added to the program and became the focus of the new Missile Garden.

The museum consists of two ninety-foot-tall forms, each with a different architectural expression, and a gantrylike viewing tower between them. The form at the east end is a plain stucco box punctured by a forty-foot-tall

View from south.

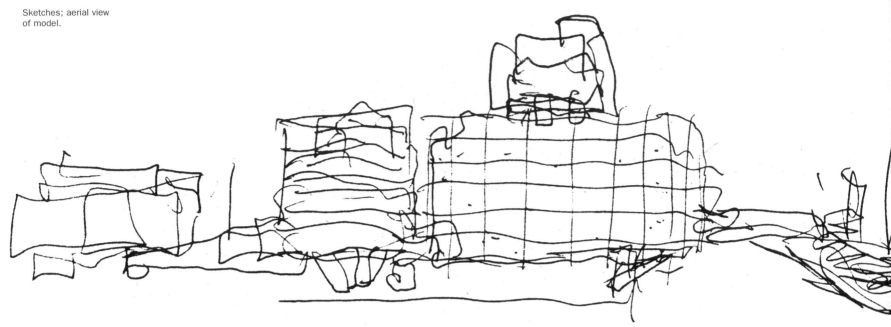

Sketches; aerial view
of model.

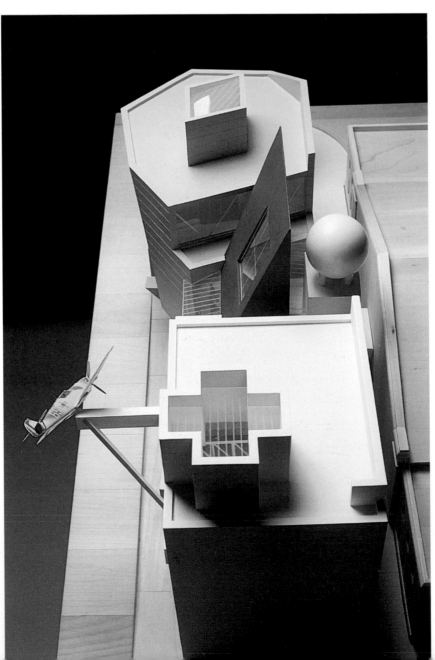

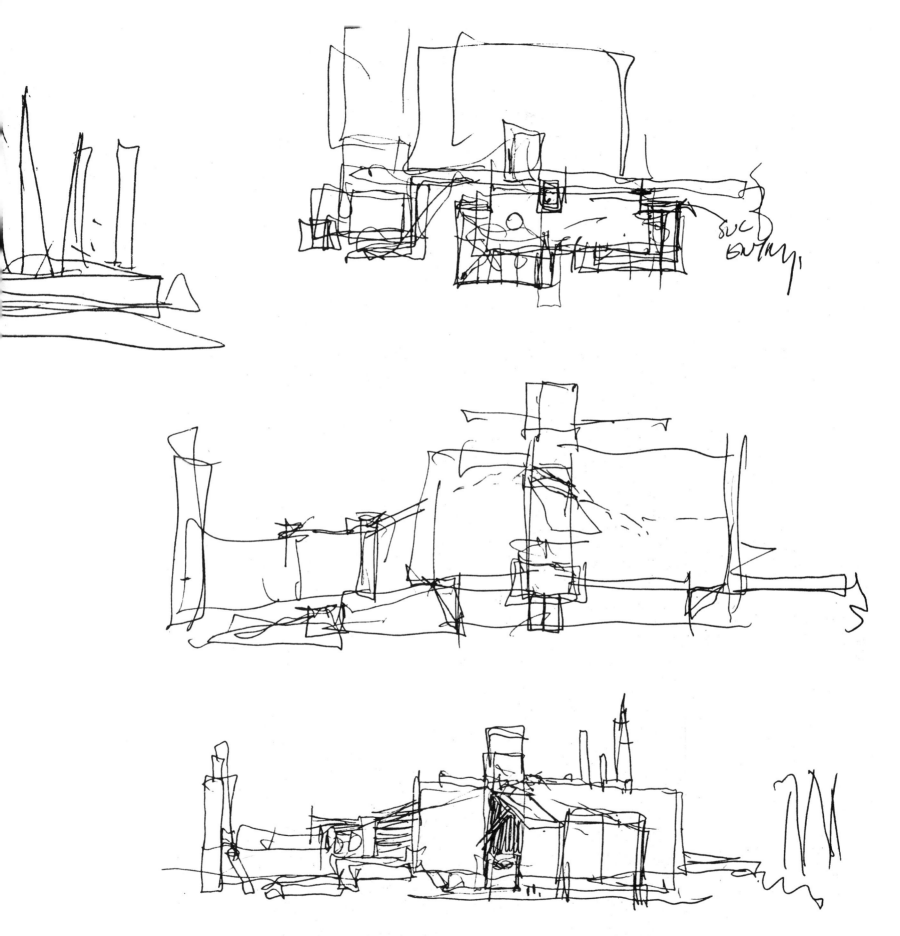

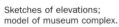

Sketches of elevations;
model of museum complex.

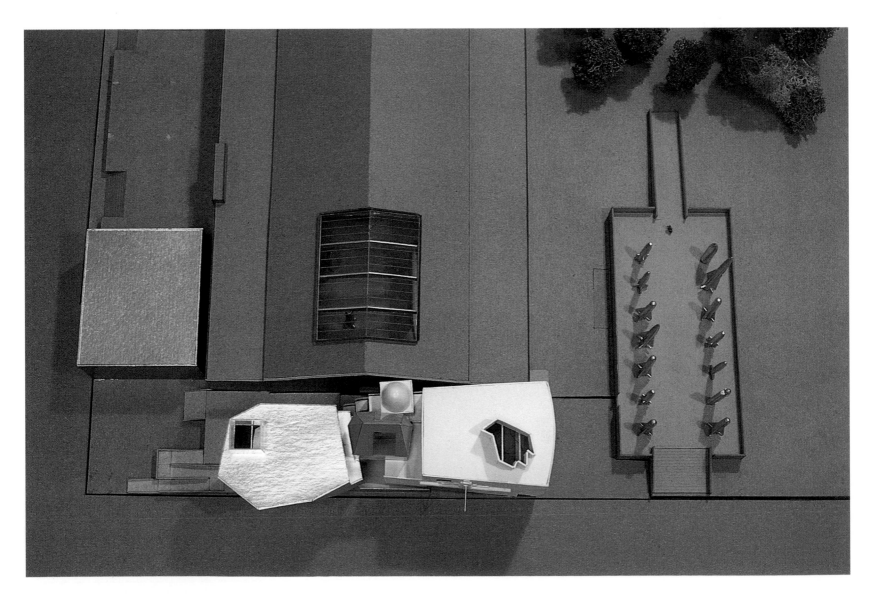

South elevation; south view of model, section through south front; mezzanine plan with reflected ceiling.

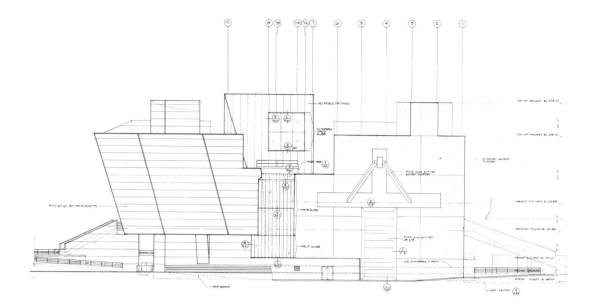

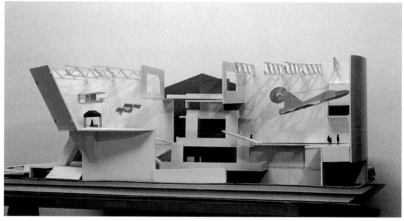

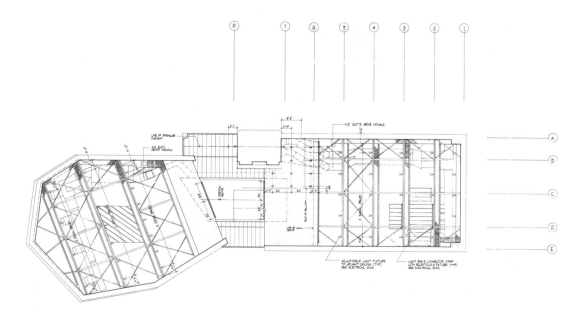

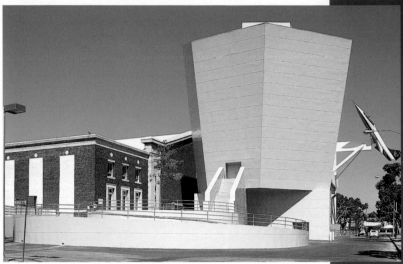

Views of polygonal
volumes; south front.

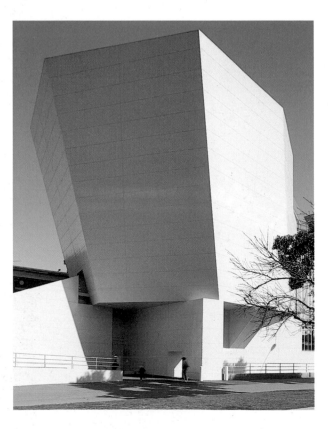

Section through two
volumes; interior views.

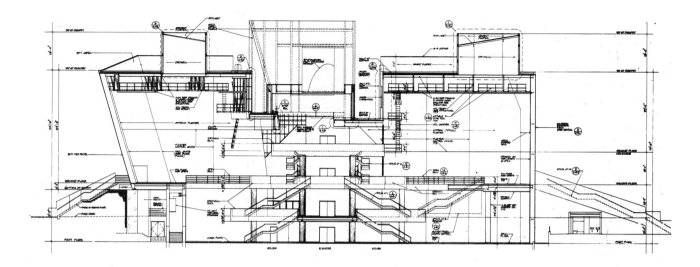

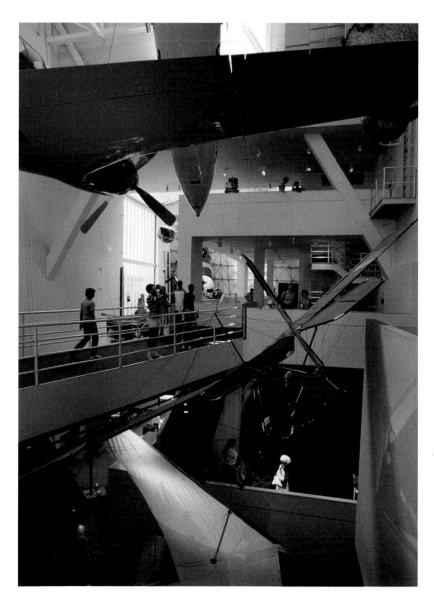

hangar door (which allows large pieces to be installed inside) over which a steel tripod suspends a Lockheed F-104. On the west end, a polygonal cone wrapped in sheet metal thrusts upward and outward. An entry ramp wraps the west end and leads visitors to the main entry, between the old armory building and the new museum.

From the outside, the two steel-frame structures appear as discrete forms; on the inside, the museum is a large singular volume pierced by gangways, ramps, skylights, and viewing platforms. Visitors enter the eighty-foot-high volume at the mezzanine level, amid space probes, satellites, and airplanes dangling from cables. The industrial scale and construction details of the interior—welded stairs, exposed beams, and giant space frames—refer plainly to the hangars and warehouses of the local manufacturing origins of the technology displayed.

Early design models show massing composed of a village or collage of separately articulated building-objects, surrounded by a landscape of scenographic and symbolic imagery. Ultimately the assemblage of forms was unified in scale and material and the imagery of flight was abstracted. The elevator shaft, for example, originally designed to resemble a missile silo, was capped instead with a less ominous sheet-metal globe.

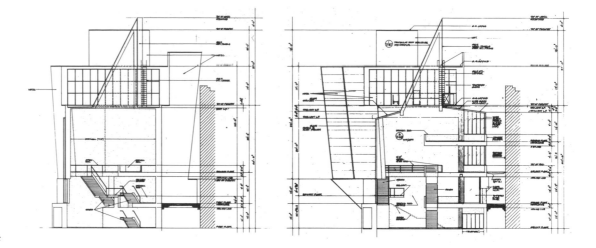

Sections; interior views.

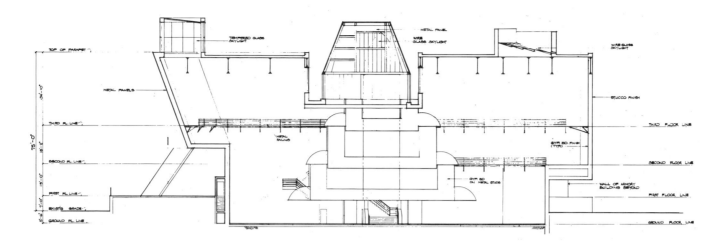

Norton Residence
Venice, California
1982–84

Client: Lynn and William Norton
Program: Single-family residence and studio/office space
Budget: $150,000
Area: 2,500 square feet
Materials: Wood frame, stucco, concrete block, glazed tile, wood logs
Project Team: Frank O. Gehry, John Clagett, David Kellen, Rene Ilustre

Gehry has referred to this three-story house as his "pride and joy." For the typically narrow beachfront lot, bounded by the heavily trafficked Venice boardwalk to the west and an alley to the rear, the owners requested that ocean views be maintained without sacrificing privacy from passersby and neighbors.

A blue-tiled box structure forms the ground-floor base for the simply stacked elements and contains a studio in the front, two bedrooms, and a double-car garage in the rear. Living and additional bedroom areas on the second and third levels are raised from the street and are set back from the beachfront walk to increase privacy and allow for ocean-view terraces. The wide second-level deck also acts as a visual buffer between the boardwalk and the living, kitchen, and dining area and is continuous with this area when the glass doors are open. The kitchen's deep skylight punches through to third-floor bedrooms and opens up the long, narrow living area. A stair leads from the western edge of the main deck to a freestanding study; this form echoes the nearby lifeguard stations and is a powerful compositional element, especially when viewed from the terrace of the third-floor master bedroom. Two terraces in the rear and easy access to the roof provide private but panoramic views of the eclectic neighborhood. Exterior materials include concrete block, glazed tile, stucco, and wood logs, with varied textures and colors intended to reflect the visual chaos of the building's complex urban context.

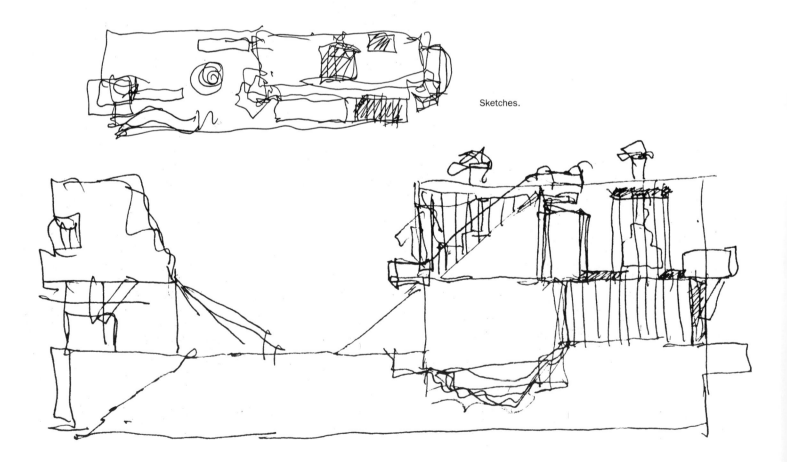

Sketches.

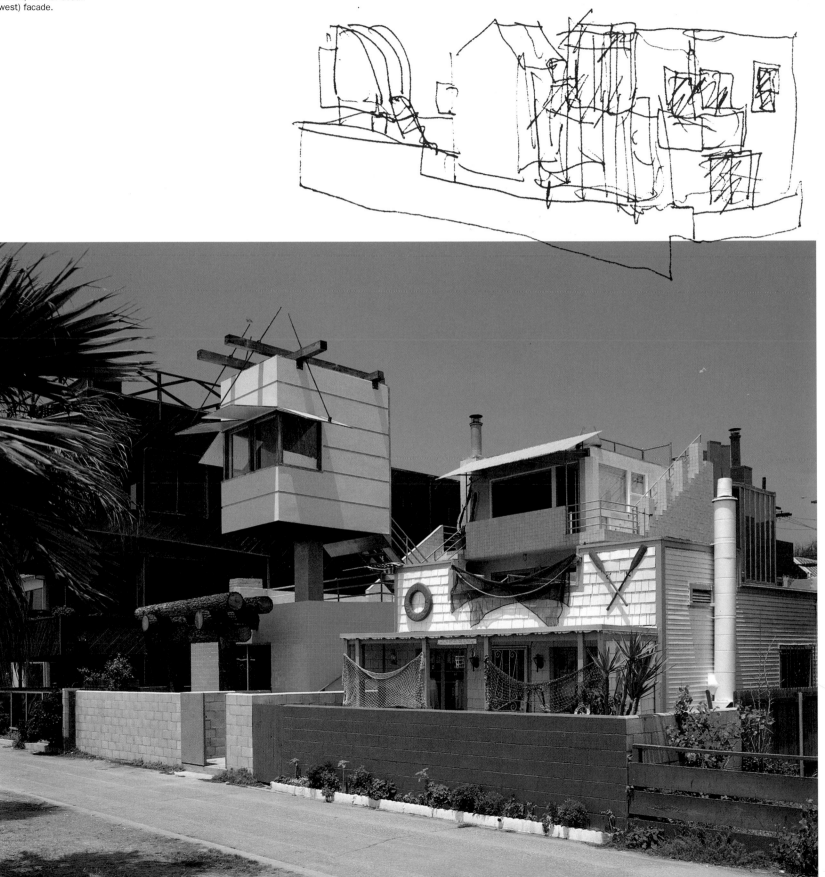

251

South elevation; east
facade; west elevation;
east elevation.

Opposite:
View of studio/office
from third-floor terrace.

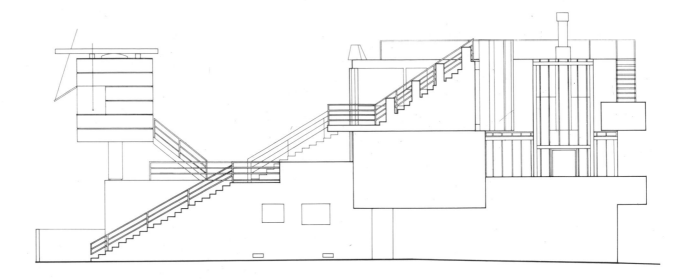

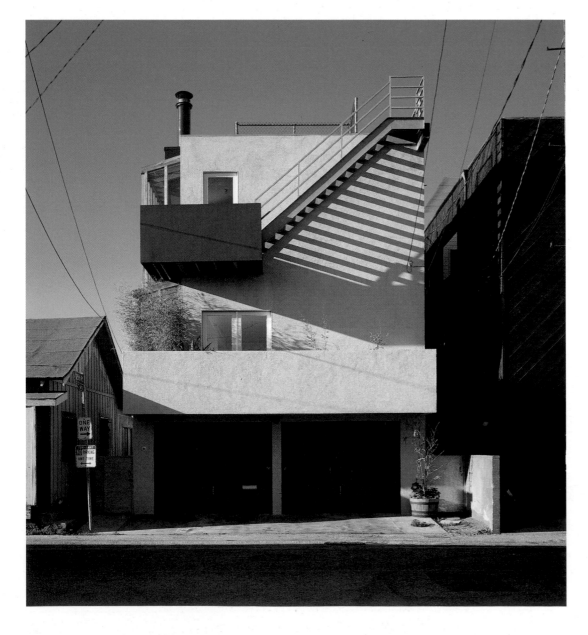

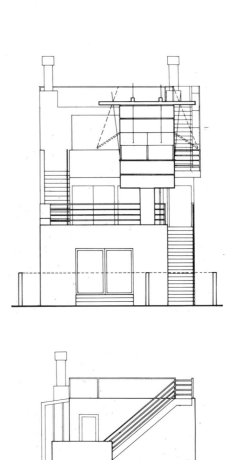

252

First- and third-floor plans; interiors.

**Rebecca's Restaurant
Venice, California
1982–85**

Client: Bruce Marder
Program: Two-hundred-seat restaurant
Budget: $1,500,000
Area: 4,450 square feet
Materials: Exposed concrete, brick, stainless
steel, glass and ceramic tile, copper, onyx, glass

Project Team: Frank O. Gehry, Robert G. Hale,
Tomas Osinski, David Kellen, C. Gregory
Walsh Jr., Carroll Stockard, Rene Ilustre;
Ed Moses, Tony Berlant, Peter Alexander,
collaborating artists

Interior.

Frances Howard Goldwyn Regional Branch Library
Hollywood, California
1982–86

Client: City of Los Angeles and Samuel Goldwyn Foundation
Program: Public library, including reading rooms, stacks, circulation and reference desks, and processing and administrative spaces
Budget: $3,000,000
Area: 19,500 square feet
Materials: Steel frame, stucco, ceramic tile, concrete, gypsum drywall
Project Team: Frank O. Gehry, Robert G. Hale, Sharon Williams, Rene Ilustre, Paul Lubowicki, C. Gregory Walsh Jr., Michael Moran, Dean Perton, Philip Okada; Kurily & Szymanski, structural engineer; Store, Matakovich & Wolfberg, mechanical engineer; Athans Enterprises, electrical engineer

For a grim stretch of urban-redevelopment area south of Hollywood Boulevard, Gehry designed a small library with a monumental presence on the street and a surprising relationship to the sky and hills from the inside. The library consists of an oasis-like massing of three towers behind a fifteen-foot stucco-covered concrete wall, giving the building not only the scale, formality, and symmetry of a civic presence but the appearance of a military compound. Passing through ten-foot steel gates, visitors enter the building via a shallow entrance plaza just below grade. Circulation and exhibition areas occupy the ground floor of the main tower. Two generously scaled reading rooms flank the tower, lit by north-facing windows facing the Hollywood Hills and overlooking reflecting pools. A grand circular stairway and elevator provide access to the upper-level reading rooms, stacks, administrative offices, and processing area. Three different textures of stucco are used with ceramic tile and concrete on the outside, and with gypsum drywall on the interiors.

Sketch; library in urban context.

East elevation; view from
east; north-south section.

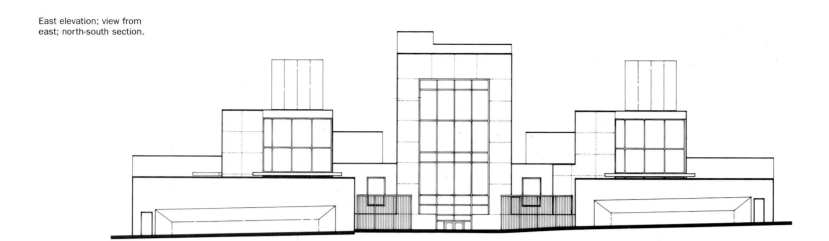

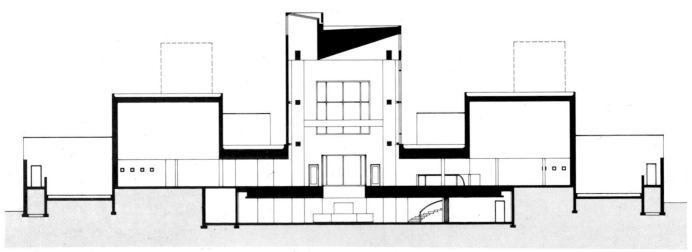

Detail of projecting
volume on second floor;
reading room on first floor;
interior of central pavilion
on first floor.

Sketches; model views.

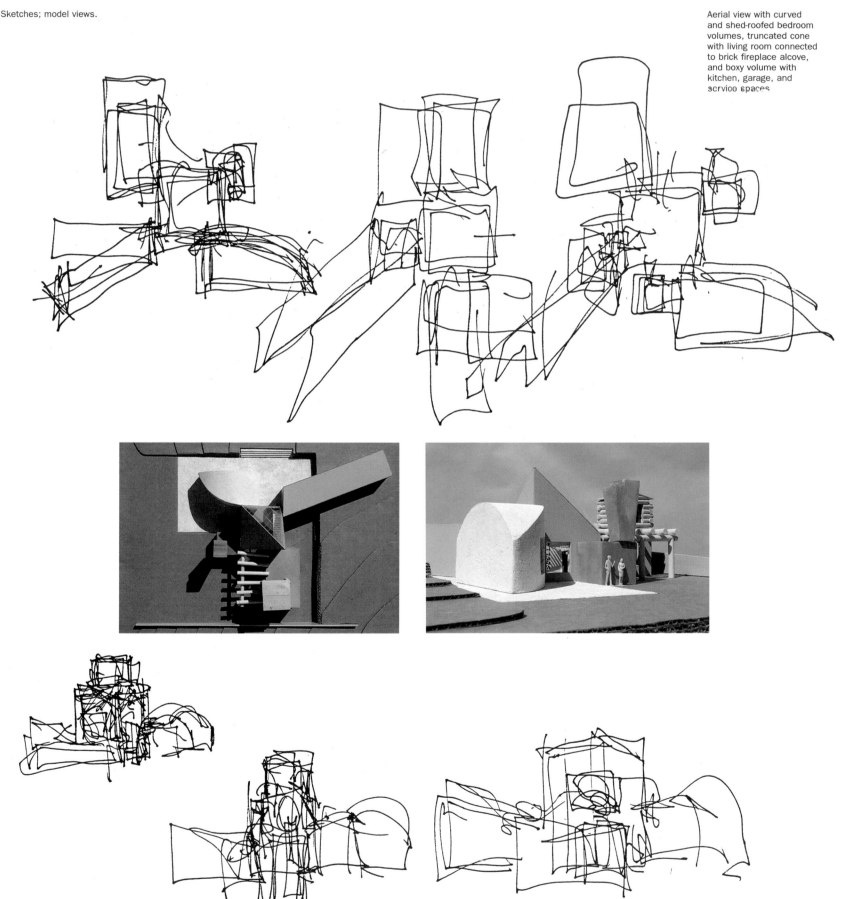

South, north, west, and east elevations; exterior view, with main house designed by Philip Johnson visible at left.

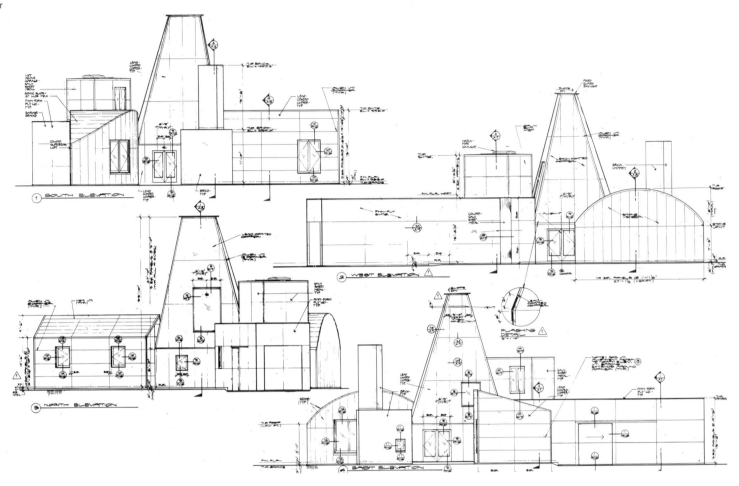

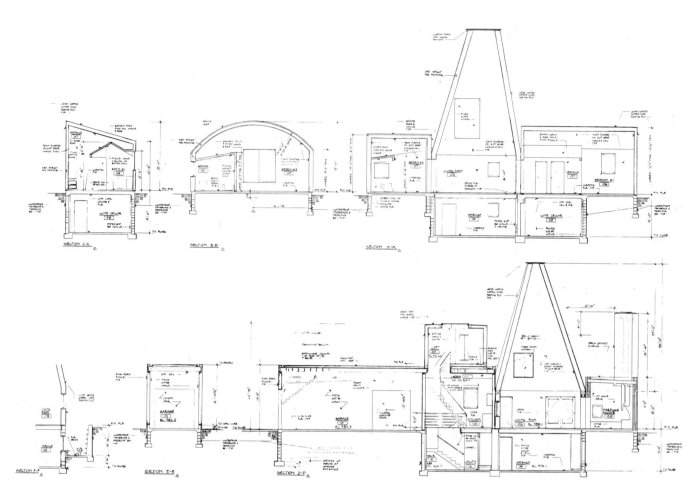

Section through first bedroom; section through second bedroom; section through two bedrooms and living area; section through entrance to lower level; section through garage; section through garage, kitchen, living area, and fireplace alcove.

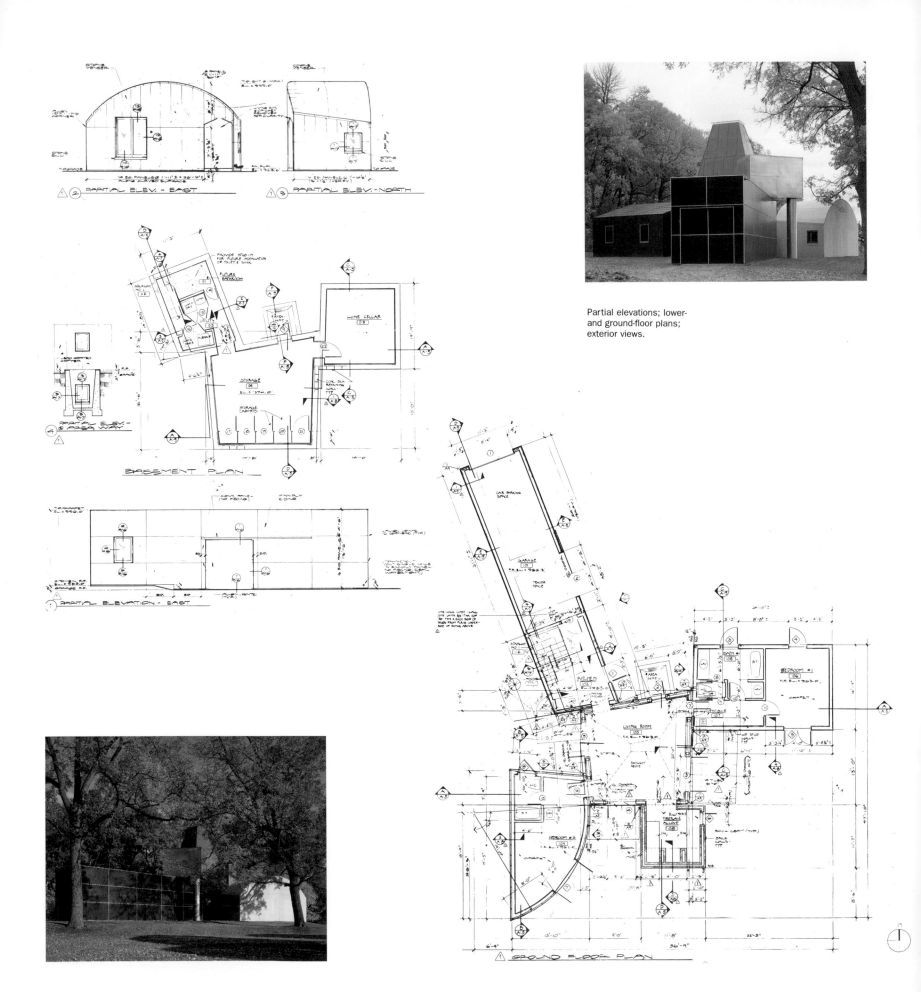

Partial elevations; lower-
and ground-floor plans;
exterior views.

Bedroom in curved volume;
details of living area.

**Kellerman-Krane Residence
Los Angeles, California
1983**

Client: Sally Kellerman and Jonathon Krane
Program: Residential remodel
Materials: Wood frame, stucco
Project Team: Frank O. Gehry, C. Gregory
Walsh Jr., Rene Ilustre

Existing house; exterior
after remodeling.

**Cricket Inn Project
Farmington, Connecticut
1983**

Client: Turnpike Properties Northeast, Inc.
Program: 126-room inn
Budget: $2,500,000
Area: 40,000 square feet
Materials: Steel frame, concrete
Project Team: Frank O. Gehry, Robert G. Hale

Model views.

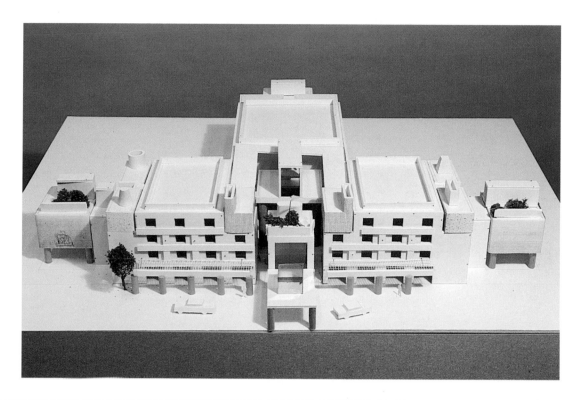

**Folly: The Prison Project
1983**

Client: Leo Castelli Gallery
Program: Snake-shaped prison and fish-shaped
viewing platform
Project Team: Frank O. Gehry

Model.

**Jencks Front Porch
1983 (project)**

Client: Charles Jencks
Program: Folly with fish, eagle, and horse
Material: Wood frame
Project Team: Frank O. Gehry

Model.

**Available Light
Temporary Museum of
Contemporary Art,
Los Angeles, California
1983**

Client: Museum of Contemporary Art,
Los Angeles
Program: Set design for performance art
Area: 2,160 square feet
Materials: Exposed wood frame, chain link
Project Team: Frank O. Gehry; Lucinda Childs,
choreographer; John Adams, composer

For the museum's opening, Gehry collaborated with the dancer-choreographer Lucinda Childs and the composer John Adams to produce a joint performance and installation piece, *Available Light*, the first in a series of mixed-media collaborations at the Temporary Contemporary. Within the vast, empty warehouse interior, Gehry designed a large double stage forty feet wide and built of rough, exposed two-by-four framing. Its lower section is thirty-six feet deep and the rear, higher platform, eighteen feet deep. A scrim of ten layers of chain-link fencing hangs on one side of the stage to dematerialize the space beyond. The audience sits in front and to one side of the stage. The building's clerestory, its source of "available light," backlights the space through layers of red gel. This red light is used in combination with temporary theatrical lighting installed on a grid hung from the ceiling to counterpoint and augment the pattern of movements created by the performers on stage. Dancers came and went on three stairways visible to the spectators in the open expanse of the warehouse space, their entrances and exits incorporated by Childs into her choreography.

The Temporary Contemporary met with such success that it remained open for nearly ten years before being closed in 1992 by the city of Los Angeles to make way for a development previously planned for the site. The planned development never reached fruition, and the Temporary Contemporary again opened its doors, in August 1995, as the Geffen Contemporary. The master plan for the renovation of the museum and for the reintroduction of the museum to the public involved three phases of construction and was completed in 1997.

Views during performance.

**German Expressionist Sculpture
Los Angeles County Museum
of Art, Los Angeles, California
1983**

Client: Los Angeles County Museum of Art
Program: Exhibition design and installation

Materials: Wood frame, drywall
Project Team: Frank O. Gehry

Installation detail.

**Boxenbaum Residence
New York, New York
1983**

Client: Charles Boxenbaum
Program: Loft/studio addition to roof of existing building
Area: 2,500 square feet
Materials: Wood frame, sheet metal, Finnish plywood
Project Team: Frank O. Gehry, C. Gregory Walsh Jr., Robert G. Hale

Studio addition seen from garden.

Médiathèque, Centre d'Art Contemporain Design Competition
Nîmes, France
1984 (project)

Client: City of Nîmes, represented by Mayor Bouscat
Program: Competition entry for contemporary art museum and library
Area: 25,000 square feet
Materials: Steel frame, concrete, glass
Project Team: Frank O. Gehry, Robert G. Hale, C. Gregory Walsh Jr., Sergio Zeballos, John Clagett, Michael Moran, Tomas Osinski, Patricia Owen, Ron Johnson, Dominic Lyon; Marc Biass, collaborating architect

Hoping to approximate the success of the Centre Georges Pompidou in Paris, the city of Nîmes in 1984 sponsored an international invitational competition for a new museum and library of contemporary art to be situated on an open site adjoining a Roman temple, the Maison Carrée.

The building was designed as a self-contained object, formally distinct from but complementary to the Maison Carrée and the city. The main building is a spiral form ending in a viewing platform overlooking the Roman temple. Stairs and ramps interconnect all levels of the exterior spaces, with facades enlivened by the sight of people on the building, exploring from top to bottom.

The small site dictated that many levels be built. Placement of the museum underground allows the building mass to be reduced in height and bulk and to relate in scale to the fabric of the city. Tall skylights provide modulated natural light for the gallery levels below. The main building mass (four levels above grade) corresponds exactly to the height of the city's prevailing cornice line. It contains the

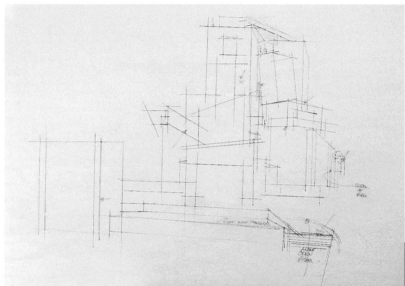

Preliminary drawing; model view.

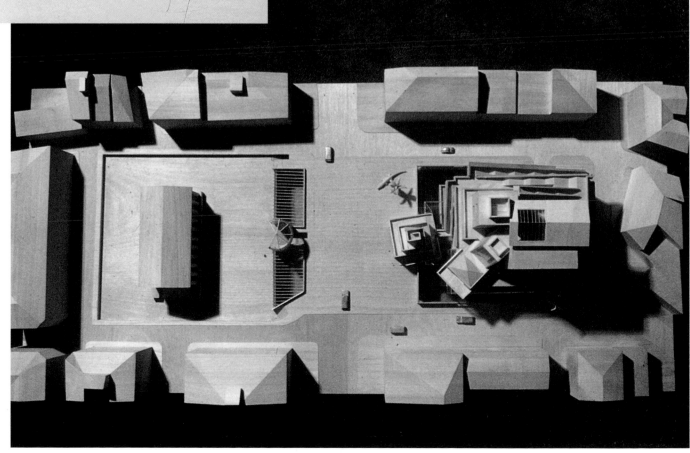

library and a special collection relating to French bullfighting. The spaces surround a tall, skylit atrium, open to the museum levels below.

A smaller rooftop structure houses the children's library and workshop, formally relating to the setback structures above the cornice found in the adjoining urban context. Gehry intended this crown, the most exuberant part of the complex, as a physical expression of a policy commitment articulated in the program brief: the future of French culture lies with the children.

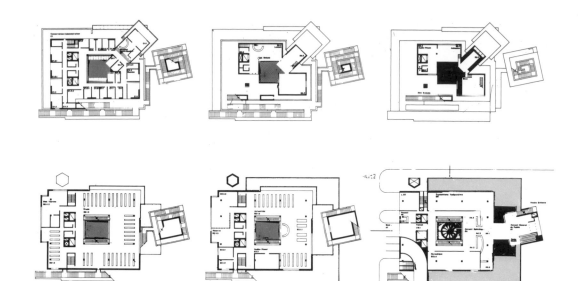

Ground-, first-, second-, third-, fourth-, and fifth-floor plans; model with the Maison Carrée; north elevation/section; south elevation.

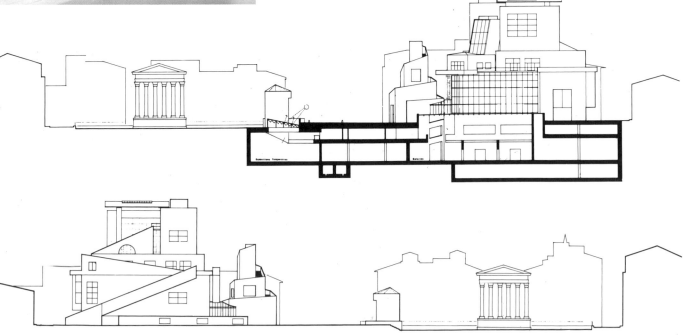

Galleria Office Building
Oklahoma City, Oklahoma
1983–85 (project)

Client: Carrozza Properties
Program: Office building
Budget: $9,900,000
Area: 180,000 square feet
Project Team: Frank O. Gehry, Ed Woll,
Hak Sik Son, Bob Cloud

Site plan.

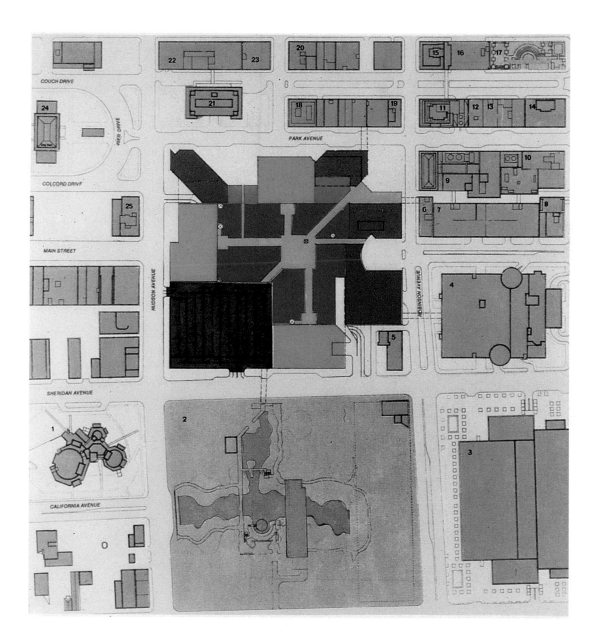

Fish and Snake Lamps
1983–86

Client: Formica Corporation and New City Editions
Program: Light-fixture prototype design
Materials: Wire frame, Formica chips
Project Team: Frank O. Gehry, Tomas Osinski; Fred Hoffman, Joel Stearns, Daniel Sachs, New City Editions

In 1983, the Formica Company initiated a competition for designers in order to illustrate the properties of a new product, Colorcore. Formica arranged to give selected designers a large quantity of material and a small grant to develop and execute their designs.

Unlike traditional Formica, Colorcore's color is integral; when viewed from the side, the edge is the same color as the surface. Interested also in the material's translucency, Gehry chose to create a lamp. After several awkward attempts, frustration built and one of the lamps was broken. On examining the wreckage, a new property was discovered: when the material broke, it didn't break along clear edges but left a sort of fissured, sheared, rough edge akin to arrowheads or shark teeth. The shards, shaped like fish scales, inspired the form of a carp.

In constructing the lamps, a wire armature was stretched over a carved wooden form. The wire was then cut, the wood removed, and the armature resoldered. Sheets of yellow Formica (the most translucent color) were shattered and the fragments sheared to size and shape and glued to the armature. A wavelike base of larger shards allows for access to the lightbulb.

Four editions of fish lamps and several snake designs—approximately three dozen lamps in total—were produced by New City Editions over three years.

Lamps; sketches.

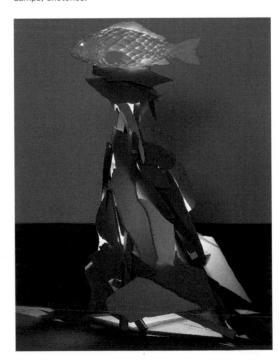

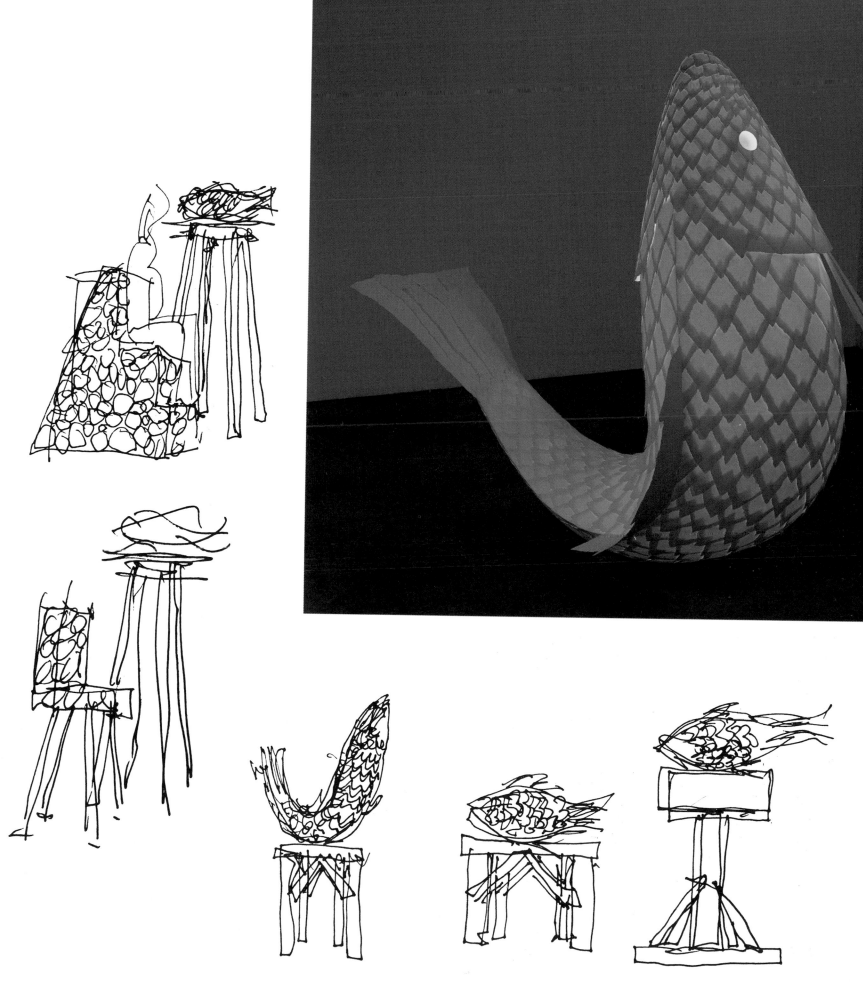

Sirmai-Peterson Residence
Thousand Oaks, California
1983–88

Client: Mark Peterson and Barbara Sirmai
Program: Single-family residence
Budget: $400,000
Area: 3,000 square feet
Materials: Wood frame, stucco, galvanized metal, concrete block, unpainted plywood
Project Team: Frank O. Gehry, C. Gregory Walsh Jr., Patricia Owen, Sergio Zeballos, Rene Ilustre

On a two-acre rural site adjacent to a ravine and a storm drain, this three-thousand-square-foot residence developed as a churchlike form, with the typical residential elements clustered around the perimeter of a central galvanized-metal cruciform block containing the core of the house.

Taking advantage of the site's varied topography, the kitchen, dining room, entry, and den meet to form a high, central cross-shaped element. The adjacent living room suggests a nave; the fireplace, an apse; and the hall to the living room, a side aisle. Two gray stucco bedroom-and-bath blocks are attached to the west side; one is reached by a bridge, the other via a sunken tunnel. Interior materials are drywall, exposed wood for the rafters, unpainted plywood, and concrete block.

The formal space between the bedrooms and the living room is expressed as an interior courtyard, visible from the entry and accessible from the living room and bedroom structures. Gehry saw the relationship of the buildings to the courtyard as similar to that of the town square of a medieval city. Rooms not fronting the courtyard face out toward a shallow lake, made by damming the existing watercourse.

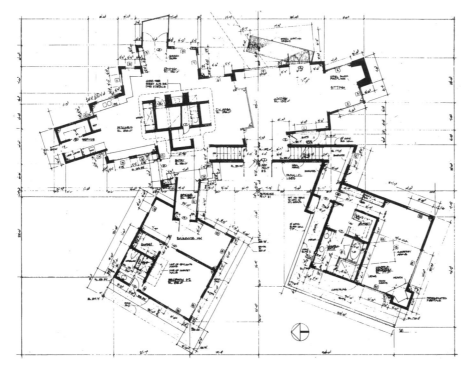

Plan; aerial view of model.

Sketches; view of model
toward water basin.

Plan sketch; view
from east; view
from northeast.

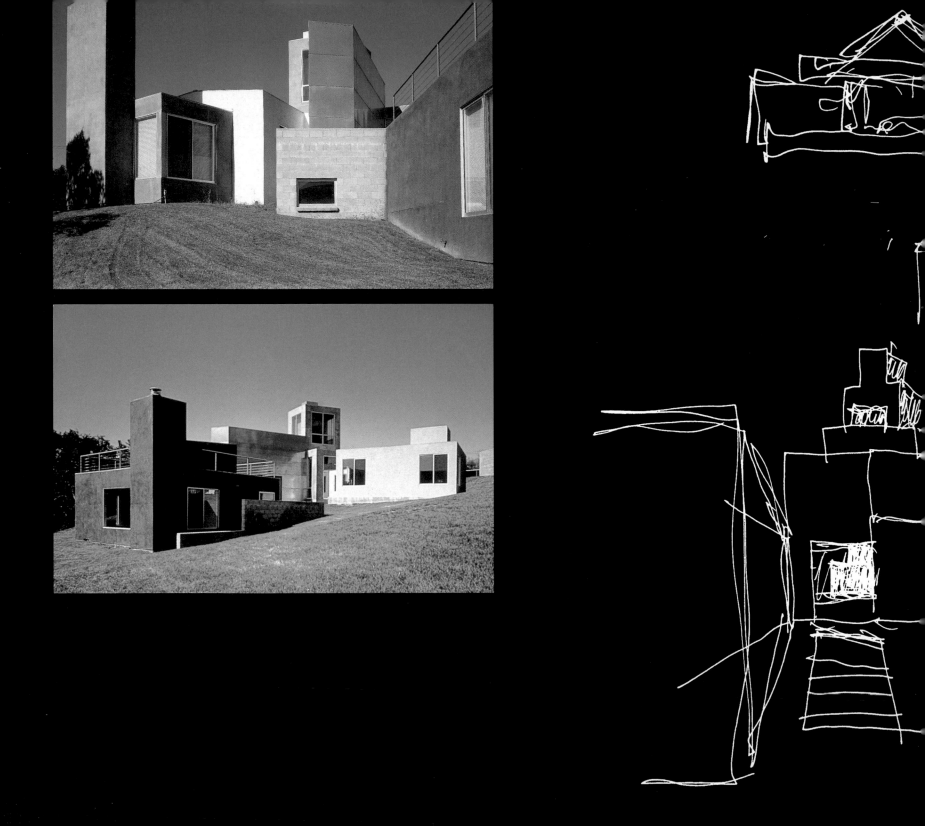

North elevation; east
elevation; sections.

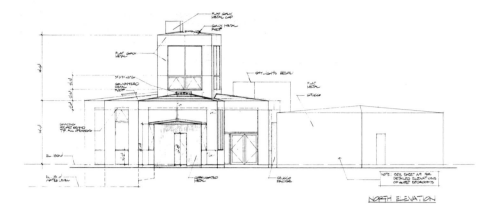

NORTH ELEVATION

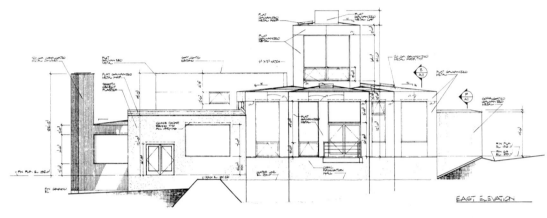

EAST ELEVATION

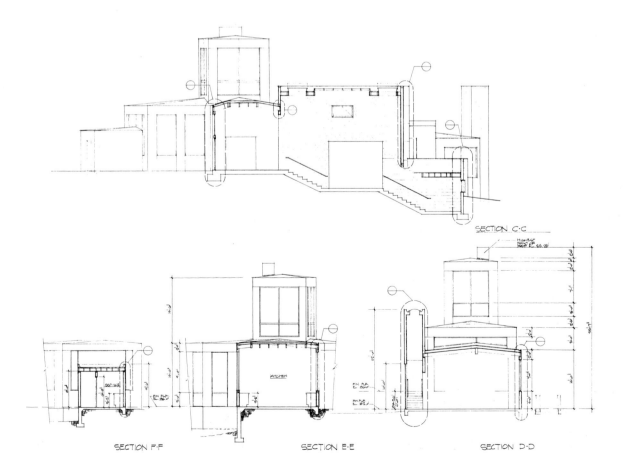

SECTION C-C

SECTION F-F   SECTION E-E   SECTION D-D

Views of living areas;
hallway.

**Camp Good Times
Santa Monica Mountains,
Malibu, California
1984–85**

Client: Pepper Abrams, Southern California Children's Cancer Services, Inc., and McDonald's Operators Association of Southern California
Program: Eleven-building, ninety-acre summer camp for children with cancer, including sleeping cabins, dining and recreation areas, infirmary, and outdoor amphitheater

Budget: $7,500,000
Area: 63,000 square feet
Materials: Wood frame, stucco, sheet metal, canvas
Project Team: Frank O. Gehry, Michael Lehrer, C. Gregory Walsh Jr., Tomas Osinski, Michael Moran; Claes Oldenburg, Coosje van Bruggen, collaborating artists

Model of service building.

**Sunar-Hauserman Showroom
Innova Design Center,
Houston, Texas
1984–86**

Client: Sunar-Hauserman, Inc.
Program: Furniture, fabric, and wall system
showroom within existing building
Budget: $350,000

Area: 7,000 square feet
Project Team: Frank O. Gehry, John Clagett,
Robert G. Hale

Exposition space.

Edgemar Development
Santa Monica, California
1984–88

Model; schematic plan
of ground floor; section.

Client: Sher Development/Santa Monica
Museum of Art
Program: Art museum, restaurant, retail shops,
office space, parking
Budget: $3,000,000
Area: 34,500 square feet
Materials: Steel, concrete, wood, ceramic tile,
stucco, chain link

Project Team: Frank O. Gehry, David Denton,
Sergio Zeballos, C. Gregory Walsh Jr., Rene
Ilustre, Roberta Weiser, David Pakshong; Kurily
& Szymanski, structural engineer; Tyler &
Cobleigh, general contractor

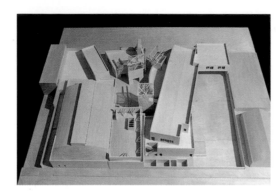

This project, an art museum and commercial
development on two levels, with both on-grade
and subterranean parking, occupies the site of a
former dairy. It consists of several structures,
each with a distinct architectural character, some
facing Main Street and others facing an internal
courtyard.

In order to maintain the small-scale character
of the existing surroundings—a commercial
zone of shops and restaurants, heavily trafficked
both day and night—parking is screened and
the existing scale maintained by lining the 250-
foot-wide street frontage with five small, visually distinct structures. Three tower elements are
positioned to enhance views and draw potential
customers into the center courtyard. The slender proportion and open character of these
higher elements interject minimally into views
of the ocean from the hillside residences behind
the project.

Along Main Street, the central element of
the complex is a wall fragment of the former
dairy, now a shop. Previously the facade was
plaster, but the original fragment collapsed during construction and was rebuilt and sheathed
in copper and green glazed tile. Also new is an
openwork tower above. Next to the tower, clad
in galvanized metal, is a curved shape containing shops and a terrace above for the office
block on the second level, surfaced in natural
gray stucco. Two other towers, a greenhouse
structure and the elevator well, the latter with a
balcony draped with chain-link mesh, are
intended to lead the eye back into the court.
The courtyard contains a ramp for disabled
access that leads up to the art museum and
restaurant, which are housed in two renovated
wood-frame dairy structures.

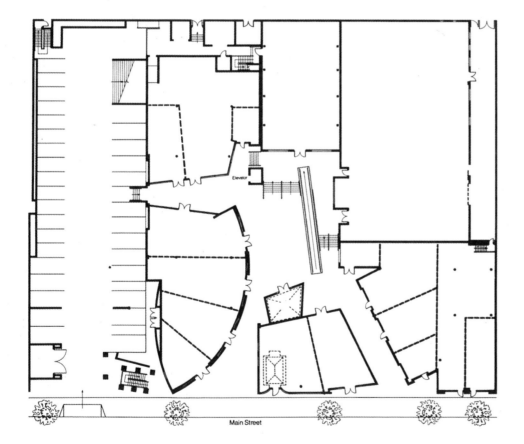

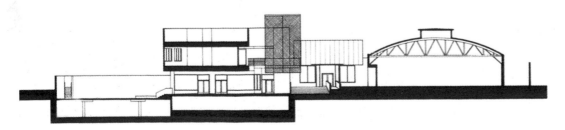

Views from Main Street.

Main Street (west) elevation; partial west elevations of office and shopping buildings in courtyard; east elevation; view from Main Street into courtyard.

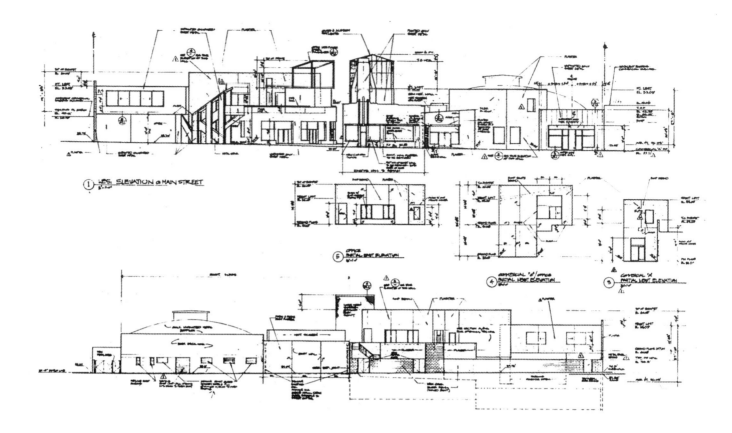

Views and construction
details of skylights atop
towers.

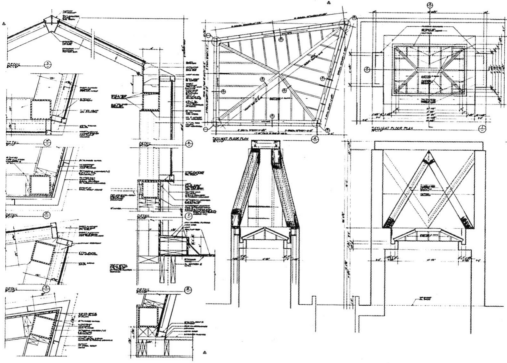

Il Corso del Coltello
Venice Biennale,
Venice, Italy
1985

Program: Performance-art piece
Project Team: Frank O. Gehry (as Frankie P.
Toronto), Germano Celant, Claes Oldenburg,
Coosje van Bruggen

Sketch.

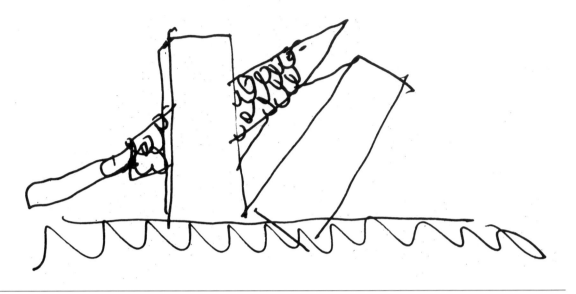

Fountain Valley School Theater
Colorado Springs, Colorado
1985

Client: Trustees of the Fountain Valley School
Program: Private school auditorium
Area: 4,000 square feet
Project Team: Frank O. Gehry, C. Gregory
Walsh Jr., David Denton, Aaron Betsky,
Robin Meierding

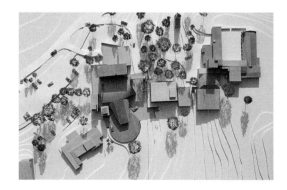

Model views.

Boylston Street Air Rights
Boston, Massachusetts
1985 (project)

Client: Cohen Properties
Program: Urban design proposal, including offices, retail, galleries, three-hundred-room hotel, and six-hundred-car parking garage
Area: 970,000 square feet
Materials: Steel, concrete
Project Team: Frank O. Gehry, Robert G. Hale, Tom Buresh, Sharon Williams

---

Pirelli Bicocca Competition
Milan, Italy
1985

Client: Industrie Pirelli, SpA
Program: Conversion of tire factory into high-tech laboratories and offices
Area: 5,000,000 square feet

Project Team: Frank O. Gehry with UCLA Graduate School of Architecture and Urban Planning

Aerial and perspective views of model.

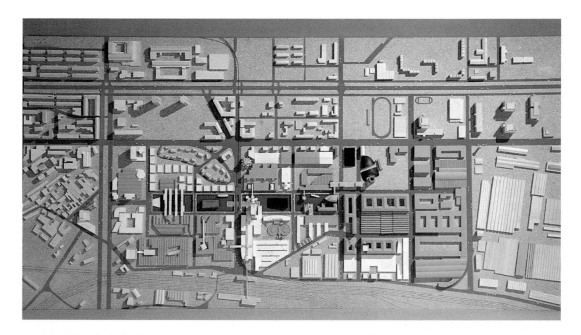

Turtle Creek Development
Dallas, Texas
1985–86 (project)

Client: Carrozza Investments Limited
Program: Mixed-use development, including
one-hundred-room hotel, office building,
twenty-three-story condominium tower, and
townhouses
Budget: $100,000,000
Area: 800,000 square feet
Materials: Concrete, steel, glass
Project Team: Frank O. Gehry, David Denton,
C. Gregory Walsh Jr., Tom Buresh

For an affluent, design-conscious area of Dallas called Turtle Creek, Gehry designed a large mixed-use project, including a 100-room luxury hotel, a 160,000-square-foot office building, a 23-story condominium tower, and 10 town-houses. These elements are grouped around a landscaped park and articulated with different skins and massing.

The location necessitated that the scale of the project be broken up, with the smaller townhouses situated to create a transitional buffer for the larger buildings. The office build-ing and hotel occupy primary locations on the corners to allow for access and visibility, but the bulk of their mass is set back from the street. A private drive and courtyard separates the town-houses from the condominiums, creating pri-vacy for both.

Clad in green glass and exhibiting a curved profile, the office building sits in an ornamental pool and is surmounted by a roof garden. The condominium tower is covered with a skin of two-story columns screening the balconies and faces a park diagonally across from the site. The hotel building and additional condominiums are housed in a faceted block posed in front of the main housing slab. The townhouses line the street's frontage and surround the complex's main entry courtyard.

Model with office tower;
schematic plan.

Model from corner with office tower; model from townhouse side.

**GFT Fish
Turin, Italy
Florence, Italy
1985–86**

Client: Gruppo Finanziario Tessile
Program: Traveling sculpture installation
Area: 37 feet long by 10 feet wide by 12 feet tall
Materials: Wood frame armature, custom-laminated plywood scales

Project team: Frank O. Gehry, Joel Stearns;
Joel Stearns, Fred Hoffman, Daniel Sachs,
New City Editions, fabrication and installation

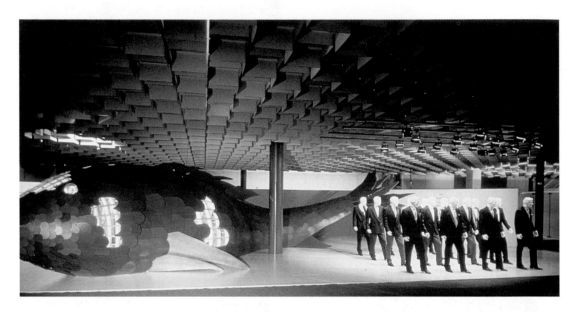

Views of installation.

360 Newbury Street
Boston, Massachusetts
1985–88

Client: Cohen Companies, Inc.
Program: Conversion of existing warehouse building in historic district to retail and offices
Budget: $10,000,000
Area: 140,000 square feet
Materials: Steel, concrete
Project Team: Frank O. Gehry, Robert G. Hale, Tom Buresh, Sharon Williams, Berthold

Penkhues, Peter Becker, Carroll Stockard, Susan Narduli, Kevin Daly, Young Kim; Schwartz/Silver Architects, Inc., associate architect; Am-Tech Engineers, Inc., plumbing, mechanical, and electrical engineer; Simpson, Gumpertz & Heger, Inc., structural consultant; Bond Brothers, Inc., construction manager

Occupying a conspicuous location in Boston's historic Back Bay area, this early-twentieth-century warehouse was converted into a 140,000-square-foot commercial retail and office building with the addition of a new lobby, elevators, and an eighth floor. The Back Bay Architectural Commission and the Boston Redevelopment Agency mandated that the two most prominent facades retain their original character, resulting in the removal and careful replacement of concrete, brick, and sculpted spandrels. A series of glass canopies was also introduced on these two street facades in order to reorient the building and provide covered entry for the ground-floor spaces. A larger, lead-coated copper canopy clearly identifies the new entrance on Newbury Street. Large struts supporting these canopies spring from the pilasters of the original building and visually reinforce its

View from northwest; study of north facade.

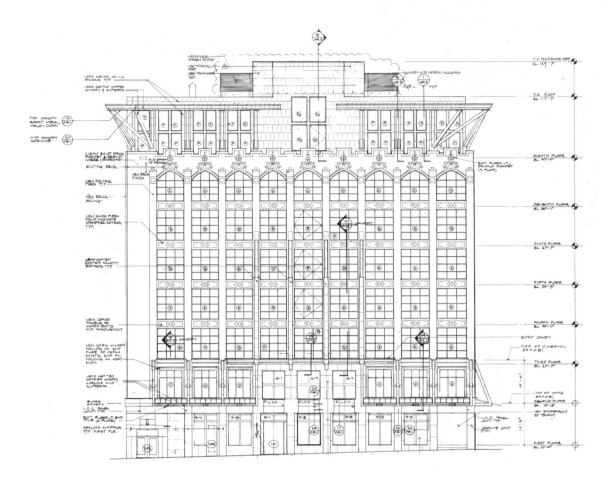

column grid. New struts support the projecting metal-clad cornice at the new penthouse level. The original crenellated cornice, an unusual feature in the Back Bay, was left visible behind the new cornice. Windows on the east and south facades are grouped in patterns that acknowledge the building's context; they are given additional detail at the head and mullions as sculptural embellishment on the wall. At the acute southeast corner of the building, the new eighth floor is set back to make room for sculpture. Claes Oldenburg and Coosje van Bruggen executed several studies for installations here, including one of a large, drooping tea bag.

The penthouse, original party-wall facades, and canopies are clad in lead-coated copper. By contrast, the lobby utilizes a rich palette of dark-stained birch wall panels with bronze joints, blue granite flooring, and a backlit yellow onyx ceiling.

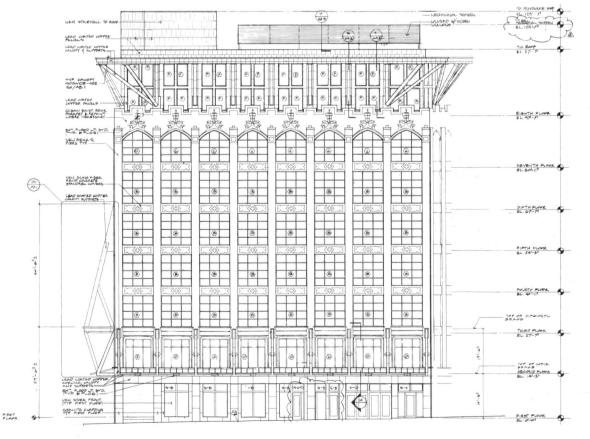

North elevation;
west elevation;
view from south.

View from southwest; section; detail and construction drawing of canopy supports.

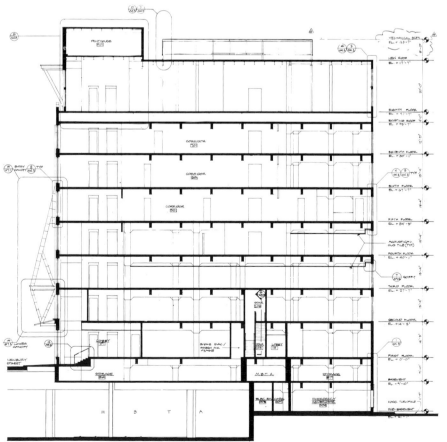

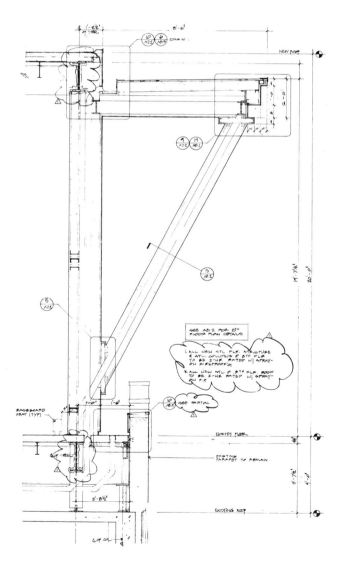

Yale Psychiatric Institute
New Haven, Connecticut
1985–89

Model view;
schematic plan.

Client: Yale University
Program: Sixty-six-bed hospital, including bedrooms, offices, therapy rooms, transitional care, and recreation areas
Budget: $10,600,000
Area: 76,000 square feet
Materials: Steel, concrete, copper and steel sheet metal
Project Team: Frank O. Gehry, David Denton, Roberta Weiser, C. Gregory Walsh Jr., Thomas Duley, Kevin Daly, Anne Greenwald, David Pakshong, Aaron Betsky, Charles Dilworth, Jane Sachs, Alex Meconi; Allan Dehar & Associates, collaborating architect; Barun Basu Associates, consulting architect; Spiegel & Zamecnik, Inc., structural engineer; Luchini, Milfort & Goodell, electrical and mechanical engineer

The Yale Psychiatric Institute is a seventy-six-thousand-square-foot, sixty-six-bed facility providing medium- and long-term care for severely disabled adolescents and young adults. Located between the large Yale–New Haven medical complex and the economically depressed Hill redevelopment area, the facility recalls Yale's colleges by transforming its city-block site into a yard surrounded by three buildings. More importantly, the design of the institute was meant to reinforce its therapeutic approach: patients begin receiving "clues" about the path back to normalcy immediately upon their arrival.

The three simply stated main buildings house most bedrooms and offices. Therapy areas and points of transition are pulled out into the courtyards and the spaces between the buildings in order to articulate the focal points of the institute and to allow the patients to recuperate in a villagelike complex of highly defined forms differing in configuration, color, texture, and scale.

The eastern and western buildings are clad in brick. The eastern building consists of three floors of offices over a commercial ground floor. By placing a bookstore and café at the entrance, it was Gehry's intention to diffuse the institutionality of the complex. The western building contains two floors of patient rooms and care facilities over a ground floor of service and therapy spaces. The central building houses offices and spaces for patients who are in transition from intensive care to reintegration with the outside environment. This recreation building is clad in lead-coated copper and natural copper and has a curved roof. Community rooms, therapy spaces, and enclosed walkways in the courtyard are clad in various combinations of Dryvit, metal, and glass.

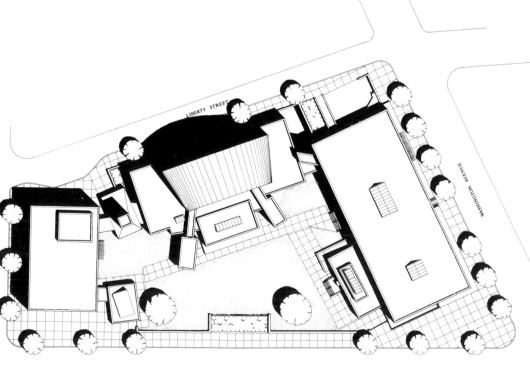

SITE PLAN

First-, second-, and
third-floor plans.

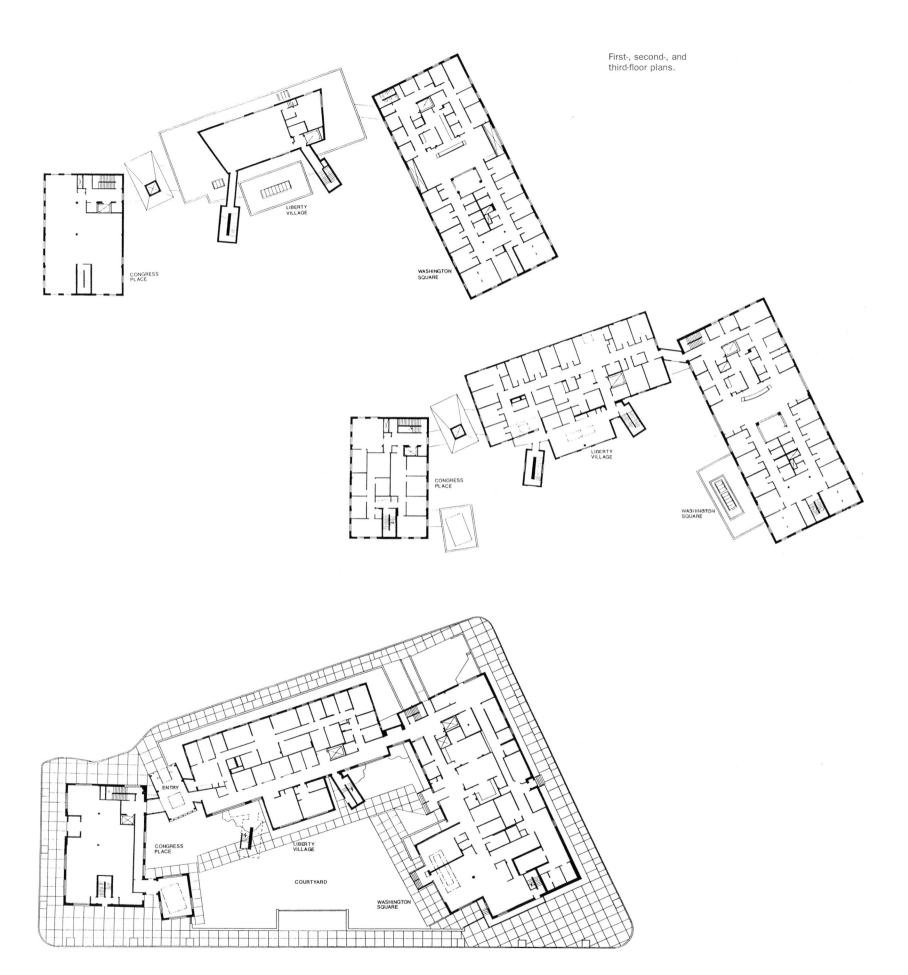

CONGRESS
PLACE

LIBERTY
VILLAGE

WASHINGTON
SQUARE

CONGRESS
PLACE

LIBERTY
VILLAGE

WASHINGTON
SQUARE

ENTRY

CONGRESS
PLACE

LIBERTY
VILLAGE

COURTYARD

WASHINGTON
SQUARE

FIRST FLOOR PLAN
NORTH

Sketches.

North elevation;
view from north.

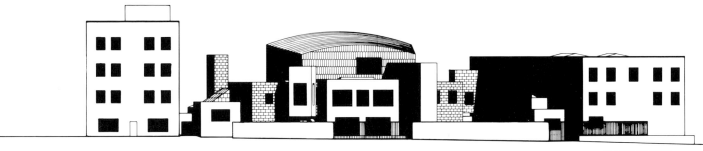

NORTH ELEVATION

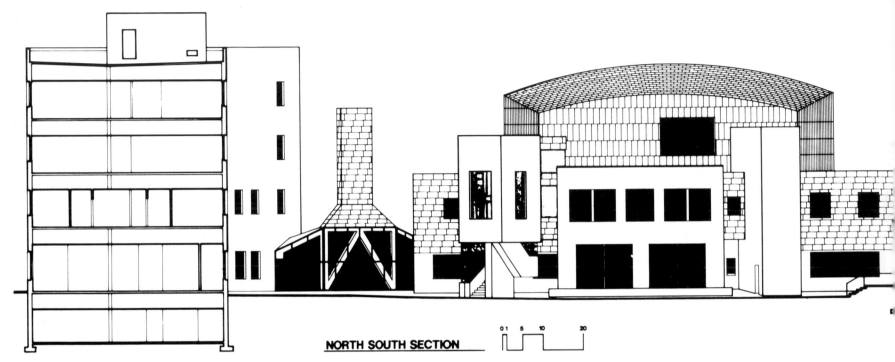

NORTH SOUTH SECTION

North-south section;
views of care facilities
in the courtyard and
between principal
buildings.

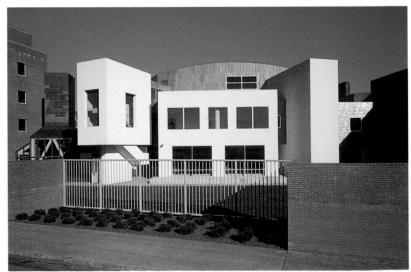

Model view;
south elevation;
view from south.

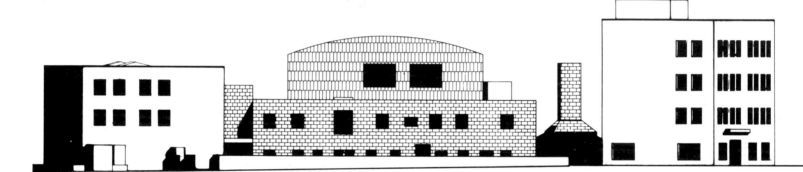

SOUTH ELEVATION

Herman Miller Western Regional Facility
Rocklin, California
1985–89

Aerial view of model; sketch.

Client: Herman Miller, Inc.
Program: Manufacturing, processing, and assembly facilities, offices, cafeteria, meeting rooms, outdoor plaza
Budget: $20,000,000
Area: 400,000 square feet
Materials: Concrete, galvanized-steel siding, stucco, copper cladding, painted aluminum
Project Team: Frank O. Gehry, Robert G. Hale, Sharon Williams, Tom Buresh, Carroll Stockard, Edwin Chan, Susan Narduli, Patricia Owen, Berthold Penkhues; Dreyfuss Blackford Engler,

associate architect; Stanley Tigerman, consulting architect for A/V Building; Capitol Engineering Consultants, mechanical engineer; Peter Walker/Martha Schwartz, landscape architect; Koch, Chun, Knobloch & Associates, Inc., electrical engineer; Buehler & Buehler, structural engineer

Twenty-one miles northeast of Sacramento, at the edge of the gently rolling Sacramento Valley plain just below the Sierra Nevada foothills, the Herman Miller Western Regional Facility occupies a 156-acre site. Gehry treated the site, strewn with wildflowers and left largely in its natural state, as an earthwork. Visitors enter through a new, hundred-foot-deep, densely planted row of redwoods. Vehicles travel a loop, with cars splitting off in one direction and truck traffic in the other, to a parking lot dotted by a field of boulders that were found on the site and placed across a grid. The main building development is located along the ridge of the site on a large, flat pad, taking advantage of views. A rocky berm defines the limits of development.

Warehouse, processing, and assembly buildings, each approximately one hundred thousand square feet, sit on either side of an outdoor material-handling corridor. Designed as neutral shells, the buildings are functionally indeterminate in order to support the changing needs foreseen by Herman Miller as the complex evolves. The manufacturing buildings, clad in flat galvanized-steel siding, are grouped informally around a central plaza fronted by a fourteen-thousand-square-foot stucco office building

Seventy-five feet above the plaza is a copper-clad, trellislike pergola, the focus of the public face of the facility and a gathering point for employees. This core area contains the main lunchroom, the kitchen, toilets and showers, outdoor eating and meeting areas, and an audiovisual meeting room designed by Stanley

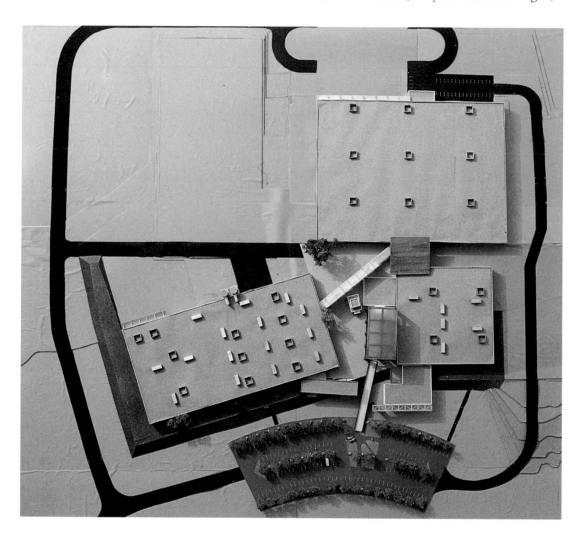

Details of model; view
of facility in context.

314

Tigerman. Each program element was designed as a sculptural object at a human scale. The big, operable window sections are painted aluminum storefronts designed in standardized configurations. Inside, floors are sealed concrete; interior walls are concrete to four feet above the floor in order to protect them from metal forklifts, with drywall on metal studs above. Gehry also developed a master plan, allowing for one million square feet of development.

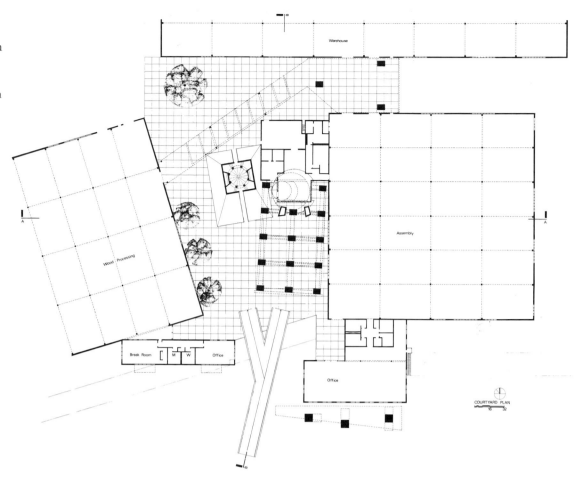

Courtyard plan; view from
south; south elevation.

Details of service building
next to entry; sections;
details of office building
with pergola.

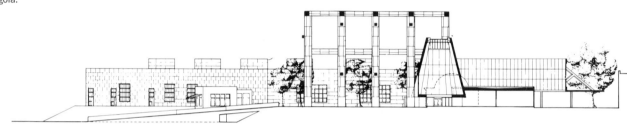

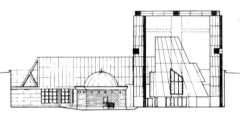

Detail of the pergola.

Chiat/Day Building
Venice, California
1985–91

Client: Chiat/Day Advertising, Inc.
Program: West coast corporate headquarters, including three-story office building and three-level parking garage.
Budget: $15,000,000
Area: 75,000 square feet
Materials: Precast concrete, steel, stucco, copper sheet metal
Project Team: Frank O. Gehry, David Denton, C. Gregory Walsh Jr., Craig Webb, Alan Au, Gerhard Auernhammer, Perry Blake, Thomas Duley, Anne Greenwald, Robert G. Hale, Victoria Jenkins, Alex Meconi, Clive Wilkinson; Leidenfrost/Horowitz & Associates, associate architect; Claes Oldenburg and Coosje van Bruggen, collaborating artists

This L-shaped site in Venice, four blocks from the Pacific Ocean, was owned by Gehry's office. Because the location falls within the Coastal Commission's jurisdiction, successive schemes were required to undergo an extensive review process. In 1978 Gehry proposed a development of nine three-story buildings containing shops and offices at ground level and apartments and artist studios above. The wood-frame, stucco, and chain-link scheme differed from the eventual Chiat/Day Building not only in program and materials but also in site strategy. The mixed-use scheme emphasized the site's dual identity: the west side of the building addressed the commercial vitality of Main Street while the east side addressed the high-density, low-income neighborhood across Fourth Street. By 1985, Gehry's design had literally turned its back on the residential neighborhood and only confronted Main Street.

Ultimately, the seventy-five-thousand-square-foot, three-story office space was designed specifically for Chiat/Day Advertising as its West Coast corporate headquarters. The building sits atop three levels of underground parking, for three hundred cars. The Main Street facade is expressed as three distinct elements intended to relate in scale and level of detail to the surrounding neighborhood. The entry to the parking structure is through the centrally placed binoculars, conceived and created in collaboration with Claes Oldenburg and Coosje van Bruggen. The binoculars contain space for private conferences and research and are tied into the main client conference room. Each cylinder is topped by one skylight oculus. On one side of the binoculars is a curved screen wall, shaped to evoke maritime imagery, which provides shade from the western sun. On the other side of the binoculars is a forestlike proliferation of branching, copper-clad columns.

Because of the configuration of the site, the height constraints imposed by the Coastal Commission, and the density required by the client, the building extends to the property line on all sides. On the third level of the south facade, a long skylight travels down through the building to the first floor. At the fork of the ell is the core of the building, adjacent to which is a large, skylit, two-story meeting room.

The Coastal Commission's height limit of thirty feet meant that the floor-to-floor heights had to be kept to ten feet, requiring flat-plate concrete framing and careful coordination between the mechanical and electrical trades. Tight ceiling spaces were mitigated by leaving

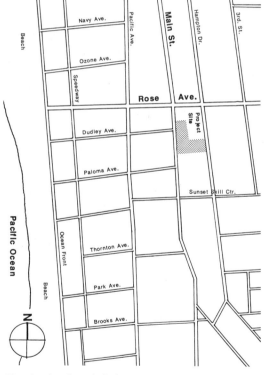

Map showing site; principal facade on Main Street.

Models and sketch for
Main Street facade.

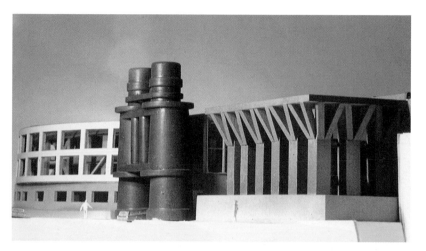

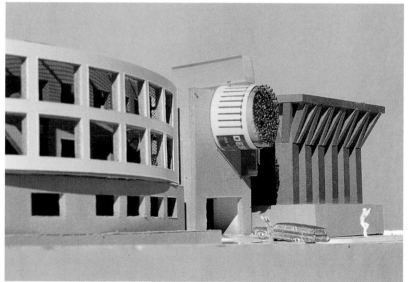

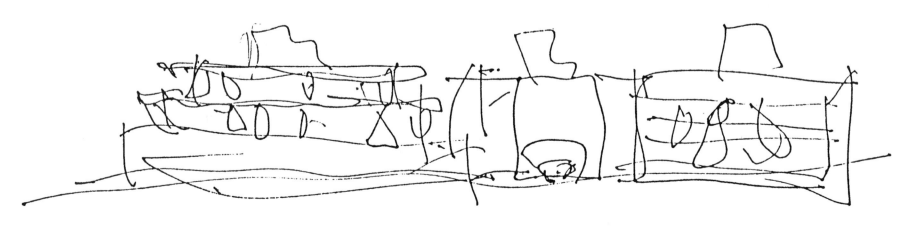

North, east, south, and
west elevations.

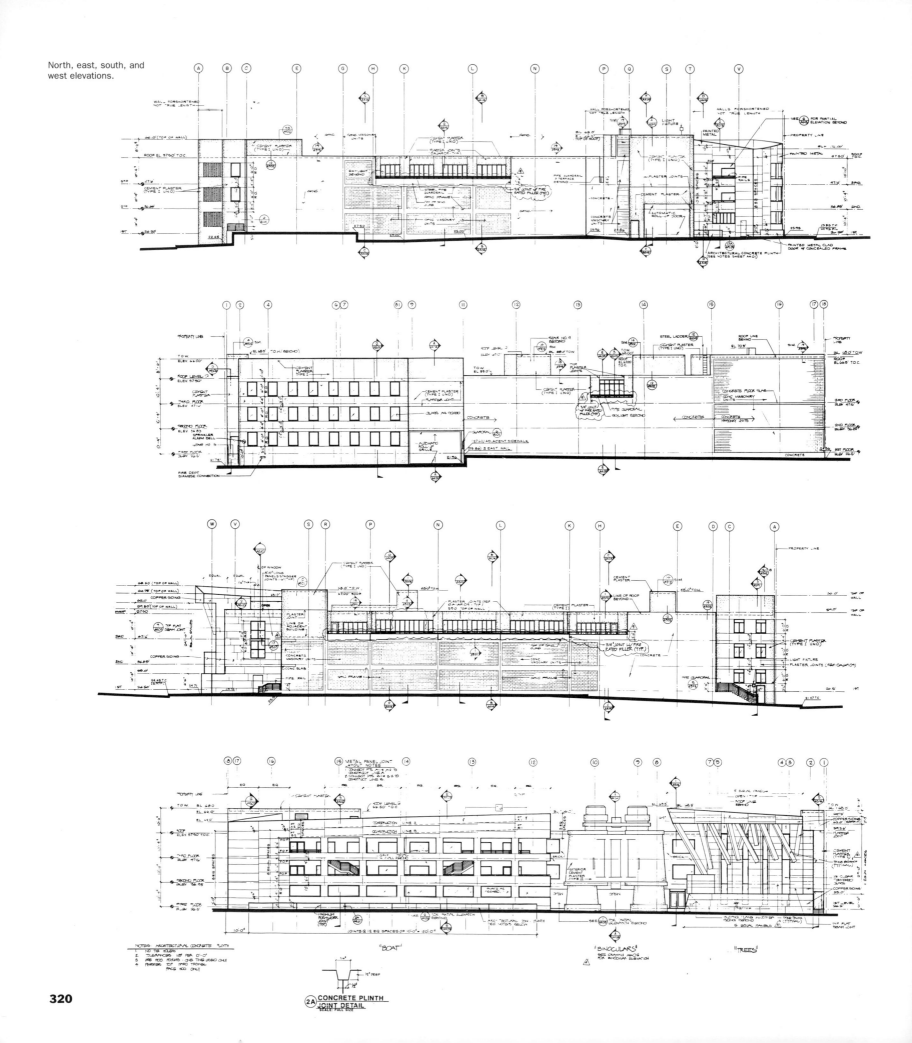

the structure exposed on the underside of the concrete deck in many places, and by position-ing light wells throughout the building to bring light down to the first and second floors. Simple built-in workstations are constructed in ply-wood.

The project was delayed for over two years because hazardous waste was discovered on the site; during this time, temporary offices were designed and fabricated in a nearby warehouse building on Hampton Avenue.

Details of facades on Main Street; second-floor plan.

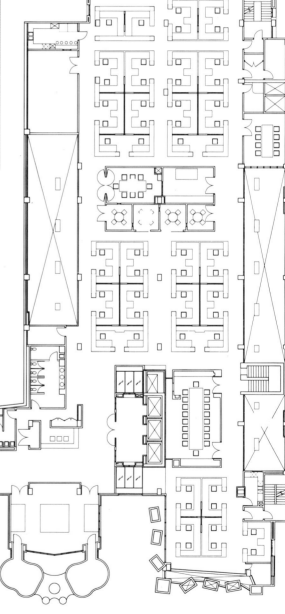

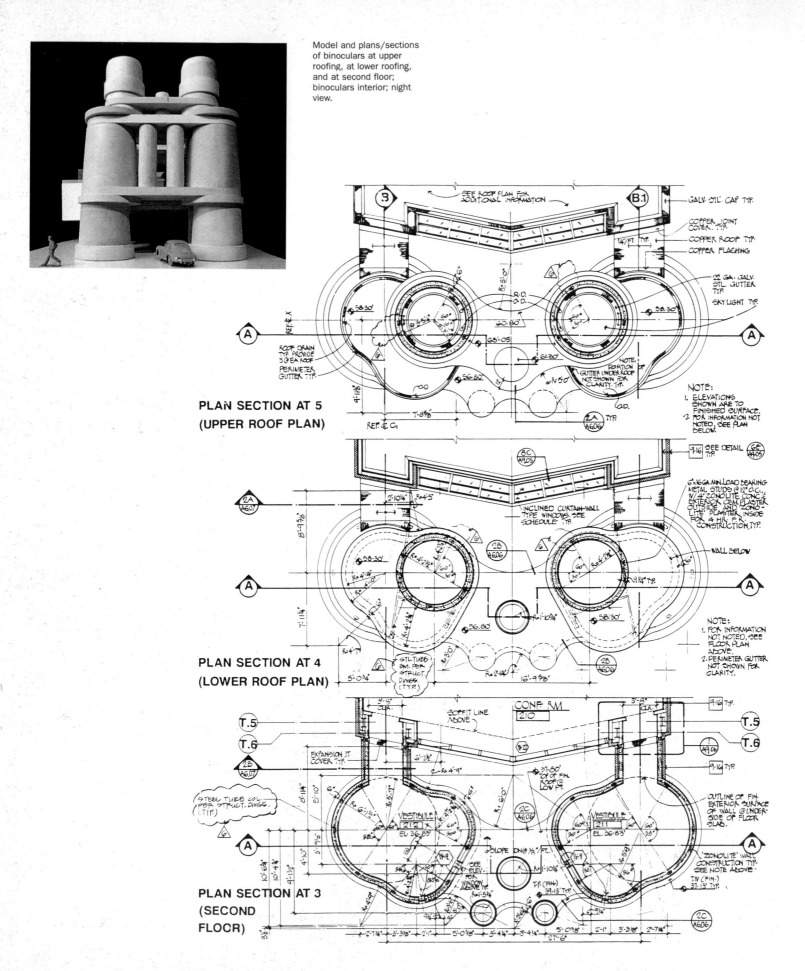

Model and plans/sections of binoculars at upper roofing, at lower roofing, and at second floor; binoculars interior; night view.

**PLAN SECTION AT 5
(UPPER ROOF PLAN)**

**PLAN SECTION AT 4
(LOWER ROOF PLAN)**

**PLAN SECTION AT 3
(SECOND FLOOR)**

**Lawrence Halprin: Changing Places
San Francisco Museum of Modern Art, San Francisco, California
1986**

Client: San Francisco Museum of Modern Art
Program: Exhibition design and installation
Project Team: Frank O. Gehry,
C. Gregory Walsh Jr.

**Hoffman Gallery
Santa Monica, California
1986**

Client: Fred Hoffman
Program: Interior remodel
Area: 2,000 square feet

Materials: Exposed wood frame, drywall
Project Team: Frank O. Gehry

Interior.

**Chiat Residence
Sagaponack, New York
1986**

Client: Jay and Donatella Chiat
Program: Single-family residence
Area: 5,000 square feet

Materials: Wood frame
Project Team: Frank O. Gehry

Model view.

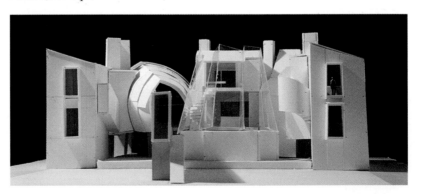

**Fan Pier, Parcel H
Boston, Massachusetts
1986**

Client: CBC Development
Program: Twelve-story, sixty-five-unit condominium tower
Area: 150,000 square feet
Materials: Steel frame
Project Team: Frank O. Gehry, C. Gregory Walsh Jr., Robert G. Hale, Robin Meierding, David Denton, Edwin Chan

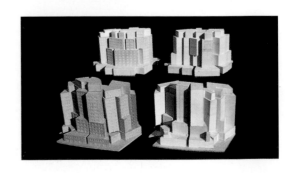

Study model.

NBC–Maguire Proposal
1986

Client: NBC and Maguire Thomas Partners
Program: Mixed-use development proposal,
including offices, studios, theaters, restaurants,
and hotel
Area: 1,800,000 square feet
Project Team: Frank O. Gehry, David
Denton, C. D. Dilworth, Doug Gardner

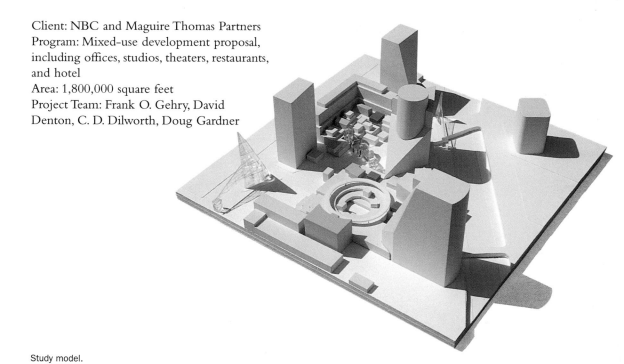

Study model.

Standing Glass Fish
Walker Art Center Sculpture
Garden, Minneapolis, Minnesota
1986

Client: Walker Art Center, Martin Friedman,
director
Program: Permanent sculpture
Area: 22 feet long by 14 feet tall by
8½ feet wide
Materials: Wood and steel-frame armature,
threaded steel rod, ¼" tempered glass shards,
clear silicon
Project Team: Frank O. Gehry; Joel Stearns,
Fred Hoffman, Daniel Sachs, New City
Editions, fabrication and installation

Standing Glass Fish.

Fishdance Restaurant
Kobe, Japan
1986–87

Client: World Company Ltd. and City of Kobe
Program: Waterfront seafood restaurant
Budget: $3,000,000
Area: 8,500 square feet
Materials: Steel frame, chain link, copper sheet metal
Project Team: Frank O. Gehry, David Denton, C. Gregory Walsh Jr., Tom Buresh, Edwin Chan, Dalia Jagger, Charles Dilworth, Sergio Zeballos, Fred Ballard, Mitchell Lawrence, Bryce Thomas; Takenaka Komuten Co. Ltd., associate architect; M. Tanaka, mechanical engineer

The fish made its first appearance in Gehry's work in 1981, as part of the colonnade in the Smith Residence project. At that time, Gehry claims to have seen the figurative element as a "kind of comment on postmodernism." In 1995 Gehry told Alejandro Zaera: "Neoclassical thinking was back and I became self-conscious about having anything to do with it. Architecture always has to do with history in some way or another, but when they started exaggerating it, the fish was kind of a joke over all these reference to the past. Everybody was quoting these old classical buildings, so I decided to quote something five hundred million years older than mankind. It was also a critique on the anthropocentrism of classical architecture, by literally referring to the body of an animal. I see it more as an experiment within the architectural culture than as a significant feature of my work."

The fish has nevertheless served as more than a one-liner for Gehry, appearing in many subsequent projects: as a monumental sculpture in his collaboration with Richard Serra for the Architectural League of New York's 1981 exhibit; in the Crosby Street Lofts (1981); in "Folly: The Prison Project" (1983); in the GFT Exhibit in Turin (1985–86); in the Walker Art Center's *Standing Glass Fish* (1986); and in the Vila Olimpica, in Barcelona (1989–92). It formed

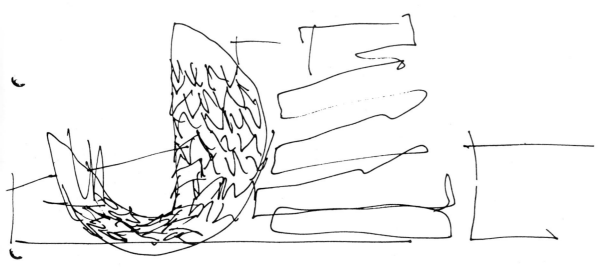

Sketch; model.

Opposite:
Views of restaurant dining room.

the basis of his 1983–86 Formica lamp designs, literally resurfaced in a bathtub in the Chiat/Day Toronto interiors (1988), and appeared again in sketches throughout the early 1980s. The fish has also been a truncated, less literal, architectural element in the roof of the Louisiana World Expo Amphitheater (1982–84), in the belly of the pool in Gehry's own backyard (1991–94), and in the skylight for Pariser Platz 3 (1994–). Gehry has also accounted for the significance of the fish in symbolic terms, as a psychological archetype dating back to his childhood, when his grandmother stored carp in the bathtub before preparing gefilte fish; and in functional terms, as architectural shorthand, a notation for some future, as-yet-undesigned building-object. Perhaps the most satisfying explanation, however, is the formal one: Gehry is perennially fascinated by the variety, flexibility, and perfection of the fish's material and structural properties.

Gehry designed and built his first large-scale fish for a Japanese restaurant set in a new public park along the Inland Sea. The clients requested that the building be an exciting place to dine, that it feel "informal" and "crowded," and that perhaps a fish be prominently incorporated into the design, relating to a preoccupation of the architect or to the waterfront location, or both.

The site's neighbors include shipyards, cranes, docks, a reconstruction of a nineteenth-century customhouse, and, at each end of the site, double-deck expressways. An adjoining warehouse, remodeled by the owners as a multipurpose hall, extends under one of the elevated highways.

In response to this industrial waterfront setting, the restaurant took shape as three large simple objects: a copper-clad tightly coiled snake, a seventy-foot-high fish sculpture made of chain-link mesh, and a sloped-roof building clad in light blue metal with a clerestory tower. The snake contains a bar and, winding above it, a *kushi-katsu* (deep fry) counter. The sloped-roof building houses the kitchen and main seafood dining area, with a bridge for the *teppan-yaki* (grill) on an upper level. All of the dining areas look through windows or glass walls at the fish, its taut, fluid form captured in a moment of upward thrust. The 8,500-square-foot project was designed and built within a ten-month period, from July 1986 to April 1987.

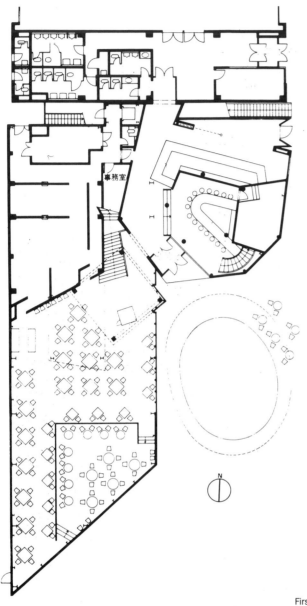

First- and second-floor plans; views from south and north.

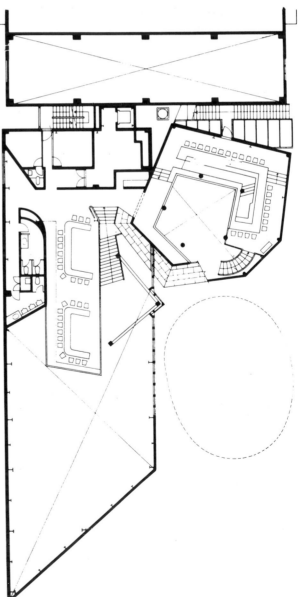

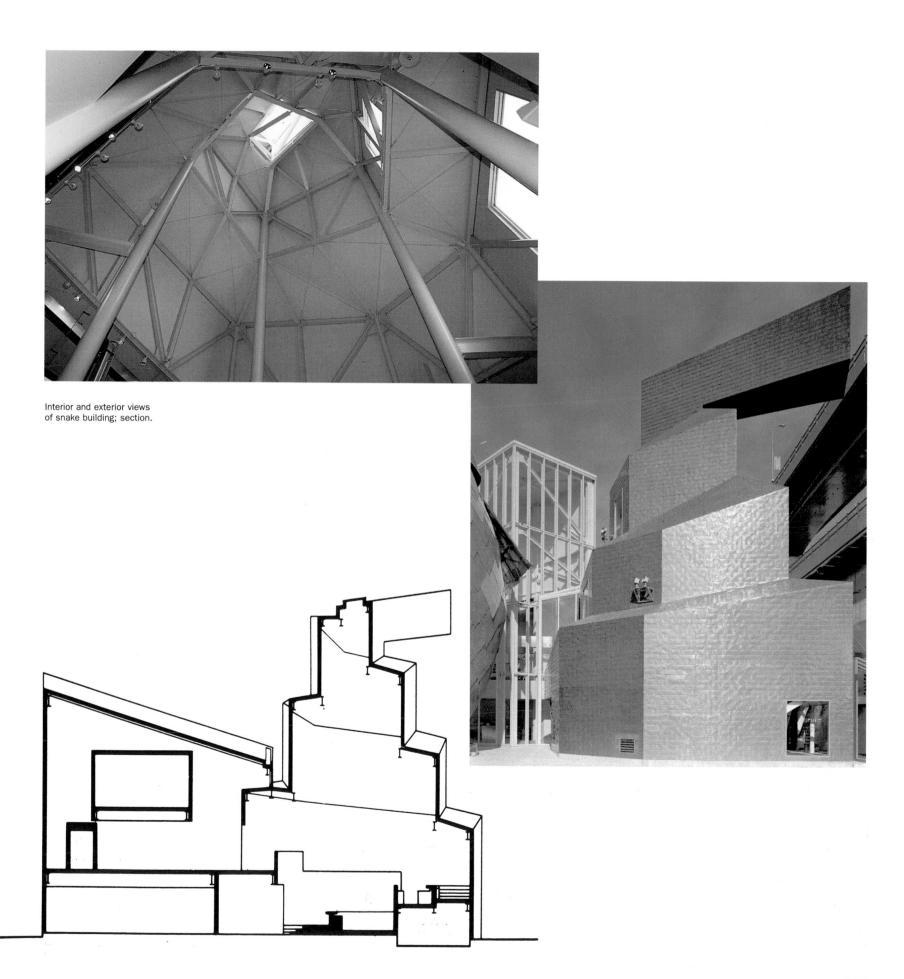

Interior and exterior views
of snake building; section.

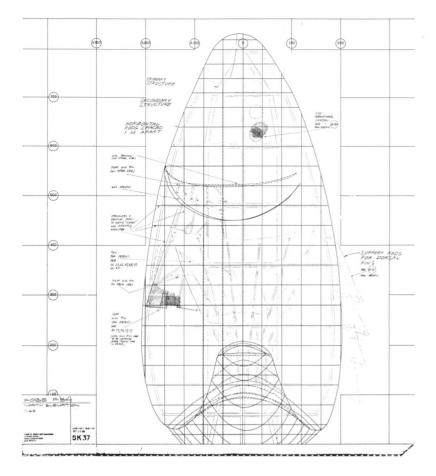

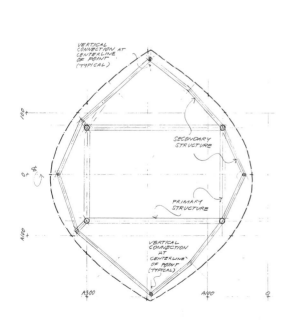

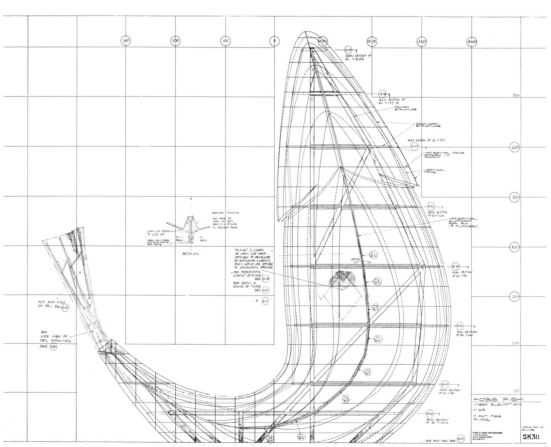

North elevation of fish;
section at six meters;
view from northeast;
west elevation.

330

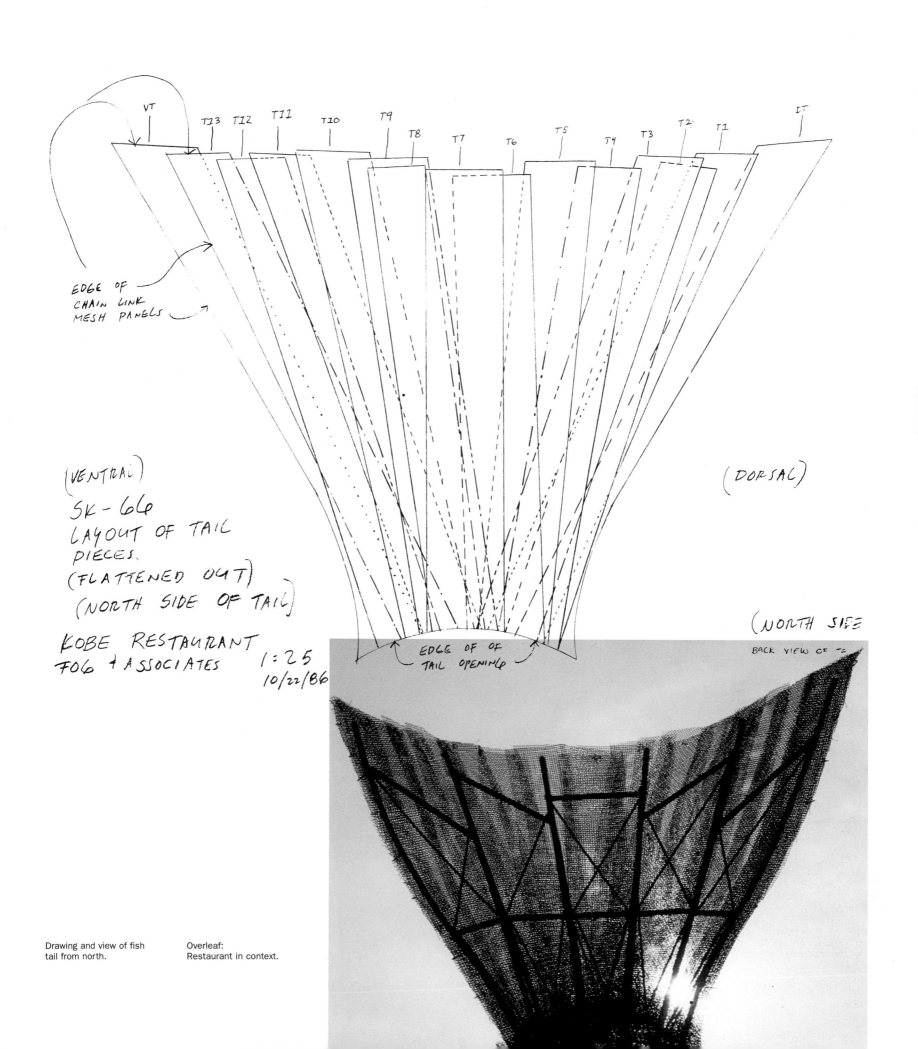

VT

T13 T12 T11 T10 T9 T8 T7 T6 T5 T4 T3 T2 T1 DT

EDGE OF
CHAIN LINK
MESH PANELS

(VENTRAL)

SK-66
LAYOUT OF TAIL
PIECES.
(FLATTENED OUT)
(NORTH SIDE OF TAIL)

KOBE RESTAURANT
FOG & ASSOCIATES   1:25
10/22/86

(DORSAL)

(NORTH SIDE

EDGE OF OF
TAIL OPENING

BACK VIEW OF TE

Drawing and view of fish
tail from north.

Overleaf:
Restaurant in context.

The Architecture of Frank O. Gehry
Walker Art Center,
Minneapolis, Minnesota
1986–87

Client: Walker Arts Center, represented by Mildred Friedman
Program: Traveling exhibition design and installation, originating in Minneapolis and traveling to Houston, Toronto, Los Angeles, and New York
Area: 7,000 square feet
Materials: Exposed wood frame, lead, copper, cardboard, Finnish plywood
Project Team: Frank O. Gehry, C. Gregory Walsh Jr., Eamon O'Mahoney, Robert G. Hale, Edwin Chan

In 1984, Mickey Friedman, design curator at the Walker Art Center, initiated a major retrospective of Gehry's work, culminating in the fall 1986 opening of a seven-thousand-square-foot exhibition. The exhibition was conceived as an attempt to bring to the museum the experience of occupying Gehry's architecture. As such, it was composed of several architectonically scaled objects, some of which enclosed smaller exhibits. These large-scale objects included a lead fish house, a Finnish-plywood snake house, a copper house, a cardboard house, and a series of "trees." A monumental fish sculpture, on permanent view at the Walker, was constructed of glass and steel. The exhibition eventually traveled to the Toronto Harborfront Museum, the Houston Museum of Contemporary Art, the Atlanta High Museum, the Los Angeles Museum of Contemporary Art, and the Whitney Museum of American Art in New York.

Installation in different cities.

Details of installation with
full-size architectonic
elements.

Chiat/Day Temporary Offices
Venice, California
1986–88

Client: Chiat/Day, Inc., Advertising
Program: Interior renovation of existing
concrete warehouse
Budget: $2,200,000
Area: 42,000 square feet
Materials: Wood frame, sheet metal, drywall,
corrugated cardboard, plywood
Project Team: Frank O. Gehry, Robert G. Hale,
Tom Buresh, Rene Ilustre, Anne Greenwald,
Carroll Stockard, Kevin Daly, Alan Au, Perry
Blake, Edwin Chan; J. A. Stewart Construction,
general contractor; Kurily & Szymanski,
structural engineer; G & W Electrical
Engineers; Western Allied Corp., mechanical
engineer; Robert Millar, Athena, lighting
engineer

The Chiat/Day Temporary Offices were
installed in renovated concrete warehouses in
Venice, around the corner from their permanent
home on Main Street. The 42,000-square-foot
main warehouse, with its twenty-four-foot ceilings, was designed to accommodate the majority of the agency's staff and activities. Building
A, 3,800 square feet, contained shipping, receiving, and storage areas, while Building B housed
a reception area, conference room, and audiovisual and kitchen facilities.

New skylights and storefront glazing at the
loading-dock doors introduced natural light
into the windowless warehouse. Electric, data,
and communication cables were housed in a
cable tray raised thirteen feet off the floor and

supported by steel columns. Wood stud construction was sheathed in a variety of finish
materials, including sheet metal, brilliantly
painted drywall, MDO plywood, and Finnish
plywood. The exterior was boldly repainted to
distinguish it from its neighbors.

Interiors of the main warehouse were organized as a villagelike landscape. A "main street"
axis ran north and south, flanked by open-plan
workstations and enclosed object-building office
spaces. A fifty-four-foot fish formed from
wooden ribs and sheathed in a galvanized sheet-
metal skin served as the principal in-house conference room. A plywood "battleship" with uplit
canopies dominated and anchored the center of
the warehouse.

In Building B, three interconnected building-objects contained within the existing concrete shed served as a conference area. The
entry was sheathed in galvanized scales, the end
pavilion in dark reddish Finnish plywood, and
the middle pavilion in sheared cardboard blocks.
A canoe light fixture hung over, and was
reflected in, the custom-built green granite conference table. A log light floating alongside illuminated the display walls, while built-in cardboard furniture formed an informal seating area
behind the conference table and a glass fish
lamp glowed in the corner. On the opposite
wall, television screens and state-of-the-art
audiovisual equipment were flush-mounted into
the cardboard walls. Remotely operated skylights allowed for control over the natural light.

Plan of lower floor of main
building with new space
allocation.

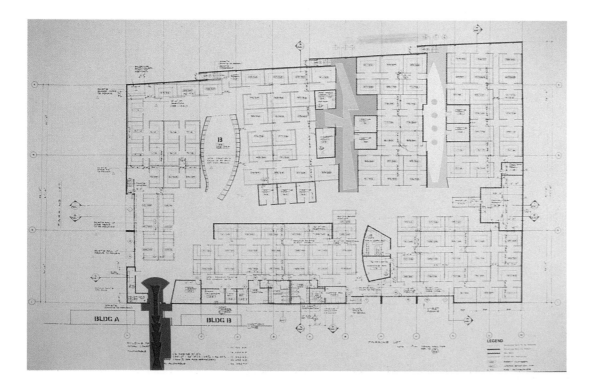

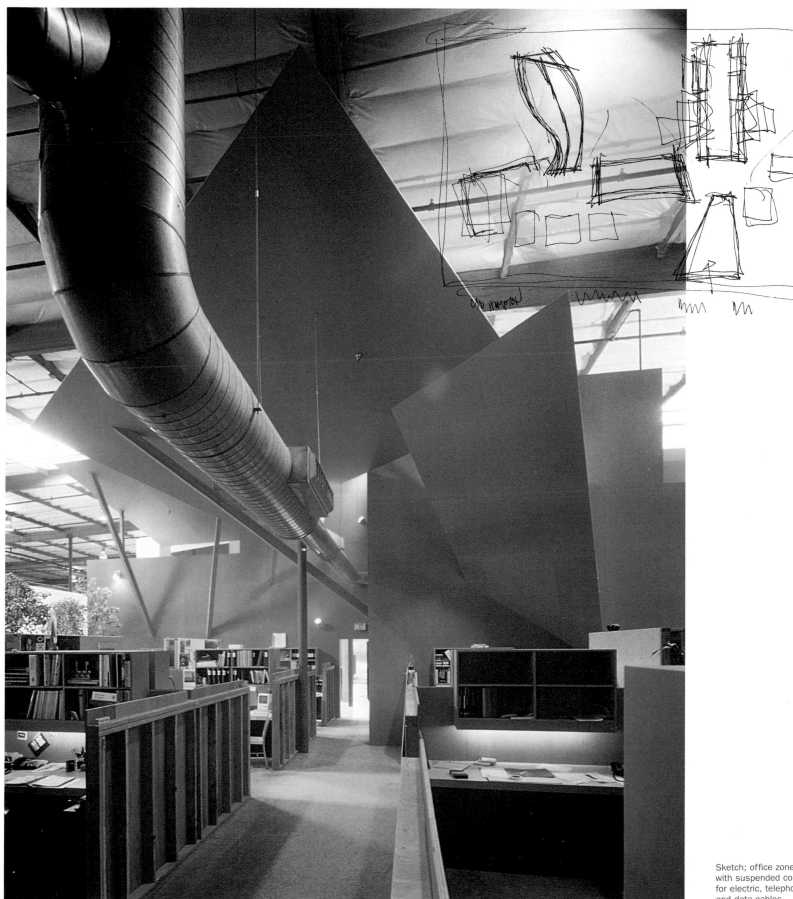

Sketch; office zone
with suspended conduit
for electric, telephone,
and data cables.

Views of fish with main conference room.

Model and exterior and interior views of the central pavilion of group of interconnected conference pavilions.

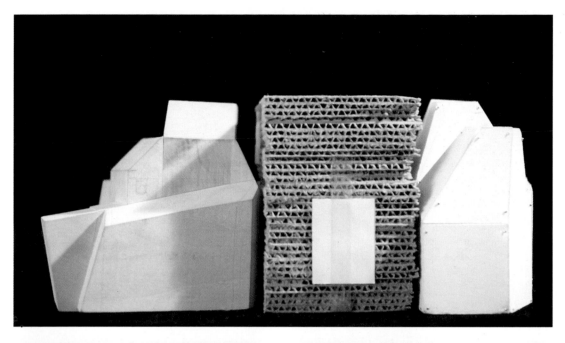

**Sheet Metal Craftsmanship:
Progress in Building
National Building Museum,
Washington, D.C.
1986–88**

Client: National Training Fund, Sheet Metal Workers' International Association; Sheet Metal and Air Conditioning Contractors National Association; National Building Museum
Program: Exhibition design and installation, including historical exhibit and demonstration workshop
Budget: Volunteer labor; donated materials
Area: 2,000 square feet
Materials: Steel frame with plywood backing, terne-coated steel, muntz brass cladding, copper and galvanized-steel cladding

Project Team: Frank O. Gehry, Robert G. Hale, Roberta Weiser, C. Gregory Walsh Jr., Tom Buresh, Adolph Ortega, Kevin Daly, Tom Duley, Nick Dermand, Berthold Penkhues, Christopher Joseph Bonura; Kurily & Szymanski, structural engineer

The purpose of this exhibit was to highlight sheet-metal materials and construction techniques in honor of the sheet metal union's centennial celebration. The exhibition was installed in a historic building recently renovated as a museum of architecture, in the museum's Great Hall, an immense volume with tall, grand columns supporting a 150-foot ceiling. The scale of the space proved the greatest design challenge; Gehry's response was to insert giant sculptural forms that would hold their own in height and massing.

The program included a historical exhibit, housed in the first of two pavilions, and a sheet-metal demonstration workshop, in the second, rear pavilion. Together, the two pavilions, located one behind the other, enclosed approximately two thousand square feet. The sixty-five-foot tower at the front was covered in terne-coated steel and muntz brass. The rear, wedge-shaped pavilion was covered in copper

Model view; views of exhibition pavilions.

with galvanized steel panels on its smaller tower. The basic shape and support for the structures was provided by plywood backing over light-gauge steel framing and structural steel tubes welded to large base plates. By engineering the structures to be built without cutting into the floor of the Great Hall, construction time was shortened to two months. The space between the two structures held a display of antique tools of the trade.

The variety and complexity of the pavilions' forms was intended to showcase the ability of the sheet-metal craftspeople and the finishes, colors, and textures with which they work. The project was constructed exclusively with donated materials and volunteer labor from various trade organizations.

Schnabel Residence
Brentwood, California
1986–89

Client: Marna and Rockwell Schnabel
Program: Single-family residence
Area: 5,700 square feet
Materials: Wood frame, stucco, lead-coated copper panels
Project Team: Frank O. Gehry, David Denton, C. Gregory Walsh Jr., Tom Buresh, Kevin Daly, Carroll Stockard, Sergio Zeballos, Rene Ilustre, Adolph Ortega; Kurily & Szymanski; Storms & Lowe, mechanical engineer; Athans Enterprises, electrical engineer; Nancy Goslee Power & Associates, landscape architect; Blackoak Development, general contractor

Aerial view from west.

Located on a quiet street in Brentwood, Los Angeles, this villagelike arrangement of forms was a direct response to the clients' elaborate building program and their desire to create a variety of outdoor spaces to extend and vary the perceptions of their standard-size suburban lot. The site was graded to create a two-tiered walled garden within which different programmatic elements were each given their own shape, surface, and architectural character, playing against one another spatially and sculpturally. The owner, trained in architecture, was an active participant in the design process.

At the west of the lot sits a plain stucco box garage with another slightly rotated box, housing staff quarters, above. A copper-clad colonnade leads along the north edge of the site to a simple two-story stucco volume containing the kitchen, a two-story family room, and two bedrooms. Like the Sirmai-Peterson Residence (1983–88), the focal point of the composition is a cruciform structure, sheathed in lead-coated copper panels, that houses the entry (accessed by a footpath directly from the east), the living and dining rooms, and a library. A three-story bottleneck skylight lights the cruciform space by day and glows by night.

Three freestanding elements dot the southern perimeter of the upper garden: a skylit guest apartment crowned with a copper dome and flanked by copper columns; a long, blue-tiled lap pool raised partially above grade; and a studio-bedroom with a sawtooth roof.

At the eastern edge of the site, the slope was cut away to create a shallow lake. One level below the rest of the site, the secluded, light-filled master bedroom pavilion with its sculptural skylight and copper-clad columns appears to float. Direct access to the master bath, dressing rooms, sauna, and exercise room is along a below-grade glazed arcade running parallel to the lake edge. A partially underground stairway connects the master bedroom pavilion to the family rooms above. Interiors throughout consist of hardwood floors, gypsum-board walls, exposed Douglas fir framing, and plywood and sheet-metal cabinetry.

The Schnabel Residence, along with the Edgemar Development (1984–88) and the Sirmai-Peterson Residence, represents a blending of the various design strategies that had been employed by Gehry thus far. Materially, the Schnabel Residence's juxtapositions are subtler than the pop collage of materials in the proposal for the Smith Residence (1981) and at the Norton Residence (1982–84), and more

Floor plans;
south elevation;
model from east.

343

Views from garden
toward entrances to
cruciform building.

sophisticated than the uniform wrapping of industrial materials seen in the Spiller Residence (1978–79) and the Indiana Avenue Houses (1979–81). Compositionally, the Schnabel Residence is made up of building-objects, but it is not the tightly composed, disembodied still life set against an open field of the Winton Guest House (1982–87), nor, although described as a clustered village, does it resemble the scattered, archetypal one-room buildings dotting the Loyola University Law School campus (1978–). The figure-ground relationship between the lot and the building forms is more continuous; the objects seem to want to come together, again reiterating the coherent wholeness of Gehry's early minimalist projects.

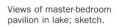

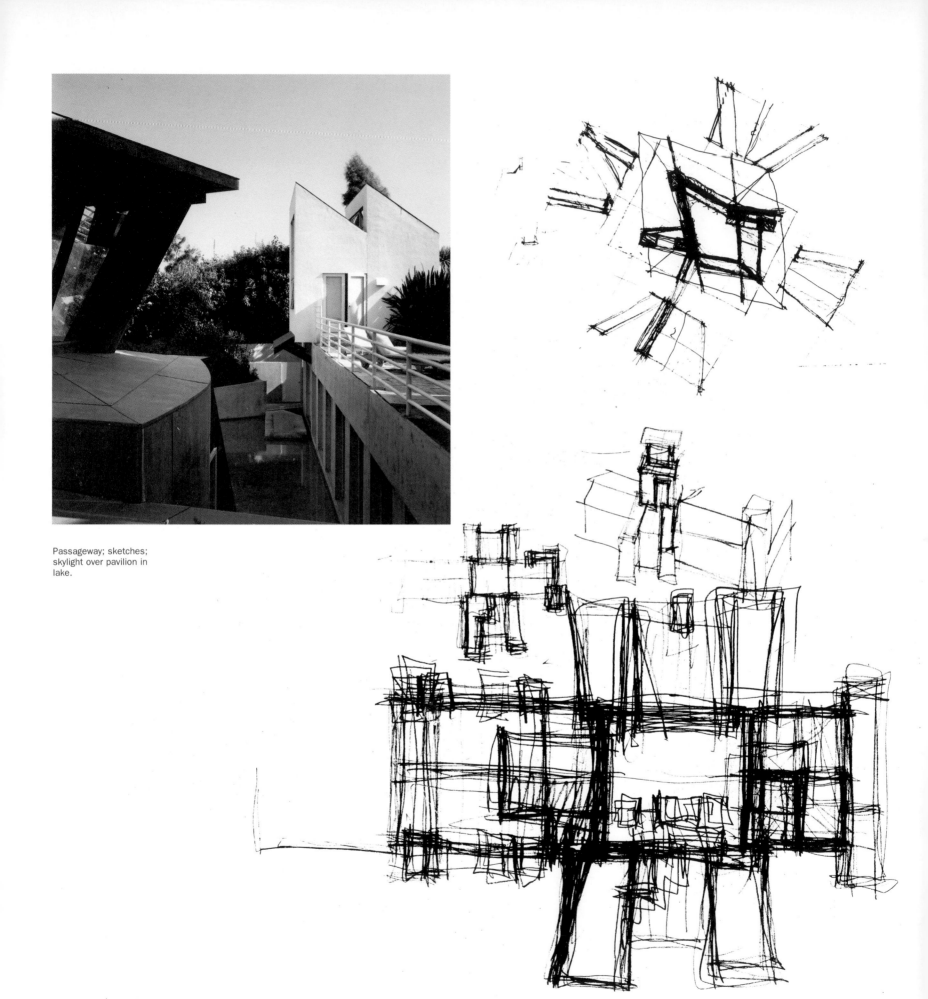

Passageway; sketches;
skylight over pavilion in
lake.

348

Living, dining, and office
areas with skylights.

Progressive Corporation Headquarters
Cleveland, Ohio
1986–91 (project)

Client: Progressive Insurance Company
Program: Corporate headquarters, including office space, art museum, scholars' library, auditorium, creativity center, cafeteria, health club, and research center
Area: 1,000,000 square feet
Materials: Steel frame, sheet-metal and stone cladding
Project Team: Frank O. Gehry, David Denton, Bruce Biesman-Simons, C. Gregory Walsh Jr., Eileen Yankowski, Susan Narduli, Andrew Alper, Christopher Joseph Bonura; Van Dijk, Johnson & Partners, associate architect

For a site at the end of Cleveland's historic Burnham Mall, Gehry designed a corporate headquarters to occupy air rights over the existing railroad tracks that separate the mall from Lake Erie. The master plan called for the end of the Burnham Mall to be flanked by the Progressive Corporation tower and a high-rise hotel, creating a gateway to the city and mirroring the positioning of City Hall and the County Building. In addition to approximately one million square feet of high-rise office space, the project included an art museum, a creativity center, a health club, and a research center.

The visual mass of the office tower is broken down into two contiguous vertical elements, one clad in metal and one in stone. Executive and mechanical penthouses as well as a restaurant are separately articulated at the top of the building by changes in both form and material. The art museum, with its scholars' library and auditorium, is located to one side of the tower and provides the entrance to the tower via an enclosed bridge. The health club, training center, and cafeteria inhabit a structure separated from the tower so that views from City Hall to the lake may be preserved.

The one-hundred-foot walkway from the mall to the lakefront was to be designed by Donald Judd, and Richard Serra was to have created a sculpture for the deck of the parking garage, the first installation in a proposed art park. Claes Oldenburg proposed a giant carpenter's C-clamp to "hold down" a part of the health club and an oversized newspaper perched atop the tower to create a skyline landmark.

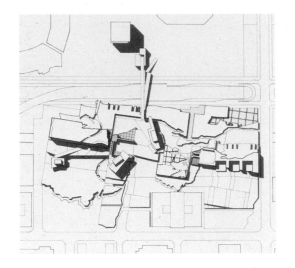

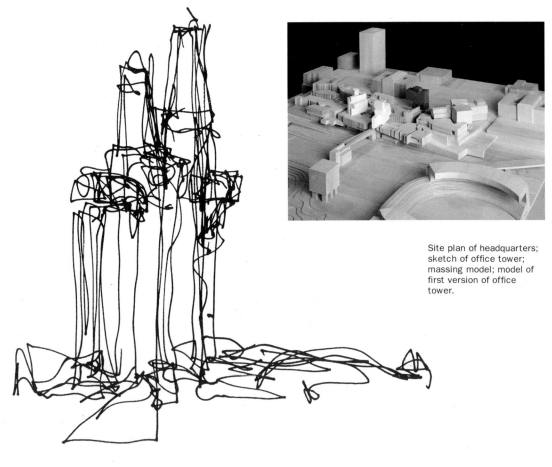

Site plan of headquarters; sketch of office tower; massing model; model of first version of office tower.

Plans of office tower
at low, middle, and high
floors; model views of
tower and surrounding
buildings; ground-floor
plan.

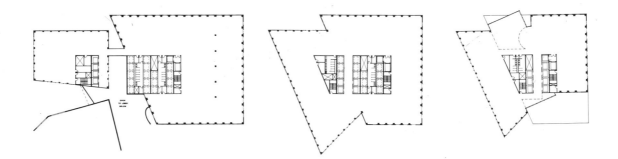

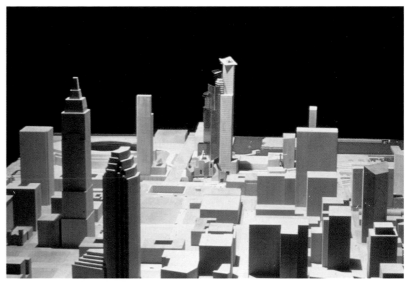

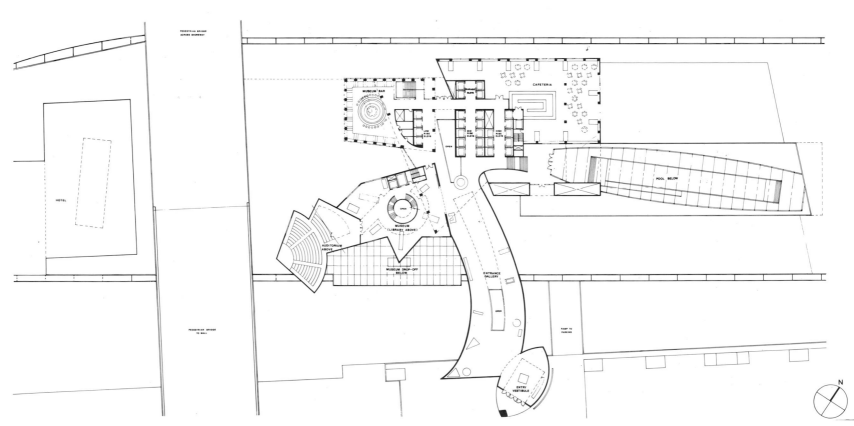

East-west section;
model views.

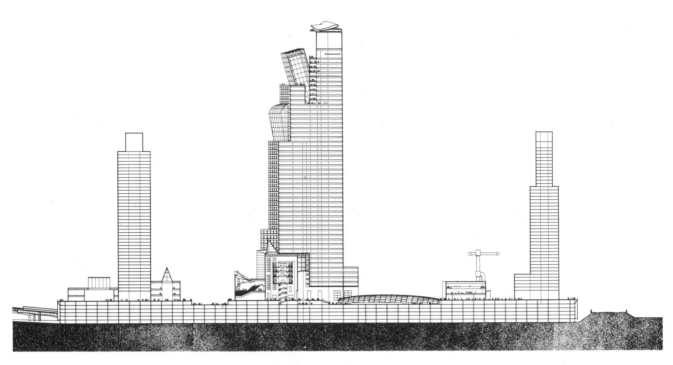

**Santa Monica Airport Park
Competition
Santa Monica, California
1987**

Client: Olympia & York, Goldrich & Kest
Program: Office park with eleven four- to
six-story office buildings, day care, restaurant,
retail, and seven-thousand-car parking
Budget: $200,000
Area: 160,000 square feet
Materials: Concrete, steel
Project Team: Frank O. Gehry; Maxwell
Starkman Associates, associate architect

Model views.

**Toronto Metropolitan
Government Headquarters
Competition
Toronto, Ontario
1987**

Client: Toronto Metropolitan Government
Program: Twenty-two-story office building with
city council chambers, public library, child care,
and cafeteria
Area: 700,000 square feet
Materials: Steel frame, concrete, sheet metal
Project team: Frank O. Gehry

Model of tower and
surrounding buildings.

**Parc de la Villette Restaurant
Competition
Paris, France
1987**

Program: Restaurant and monumental fish
Area: 3,500 square feet
Materials: Steel frame, glass, sheet metal
Project Team: Frank O. Gehry, C. Gregory
Walsh Jr., Robert G. Hale

Model view.

**Culver Center
Culver City, California
1987**

Client: Culver City Redevelopment Agency
Program: Development of site master plan for
mixed-use urban redevelopment

Project Team: Frank O. Gehry, David Denton,
Bruce Biesman-Simons, Michael Maltzan

Model view.

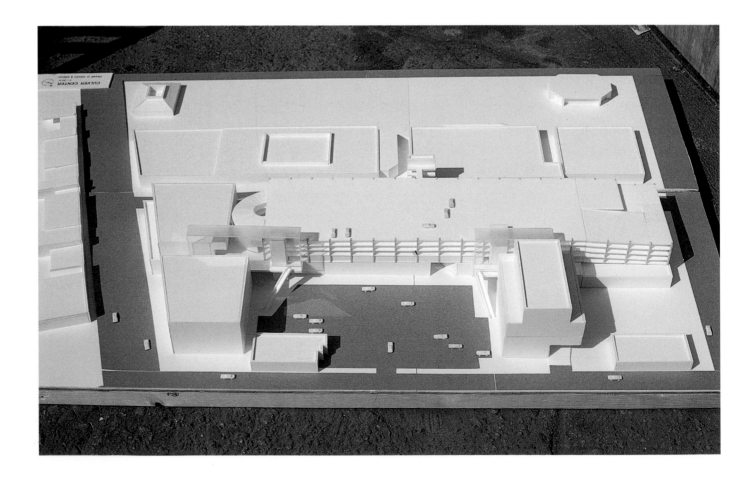

Kings Cross Competition
London, England
1987 (project)

Client: Rosehaugh Stanhope
Program: Mixed-use urban redevelopment proposal, including retail, residential, hotel, offices, pedestrian paths, and restoration of historic structures
Area: 12,000,000 square feet
Project Team: Frank O. Gehry, David Denton, Edwin Chan, Susan Narduli

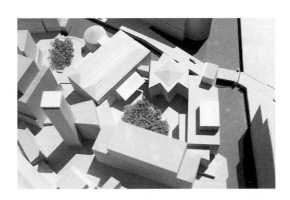

**Borman Residence
Malibu, California
1987**

Client: Borman family
Program: Single-family residence including five
bedrooms, tennis court, pool, exercise room
Area: 12,000 square feet

Materials: Wood frame, stucco, copper sheet
metal
Project Team: Frank O. Gehry, C. Gregory
Walsh Jr., Ron Johnson, Carl Davis, Peter Becker

Exterior.

**Madison Square Garden
Competition
New York, New York
1987 (project)**

Client: Olympia and York Development
Corporation
Program: Mixed-use addition to existing rail
station, including three office towers, retail
complex, and new grand hall entry with canopy
joining the three towers at the base
Area: 4,500,000 square feet

Materials: Steel frame, sandblasted stainless-steel
panels
Project Team: Frank O. Gehry, David Denton,
Bruce Toman, C. Gregory Walsh Jr., Tom
Buresh, Bruce Biesman-Simons; Skidmore,
Owings & Merrill, collaborating architect

Study models of tower.

**Fine Arts Center Planning Study
Los Angeles County Museum of
Art, Los Angeles, California
1987**

Client: Los Angeles County Museum of Art
Program: Schematic planning study for museum
expansion
Project Team: Frank O. Gehry

Ground-floor plan (museum
in yellow, shopping center
in red, stores in blue);
sections; model views.

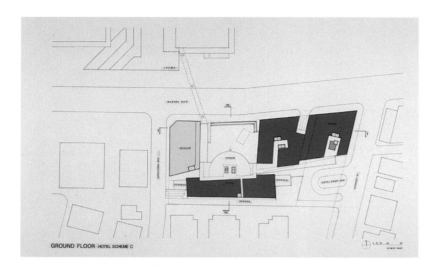

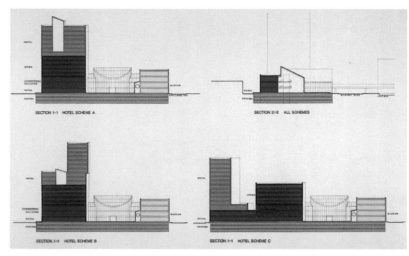

San'wiches 1 and 2
San Diego, California
1987–89

Client: Joe Baum/Michael Whiteman Co., and Chiat/Day, Inc.
Program: Fast-food restaurant chain pilot stores
Budget: $65,000
Area: 1,500 square feet

Materials: Exposed wood frame, painted plywood, aluminum and stainless-steel sheet metal, animated robot
Project Team: Frank O. Gehry; Alejandro Gehry, robot designer

Restaurant interiors; model view with furniture.

St. James Office Building
Boston, Massachusetts
1987–90 (project)

Client: Cohen Properties
Program: Conceptual site plan and floor plans for office tower with retail and parking

Area: 420,000 square feet
Project Team: Frank O. Gehry, David Denton, Robert G. Hale

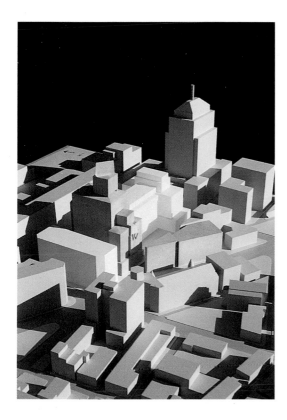

Site model; tower model.

Vitra International Furniture Manufacturing Facility and Design Museum
Weil am Rhein, Germany
1987–89

Client: Vitra International, Ltd., represented by Rolf Fehlbaum
Program: Furniture assembly plant with adjacent office, mezzanine, and distribution areas; small furniture museum with library and offices; master plan including new entrance road and gate house, future expansion of the factory, museum parking, and ancillary facilities
Budget: $10,000,000
Area: 98,000 square feet
Materials: Concrete frame, stucco, plaster over masonry, titanium-zinc panels
Project Team: Frank O. Gehry, Robert G. Hale, C. Gregory Walsh Jr., Berthold Penkhues, Liza Hansen, Edwin Chan, Christopher Joseph Bonura; Gunter Pfeifer Associates, associated architect; Claes Oldenburg and Coosje Van Bruggen, collaborating artists

Situated in a rural landscape bordered by Switzerland and France, this complex and its design comprises three major parts: a furniture assembly plant with adjacent office, mezzanine, and distribution areas; a small museum to house the owner's collection of furniture and his library of manufacturers' catalogs; and a master plan for the site, to include a new entrance road and gatehouse, space for future expansion of the factory, museum parking, and ancillary facilities.

The factory consists of concrete-frame construction with a stucco finish, skylights, and large windows. The offices on the north mezzanine have spectacular views of the adjacent mountains, the museum, and Claes Oldenburg and Coosje van Bruggen's *Tool Gate* sculpture. The north facade faces the main road and represents the public face of the factory as well as a backdrop for the museum. Ramps and entrance canopies flank this factory facade, creating an effect of sculptural bookends. These forms relate to each other and extend the visual impact of the project as a whole, functioning as scale-giving decoration for the big, simple factory shed. To create a campuslike environment at a human scale, Gehry employed a consistent, albeit differentiated, formal vocabulary in tying the various pieces together. Skylights and clerestories create various natural lighting conditions within these forms.

The museum building includes a library, office, and storage and support spaces in addition to exhibition space. The galleries are treated as connected volumes that interpenetrate one another spatially; each has a different character according to its natural light, volume, surface, and scale. Although visually linked, the galleries may all be secured separately. Skylights are shaped to soften, bounce, and diffuse the ample natural light.

The construction is smooth white plaster over masonry on vertical and inverted surfaces and titanium-zinc roofing panels on sloped water-shedding surfaces. The master plan calls for several independent galleries to be added to the initial museum building and additional factories to be added to the west side of the new entrance road. Parking will eventually be expanded at the west and south ends of the site.

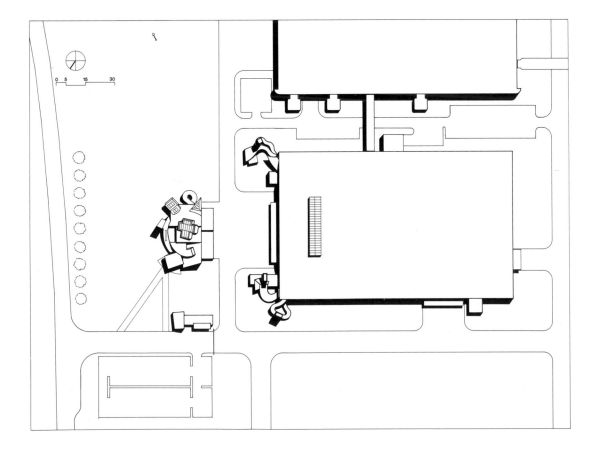

Site plan.

362

Model and view of
manufacturing facility
and museum, with
sculpture by Oldenburg
and van Bruggen in
foreground.

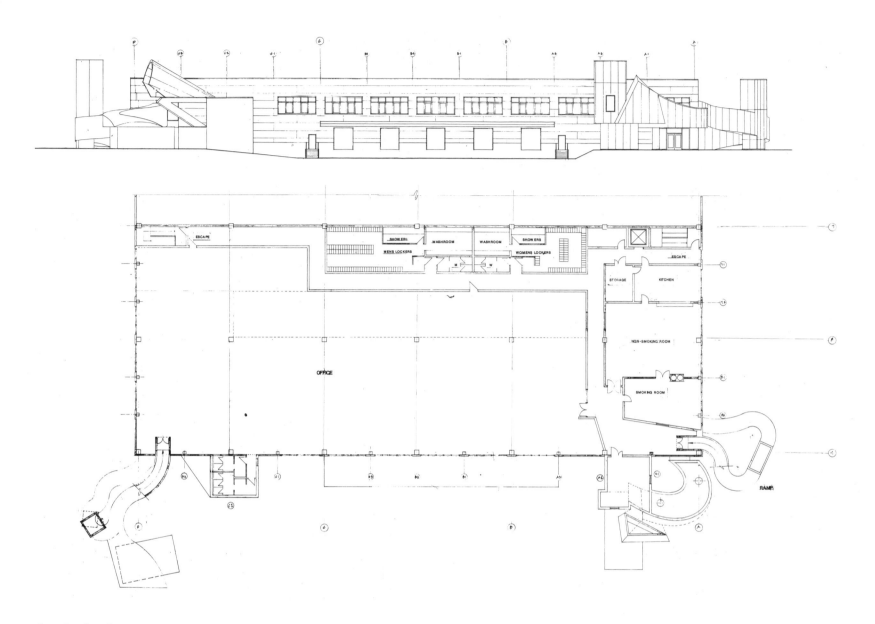

East elevation; plan
of factory mezzanine;
views to courtyard.

Aerial view of model;
roof plan; elevations.

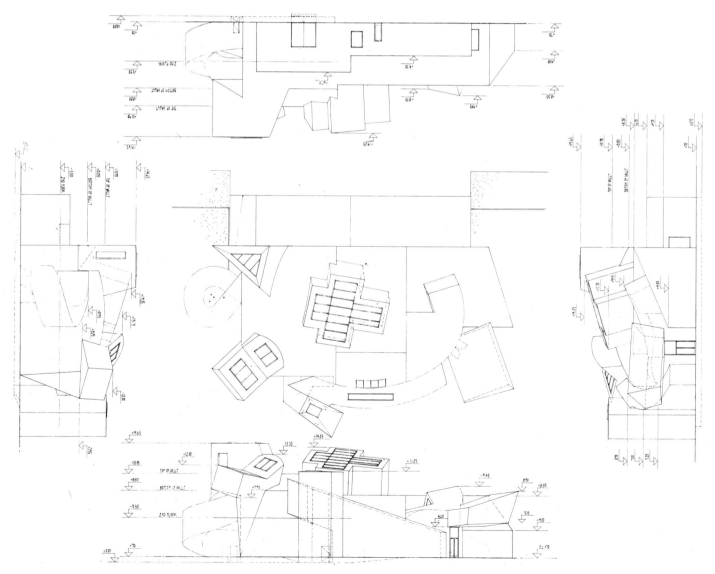

South elevation;
view from south.

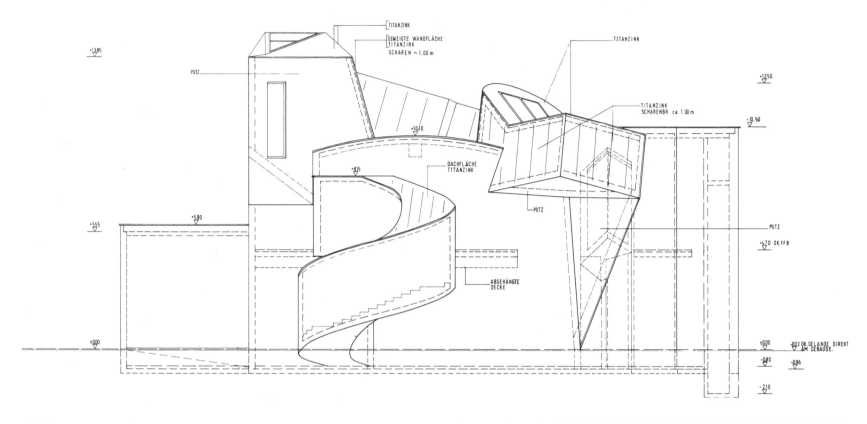

Detail of roof; east facade.

View from south;
interiors.

Iowa Laser Laboratory
Iowa City, Iowa
1987–92

Client: University of Iowa
Program: Research laboratories, offices, conference rooms
Budget: $17,500,000
Area: 136,000 square feet
Materials: Steel frame, limestone block, copper, and stainless-steel sheet-metal cladding
Project Team: Frank O. Gehry, David Denton, Roberta Weiser, Thomas J. Hoos, C. Gregory Walsh Jr., Bruce Biesman-Simons, Tom Buresh, Christopher Joseph Bonura, Kevin Daley, Tom Duley, Alex Meconi, David Pakshong, Carroll Stockard; Herbert Lewis Kruse Blunck, associate architect; Structural Consultants, PC, structural engineer; Kimmell-Jensen-Wegerer-Wray PC, mechanical and electrical engineer; Cost-Planning-Management-International, Inc., construction management

Occupying a site along the Iowa River, this 136,000-square-foot addition to the University of Iowa campus unites five functionally and visually distinct structures, designed to operate both independently and in support of each other. Three floors of research laboratories, faced with Anamosa limestone quarried from Stone City, Iowa, represent the largest programmatic element of the complex. Adjacent to this building is a long, low single-story facility, clad completely in copper and containing support laboratories and major mechanical spaces for the research building. The necessity for strict light, temperature, and humidity control within these two structures resulted in sheet facades without window openings.

To the east of the laboratory building is the long narrow bar through which the public enters the complex. Housing an exhibition space, information desk, and administrative offices, the building is clad in matte-finished stainless steel. It serves as a backdrop for the village of scientists' offices that fans out to the west toward the river. The offices are organized around a five-story, irregularly shaped atrium topped with flat, peaked, and angled skylights. The crystalline forms are surfaced in mirror-finish stainless steel, refracting sunlight and reflections off the river.

Nestled between the entrance and the offices stands the fifth element in the composition of forms, a freestanding structure that functions as a conference room. Its curving form is distinguished by its thirty-foot-high atrium and large windows overlooking the patio and the river.

The ghost of a sixth building, a concrete outline now planted with ornamental pear trees, indicates where four floors of office space would have been located had the building not been abandoned partway into the construction process due to budget restrictions.

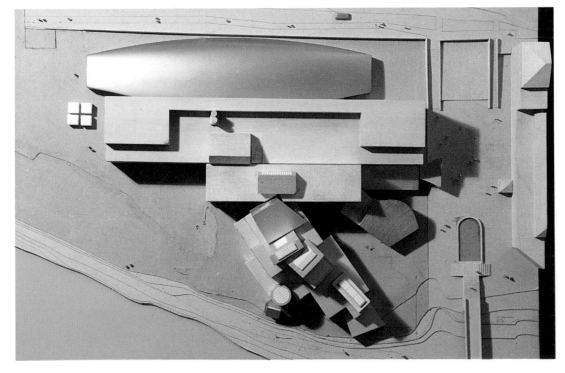

View from river;
aerial view of model.

370

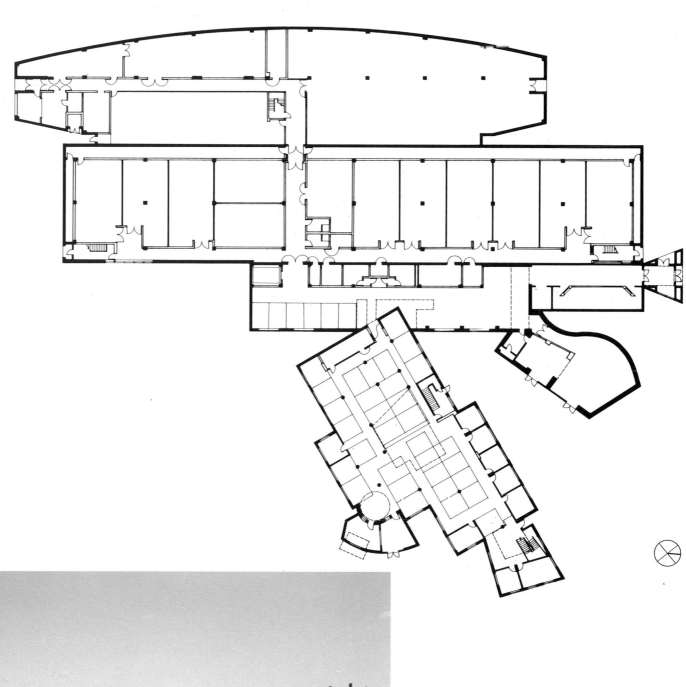

Ground-floor plan (top to bottom, support laboratories, laser laboratories, entrance corridor, conference room, offices); view from northwest.

East and west elevations;
view from east.

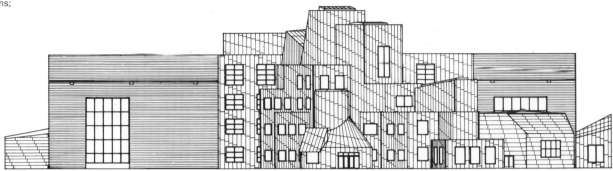

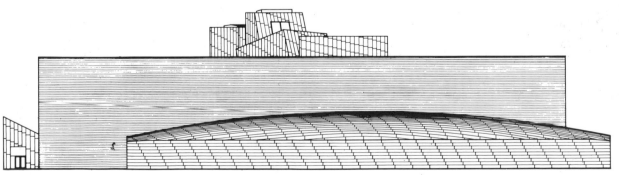

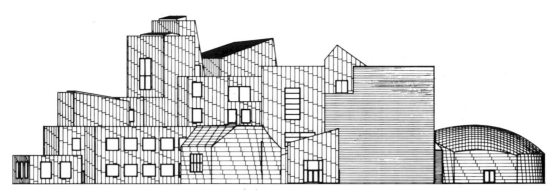

North and south
elevations; view from
northwest.

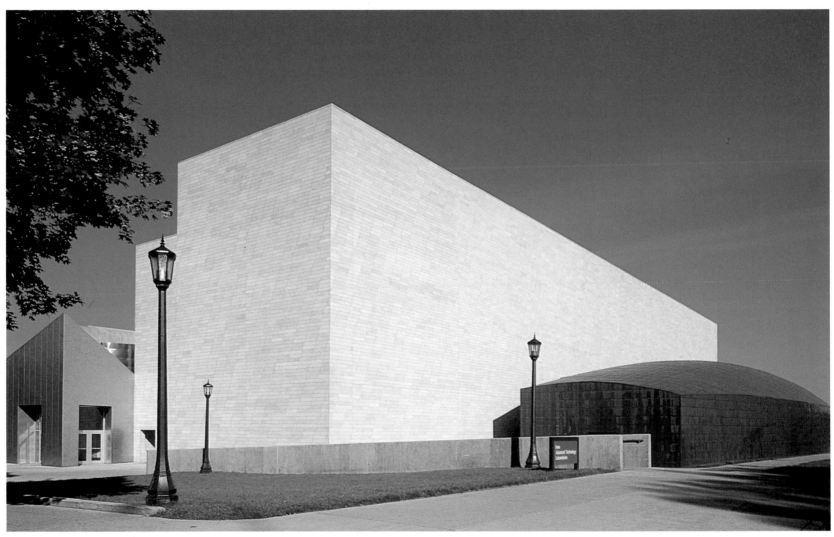

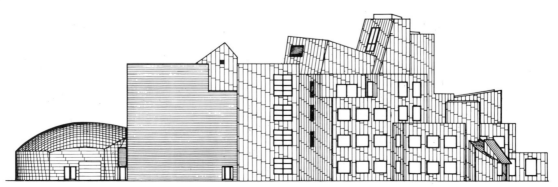

Views of north facade.

Views of east facade.

Overleaf:
Interiors.

Team Disneyland Administration Building
Anaheim, California
1987–95

Client: Disney Development Company
Program: Office building with cafeteria, exercise facility, two-hundred-seat auditorium, and parking garage
Area: 333,000 square feet
Materials: Steel frame, stucco, galvanized-stainless-steel sheet metal
Project Team: Frank O. Gehry, Randy Jefferson, Bruce Biesman-Simons, Edwin Chan, Kevin Daly, Jonathan Davis, Jim Dayton, David Gastrau, Robert G. Hale, Patricia McCaul, Michael Resnic, Todd Spiegel, Randall Stout, Lisa Towning, C. Gregory Walsh Jr., Josh White, Tim Williams; Langdon Wilson Associates, associate architect, Jim House, Douglas Gardner, Behrooz Kooklan, Nial Kelly; Martin & Associates, structural engineer; Rosenberg & Associates, mechanical engineer, Kocher & Schirra, electrical engineer; Lam Partners, lighting consultant; Dinwiddie Construction Company, preconstruction services

To house Disneyland's 1,100-person administrative staff, Gehry designed an office building at the edge of the theme park parallel to the Santa Ana Freeway. As he did at the Euro-Disneyland Retail and Entertainment Center (1988–93),

the architect captured the pop playfulness of the client's corporate identity not by resorting to figurative forms but by using an abstract formal vocabulary with a strong material presence.

The four-story building stretches and undulates for almost nine hundred feet along the freeway, iridescent in blue-green quilted-stainless-steel panels that have been treated with acid and blasted with glass beads to refract light. Staggered window openings on the highway facade emphasize the scaly shingled quality of the metal panels, and a long steel rake that Gehry calls the "cowcatcher" sits along the ground plane, threatening to peel the facade's skin away from the steel frame beneath.

On the east facade, facing the amusement park, the building reveals its second identity. This side is clad in brightly painted stucco at the approaches and entries, and the scale of the office building is broken down by a series of curved and sculptured forms denoting the main staff and auditorium lobby and endpoints. A series of sculpted galvanized-metal canopies cantilever out above the ground-floor windows along the walkway from the parking structure, which leads to the offices, a separate cafeteria, and a two-hundred-seat auditorium.

By separating special functions from the office building, a landscaped village of smaller buildings is created in the scale of other park facilities. The cafeteria building is a straightforward, preengineered type of structure, clad in galvanized sheet metal to relate to the existing adjacent buildings. The entrance to the garage is marked by a sculpted and painted stucco-and-metal canopy, in the same language as the forms on the main building. The walkway connecting the elements is free of vehicular traffic and, as at the Temporary Contemporary (1982–83) and the Disney Community Ice Center (1993), the surface of the plaza has been treated with boldly colored concrete. The only part of the interior designed by Gehry's office is the four-story entry atrium; the remainder was designed by the project's executive architect, Langdon Wilson.

Model from amusement park.

378

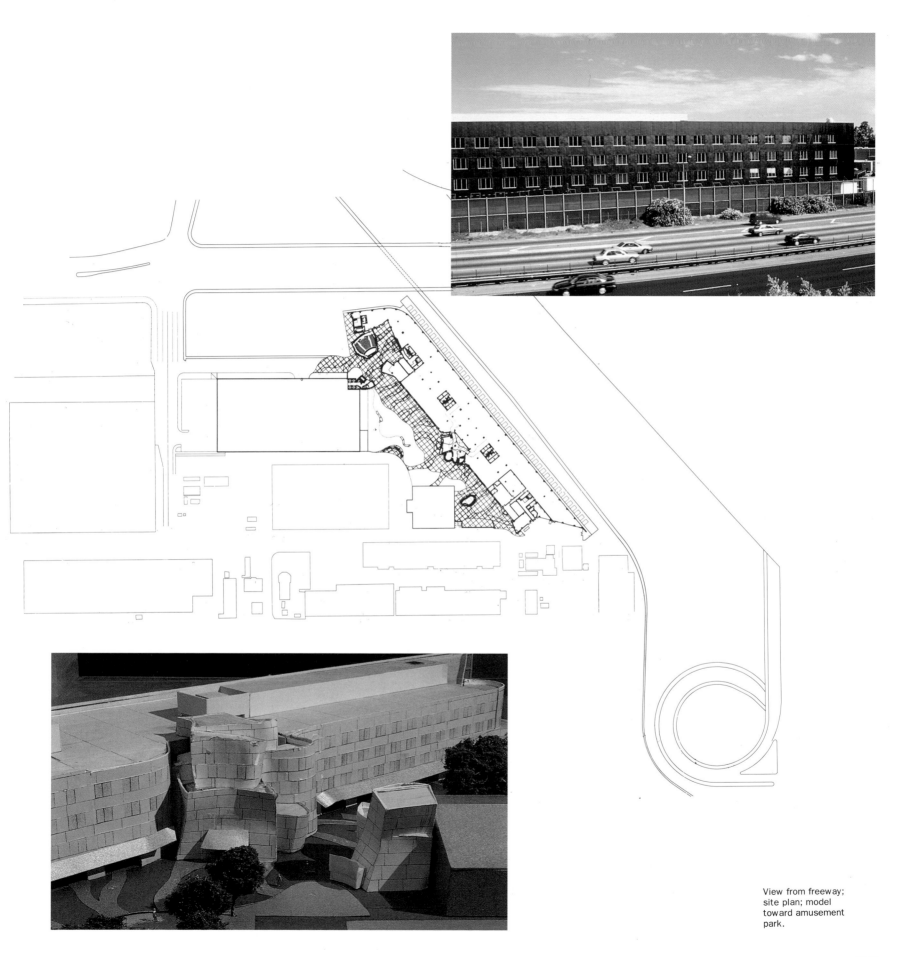

View from freeway;
site plan; model
toward amusement
park.

379

Views of amusement-park facade.

Views of atrium stairs.

**Cloverfield Alterations for
Frank O. Gehry and Associates
Santa Monica, California
1987–96**

Client: Schuminsky Investments and
Frank O. Gehry and Associates
Program: Warehouse remodel, including studio,
offices, model shop, library, conference room,
reprographics, and storage
Area: 10,000 square feet
Materials: Exposed wood frame, steel, plywood,
drywall, sheet-metal cladding
Project Team: Frank O. Gehry, David Denton,
James M. Glymph, Robert G. Hale, Bruce
Biesman-Simons, Kevin Daly, Jon Drezner,
Anne Greenwald, Michael Resnic, Bruce Toman

Office area; model shop.

Chiat/Day Toronto
Toronto, Ontario
1988

Client: Chiat/Day, Inc., Advertising
Program: Advertising agency offices
Budget: $1,500,000
Area: 16,000 square feet
Materials: Glass, plywood, untrimmed logs, pink
Minnesota dolomite pavers, wool felt
Project Team: Frank O. Gehry, Robert G. Hale,
Bobbie Weiser, Carroll Stockard, Christopher

Joseph Bonura, Anne Greenwald; David
Fujiwara and Associates, associate architect

The Toronto offices of Chiat/Day are located
on the top two floors of a seven-story building
on Lake Ontario. Each floor is roughly eight
thousand square feet in area, with eleven-foot
ceilings. The low floor-to-ceiling height was
visually extended by suspending a reflective glass
ceiling below the existing concrete deck. The
perimeter of each floor is lined with plywood
divider walls and workstations. The divider walls
have punched openings glazed with wire-rein-
forced glass in metal frames, located in series
along sight lines through the space.

The exterior walls of two meeting rooms are
sheathed in Douglas fir plywood, as is a third
plywood wall at the elevator's lobby. Together,
the plywood walls enclose the reception area
and frame a screen of full-height glass panels
surrounding the lead-clad client conference
room and sculpture platform. The warmth of
the plywood in this area is complemented by
three bark-covered maple log columns and pink
Minnesota dolomite pavers on the floor.

A lead fish suspended in a white enameled
bathtub adorns the sculpture platform. Inside
the conference room, wire glass is clipped onto
galvanized-steel studs along three walls. A fourth
wall, used for presentations, is covered by strips
of industrial wool felt. Above the wool-and-ply-
wood conference table hangs a sculptural light
fixture made of looped strips of the same felt.

Atrium; platform
with sculpture.

Axonometric showing
both floors; conference
room; sketch.

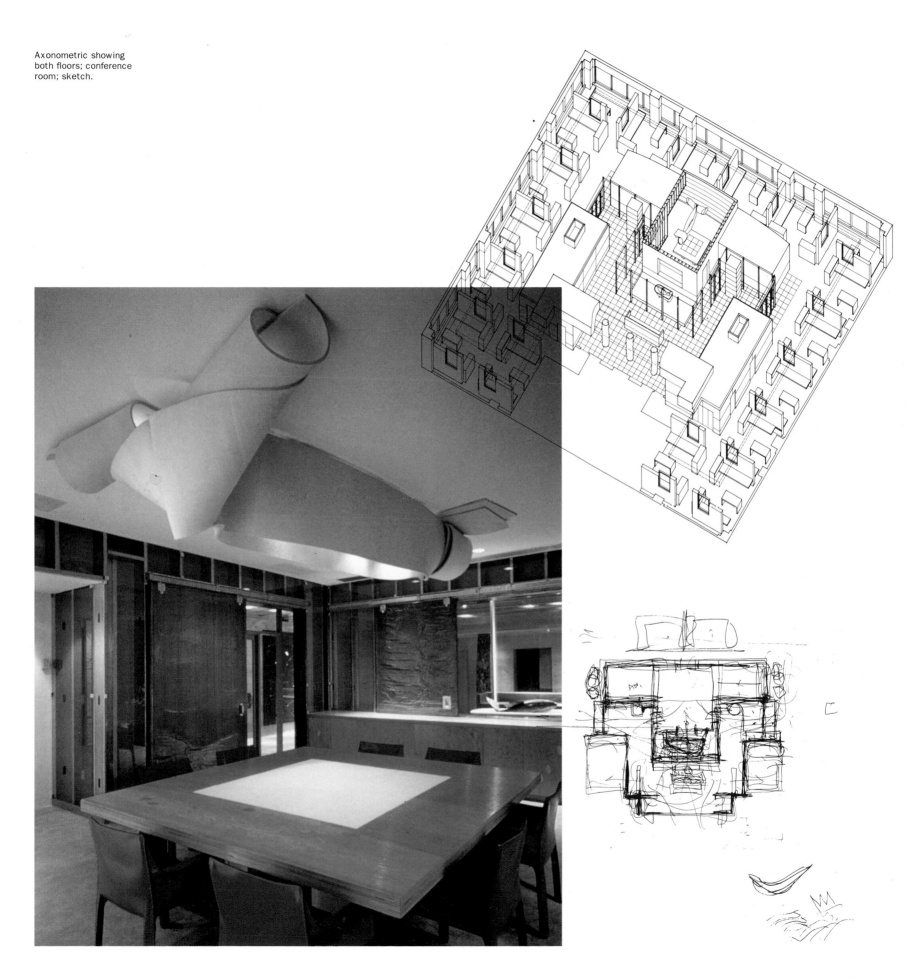

Milan Triennale
Milan, Italy
1988

Client: Art in Public Places Trust
Program: Exhibition design and installation
Materials: Exposed wood frame, plywood,
hardwood veneer

Project Team: Frank O. Gehry, C. Gregory
Walsh Jr., David Denton, Edwin Chan;
Claes Oldenburg and Coosje van Bruggen,
collaborating artists

Views of installation.

Port Imperial Competition
Weehauken, New Jersey
1988 (project)

Client: ARCORP Properties
Program: Mixed-use waterfront redevelopment
Project Team: Frank O. Gehry, David Denton;
Venturi, Scott Brown and Associates,
collaborating architect

Canary Wharf Competition
London, England
1988 (project)

Client: Olympia and York
Program: Urban development proposal,
including residential and hotel
Area: 6,000,000 square feet
Project Team: Frank O. Gehry; Skidmore,
Owings & Merrill

View of model
from Thames.

**Library Square
Los Angeles, California
1988 (project)**

Client: Maguire-Thomas Partners–
Library Square Ltd.
Program: Monumental outdoor snake sculpture
Budget: $1,500,000
Materials: Steel frame, copper cladding

Project Team: Frank O. Gehry, David Denton,
C. Gregory Walsh Jr., Edwin Chan

Models of sculpture
and installation.

**Hollywood Sign
Barcelona, Spain
1988**

Client: Barcelona Film Festival
Program: Signage
Area: 175 feet long by 50 feet wide by
25 feet high
Materials: Steel frame, copper and stainless-steel
sheet metal
Project Team: Frank O. Gehry, Michael Maltzen

Model views; installed
sign.

**Weisman Center
Venice, California
1988 (project)**

Client: Frederick Weisman
Program: Art galleries, offices, study center
Area: 20,000 square feet

Project Team: Frank O. Gehry, David Denton,
Robert G. Hale, Roberta Weiser

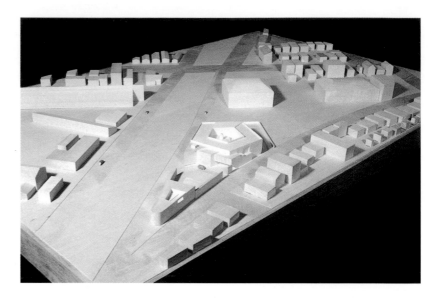

Model in context.

**Massachusetts Museum
of Contemporary Art
North Adams, Massachusetts
1988**

Client: Massachusetts Museum of
Contemporary Art
Program: Renovation of existing mill buildings
to house contemporary art museum
Materials: Steel frame, sheet–metal cladding
Project Team: Frank O. Gehry

Renovation proposals.

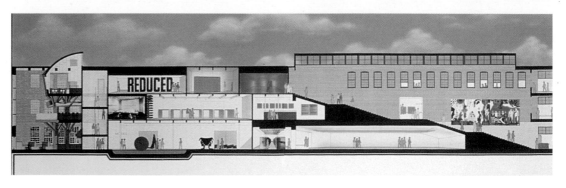

New York Bagel Shop
Los Angeles, California
1988–90

Client: G. David Rosen
Program: Fifty-seat delicatessen
Area: 1,600 square feet
Materials: Concrete, stainless steel, painted sheet metal, Finnish plywood, Douglas fir
Project Team: Frank O. Gehry, C. Gregory Walsh Jr., Kevin Daly, Tomas Osinski; Anita Berry, Marion Sampler, graphic design

In a typically Californian auto-oriented tenant space, the challenge of this project was to create a place that would feel like a New York City delicatessen. The design was treated very simply: the exterior storefront consists of a large glass window and door, surrounded by panels of Finnish plywood. Inside, the walls and ceiling are covered with panels of natural-finish Douglas-fir plywood in a staggered pattern. The floor repeats the same pattern, but with the plywood defining inlaid panels of gray concrete.

Two theatrical objects dominate the dining room. A model of New York City's Chrysler Building, fabricated in galvanized metal, slants down from the ceiling, hiding air-conditioning ducts and adjustable track-light fixtures within. Playing off this sculpture is a stainless-steel sign and seating counter with "New York" in cutout letters. All other elements of the interior—delicatessen cases, traditional Formica pedestal tables, aluminum chairs, and red naugahyde upholstered booths—were chosen or selected to appear conventionally off-the-shelf.

Views of dining room.

Views of dining room
with galvanized-metal
Chrysler Building.

**Euro-Disneyland Retail and
Entertainment Center
Villier-sur-Marne, France
1988–93**

Client: Euro-Disneyland, S.C.A.
Program: Entertainment complex including
shops, bars, nightclub, restaurants, dinner theater,
administrative and support offices
Area: 185,000 square feet
Materials: Poured concrete, laminated wood
structure, stainless steel, natural zinc, painted
sheet metals, plaster

Project Team: Frank O. Gehry, Robert G. Hale,
Bruce Biesman-Simons, Vince Snyder, Andy
Alper, Gaelle Breton, Michael Sant, Marc
Salette; Saubot et Jullien, associate architect

Exterior views, with
pointed-arch building
housing nightclub.

American Center
Paris, France
1988–94

Sketch; study model.

Client: American Center
Program: Cultural center, including multi-purpose performance, rehearsal, and exhibition spaces, bookstore, restaurant, four-hundred-seat theater, great hall, duplex apartments, language school, administrative offices, visual arts and dance studios, sculpture terrace
Budget: FFr 130,000,000

Area: 198,000 square feet
Materials: Steel frame, limestone block, natural zinc sheet metal
Project Team: Frank O. Gehry , Robert G. Hale, James M. Glymph, Edwin Chan, C. Gregory Walsh Jr., Marc Salette, Thomas J. Hoos, Brian Yoo, David Gastrau, David Pakshong, Kevin Daly; Saubot & Jullien, associate architect; Xu Acoustique, acoustical engineer; Rioualec Scènographie, theater consultant

The American Center existed as a venue for expatriate American artists, musicians, and performers from 1931 to 1987 in a remodeled Beaux-Arts building in Montparnasse. In 1987, the original building was sold and a new lot secured at 51, rue de Bercy, in the twelfth arrondissement, across the Seine from the new French library and not far from the Palais Omnisport. At the recommendation of Martin and Mildred Friedman of the Walker Art Center in Minneapolis, Henry Pillsbury, a former executive director of the American Center, invited Gehry to design the new building, his first design for a large cultural institution outside the United States.

The site is located in a formerly industrial area currently under rehabilitation—rail lines lie to the north, a new park to the south, housing to the east, and a public plaza to the west—but the area is most often associated with blocks of wine warehouses. The program called for 198,000 square feet of performance and exhibition spaces, administrative offices, and visiting-artist apartments that would celebrate French-American cultural dialogue. The context called for a density of form, continuity of materials, and intense, accessible visibility. Formally, the building's massing assertively responds to the Parisian roofscape; materially, limestone, glass, and zinc acknowledge the historical traditions of Parisian architecture and the complex contextual conditions of the immediate urban environment. Gehry saw the building as a "*petite ville*, full of dance and music and activity and a lot of energy like the city . . . an American interpretation of Paris as I see it, without trying to make a French building."

The north facade, seen from the street, maintains a geometric regularity. Gehry describes it as "calm" and "polite" on first approach, with a mansard roof slipping down the side of the building all the way to the ground. The southwest corner, however, dissolves and unfolds over a public plaza facing the Parc Bercy and leads inside to a great hall, around which are orga-

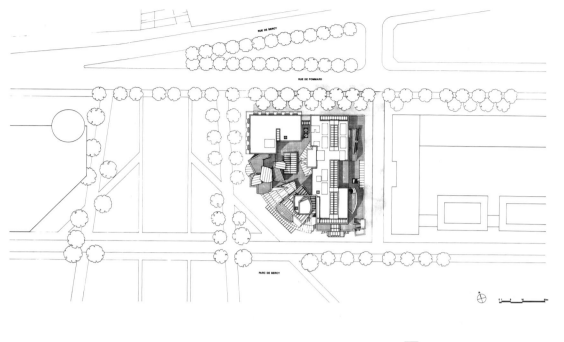

nized the center's most public functions. Multi-purpose performance, rehearsal, and exhibition spaces, a bookstore, a restaurant, and a four-hundred-seat theater are organized along the edges of the site, taking advantage of easy accessibility from the street as well as from the great hall. Also linked to the hall is a raised gallery area that provides over two thousand square feet of flexible space for special exhibitions.

The more exclusive functions of the center are expressed on the upper levels of the building as two distinct forms. To the west, an L-shaped tower is crowned by duplex apartments, a form Gehry refers to as "the pineapple," taking advantage of full views of the Parisian skyline. To the east, an articulated block houses the fly gallery of the theater, as well as a language school, administrative offices, and studio spaces for art and dance classes. Animating the top level of the block is six thousand square feet of flexible exhibition space with twenty-foot ceilings punctuated by monumental skylights. This exhibition area opens onto a sculpture terrace overlooking the park and the skyline.

Complicated site lines and circulation paths animate the building. The great hall, a two-level atrium, was intended to be opened to the outdoors in fair weather. The mezzanine level of the hall has a glass roof that allows views of the sky, rooftops, and sculptural elements of the building. Balconies, stairways, and terraces provide views of the interior's multidisciplinary activities as well as to the outdoors. Such animation by human activity remains to be seen, however; the American Center closed as an institution on February 12, 1996, and the building was put up for sale.

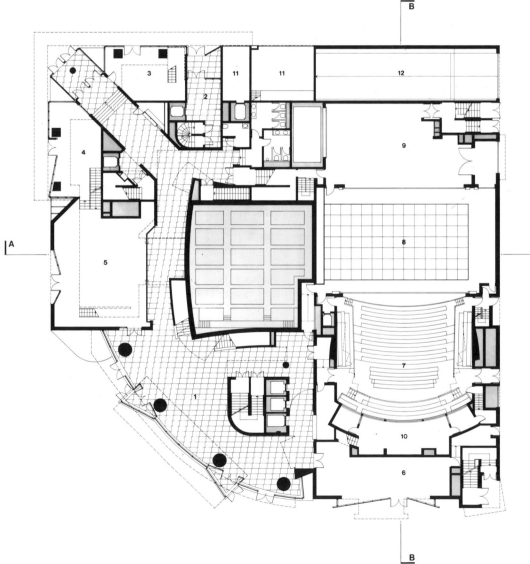

Site plan; ground-floor plan:
1. atrium
2. apartment atrium
3. bookstore
4. store
5. restaurant
6. travel agency
7. theater
8. stage
9. backstage area
10. control area
11. store
12. ramp

Overleaf:
Study model; sketches; final model.

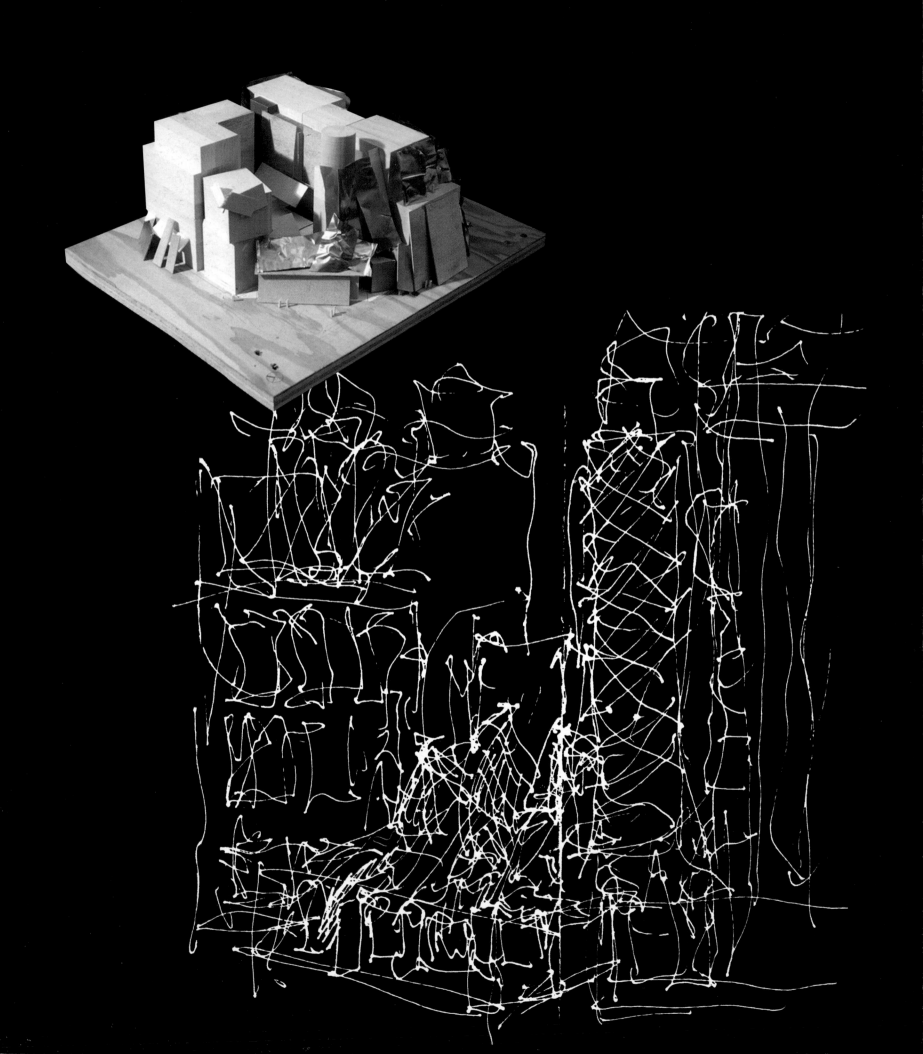

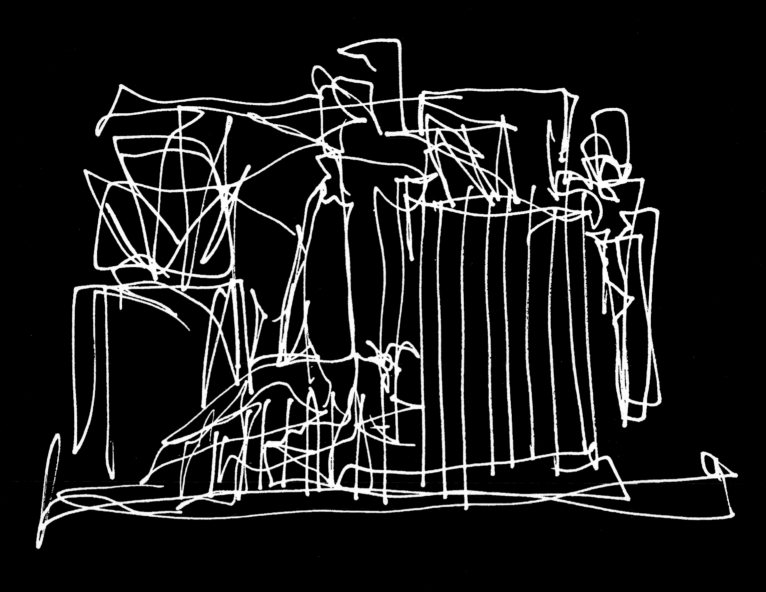

View from west;
west elevation.

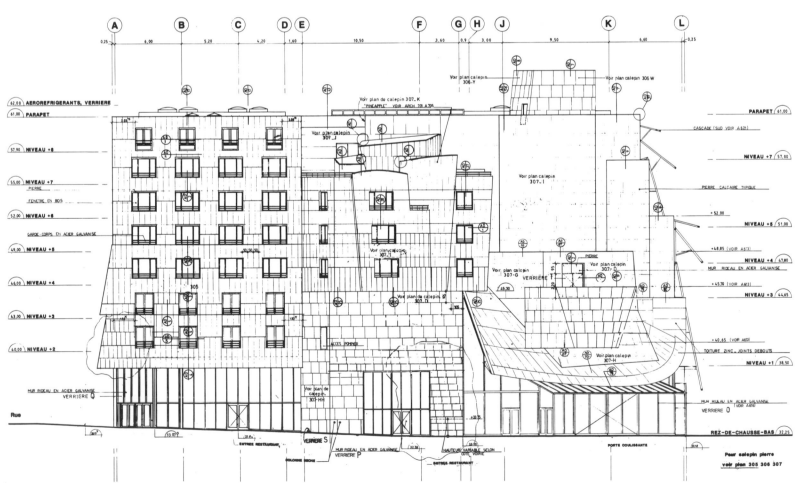

View from south;
south elevation.

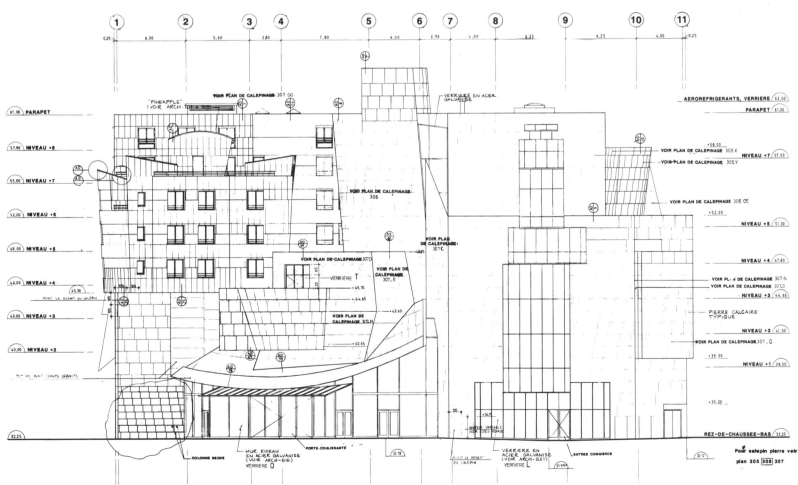

View of southwest corner
looking toward atrium;
sketch; panoramic terrace.

Skylights on roof; terraces; volumes above atrium.

404

Views of exhibition space;
stairs.

Section and view of
theater:
1. foyer
2. theater
3. stage
4. backstage area
5. control area
6. orchestra pit
7. travel agency
8. dance studio
9. visual-arts studio
10. exhibition spaces
11. language school
12. administration
13. theater laboratory
14. offices
15. conference room
16. dressing room
17. darkroom
18. exhibition store
19. mechanical system
20. parking
21. ramp

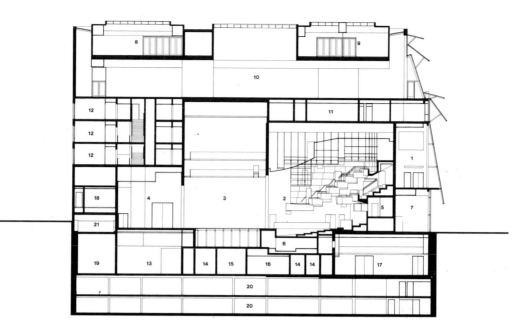

Vitra International
Biersfelden, Switzerland
1988–91

Client: Vitra International Ltd.
Program: Corporate headquarters, including flexible work spaces, conference and meeting rooms, main entrance/reception, cafeteria, switchboard, and mailroom
Budget: SFr 15,000,000
Area: 60,000 square feet
Materials: Steel frame, concrete, masonry, stucco, zinc panels
Project Team: Frank O. Gehry, Robert G. Hale, James M. Glymph, Vincent Snyder, Randall Stout, Liza Hansen, Peter Locke, Eva Sobesky, David Stein, Laurence Tighe, Dane Twichell, Brian Yoo; Gunter Pfeifer Associates, associate architect, Roland Mayer, Elke Hudetz, Jurgen Roth

Part of a master-planned development on a suburban site outside Basel, this sixty-two-thousand-square-foot corporate office building is bounded by a low-rise Vitra manufacturing building on one side and a small converted office structure on the other. The surrounding neighborhood contains a mixture of light manufacturing, offices, houses, and garden apartments. To the east is a dense forest reserve, visually tied to but physically severed from the site by an autobahn submerged well below grade.

The existing zoning required a building less than thirty feet in height. Parking was limited to one car for every three employees on the site.

The building houses various working groups in spaces that are flexible enough to allow for experimentation with their own furniture lines and neutral enough to serve as showrooms. Gehry's office invested much research into state-of-the-art office space, resulting in a sampling of "combi-office" and "office landscape" types as well as more traditional closed and open offices. Switzerland's strict energy codes mandated that there be no air-conditioning, so natural ventilation is provided through operable windows and the entire south wall is shaded beneath a large wing-shaped canopy.

In addition to the flexible office block, more permanent communal support areas such as the main entrance and reception, cafeteria, switchboard, mail, meeting, and conference rooms form a central core, allowing for future expansion of offices around them. These spaces took on richer, sculpted shapes, similar to the scale of some of the houses nearby; the core was thus dubbed "the villa." Inside the villa, conference and meeting rooms are enhanced by strong colors and custom light fixtures of sculptural shapes, including a fish form. The wing canopy houses a "living room" atrium and formally mediates between the simple office block and the central, energetic villa.

The structure of the building is concrete and masonry. External materials are a combination of painted stucco, zinc panels, wood-framed doors, and operable windows.

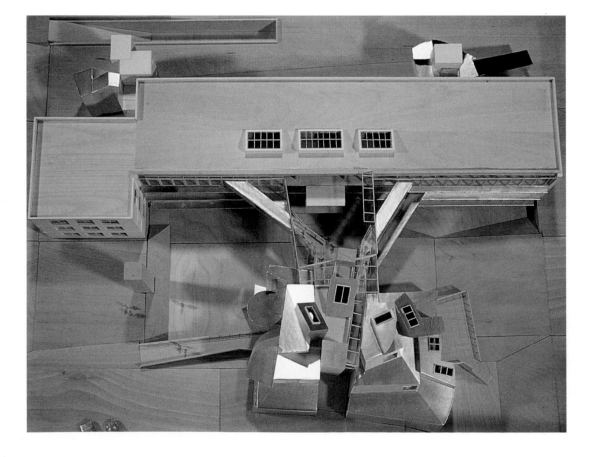

Aerial view of model.

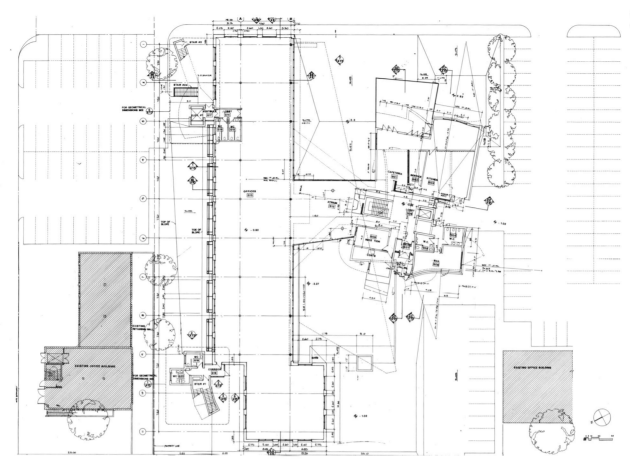

Detail of the shell of the "villa"; view of north facade.

〈

411

North and east elevations;
view from southeast.

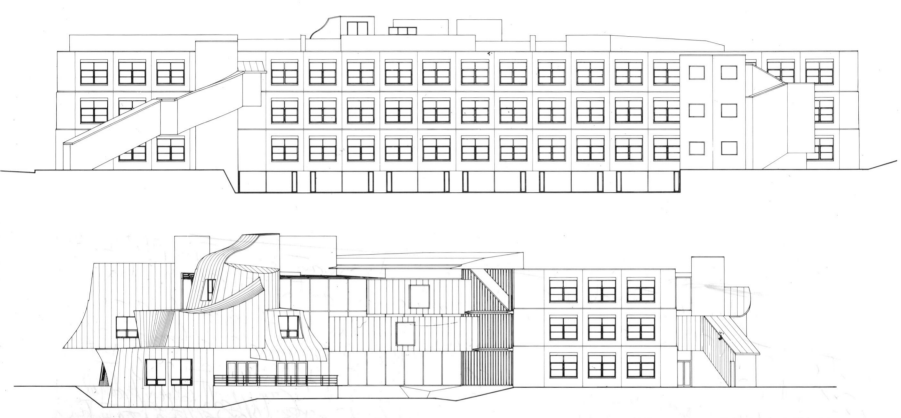

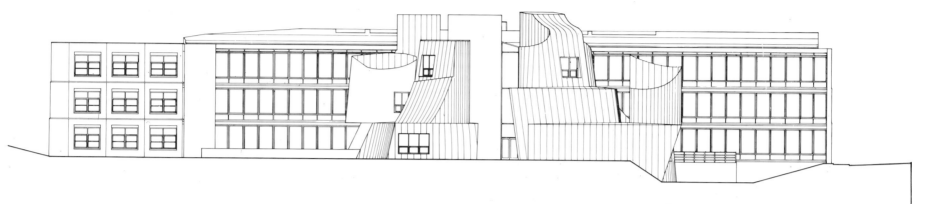

West elevation; view
from southwest; detail
of shell of "villa."

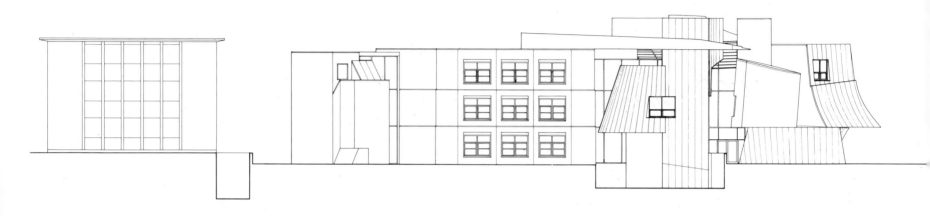

**Federal Triangle Competition
Washington, D.C.
1989 (project)**

Project Team: Frank O. Gehry

Section through World
Link.

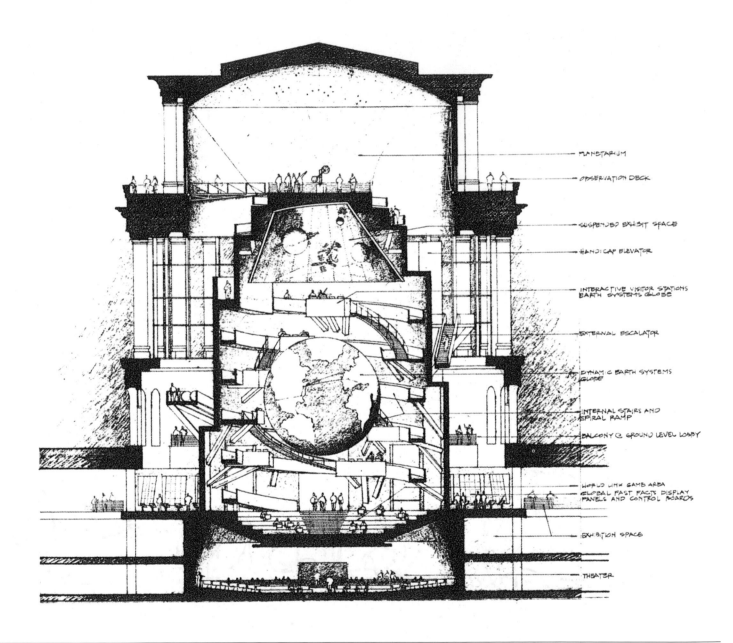

PLANETARIUM

OBSERVATION DECK

SUSPENDED EXHIBIT SPACE

HANDICAP ELEVATOR

INTERACTIVE VISITOR STATIONS
EARTH SYSTEMS GLOBE

EXTERNAL ESCALATOR

DYNAMIC EARTH SYSTEMS
GLOBE

INTERNAL STAIRS AND
SPIRAL RAMP

BALCONY @ GROUND LEVEL LOBBY

WORLD LINK GAME AREA
GLOBAL FAST FACTS DISPLAY
PANELS AND CONTROL BOARDS

EXHIBITION SPACE

THEATER

**12th Street Project
Santa Monica, California
1989**

Client: Development project
Program: Artists' studios
Area: 6,500 square feet
Materials: Wood frame, corrugated galvanized
steel
Project Team: Frank O. Gehry

**Center for the Visual Arts
University of Toledo,
Toledo, Ohio
1989**

Sketch.

Overleaf:
View from east.

Client: Toledo Museum of Art
Program: Three-story studio and classroom
building including gallery, library, and
administration
Budget: $10,000,000
Area: 51,000 square feet
Materials: Steel frame, lead-coated copper
cladding, green-tinted glass
Project Team: Frank O. Gehry, James M.
Glymph, David Denton, Peter Locke, Randall
Stout, C. Gregory Walsh Jr., Michael Maltzan,
Andrew Alper, Jon Drezner, Michael Resnic,
Tami Wedekind; Collaborative, Inc., executive
architect

Formerly housed in the Toledo Museum of Art,
the new Center for the Visual Arts is now situated immediately adjacent to the museum. The
project's placement in the park to the east of
the museum was chosen over potential sites to
the south and west in order to allow for future
expansion. The building is L-shaped in plan,
forming a courtyard next to the museum building. It is an object, sculpturally and visually
complete, next to the elegantly detailed, neoclassical museum. A later phase is planned in

which a bar-shaped building will form a backdrop to the first phase of the project.

The strategy for the compact, three-story
building consisted of placing the studios and
classrooms requiring natural light on the upper
two floors. Other functions—student gallery,
library, and administrative services—occupy the
ground floor. The basement level houses those
areas not requiring natural light, such as photography studios, a lecture hall, and mechanical
rooms. Circulation through the building occurs
along a glass-walled corridor surrounding the
courtyard. Vertical circulation is at the ends of
the corridor in two glass-enclosed stair towers.

Generally relating to the height of the plinth
of the museum building, a grass-covered berm
slopes up toward the north side of the building,
engaging it with the landscape while screening
the library from street noise. The new building
is clad in lead-coated copper and glass. The
green-tinted glass of the entry and courtyard
facades relates to the patinated copper of the
museum. The lead-coated copper cladding has
an aged appearance while its iridescent quality
lends life to the building. Mature trees on the
site were integrated into the design.

417

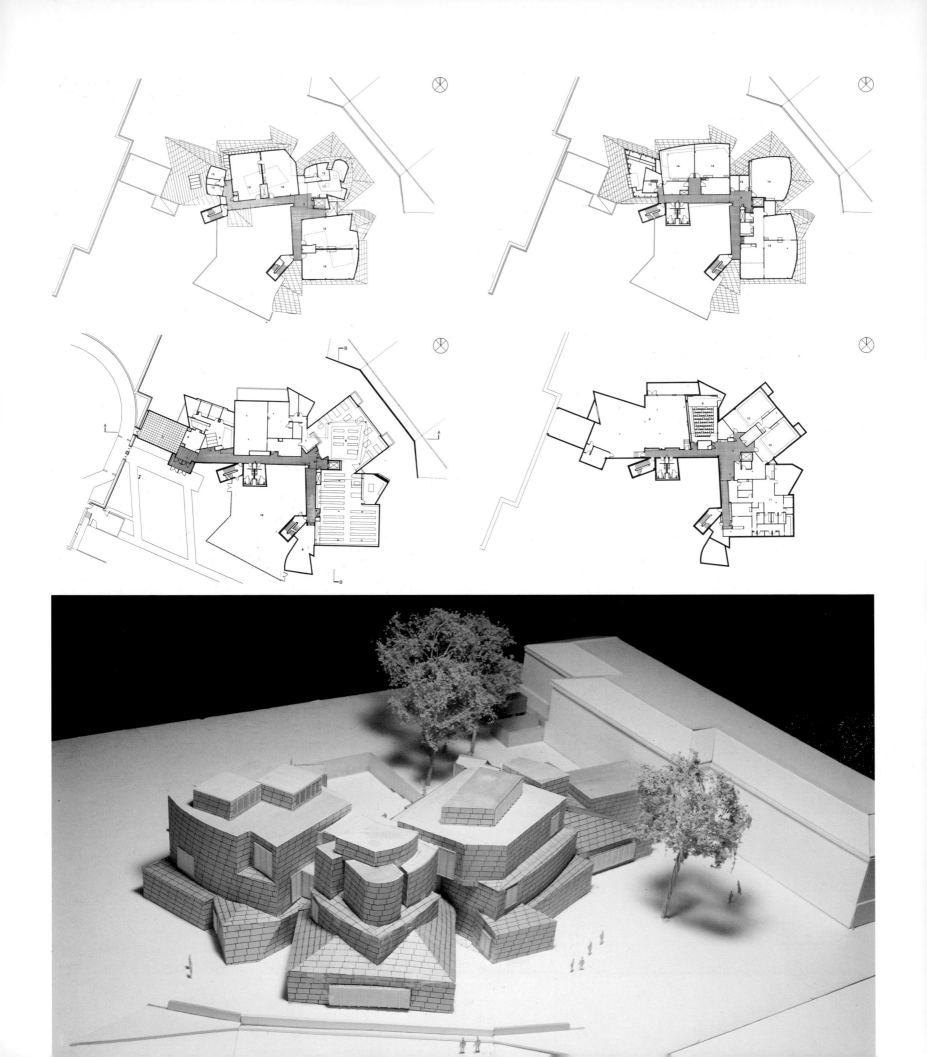

Lower-, ground-, second-,
and third-floor plans;
northeast view of model.

Aerial view from adjacent
museum; west elevation.

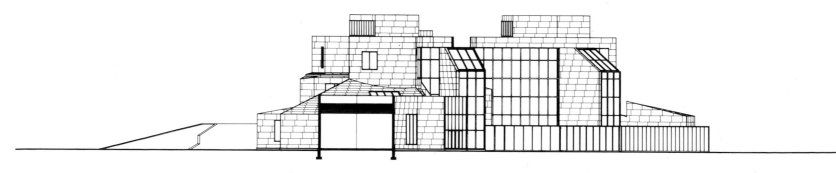

Sketches; view
toward south.

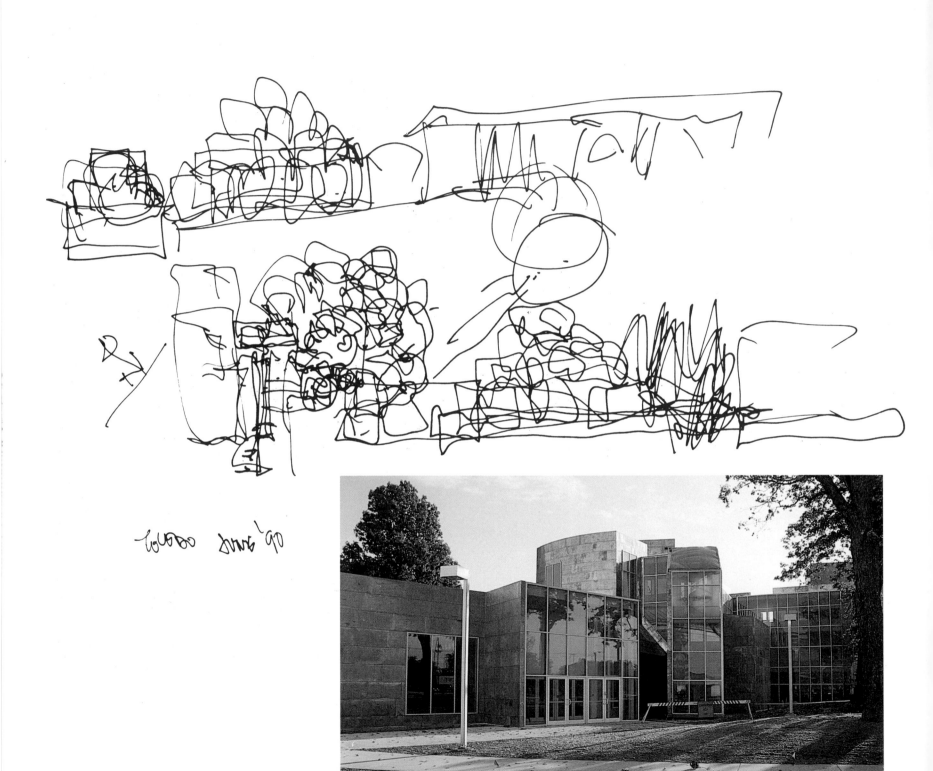

Pito Tea Kettle
1989

Client: Officina Alessi, Milan
Retail Price: $300
Materials: Stainless steel, mahogany
Project Team: Frank O. Gehry

Model view.

New Zealand Museum
Competition
Aukland, New Zealand
1989

Program: Waterfront urban development
proposal
Project Team: Frank O. Gehry

Aerial view of model.

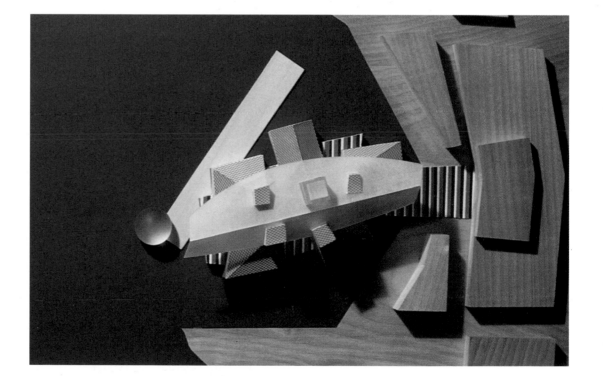

Bentwood Furniture
1989–92

Client: Knoll Group, Maurice C. Sardi, Andrew Cogan
Program: Lightweight wooden chairs and tables
Retail Prices: $900–$4,000
Materials: Maple veneer laminated strips, glue

Project Team: Frank O. Gehry, Daniel Sachs, Tom MacMichael, Kevin Lindores, Tom Sachs, Michelle Lambson, Christopher Tandon, Alexander Platt

Sketches; prototypes; various stages of design.

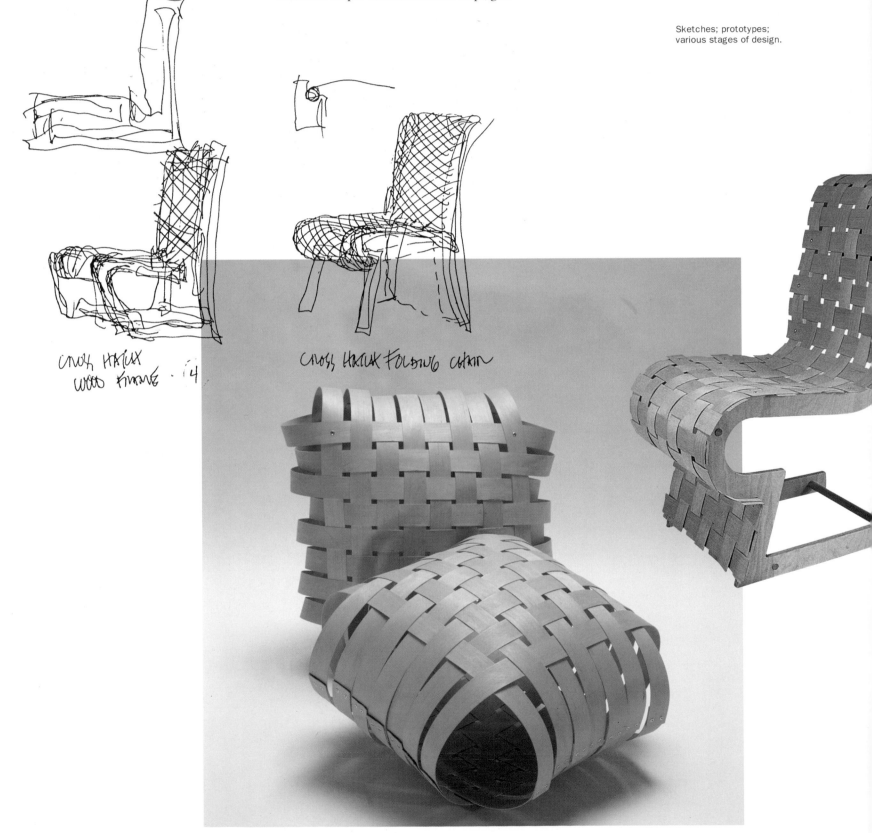

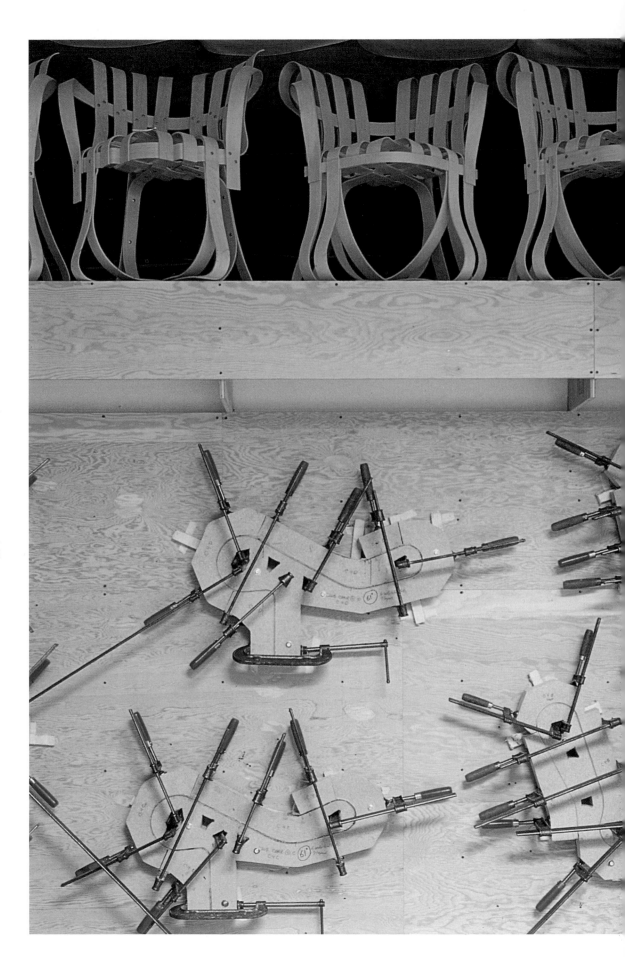

Gehry had been thinking for almost a decade prior to the development of his Knoll furniture line about how to make lightweight wood furniture. Early sketches illustrate his concept of weaving wood strips to overcome the artificial separation of support structure and seat that had characterized much laminated furniture, and he cites as his inspiration the bushel baskets on which he played as a child in Toronto.

Gehry believes that the lighter a piece is, the easier it is to make, and that by paring something to its essence, the structure is at its ultimate expression. Furniture based on these ideas, however, failed to find the support of manufacturers. It was not until spring 1989 that Gehry had a means to verify his concept in full scale, when Knoll visited him to discuss the creation of a new line of furniture.

In fall 1989, Knoll opened a workshop next door to Gehry's studio, affording him the kind of hands-on, day-to-day involvement he wanted with the project. After a few months, Gehry discovered that by laminating thin strips of maple veneer and weaving them like a basket, he was able to create continuous structures that integrated the chair's seat, back, and frame. One hundred twenty prototypes were produced over the next two years, culminating in the development of the Hat Trick, High Sticking, Cross Check, Power Play, Icing, and Offside chairs and the Face-Off table, all of which were introduced to the public in spring 1992.

Sketches; prototypes.

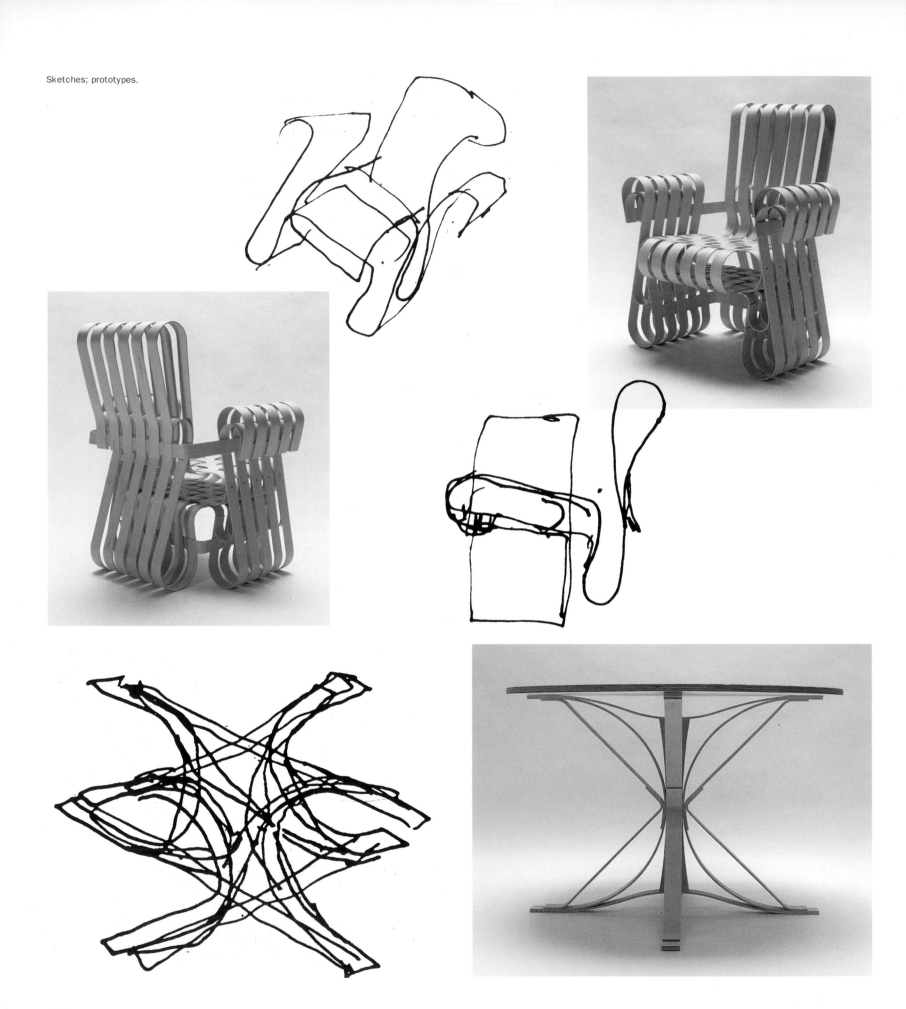

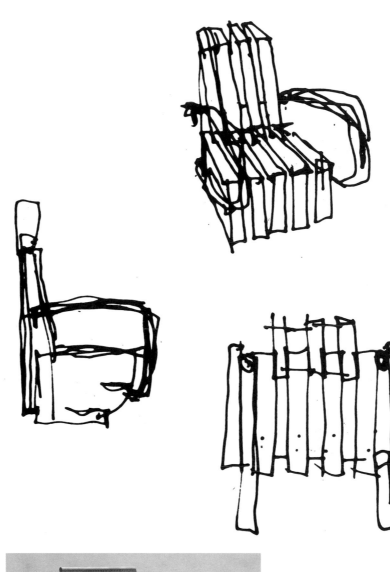

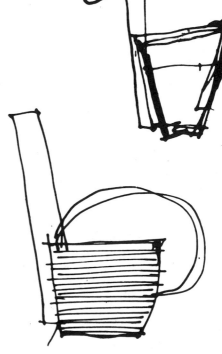

Vila Olimpica
Barcelona, Spain
1989–92

Sketches of sculpture; final drawings made using CATIA.

Client: Travelstead Group
Program: Waterfront retail and commercial complex, including monumental fish sculpture
Area: 150,000 square feet; fish sculpture: 160 feet long by 100 feet tall
Materials: Stone, steel, glass
Project Team: Frank O. Gehry, David Denton, James M. Glymph, Michael Maltzan, C. Gregory Walsh Jr., Douglas Hanson, David Reddy, Rick Black, Karl Blette, Christopher Joseph Bonura, Kevin Daly, Peter Locke, Michael Sant, Dane Twichell

The Vila Olimpica hotel project is located in Barcelona's 1992 Olympic Village redevelopment site adjacent to the Passeig de Carlos I, a primary artery terminating at a marina and conference center on the Mediterranean. Within a master plan executed by Martorell, Bohigas and Mackay, the project includes a hotel, apartment, and office tower designed by Bruce Graham of Skidmore, Owings & Merrill, as well as 150,000 square feet of commercial structures designed by Gehry.

Gehry's retail portion of the project is bounded by the hotel tower to the north and the beach to the south and includes a portion of the Pasco Maritimo—the waterfront promenade—winding from the old harbor through the Olympic Village and up the coast to the northeast. Shops are arranged around a central court linking the development to the waterfront at both the beach and the promenade. A variety of sculptural elements, including a monumental fish sculpture floating over the retail court, serve as highly visible landmarks. The palette of materials—stone, steel, and glass—was drawn from the hotel tower in order to reinforce the unity of the project as a whole. At the same time, the expressed structure of the fish sculpture, pedestrian bridges, and the trellis elements of the public spaces are more liberated extensions of the tightly ordered structural language of the Skidmore, Owings & Merrill tower.

The fish sculpture, approximately 160 feet long and 100 feet tall, provides an abstract foreground element when viewed from the hotel terraces, and is a shading and enclosing device

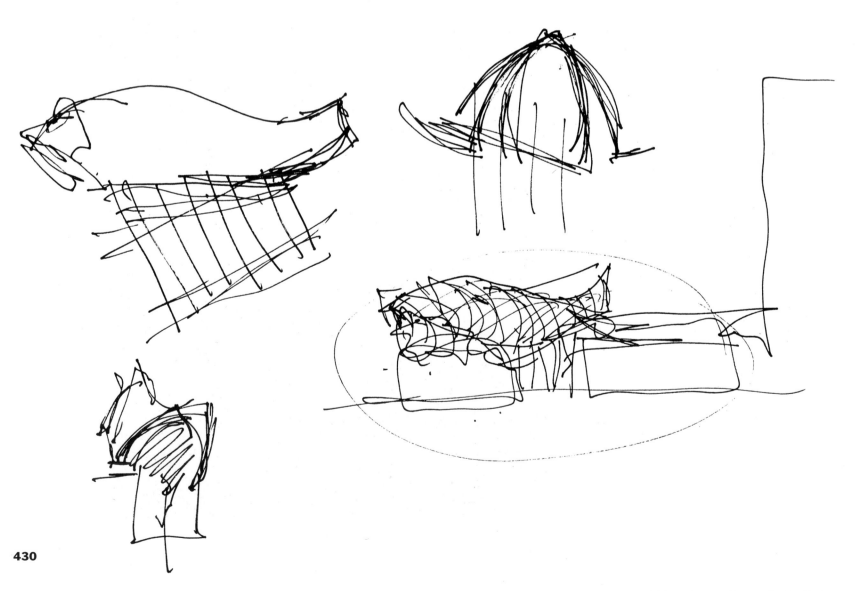

for the retail court. Elevators and escalators connect the shops with below-grade parking.

The construction of the fish represents the first time Gehry's office employed a computer in the building process. On a tight budget and schedule, the search for an appropriate software and hardware package was driven by the need to assist manufacturers and contractors in building the structure quickly and economically. The computer was not needed as a design or presentation tool, but rather as a tool for facilitating production, augmenting a three-dimensional design process that had been in place for thirty years. Although Gehry's office had previously built fish and other complex curvilinear structures, designs had been limited by what could be described in traditional two-dimensional drawings. In looking for the appropriate three-dimensional medium, Gehry's office sought a system that would allow them to continue working in physical models and at the same time describe to contractors how to build the unique structures, demystifying the material behavior, surface geometries, and structural principles of complex curves so that the time and money expended on the project would reflect the true cost of assembly rather than the costs associated with misunderstanding.

Software research, led by James Glymph, a principal at the firm, began in the aerospace and automotive industries, both of which design and fabricate in three dimensions rather than with layered views in two dimensions. Both industries also design, like Gehry, from the skin inward. Ultimately the firm adopted CATIA by Dassault Systèmes of Paris, a program originally developed for the design of Mirage fighter jets, distributed by IBM, and run on IBM workstations. In Gehry's office, the dimensions of physical models are digitized by tracing their forms with a laser stylus, attached to a six-foot-tall three-dimensional point digitizer. This data is then fed into CATIA, where design and engineering are refined.

By working closely with the contractor on full-scale mockups of the Barcelona fish sculpture and extracting data from the computer model, the firm developed a set of flexible but nonetheless standardized component fittings, adjustable to different geometries and rotation angles. The database provided the contractor with each fitting's position and orientation, making a complex structure relatively easy to assemble. CATIA was integral to the design development and construction documents for the Disney Concert Hall (1989–), and has been so for all subsequent projects.

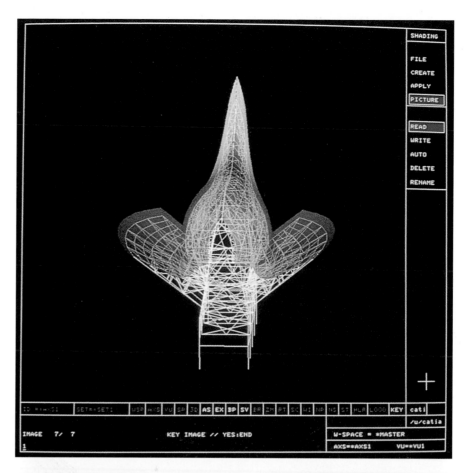

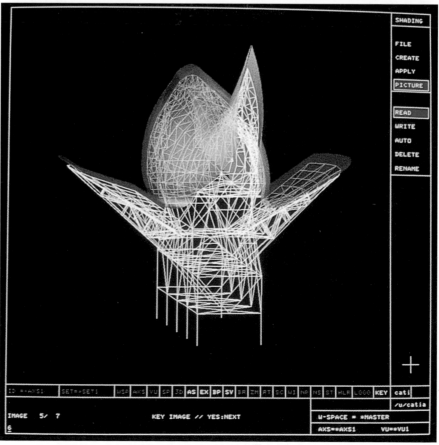

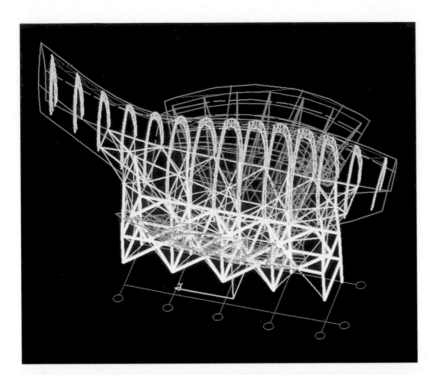

Final design; exterior view; model views with sculpture.

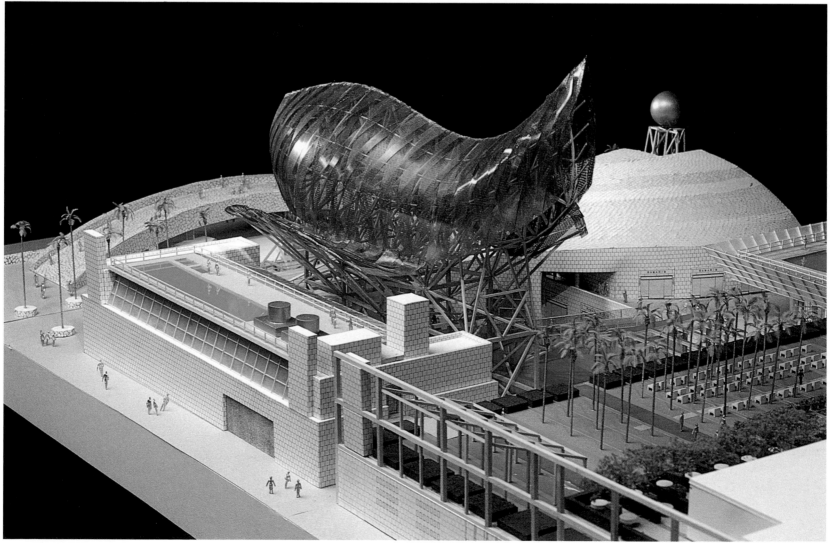

Lewis Residence
Lyndhurst, Ohio
1989–95 (project)

Study model;
volumetric plan;
plan of first scheme.

Client: Peter B. Lewis
Program: Single-family residence, two guest houses
Area: 22,000 square feet
Materials: Concrete shell, steel frame, limestone, stainless-steel sheet metal
Project Team: Frank O. Gehry, James M. Glymph, Craig Webb, Susan Desko, Vincent L. Snyder, Terry Bell, George Metzger, Laurence Tighe, Rich Barrett, Karl Blette, Naomi Ehrenpreis, John Goldsmith, Michael Jobes, Michael Mantzoris, Jay Park, David Reddy, Philip Rowe, Eva Sobesky, Kevin Southerland, Tensho Takemori, Robert Thibodeau, Lisa Towning, Dane Twichell, Scott Uriu, Jeff Wauer, Josh White, Kristin Woehl, Nora Wolin, Brian Yoo; Philip Johnson Architects, collaborating architect, Philip Johnson, John Manley; Richard Serra, Larry Bell, Claes Oldenburg and Coosje van Bruggen, Maggie Cheswick-Jencks, collaborating artists; Hanna/Olin, Ltd., landscape architect; Van Dijk, Pace, Westlake, & Partners, associate architect; DeSimone, Chaplin and Dobryn Consulting Engineers, P.C., structural engineer; Cosentini Associates, mechanical/electrical engineer; Lewis Wallack & Associates, Inc., interior programming consultants C-cubed, computer design, Rick Smith

The program for the Lewis Residence, a twenty-two-thousand-square-foot home for a bachelor outside of Cleveland, called for a commercial-grade kitchen, a dining room, a living room, an art gallery, two master bedrooms, a study, a conservatory, an enclosed lap pool, two separate guest houses, staff quarters, and a five-car garage. The designs of the house, landscape,

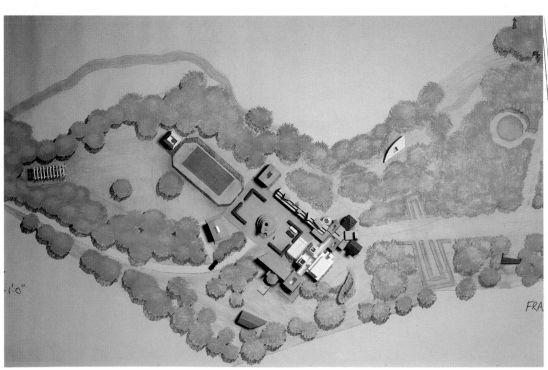

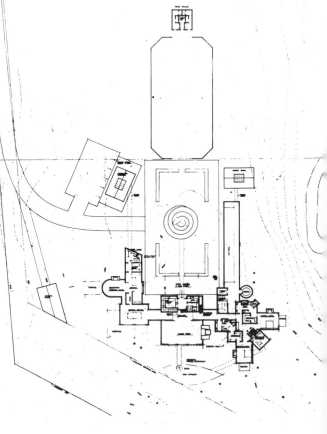

Study models of
second scheme.

Overleaf:
Sketches.

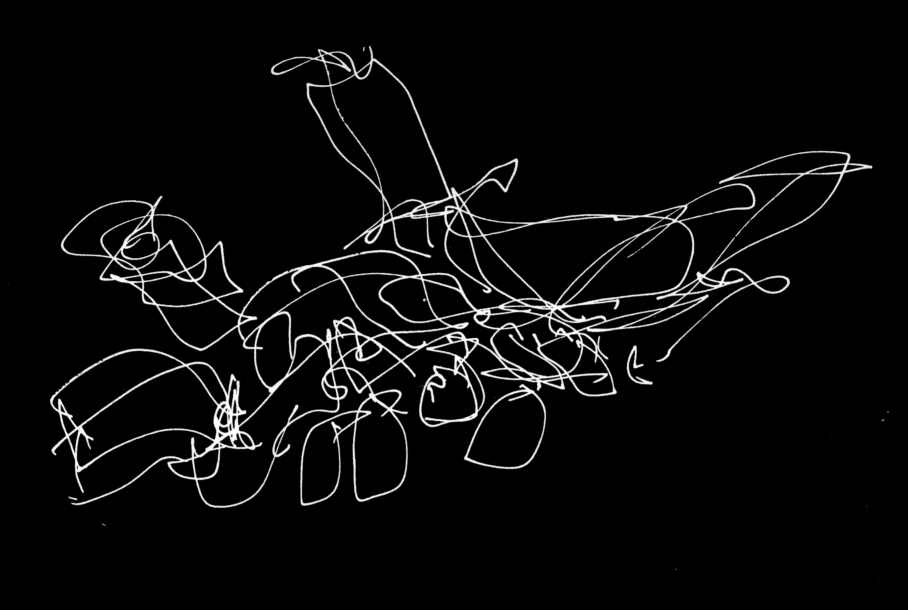

Models of second scheme.

438

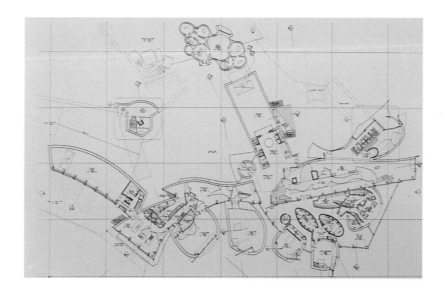
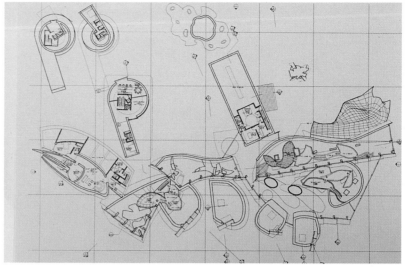

Plans and model
of final scheme.

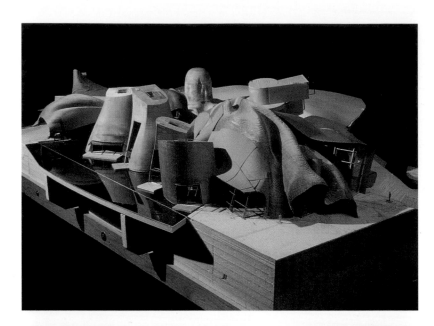

Models views
of final scheme.

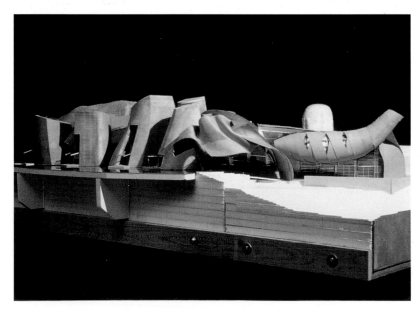

and surrounding sculptures were the result of a collaborative exploration of forms and ideas between Gehry, Philip Johnson, and several celebrated artists. Located on nine acres of woodland, the house was to be bounded by two large reflecting pools, bronze figures, steel plates, a tower, and a light-and-water sculpture. All were to play an integral role in the composition and form of the project. The resulting composition of complex forms and geometries was to be constructed from a variety of materials, including plaster, stone, metal, and glass. After six years of design and dozens of largely zoomorphic iterations, the project was ultimately canceled.

Details of interior
and exterior of model
of final scheme.

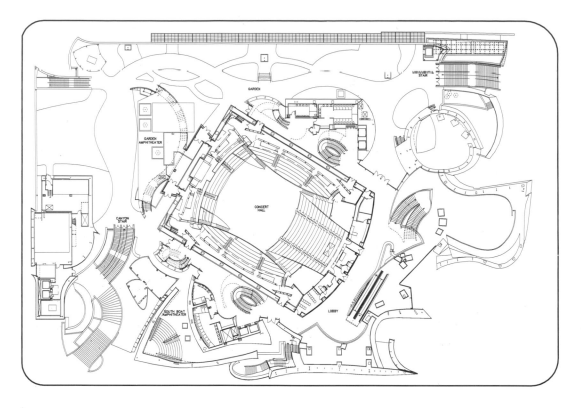

Garden-level plan;
aerial view of model.

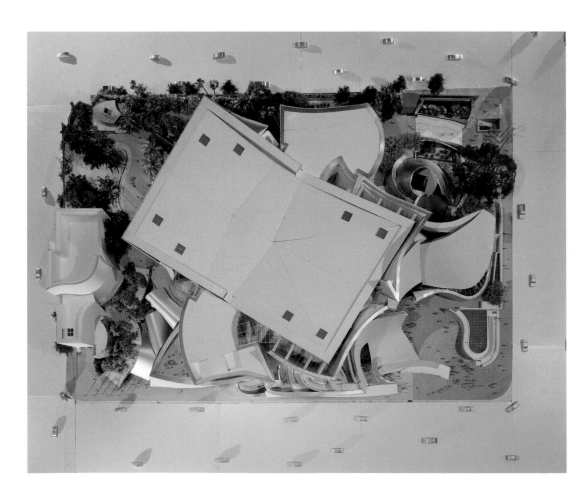

After the competition, significant changes in the program occurred. The chamber hall was eliminated and the size of the foyer reduced. Further design studies suggested a solution for the foyer that included a five-hundred-seat performance area to accommodate most of the objectives of the original program. A four-hundred-room hotel with a ballroom, meeting rooms, two restaurants, and retail shops was added to the program, leading to extensive design studies, and later eliminated for financial and scheduling reasons.

Most important to the long design process following the competition was establishing the hall's final acoustical parameters and resolving their resulting architectural expressions. The building committee visited the Boston Symphony, the Amsterdam Concertgebow, the Berlin Philharmonic, and Tokyo's Suntory Hall; Gehry's office built and studied scale models of each. Ultimately, Minoru Nagata, Suntory Hall's acoustician, was selected to consult on the final design. Nagata's input had radical repercussions for the interior architecture of the concert hall, which in turn shaped the final sculpture of the forms enclosing it.

The science of acoustics is inexact, with two prevailing architectural strategies for producing great sound: one calls for the curves of organic form, as seen in Hans Scharoun's Berlin concert hall; the other strives for the perfectly proportioned "shoe box," perhaps best approximated in Boston's Symphony Hall. Through his discussions with Nagata, Gehry adopted a third strategy, that of a modified shoe box. The modifications resulted from Nagata's observations that the concert hall's far corners, for example, were acoustically unnecessary, and could therefore open to skylights; that the ends of the box should incline upward, following the path traveled by the sounds of violins and violas; that convex surfaces disperse sound, shaping the billowing arc of the ceiling and the high bowed walls, known as the "starched collar," at the sides of the orchestra; and that balconies, acoustically problematic as well as socially divisive, could be eliminated. Perhaps as important as Gehry's discussions with Nagata were those with musicians and conductors. Esa-Pekka Salonen, Pierre Boulez, Zubin Mehta, Simon Rattle, and numerous Los Angeles Philharmonic musicians all articulated an important psychological factor that influences their performances: exalted space produces exalted musical ambitions.

Larger-scale models—specifically the orchestra platform configuration, the ceiling form, and

Sketch; study models.

Overleaf:
Elevation along First
Street; model view.

Second overleaf:
Elevation along Grand
Street; model view.

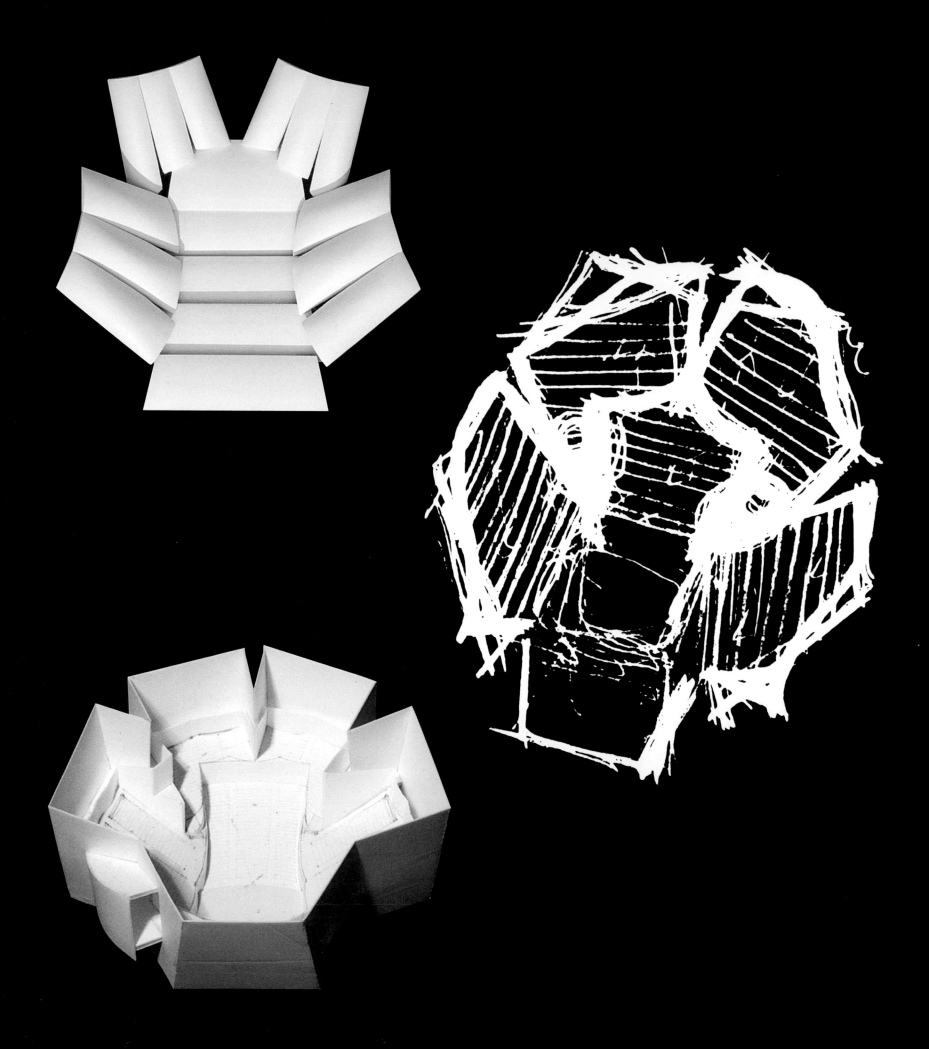

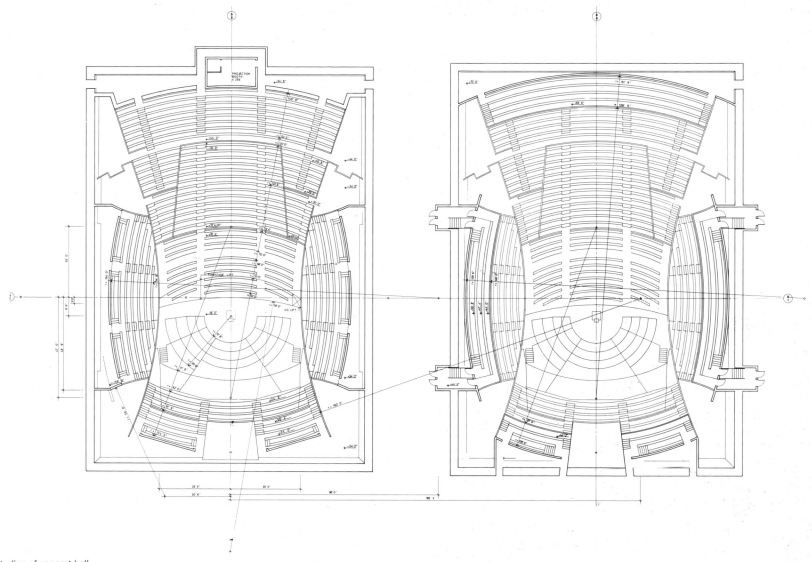

Studies of concert-hall
configuration; plans; views
of model toward audience
and balconies and toward
stage, with great central
organ.

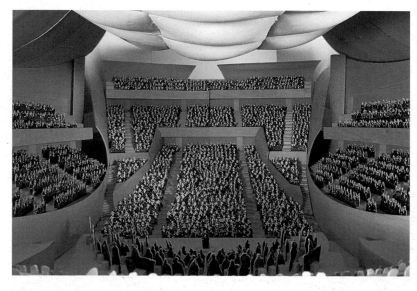

the pipe organ—were built to test the relation-ship of sound and space using laser and com-puter technology as well as the reactions of musicians and conductors. In the final design, Douglas fir seating blocks surround the orches-tra platform and, together with the sail-like ceil-ing forms, give the impression of a great ship within the plaster walls of the container. The pipe organ occupies a central position between seating blocks at the rear of the stage. Skylights and a large window at the back of the hall allow natural light to enhance daytime concerts.

The hall's interior architecture produced a form resembling a saddle from the outside. Gehry chose to repeat the saddle's peaks in tall, curving limestone "wrappers," leaving pockets and "saddlebags" between the exterior skin and the interior volumes. His approach in resolving the incongruity between the interior volumes and the exterior form—countering the asser-tion that the building is nothing more than a "decorated shed"—was to fill the spaces between the limestone wrapper and the shoe box inside with surprises: terraces, gardens, pre-concert gathering areas, and the café, gift shop, and Founder's Room all are located within the crevices and pavilions created by the limestone, titanium, and glass pockets. Two larger "saddle-bags" at the side contain elevators, stairways, and restrooms. The intention was to craft a festive and alluring vessel that cannot be understood, or experienced fully, from a single point of view. Not so much a singular culture palace with a front entrance and a back-of-house, the building can be seen as a terraced geological outcropping on which the city might picnic.

The majority of the site will be devoted to gardens, accessible not only from the hall but from adjacent streets, providing an oasis within the surrounding urban environment. An entry plaza will be located at the corner of First and Grand to relate to the existing Music Center, with a secondary entry plaza located at the cor-ner of Second and Grand to provide primary access to the gardens. Unlike most concert halls, the building lobby will be dispersed along the street and will remain open during the day. Large, operable glass panels will provide maxi-mum accessibility to various amenities, includ-ing a gift shop, a restaurant, a museum of Phil-harmonic and Walt Disney memorabilia, the underground parking garage, and a preconcert amphitheater. The amphitheater area is to be used for performance-related lectures, educa-tional programs, and other scheduled and impromptu performances throughout the day.

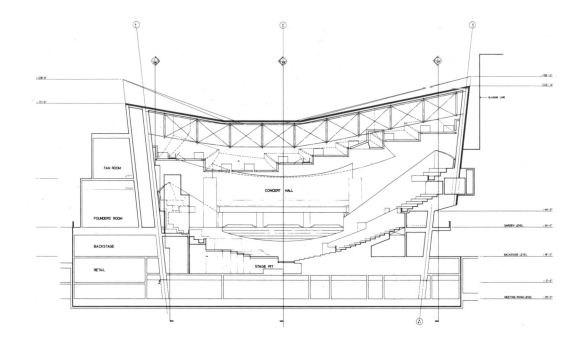

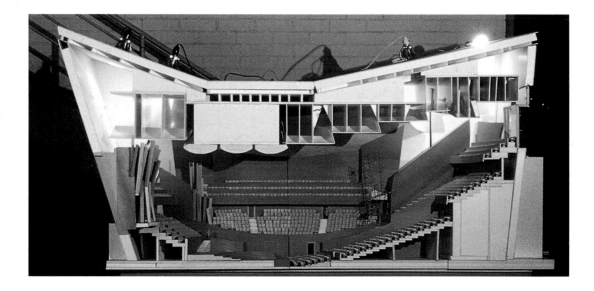

Section; model section through concert hall; views of concert-hall model with cloth ceiling over orchestra.

Chiat/Day New York Offices
New York, New York
1990 (project)

Client: Chiat/Day/Mojo, Inc. Advertising
Program: Office lobby remodel
Project Team: Frank O. Gehry, Victoria Jenkins

Study models.

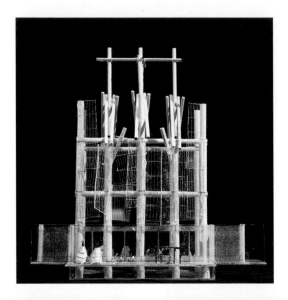

Frederick R. Weisman Art and Teaching Museum
Minneapolis, Minnesota
1990–93

Sketch; plan at museum level.

Client: University of Minnesota
Program: Exhibition galleries, auditorium, sales shop, rental gallery, print study room, administrative offices, frame shop, carpentry shop, storage
Budget: $10,500,000
Area: 41,000 square feet
Materials: Concrete, steel frame, brick, painted and mill-finish stainless-steel panels
Project Team: Frank O. Gehry, Robert G. Hale, Edwin Chan, Victoria Jenkins, Matt Fineout, David Gastrau, Richard Rosa; Meyer, Scherer & Rockcastle, associate architect; Ericksen, Ellison & Associates, mechanical and electrical engineer; Meyer, Borgman & Johnson, Inc., structural engineer; Progressive Consulting Engineers, civil engineer; Pha Lighting Design Inc., lighting consultant; Lam Partners, opening exhibition lighting; Damon Farber & Associates, Inc., landscape architect; Strgar-Roscoe-Fausch, Inc., transportation/parking engineer; Ted Jage and Associates, cost consultant; Jack Lindeman, specification consultant

For a site on a bluff overlooking the Mississippi River, Gehry designed his first all-new art museum. Located at the western edge of the University of Minnesota's core, the building connects the campus with the skyline of downtown Minneapolis. A four-story brick box was inserted into the context of the university's classical mall, its program distributed to accommodate dual access to the site: cars approach from the east and enter a 120-car parking garage below grade, while pedestrians, including some of the ten thousand students who walk by the site each day, enter from a walkway on the north side that connects the Washington Avenue Bridge with Coffman Memorial Plaza.

On the lowest level are the freight elevator, art storage spaces, a frame shop, and mechanical and electrical rooms. The next level is occupied by a carpentry shop and general storage, accessible from the freight and passenger elevators as well as from the intermediate parking levels. The top level of the museum houses administrative offices and the mechanical and electrical space for the galleries.

On the main museum level, the gallery spaces, including the Weisman Collection, are large, rectilinear spaces in the southeast corner, lit by a combination of halogen lamps and sunlight from three sculptural skylights floating above partition walls and massive, partially exposed trusses. Adjacent to the galleries is a 1,500-square-foot black-box auditorium. Large sliding doors on its west wall enable the auditorium to open to the surrounding lobby, which wraps continuously around the north, west, and south, providing an internal "street" from which to glimpse the galleries as well as the Mississippi. The sales shop, rental gallery, registrar, and print study room are also located on this level, with frontage along the pedestrian bridge. Oversize picture windows provide with views into these spaces through the interior street to the galleries beyond. The main level can be secured to operate independently from the rest of the building for special receptions and events.

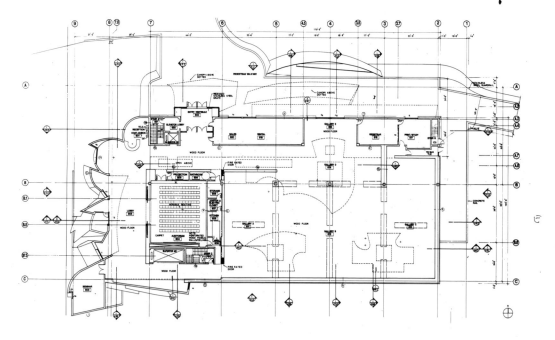

455

North elevation;
view from north.

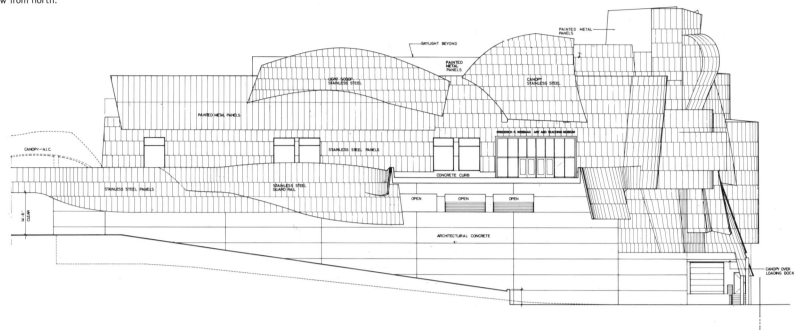

Exterior; construction
details; elevations
of pedestrian bridge.

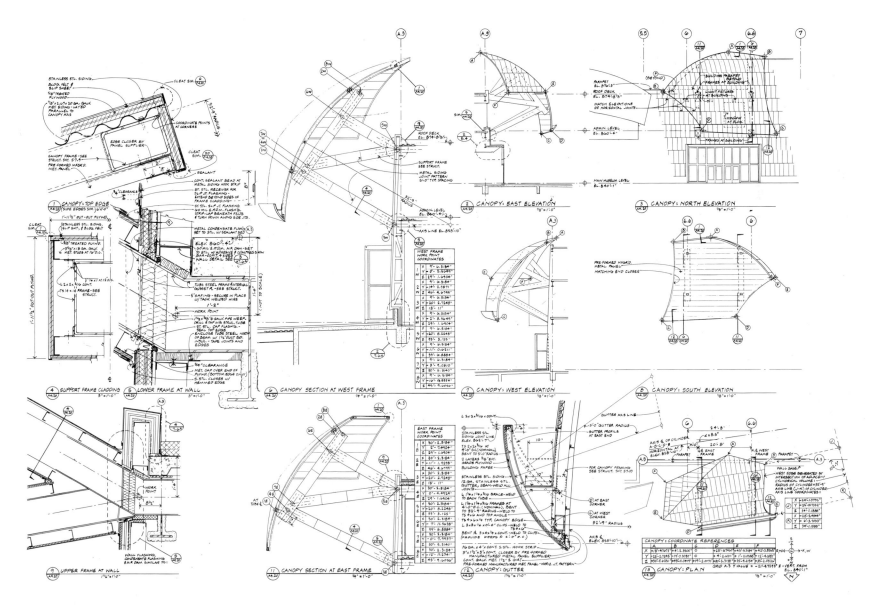

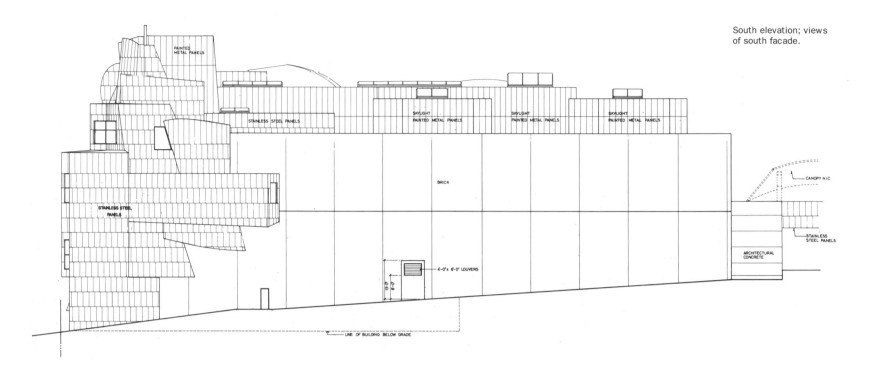

South elevation; views
of south facade.

PAINTED
METAL PANELS

STAINLESS STEEL PANELS   SKYLIGHT   SKYLIGHT   SKYLIGHT
PAINTED METAL PANELS   PAINTED METAL PANELS   PAINTED METAL PANELS

STAINLESS STEEL
PANELS

BRICK

CANOPY N.I.C.

STAINLESS
STEEL PANELS

ARCHITECTURAL
CONCRETE

4'-0" x 6'-0" LOUVERS

LINE OF BUILDING BELOW GRADE

The most startling element of the otherwise straightforward building is its west facade. A cubist composition of sliced cylinders and cones rises one hundred feet above the riverbank, reflecting the changing light and the river from its rippled, mill-finished stainless-steel skin. Ribbons of stainless steel, some mill finished and some painted, extend laterally along the north facade, wrapping the walkway and entry. Only the interiors of the director's and the curator's offices at the southwest and northwest corner towers correspond to the exterior forms; otherwise the west facade is essentially a decorative, sculptural application on the rectilinear form behind.

For the museum's opening, Gehry was asked to curate a show entitled "A New View: The Architect's Eye." Gehry selected a sampling of work, primarily from the 1960s and early 1970s, that included pieces by Billy Al Bengston, Ron Davis, Donald Judd, Ed Moses, Claes Oldenburg, and Frank Stella, paying tribute to and drawing connections between artists whose work has informed and shaped some of Gehry's own explorations of ordinary materials, popular imagery, and minimalist sculpture.

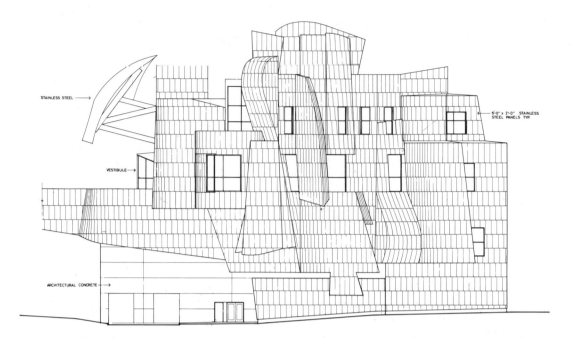

West elevation;
west facade;
detail of cladding.

Exhibition room.

Bonames Housing Project
Frankfurt, Germany
1991

Client: Bonames City Planning Department
Program: Residential development master plan including housing, schools, retail, park, and community center
Project Team: Frank O. Gehry, David Denton, Robert G. Hale, Randall Stout, Eva Sobesky

Griesheim (Lancia Study)
Frankfurt, Germany
1991

Client: City of Frankfurt
Program: Urban redevelopment study
Project Team: Frank O. Gehry, David Denton, Robert G. Hale, James M. Glymph

Model view.

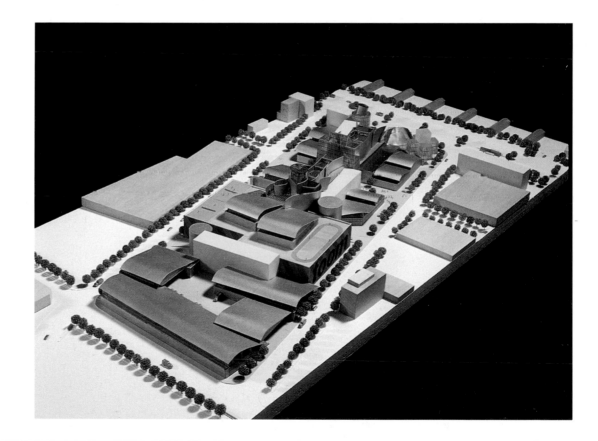

Parc del Delta
Barcelona, Spain
1991 (project)

Client: Travelstead Group
Program: Master plan for hotel and entertainment development
Project Team: Frank O. Gehry, David Denton, James M. Glymph, Doug Hanson, Tomaso Bradshaw

**The Walt Disney Concert Hall
Design Process
Venice Biennale, Venice, Italy
1991**

Client: La Biennale di Venezia
Program: Exhibition design and installation
Project Team: Frank O. Gehry, Michael Maltzan,
Randall Stout

Views of installation.

**Los Angeles Rapid Transit
District Headquarters
Competition
Gateway Center, Union Station,
Los Angeles, California
1991 (project)**

Client: Catellus Development Corporation and
Southern California Rapid Transit District
Program: Office tower including RTD offices,
child care, retail, transit police station, cafeteria,
and special functions spaces
Budget: $120,000,000
Area: 595,000 square feet

Materials: Steel frame, concrete, glass, sheet
metal
Project Team: Frank O. Gehry, David Denton,
Randall Stout, Edwin Chan, Christopher
Joseph Bonura, Jon Drezner, Michael Resnic,
Dane Twitchell, Craig Webb, Gretchen Werner,
Brian Yoo

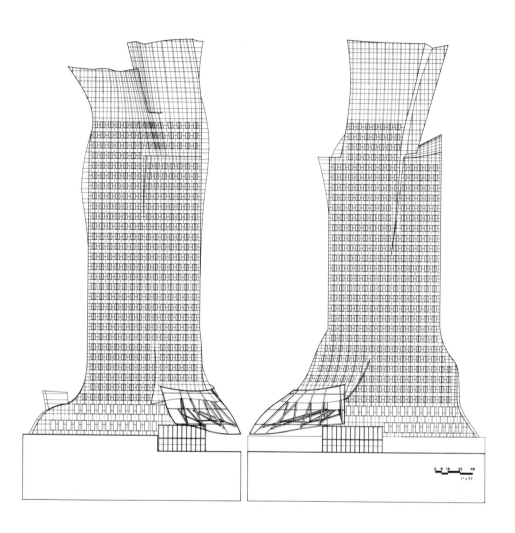

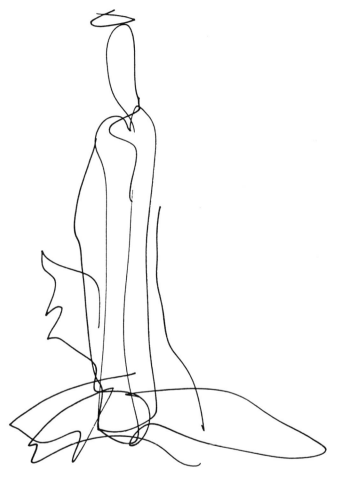

West and south
elevations; sketch; plan at
atrium level; plan at
public-access level; typical
office-floor plan.

Views of site model;
tower study model.

**Hannover Bus Stop
Hannover, Germany
1991–94**

Client: Stiftung Niedersachsen, Foundation of Lower Saxony, represented by Peter Ruthenburg
Program: Public bus shelter
Budget: $170,000
Area: 300 square feet
Materials: Galvanized steel frame, stainless-steel panels, glass
Project Team: Frank O. Gehry, James M. Glymph, Randall Stout, Mara Dworsky, David Reddy, Eva Sobesky, Tami Wedekind, Tim Williams; Leonhardt Schirmer Meyer, associated architect; Permasteelisa, fabrication

Model view; exterior.

Views from south; section through exhibition gallery; section through garage; sketches.

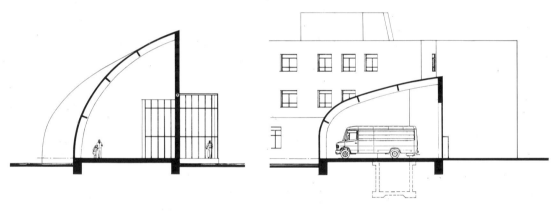

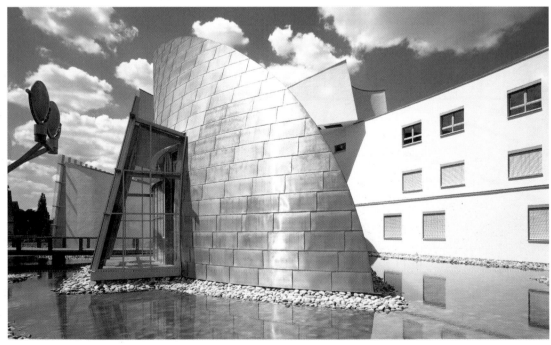

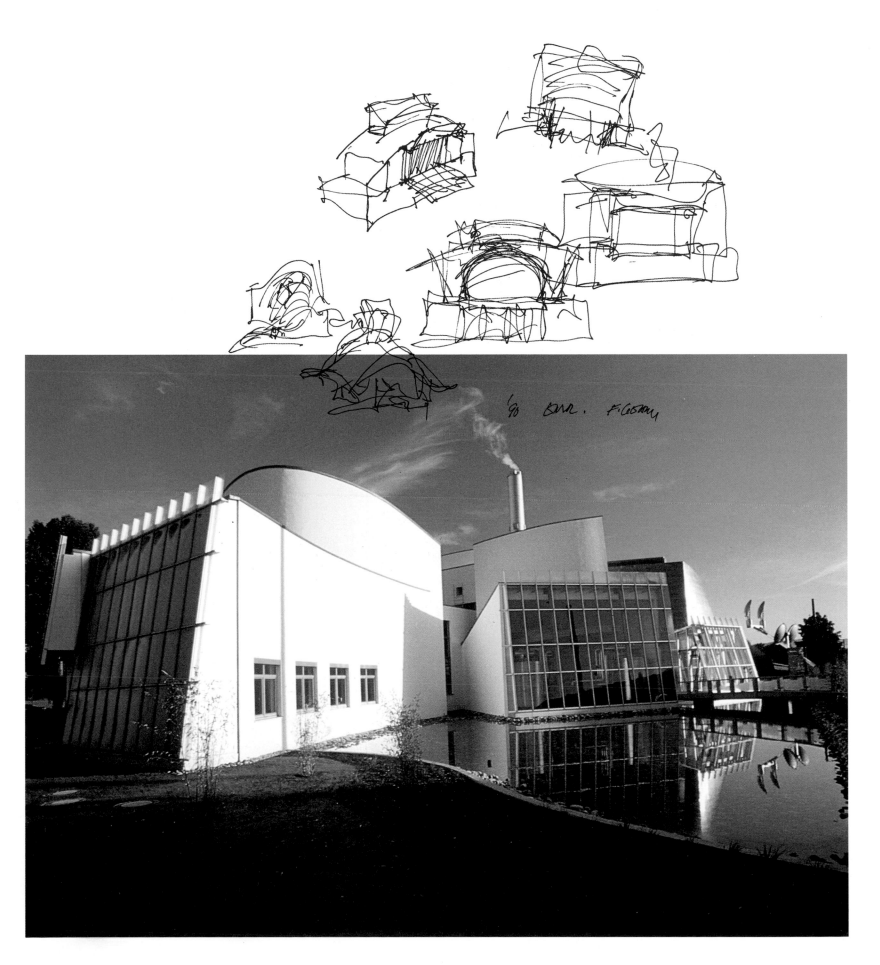

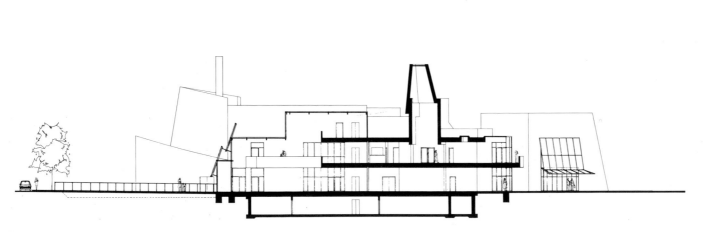

Sections; view from
north; view from west.

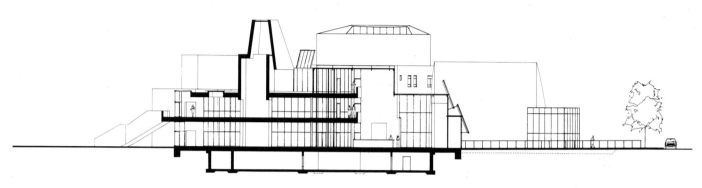

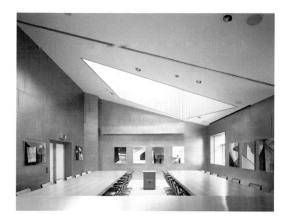

and Dehmer Strasse to the south and east. West of the site is an industrial warehouse area planned for conversion to a new retail and commercial complex. To the north of the site is a greenbelt along the Werre River. Further north is rural housing and farmland along the foothills of the Wiehew Mountains. Located on a prominent entry road into Bad Öynhausen, the building was conceived as a gateway to the community.

The organization of the building program responds to the urban context of the Mindener Strasse frontage. The office and technical facilities were placed in a linear building along the street, creating an urban edge while forming garden spaces on the north and west sides of the building. The office portion of the linear building occupies three levels. The technical facilities containing the network control center for regional power distribution occupy two levels. At the center of the linear building is an atrium containing entry, reception, and circulation. Other major building components, of a size and shape responding to urban conditions, are accessible from the atrium. Directly attached on the southeast is a hall for an exhibition about renewable resources, energy conservation, and new technologies. Also attached on the southeast is an energy center housing state-of-the-art mechanical equipment. These components are visible from the atrium and from the street and neighborhood. On the north side of the atrium, corridors lead to a two-level pavilion housing an employee dining facility and conference center. In addition to the exhibit hall, the building itself is planned to demonstrate energy technologies and systems appropriate to this building type. The office wing utilizes daylighting, natural ventilation, and thermal cycles. The technical wing, which has continuous occupancy, incorporates a thermal storage wall on the south facade, as does the exhibit center.

Roof forms integrate photovoltaic cells for supplementary power production, as well as solar collectors for hot-water use in the kitchen facility. A solar air heater is also planned, to preheat air entering the mechanical system.

The building exterior integrates the energy systems and existing context through forms clad with plaster, metal panels, and glass. A garden setting, opening toward the river and mountains to the north, enhances the site from the Mindener Strasse approach. An additional pedestrian entry located on the south side of the atrium consists of a bridge crossing a lake built to retain surface-water runoff.

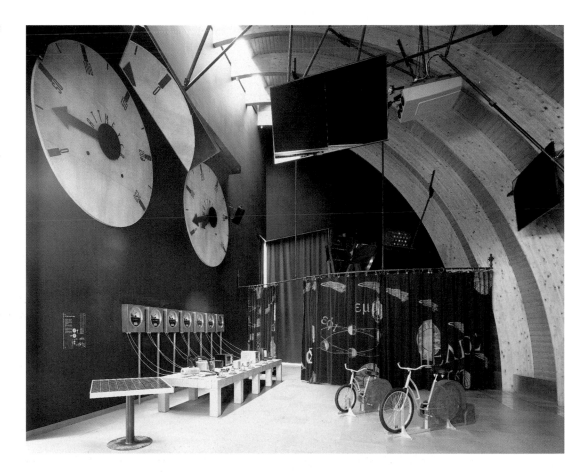

Goldstein Housing Project
Frankfurt, Germany
1991–96

Client: Nassauische Heimstatte
Program: 162-unit public housing
Budget: $23,000,000
Area: 110,000 square feet
Materials: Masonry, zinc panels, colored plaster
Project Team: Frank O. Gehry, James M. Glymph, Randall Stout, Michael Maltzan, Tomaso Bradshaw, Jonathan Davis, David Denton, Mara Dworsky, Robert G. Hale, Michael Resnic, Matthias Seufert, Eva Sobesky, Hiroshi Tokumaru, Keith Wiley, Tim Williams; Nassauische Heimstatte, associate architect; Andreas Varnai, retail space architect; Hanna/Olin, landscape design; Corinna Endress, BWN&P, executive landscape architect

On a parcel of land approximately five miles west of downtown Frankfurt, the Goldstein Housing Project is situated between an existing park to the south, Frankfurt's forested greenbelt to the north, existing public housing to the west, and transportation lines to the east. As the last undeveloped public housing tract in the area, the project integrates and connects the new housing with old, as well as with sports fields, transportation lines, and schools. The site strategy of the 162-unit housing complex was organized around the two principal axes, each given its own distinct landscaping identity. The meandering north-south recreational path is dense with trees, seating, and play areas, while the east-west transportation path is a linear grid of hardscape, accommodating frequent bicycle travel. A tree-lined stream cuts through the north courtyard. As the path enters the south courtyard, it splits to reveal a theater-shaped space with perimeter seating areas and a sloped grass floor oriented toward the greenbelt.

In contrast to the modernist housing that surrounds the eleven-acre site, Gehry's low-rise masonry buildings are arranged in irregular L-shapes around paths, terraces, and private gardens. Buildings are individualized with boldly colored plaster facades in red, white, and yellow. Zinc-covered stairs, balconies, and penthouse gardens modulate facade surfaces and break down the scale. Apartments, ranging from studios to four-bedrooms, are sited for maximum sunshine and views to the parks and landscaped courtyards.

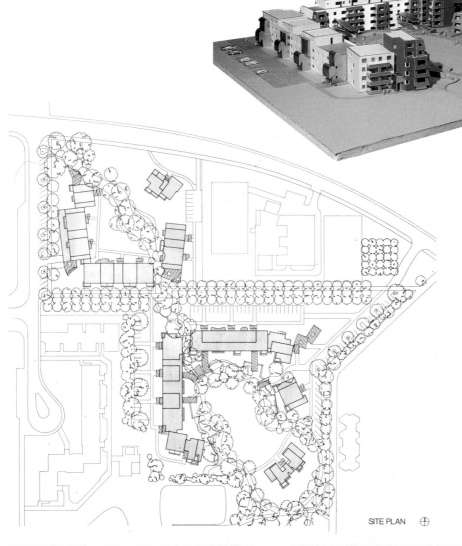

SITE PLAN

Model of a courtyard; site plan; models of two buildings.

**Guggenheim Museum
Bilbao, Spain
1991–97**

Client: Consorcio del Proyecto Guggenheim
(Basque Country Administration) and
Solomon R. Guggenheim Foundation
Program: Museum of contemporary art,
including permanent collection and temporary
exhibition spaces, administrative offices, three-
hundred-seat auditorium, restaurant, retail,
public plaza and water garden
Budget: 10,859 million pesetas
Area: 265,000 square feet

Sketch; approach to
museum from south.

Model view; site plan.

Overleaf:
Exterior views; sketch.

Materials: Concrete, steel, Spanish limestone, titanium, glass

Project Team: Frank O. Gehry, Randy Jefferson, Vano Haritunians, Douglas Hanson, Edwin Chan, Robert G. Hale, Rich Barrett, Karl Blette, Tomaso Bradshaw, Steve Butts, Padraic Cassidy, Naomi Ehrenpreis, Matt Fineout, Doug Giesey, Dave Hardie, Michael Hootman, Grzegorz Kosmal, Mark Lefitz, Sara MacDonald, Mehran Mashayekh, Patricia McCaul, Chris Mercier, George Metzger, Brent Miller, David Reddy, Marc Salette, Charles Sanchez, Eva Sobesky, Derek Soltes, Todd Spiegel, Tom Stallman, Jeff Wauer, Tami Wedekind, Josh White, Kristin Woehl; IDOM, Bilbao, associate architect and engineer; Skidmore, Owings & Merrill, Chicago, structural engineer; Cosentini Associates, New York, mechanical engineer; Lam Partners, Boston, lighting consultant

The Guggenheim Museum in Bilbao, completed in 1997, is the result of a collaboration between the Basque Country Administration, which finances and owns the project, and the Solomon R. Guggenheim Foundation, which will operate the museum and provide the core art collection. The museum represents the first step in the redevelopment of the former trade and warehouse district along the south bank of the Nervion River. Directly accessible from the business and historic districts of the city, the museum marks the center of a cultural triangle formed by the Museo de Bellas Artes, the university, and the Old Town Hall. The Puente de la Salve Bridge, which connects the nineteenth-century city center with outlying areas, passes over the site at its eastern edge, transforming the museum into a gateway to the city.

A public plaza located at the entrance of the museum encourages pedestrian traffic between the Guggenheim and the Museo de Bellas Artes, and between the old city and the riverfront. Public facilities, including a three-hundred-seat auditorium, a restaurant, and retail spaces, are accessible from the main public plaza as well as from within the museum itself. This dual access enables the spaces to operate

483

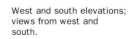
West and south elevations;
views from west and
south.

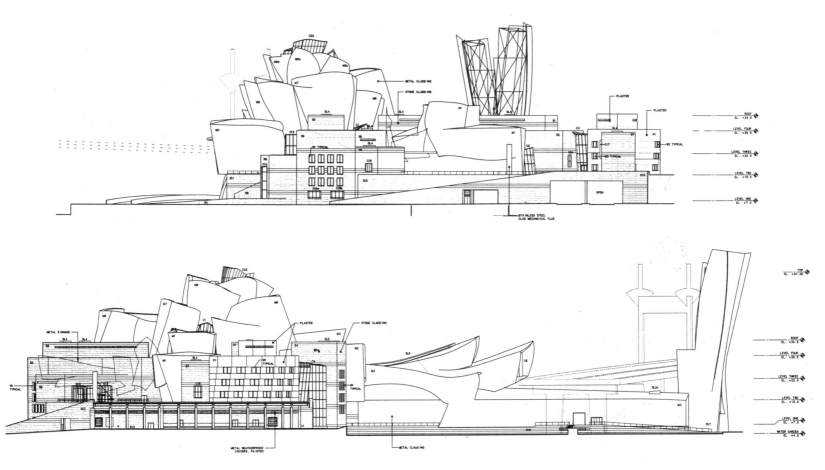

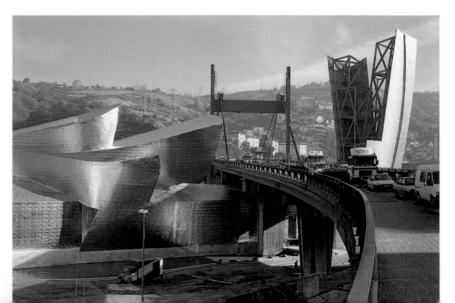

East elevation;
views from east.

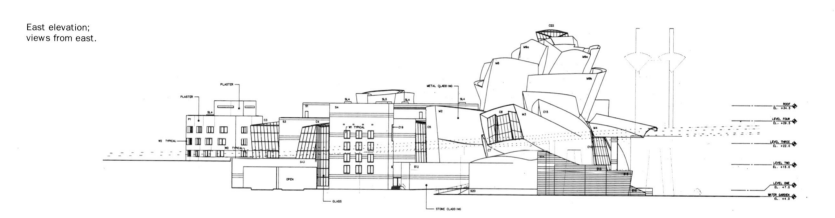

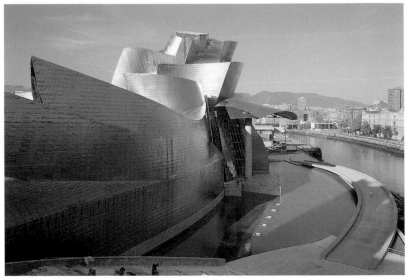

North elevation;
views from north.

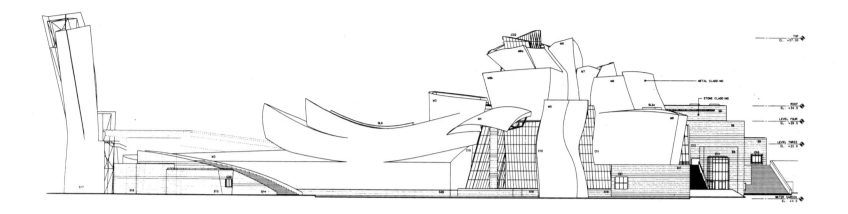

Computer drawings;
details of cladding.

Overleaf:
Cladding detail.

488

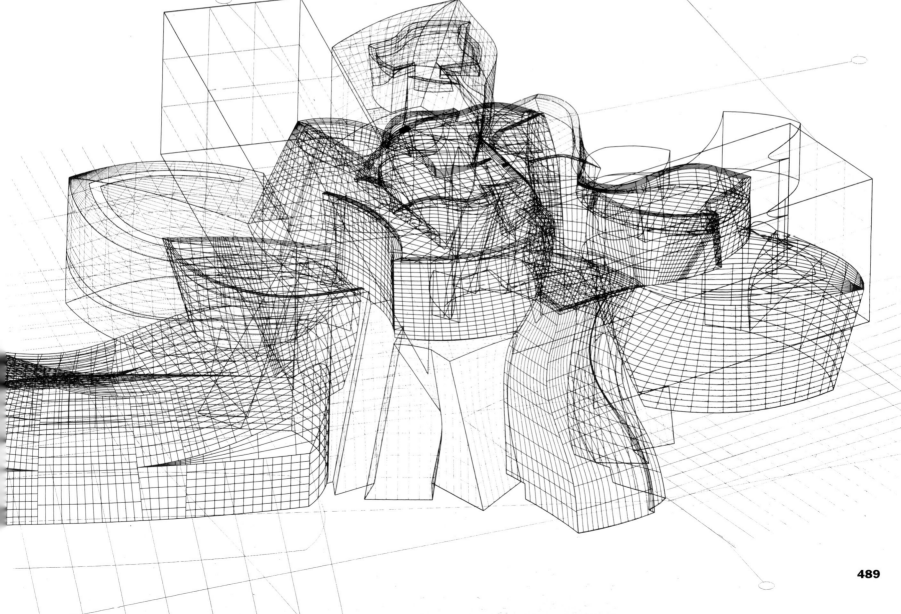

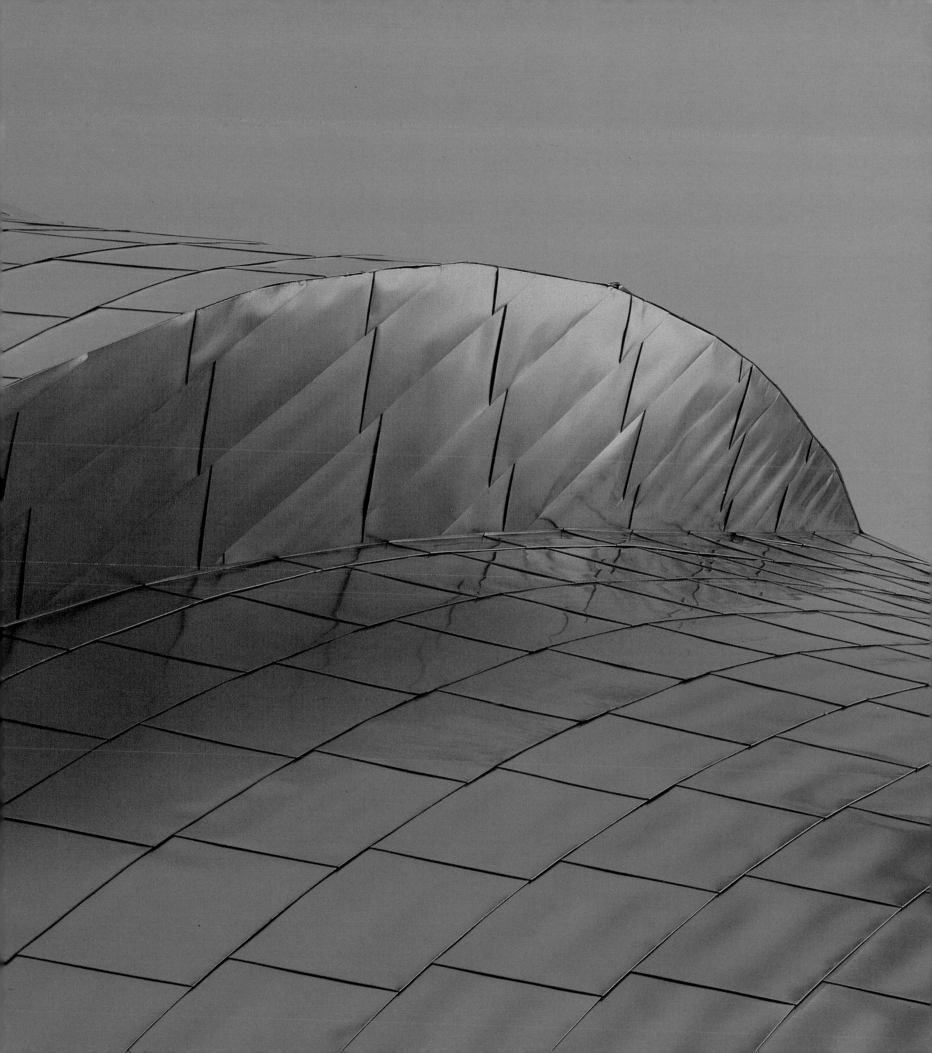

Interiors.

independently from the museum, allowing them to play an integral part in the urban life of Bilbao.

The main entrance to the museum is through a large central atrium, where a system of curvilinear bridges, glass elevators, and stair towers connects the exhibition galleries concentrically on three levels. A sculptural roof form rises from the central atrium, flooding it with light through glazed openings. The scale of the central atrium, rising more than 150 feet above the river, is an invitation to monumental site-specific installations and special museum events.

The Guggenheim Foundation required gallery spaces to exhibit a permanent collection, a temporary collection, and a collection of selected living artists; in response, three distinct types of exhibition space were designed. The galleries for the exhibition of the permanent collection are relatively conservative in design. This collection is housed in two sets of three consecutive square galleries stacked on the second and third levels of the museum. The temporary collection is housed in a more dramatic, elongated rectangular space that extends to the east. This space passes underneath the Puente de la Salve Bridge and terminates in a tower on its far side, integrating the bridge into the overall composition of the museum. The interior of the space is entirely free of support columns, permitting the museum to stage large-scale art installations that would otherwise not be feasible. The exhibition of the work of selected living artists is housed in a series of eleven distinct galleries, each of unique spatial quality and generous ceiling height. Back-of-house functions, such as loading, art staging, storage, and conservation, are housed in the lower level of the museum.

The major exterior material on the rectangular buildings of the museum is Spanish limestone, while the more sculptural shapes of the building are clad in titanium panels. The interior walls of the galleries are a smooth-finish plaster. Large, glazed curtain walls open to views of the river and surrounding city. Mechanical systems maintain a strict temperature and humidity control. The galleries for the permanent collection are lit by direct exhibition lights with a flush-mounted power system, while the galleries for the temporary collection and for the living-artists collection are lit by a theatrical catwalk-mounted lighting system. In addition, custom-designed wall-wash fixtures create an even illumination of ten to twenty footcandles at eye level in all the galleries. Natural light is

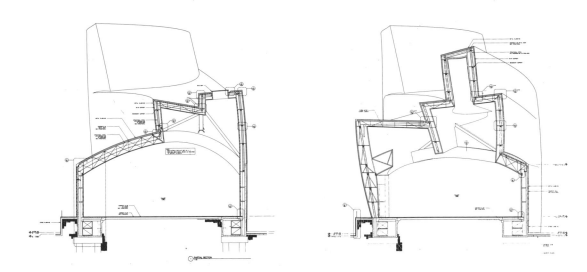

introduced through skylights with supplemental blackout shades for daylight control.

The 256,000-square-foot, one-hundred-million-dollar project is one of many redevelopment projects the Basque city is undertaking to commemorate its seven-hundredth birthday, in the year 2000. Other projects include a footbridge over the river by Santiago Calatrava, new metro stations by Sir Norman Foster, a transportation hub by Michael Wilford and Partners, a new airport terminal by Calatrava, and a master plan of the city's business district by Cesar Pelli.

Model of an exhibition
room; partial sections with
construction details,
gallery; exhibition room.

Overleaf:
Views up to glazed
atrium roof.

Degenerate Art: The Fate of the Avant-Garde in Nazi Germany
Los Angeles, California, and Berlin, Germany
1992

Client: Los Angeles County Museum of Art
Program: Exhibition design and installation
Materials: Douglas fir, drywall
Project Team: Frank O. Gehry

Views of installation in Los Angeles.

**Metal Crafts Building
University of Toledo,
Toledo, Ohio
1992–94**

Client: University of Toledo
Program: Departments of sculpture and
metalsmithing, including workshops, tool
storage, forges, woodshop, and staff offices
Budget: $900,000
Area: 7,000 square feet
Materials: Precast concrete, steel, wolmanized
telephone-pole columns, translucent
corrugated-acrylic roofing, sheet metals
Project Team: Frank O. Gehry, James M.
Glymph, Randall Stout, Michael Maltzan,
Tomaso Bradshaw; Collaborative, Inc. executive
architect; Ruddolph/Libbe, Inc., construction
manager

Model view;
exterior; interior.

Children's Museum
Boston, Massachusetts
1992–96

Site plan.

Client: The Children's Museum
Program: Renovation of and addition to
existing children's museum, including improved
entry, expanded indoor and outdoor exhibition
spaces
Budget: $7,500,000
Area: Barge and bridge: 7,400 square feet;
Wave: 5,900 square feet; interior renovation:
10,900 square feet
Materials: Concrete and steel frame, stainless
steel, glass
Project Team: Frank O. Gehry, Randy Jefferson,
Edwin Chan, Robert G. Hale, Jonathan Davis,
David Gastrau, Michael Gale, Patricia McCaul,
Bruce Biesman Simons, Lisa Towning, Kristin

Woehl, Philip Rowe; Schwartz/Silver
Architects, Inc., executive architect; Boston
Building Consultants, structural consultant;
T.M.P. Consulting Engineers, Inc., mechanical
engineer; Lottero & Mason Associates, Inc.,
electrical engineer; Childs Engineering Corp.,
marine engineer; Barr & Barr Builders, Inc.,
preconstruction services

This project entailed the expansion of an
existing brick warehouse building occupied by
both the Children's Museum and a separate
entity, the Computer Museum, located across
from Boston's financial district on the Four
Point Channel off Boston's Inner Harbor. The

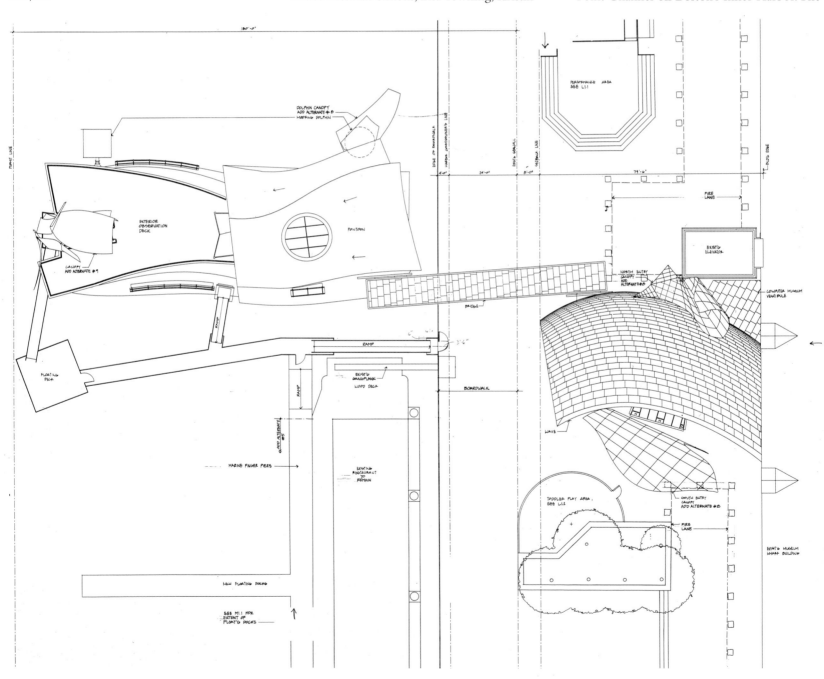

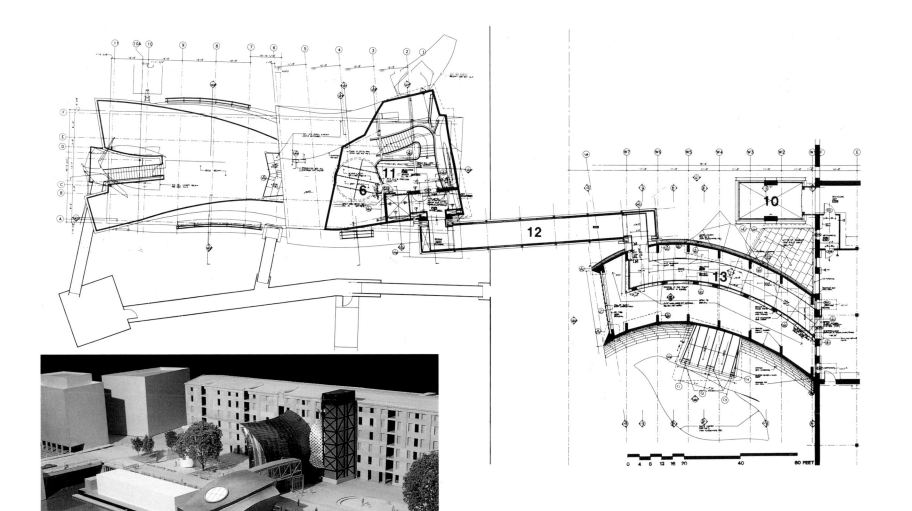

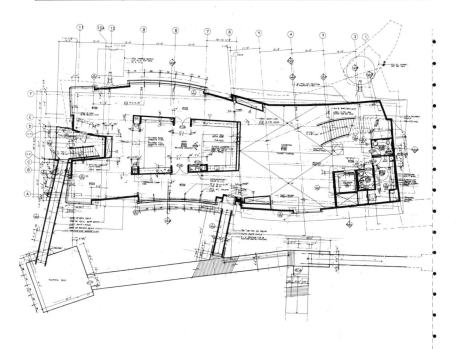

Bridge-level plan;
lower-level plan;
model views.

Sketch; section
through barge.

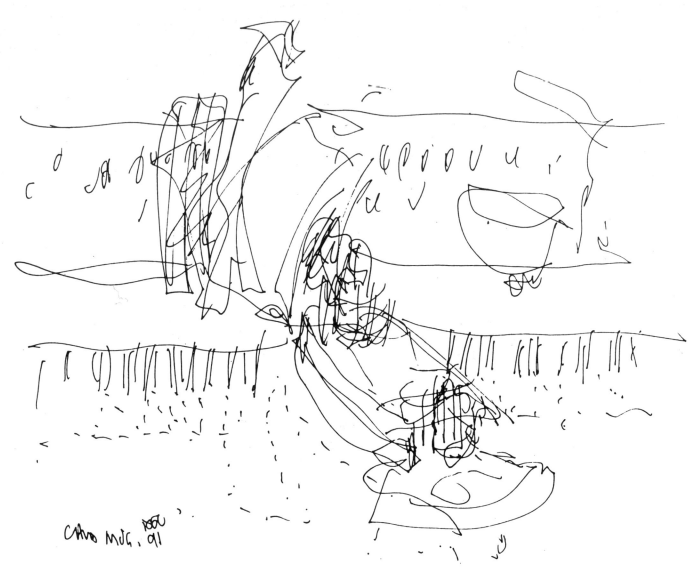

CARO MUG, DOU '91

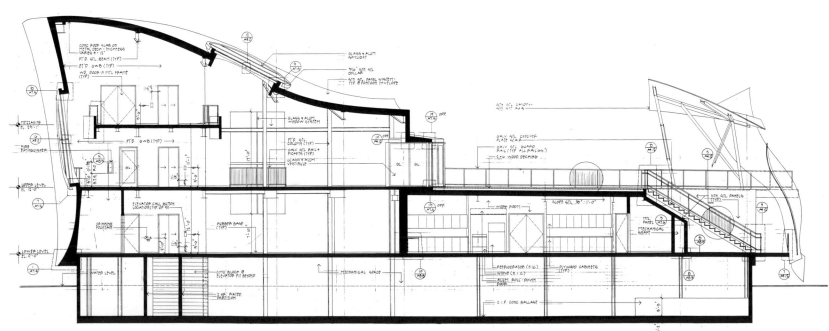

Model seen from canal.

expansion program of the Children's Museum required a new lobby entry sequence with a greater presence on the boardwalk. In response to the clients' desire to expand the focus of the exhibits to include the waterfront environment, Gehry proposed floating exhibition spaces on the water connected to the boardwalk by an articulated bridge that would accommodate the large tidal surge in the channel. The architectural intervention consists of a floating barge structure, a hinged bridge, and a "wave" form composed against the long brick facade of the existing building.

The new lobby functions as a shared entrance for the two museums, and the existing lobby has been reworked to accommodate the revised circulation requirements. A large glass window fronts the boardwalk, focusing views past the barge to the city skyline beyond. The upper balcony and the ramped gallery, joining the articulated bridge to the existing second

floor, activate the space within the wavelike, heavy timbered structure. The wave form is clad in natural copper panels that are intended to patinate over time. Connecting to the second floor of the wave, the glass and steel-framed bridge takes visitors across the boardwalk to the mezzanine level of the floating exhibit spaces.

The urban waterfront context inspired the development of both interior and exterior spaces, and Gehry emphasized interaction, observation, and experimentation. A free-form climbing structure, the *Cloud Climb*, rises past a south-facing window to the mezzanine level and up to a large circular skylight in the undulating roof above. At the prow of the barge, large windows allow the visitor to observe and control experiments in the Four Point Channel. Above this space, the exterior observation deck with its flowing stair canopy brings the visitor outside to the channel. The barge is constructed of stainless-steel-clad sculptural forms framed in

steel and concrete built on a floating pontoon.

At a smaller scale, solid and woven free-form sheet-metal canopies, such as the one at the barge prow, signify distinct areas of the museum. One of the canopies fronts the wave, allowing entry under its crest. The other wave canopy engages the existing steel-frame-and-glass elevator marking the internal entrance to the Computer Museum.

To document the sculptural geometries of the project, various methods were used. The complex surfaces and forms were modeled in the CATIA computer program and then transferred into AutoCad for use by the project's executive architect. The more regular forms were shaped in AutoSurf, and the wave was rigorously controlled by traditional hand-calculated, circular geometries. These differing descriptive systems each eventually returned the dimensional information to standard architectural drawing format.

Nationale-Nederlanden Building
Prague, Czech Republic
1992–96

Client: Nationale-Nederlanden/International Netherlands Group, represented by Yan Scheere, Paul Koch
Program: Office building with conference rooms, café-bar, restaurant
Budget: $9,000,000
Area: 58,000 square feet
Materials: Steel, glass, precast concrete with plaster finish

Project Team: Frank O. Gehry, James M. Glymph, Marc Salette, Edwin Chan, Douglas Giesey, Masis Mesropian, Eva Sobesky, Thomas Stallman, Lisa Towning, Philip Rowe, Kristen Woehl; Studio Vlado Milunić, collaborating architect; Kappa, S.R.O., executive architect; Atipa, S.R.O., engineering; Les Entreprises SBBM, Six Construction SA, general contractor; Permasteelisa, curtain-wall contractor; Croon, services contractor

Located along the Vltava River, within walking distance of the National Theater and other prominent cultural facilities, the site for the Nationale-Nederlanden Building is one of only three in the historic district of central Prague on which new construction has been permitted. On the ground level of the building, directly accessible from the riverfront and from the public square opposite, sits a café and shops. Offices occupy the second through seventh floors, and a restaurant on the top level takes full advantage of the view of Prague's skyline and the nearby castle.

Known within Gehry's office as the Wave, the principal facade, overlooking the riverbank, extends the scale and rhythms of the adjacent rowhouses. Its staggered windows and horizontal striations gradually break into a pattern of undulating cornice lines. As the building turns the corner, two towers, one a solid cylindrical volume, the other a tapering glass tower, are supported by a number of sculptural columns,

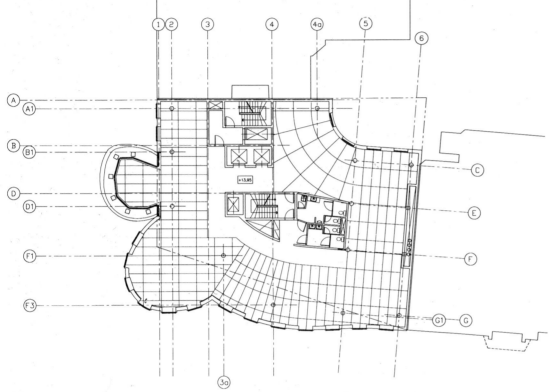

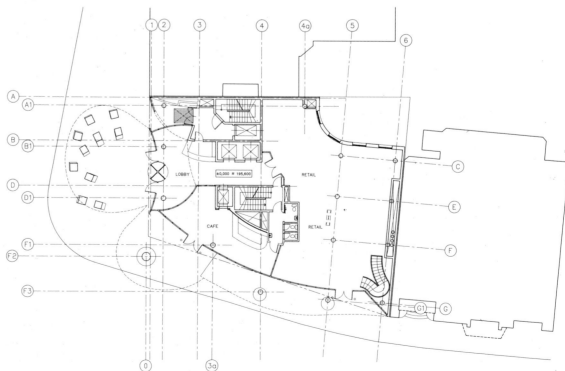

Ground- and fifth-floor plans.

Opposite:
Computer rendering; sketch; model view.

504

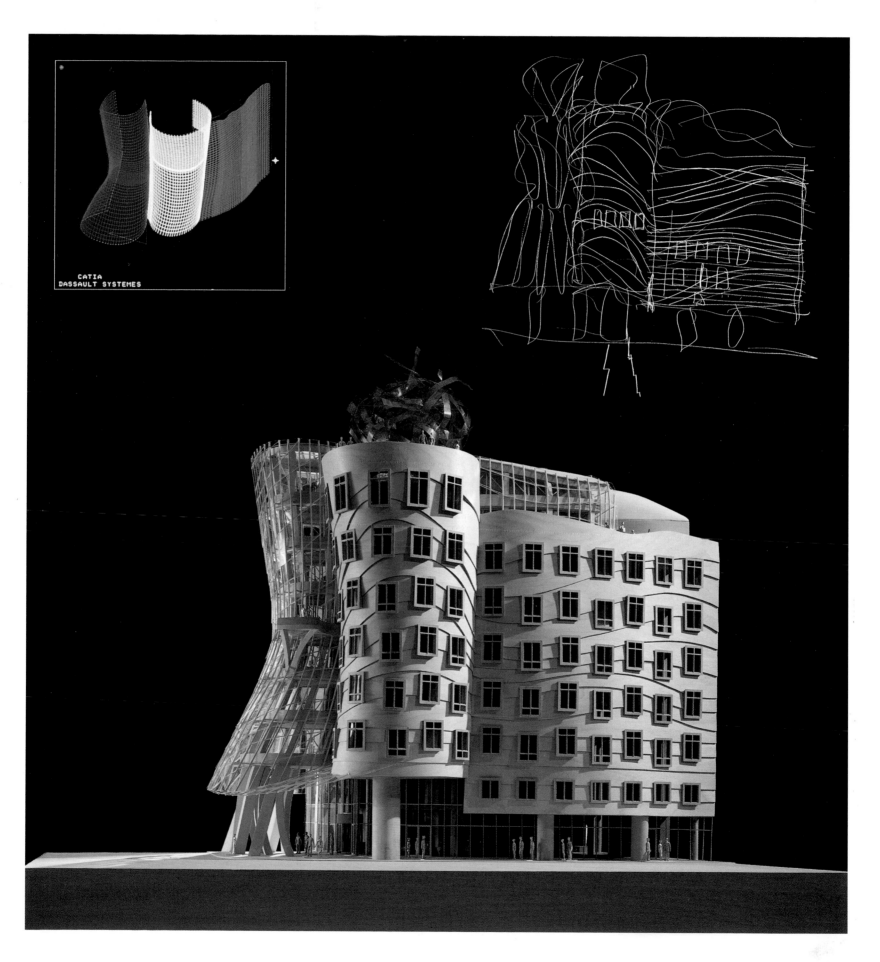

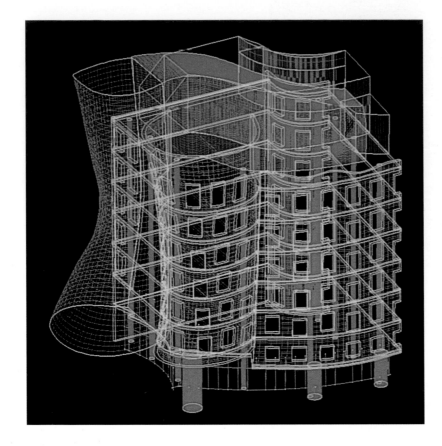

creating a small, covered entrance plaza. The opaque tower, known as Fred, is formed from precast concrete panels with a shaped insulation and plaster system, as is the Wave. The glass tower, Ginger, consists of two layers of steel-supported glass curtain wall. The interior layer, or underskirt, is the actual wall of the building, while the outer layer acts as a screen for the office spaces underneath. Ginger's vertical steel T-members curve in two directions and also twist.

Three-dimensional computer modeling not only supplemented the traditional methods of documentation, bidding, and quality control but also allowed Gehry's office to refine and elaborate complex, irrational, and nonrepetitive geometries in three-dimensional physical models. Plaster casts of the two towers, for example, were digitized, refined in virtual models, and output again into physical form with the help of a three-axis computer-controlled milling machine. By providing final computer models to various contractors and fabricators, the computer also linked the design and construction processes more closely and more economically. For example, to cast each of the concrete panels for the facade, none of which are identical, the computer sorted the panel geometries into five or six categories based on their surface curvature. Each group was cast from the same form, which was modified slightly after each pour for the next unique shape.

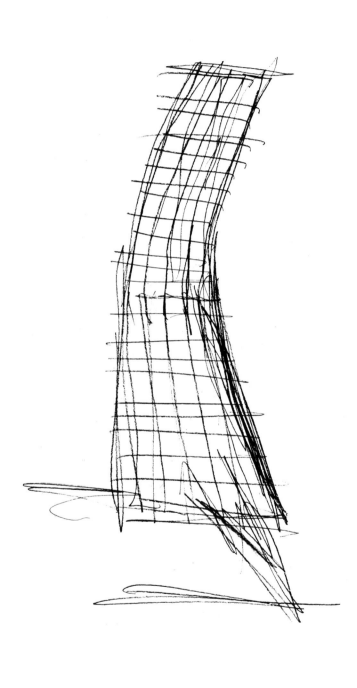

Overleaf:
Colonnade defining
entrance area; detail of
concrete-panel cladding.

510

**Alameda Redevelopment
Mexico City, Mexico
1993 (project)**

Client: Reichmann International
Program: Urban redevelopment proposal,
including high-rise office tower; mid-rise
offices, apartments, and hotels; and small-scale
retail and restaurants
Area: 3,300,000 square feet

Project Team: Frank O. Gehry, Randy Jefferson,
Michael Maltzan, Tomaso Bradshaw; Skidmore,
Owings & Merrill, New York, Ricardo
Legorreta, Mexico City, collaborators

Sketch; model views.

Disney Community Ice Center
Anaheim, California
1993

Client: Disney Development Corporation
Program: Two-hundred-seat community ice rink, eight-hundred-seat professional ice rink, snack bar, skate rental counter, equipment shop, restaurant
Area. 85,000 square feet
Materials: Wood frame, plywood, corrugated-aluminum cladding
Project Team: Frank O. Gehry, Randy Jefferson, Michael Maltzan, Tomaso Bradshaw, Mok Wai Wan, Gaston Nogues, Stefan Helwig, Josh White; Langdon Wilson Associates, executive architect; John A. Martin & Associates, structural engineer; Kocher & Schirra, electrical engineer; Matt Construction Corp., general contractor; Rosenberg & Associates, HVAC consultant

Designed as both a community recreation facility and a permanent training facility for a professional hockey team, the Disney Community Ice Center expresses its dual purpose in the two vaulted, swelling arcs that undulate beneath its anodized aluminum sheathing. With important frontages on both Lincoln Boulevard and the Anaheim Civic Center, the utilitarian structure provides Anaheim's downtown area with a strong sculptural focus, while the painted surface of the large plaza at the front entrance extends a colorful invitation to the public.

From the entry, a curvilinear, skylit lobby containing the snack bar, rental counter, and equipment shop leads to the NHL- and Olympic-regulation-size ice rinks. The central spine of the bicameral building houses locker rooms on the first floor and supports bleachers overlooking both rinks (eight hundred seats for the NHL rink and two hundred seats for the Olympic rink). The transparent upper story of the spine unites the two rinks: a restaurant looks out over both, providing a warm area from which to view the skating, similar to the bridge of a ship. The vaulted spaces are supported by massive curving glue-laminated ribs intended to echo the movements of skaters. An exposed plywood ceiling recalls traditional wooden rinks and adds visual warmth.

Sketches; plans; model of first scheme.

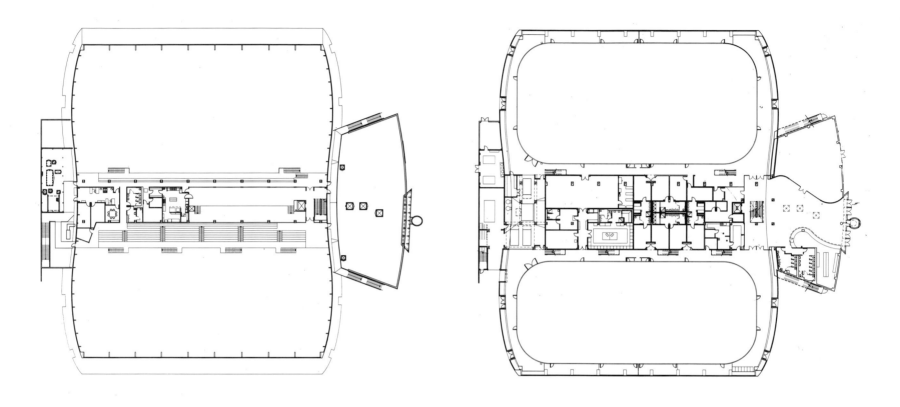

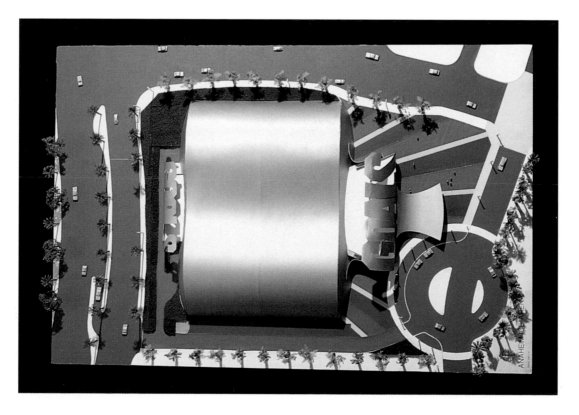

515

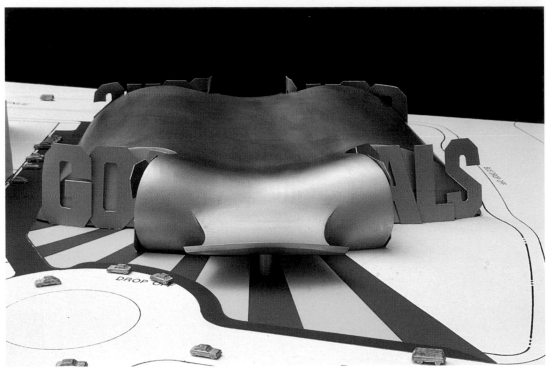

Sketches; models
of various versions;
section.

Overleaf:
Sketches.

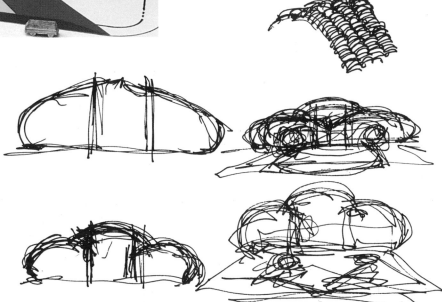

516

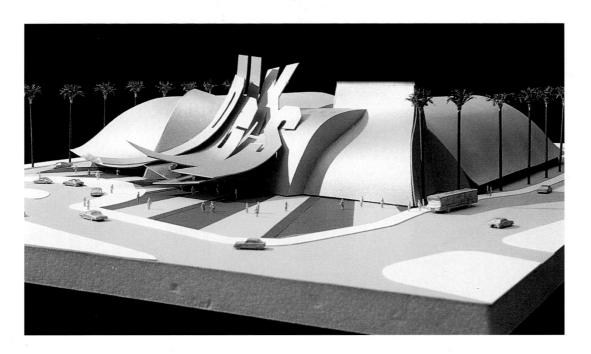

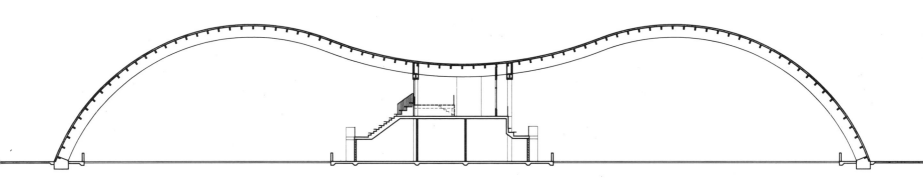

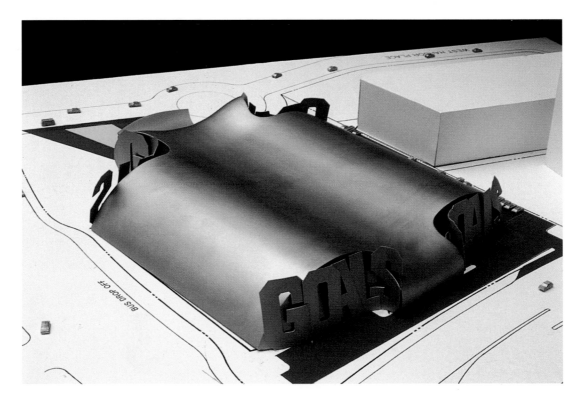

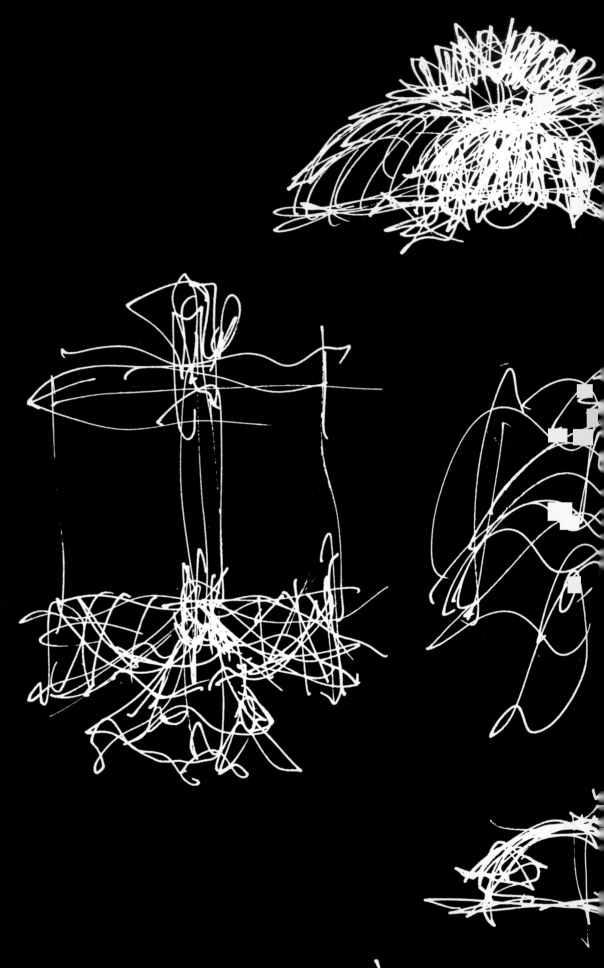

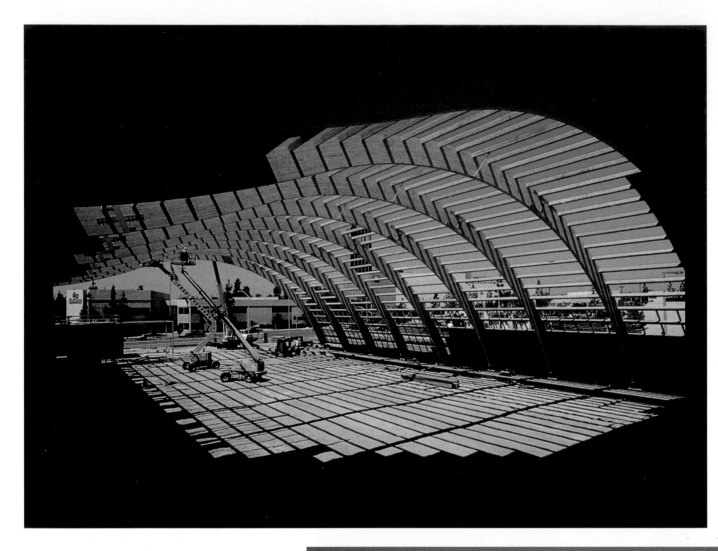

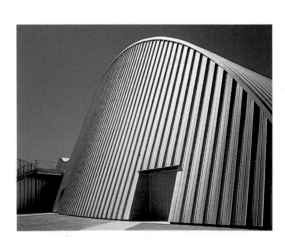

**Telluride Residence
Telluride, Colorado
1993–**

Client: Jay and Donatella Chiat
Program: Single-family residence and two
guest houses
Materials: Wood frame, stone cladding, cedar
shingles
Project Team: Frank O. Gehry, Randy Jefferson,
Michael Maltzan, Jonathan Davis, Larry Tighe

Model views.

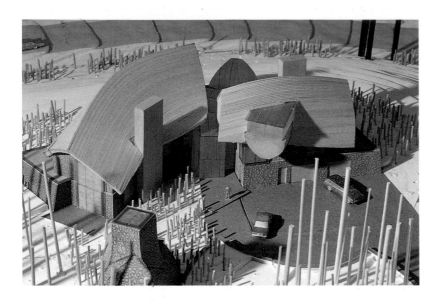
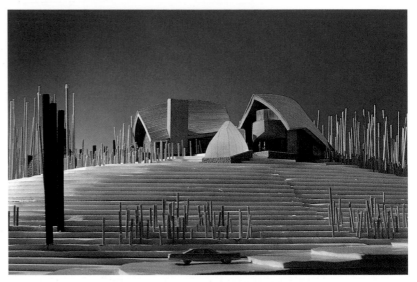

Center for Molecular Studies
University of Cincinnati, Cincinnati, Ohio
1993–

Plan; sections through
offices and through
laboratories; site model.

Client: University of Cincinnati
Program: Research laboratories, offices, and
academic spaces
Budget: $27,000,000
Area: 128,000 square feet
Materials: Steel frame, brick
Project Team: Frank O. Gehry, James M.
Glymph, Randall Stout, Michael Maltzan,
Hiroshi Tokumaru, Terry Bell, Richard Claridge,
Michael Gale, John Goldsmith, Stefan Hellwig,
Wai Wan Mok, Gaston Nogues, Jay Park, Todd
Spiegel, Tensho Takemori, Nora Wolin; Baxter
Hodell Donnelly Preston, Inc., executive
architect; Earl Walls Associates, laboratory
consultant; THP Limited, structural engineer;
H. A. Williams Associates, mechanical/electrical
engineer; LAM Partners, Inc., lighting
consultant

One of six buildings added to the University of Cincinnati as part of a $130-million master plan, the Center for Molecular Studies was designed to act as a gateway to the campus. The five-story building, which houses state-of-the-art laboratories for two hundred researchers in the neurosciences, is located at the intersection of two principal arteries, adjacent to the school's medical center, hospital, entry plaza, and an as-yet-undeveloped parcel of green space.

In plan, the building is cruciform, with laboratories forming the north-south arm and offices the east-west. At the center is a skylit atrium with shared staff lounges and meeting areas, stairs, toilets, and elevators. Designed for maximum flexibility, each laboratory floor's mechanical systems are contained within an interstitial level above; as equipment and methodologies evolve, systems can be remodeled or customized while laboratories remain occupied and functional below.

The building exteriors, in varying shades of brick, bulge outward both vertically and laterally. Oversize bay windows in aluminum frames expose multiple stories within.

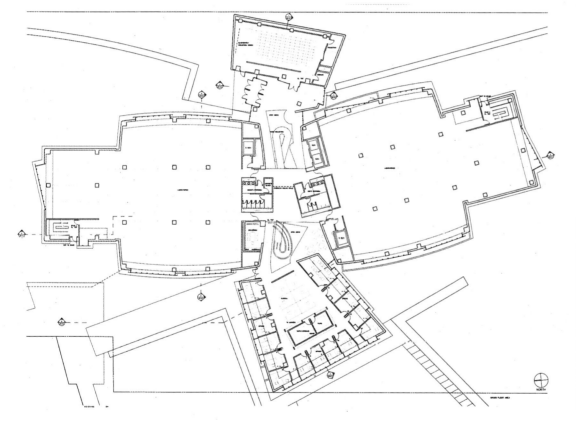

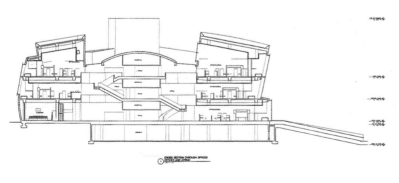

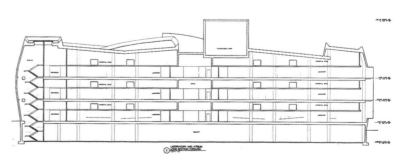

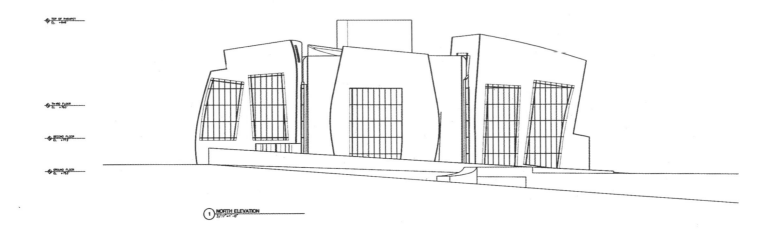

① NORTH ELEVATION

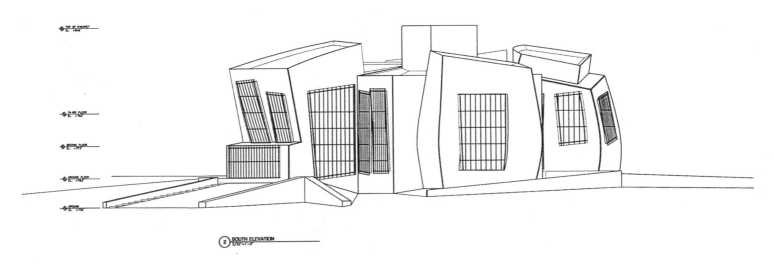

② SOUTH ELEVATION

East and west elevations; model views.

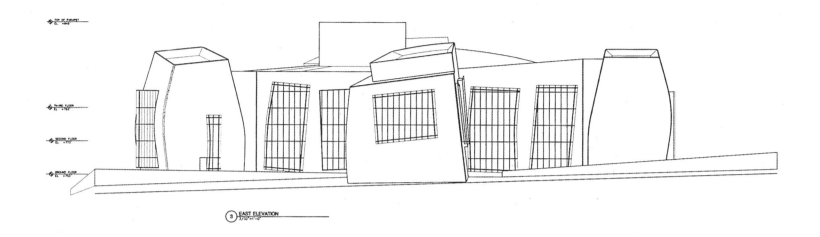

3 EAST ELEVATION
3/32"=1'-0"

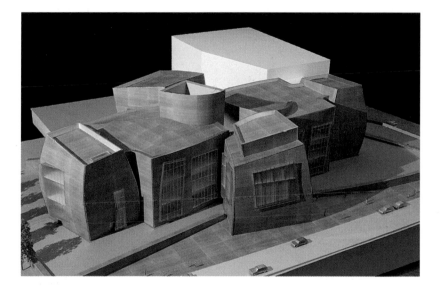

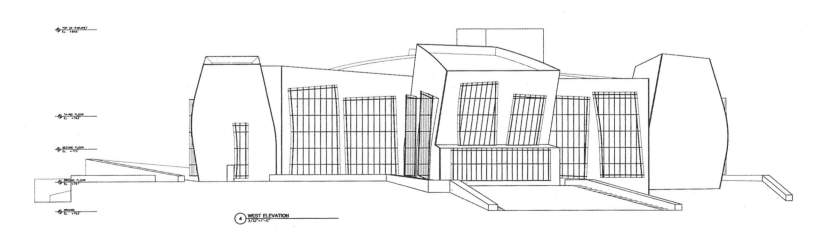

4 WEST ELEVATION
3/32"=1'-0"

Berlin Museum Competition
Berlin, Germany
1994 (project)

Site plan; model view.

Opposite:
Model views; sections.

Client: Staatliche Museum zu Berlin/
Preussischer Kulturbesitz
Program: Addition to and connections between
existing museums, including permanent and
temporary exhibition spaces, technical support,
café, restaurant, bookstore, public plaza
Area: 135,000 square feet
Materials: Steel frame, stone cladding, sheet
metal, glass
Project Team: Frank O. Gehry, James M.
Glymph, Edwin Chan, Tomaso Bradshaw,
Kenneth Ahn, Kamran Ardalan, Maria Arroyo,
Herwig Baumgartner, Mark Baez, Helena

Berge, Jackson Butler, Jonathan Davis, Michael
Gale, Doug Giesey, Michelle Kaufmann, Axel
Korn, Milana Kosavec, Patricia McCaul, Talbot
McClanahan, Michael Mantzoris, Chris
Mercier, Mok Way Wan, David Nam, Gaston
Nogues, Jay Park, Reg Prentice, Elissa Scrafano,
Matthias Seufert, Tadao Shimizu, Derek Soltes,
Kevin Southerland, Tensho Takemori, Hiroshi
Tokumaru, Lisa Towning, Scott Uriu, Eric
Wegerbauer, Kristin Woehl

With his competition entry for Berlin's Museums-
insel, Gehry intended to create a unified suite of
museum buildings relating in scale, density, and
detail to the surrounding context of Berlin's
embankment. Gehry saw the main task of the
design as harmonizing the island's existing components with a modern architecture as well as
improving access and movement among its
parts. Gehry's submission articulated the following goals: to mediate between the major domed
structures of the Bodemuseum and the Dom; to
activate the Kupfergraben; to preserve the proportions of Schinkel's Altes Museum by reposi-
tioning the bridge to the Neues Museum; and
to highlight the Neues Museum as the main
entry to the unified museum complex from
both the east and the west.

The planning components of the proposal
attempted to reinforce public activity along the
Kupfergraben by siting new exhibition buildings adjacent to the existing structures along the
water's edge. Access to the complex occurs via
a bridge relocated from the Pergamon Museum
to a new axis linking Clara-Zetkin-Strasse to
the Neues Museum, reinforcing the central
position of the latter and allowing it to become
the major entry point to the six existing
museums.

Architecturally, the proposal is comprised of
three separate but linked curved, stone-clad volumes along the southern edge of the site, housing the collections of classical Greek and
Roman sculpture. A canted, metal-clad cubic
building housing temporary exhibition spaces
and the bookstore sits to the north of the three
stone structures. Between these additions, a large
public-entry plaza fronts the entry of the Neues
Museum and the new bridge. Farther north, the
large courtyard of the Pergamon Museum is
fully enclosed and roofed in glass, serving as a
great hall, naturally lit by a vast elliptical skylight, for the Egyptian collection. Other interventions include a glass-covered circulation and
exhibition space linking the Pergamon and
Neues Museums, terminating in a glass stair and

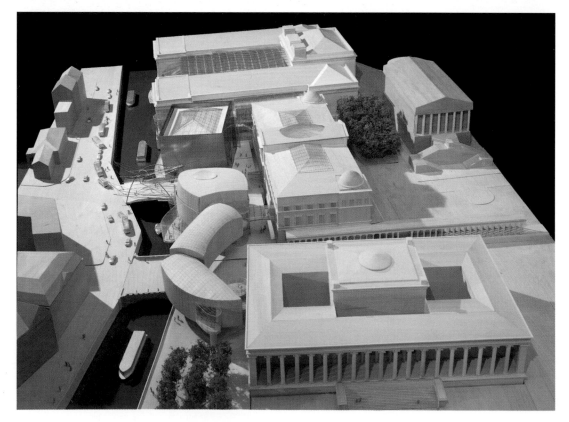

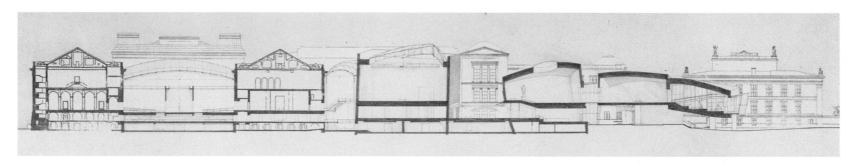

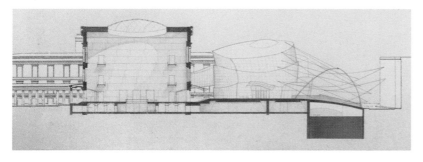
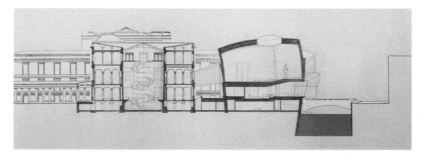

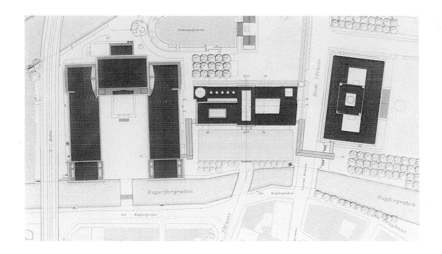

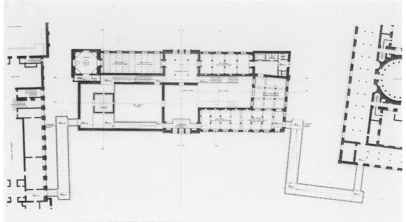

Site plan; entry-level plan; section; model of second phase, first scheme.

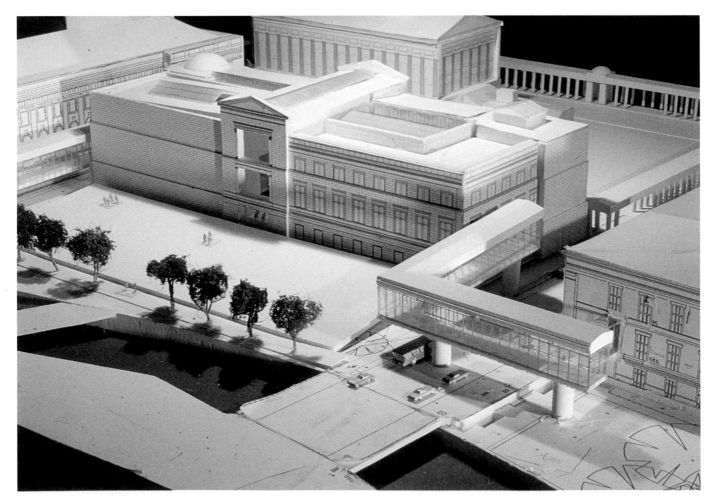

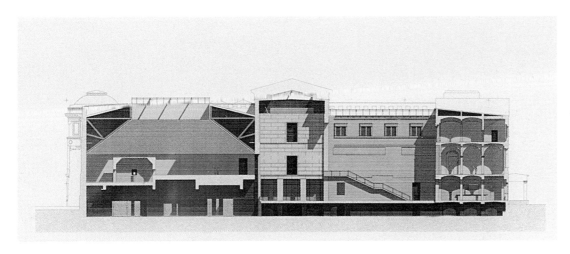

Longitudinal section;
sections toward Pergamon
and toward Altes Museum;
study models of internal
disposition of Neues
Museum (second phase,
first scheme).

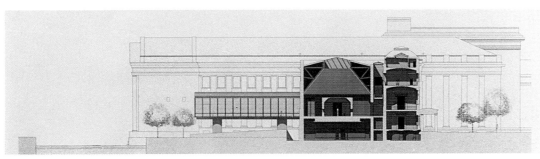

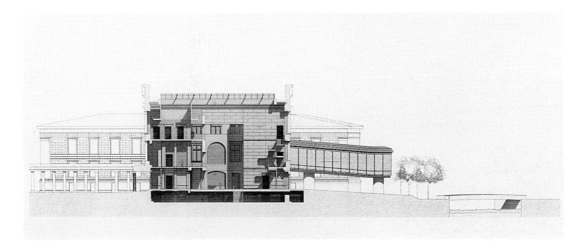

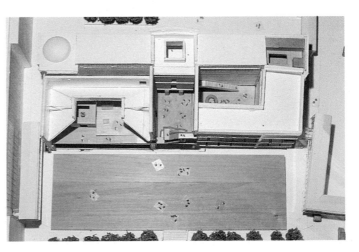

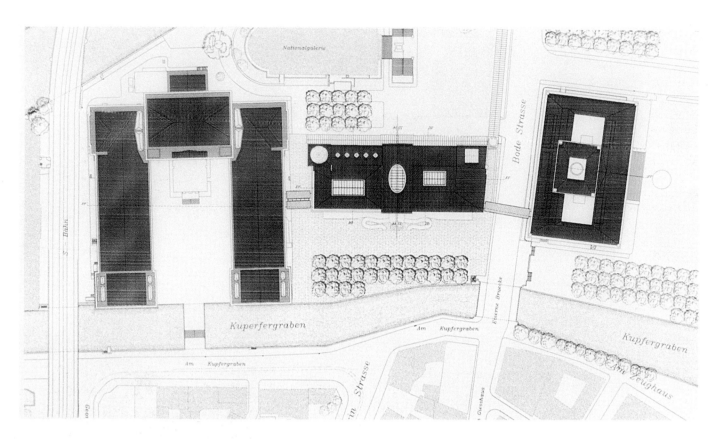

Site plan; entry-level plan; elevation along Kupfergraben (second phase, second scheme).

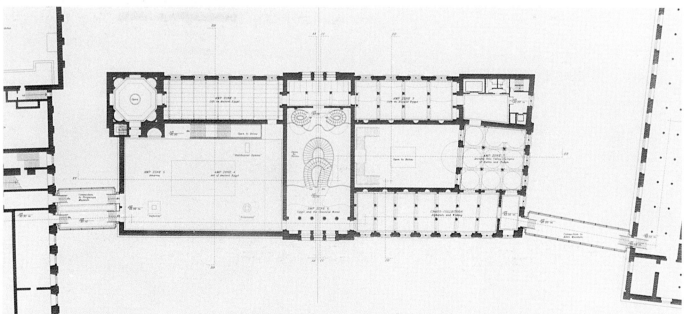

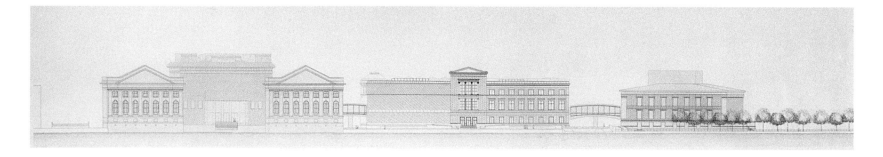

elevator tower at the Kupfergraben and an inclined grove of trees above the lecture halls adjacent to the National Galerie, in the Court of Colonnades garden area. The gallery housing the Pergamon Altar is enlarged and reconfigured, allowing the altar to be viewed in its correct orientation. A new café and restaurant, boat deck, and entry are located along the Spree Canal at the northern side of the site.

Gehry's design attempted to interweave the collections, challenging traditional museum demarcations and hierarchies, through a series of grand and intimate flexible spaces. The vaulted glass roof of the Pergamon court and the arcade linking the Pergamon, Neues Museum, temporary-exhibit gallery, and auditorium were intended to touch lightly on their neighbors, respecting the original architecture and allowing its character to read through the composition. The glass-enclosed arcade provides a variety of adjustable vertical and horizontal links between individual collections and thematic, cross-cultural, or temporary exhibits; it also provides increased visibility to collections on all levels of the Pergamon.

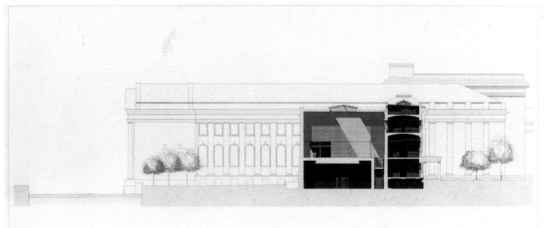

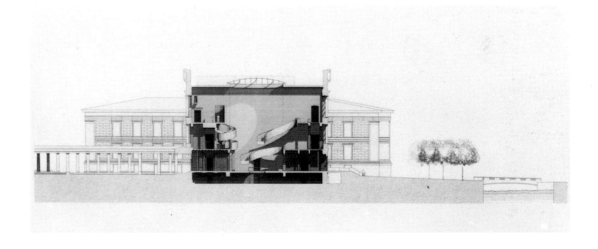

Longitudinal section; section through Neues Museum toward Pergamon; section through Neues Museum toward Altes Museum (second phase, second scheme).

Overleaf:
Study models of stairs in central atrium of Neues Museum (second phase, second scheme).

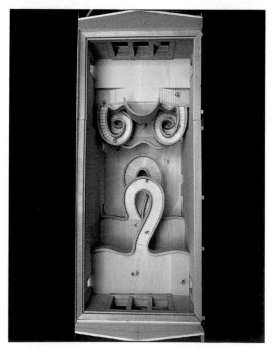

Kunsthalle Bielefeld
Bielefeld, Germany
1994

Client: Kunsthalle Bielefeld
Program: Addition to existing museum
by Philip Johnson
Area: 100,000 square feet
Materials: Steel frame, titanium sheet metal,
glass

Project Team: Frank O. Gehry, Edwin Chan,
Masis Mesropian, Mehran Mashayekh, Derek
Soltes, Rich Barrett

Model views.

Pferdeturm USTRA Bridge
Hannover, Germany
1994–95 (project)

Client: USTRA, Hannover Public Transportation Company
Program: Light-rail overpass
Materials: Stainless steel, translucent glass
Project Team: Frank O. Gehry, Randy Jefferson, Randall Stout, Michael Maltzan, Karl Blette; John A. Martin & Associates, Inc., structural engineer

Intended to relieve traffic congestion at an important intersection in Hannover, this glass-and-steel long-span bridge was designed as a scaffolding from which to suspend images, signage, and graphics to promote major public events, particularly Hannover's Expo 2000. The bridge design allows light-rail trains to pass over the surface street, thereby avoiding signal delays and traffic congestion with cars. The overpass corresponds to a new automobile underpass for Messe-Schnellweg Strasse, the major artery from the autobahns to the Expo 2000 fair site.

The two principal elements of the design are inclining planes holding the track and the long-span structure over Messe-Schnellweg. The inclining planes have been treated as a minimalist object of kinetic sculpture, with curved edges of stainless steel reflecting images of passing trains. The long-span segment, sheathed in translucent glass held by structural beams, creates a monumental and symbolic gateway arch.

Model views,
with underpass.

Der Neue Zollhof
Düsseldorf, Germany
1994–

Client: Kunst- und Medienzentrum Rheinhafen GmbH

Program: Three-tower commercial complex, including advertising, insurance, and media-related offices, public plaza, and below-grade parking.

Budget: DM 95,000,000

Area: 260,000 square feet

Materials: Concrete, steel, glass, plaster, sheet metal

Project Team: Frank O. Gehry, Randy Jefferson, Randall Stout, Edwin Chan, Michael Maltzan, Craig Webb, Tomaso Bradshaw, Terry Bell, Kirk Blashke, Verena Braun, Douglas Dahlkemper, Jim Dayton, John Goldsmith, Jeff Guga, Leigh Jerrard, Michael Jobes, Naomi Langer, Toni Lewis, Brent Miller, Jay Park, Steven Pliam, Reg Prentice, Jorg Ruegemer, Charles Sanchez, Bruce Shepard, Rick Smith, Eva Sobesky, Todd Spiegel, Tensho Takemori, Larry Tighe, Lisa Towning, William Ullman, Scott Uriu, Flora Vara, Jeff Wauer, Josh White, Keith Wiley, Kristin Woehl, Adam Woltag

Model views toward port and riverfront.

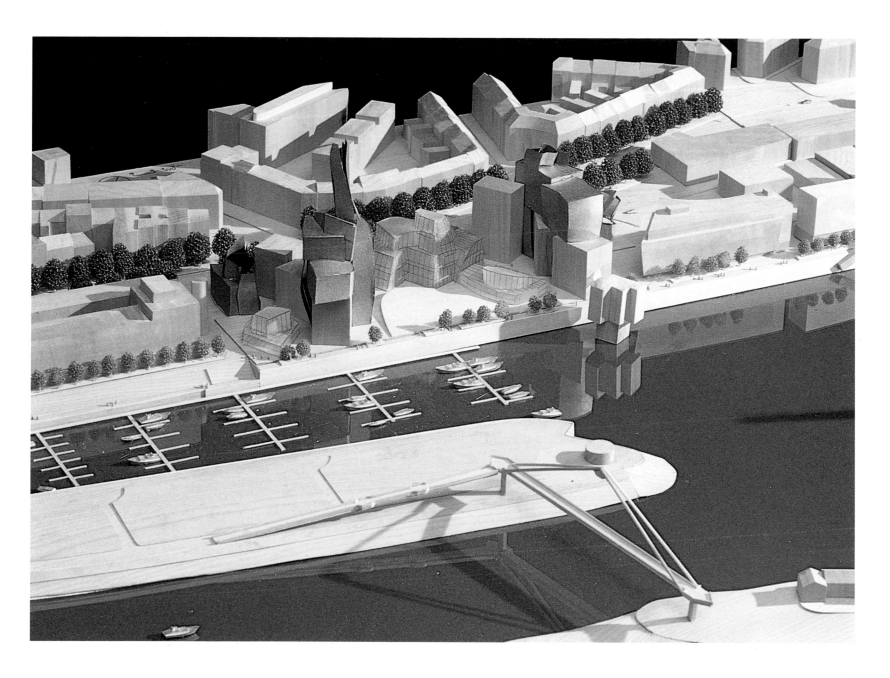

This project is situated in a redeveloping waterfront area of Düsseldorf where warehouses are steadily being replaced by arts- and media-related agencies. With a residential district to the south and the municipal and finance district farther east, the rehabilitation of the harborfront is seen as crucial to expressing the emergence of Düsseldorf as a cultural and business center.

The program called for 260,000 square feet of commercial space, including advertising, insurance, and media-related offices, a public plaza, and below-grade parking. The flat site runs along a waterfront promenade with extensive views up and down the Rhine. Gehry responded by proposing a complex of three separate towers, thus allowing a highly open site

plan and minimizing the overall bulk of the project. The placement of the buildings acknowledges the convergence of Brueckenstrasse and Wupperstrasse toward the site, leaving it open to the residential district across Stromstrasse. The clustered, mid-rise massing was intended to give high visibility to each of the three principal tenants, and also to provide a counterpoint to the typical horizontal development of the adjacent districts.

The three towers consist of "finger blocks" ranging from thirty thousand to fifty thousand square feet grouped around a central core, allowing for flexible leasing arrangements within an articulated massing. The towers rest on an expansive plaza, with paths connecting

the street to the harbor and parking below grade. The construction is concrete flat slab and frame, with punched window openings. All floor plates accommodate open or modular office planning. The buildings have operable windows for natural ventilation, with the clustered organization allowing for as many water-view offices as possible. Each finger of the tower blocks contains office space, while the joints between allow for the reception and ancillary spaces. The central building is essentially a grouping of concrete volumes clad in a faceted floating glass skin; the easternmost, tallest tower is composed of curvilinear volumes clad in plaster, while the west tower is clad entirely in metal panels with punched openings.

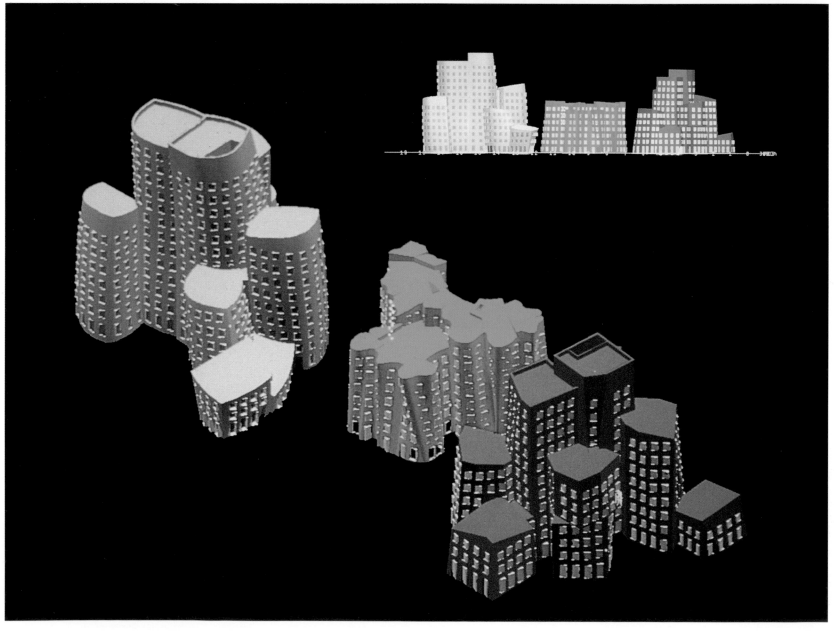

Models and studies
of the office towers.

**Pariser Platz 3
Berlin, Germany
1994–**

Client: Hines Grundstucksentwicklung GmbH and DG Immobilien Management GmbH
Program: Ten-story office building, including bank headquarters, auditorium, forty apartments
Area: 200,000 square feet
Materials: Steel, limestone, glass, alabaster, sheet metal
Project Team: Frank O. Gehry, Randy Jefferson, Craig Webb, Marc Salette, Herwig Baumgartner, Kirk Blashke, Sam Blower, Padraic Cassidy, Nida Chesonis, Tom Cody, Jim Dayton, John Goldsmith, Jeff Guga, Stephan Helwig, Blayne Imata, John Jennings, Leigh Jerrard, Michael Jobes, Jason Kuperman, Michael Mantzoris, George Metzger, Jorg Ruegemer, Charles Sanchez, Bruce Shepard, Tadao Shimizu, Rick Smith, Eva Sobesky, Tensho Takemori, Larry Tighe, Hiroshi Tokumaru, Scott Uriu, Flora Vara, Josh White, Gudrin Wiedemer, Keith Wiley

Model of Behrenstrasse facade; sketch.

Not long after losing the Berlin Museum competition, in 1994, Gehry received his first commission in Berlin: Pariser Platz 3 is a mixed-use building that will house the DG Bank headquarters and forty apartments. Because the site is adjacent to the recently reconstructed square and gardens in an area designated as the heart of Berlin's new diplomatic zone, the design of the building's exterior was tightly circumscribed by zoning requirements. The building fills the entire volume of the zoning envelope, maintaining the form of Pariser Platz to the north and reinforcing the Behrenstrasse streetscape to the south. A cornice line extends from the adjacent building across the seven-story facade on the Pariser Platz, and both the front and rear facades of the building are clad in limestone, close in color to the Brandenburg Gate. Window openings along the Pariser Platz are deeply recessed and continuous with the rhythms and proportions of surrounding buildings; the deep window bays model the facade, lending it mass, thickness, and weight. At the rear, the facade of the ten-story apartment tower is a denser, more dynamic composition of curves and terraced setbacks.

The restraint of the facades, however, is deceptive. Behind its carefully constructed contextual facades, Pariser Platz 3 is a reversal of solids and voids: the skin and vestibule are all "mass"; the interior is a fluid and transparent singular space. Inside, offices ring the perimeter

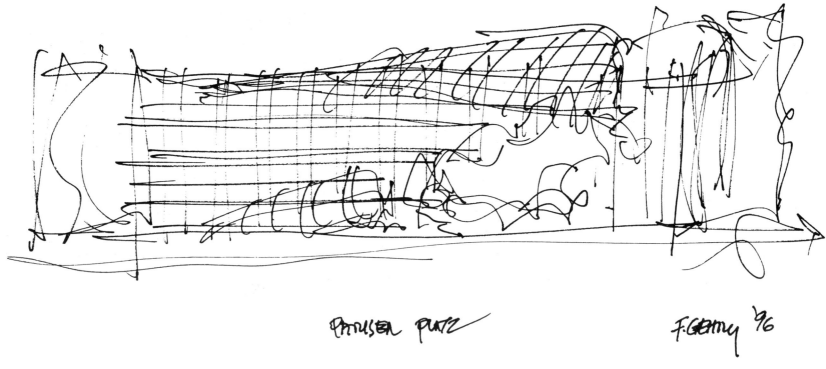

PARISER PLATZ   F. Gehry 96

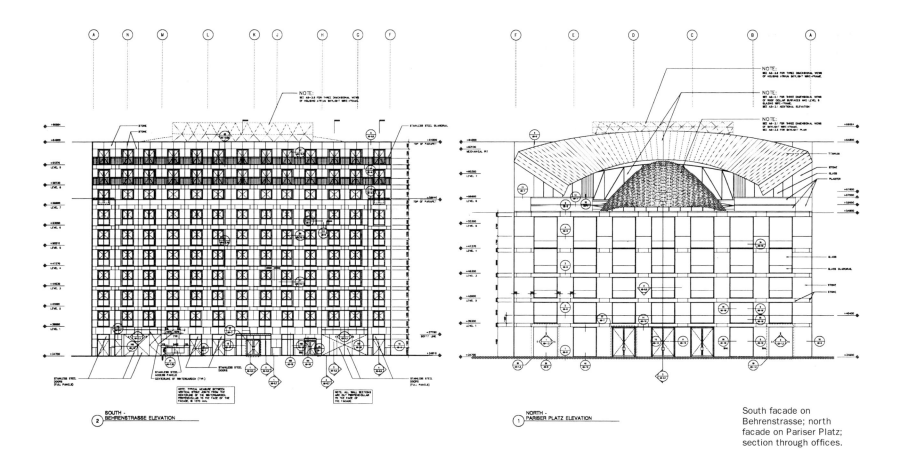

SOUTH -
BEHRENSTRASSE ELEVATION

NORTH -
PARISER PLATZ ELEVATION

South facade on
Behrenstrasse; north
facade on Pariser Platz;
section through offices.

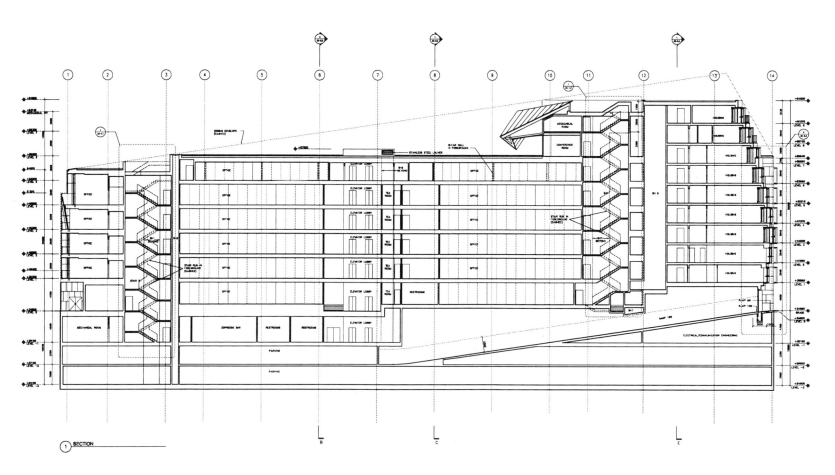

SECTION

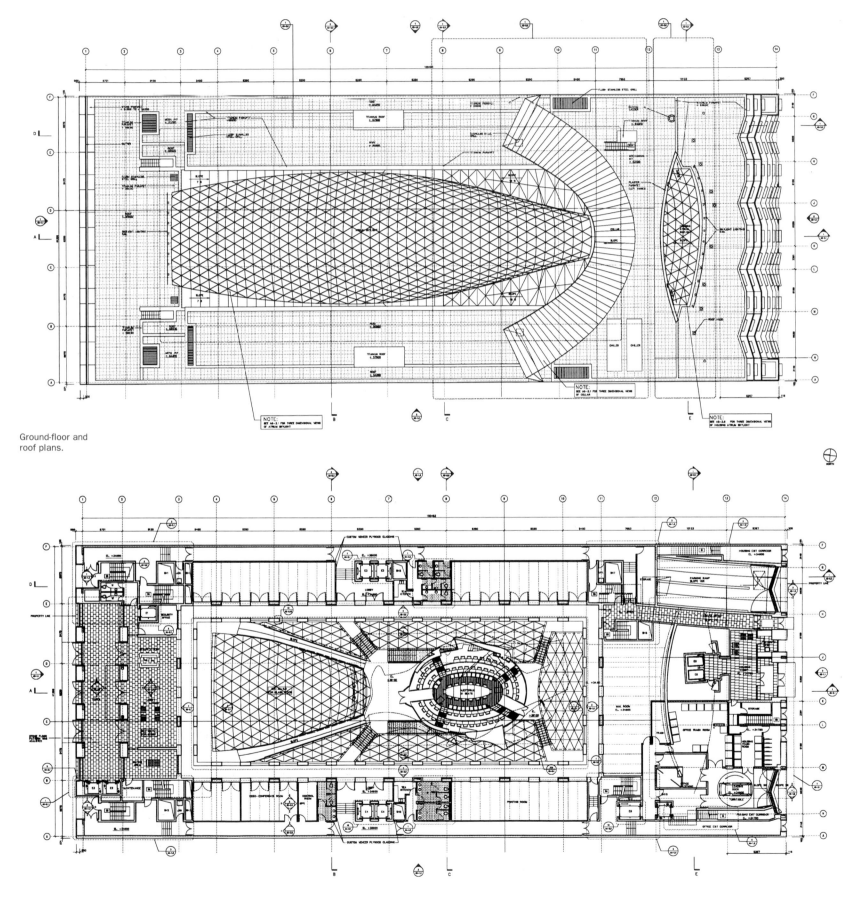

Ground-floor and
roof plans.

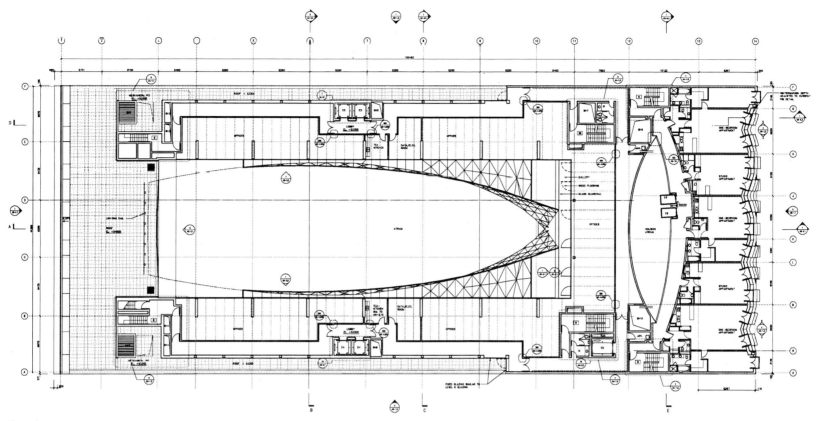

Fourth- and
fifth-floor plans.

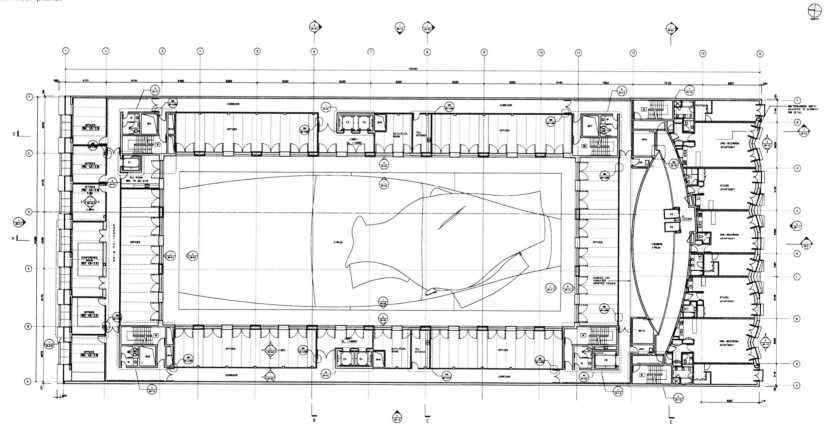

Views of study model;
cross-section; section
through atrium.

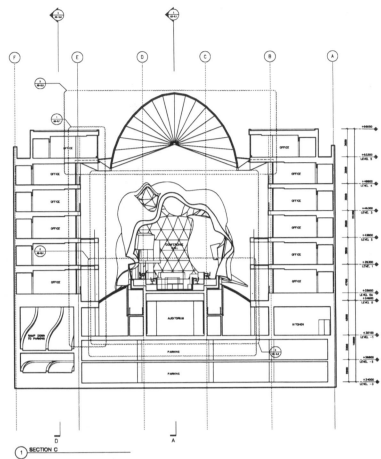

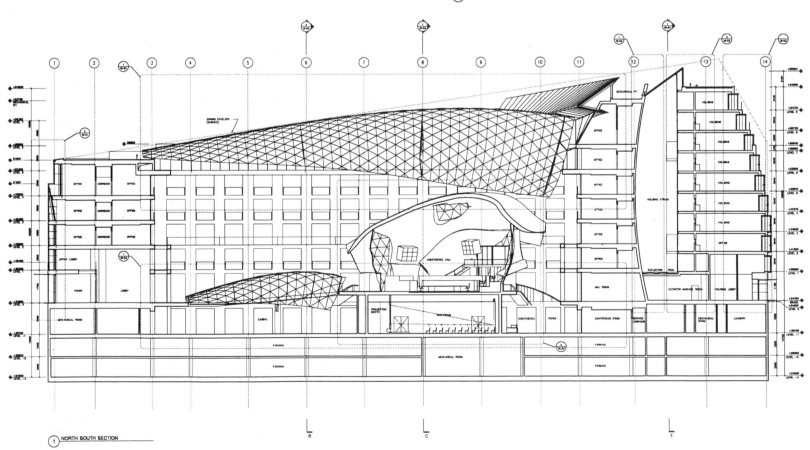

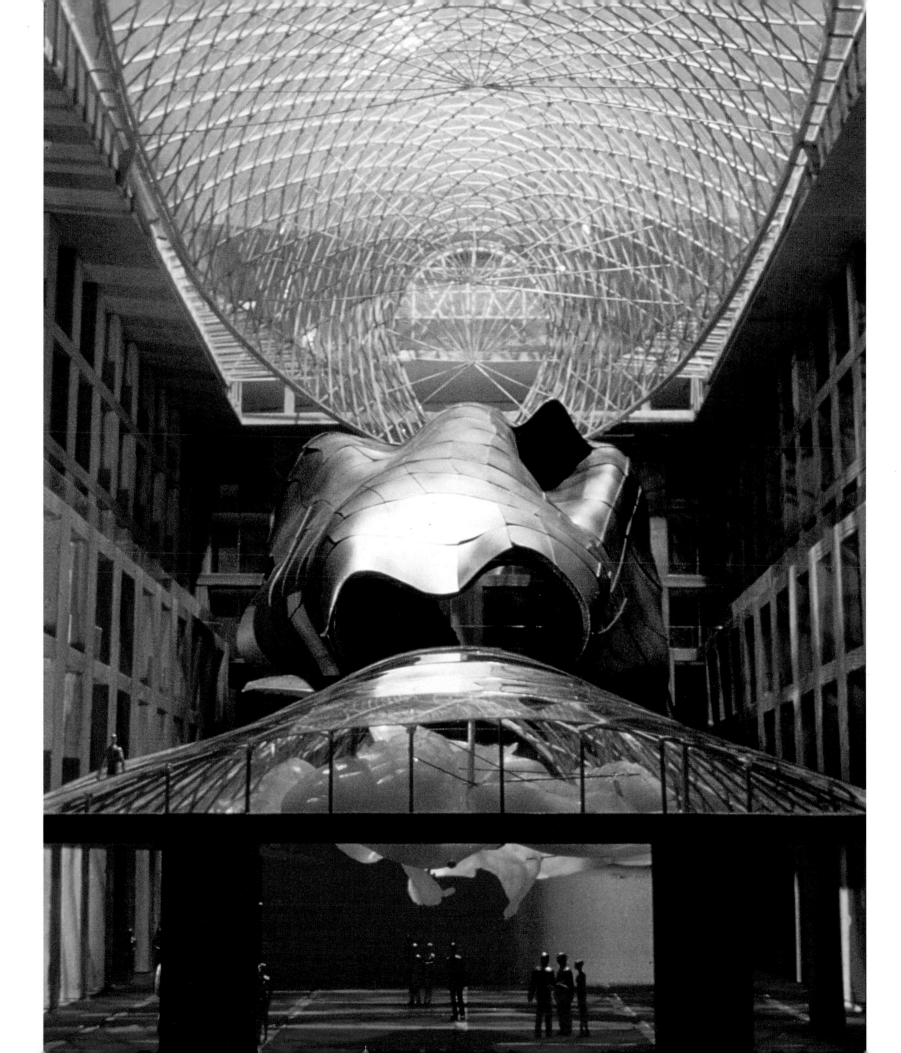

Three-dimensional study renderings of atrium roofing; models of structure for conference room.

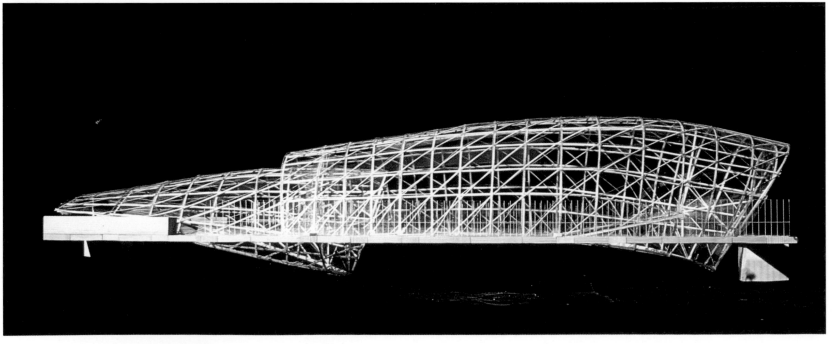

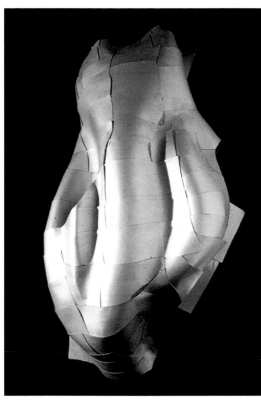

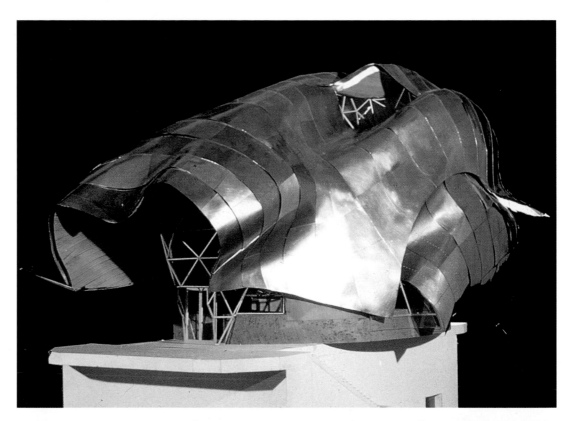

of a dramatic seven-story atrium. A fish-bodied skylight of glass on a steel-wire frame stretches over the full two-hundred-foot length of the interior court. At the rear of the court, like a statuary god at the heart of an animist temple, sits a one-eyed, steel-skinned horsehead, seventy-five feet long and fifty feet tall. The transparent floor plane leading to it is glass tile over a convex wire frame, with ramps leading up to the inner sanctum of the horse's skull, an oval conference room.

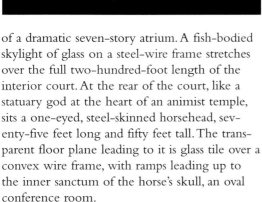

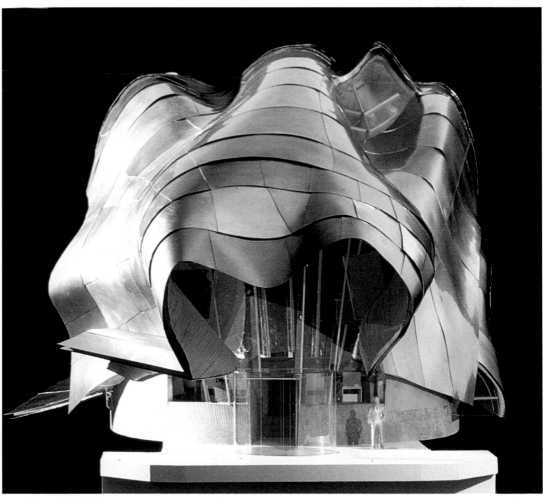

Beneath the glass floor is a 225-seat casino; a 100-seat auditorium is housed beneath the base of the horse's skull. A wood-clad arcade leads to the office elevator lobbies on either side of the main atrium. Offices on the first and second floors have glass-floored balconies overlooking the atrium. Offices, meeting rooms, and private dining rooms on the top floors of the building were designed with high ceilings and inclined north-facing glass walls to take advantage of spectacular views of the Brandenburg Gate and the Reichstag.

A second, smaller atrium space backlights the residential area, located in a thin ten-story tower facing Behrenstrasse. The tall, compressed atrium serves as a lobby to the apartments, providing both natural light and ventilation to the housing block.

**Temporary Contemporary
Renovations
Museum of Contemporary Art,
Los Angeles, California
1995–96**

Client: Museum of Contemporary Art,
Los Angeles
Program: Museum renovation, including
studio/classrooms, interactive media research
room, administrative offices, renovated
exhibition space, new security system,
orientation room, reading room, and renovation
of exterior street plaza with bookstore, café, and
outdoor performance areas
Area: 62,000 square feet

Project Team: Frank O. Gehry, Randy Jefferson,
Edwin Chan, Vano Haritunians, Chris Mercier;
Kurily & Szymanski, structural engineer;
Sullivan and Associates, mechanical engineer;
Athans Enterprises, electrical engineer

The first phase of the renovation, completed for
the 1995 reopening, consisted of two new
visitor-education facilities and the first stage of
a fully integrated security system. A guest-
orientation room introduces visitors to museum
events and current installations with video and
slide presentations while a plywood-clad reading
room invites visitors to browse through books
and catalogs related to the museum's exhibitions. A versatile ticketing and information desk
contains a small retail counter.

The second phase focused on revitalizing the
existing exterior street plaza below the entrance
canopy. The plaza, evoking an urban village,
contains a bookstore, coffee bar, and outdoor
seating and performance areas. A new signage
tower greets visitors upon arrival.

The third phase of the renovation, completed
in August 1996, entailed the design and construction of a studio and classroom facility and
an interactive media space with full research
capabilities. The studio and classroom area provides space for the museum's teaching programs
and commands views into the exhibition spaces.
Also included in the third phase are the construction of new administrative offices and the
completion of the security-system control
room. These additions serve as the backdrop to
the newly renovated exhibition space created by
clearing the existing concrete dock and bunker.
Large roll-up doors allow the museum direct
access to the outdoor plaza space.

Exterior space;
exhibition spaces.

Decorative Arts Museum of Montreal
Montreal, Quebec
1995–

Client: Musée des Arts Décoratifs de Montréal
Program: Museum remodel, including decorative arts galleries and administrative offices
Budget: $2,500,000
Area: Gallery: 93,000 square feet
Materials: Douglas fir, plaster, glass
Project Team: Frank O. Gehry, Randy Jefferson, Jon Drezner, Jim Dayton, Blayne Imata, Michael Mantzoris, Stephen Paddock, Eva Sobesky, Scott Uriu; Provencher/Roy, associate architect; Bouthillette Parizeau & Associates, mechanical and electrical engineer

The Decorative Arts Museum of Montreal is located within the existing Museum of Fine Arts building at street level, in an area originally designated to house retail shops. The Decorative Arts Gallery is adjacent to an existing glass "cultural corridor" linking Crescent Street and Bishop Street.

The Decorative Arts Gallery is approximately eighty thousand square feet, divided into permanent and temporary exhibition spaces. The permanent exhibition space is distinguished by tall vitrines extending up to sixteen feet into the high-ceiling voids. The temporary space consists mainly of small, movable vitrines, with the exception of several tall, permanent vitrines located at the west end of the gallery. Art can be displayed either on or in the vitrines.

The vitrines and the floor of both the permanent and the temporary exhibition spaces are made of vertical-grain Douglas fir; the wood's texture and hue is intended as a warm backdrop for the color of the art on display. An exceptionally clear Starphire glass is used to encase any art requiring protection. The glass is seamed together at the corners without fasteners.

Exhibited art is illuminated from ceiling spotlights; when resting on optional sandblasted glass surfaces, the art can also be illuminated from a light within the vitrine. Ceilings of both exhibition spaces expose the building's mechanical systems to accentuate gallery height. A flexible ceiling lighting design allows light sources to be located anywhere between the mechanical components, and only in locations as required for particular exhibitions. All ceiling material surfaces are white, increasing ambient light for the wooden gallery.

The museum's administrative offices are located on the mezzanine level, at the west end of the gallery. Three double-height windows provide views from the mezzanine and gallery toward Bishop Street.

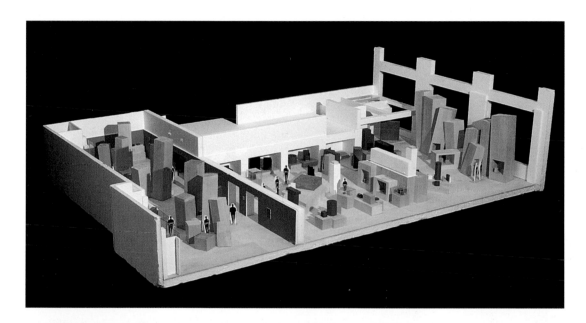

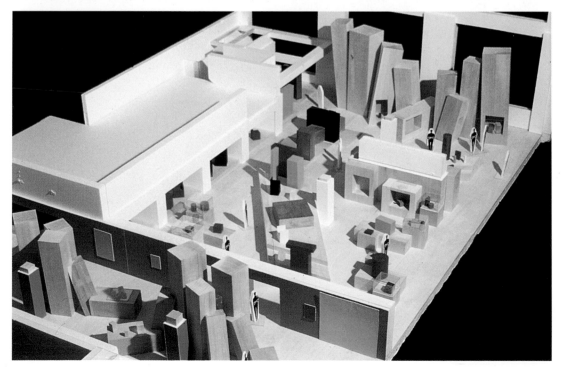

Model views showing internal disposition.

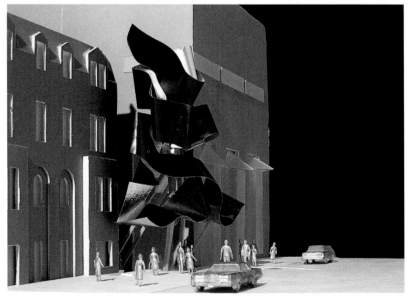

Samsung Museum of Modern Art
Seoul, Korea
1995–

Client: Samsung Foundation
Program: Museum of traditional and contemporary Korean and international art, including galleries, offices, shops, auditorium, storage, and parking
Area: 470,000 square feet
Materials: Steel frame, concrete, stainless-steel sheet metal, glass
Project Team: Frank O. Gehry, James M. Glymph, Edwin Chan, Doug Hanson, Kamran Ardalan, Juan Azulay, Richard Barrett, Bruce Beisman-Simons, Terry Bell, Kirk Blashke, Karl Blette, Damien Blower, Robert Brown, Glenn Butler, Nida Chesonis, Richard Claridge, Tom Cody, Joshua Coggeshal, Douglas Dahlkemper, Jim Dayton, Emil Dilanian, Jon Drezner, Anthony Fontenot, Alex Gentile, Timothy Gratkowski, Jeff Guga, Bo Sook Han, Timothy Hosbein, John Hreno, Blayne Imata, Leigh Jerrard, Michael Jobes, Mickey Johnson, Ann Koshalek, Jason Kuperman, Naomi Langer, Toni Lewis, Yannina Manjarres-Weeks, Christopher Mercier, George Metzger, Brent Miller, Pedro Morales Jr., David Nam, Jay Park, Daniel Parks, Steven Pliam, Reg Prentice, Charles Sanchez, Christopher Seals, Habibou Sissoko, Bruce Shepard, Rick Smith, Derek Soltes, Jeff Stern, Hiroshi Tokumaru, Lisa Towning, Scott Uriu, Flora Vara, Frederick Vogel IV, Mok Wei Wan, Jeff Wauer, Craig Webb, Frank Weeks, Josh White, Elizabeth Whittaker, Keith Wiley, Kristin Woehl, Adam Woltag, Brian Yoo, Kevin Yoshikawa

The Samsung Museum of Art, to be located on Yul-Gok Road in the Un-Ni Dong district of Seoul, will house the Samsung Foundation's Ho-Am Museum, for traditional Korean art, and the Ho-Am Gallery, for contemporary Korean and European art. Twice the size of the Guggenheim Museum in Bilbao (1991–97), the Samsung Museum is intended as a great civic presence in a congested, chaotic urban landscape.

The site is surrounded by multiple urban conditions: the Hyundai high-rise and a major artery to the north; middle- and low-rise commercial buildings to the northwest; a Japanese cultural center to the west; very high-density residential neighborhoods, a park, and a kindergarten to the south; an ancient imperial palace and shrine, both sacred locations heavily trafficked by tourists, to the southeast; and office towers to the east. The site's footprint, already small in relation to the complexity and size of the 470,000-square-foot program, is further reduced by zoning requirements that restrict the building to 60 percent of the site's area.

Six months of conceptual design, from June to December 1995, resulted in the winning proposal for the invited competition. The scheme diagrams the museum's massing, in an almost literal manifestation of the maximum allowable building envelope, as one high-rise, one mid-rise, and one low-rise volume arranged in an L-shape. The model shows an orthogonal arrangement of glowing, glass-

Urban context.

Site model; ground-floor plan; plan of lower level of final project.

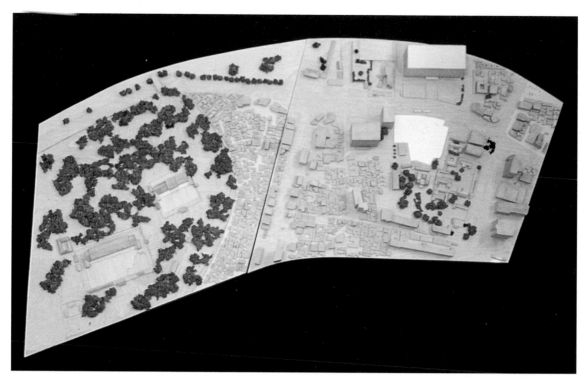

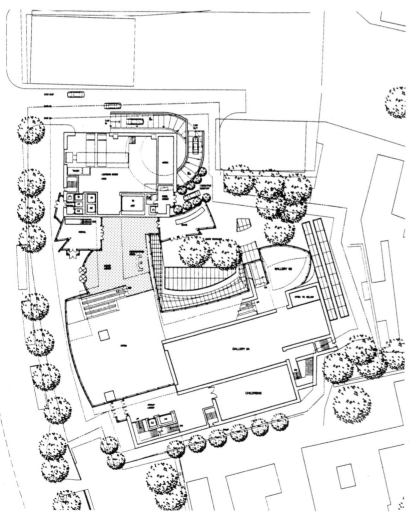

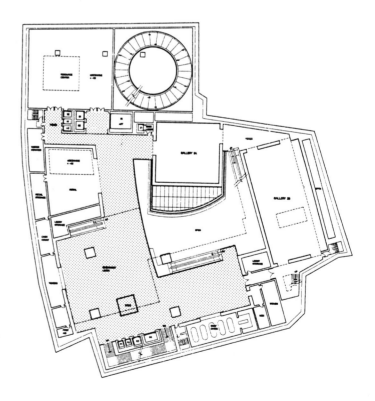

-00M LEVEL
SCHEMATIC DESIGN
14 JUNE 1995

-08M LEVEL
SCHEMATIC DESIGN
14 JUNE 1995

Study model of east
building; plans at
+42 and +30 meters.

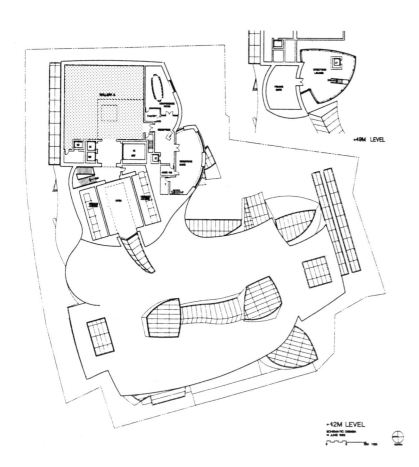

+42M LEVEL
SCHEMATIC DESIGN
10 JUNE 1988

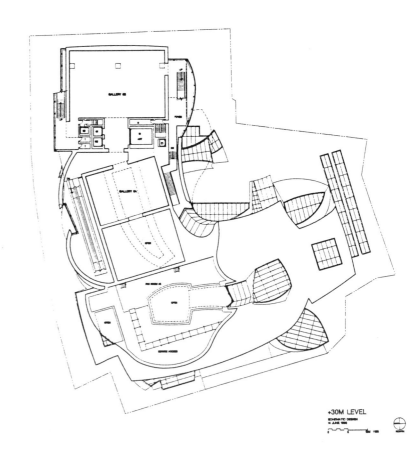

+49M LEVEL

+30M LEVEL
SCHEMATIC DESIGN
10 JUNE 1988

Study model from west; plans at +20 and +10 meters.

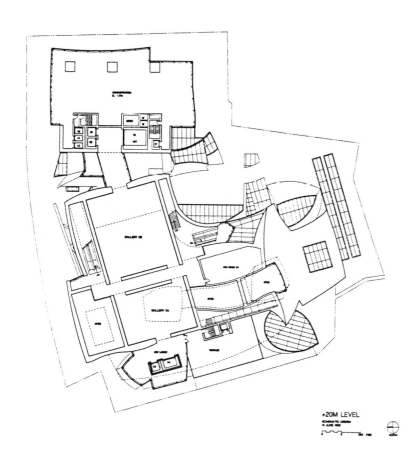

+20M LEVEL
SCHEMATIC DESIGN
14 JUNE 1998

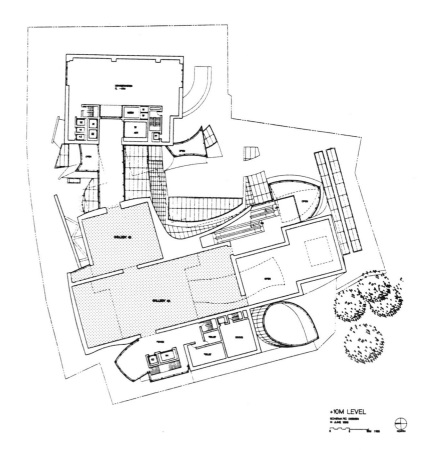

+10M LEVEL
SCHEMATIC DESIGN
14 JUNE 1998

Sections; study models.

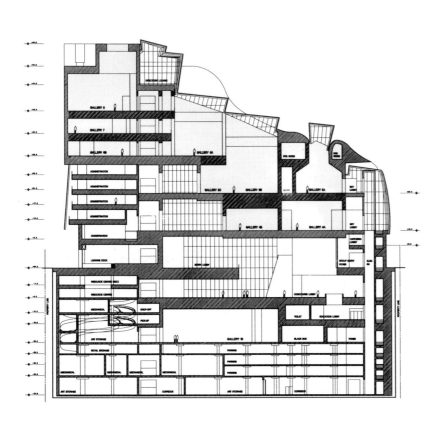

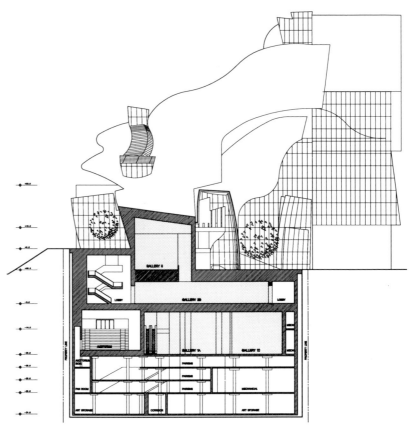

SECTION AA
SCHEMATIC DESIGN
14 JUNE 1996

SECTION CC
SCHEMATIC DESIGN
14 JUNE 1996

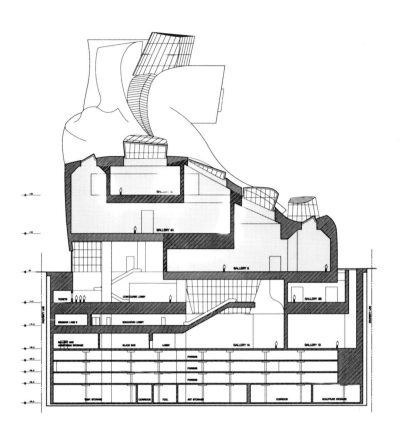

SECTION BB
SCHEMATIC DESIGN
14 JUNE 1996

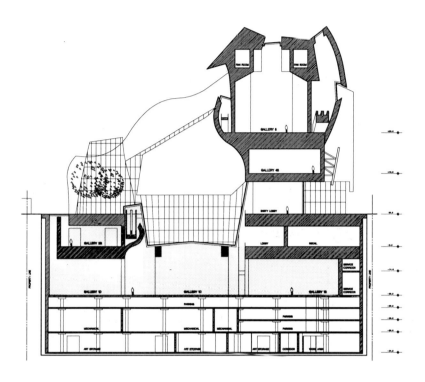

SECTION DD
SCHEMATIC DESIGN
14 JUNE 1996

West and southeast
views of final model.

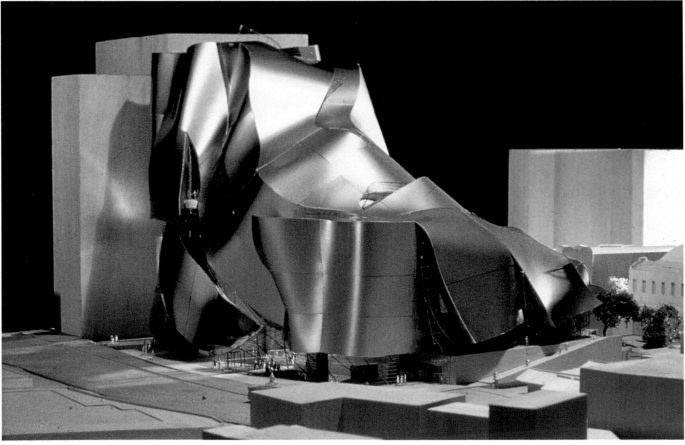

West and northeast
views of final model.

wrapped towers with gardens and freestanding sculptural enclosures on the roofs; the transparent skin of the towers reveals the building's guts as well as circulation and activity within. The transparency was seen as a way of approaching, and perhaps resolving, a consistency of image from all sides, providing a foil to the multiple urban identities on each frontage.

The L-shaped diagram indicates important points of access at two corners, and leaves the south face open-ended, possibly to be developed later as a cultural park. It also provides the symbolic forms of twin mountains, important imagery in Seoul's physical and cultural landscape and a powerful body language for the specific site. The exterior of the competition project still resembled a commercial building type rather than a cultural one, however, and the provision of natural light and the accommodation of the entire program were still problems. By placing a large portion of the program below grade, an unfortunate hierarchy—above-ground versus underground, seen versus unseen, important versus unimportant—had emerged.

During schematic design, from December 1995 to June 1996, Gehry carefully considered the building's symbolic imagery. By studying Korean landscape paintings and traditional Korean architecture, he tried to understand what he described as "the yearnings and aspirations" of the contemporary culture as well as the ancient. The "peaks" of the building acknowledged not only the importance of the natural landscape to the people of Seoul but, in a modified version, also began to echo the proportions and scale of traditional Korean temples, with their massive, overscaled roofs hovering over light structures, as at the Temple of the Floating Rock. Gradually the cluster of towers was transformed into a continuous gesture, a mountainscape wrapped in ephemeral clouds of glass, in a cascading spiral of galleries that floats above a transparent glazed band at ground level.

Gehry mitigated the above-grade/below-grade dichotomy by anchoring the spiral with one major gallery—among the largest and most flexible contemporary-art exhibition spaces in Asia—sixty feet below grade. At the heart of the spiral, the twenty-three-thousand-square-foot temporary-exhibition gallery is lit by a giant light well. Circulation spirals upward through the gallery for young Korean artists to the concourse level and continues through the galleries for modern and contemporary Korean and international art seven levels above. Vertical and horizontal openings penetrate the galleries

Study models of interiors.

along sight lines, allowing glimpses ahead and behind. Controllable levels of natural light illuminate most galleries through skylights, while several galleries are left dark for fragile works on paper. Most ceiling heights are forty-five to fifty feet, with breaks that open to views of the ancient palaces and gardens in the distance.

The museum's entry at ground level is open and transparent. Visitors descend to the large concourse twenty-five feet below grade. Through the entry are views to galleries, the street, the retail and public functions of the concourse, and, through a crevasse opening to the rear of the site, the garden and café.

The design-development phase has been spent exploring the building's ephemeral imagery and articulating the separate architectural elements accordingly: glass, for example, is seen as a unifying layer of clouds, rather than as curtain wall. Initially the glass clouds were considered the most active element of the composition; one important model, however, shows the sheet-metal skin as cascading ribbons, asserting a formal presence as visible as that of the glass clouds. One other central issue of the design-development phase has been the issue of interrelating the interior volumes with the exterior forms. The client requested rectilinear galleries, raising a question as to whether the interior and exterior will offset each other (as at Bilbao) or whether the building will be engineered as a "decorated shed" (as at the Disney Concert Hall, 1989–)?

Perhaps more importantly, Gehry continues to ask the question, What are the needs of the twenty-first-century museum? If art comments on the world, and the future of world is unpredictable, then, Gehry contends, art of the next century is surely unpredictable as well. While the forms and spaces Gehry proposes for viewing art may be unfamiliar, he continues to stress the historical importance of the building's iconic identity, its civic presence. As Korea reasserts an artistic and architectural identity for future generations with the same confidence it has asserted its economic identity, Gehry feels it is crucial to face the uncertainty of the future and the chaos of the urban context with an open, inclusive, democratic optimism. For him, the essential task remains the creation of a building on a particular site that maintains a relationship with its neighbors and at the same time has its own body language—formally idiosyncratic, visible, and independent, and, therefore, socially inviting, accessible, and pluralist.

**USTRA Office Building
Germany
1995–**

Client: USTRA, Hannover Public
Transportation Company
Program: Nine-story mixed-use tower,
including offices and advertising
Area: 21,000 square meters

Materials: Steel frame and stainless-steel cladding
Project Team: Frank O. Gehry, Randy Jefferson,
Randall Stout, Michael Maltzan, Laurence
Tighe, Naomi Ehrenpreis, Jeff Guga, John
Jennings, Tensho Takemori, Kevin Yoshikawa

Model views showing new
office tower.

**Church of the Year 2000
Competition
Rome, Italy
1996 (project)**

Client: Vicariato di Roma
Program: Church, chapel, offices, cleric's
residence, community center, and auditorium
Budget: $5,000,000
Area: 20,000 square feet
Materials: Concrete and masonry shell, exterior
plaster, stone, sheet-metal cladding

Project Team: Frank O. Gehry, Edwin Chan,
Chris Mercier, Adam Woltag, Hiroshi
Tokumaru, Jeff Guga, Kamran Ardalan,
Michael Jobes, Nida Chesonis, Tadao Shimizu,
Doug Dahlkemper, Rob Brown, Flora Vara,
Alex Gentile, Keith Wiley, Josh White

Site model; sketch.

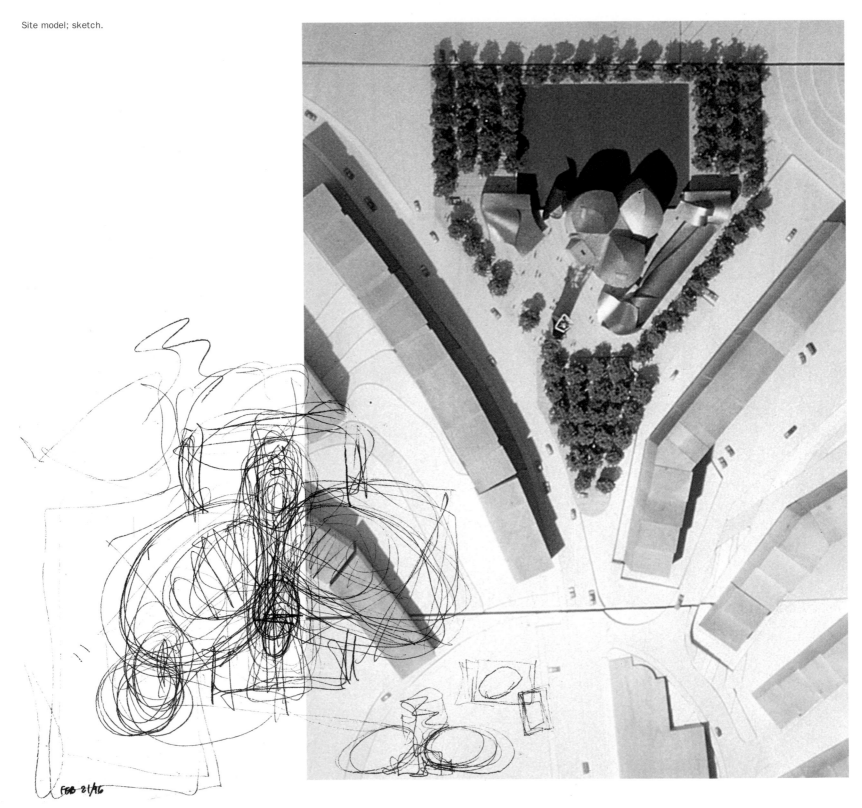

564

Sketch; ground- and
first-floor plans.

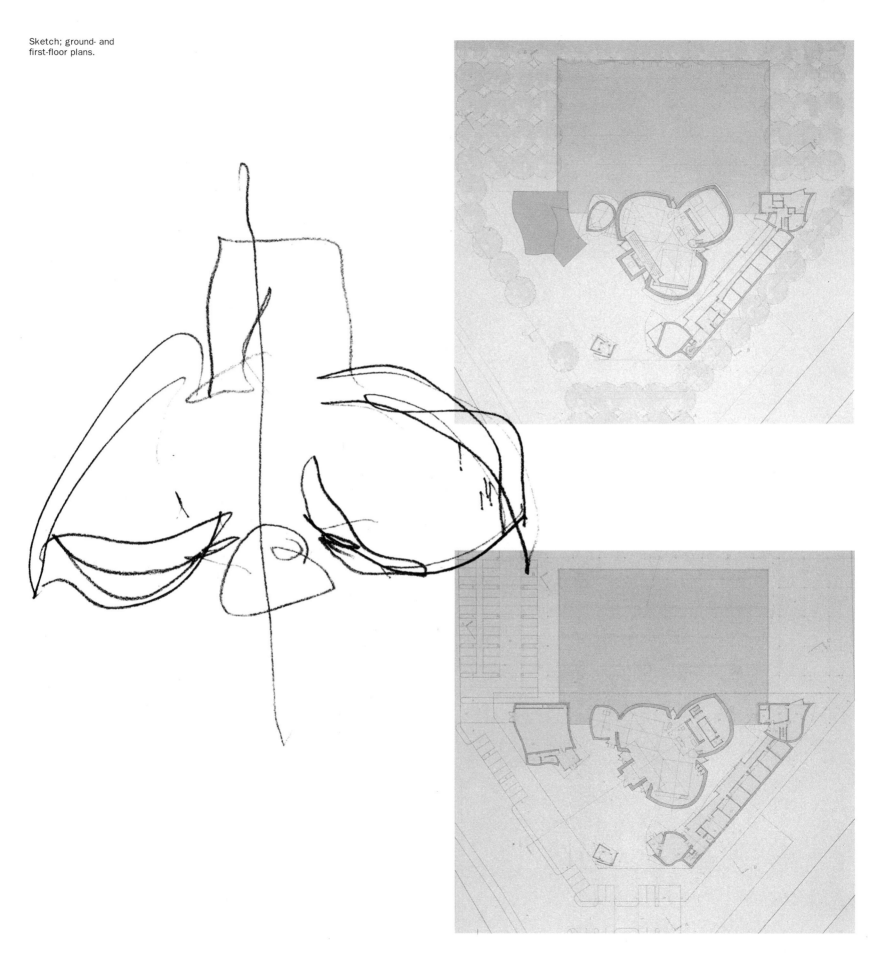

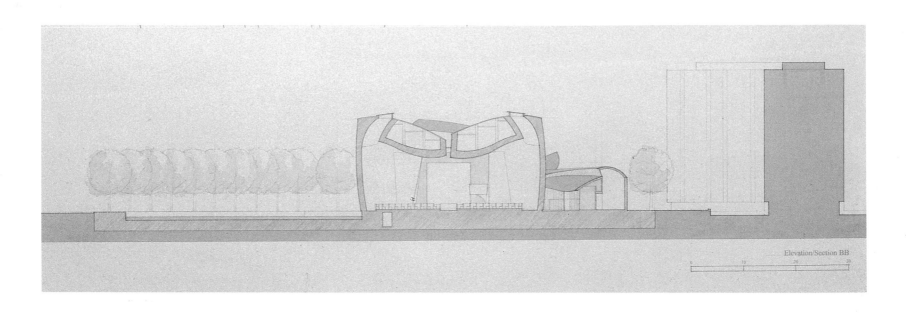

Elevation/Section BB

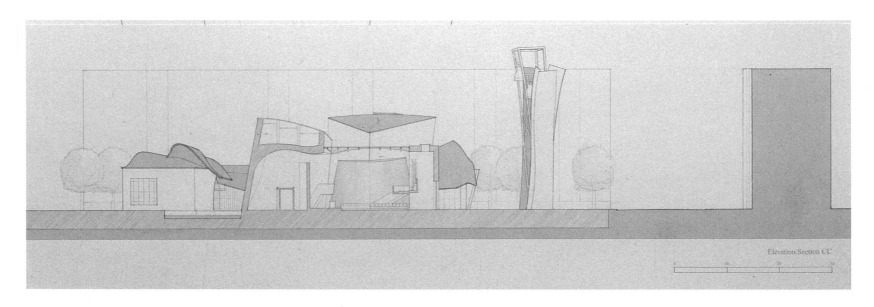

Elevation/Section CC

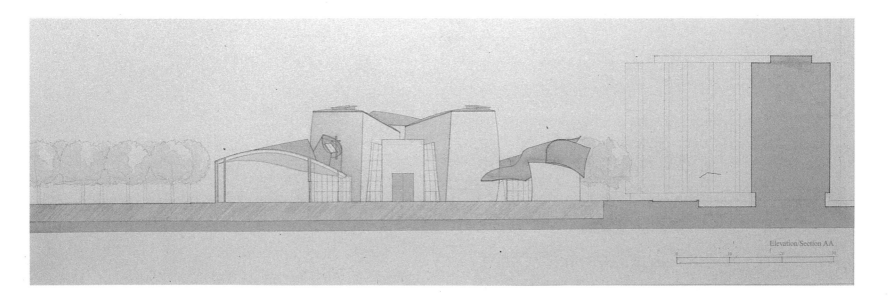

Elevation/Section AA

Elevations/sections;
entrance elevation;
exterior views of model
of church and complex.

Experience Music Project
Seattle Center Campus,
Seattle, Washington
1996–

Client: Experience Music Project, represented by Paul Allen
Program: Museum of contemporary music, including exhibition galleries, electronic library, sound laboratories, performance hall, screening room, administration, archival storage, store, and café
Area: 110,000 square feet
Materials: Steel frame, concrete shell, epoxy-based colored-glass terrazzo, autobody-finish-coated concrete, interference-colored stainless steel, cast-glass tiles, titanium wire, stainless-steel sheet metal
Project Team: Frank O. Gehry, James M. Glymph, Craig Webb, George Metzger, Herwig Baumgartner, Elizabeth Beasley, Helena Berge, Nida Chesonis, Rebeca Cotera, John Drezner, Jeff Guga, David Herrera, Leigh Jerrard, Michael Jobes, Naomi Langer, David Pakshong, Bruce Shepard, Rick Smith, Randall Stout, Larry Tighe, Hiroshi Tokumaru, Lisa Towning, Scott Uriu

Sketch; study model.

Overleaf:
Mezzanine-, second-, and third-floor plans; model views, with study models at top and final model at bottom.

Second overleaf:
Study models, with final model at bottom right; three-dimensional renderings.

The Experience Music Project, located on Fifth Avenue adjacent to the Space Needle at Seattle Center, is a 110,000-square-foot facility intended to celebrate creativity and innovation as expressed in American popular music and culture. The building provides, in an educational museum and exhibition environment, opportunities for visitors to explore the history and traditions of American popular music, participate in the music-making process, and learn the secrets of musical composition and performance. The project places a special emphasis on music-related traditions of the Pacific Northwest and will specifically commemorate Jimi Hendrix, one of American music's most creative and influential artists.

The exhibits and public programs are envisioned as a three-dimensional floating puzzle, with each piece critical to the shape and the nature of the whole. Six elements—the Sky Church, the Crossroads, the Sound Lab, the Artist's Journey, the Electric Library, and the Ed. House—form the basis of the exhibits and public programs. The Sky Church, a concept inspired by Jimi Hendrix, represents all types of people being united by the power and joy of music and music-making; it is physically embodied in the building's central public gathering area.

The building itself consists of a cluster of colorful curving elements clad in a variety of materials. The fragmented and undulating forms of the building are inspired in part by the image of a shattered Fender Stratocaster. The Seattle Center Monorail, a remnant of the 1962 World's Fair that continues to provide transportation between Seattle Center and downtown Seattle, passes through the building, allowing monorail riders a glimpse inside. In addition to the thirty-five thousand square feet of exhibition space, the building houses a restaurant, a bookstore, and administrative spaces, with support spaces and storage areas located below grade.

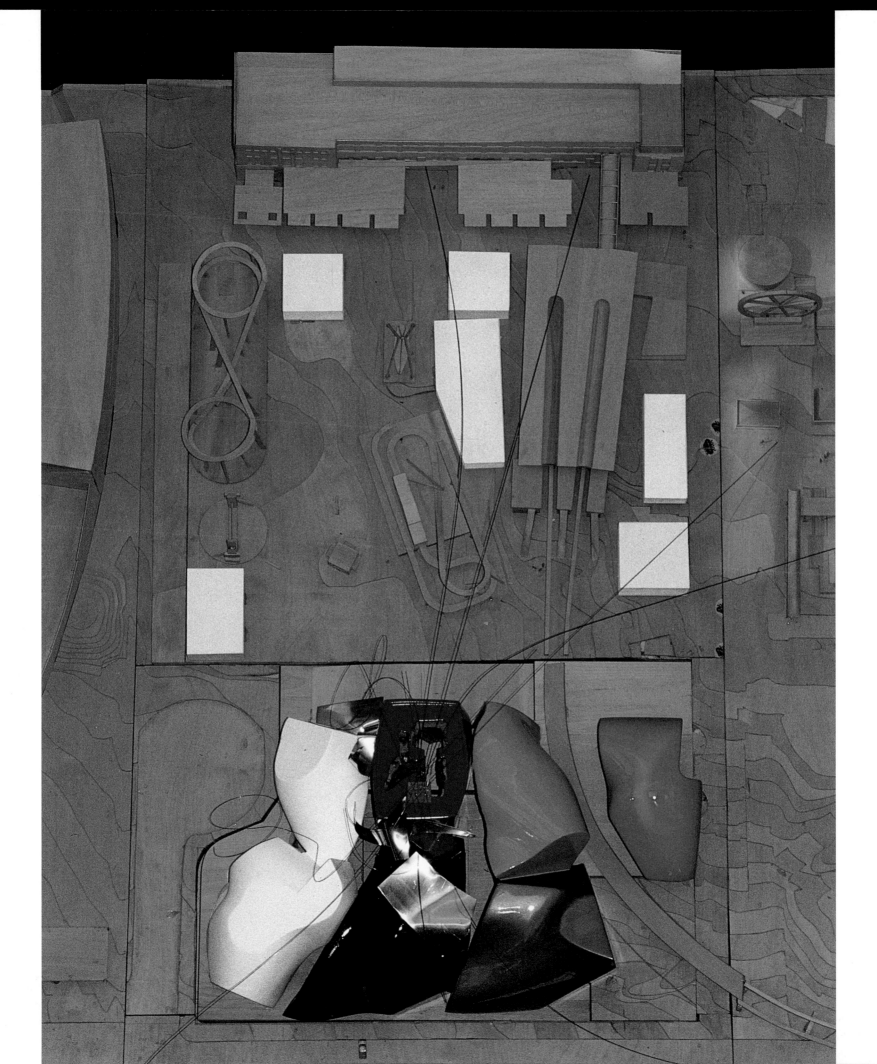

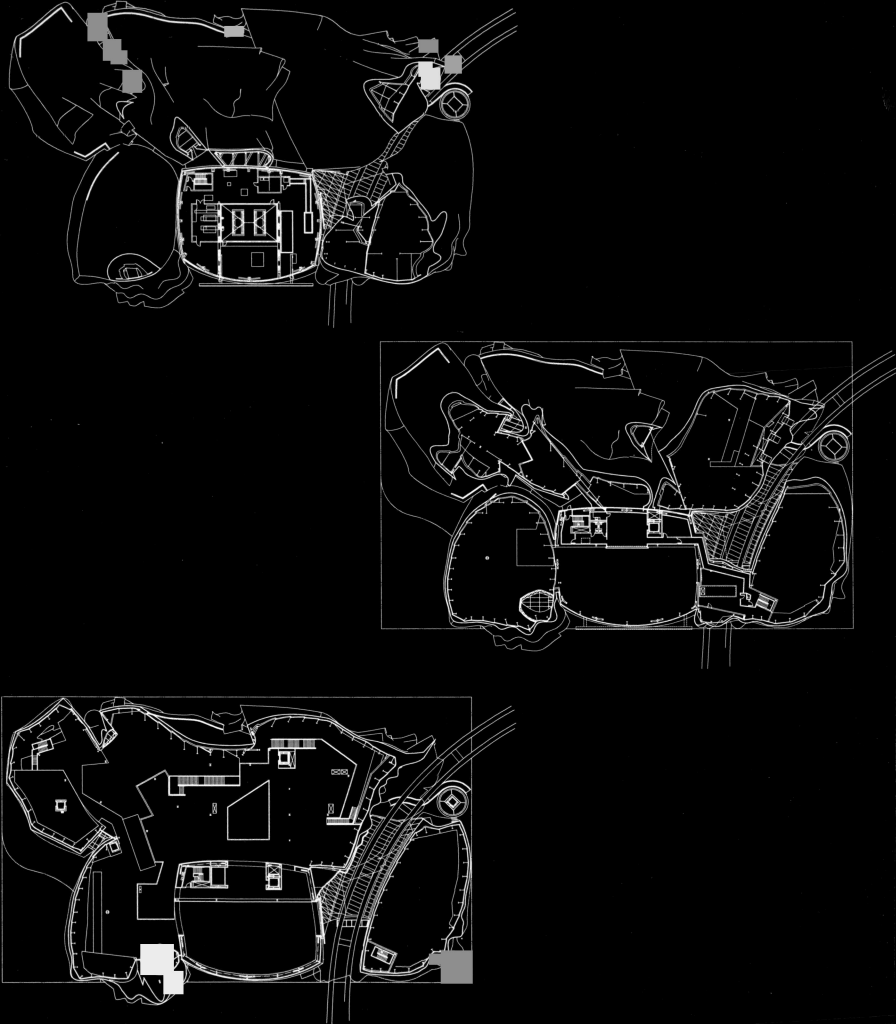

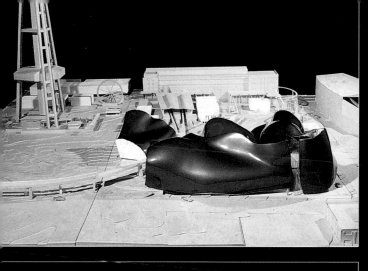
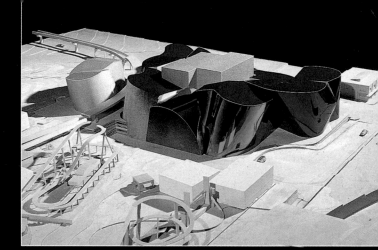
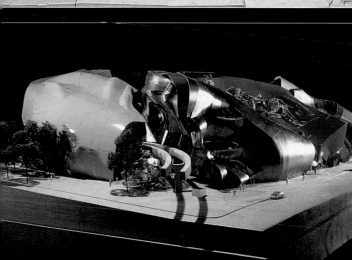

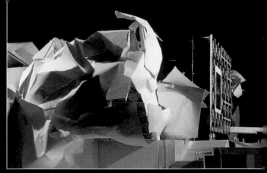
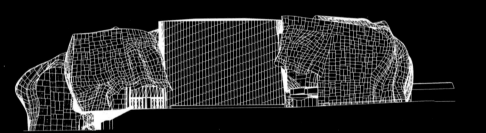

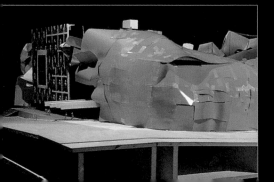

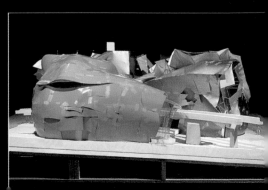

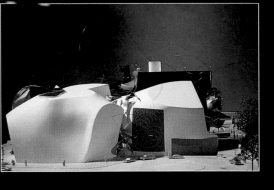
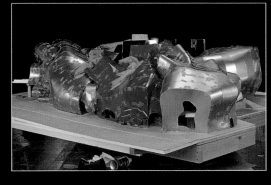
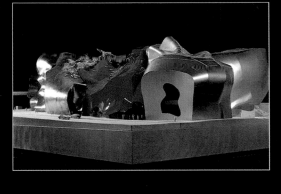

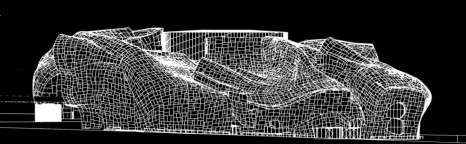
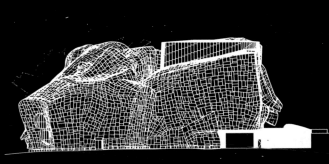

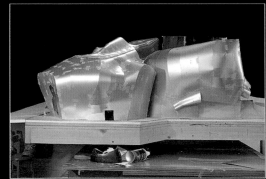
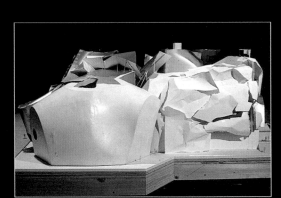

**Financial Times Millennium
Bridge Competition
London, England
1996 (project)**

Client: Royal Institute of British Architects
Competition Office
Program: Pedestrian bridge
Project Team: Frank O. Gehry, Richard Serra,
Randy Jefferson, Chris Mercier, Elizabeth
Beasley, Karl Blette, Nida Chesonis, David
Herrera, Leigh Jeffard, Charles Sanchez, Tadao
Shimizu, Rick Smith; Jorg Schlaich, structural
engineer

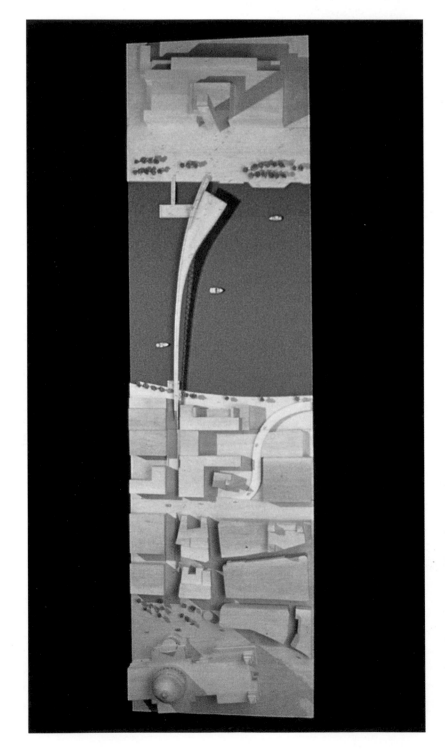

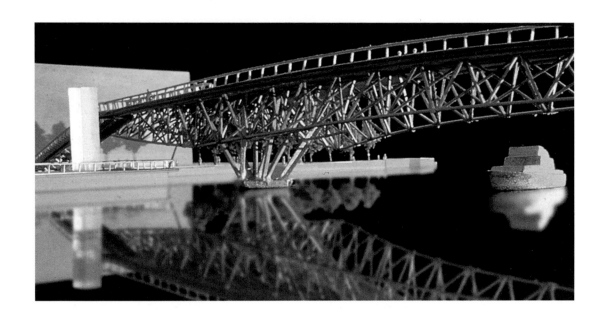

Model views; sketch.

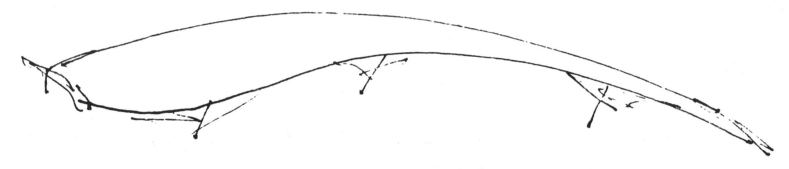

**Chapel for Father Serra,
Cathedral Square Competition
Los Angeles, California
1996**

Client: Roman Catholic Archdiocese
of Los Angeles
Program: Chapel
Materials: Wood, concrete, glass

Project team: Frank O. Gehry, Randy Jefferson,
Craig Webb, Nida Chesonis, James Dayton, Jeff
Guga, Chris Mercier, Tadao Shimizu, Flora Vara

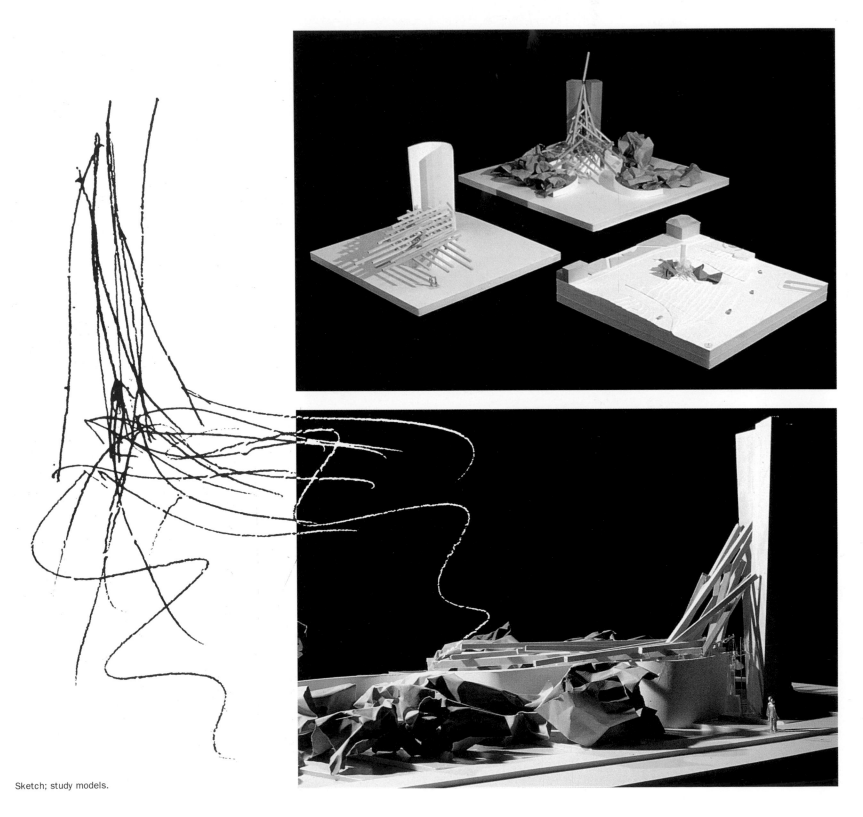

Sketch; study models.

**Telluride Residence
Telluride, Colorado
1996–**

Client: Jay Chiat
Program: Private residence
Area: 3,500 square feet
Materials: Blackened copper panels, glass, wood frame

Project team: Frank O. Gehry, Randy Jefferson, Edwin Chan, Rachel Allen, Kenneth Ahn, Kamran Ardalan, David Nam

Study models.

Condé Nast Cafeteria
New York, New York
1997–

Client: Condé Nast Publications
Program: Employee cafeteria with private dining areas for meetings and presentations
Area: 8,800 square feet
Materials: Blue titanium panels, glass panels, ash

Project Team: Frank O. Gehry, Randy Jefferson, Edwin Chan, Michelle Kaufmann, Leigh Jerrard, Kamran Ardalan, David Herrera, Chris Mercier, David Nam, Bruce Shepard, Rick Smith, Kristin Woehl

Model views.

One Times Square
New York, New York
1997

Client: Warner Brothers
Program: Animated architectural attraction, including retail spaces and bar/restaurant
Materials: Custom-fabricated wire mesh, mechanical systems for animated architectural attraction
Project Team: Frank O. Gehry, Randy Jefferson, Edwin Chan, David Herrera, Leigh Jerrard

One Times Square, originally known as Times Tower, is on a triangular lot between Forty-second and Forty-third Streets and Broadway and Seventh Avenue in Manhattan. Originally designed for the *New York Times* in 1904, the building later became the site of an annual rite drawing thousands of visitors to Times Square: the motorized ball drop from the roof of the

Model view.

building heralding the start of the new year. In 1964 the building underwent a renovation in which the original terra-cotta exterior was resheathed in white marble. In 1990 the Sony Jumbotron, an oversized television, was hung on the building's north facade.

In 1996 Warner Brothers signed a long-term lease for the entire 22-story, 110,000-square-foot building and asked Gehry to renovate the building and create a major symbolic presence in Times Square for Warner Brothers and for its parent company, Time Warner. Because the building's useable floor plates are extremely small, due to the unique, triangular geometry of the site, the concept of redeveloping the building as traditional offices was rejected. The alternate program proposed

involves the creation of an open public plaza directly accessible from Times Square. A Warner Brothers retail store is located below grade and a theme restaurant and bar mark the entrance to the below-grade retail area, accessed via escalators. The restaurant and bar are reached with express elevators on the exterior of the building. The white marble that currently covers the facades of the building is removed, and the exposed structural skeleton is covered with a translucent metallic fabric that keeps the existing billboard signage intact.

Between the underground retail store and the restaurant and bar above, an architectural attraction based on the concept of a mechanized clock tower is created by removing eight

floor plates from the lower levels of the building. Visible on the exterior of the building from Times Square and on the interior of the building from the open public plaza below, Warner Brothers animated cartoon characters emerge hourly and move in and around the building on a track system. Preprogrammed by computer to perform several different scenarios highlighted with the use of lasers, smoke machines, and other advanced technologies, the characters interact with the building's exposed structural skeleton and with the translucent metallic fabric, creating an hourly urban spectacle on Times Square that solidifies the significance of the building as the area's most important entertainment destination.

Model views.

Project Register

1954
Senior Thesis, University of Southern California

Romm Residence, Los Angeles, California (project)

1956
Third Army Day Room Improvements, Fort Bragg, North Carolina

1958
David Cabin, Idyllwild, California

Steeves Residence, Brentwood, California (1958–59)

1960
Clifton Springs Resort, Port Phillip Bay, Clifton Springs, Australia

Marais & Miranda Residence, Los Angeles, California (1960–61)

1961
Hillcrest Apartments, Santa Monica, California (1961–62)

1962
Kay Jewelers Office and Warehouse, Los Angeles, California (1962–63)

Kay Jewelers Store, South Bay Shopping Center, Redondo Beach, California (1962–64)

Kay Jewelers Store, Buena Park Shopping Center, Buena Park, California (1962–64)

1963
Sixth and Hill Apartments, Santa Monica, California (project)

SMIV Apartments, Santa Monica, California (project)

Steeves Office Building, Santa Monica, California (project)

Kenmore Apartments, Los Angeles, California (1963–64)

Faith Plating Company, Hollywood, California (1963–64)

Atkinson Park Recreation Center, Santa Maria, California (1963–64)

1964
Hauser-Benson Health Resort, Yucca Valley, California (project)

Kline Residence, Bel Air, California

Kay Jewelers Store, San Fernando, California (project)

Kay Jewelers Store, Alameda, California (project)

Los Angeles County Museum of Science and History Planning Study, Los Angeles, California (project)

Newburgh Feasibility Study, Newburgh, New York (project)

Office Building, Beverly Hills, California (project)

Danziger Studio and Residence, Hollywood, California (1964–65)

1965
"Art Treasures of Japan," Los Angeles County Museum of Art, Los Angeles, California

Clinton Laboratories, Torrance, California (project)

Reception Center, Columbia, Maryland (1965–67)

1966
"Assyrian Reliefs," Los Angeles County Museum of Art, Los Angeles, California

Hotchkiss Residence, Santa Monica, California

Merriweather-Post Pavilion, Columbia, Maryland (1966–67)

1967
Ahmanson Gallery Planning Study, Los Angeles County Museum of Art, Los Angeles, California (project)

Marr Ranch Land Use Study, Simi Valley, California (project)

Central Business District Planning Study, Hermosa Beach, California (project)

Vernon-Central Redevelopment Project, Los Angeles, California (project)

Greber Studio, Beverly Glen, Los Angeles, California (project)

Watts Automotive Park, Los Angeles, California (project)

Public Safety Building, Columbia, Maryland (1967–68)

1968
Norton Simon Sculpture Courtyard, Los Angeles County Museum of Art, Los Angeles, California

Rockdale Urban Renewal Study, Rockdale, Georgia (project)

"Billy Al Bengston," Los Angeles County Museum of Art, Los Angeles, California

O'Neill Hay Barn, San Juan Capistrano, California

Clark County Family Housing, Henderson, Nevada (project)

Rose Gardens, North Las Vegas, Nevada (project)

Joseph Magnin Store, Costa Mesa, California (1968–69)

Joseph Magnin Store, San Jose, California (1968–69)

Bixby Green, Garden Grove, California (1968–69)

Davis Studio and Residence, Malibu, California (1968–72)

1969
American School of Dance, Los Angeles, California (project)

Easy Edges Cardboard Furniture (1969–73)

Rouse Company Headquarters, Columbia, Maryland (1969–74)

1970
University Park Apartments, Irvine, California

Hollywood Bowl Renovation: Temporary Renovation, Hollywood, California

1971
Handler Residence, Santa Monica, California (1971–73; project)

Hollydot Park Townhouses, Hollydot Park, Colorado (1971–73)

Hollywood Bowl Renovation: Master Plan, Hollywood, California (1971–73)

1972
Recreation Center, Cochiti Lake, New Mexico (1972–73)

Janss Residence, West Los Angeles, California (1972–74)

Woodlands Metro Center, Woodlands, Texas (1972–77; project)

Santa Monica Place, Santa Monica, California (1972–80)

1973

Larkspur-Greenbrae Mall, Marin County, California (project)

Illinois Center, Chicago, Illinois (project)

Golden Cove Shopping Center, Palos Verdes Estates, California

Placement and Career Planning Center, University of California, Los Angeles (1973–75)

Concord Performing Arts Center, Concord, California (1973–76)

1974

Westinghouse Distribution Services Office Building, Flair Industrial Park, El Monte, California

Horton Plaza, San Diego, California (project)

The Atrium, Rudge and Guenzel Building, Lincoln, Nebraska (1974–76)

Norton Simon Gallery and Guest House, Malibu, California (1974–76)

1975

Shoreline Aquatic Park Pavilions, Long Beach, California

1976

Harper House, Village of Cross Keys, Maryland

Thornwood Mall, Park Forest South, Illinois (project)

Santa Monica Pier Renovation, Santa Monica, California (project)

Manhattan Tower, Los Angeles, California (project)

Jung Institute, Los Angeles, California (project)

The Vineyard, Escondido, California (project)

Hollywood Bowl Renovation: Phase I, Hollywood, California

St. Ives Residence, Santa Monica, California (1976–78)

Mid-Atlantic Toyota, Glen Burnie, Maryland (1976–78)

Gemini G.E.L., Los Angeles, California (1976–79)

1977

Weisman Beach House, Trancas, California

Trancas Beach House, Trancas, California

Berger, Berger, Kahn, Shafton & Moss Law Offices, Los Angeles, California (1977–78)

Gehry Residence, Santa Monica, California (1977–78)

Cabrillo Marine Museum, San Pedro, California (1977–79)

1978

Cheviot Hills Residence, Los Angeles, California

Nelson Residence, Westwood, California

"Treasures of Tutankhamen," Los Angeles County Museum of Art, Los Angeles, California

Nasli M. Heeramaneck Collection, Los Angeles County Museum of Art, Los Angeles, California

Main Street Development Project, Venice, California (project)

Wagner Residence, Malibu, California (project)

Gunther Residence, Encinal Bluffs, California (project)

Familian Residence, Santa Monica, California (project)

Carriage House, New York, New York (project)

Valley Cultural Center, Warner Ranch Park, Woodland Hills, California (project)

Arts Park, Van Nuys, California (project)

Hollywood Bowl Renovation: Phase II, Hollywood, California (project)

Spiller Residence, Venice, California (1978–79)

Loyal Heights Manor, Seattle, Washington (1978–80)

Centerpoint Mall, Oxnard, California (1978–80)

Loyola University Law School: Phase I, Fritz B. Burns Student Center, Los Angeles, California (1978–82)

Loyola University Law School: Phase II, Merrifield Hall, Donovan Hall, Hall of the 70s, and Chapel, Los Angeles, California (1978–84)

1979

Children's Museum, Los Angeles, California (1979–80)

Indiana Avenue Houses, Venice, California (1979–81)

Experimental Edges Cardboard Furniture (1979–82)

Benson Residence, Calabassas, California (1979–84)

1980

Late Entry to the Chicago Tribune Tower Competition (project)

Stolte Office Building, Portland, Oregon (project)

"In the Presence of the Past: Strada Novissima," Corderia of the Arsenale, Venice, Italy

"The Avant-Garde in Russia, 1910–1930," Los Angeles County Museum of Art, Los Angeles, California

Angel's Place, Los Angeles, California (project)

United States Embassy & School, Damascus, Syria (project)

Bubar's Jewelers, Santa Monica Place, Santa Monica, California

World Savings and Loan Association, North Hollywood, California

Hollywood Bowl Renovation: Phase III, Hollywood, California

House for a Filmmaker, Santa Monica Canyon, California (1980–81)

Lafayette Square, New Orleans, Louisiana (1980–84; project)

1981

Smith Residence, Brentwood, California (project)

"Collaborations: Artists and Architects," Architectural League of New York, New York, New York (project)

Westlake–Thousand Oaks Industrial Park, Thousand Oaks, California

14th Street Housing, Atlanta, Georgia

Fish Sculpture, New York, New York (project)

"Seventeen Artists in the Sixties," Los Angeles County Museum of Art, Los Angeles, California

Paramount Theater Shell, Oakland, California (project)

Screen Actors Guild, Studio City, California

Binder House, Los Angeles, California

Central Business District, Kalamazoo, Michigan

Galleria Shopping Mall, Oklahoma City, Oklahoma

Brooks Avenue Development Project, Venice, California

Frank O. Gehry and Associates Office, Venice, California

Hollywood Bowl Renovation: Phase IV, Hollywood, California

Wosk Residence, Beverly Hills, California (1981–84)

1982

Fleck Residence, Los Angeles, California (project)

Fleck Office Building, Los Angeles, California

Tract House (project)

World Savings Bank, Denver, Colorado (project)

Century View Office Building, Los Angeles, California

Civic Center Competition, Beverly Hills, California

Hollywood Bowl Renovation: Phase V, Hollywood, California

Hollywood Bowl Renovation: Phase VI, Hollywood, California

The Temporary Contemporary, Los Angeles, California (1982–83)

World Expo Amphitheater, New Orleans, Louisiana (1982–84)

California Aerospace Museum and Theater, Los Angeles, California (1982–84)

Norton Residence, Venice, California (1982–84)

Rebecca's Restaurant, Venice, California (1982–85)

Frances Howard Goldwyn Regional Branch Library, Hollywood, California (1982–86)

Winton Guest House, Wayzata, Minnesota (1982–87)

1983

Kellerman–Krane Residence, Los Angeles, California

Cricket Inn Project, Farmington, Connecticut

"Folly: The Prison Project"

Jencks Front Porch (project)

Available Light, Temporary Museum of Contemporary Art, Los Angeles, California

"German Expressionist Sculpture," Los Angeles County Museum of Art, Los Angeles, California

Boxenbaum Residence, New York, New York

Galleria Office Building, Oklahoma City, Oklahoma (1983–85; project)

Loyola University Law School: Phase III, Rains Library Renovation, Los Angeles, California (1983–85)

Fish and Snake Lamps (1983–86)

Information and Computer Science/Engineering Laboratory and Engineering Center: Phase I, University of California, Irvine, Irvine, California (1983–86)

Sirmai-Peterson Residence, Thousand Oaks, California (1983–88)

1984

Médiathèque, Centre d'Art Contemporain Design Competition, Nîmes, France (project)

Camp Good Times, Santa Monica Mountains, Malibu, California (1984–85)

Sunar-Hauserman Showroom, Innova Design Center, Houston, Texas (1984–86)

Edgemar Development, Santa Monica, California (1984–88)

1985

Il Corso del Coltello, Venice Biennale, Venice, Italy

Fountain Valley School Theater, Colorado Springs, Colorado

Boylston Street Air Rights, Boston, Massachusetts (project)

Pirelli Bicocca Competition, Milan, Italy

Turtle Creek Development, Dallas, Texas (1985–86; project)

GFT Fish, Turin, Italy, Florence, Italy (1985–86)

360 Newbury Street, Boston, Massachusetts (1985–88)

Yale Psychiatric Institute, New Haven, Connecticut (1985–89)

Herman Miller Western Regional Facility, Rocklin, California (1985–89)

Chiat/Day Building, Venice, California (1985–91)

1986

"Lawrence Halprin: Changing Places," San Francisco Museum of Modern Art, San Francisco, California

Hoffman Gallery, Santa Monica, California

Chiat Residence, Sagaponack, New York

Fan Pier, Parcel H, Boston, Massachusetts

NBC-Maguire Proposal

Standing Glass Fish, Walker Art Center Sculpture Garden, Minneapolis, Minnesota

Fishdance Restaurant, Kobe, Japan (1986–87)

"The Architecture of Frank O. Gehry," Walker Art Center, Minneapolis, Minnesota (1986–87)

Chiat/Day Temporary Offices, Venice, California (1986–88)

"Sheet Metal Craftsmanship: Progress in Building," National Building Museum, Washington, D.C. (1986–88)

Information and Computer Science/Engineering Laboratory and Engineering Center: Phase II, University of California, Irvine, Irvine, California (1986–88)

Schnabel Residence, Brentwood, California (1986–89)

Progressive Corporation Headquarters, Cleveland, Ohio (1986–91; project)

1987

Santa Monica Airport Park Competition, Santa Monica, California

Toronto Metropolitan Government Headquarters Competition, Toronto, Ontario

Parc de la Villette Restaurant Competition, Paris, France

Culver Center, Culver City, California

Kings Cross Competition, London, England (project)

Borman Residence, Malibu, California

Madison Square Garden Competition, New York, New York (project)

Fine Arts Center Planning Study, Los Angeles County Museum of Art, Los Angeles, California

San'wiches 1 and 2, San Diego, California (1987–89)

Vitra International Furniture Manufacturing Facility and Design Museum, Weil am Rhein, Germany (1987–89)

St. James Office Building, Boston, Massachusetts (1987–90; project)

Iowa Laser Laboratory, Iowa City, Iowa (1987–92)

Team Disneyland Administration Building, Anaheim, California (1987–95)

Cloverfield Alterations for Frank O. Gehry and Associates, Santa Monica, California (1987–96)

1988

Chiat/Day Toronto, Toronto, Ontario

Milan Triennale, Milan, Italy

Port Imperial Competition, Weehauken, New Jersey (project)

Canary Wharf Competition, London, England (project)

Library Square, Los Angeles, California (project)

Hollywood Sign, Barcelona, Spain

Weisman Center, Venice, California (project)

Massachusetts Museum of Contemporary Art, North Adams, Massachusetts

New York Bagel Shop, Los Angeles, California (1988–90)

Euro-Disneyland Retail and Entertainment Center, Villier-sur-Marne, France (1988–93)

American Center, Paris, France (1988–94)

Vitra International, Biersfelden, Switzerland (1988–94)

1989

Federal Triangle Competition, Washington, D.C. (project)

12th Street Project, Santa Monica, California

Center for the Visual Arts, University of Toledo, Toledo, Ohio

Pito Tea Kettle

New Zealand Museum Competition, Aukland, New Zealand

Loyola University Law School: Phase IV, Casassa Building, Los Angeles, California (1989–91)

Bentwood Furniture (1989–92)

Vila Olimpica, Barcelona, Spain (1989–92)

Lewis Residence, Lyndhurst, Ohio (1989–95; project)

Walt Disney Concert Hall and Hotel, Los Angeles, California (1989–)

1990

Chiat/Day New York Offices, New York, New York (project)

Frederick R. Weisman Art and Teaching Museum, Minneapolis, Minnesota (1990–93)

1991

Bonames Housing Project, Frankfurt, Germany

Griesheim (Lancia Study), Frankfurt, Germany

Parc del Delta, Barcelona, Spain (project)

"The Walt Disney Concert Hall Design Process," Venice Biennale, Venice, Italy

Los Angeles Rapid Transit District Headquarters Competition, Gateway Center, Union Station, Los Angeles, California (project)

Hannover Bus Stop, Hannover, Germany (1991–94)

Gehry Residence, Santa Monica, California (1991–94)

EMR Communication and Technology Center, Bad Öynhausen, Germany (1991–95)

Goldstein Housing Project, Frankfurt, Germany (1991–96)

Guggenheim Museum, Bilbao, Spain (1991–97)

1992

"Degenerate Art: The Fate of the Avant-Garde in Nazi Germany," Los Angeles, California, Berlin, Germany

Metal Crafts Building, University of Toledo, Toledo, Ohio (1992–94)

Loyola University Law School: Phase V, Parking Garage, Los Angeles, California (1992–94)

Children's Museum, Boston, Massachusetts (1992–96)

Nationale-Nederlanden Building, Prague, Czech Republic (1992–96)

1993

Alameda Redevelopment, Mexico City, Mexico (project)

Disney Community Ice Center, Anaheim, California

Telluride Residence, Telluride, Colorado (1993–)

Center for Molecular Studies, University of Cincinnati, Cincinnati, Ohio (1993–)

1994

Berlin Museum Competition, Berlin, Germany (project)

Kunsthalle Bielefeld, Bielefeld, Germany

Pferdeturm USTRA Bridge, Hannover, Germany (1994–95; project)

Der Neue Zollhof, Düsseldorf, Germany (1994–)

Pariser Platz 3, Berlin, Germany (1994–)

1995

Temporary Contemporary Renovations, Museum of Contemporary Art, Los Angeles, California (1995–96)

Decorative Arts Museum of Montreal, Montreal, Quebec (1995–)

Samsung Museum of Modern Art, Seoul, Korea (1995–)

USTRA Office Building, Germany (1995–)

Loyola University Law School: Phase VI, Los Angeles, California (1995–)

1996

Church of the Year 2000 Competition, Rome, Italy (project)

Financial Times Millennium Bridge Competition, London, England (project)

Chapel for Father Serra, Cathedral Square Competition, Los Angeles, California

Experience Music Project, Seattle Center Campus, Seattle, Washington (1996–)

Telluride Residence, Telluride, Colorado (1996–)

1997

One Times Square, New York, New York

Condé Nast Cafeteria, New York, New York (1997–)

Biography

February 28, 1929

Born in Toronto, Ontario, with the name Frank Owen Goldberg.

1947

Moves with his family to Los Angeles, California.

September 1949–May 1951

College of Architecture, University of California, Los Angeles: Studies ceramics with Glen Lukens; attends evening courses in drawing.

September 1951–May 1954

College of Architecture, University of California, Los Angeles: Receives degree in architecture; encouraged by Lukens, attends second year of graduate school in architecture.

May 14, 1954

Changes his last name to Gehry.

June 1953–January 1955

Victor Gruen Associates, Los Angeles, California: Project architect for residential and commercial buildings.

1954–55

Collaborative Professional Planning Group, Los Angeles, California: Project architect.

January 1955–October 1956

United States Army, Special Service Division, Atlanta, Georgia: Architect in charge of recreational services for the army.

Robert and Company, Architects, Atlanta, Georgia: Architect and planner for urban-renewal projects.

September 1956–February 1957

Graduate School of Design, Harvard University, Cambridge, Massachusetts: Encouraged by Garrett Eckbo to undertake advanced studies in urban planning, attends Harvard for one semester.

January–May 1957

Perry, Shaw, Hepburn, and Dean, Boston, Massachusetts: Architect and planner.

Hideo Sasaki, Landscape Architect, Boston, Massachusetts: Architect and planner.

June–September 1957

Pereira and Luckman, Architects, Los Angeles, California: Architect.

October 1957–March 1961

Victor Gruen Associates, Los Angeles, California: Architect, planner, architect-in-charge.

April 1961–September 1962

André Rémondet, Architecte, Paris, France: Architect and planner.

1962–65

Gehry and Walsh, Architects, Santa Monica, California: Principal.

1966–67

Gehry, Walsh, and O'Malley, Baltimore, Maryland, and Los Angeles, California: Principal.

1967

Receives Merit Award for the Merriweather-Post Pavilion from the Baltimore Chapter of the American Institute of Architects.

1967–

Frank O. Gehry and Associates, Santa Monica, California: Principal.

1969

Receives Honor Award for the Joseph Magnin Store, Costa Mesa, California, from the Southern California Chapter of the American Institute of Architects.

1969–72

Junior Arts Center, Barnsdall Park, Los Angeles, California: Teaches the class "Fantastic City" for students in public elementary schools.

Smithsonian Institute, Washington, D.C.: With his sister, Doreen Nelson, organizes an experimental course in urbanism for elementary-school students.

Los Angeles Public School System, California: Consultant and teacher in the city's construction education program, supported by the National Endowment for the Arts in six city elementary schools.

1971

Los Angeles County Museum of Art and NASA: Works with the Garrett Corporation on the "Art and Technology" program for the study of principles of livability in space and subsequent implications on the Earth.

1971–72

College of Architecture, University of Southern California, Los Angeles: Assistant professor.

1974

Elected to College of Fellows, American Institute of Architects.

1975

Receives Honor Awards for the Concord Performing Arts Center and the Cochiti Lake Recreation Center and Merit Award and Special Award for the Davis Studio and Residence from the Southern California Chapter of the American Institute of Architects.

1975–76

Southern California Institute of Architecture, Santa Monica: Instructor.

1976

Rice University, Houston, Texas: Visiting critic.

Receives Honor Award for the Rouse Company Headquarters from the Southern California Chapter of the American Institute of Architects.

1977

Receives Arnold W. Brunner Memorial Prize from the American Academy of Arts and Letters.

Receives Honor Award for the Concord Performing Arts Center and Merit Award for the Westinghouse Distribution Services Office Building from the Southern California Chapter of the American Institute of Architects.

1977–79

University of California, Los Angeles: Visiting critic.

1978

Cooper Union, New York: Lecturer and visiting critic.

University of Texas, Houston: Lecturer and visiting critic.

Receives Honor Award for the University of California Placement and Career Planning Center and Honorable Mention for the Gehry Residence from the Southern California Chapter of the American Institute of Architects.

1979

University of California, Los Angeles: Visiting critic.

School of Architecture, Yale University, New Haven, Connecticut: William Bishop Chair.

Receives Honor Award for Mid-Atlantic Toyota from the Southern California Chapter of the American Institute of Architects.

1980

Graduate School of Design, Harvard University: Visiting critic.

Receives Honor Award for the Gehry Residence from the American Institute of Architects.

Receives Citation for the exhibition "The Avant-Garde in Russia, 1910–1930" from the Southern California Chapter of the American Institute of Architects.

1981

Receives prizes for Santa Monica Place and Indiana Avenue Houses from the Los Angeles Chapter of the American Institute of Architects.

1982

School of Architecture, Yale University, New Haven, Connecticut: Charlotte Davenport Professorship in Architecture.

Receives prize for the Norton Residence from *Architectural Record*.

Receives Honor Award for Fritz B. Burns Student Center, Loyola University Law School, from the Los Angeles Chapter of the American Institute of Architects.

1983

Graduate School of Design, Harvard University, Cambridge, Massachusetts: Visiting critic.

Receives prize for the Spiller Residence from *Architectural Record*.

1984

Graduate School of Design, Harvard University, Cambridge, Massachusetts: Eliot Noyes Chair.

Receives Honor Award for the Temporary Contemporary and Citations for the California Aerospace Museum and Theater and Loyola University Law School, Phase II, from the Los Angeles Chapter of the American Institute of Architects.

Receives Awards of Distinction for Santa Monica Place, the Spiller Residence, and Cabrillo Marine Museum from the California Coastal Commission.

1985

School of Architecture, Yale University, New Haven, Connecticut: Charlotte Davenport Professorship in Architecture.

Receives Honor Awards for the Norton Residence and the Wosk Residence from the Los Angeles Chapter of the American Institute of Architects.

1986

Receives Honor Award for Loyola Law School from the American Institute of Architects.

Receives Honor Awards for the Frances Howard Goldwyn Regional Branch Library and the Winton Guest House, Merit Award for the Fishdance Restaurant, and Distinguished Architect Award from the Los Angeles Chapter of the American Institute of Architects.

1987

Elected to College of Fellows, American Academy of Arts and Letters.

Receives Honorary Doctorate of Visual Arts from California Institute of the Arts.

Receives Honorary Doctorate of Fine Arts, Rhode Island School of Design.

Receives Honor Award from the School of Architecture, University of Southern California.

Receives architecture prize from *House and Garden*.

Receives Honor Awards for the Information and Computer Science/Engineering Laboratory and Engineering Center, University of California, Irvine, the California Aerospace Museum and Theater, and the Norton Residence from the American Institute of Architects.

Receives Honor Awards for the Information and Computer Science/Engineering Laboratory and Engineering Center, University of California, Irvine, from the Los Angeles Chapter of the American Institute of Architects.

1987–89

School of Architecture, Yale University, New Haven, Connecticut: Charlotte Davenport Professorship in Architecture.

1988

Receives Honor Award for the Winton Guest House from the American Institute of Architects.

Receives Merit Award for the exhibition "Sheet Metal Craftsmanship: Progress in Building" from the Los Angeles Chapter of the American Institute of Architects.

1988–89

University of California, Los Angeles: Assistant professor.

1989

Receives Pritzker Prize in Architecture.

Elected a trustee of the American Academy in Rome.

Receives Honorary Doctorate of Engineering from the Technical University of Nova Scotia.

Receives Honorary Doctorate of Fine Arts from Otis Art Institute.

Receives Merit Award for 360 Newbury Street from the Southern California Chapter of the American Institute of Architects.

Receives Gold Medal Honor Award for the Edgemar Development and Merit Award for the Herman Miller Western Regional Facility from the Los Angeles Chapter of the American Institute of Architects.

Receives Merit Award for the Herman Miller Western Regional Facility from the American Society of Landscape Architects.

1990

Receives the Gold Key of the Country of Panama from the president of Panama.

Receives architecture award from the California Arts Council.

Receives Distinguished Artist Award from Club 100 of the Los Angeles Music Center.

Receives Honor Award for the Schnabel Residence from the American Institute of Architects.

Receives Design Awards for Chiat/Day Toronto and Edgemar Development from the Southern California Chapter of the American Institute of Architects.

Receives Honor Award for Vitra International Furniture Manufacturing Facility and Design Museum from the Los Angeles Chapter of the American Institute of Architects.

1991

Elected to the College of Fellows of the American Academy of Arts and Sciences.

Recognized by the Senate of Ohio for his career.

Receives *Progressive Architecture* Awards for the Frederick R. Weisman Art and Teaching Museum and the American Center.

Receives Hugo-Häring-Preis for Vitra International Furniture Manufacturing Facility and Design Museum.

Receives Parker Prize for 360 Newbury Street.

Receives Honor Awards for 360 Newbury Street, the Herman Miller Western Regional Facility, and Vitra International Furniture Manufacturing Facility and Design Museum from the American Institute of Architects.

Receives Honor Award for the Yale Psychiatric Institute from the Connecticut Society of Architects.

Receives Honor Award for Vitra International Furniture Manufacturing Facility and Design Museum from the Southern California Chapter of the American Institute of Architects.

Receives Honor Award for Progressive Corporation Headquarters from the Los Angeles Chapter of the American Institute of Architects.

1992

Receives Praemium Imperiale Award from the Japan Art Association.

Receives Wolf Prize in Art (Architecture) from the Wolf Foundation.

Bartlett School of Architecture and Planning: Sir Bannister Fletcher Visiting Professorship.

Receives *Progressive Architecture* Honor Award for Walt Disney Concert Hall and Hotel.

Receives Gold Award for Bentwood Furniture from *I.D.*

Receives Roscoe Award for Bentwood Furniture from *Interior Design*.

Receives Honor Award for Euro-Disneyland Retail and Entertainment Center from the American Institute of Architects.

Receives Honor Award for Chiat/Day Building from the California Council of the American Institute of Architects.

Receives Honor Award for the Frances Howard Goldwyn Regional Branch Library from the California Central Valley Chapter of the American Institute of Architects.

1993

Receives Honorary Doctorate of Humanities from Occidental College.

Receives Merit Award for the University of Toledo Center for the Visual Arts from the Metal Construction Association.

Receives Honor Award for the University of Toledo Center for the Visual Arts from the California Chapter of the American Institute of Architects.

Receives Merit Award for the University of Toledo Center for the Visual Arts from the Ohio Chapter of the American Institute of Architects.

Receives Honor Award for the Iowa Laser Laboratory from the Los Angeles Chapter of the American Institute of Architects.

1994

Receives Dorothy and Lillian Gish Award for lifetime contribution to the arts.

Elected as Academician by the National Academy of Design.

Receives Thomas Jefferson Medal of Architecture from the University of Virginia.

Receives *Progressive Architecture* Honor Award for the Boston Children's Museum.

Receives Honor Award for the Frederick R. Weisman Art and Teaching Museum from the American Institute of Architects.

1995

Receives honorary degree from Whittier College.

Receives John M. Olguin Marine Environment Award for Cabrillo Marine Museum.

Receives Golden Plate Award from the American Academy of Achievement.

Receives Chrysler Award for Innovation in Design.

1996

Receives Honorary Master of Architecture from the Southern California Institute of Architecture.

Federal Institute of Technology (ETH), Zurich, Switzerland: Visiting scholar.

Receives Honorable Mention for Team Disneyland Administration Building from *I.D.*

Receives Honor Award for the University of Toledo Center for the Visual Arts from the American Institute of Architects.

1997

Elected as Honorary Consul of the City of Bilbao.

Receives Honorary Doctorate of Architecture from the Southern California Institute of Architecture.

1998

University of California, Los Angeles: Visiting professor.

Receives the Friedrich Kiesler Prize.

Elected Honorary Academician by the Royal Academy of Arts.

Receives Gold Medal from the Royal Architectural Institute of Canada.

Elected Chancellor of the City of Bilbao.

Bibliography

1963

"After the Kids," *Los Angeles Herald Examiner*, August 18.

1964

"Picture Preview of Progress in Construction," *Southwest Building and Contractor*, January 24.

"Apartment Planned," *Los Angeles Times*, April 19.

"Japanese Garden Shared with Public," *Architecture/West*, September.

"Architect Explains Leisure," *Santa Maria Times*, October 30.

1965

"Where Architects Hang Their Hats," *Architecture/West*, August.

1966

"Wilde Lake Village Development Begins," *Baltimore Sun*, July 19.

"Exhibition Installation by Gehry and Walsh, Architects," *Arts and Architecture*, July.

"The Architect's Own Office: Showplace and Workplace," *Progressive Architecture*, September.

1967

"D.C. Symphony Pavilion to Be 'Giant Umbrella,'" *Washington Evening Star*, June 21.

"Columbia Seeks to Revive 'Village Life,'" *Baltimore Sun*, June 28.

Elliot W. Galkin, "Music Festivals: Unique . . . ," *Baltimore Sun*, July 9.

Frederic B. Hill, "Wet Throng Hails Columbia, Rouse, Humphrey, and Music," *Baltimore Sun*, July 15.

"Music Fete Marred by Mud, Rain," *Baltimore Evening Sun*, July 15.

Myra MacPherson, "Symphony Gala Ends as Okefenokee of the Arts," *New York Times*, July 16.

"Rain Christens Culture in New Columbia Pavilion," *Washington Post*, July 16.

Harold C. Schonberg, "Music: Columbia Festival is Baptized," *New York Times*, July 16.

Paul Hume, "New Symphony Pavilion Has Gay Nineties Aura," *Washington Post*, July 17.

Harold C. Schonberg, "Music: Hurtling from Famine to Feast," *New York Times*, July 23.

Myra MacPherson, "Maryland Partygoers Refused to Be Rained Out Again," *New York Times*, August 5.

James Hibbard, "Cheer the Pavilion Hear, Hear," *Washington Daily News*, August 11.

Lou Desser, "Ponte Vecchio Theme: Architect Envisions Seaside Tourist Spot," *Los Angeles Times*, August 27.

"The Merriweather Post Pavilion of Music," *Architectural Forum*, November.

"Architect—The Award-Winning Scheme: Merriweather-Post Pavilion, Columbia," *Maryland Living*, November 12.

1968

"South Coast Plaza, Joseph Magnin Store Features Thin Coast Plaster by Varner," *California Plasterer*, May.

Kenward S. Olyshant, "Unique Acoustical Control by Bixby Green," *California Drywall Industry*, July.

Hector Aree, "Things to Come . . . Now," *Home Furnishings*, July 2.

"'Sound Barrier' Solves Noise Problem," *Los Angeles Times*, August 11.

William F. Hallstead, "Music Comes to the Woodlands," *Maryland Magazine*, autumn.

"Conversation with Indrani," *Dance Magazine*, September.

"Store Openings: Joseph Magnin," *Fashion Week*, November 25.

"Eye on Architecture," *Home Furnishings Daily*, December 16.

1969

Harold C. Schonberg, "Acoustician Hits a High Note with His Slide Rule," *New York Times*, July 19.

"Architects Win Awards for 12 Building Designs," *Los Angeles Times*, November 16.

"Guidance by New Towns," *Baltimore Sun*, November 23.

"Architects Report New Towns Need Public Guidance," *Home Builder News*, December 8.

1970

Hector Aree, "Store Packaging in Display," *Women's Wear Daily*, January 13.

John Rockwell, "A Different Bowl Awaits Summer Concert Goers," *Los Angeles Times*, April 22.

Gay Scott, "Bowl Gets Facelifting to Tune of $160,000," *S.C. Citizen News*, April 25.

Martin Bernheimer, "A New Look, a New Sound for an Old Bowl," *Los Angeles Times*, May 24.

David LePage, "First Apartments at Irvine Put Focus on Space," *Los Angeles Times*, July 5.

Dick Turpin, "Child Planners Build City of Dreams . . . More Space for Recreation," *Los Angeles Times*, July 5.

Martin Bernheimer, "Krips Conducts Opener at the Revamped Bowl," *Los Angeles Times*, July 9.

Sharon Fay Koch, "First-Nighter Picnic, Hear Beethoven," *Los Angeles Times*, July 9.

Karen Mouson, "Sound Mars Festive Hollywood Bowl Opening," *Los Angeles Herald Examiner*, July 9.

John Pastier, "Design Team Makes Notable Contribution to Hollywood Bowl," *Los Angeles Times*, July 19.

1971

Reyner Banham, *Los Angeles: The Architecture of Four Ecologies* (Harmondsworth, England: Penguin).

"School Children Build Models to Learn City Problems," *Los Angeles Herald Examiner*, November 15.

1972

"Institute Is Host to Young City Builders," *Institute News, California Institute of the Arts*, January 5.

Alexander Fried, "Concord Readies Pavilion," *San Francisco Examiner*, February 19.

Jean Murphy, "From Sand Castles to Cities of Future," *Los Angeles Times*, March 14.

Patricia McCormack, "Award Winning Architect Designs New Furniture," *Lexington Leader*, March 25.

"Different Kind of Lib," *Montreal Sunday Express*, March 26.

"Here It Is: Low Cost, No Upkeep Furniture," *Miami Herald*, March 26.

"Furniture for a Revolution," *San Francisco Examiner*, March 27.

"Bar, Desk Unit or Perch," *Rocky Mountain News*, April 1.

"The Squiggly Look," *Baltimore Sun*, April 3.

"Easy Pieces," *Home Furnishings Daily*, April 7.

Norma Skura, "Paper Furniture for Penny Pinchers," *New York Times Magazine*, April 9.

Mary Meyers, "Bloomingdales . . . Living Naturally," *Home Furnishings Daily*, April 12.

Rita Reif, "Mediterranean Style Upstaged," *New York Times*, April 12.

Susan Rogers, "That's Right . . . Cardboard," *New York Post*, April 13.

"Easy Edges Marks the Next Step in Furniture Design," *Chicago Tribune*, April 17.

Marilyn Hoffman, "Liberated Design: Cardboard Moves in on Furniture World," *Christian Science Monitor*, April 19.

"Cardboard Furniture: Chic and Low Cost," *Baltimore Sun*, April 30.

Dan MacMasters, "Easy Edges: Why Didn't Somebody Think of This Before?," *Los Angeles Times Home Magazine*, April 30.

Judy Hazlett, "Lifestyle: New Concept Is Easy to Live With," *Long Beach Independent Press-Telegram*, May 30.

"The Cardboard Furniture Is Here," *Riverside–San Bernadino Press-Enterprise*, June 4.

"Fiberboard Furniture: Easy on the Eye, Easy on the Wallet," *Chicago Tribune*, June 11.

"Paper Chairs? Fashioned Furniture," *Biloxi-Gulfport Daily Herald*, June 12.

Madeline McDermott, "It's Different, Curvy and Cardboard," *Houston Chronicle*, June 22.

Amy Manning, "The Corrugated Comeback," *Washington Sunday Star*, July 9.

Blair Sabol, "Teacher Chauvinism Not Tolerated: The City That 20 Children Built," *Village Voice*, August 31.

Amy Holmes, "The Spotlight: New Looks in Now Design," *Houston Chronicle*, December 1.

1973

James Hennesy, *Nomadic Furniture* (New York: Pantheon).

Innovations: Contemporary Home Environs (exhibition catalog, La Jolla: La Jolla Museum of Contemporary Art).

Ed Moosbrugger, "SM Picks Rouse Plan for Center," *Santa Monica Evening Outlook*, May 23.

Seymour Beubis, "Firm Named for $100 Million Project in Santa Monica," *Los Angeles Times*, May 24.

Ed Moosbrugger, "Imagination Wins in Santa Monica: Openness Counts," *Santa Monica Evening Outlook*, May 25.

Robert Hollis, "Proposal May Halt Bay Fill," *San Francisco Examiner and Chronicle*, June 3.

John Pastier, "A Vote for Innovation in Santa Monica," *Los Angeles Times*, June 4.

"Greenbrae Mall Plan to be Aired," *Los Angeles Times*, June 4.

Patricia Perry, "Shopping Center Vote Is Cheered," *San Rafael Independent Journal*, June 6.

"Shopping Center Action Is Taken," *San Rafael Independent Journal*, June 19.

"Water Issue Stirs Anger in March County," *Los Angeles Times*, June 20.

Joanne Norris, "Dining at the Hollywood Bowl," *Long Beach Independent Press-Telegram*, June 24.

Leonard Feather, "No Dissonance: Jazz Festival in Concord," *Los Angeles Times*, August 1.

"Renovation Study of Hollywood Bowl Set," *Los Angeles Times*, September 26.

Erik M. Ingram, "Lack of Public Transport for Proposed Center Hit," *San Rafael Independent Journal*, November 15.

"Santa Monica Officials in High Praise of Redevelopers," *Los Angeles Times*, November 16.

"Desert Facility," *Los Angeles Times*, December 2.

1974

Ed Moosbrugger, "For Redevelopment: Santa Monica Agency Picks Three Consultants," *Santa Monica Evening Outlook*, January 24.

"Ferry Foes Beaten by Full Board," *San Rafael Independent Journal*, February 5.

Ed Moosbrugger, "Environmental Impact: Shopping Center Consultant Picked," *Santa Monica Evening Outlook*, February 15.

Anne Morgenthaler, "Santa Monica Development: Shopping Center Faces Obstacles," *Santa Monica Evening Outlook*, February 20.

Ken Fanucchi, "Planners Will Tackle Mandate: Improve Quality of Life in Santa Monica," *Los Angeles Times*, February 24.

Anne Morgenthaler, "Downtown Center Redesign Weighed," *Santa Monica Evening Outlook*, March 8.

"Energy Saving Concepts: SM Center Change Detailed," *S. C. Roberts News*, March 13.

Ed Moosbruger, "Rouse Company Report," *Santa Monica Evening Outlook*, March 13.

Ed Moosbruger, "Shopping Center: Redevelopment Project Development Delayed," *Santa Monica Evening Outlook*, March 27.

"Santa Monica Shopping Center—Hahn, Inc. to Join in Development," *Santa Monica Evening Outlook*, April 5.

Camilla Snyder, "New Contemporary Museum Will Open for Los Angeles," *Los Angeles Herald Examiner*, June 13.

"Concord Pavilion Near Completion," *Oakland Tribune*, October 27.

1975

Bruce Adams, "Concord Pavilion Acoustics Will Aid Concerts, Theater," *Contra Costa Times*, March 19.

"Editorial: Concord Opening Key to Future," *Contra Costa Times*, May 1.

Heuwell Tircuit, "Music World: An Acoustical Reason to Celebrate," *San Francisco Chronicle*, May 13.

John Dengel, "Jazzy Debut for a New Pavilion," *Oakland Tribune*, May 16.

"Editorial: Concord Pavilion Comes Alive Tonight," *Contra Costa Times*, May 16.

William C. Glackin, "Arts in Review: A Place for All Reasons," *Sacramento Bee*, May 18.

"Concord Pavilion: An Exercise in Acoustics," *Berkeley Gazette*, May 19.

"Pavilion Christened by Jazz," *Oakland Tribune*, May 19.

"Perfect Weather for the Pavilion," *Oakland Tribune*, May 19.

"Fiery, Jazzy Dramatics at the Concord Pavilion," *San Francisco Chronicle*, May 20.

Anne Morgenthaler, "Facelifting of Santa Monica Pier Approved," *Santa Monica Evening Outlook*, May 28.

Ed Moosbruger, "Indirect System Used; New Light Shed on Offices," *Santa Monica Evening Outlook*, May 30.

"Santa Monica Architect Wins Awards for Design," *Santa Monica Evening Outlook*, May 30.

Philip Elwood, "Tanya Earns a Rave at Concord," *San Francisco Examiner*, June 2.

Benjamin Clavan, "Architecture: Sounds from the Hillside," *Daily Californian*, June 6.

Dick Turpin, "Southland AIA Chapter Will Present 20 Awards," *Los Angeles Times*, June 8.

Dan MacMasters, "Q and A— Ron Davis: He Plays Tricks with Dimensions," *Los Angeles Times Home Magazine*, August 17.

Daryl Lembke, "Concord: Start of Something Big?," *Los Angeles Times*, August 21.

Joseph Simpson, "The Greening of the Offices," *Baltimore Sun*, September 28.

1976

Paul Goldberger, "Studied Slapdash," *New York Times Magazine*, January 18.

"A Rousing Place," *Progressive Architecture: Interior Architecture*, February.

Pat Morrison, "Environmentalist Will Design Museum," *Los Angeles Times*, February 1.

Art Seidenbaum, "A Bowlful of Musical Chairs," *Los Angeles Times*, February 20.

Martin Bernheimer, "An Overdue Face-Lift for a Musical Landmark," *Los Angeles Times: Calendar*, February 22.

Bruce Lewis, "Councilmen Plan Look at Speaker Cost," *Contra Costa Times*, March 14.

"Pavilion Program Previews Tonight," *California Transcript*, March 17.

Phillip Elwood, "Weekend of Opening Concerts: Concord's Sunny New Pavilion," *San Francisco Examiner,* March 19.

"Council to Eye Speakers," *Contra Costa Times,* March 21.

Brooks Keuhl, "Pavilion Termed 'Great' by Mitch," *California Transcript,* April 15.

Paul Hertelendy, "Oakland Symphony Opener," *Oakland Tribune,* April 19.

Lou Desser, "AIA Jury Picks Best-Designed Buildings for 1976: 10 Southland Companies Capture Design Awards—Gruen, Gehry Win Highest Honors," *Los Angeles Times,* October 31.

"Concord Pavilion: Concord, California," *Baumeister,* November.

Art Seidenbaum, "Filling in the Centers," *Los Angeles Times,* November 5.

1977

"Davis Residence: Malibu, California," *GA Houses* 2.

David Gebhard and Deborah Nevins, *200 Years of American Architectural Drawings* (New York: Watson-Guptill).

David Gebhard and Robert Winter, *A Guide to Architecture in Los Angeles and Southern California* (Santa Barbara: Peregrine Smith).

A View of California Architecture, 1960–1976 (San Francisco: San Francisco Museum of Art).

John Dreyfuss, "Job Center Does Its Job . . . and Architecture Excels," *Los Angeles Times,* January 23.

"Plans Finished for Cabrillo Marine Museum," *Southland,* March 27.

John Dreyfuss, "Pavilion: Crater with a Stage at Bottom," *Los Angeles Times,* May 15.

"Concord Pavilion Tops Nation in Architectural Design," *San Francisco Examiner Home,* May 22.

Jeannette Hartman, "Design Stressed over Materials," *Santa Monica Evening Outlook,* June 8.

Don Martinez, "Concord's Invaluable, Indebted Arena," *San Francisco Examiner,* July 21.

George Shaffer, "Model Exhibited in Preview of Valley Cultural Center," *Los Angeles Times,*

August 7.

Art Seidenbaum, "Opening Our Eyes to Buildings," *Los Angeles Times,* December 28.

1978

"Arts Park Los Angeles Up for Debate," *Los Angeles Times,* February 10.

John Dreyfuss, "Gehry's Artful House Offends, Baffles, Angers His Neighbors," *Los Angeles Times,* July 23.

Ann Holmes, "Disregarding the Rules," *Houston Chronicle,* August 20.

Will Thorne, "House that Gehry Built Stirring up SM Controversy," *Santa Monica Evening Outlook,* August 22.

"Where Categories Collide," *Architecture,* September.

Sally Koris, "Architect Gehry Does Own Thing," *Los Angeles Herald Examiner,* September 17.

"Legal Establishment," *Interiors Magazine,* October.

1979

Frank Gehry, "Frank Gehry's Suburban Changes: Architect's House in Santa Monica 1978," *International Architect.*

Robert Hughes, "U.S. Architects Doing Their Own Thing," *Time,* January 8.

Sally Koris, "Renegade Frank Gehry Has Torn Up His House—and the Book of Architecture," *People,* March 5.

John Dreyfuss, "A New Museum for Children," *Los Angeles Times,* April 5.

Tia Gindick, "The Power of Positive Organizing," *Los Angeles Times,* April 5.

Barbara Goldstein, "All Glorious Within," *Architectural Review,* May.

Paul Goldberger, "A House Slipcovered in Metal," *New York Times,* May 17.

Robert Smaus, "Will It Ever Be Finished?," *Los Angeles Times,* May 20.

"Building of the Quarter (Gehry Residence)," *Archetype,* summer.

William Georgis, "An Interview with Frank Gehry," *Archetype,* summer.

Camilla Snyder, "A Museum for Kids to Romp Through," *Los Angeles Herald Examiner,* June 5.

Sam Kaplan, "Los Angeles Children's Museum: It's Child's Play," *Los Angeles Times,* June 11.

Martin Filler, "Perfectly Frank: Mid-Atlantic Toyota Distributors Warehouse and Offices," *Progressive Architecture,* July.

Edward Gunts, "Parts, Arts and Architecture," *News American,* July 22.

"Mid Atlantic Toyota Offices, Glen Burnie, Maryland," *Domus,* August.

Paul Goldberger, "Architects Move into the Office," *New York Times Magazine,* August 5.

"Gehry Residence and Other Residential Projects," *GA Houses* 6 (fall).

"Stanley Tigerman vs. Frank O. Gehry," *GA Houses* 6 (fall).

"Gehry Residence: Santa Monica, California," *Domus,* October.

Joseph Giovannini, "Photography the Final Winner of the Architectural Competition," *Los Angeles Herald Examiner,* October 24.

Don B. Campbell, "Warehouse Among Top 4 AIA Awards," *Los Angeles Times,* October 28.

Jo Werne, "Architects Clash on 'Morality' of U.S. Design," *Miami Herald,* October 28.

John Dreyfuss, "Gehry: The Architect as Artist," *Los Angeles Times,* November 7.

"1979 Design Awards," *LA Architect,* December.

"Maison d'architecture," *L'Architecture d'Aujourd'hui,* December.

Sharon Lee Ryder, "Brutally Frank," *Residential Interiors,* December.

Anne Troutman, "A Delicate Balance," *Residential Interiors,* December.

Joe W. Anguiano, "Loyola Law School Plans Expansion," *Los Angeles Times,* December 16.

1980

"La Biennale di Venezia, Venice: Edizione La Biennale di Venezia," *La Presenza del Passato.*

Barbaralee Diamonstein, *American*

Architecture Now (New York: Rizzoli).

"Gehry Residence: Santa Monica, California," *GA Document: Special Issue, 1970–80.*

Brendan Gill, *The Dream Come True: Great Houses of Los Angeles* (New York: Lippincott and Crowell).

Jack Brogan: Projects (exhibition catalog, Baxter Art Gallery, California Institute of Technology).

Stanley Tigerman, ed., *The Chicago Tribune Tower Competition, vol. 2: Late Entries to the Chicago Tribune Tower Exhibition* (New York: Rizzoli).

"The 27th Annual P/A Awards," *Progressive Architecture,* January.

S. C. Larsen, "Imagine a Space, a Form, a World: The Paintings of Ron Davis," *Art News,* January.

Thomas Hine, "A Careless Design—Carefully Done," *Philadelphia Inquirer,* January 13.

Tricia Crane, "At the Children's Museum, Touches Join Looks," *Valley News,* January 19.

Patricia Willard, "Jazz Artists Agree on Outdoor Pavilion," *Federal Design Matters,* spring.

Olivier Boissière, "Ten California Architects," *Domus,* March.

Barbara Goldstein, "Frank O. Gehry and Associates: Firm Profile," *Progressive Architecture,* March.

Barbara Goldstein, "Spaces in Between," *Progressive Architecture,* March.

"Une Maison qui joue l'ouverture," *Maison Française,* March.

A. Mendini, "Dear Frank Gehry," *Domus,* March.

Jim Murphy, "Art on Melrose," *Progressive Architecture,* March.

Suzanne Stephens, "Out of the Rage for Order," *Progressive Architecture,* March.

"Ten California Architects," *Domus,* March.

John Dreyfuss, "Bunker Hill Project Under Wraps," *Los Angeles Times,* March 16.

Susan Doubilet, "Gehry Wraps Old Homes in New Ideas," *Globe and Mail,* March 27.

Martin Filler, "Tradition Transformed Knockout Kitchen," *House and Garden,* April.

A. Jeffrey Skorneck, "Bunker Hill Development Competition," *LA Architect*, April.

Joseph Giovannini, "Big New Proposal for Bunker Hill," *Los Angeles Herald Examiner*, April 16.

Giovanni Odoni, "Un Arredo in Prospettiva," *Casa Vogue*, May.

John Pastier, "The Art of Being Different," *Pacific Southwest Airways Magazine*, May.

John Pastier, "Of Art, Self-Revelation and Iconoclasm," *AIA Journal*, mid-May.

Clifford Berman, "An Artist's Studio in the Malibu Hills Balances Aesthetics and Function, Home and Work," *Residential Interiors*, May–June.

"Casa Gehry, Santa Monica, California," *Arquitectura*, May–June.

Sarah Booth Conroy, "The Remodeled American Dream, East, West," *Washington Post*, May 25.

Martin Filler, "Eccentric Space: Frank Gehry," *Art in America*, summer.

Jayne Merkel, "Awards Reflect Trends and Issues," *Cincinnati Inquirer*, June 8.

"Architect's House, Los Angeles," *A+U*, July.

"Chiudi (e apri) la casa (a Santa Monica)," *Architettura*, July.

Barbara Goldstein, "Frank Gehry," *Architectural Review*, July.

"A New Wave in American Architecture: Frank O. Gehry," *Space Design*, July.

Michael Franklin Ross, "Paper Architecture: Late Entries to the Chicago Tribune Tower Competition," *LA Architect*, July.

Hilton Kramer, "Art: Russian Avant-Garde in Los Angeles," *New York Times*, July 7.

Daniel Cariaga, "'Phoenix' Helps Launch 59th Summer Season for the Bowl," *Los Angeles Times*, July 10.

Hilton Kramer, "The Daring of the Russian Avant-Garde," *New York Times*, July 12.

William Wilson, "Isms, Schisms, and Russian Avant-Garde," *Los Angeles Times*, July 13.

Joseph Giovannini, "The Last Draw on Bunker Hill," *Los Angeles Herald Examiner*, July 16.

Wolf von Eckhardt, "The Good, the Bad, and the Tricky," *Los Angeles Times*, July 18.

Clara McClure, "Little Ones Stand Tall at the Children's Museum," *Weekend Outlook*, July 19.

Hilton Kramer, "The Mystical Basis of the Russian Avant-Garde," *New York Times*, July 20.

Jayne Merkel, "It's Just a Colonial Turned Outside-In," *Cincinnati Inquirer*, August 3.

Mark Stevens, "The Russian Visionaries," *Newsweek*, August 4.

Joseph Giovannini, "In Venice, an Idea House That's Not for the Timid," *Los Angeles Herald Examiner*, August 6.

Joseph Giovannini, "The Architect-Owner-Contractor Axis," *Los Angeles Herald Examiner*, August 13.

Joseph Giovannini, "Biennale Lays Bare Threat of Classical Revivalism," *Los Angeles Herald Examiner*, August 20.

Martin Filler, "Breaking the Rules and Getting Away with It," *House and Garden*, September.

Cathleen McGuigan, "The Architect," *TWA Ambassador*, September.

John Vinci, "Better Never Than Late: The Late Entries to the Chicago Tribune Competition," *Artforum*, September.

Roger Green, "Arts Laying Claim to Lafayette Square," *Times-Picayune*, September 6.

Charles Jencks, "The Presence of the Past," *Domus*, October.

Barbara Goldstein, "Constructivism in L.A.," *Progressive Architecture*, October.

"The Extension that Encompassed the House," *House and Garden*, October.

B. J. Archer, "First Architectural Biennale in Venice," *International Herald Tribune*, October 4–5.

DeDe Bazyk, "Frank Gehry," *Soho Weekly News*, October 15.

Ed Moosbrugger, "Santa Monica Place to Open Thursday," *Santa Monica Evening Outlook*, October 15.

Joseph Giovannini, "Shopping Center Well Place-ed in Santa Monica," *Los Angeles Herald Examiner*, October 20.

Kenneth Fanucchi, "Mall's Pros, Cons Remain," *Los Angeles Times*, October 26.

Barbara Baird, "Santa Monica Has a Place for Seaside Shopping," *Los Angeles Times*, October 26.

Deirdre Childress, "Clutter Is Creative at Kids Museum," *Los Angeles Times*, October 28.

Tim Street-Porter, "The Outside-In House," *Belle*, November–December.

"Accolades Presented by AIA Chapter," *Los Angeles Times*, November 2.

"25th Annual Design Awards," *LA Architect*, December.

Germano Celant, "Strada Novissima," *Artforum*, December.

Joseph Giovannini, "New West Side Story," *Interiors*, December.

"Retail Complex Renews City Commerce," *Contract*, December.

John Dreyfuss, "L.A. Will Get Two Modern Art Museums," *Los Angeles Times*, December 5.

Dan Healy, "Cabrillo Museum—Avant Garde Design in San Pedro," *Random Lengths*, Christmas.

Joseph Giovannini, "Mural, Mural on the Wall," *Los Angeles Herald Examiner*, December 29.

1981

Olivier Boissière, *Gehry/Site/Tigerman: Trois Portraits de l'Artiste en Architects* (Paris: Editions du Moniteur).

Barbaralee Diamonstein, ed., *Collaborations: Artists and Architects* (New York: Watson-Guptill).

"Frank Gehry: Counter Statements," PAV Publications 6/8106, World Microfilms Publications (recorded slide lecture).

Esther McCoy and Barbara Goldstein, *Guide to U.S. Architecture 1940–1980* (Los Angeles: Art and Architecture Press).

Ted Williams and Ricardo Scoficio, *Window Room Furniture* (New York: Rizzoli).

Richard Saul Wurman, *L.A. Access* (Los Angeles: Access Press).

"A Place in Santa Monica," *Progressive Architecture*, July.

"The Play of the Roles," *Domus*, September.

"Siège Administratif de Toyota à Glen Burnie, U.S.A.," *Techniques et Architecture*, September.

"AIA Convention: Reality and Fantasy," *Los Angeles Herald Examiner*, October.

"Architecture: The Mall of Them All," *House & Garden*, October.

"Cabrillo Marine Museum," *Los Angeles Times*, December.

1982

"Cabrillo Marine Museum, Santa Monica Place, Loyola Law School," *GA Document*.

Frank Gehry: Selected Works (USC Atelier, University of Southern California).

Frank O. Gehry: An Exhibition of Recent Projects (Boston: Institute of Contemporary Art).

"New Waves in American Architecture, Indiana Project, Spiller Residence," *GA Houses* 11.

Shape and Environment: Furniture by American Architects (New York: Whitney Museum of Art).

"The Corporate Dilemma: To Move or Renovate?," *Designers West*, January.

"Inside and Out, Irrespectively," *Domus*, January.

John Mutlow, "Loyola Law School," *LA Architect*, January.

"Santa Monica Place," *A+U*, January.

"Vertriebsburo in Glen Burnie," *Baumeister*, January.

"Agritrop's Legacy," *Progressive Architecture*, March.

"Fish and Flying Cubes Leads Gehry's Assault," *Globe and Mail*, March.

"Frank O. Gehry: House in Santa Monica," *Evening Outlook*, April.

"A Vision Made Real, A Contemporary Look at the American Dream," *United: The Magazine of the Friendly Skies*, May.

Joseph Morgenstern, "The Gehry Style," *New York Times Magazine*, May 16.

"Architecture Outside the Rules," *Belle*, May–June.

Carol King, "Getting Tough with Economics," *Designers West*, June.

"Shopping Centers in America," *Japan Interior Design,* July.

"Cardboard Furniture Reborn," *New York Times,* July 22.

"Mid-Atlantic Toyota Leads the Way," *Corporate Design Magazine,* July–August.

"People Are Talking About," *Vogue,* September.

"Furniture as Sculpture: The Art of Frank O. Gehry," *Middlesex News,* September 12.

"Opening at the ICA," *Patriot Ledger,* September 14.

Martin Filler, "Gehry's Urbanism: Critique of Loyola Law School and Spiller House," *Skyline,* October.

"Frank Gehry's Pop Perspective," *Boston Globe,* October 5.

"Gehry's Cardboard: Bargain Elegance," *Boston Globe,* October 8.

Peter Cook, "Frank Gehry Los Angeles: Links in a Context of Fragmentation," *Architectural Journal,* December 22–29.

1983

Available Light (Los Angeles: Museum of Contemporary Art).

B. J. Archer and Anthony Vidler, eds., *Follies: Architecture for the Late-Twentieth-Century Landscape* (New York: Rizzoli).

Roselee Goldberg, "Dance from the Music: Performance in the Age of Communications, Contemporary Collaborations between Choreographers and Other Artists," *Next Wave Festival* (souvenir program, New York: Brooklyn Academy of Music).

Paul Goldberger, *On the Rise* (New York: Times Books).

Ten New Buildings (London: Institute of Contemporary Arts).

"Obsession of an Architect with Fish on a Grand Scale," *Los Angeles Herald Examiner,* March 4.

"Post Modernism has Arrived . . . ," *Los Angeles Herald Examiner,* March 30.

"Gehry Unveils Plans for Temporary MoCA," *Los Angeles Herald Examiner,* April 14.

"Temporary Museum May Stay Around," *Los Angeles Times,* April 14.

"Spiller House," *Architectural Record: Houses,* mid-May.

"Today We Have a Kind of Free-for-all Architecture," *U.S. News and World Report,* May 30.

"A Minimalist Architecture of Allusion: Current Projects of Frank Gehry," *Architectural Record,* June.

"Bells Are Ringing," *Village Voice,* August.

"Critics Choice: Available Light," *Los Angeles Reader,* September 23.

"MoCA & Available Light," *Los Angeles Weekly,* September 23.

"Abstracting Time, Space with Childs," *Los Angeles Times: Calendar,* September 25.

"A Museum at Home Away From Home," *Los Angeles Times: Calendar,* September 25.

David Bither, "California Dreamin': West Coast Artists in the Next Wave," *Next Wave,* October.

1984

"LA Style/LA School," *AA Files,* January.

"Shack of the New," *House & Garden,* February.

"Genius or Eccentric?," *New York Times Magazine,* April 15.

"Reality Squeezes Out Fantasy in Louisiana Fair's Architecture," *New York Times,* May 13.

"Frank Gehry's Buildings Invent Their Own Order," *Los Angeles Herald Examiner,* July 29.

"Los Angeles Museum Shows How," *San Francisco Chronicle,* July 29.

"Frank Gehry," *Werk, Bauen + Wohnen,* July–August.

"An Architect Captures Los Angeles Tensions in Solid Form," *Los Angeles Herald Examiner,* August 26.

"Waiting for Dr. Coltello," *Artforum,* September.

"Frank O. Gehry," *City Magazine International,* November.

"Projects and Realizations," *L'Architecture d'Aujourd'hui,* December.

1985

Peter Arnell and Ted Bickford, eds., *Frank Gehry: Buildings and Projects* (Rizzoli: New York).

"The Right Stuff," *Architectural Record,* January.

"Form Follows Ferment," *Progressive Architecture,* February.

"Frank Gehry's Sculptural Vision," *United Magazine,* February.

"Frank O. Gehry and Associates," *GA Document,* February.

"Positive Space," *Arts & Architecture,* February.

"Wosk Residence," *GA Houses,* February.

"Architect's Playful Hand Seen in Loyola's New Campus," *Los Angeles Daily Journal,* April 1.

"Distillation of a Paradoxical City," *Architecture,* May.

"Frank Gehry: The Deconstructionist," *Art & Design,* May.

"Libero di Volare," *L'Espresso,* May.

"Frank O. Gehry & Associates," *Casabella,* June.

"Frank O. Gehry: Avis de Tempête sur le Pacifiques," *L'Architecture d'Aujourd'hui,* June.

"Una casa che non si fa Inghiottire," *Abitare,* October.

"Mummery and Flummery in Venice," *Arts,* November.

"Rooms at the Top," *Progressive Architecture,* December.

1986

The Architecture of Frank Gehry, foreword by Henry N. Cobb, essays by Rosemarie Haag-Bletter et al. (Rizzoli: New York).

"GFT e Frank O. Gehry: La Fantastica Casa-Pesce," *Vogue Italia* 14.

Paul Goldberger and Pilar Viladas, "Essays," *Freestyle: The New Architecture and Interior Design from Los Angeles.*

Joseph M. Montaner, Jerdi Oliveras, *The Museums of the Last Generation* (Barcelona: Gustavo Gili).

Peuua Suhonen and Marja-Riitta Norri, "Tilojen Yhteenyörmäyusiä Rauenneyuissa Luonnousissa," *Arkkitehti Arkitekten* 5.

"Frank O. Gehry and Associates," *A+U,* January.

"Masce in Riva All'Arno La Casa: Pesce di Gehry," *La Stampa,* January 3.

"Per Tre Giorni la Moda Sara Padrona di Firenze," *La Città,* January 10.

Luigi Saitta, "Iter sperimentale di un Pesce Simbolo," *Il Tempo,* January 13.

"Gehry, Fantasie della California," *Il Corriere della Sera,* February 2.

Lars Lerup, "Frank O. Gehry: American Architect," *Design Book Review,* spring.

"La Casa pesce del Gruppo Finanziorio Tessile," *Modaviva,* March.

"Architecture that Harbors Obsession and Intuition," *Globe and Mail,* March 8.

"L'Architettura di Gehry a Rivoli Ritorno al Mare Culla Della Vita," *Stampa Sera,* March 25.

"La Casa Pesce e il Terremoto," *La Stampa,* March 27.

"Collezioni e Scenografie," *Linea Capital,* March–April.

"AIA Honor Award for Brooks/Collier," *Texas Society of Architects Report,* April.

John Boal and Tom Peters, "60 Winners," *Western World's Magazine,* April.

Aleks Istanbullu, "Gehry Deserves Better," *Los Angeles Architect,* April.

Leon Whiteson, "The Image Is the Message During Westweek '86," *Los Angeles Herald Examiner,* April 6.

Cesere De Seta, "Architettura di Reperti," *Il Mattino,* April 8.

Floriana Pique, "Castello di Rivoli," *Flash Art,* April–May.

George Christy, "The Great Life," *Hollywood Reporter,* May.

"Un Projetto al Plastico," *Casabella,* May.

Leon Whiteson, "Frank Gehry Grows up with Civil Civic Design for Hollywood Library," *Los Angeles Herald Examiner,* May 25.

Leon Whiteson, "Mix and Match Architecture," *Los Angeles Herald Examiner,* May 28.

Joaquinn Maestre, "Frank O. Gehry," *El Paseante,* summer.

William Hubbard, "University of California Irvine," *Los Angeles Architect,* June.

Heinrich Klotz, "Die Neve Suche Nach Sinn," *Architektur und Symbol Heure,* June.

Esa-Pekka Salonen, "Frank O. Gehry Suunnilelee Suomessa/ Frank O. Gehry Designs in

Finland," *Helsingin Sanomat,* June 18.

Bruno Zevi, "Pesce d'Autore," *L'Espresso,* June 22.

"Architetti Frank O. Gehry," *Il Giornale dell'Arte,* July.

Claudio Castellacci, "Frank Gehry," *Max,* July.

Marco Pastonesi, "Moda e Arte: Frank Gehry per il GFT," *Mondo Vomo,* July.

Ruth Reichl, "The Look, The Feel . . . Oh Yes, and the Food," *Los Angeles Times,* July 13.

Allen Temko, "Lawrence Halprin, Changer of Cities," *San Francisco Chronicle,* July 13.

Leon Whiteson, "Tonic to the Eye or the Ugliest Building," *Los Angeles Herald Examiner,* July 20.

Robert Campbell, "A Bold Makeover," *Boston Globe,* July 22.

"National AIA Honor Awards 1986," *Architecture California,* July–August.

Hunter Drohojawska, "An Appetite for Design," *Los Angeles Style,* August.

Adele Freedman, "Gehry Still Swimming Against the Tide," *Globe and Mail,* September.

Charles K. Gandee, "Frank Gehry's Building Reputation," *Vanity Fair,* September.

Paul Goldberger, "Housing the Revolution," *California Magazine,* September.

"Review on New Restaurants," *Food & Wine,* September.

Gene Stone, "In with the Din," *California Magazine,* September.

Charles K. Gandee, "That Was Then, This Is Now," *Architectural Record,* mid-September.

Mary Abbe Martin, "Critics Choice/Exhibition," *Minneapolis Star and Tribune,* September 19.

Susanne Muchnic, "Oldenburg's Ladder Has a Leg to Stand in Los Angeles," *Los Angeles Times,* September 24.

Linda Mack, "Frank Gehry: Inside the Architect, You'll Find an Artist," *Minneapolis Star and Tribune,* September 28.

Larry Millett, "Off the Wall Architect Gehry Puts on a Fascinating Show," *St. Paul Pioneer Press and Dispatch,* September 28.

Frank Peters, "Frank Gehry's Livable Art," *St. Louis Post-Dispatch,* September 28.

"Frank O. Gehry: Maison Sirmai-Peterson et Maison Winton," *A.M.C. Revue d'Architecture,* October.

Adele Freedman, "Frank O. Gehry and Associates: Due Opere Recenti," *Casabella,* October.

Adele Freedman, Joseph Giovannini, Esther McCoy, Pilar Viladas, and Leon Whiteson, "Special Issue: Frank O. Gehry," *Progressive Architecture,* October.

Jill Spalding, "Fishing for Pale Compliments," *Vogue Australia,* October.

Eric Wieffering, "From Junki-tecture to Art, Blurring the Edges," *Twin Cities Reader,* October 1.

Jim Bilings, "Architect Defies Conventions," *Echo,* October 3.

Paul Goldberger, "A Show that Gets Inside the Work of Frank Gehry," *New York Times,* October 5.

Frank Peters, "Shedding the Burden of Culture for Architectural Freedom," *St. Louis Post-Dispatch,* October 5.

Rob Silberman, "Don't Fence Me In," *City Pages,* October 8.

Sam Hall Kaplan, "Eclecticism Shown in AIA Judging," *Los Angeles Times,* October 12.

Kurt Anderson, "Building Beauty the Hard Way," *Time,* October 13.

Patricia Leigh Brown, "A Mecca of Eclectic Food and Underwater Fantasy," *New York Times,* October 17.

Martin Filler, "Maverick Master," *House & Garden,* November.

"Los Angeles AIA Design Awards" *Los Angeles Architect,* November.

John Mariani, "America's Best New Bars & Restaurants," *Esquire,* November.

Clark McCann, "Making Friends with Anenomes," *PSA Magazine,* November.

John Pastier, "Retrospective: Frank O. Gehry," *Architecture,* November.

Jill Spaulding, "Rivalry Rises to New Heights," *Vogue Australia,* November.

Ellen Posner, "From 'Forests' to Fish: An Architect's Evolution," *Wall Street Journal,* November 11.

Carlton Knight, "Architecture Inspired by Art," *Christian Science Monitor,* November 12.

1987

"Fish Dance," *Japan Architect.*

"Winton Guest House," *GA Houses* 22.

Victorio Magnago Lampugnani, "ERL—University of California at Irvine," *Domus,* January.

Anne Holmes, "Earthshaking Architect," *Houston Chronicle,* January 19.

Susan Chadwick, "The Architecture of Frank Gehry at the Contemporary Arts Museum," *Houston Post,* January 25.

Barnaby Conrad III, "Los Angeles: The New Mecca," *Horizon,* January–February.

Roy Strickland, "No Little Plans: An Ambitious Mixed-Use Scheme for Boston," *Architectural Record,* February.

Bill Marvel, "The Architecture of Frank Gehry," *Dallas Morning News,* February 16.

Albert Pope, "The Architecture of Frank Gehry," *Cite,* spring.

John Farrell, "Frank Gehry's Temporary Contemporary: The Ultimate Cinderella Story," *U.S.C. Trojan Family,* March.

Donna Tennant, "Frank Gehry's Innovative Architecture and John Kessler's Surrealist Wall Sculptures at CAM," *Houston City Magazine,* March.

Paul Gapp, "Architecture's Hottest Guru," *Chicago Tribune,* March 15.

Gabriella De Ferrari, "The Passions of Architect Frank Gehry," *Art New England,* April.

John Pastier, "Frank O. Gehry Exhibition at the Walker Art Center," *GA Document,* April.

Michael Webb, "What Will Frank Gehry Come up with Next," *Smithsonian,* April.

Rick Cziment, "Gehry Art Provokes, Impresses," *Evening Outlook,* April 10.

John Pastier, "The Norton Residence," *Architecture,* May.

Elizabeth Venant, "Grand Design: Frank Gehry, Los Angeles's Hottest Architect," *Los Angeles Times Magazine,* May 3.

Ben Forgey, "Architecture On the Edge," *Washington Post,* May 12.

Janice Fillip, "The Illusion of Chaos," *Architecture California,* September–October.

Martin Filler, "The House as Art," *House & Garden,* October.

J. J. Navarro Arisa, "La Arquitectura es Expresión de Progreso y Habla Para el Futuro (Architecture Is Expression of Progress and Speaks of the Future)," *El País,* November 26.

Sergio Vila-San Juan, "Frank O. Gehry: La Arquitectura Californiana de la Cúpula, la Garita Playera y la Forma de Pez (Frank O. Gehry: Californian Architecture, Dome, Lifeguard Tower, and Fishdance Sculpture)," *La Vanguardia,* November 26.

Olivier Boissière, "Gehry a Hollywood," *L'Arca,* December.

Pilar Viladas, "The Image of the House," *Progressive Architecture,* December.

1988

Charles Gandee, "Catch of the Day," *Architectural Record,* January.

Judith Michaelson, "6 Architects Are Candidates for Disney Hall," *Los Angeles Times,* January 15.

Judith Michaelson, "Architect Candidates for Disney Hall Share Their Views," *Los Angeles Times,* January 21.

Horst Rasch, "A Work of Art for Guests," *Häuser,* February.

Larry Albert, "Fitting In, Standing Out," *Boston Phoenix,* February 12.

Olivier Boissière, "Fragmented Architecture," *L'Arca,* March.

Kurt Forster, "Volumini in Liberta," *Archithese,* March.

"Completata la Winton Guest House di Frank O. Gehry," *Casabella,* April.

"Das eigene Haus in Santa Monica," *Baumeister,* May.

Pilar Viladas and Susan Doubilet, "UC Builds," *Progressive Architecture,* May.

"Du cedve de Chateaubriand aux plantanes des pinardiers," *Le Monde,* May 14.

Pilar Viladas, "Frank Gehry," *Exhibitions,* May–June.

Andrea Oppenheimer Dean,

"Deconstructivist Construction," *Architecture*, June.

Deborah K. Dietsch, "Sheet Metal Exhibit, National Building Museum, Washington, D.C.," *Architectural Record*, June.

Lawrence Biemiller, "California Campuses in the 80's," *Chronicle of Higher Edication*, June 8.

Erwin Leiser, "Frank Gehry," *Frankfurter Allgemeine Magazine*, June 10.

Paul Goldberger, "Theories as the Building Blocks for a New Style," *New York Times*, June 26.

Llatzer Moix, "Frank Gehry, la intuicion y los peces (Frank Gehry: Fishes and Intuition)," *La Vanguardia*, June 29.

Peter Blake, "Orders and Chaos," *Interior Design*, July.

"Deconstructivist Architecture," *A+U*, July.

Paul Goldberger, "An Architect at Mainstream's Edge," *New York Times*, July 7.

Carter B. Horsley, "Gehry at the Whitney," *New York Post*, July 14.

Sam Hall Kaplan, "Architecture as Sculptural Objects," *Los Angeles Times*, July 14.

Mimi Read, "Frank's Place," *New York Newsday*, July 17.

Peter Cook, "LA Magician," *RIBA Journal*, August.

Ziva Freiman, "What is Deconstructivism?," *Metropolitan Home*, August.

Sara Nolan, "Gehry Go-Around," *Vanity Fair*, August.

Vera Graaf, "Die Kalkulierte Disharmonic," *Feuilleton*, August 8.

Paul Goldberger, "Unplanned Stop for Frank Gehry's Iconoclastic Designs," *New York Times*, August 16.

Margo Kaufman, "A Striped Warehouse Joins the Local Color," *New York Times*, August 18.

Ellen Steese, "When Is a Building not a Building," *Christian Science Monitor*, August 24.

Dolores A. Long, "Architect Interprets World from a Different Perspective," *California Canadian*, August 25.

"Santa Monica's Gallery of Functional Art," *Angeles*, September.

Michael Kimmelman, "An Old Ice Warehouse Is Sculpted into a Museum," *New York Times*, September 4.

Hunter Drohojowska, "Frank Gehry's Grand Illusions," *Artnews*, October.

Shira Rosan, "Southern California Triumphant," *World and I*, October.

Brooke Adams, "Frank Gehry's Merzbau," *Art in America*, November.

Andrea Nulli, "Casa per Ospiti, Minneapolis," *Domus*, December.

Leon Whiteson, "Four Different Visions of Disney Concert Hall," *Los Angeles Times*, December 8.

Sam Hall Kaplan, "A Competition in Spirit of Disney," *Los Angeles Times*, December 11.

Marc Porter Zasada, "Choosing the Disney Concert Hall Finalist," *Los Angeles Downtown News*, December 12.

Tom Jacobs, "Los Angeles Life: Frank Gehry Named Disney Hall Architect," *Daily News*, December 13.

Michael Kimmelman, "Gehry Is Named Designer for Disney Hall," *New York Times*, December 13.

Susan King, "Disney Gift," *Los Angeles Herald Examiner*, December 13.

Judith Michaelson, "Gehry's Disney Hall Design," *Los Angeles Times*, December 13.

Judith Michaelson, "Happy Note: Los Angeles Architect Has Winning Design for Disney Concert Hall," *Los Angeles Times*, December 13.

Nancy Reed, "SM Architect Gehry to Design New Concert Hall," *Outlook*, December 13.

Allan Temko, "Gehry Wins Disney Concert Hall Job," *San Francisco Chronicle*, December 14.

Alan Rich, "Hopes Are High for Gehry's Disney Hall Design," *Los Angeles Herald Examiner*, December 18.

Leon Whiteson, "Frank Gehry Always Wanted to Work Big," *Los Angeles Times*, December 18.

Joseph Morgenstern, "Los Angeles Turns to One of Its Own," *Wall Street Journal*, December 23.

1989

"Frank O. Gehry: Laser Laboratory Building, University of Iowa," *GA Document*.

"Walt Disney Concert Hall, Los Angeles: Frank Gehry," *Architectural Design*.

Aaron Betsky, "Trugerisch im Detail," *Archithese*, January.

Martin Filler, "In Compagnia del Cubo e dei Suoi Amici," *Casa Vogue*, January.

"Gehry Awarded Concert Hall," *Los Angeles Architect*, January.

Robert Campbell, "Trends and Movements Came and Went," *Boston Globe*, January 1.

William Wilson, "The Blossoming of Los Angeles Artists in '88," *Los Angeles Times*, January 1.

Michele Saee, "Gehry on Main Street," *Architects' Journal*, January 18.

John Pastier, "Hall in the Family," *Los Angeles Weekly*, January 20.

Peter M. Bode, "Frank Gehry: Manner Mit Mut," *Deutsch Vogue*, February.

Olivier Boissière, "Les Tribulations de FOG," *L'Architecture d'Aujourd'hui*, February.

Birgit Dietsch, "Welcome to the Pleasuredome," *Bauwelt*, February.

"Frank O. Gehry Selected as Architect of Walt Disney Concert Hall," *News From the Music Center*, February.

Barbara Goldstein, "Gehry Awarded Disney Hall," *Progressive Architecture*, February.

Jane Holtz Kay, "News on Newbury Street," *Progressive Architecture*, February.

"Los Angeles Lilt," *Architectural Record*, February.

John Pastier, "Gehry Wins Competition for Los Angeles's Disney Concert Hall," *Architecture*, February.

Adele Freedman, "Fillets of Soul," *Globe and Mail*, February 25.

"Frank Gehry Detailing," *Terrazzo*, spring.

"Frank Gehry to be U.W. Author/Artist," *Direction*, spring.

Sarah Milroy, "Fast Forward," *Canadian Art*, spring.

"Architektur: Shopping Center als Kunstwerk," *Häuser*, March.

Aaron Betsky, "Von Fishen und Schlangen," *Archithese*, March.

C. Casey and M. Mathewson, "Lobgesang auf die Kunstlichkeit," *Bauwelt*, March.

"Los Angeles Architect to Design Disney Concert Hall," *Music Center News*, March.

Anthony Vidler, "Opere Recenti di Frank O. Gehry," *Casabella*, March.

"Walt Disney Concert Hall in Los Angeles," *Baumeister*, March.

Aaron Betsky, "No More Cartoons: Gehry Designs Disney Hall," *Art Coast*, March–April.

"A Holistic Environment," *Contract Magazine*, March–April.

Arnold Schrier and Artin Knadjian, "Art and Architecture Go Hand in Hand in Gehry's World," *Montreal Gazette*, April 22.

Wolfgang Bachmann, "Los Angeles: Paradise and Limbo," *Bauwelt*, April 28.

"Frank Gehry," *Architectural Design*, April–May.

Mark Alden Branch, "Pritzker Prize to Frank Gehry," *Progressive Architecture*, May.

Nora Richter Greer, "Frank Gehry Named Recipient of Eleventh Pritzker Prize," *Architecture*, May.

Larry Richards, "Mocking Up Life: Chiat/Day Offices, Toronto," *Canadian Architect*, May.

Sam Hall Kaplan, "Architect Gehry Named Pritzker Prize Laureate," *Los Angeles Times*, May 1.

Christopher Knight, "Frank Gehry Wins 1989 Pritzker Prize," *Los Angeles Herald Examiner*, May 1.

Daryl H. Miller, "Los Angeles's Artful Builder," *Daily News*, May 1.

Bonnie Churchill, "Pritzker Prize Winner Is Joining the Giants," *Christian Science Monitor*, May 2.

"Gehry Gets Top Prize for Architecture," *San Francisco Chronicle*, May 2.

Paul Goldberger, "Gehry Wins Pritzker Architecture Prize," *New York Times*, May 2.

Sam Hall Kaplan, "Gehry Shuns the Architectural Rut," *Los Angeles Times*, May 7.

Leon Whiteson, "Santa Monica's Edgemar Improves upon the Mini-Mall," *Los Angeles Times*, May 7.

"U.S. Architect Gets Pritzker at

Ceremony in Nara Temple," *Japan Times*, May 19.

Cathleen McGuigan, "A Renegade Takes the Prize," *Newsweek*, May 22.

Jim Johnson, "Herman Miller," *Sacramento Bee*, May 28.

"Geometric Gehry," *Architecture Minnesota*, May–June.

Ben Marks, "Los Angeles Diary," *New Glass Work*, summer.

"Gehry Awarded Pritzker Prize," *Los Angeles Architect*, June.

"Gehry Wins 1989 Pritzker," *Architectural Review*, June.

Elena Marcheso Moreno, "What Makes a Museum Environment Successful," *Architecture*, June.

"Preisgewinner 1989: Frank O. Gehry," *Architektur und Technik*, June.

"The Pritzker: Architecture as Frozen Jazz," *Architectural Record*, June.

"Pritzker Prize Goes to Gehry," *Artworld*, June.

David Hay, "Cardboard Chairs and Formica Fish," *Bulletin*, June 6.

Dennis Fawcett, "Architects Find Strength in Collaboration," *Register*, June 11.

"Interview," *Nikkei Architecture*, June 26.

"Pritzkerprijs Voor Frank Gehry: Werk Van Een Amerikaanse Optimist," *Architectuur/Bonwen*, June–July.

"Art Forum," *Hiroba*, July.

"Herman Miller," *Progressive Architecture*, July.

Karen Stein, "Main Street," *Architectural Record*, July.

Bob Howard, "It's New, It's Not, It's Cool, It's Hot, It's the Westside," *Los Angeles Business Journal*, July 3.

Leon Whiteson, "Los Angeles's New Wave Designers Draw Global Attention," *Los Angeles Times*, July 11.

"Les Hotels du Royaume de Mickey," *Le Moniteur*, July 14.

"Perception Og Pragmatisme," *Arkitekten*, July 25.

"Wearing It," *Ion*, July 30.

"Anspruch Auf Eine Unsichtbare Architektur," *Werk, Bauen + Wohnen*, July–August.

"Chiat/Day, Toronto," *Interior Design*, August.

"Frank O. Gehry Fick Arets Pritzkers Architecture Prize," *Bygg and Teknik*, August.

Joseph Giovannini, "Will Success Spoil Frank Gehry?," *Metropolitan Home*, August.

"Herman Miller, Inc.," *GA Document*, August.

Richard J. Pietschmann, "Santa Monica Main-Lining," *Los Angeles Magazine*, August.

"State of the Art: New Corporate Design, Chiat/Day, Toronto," *Interior Design*, August.

Dan Schifrin, "Visiting Professor Earns Prestigious Architecture Award," *UCLA Bruin*, August 17.

Kurt Forster, "Visions of Urban Transparency: On Frank Gehry's Concert Hall Project for Los Angeles," *Daidalos*, September.

"Frank Gehry," *A+U*, September.

"Frank Gehry: Fish on a Line," *Newsline*, September.

"Frank Gehry Reçoit Le Prix Pritzker," *Maison Française*, September.

Carol McMichael Reese and Thomas Ford Reese, "Progetti per il Concorso della Walt Disney Concert Hall," *Zodiac*, September.

Leon Whiteson, "From Eggs to Art," *Angeles*, September.

Judith Michaelson, "The Crown Jewel," *Encore*, September 10.

David Galloway, "Museum for Chairs: Sitting in Judgement," *International Herald Tribune*, September 16.

"American Award," *Il Bagno*, September–October.

Gary Michael Dault, "The Office: User Friendliness," *Toronto Life*, October.

Doriana O. Mandrelli, "Frank O. Gehry," *Artnumbria*, October.

Katherine van Sittart, "Frank Gehry: Interview," *House and Home*, October.

Paul Goldberger, "The Quest for Comfort: Architecture Eases into the 90's," *New York Times Magazine*, October 15.

Peter Slatin, "Castles in the Air," *Forbes*, October 30.

Leon Whiteson, "Frank Gehry: The Evolution of a Master," *Los Angeles*

Times, October 30.

Frances Anderton, "A Passion for Chairs," *Architectural Review*, November.

Frizo Broeksma, "Dispatches from California," *Forum*, November.

Robert Campbell, "In Boston, Adding Floors and Flair," *Architecture*, November.

"Neue Fabrik und Stiehl-Museum für Vitra in Weil am Rhein," *Jahrbuch für Architektur*, November.

"One Man and His Museum," *Blueprint*, November.

"A 'Village' of Hope," *Yale Alumni Magazine*, November.

Patricia Leigh Brown, "A Museum for Lovers of Modern Furniture," *New York Times*, November 2.

Hugh Pearman, "Rebuilding the Terms of the Design Debate," *London Sunday Times*, November 5.

"Interview with Frank Gehry," *Ambiente*, November 11.

Paul Goldberger, "Frank Gehry's Village of Geometric Forms at Yale," *New York Times*, November 12.

Colin Amery, "Museum Through the Looking-Glass," *London Financial Times*, November 20.

Liz Jobey, "Up Against the Prince," *Independent Magazine*, November 25.

Luc Verstraete, "Architektur Met Het Mes," *De Standaard*, November 25.

H. A. Shirvani, "Gehry and Deconstructivism: A Matter of Difference in Text," *Avant Garde*, winter.

"An den Grenzen der Geometrie," *Bauwelt*, December.

"Design Als Poessie," *Elle*, December.

"Edgemar Project," *Nikkei Architecture*, December.

"Frank O. Gehry in Germania," *Casabella*, December.

Francis Rambert, "Gehry, Le Malade du Design," *D'Architectures*, December.

Pilar Viladas, "House(s) on the Lakeside," *Progressive Architecture*, December.

Martine Esquirou, "Gehry: I Love Paris," *L'Express Paris*, December 8.

Odile Fillion, "Un Amercain à Paris," *Le Moniteur*, December 8.

Emmanuel de Roux, "Les Habits Neufs du Centre Americain," *Le Monde*, December 9.

"Design Unveiled for Paris' New American Center," *International Herald Tribune*, December 9–10.

Nicholas Powell, "American Center Gets Some California Feeling," *Wall Street Journal*, December 22–23.

1990

Tadeusz Barucki, "Frank O. Gehry w Warzawie," *Projekt* 194.

"La musica de Los Angeles, Sala de conciertos Walt Disney," *A+U*.

"Opera Recenti di F. O. Gehry," *Casabella*.

"Schnabel House," *GA Houses* 28.

"Architekturinssenierung," *Deutsche Bauzeitung*, January.

"Best of the Decade: Loyola Law School," *Time*, January.

"Il Caos Ben Temperato," *Casa Vogue*, January.

Aldo Castellano, "Una Sculptura Per Il Design," *L'Arca*, January.

"Gehry a Bercy: Le Futur American Center," *Techniques et Architecture*, January.

Vera Graof, "Die Trend Story: Los Angeles Style," *Architektur & Wohnen*, January.

Ross Miller, "The Master of Mud Pies," *Interview*, January.

Florian Musso, "Vitra: I Did It My Way," *Archithese*, January.

"Un Ordre Polyphonique: Musée Vitra," *Techniques et Architecture*, January.

Heiner Scharfenorth, "Gehry Was Here," *Architektur & Wohnen*, January.

Judith Sheine, "Engineered Refinements," *Architecture*, January.

Karen D. Stein, "City on a Hill," *Architectural Record*, January.

Michael Webb, "Frank Gehry's Architecture of Improvisation," *Dialogue*, January.

Marc Wortman, "A Model City Remodeled," *Progressive Architecture*, January.

Linda Mack, "Gehry to Design 'U' Art Museum," *Star Tribune*, January 12.

Mary Blume, "Frank Gehry: An Architectural Force for the Age,"

International Herald Tribune, January 15.

Kurt W. Forster, "El Auditorio de Gehry (Gehry's Auditorium)," *Arquitectura Viva,* January–February.

"Chair Man's Report," *Times Magazine,* February.

Marc Emery, "Frank Gehry en Europe," *Architecture Interieure Créé,* February.

"Frank O. Gehry & Associates: Vitra Design Museum," *Progex,* February.

"Le Musee Vitra," *L'Architecture d'Aujourd'hui,* February.

Olivier Boissière, "Frank Gehry," *Vogue Decoration,* February–March.

"Frank Gehry Exhibition Tours Europe," *Art Sphere,* spring.

Warren James, "Entrevista Frank O. Gehry (Interview with Frank O. Gehry)," *Arquitectura,* March.

"A Village of Healing," *Architecture,* March.

Gebaudén Bestehen, "Wir Wollen Ein Dorf," *Häuser,* April.

Aaron Betsky, "The Academic Village of Exurbia," *Architectural Record,* April.

"Elements of Style: Design 100," *Metropolitan Home,* April.

"Highway Haven," *Architecture,* April.

Richard Pietschmann, "Winning Maverick: Frank Gehry," *Vis A Vis, United Airlines Magazine,* April.

Sophie Rucker, "Taking the Chair," *Departures,* April.

Patricia Leigh Brown, "Disney Deco," *New York Times Magazine,* April 8.

Christopher Knight, "Is Los Angeles a World Class Art City?," *Los Angeles Times: Calendar,* April 9.

Arthur Goldgaber, "Construction of Disney Concert Hall Stalls as Engineers and Architects Modify Design," *Los Angeles Business Journal,* April 30.

"Frank O. Gehry: A to Z," *Quaderns,* April–June.

Martin Filler, "The Well Furnished Museum," *House & Garden,* May.

John Howell, "America in Paris," *Elle Decor,* May.

"Jay Chiat Order and Mystery," *Artnews,* May.

Roger Moore, "Mr. Gehry Goes to Hollywood," *Blueprint,* May.

"Des Rituels de Foundation," *Art Press Architecture,* May.

"Une Usine a Reves, Usine Herman Miller a Rocklin, Californie," *Architecture Interieure Créé,* May.

Pilar Viladas, "Cranked, Curled and Cantilevered," *Progressive Architecture,* May.

Michael Webb, "High Gehry," *LA Style,* May.

Ruth Reichl, "Top 40 Restaurants," *Los Angeles Times Magazine,* May 6.

Paul Goldberger, "Frank Gehry Project to Build a Vision from the US in Paris," *New York Times,* May 15.

Paul Goldberger, "Frank Gehry to Create a Bit of the US in Paris," *New York Times,* May 15.

Leon Whiteson, "Gehry: An American in Paris," *Los Angeles Times: Calendar,* May 22.

"1990 Design Awards California AIA," *Architectural Record,* June.

Joseph Giovannini, "Los Angeles Original," *Eastern Review,* June.

John Gregorson, "Building to a Crescendo," *Building Design & Construction,* June.

Patsy Klein, "That House that FAX Built," *Town & Country,* June.

Nic Mills, "90's Payback Decade," *New York Times,* June.

Chris Reinewald, "Een Kathedraal Voor Het Zitten, Het Vitra Design Museum," *Man,* June.

Claudia Steinberg-Heys, "Provocateur van Goede Smaak," *O,* June.

Teri Appel, "Inside Out: Frank O. Gehry," *Scape,* June–July.

"American Center," *Engineering News Record,* July.

"American in Paris Gets a New Home" *Architectural Record,* July.

Paul Gapp, "American Center," *Chicago Tribune,* July.

Kathleen Neumeyer, "The 30 Most Powerful," *Los Angeles Magazine,* July.

Dean Sebastien Stehli, "Un Américain à Paris," *Architecture,* July.

Pilar Viladas, "Pavilions on the Edge," *House & Garden,* July.

"Project: Frank Gehry, An American in Paris," *Architecture Today,* July 1.

Evaristo Nicolao, "Frank Goes to Hollywood . . . Bowl," *Arredo Urbano,* July–August.

"Yale Psychiatric Institute," *International Design,* July–August.

Aaron Betsky, "Designs on the World: Los Angeles Architects Go Global," *Angeles,* August.

Kurt W. Forster, "The Snake and the Fish on the Hill," *A+U,* August.

Sylvia Lavin, "Perspectives," *Progressive Architecture,* August.

Karen Stein, "Master Builders," *Harper's Bazaar,* August.

"That's Entertainment," *Architectural Record,* August.

Stanislaus von Moos, "Chapel for Chairs," *A+U,* August.

Michael Webb, "Kentucky Fried Mod.," *Los Angeles Times Magazine,* August 5.

"American Center a Parigi 1989," *Phalaris,* August 9.

Aaron Betsky, "The Tower," *Los Angeles Weekly,* August–September.

"An American in Paris," *France,* fall.

"Gehry Exhibit Opens in Warsaw," *Art Sphere,* fall.

Liz Brody, "Like Art for the Bay's Sake," *Los Angeles Magazine,* September.

Mary Chesterfield, "Frank O. Gehry: Snake Lamp," *Angeles,* September.

Neil Cohen, "Work in Progress," *Continental,* September.

Andrea Oppenheimer Dean, "American Architects Abroad: American Center, Vila Olimpica," *Architecture,* September.

"Frank O. Gehry: Vitra Design Museum," *GA Document,* September.

"Heavy Metal für Herman Miller," *Bauwelt,* September.

Julie Iovine, "American Center: Freeze Frame Art," *Metropolitan Home,* September.

Robert Maxwell, "Frank Gehry: Il Museo Vitra a Weil am Rhein," *Ottagono,* September.

"People in Review," *Art in America,* September.

Mayer Rus, "N.Y. Bagel," *Interior Design,* September.

"Il Vitra Design Museum, Weil am Rhein," *Abitare,* September.

Beth Kleid, "California Honors: Frank O. Gehry," *Los Angeles Times,* September 7.

Alan Rich, "Distinguished Artists Awarded for Music Center Work," *Daily News,* September 7.

"Los Angeles Architects Go Global: Fishdance Restaurant," *Los Angeles Times,* September 22.

"Frank Gehry: De Singh," *Auxipress,* September 27.

Petra Maclot, "Sculpture Habitable," *Nieuwe Gazet,* September 30.

"Beaty is Beautiful," *Los Angeles Magazine,* October.

Olivier Boissière, "Frank O. Gehry Chroniques Gehriennes," *L'Architecture d'Aujourd'hui,* October.

Olivier Boissière, "Maison Schnabel a Los Angeles," *L'Architecture d'Aujourd'hui,* October.

Ross Miller, "Why and How Does Disney Do It?," *Progressive Architecture,* October.

"De Singel Toont Frank Gehry," *Nieuwsblad,* October 3.

Guy Goethals, "De architect van de geprogrammeerd e chaos," *Dinsdag,* October 16.

Marc Dubois, "Architektuur als Skulptuur," *Knack,* October 17.

"Les Nouveaux Adventuriers," *Figaroscope,* October 31–November 6.

"Architect Hired for U's New Art Museum," *Minnesota Daily,* November.

"Christopher Columbus' French Connection," *Sites,* November.

"Designs with Sites in Mind," *Angeles Times,* November.

"Frank Gehry Arquitecto (Architect Frank Gehry)," *La Prensa,* November.

"Frank O. Gehry," *El Croquis,* November.

"Main Street: Edgemar," *Angeles,* November.

"University Art Museum Design Is an Eye Opener," *Star Tribune,* November.

"Unpredictable, But Just Right!

Toledo's Way," *Detroit Free Press*, November.

Jesus Ramon, "Aniversario del Colegio de Arquitectos (College of Architects Anniversary)," *El Mexicano*, November 7.

"Requests Approve Spectacular Design for New Art Museum," *Pioneer Press*, November 9.

Pat Griffith, "U.T.O. New Art Building Moves Closer to Reality," *Blade*, November 14.

Sally Vallongo, "An Optimistic Man of Design," *Blade*, November 18.

Barbara Isenberg, "On the Run With the Next Man About Town," *Los Angeles Times: Calendar*, November 25.

"Editorials," *Minnesota Daily*, November 27.

"For Those Who Wouldn't Settle for Second Best," *Architects India*, November 27.

Suzanne Slesin, "Architects Show How to Set a Grand Table," *New York Times*, November 29.

Isabella Cywinska, "A Revolution within a Revolution," *Artnews*, December.

"FOG, LA, Darf in Paris ein Neues Amerikanisches Kulturzentrum," *Baumeister*, December.

Karrie Jacobs, "The Art of the Design Museum," *Metropolis*, December.

Hans Lutz, "Tweede Utrechtre Rielveldlezing door, Frank O. Gehry," *Utrechts Nieuwsblad/NZC*, December 1.

William Wilson, "Filling up with Ed Ruscha," *Los Angeles Times*, December 10.

Paul Goldberger, "The Important Things Were What Didn't Happen," *New York Times*, December 30.

1991

"Architectuur: Frank Gehry," *Mit Jiobs Voor Antwerpen*.

Aaron Betsky, John Chase, and Leon Whiteson, *Experimental Architecture in Los Angeles*, introduction by Frank Gehry (Rizzoli: New York).

"Frank O. Gehry: American Center," *GA Document* 29.

"Frank O. Gehry, Projects en Europe," *Votre Logement* 54.

"Frank O. Gehry: Vitra Museum," *European Masters* 3.

Christine Karich, "Frankie Was Here," *Ambiente: Special Issue*.

"Winton Guest House," *Architecture Contemporaine*.

Aldo Castellano, "Una Scultura per il Design," *L'Arca*, January.

"Comme Par Hasard," *Archithese*, January.

"Now and Then," *Vogue*, January.

"Scheinbar Zufallig," *Archithese*, January.

Bruce N. Wright and Mark Alden Branch, "Two New Museums," *Progressive Architecture*, January.

Patricia Leigh Brown, "Whither Design? Thithers Aplenty," *New York Times*, January 10.

"Frank's Place," *Adweek*, January 28.

"Frank Gehry," *Experimenta*, January March.

"Kunst Gegenkrebs," *Stern*, spring.

"Frank Gehry," *Blueprint*, March.

Robert Campbell, "Living Arts," *Boston Globe*, March 5.

B. Rudolph, "EuroDisneyland Is on Schedule," *Monsieur Mickey*, March 25.

"Frank Gehry L'Europeen," *Le Moniteur*, March 29.

D. Picabia, "L'Atterragio Diicaro," *Phalaris*, March–April.

"Un Californien en Europe," *Urbanism et Architecture*, April.

"Frank Gehry," *Designers' Journal*, April.

Joseph Montanes, "Temporary Contemporary Museum," *Nuevos Museos*, April.

Ruth Ryon, "11 Southland Projects Win AIA Design Awards," *Los Angeles Times*, April.

"Architect to Share Plan with the Public," *Topics*, April 4.

"Architect of New University Art Museum Shows Plans," *Minnesota Daily*, April 5.

"Frank Gehry: Un Americain à Paris," *Libération*, April 7.

Barbara Isenberg, "Frank Gehry's Creative Journey," *Los Angeles Times: Calendar*, April 7.

"Architect Frank Gehry's Structures Are Built on the Edge of Imagination," *Star Tribune*, April 11.

"Boston Building Garners Award for Gehry Designers," *California Real Estate Journal*, April 15.

Jill Stewart, "The Capital of Hip," *Los Angeles Times*, April 28.

"The Skyline: Disneyitis," *New Yorker*, April 29.

"Cubist Village," *Inside*, April–May.

"Architektur Heute," *Ambiente*, May.

"Ausstellungen," *Deutsche Bauzeitung*, May.

John Brody, "Gehry's Credo: Master Philip and the Boys," *Spy*, May.

"Central Intelligence," *Travel and Leisure*, May.

"A Gehry Museum in Minnesota," *Home*, May.

"Los Angeles Projects Win State Architectural Awards," *Design Los Angeles*, May.

"Modern Mobilyanim Tarihcesini Iceren: Vitra Design Museum," *Tasarim*, May.

"Parigi," *Ambiente*, May.

Christine Richard, "Evènement," *Le Quotidien*, May.

Susan Shapiro, "The Screwball Classic," *Avenue*, May.

Leon Whiteson, "Young Turks," *Angeles*, May.

"Un American à Paris," *Monuments Historiques*, May–June.

"Disney Entertainment Center," *Euro Disney*, spring–summer.

Alastair Gordon, "I Dream of Gehry," *Architecture*, summer.

"Frank Gehry," *BAT*, June.

Ester Laushway, "America Participates in the New Europe," *Europe*, June.

Jean-Pierre Menard, "Details: Les Facades Metalliques," *Le Moniteur Architecture*, June.

"Ralf Hotchkiss," *San Francisco Magazine*, June.

Frederic Edelmann, "Le Jeu de Construction," *Le Monde*, June 4.

"Arquetipos y Abstracciones (Prototypes and Abstractions)," *Arquitectura & Construcción*, June 6.

"Groundbreaking for Museum Campus Begins Construction," *Collegian*, June 6.

"Spirits Soar at Groundbreaking for UT Art Building at Museum,"

Blade, June 6.

"University of Toledo Begins Work on Arts Center," *Cleveland Plain Dealer*, June 6.

Carol Vogel, "Playing Favorites," *New York Times Magazine*, June 9.

Edward M. Gomez, "Blueprint for Success," *San Francisco Examiner*, June 10.

"A Transition Based on Transit," *Downtown News*, June 10.

Cathleen McGuigan, "A Maverick Master," *Newsweek*, June 17.

"New Faces Will Change Twin Cities Museum Landscape," *Star Tribune*, June 30.

"Gehry na Europa," *A+U*, June–July.

"The Century Club," *Architectural Record: Centennial Issue*, July.

Louis Sahagun, "Long Delayed Disney Concert Hall Complex Gets Council's Approval," *Los Angeles Times*, July.

"The Bowl and Beyond," *International Arts Manager*, July 7.

"Don't Trivialize the Original," *New York Times*, July 7.

Martin Filler, "Money Changers in the Temple: Commerce and the Custodians of Culture," *Times Literary Supplement*, July 19.

"Metro Digest: Visionary Design," *Los Angeles Times*, July 26.

"Look Mickey, No Kitsch," *Time*, July 29.

"Architect Gehry to Address VAC," *Argonaut*, July 31.

Sandro Marpillero, "Gehry in Sequenza," *Casabella*, July–August.

"La ZAC Bercy," *Casabella*, July–August.

"Das Leben Ist Nicht Ordentlich," *Die Zeit Feuilleton*, August.

"The AD 100 Architects," *Architectural Digest*, August 15.

Beth Kleid, "Modeling in Italy," *Los Angeles Times*, August 19.

Jack Skelly, "Shoebox in a Rose Unveiled as Phil's New Home," *Los Angeles Downtown News*, August 19.

"Sacramento, California: Herman Miller," *Abitare*, September.

Karen Salmon, "American Architects at Venice Biennale," *Architecture*, September.

Barbara Isenberg, "Curtain Rises

on Final Design for Disney Hall," *Los Angeles Times,* Valley Edition, September 5.

"Go to Venice and See the Whole World," *Independent,* September 11.

Leon Whiteson, "High Note," *Los Angeles Times,* September 15.

Gordon Dillow, "Stop the Disney Concert Hall," *Downtown News,* September 16.

"City Snaps," *Angeles,* September 19.

Gilbert Luigi, "Gehry-Botta: De Sourire de Gehry à la Severite de Botta," *Neuf Neiuw,* September–October.

"American Center Building Project," *GA Document,* October.

Claire Downey, "An American in Paris," *Metropolis,* October.

"Gehry: Turtle Creek Development," *Materia,* October.

Marinetta Nunziante, "L'Immagine, Il Gesto, La Visione," *Ville Giardini,* October.

Marinetta Nunziante, "Il Nostro Ritratto In Pietra (Abitare il Moderno)," *Ville Giardini,* October.

"Vitra, International Furniture Manufacturing Facility," *GA Document,* October.

Paul Goldberger, "Beyond the Master's Voice," *New York Times Magazine,* October 13.

Aldo Castellano, "Quinta Mostra Internazionale di Architettura," *Abitare,* November.

"Guggenheim Asks Gehry to Design New Expansion Museum for Bilbao," *Architectural Record,* November.

"LA Architect at Large," *LA Architect,* November.

Suzanne Stephens, "US Pavilion a Biennale Standout Amid Exhibit Excesses," *Architectural Record,* November.

"F. O. Gehry, Excerpts from the Rietveld Lecture," *Kunst & Museum Journaal,* November 6.

Leena Maunula, "Walt Disneyn Konsettitalosta Kasvaa Kalifornian Kulttuurin Kuva," *Helsingin Sanomat Kultturi,* November 22.

Mark Alden Branch, "Estrategias del ocio: La Arquitectura de Disney (Disney's Architecture: Leisure Craftness)," *Arquitectura Viva,* November–December.

Victoria Geibel, "Framing the Dance," *Dance Ink,* winter.

Hernán Garfias, "Vitra Design Museum," *Diseño,* December.

"Gehry's Guggenheim Unveiled," *Architecture,* December.

Nonie Niesewand, "Biennale Build-Up: How the Architects Stole the Show in Venice," *British Vogue,* December.

Cathleen McGuigan, "The Barcelona Way," *Newsweek,* December 9.

Olga Spiegel, "Gehry y Miyawaki exponen obras y proyectos en la Miró (Gehry and Miyawaki Exhibit Projects and Designs at the Miró)," *La Vanguardia,* December 13.

S. Vales, "El Proyecto del Museo de Arte Moderno Guggenheim, se presenta hoy en Bilbao (Guggenheim's Museum of Modern Art Project Presented in Bilbao Today)," *El Correo Español—El Pueblo Vasco,* December 13.

J. A. Gonzales Carrera, "El Museo de Bilbao Tiene el Apoyo de Todos los Miembros de la Fundación (Bilbao's Museum Has the Support of All Foundation Members)," *El Correo Español—El Pueblo Vasco,* December 14.

"Las Instituciones y la Fundación Guggenheim rubrican el acuerdo para instalar el Museo en Bilbao (Guggenheim Foundation and the Institutions Sign Agreement for Bilbao Museum)," *El Correo Español—El Pueblo Vasco,* December 14.

Nekane Lauzirika, "El Museo Guggenheim de Bilbao Reunirá Condiciones más que Suficientes para Albergar el 'Gernika' de Picasso (Bilbao's Guggenheim Museum Will Be More than Adequate to Store Picasso's Guernica)," *DEIA Diario de Euskadi,* December 14.

"El Museo Guggenheim, en Bilbao Dentro de Cuatro Años (Bilbao's Guggenheim Museum Will Be Completed in Four Years)," *El Mundo del País Vasco,* December 14.

Sonia Nanclares, "Las Instituciones Vascas y la Fundación Neoyorquina Sellan un Pacto Para 20 Años (New York Foundation and Basque Institutions Sign a Twenty-Year Agreement)," *El Correo Español—El Pueblo Vasco,* December 14.

"Escultures del buit i arquitectures dels volums," *Diari de Barcelona,* December 19.

Mike Davis, "Los Angeles Ciudad-Fortaleza, Metáforas de la Reclusión (Metaphors of Reclusion: Los Angeles, Fortress City)," *A & V,* November–December.

Diane Ghirardo, "Entre el terremoto y la sequía, Las dos últimas décadas (The Last Two Decades: between Drought and Earthquake)," *A & V,* November–December.

"Propileros Binoculares, Nueva Sede de Chiat/Day, Venice (Binoculars Propilaea: Chiat/Day's New Headquarters, Venice)," *A & V,* November–December.

1992

B. J. Archer, "Die Busfahrkarte: Ein Abstecher zu Frank O. Gehry," *Internationales Design-Projekt* (Hannover: Busstops).

"La Ballena Verada Zona Comercial del Hotel de las Artes: Frank Gehry (Frank O. Gehry: Standing Whale, Hotel de Las Artes Commercial Zone)," *A&V.*

Alan Cohl, "Fashion and Uncertainty: Interview with Wolf Prize Recipients, 1992," *Architecture of Israel: Towards the Year 2000.*

"Frank Gehrys Neue Stuhlklassiker," *Mensch & Buro.*

François Chaslin, "Frank O. Gehry," *L'Architecture d'Aujourd'Hui.*

"Interview: Frank on Frank," *Knoll Talk* 2, no. 2.

"P.S. Designer Flechten Möbel," *Elle Decoration.*

"Abd ve Kanada'dan: Muze Binalari," *Mimarlik,* January.

Patricia Beard, "The Escape Artists," *Mirabella,* January.

"PA Awards: American Center in Paris," *Progressive Architecture,* January.

Vincente Verdú, "El Hombre Intraquilo (Restless Man)," *El Europeo,* January.

Michael Webb, "A Monument to Vision," *LA Style,* January.

Anatxu Zabalbeascoa, "Frank Gehry, Como Pez en el Agua (Frank Gehry, Like Fish in Water)," *El Europeo,* January.

Luis J. Grossman, "Críticos: Cita de Honor en Los Angeles (Critics: Rendezvous of Honor in Los Angeles)," *La Nacion,* January 2.

Juan Luis Laskurian Argarete, "Del Guggenheim, Costos y Prudencias (Guggenheim's Costs and Discretions)," *El Correo Español—El Pueblo Vasco,* January 12.

"Three Architects Share Wolf Prize for Arts," *Jerusalem Post,* January 16.

"Un Guggenheim para Bilbao (A Guggenheim for Bilbao)," *El Correo Español—El Pueblo Vasco,* January 18.

Morris Newman, "Public and Civic Projects Around in the Office Lull," *New York Times,* January 19.

Patricia Leigh Brown, "With the Glue Hardly Dry, This Chair Is a Classic," *New York Times,* January 23.

Javier Munoz, "El 'elefante' Krens acampa en Bilbao (The Krens 'Elephant' Camping in Bilbao)," *El Correo Español—El Pueblo Vasco,* January 26.

"Ausschrei der Emporung (Cry of Indignity)," *Umriss,* January–February.

"Chiat Day à Venice," *L'Architecture d'Aujourd'hui,* February.

Judith Davidsen, "Birth of a Chair," *Architectural Record,* February.

Adele Freedman, "Man of Steel and Cardboard and Chain Link and Wallpaper and Fish," *Saturday Night,* February.

Francesca Garcia-Marquez, "Office Building, Venice, California," *Domus,* February.

"Making a Proposal for the 'Super Museum,'" *Scape* 21 (February).

Susan Goldman Rubin, "Frank Gehry on Survival x 2," *Designers West,* February.

Mark Swed, "Pacific Overtures," *Connoisseur,* February.

Pilar Viladas, "Gehry in Focus," *House & Garden,* February.

Michael Webb, "Through the Looking Glass," *Blueprint,* February.

J. A. Gonzales Carrera, "El Proyecto Guggenheim Puede ser Reducido en una Cuarta Parte (Guggenheim Project Could be Reduced One Fourth)," *El Correo Español—El Pueblo Vasco*, February 12.

J. A. Gonzales Carrera, "Guggenheim y las Instituciones Sellarán su Acuerdo el día 27 (Guggenheim and the Institutions to Seal Agreement on the 27th)," *El Correo Español—El Pueblo Vasco*, February 18.

Brigitte Fitoussi, "L'Entreprise Architecture: Florilèdge d'architectes pour usine de meubles," *L'Expansion*, February 20.

J. A. Gonzalez Carrera, "Ardanza dice que el Museo Guggenheim Será Un Foco de Proyección al Mundo (Ardanza Predicts Guggenheim Museum Will Be a Projection Center to the World)," *El Correo Español—El Pueblo Vasco*, February 28.

Jon Spayde, "In Profile: Perfectly Frank," *Departures*, February–March.

Martin Filler, "Sticks and Stains," *Design Quarterly*, spring.

Frank Gehry, "Up Everest in a Volkswagen," *Design Quarterly*, spring.

"Notable and Noteworthy," *Loyola Lawyer*, spring.

Geert Bekaert, "De Mythe de Banalisering," *Archis*, March.

Yukio Futagawa, "F.O.G. & A, Chiat/Day Main Street; Chiat/Day Hampton Drive," *GA Document*, March.

Jeremy Levine, "Ode to the Chair," *Los Angeles Architect*, March.

Tiziana Lorenzelli, "Beyond Brentwood," *Los Angeles Architect*, March.

Jim Murphy, "A Venice Collaboration," *Progressive Architecture*, March.

Yves Nacher, "Frank Gehry: L'Artiste," *Jardin des Modes*, March.

Christine Pittel, "Frank Gehry: Architect on the Edge," *House Beautiful*, March.

Terence Riley, "Frank Gehry: New Furniture Prototypes," *MOMA Members Quarterly*, March.

"The Rink Cycle," *Esquire*, March.

Guy Sorman, "Frank Gehry, L'Architecte du Mouvement," *Le Figaro Magazine*, March.

Suzanne Stephens, "MOMA's Power Play," *Oculus*, March.

Pilar Viladas, "Gestaltung der Ausstellung," *Entartete Kunst*, March.

Marilyn Zelinski, "A Twist on Convention," *Interiors*, March.

Aaron Betsky, "Bent on Comfort," *Los Angeles Times Magazine*, March 1.

Evelyn De Wolfe, "State Architects Prevail at Coveted Awards," *Los Angeles Times*, March 8.

Judith Nasatir, "Hail Gehry, Full of Grace," *Interior Design: Show Daily*, March 18.

Christine Pittel, "Architecture at the Outer Limits," *San Francisco Examiner*, March 26.

Adele Freedman, "Gehry Makes Us Sit Up and Take Notice," *Globe and Mail*, March 28.

Ann Jarmusch, "Classic Zing!," *San Diego Union*, March 29.

Emilio Ambasz, "Stickhandling," *I.D.*, March–April.

Claudine Mulard, "Optique Architecturale: Chiat/Day/Mojo," *Architecture Interieur Créé*, March–April.

C. Abdi Guzer, "Mimariligin Uç Noktasi Artik Daha Yakin," *Arredamento Dekorasyon*, April.

Claire Booney, "Vitra Design Museum," *City & Country Home*, April.

"Designing with Nature," *Art in America*, April.

Iç Dünyalar, "Schnabel Evi: Geleneksel Geometriye Bir 'Reddiye,'" *Arredamento Dekorasyon*, April.

Irem Erez and Ömer Madra, "Soylesi/Interview: Frank Gehry," *Arredamento Dekorasyon*, April.

"Go-Ahead for Bilbao Guggenheim," *Art in America*, April.

Philip Jodidio, "The Architects of Euro Disney Resort," *Connaissance des Arts: Euro Disney*, April.

Philip Jodidio, "Euro Disney: Le Pari et le Rêve," *Connaissance des Arts: Euro Disney*, April.

Philip Jodidio, "Festival Disney," *Connaissance des Arts: Euro Disney*, April.

Michael Muffler, "Watum Metropoleist Kultur nicht uberall?," *Der Architekt*, April.

"Möbelhit: Frank Gehrys "Web"-Stühle," *Häuser*, April.

"Philip Johnson'A Göre Gehry," *Arredamento Dekorasyon*, April.

"Profil: Frank O. Gehry: Sinirsiz Özgurlugun Pesinde," *Arredamento Dekorasyon*, April.

Ugur Tanyeli, "Gehry'Nin 'Karsi-Dil' i," *Arredamento Dekorasyon*, April.

Fernando Iturribarria, "A la caza del Ratón Mickey (In Pursuit of Mickey Mouse)," *El Correo Español—El Pueblo Vasco*, April 12.

Patricia Leigh Brown, "Sinuous Chairs Become Instant Classics," *Milwaukee Journal*, Home Section, April 19.

Robert Campbell, "Children's Museum Sees New Wing as Wave of Future," *Boston Globe*, April 22.

Marie Gendron, "Children's Museum Looks to Ride Expansion Wave," *Boston Herald*, April 22.

Charles-Arthur Boyer, "Frank Gehry: Une Architecture douce pour EuroDisneyland," *Jardin des Modes*, May.

Akiko Busch, "Why We Love Frank," *Metropolis*, May.

Robin Cembalest, "The Guggenheim's High-Stakes Gamble," *ArtNews*, May.

"Techniques of Approach: Frank O. Gehry's Redesign," *Lotus*, May.

Tom Whitlock, "Binocular Vision: Chiat/Day/Mojo," *Los Angeles Architect*, May.

Judy Siegel, "Eight Receive Wolf Prize in 5 Categories," *Jerusalem Post*, May 18.

Francisco Chacon, "El Redimensionamiento no Tiene por que Afectar a mi Proyecto para el Guggenheim (Redimensioning Should Not Have to Affect My Guggenheim Project)," *El Mundo*, May 19.

J. A. Gonzales Carrera, "La Mayor parte de los museos son edificios intimidatorios (Most Museums Are Intimidating Buildings)," *El Correo Espanol—El Pueblo Vasco*, May 19.

Alain Guiheux, "Frank O. Gehry: Le Centre Culturel Americain, Paris, France, 1991," *Centre Georges Pompidou: Trente Ans D'Architecture*, May 27.

Joseph Giovannini, "Im Fernglas keimen die Ideen," *Frankfurter Allgemeine Zeitung*, May 29.

Adolfo Morán, "Frank Gehry: El Arquitecto Punk (Frank Gehry: Punk Architect)," *Suplemento*, May 31.

Luis Fernández-Galiano, "Un Pulpo De Acero (Steel Octopus)," *Arquitectura Viva*, May–June.

José Ignacio Wert, "Las Musas y Las Masas (Masses and Muses)," *Arquitectura Viva*, May–June.

"In & Ex-terior, Chiat/Day," *Brutus*, spring–summer.

"Knitting with Wood," *Design Review*, summer.

"Trustees Take First Trip to LA," *Newsletter of the American Academy of Rome*, summer.

Philip Jodidio, "Festival Gehry," *Connaissance des Arts*, June.

Terence Riley, "Frank Gehry: New Furniture Prototypes," *A+U*, June.

Marco Romanelli, "Frank O. Gehry sedule intrecciate in laminato di acero curvato," *Domus*, June.

Karen Salmon, "The Children's Museum," *Architecture*, June.

Suzanne Stephens, "Festival Disney," *Architectural Record*, June.

Jean Webb, "Furniture with a Twist," *Furniture Design and Manufacturing*, June.

Michael Webb, "Los Prismaticos de Venice (Venice Binoculars)," *Diseño Interior*, June.

Llatzer Moix, "Los roces en la zona comercial del hotel Arts se deben a un malentendido cultural (Friction in the Commercial Zone of the Arts Hotel Is the Result of Cultural Misunderstanding)," *La Vanguardia*, June 5.

J. J. Navarro Arisa, "Frank Gehry califica de 'malentendido cultural' el conflicto del hotel de las Arts (Frank Gehry Calls Conflict at the Arts Hotel 'Cultural Misunderstanding')," *El País*, June 5.

"Architect Gehry Wins Japanese Arts Prize," *Washington Post*, June 12.

"Arts Premium," *USA Today*, June 12.

Mauretta Capuano, "Como un Nobel, Senza Confini, per Un'Arte Universale," *Il Tempo*, June 12.

Shcila Rule, "Major Arts Prizes for Gehry and Kurosawa," *New York Times*, June 12.

John T. Daxland, "U.S. Architect Hailed," *Daily News*, June 15.

"Frank Gehry's 'Nobel Prize,'" *Architects' Journal*, June 17.

J. A. Gonzalez Carrera, "Una misión Vasca Viaja a EE UU a la Reapertura del Guggenheim (Basque Mission Travels to U.S.A for Guggenheim's Reopening)," *El Correo Espanol—El Pueblo Vasco*, June 20.

"EuroDisneyland: Festival Disney," *Nikkei Architecture*, June 22.

Shlomit Shakked, *Maariv*, June 22.

Barbara Isenberg, "Disney Concert Hall Plan Advances," *Los Angeles Times*, Metro, June 26.

Frank Gehry, "Creating Housing," *Los Angeles Times*, June 28.

"Guggenheim Museum Bilbao," *Guggenheim Commemorative Magazine*, June 28.

Barbara Isenberg, "Disney Concert Hall Project Gets Final OK," *Los Angeles Times*, June 30.

"All That Fun: Mickey, Grand Urbaniste," *Architecture Interieure Créé*, June–July.

Patrick Grace, "Frank O. Gehry Lecture, April 24, 1992, Milwaukee Art Museum," *Art Muscle*, June–July.

"Frank Gehrys Neue Stuhl-klassiker: Revolution Im Bugholzwald," *Mensch & Buro*, June–August.

Judith Davidsen, "Light-Hearted Models for Serious Results," *Architectural Record*, July.

John Morris Dixon, "Disney Over There," *Progressive Architecture*, July.

Gabriella De Ferrari, "Frank Gehry: The Architect Gives Children a Floating World to Learn On," *Mirabella*, July.

Joseph Giovannini, "Olympic Overhaul," *Progressive Architecture*, July.

"Ein Klassischer Seitensprung," *Playboy*, July.

Mildred F. Schmertz, "Eclectic Avenue," *Architecture*, July.

Philip Wesselhöft, "Architektur: Tief Durchs Glas Geschaut," *Schöner Wohnen*, July 7.

J. A. Gonzalez Carrera, "Gehry

Podría Colegiarse en Vizcaya para Firmar el Proyecto del Museo Guggenheim (Gehry Could Be Licensed in Vzscaya to Sign Guggenheim's Museum Project)," *El Correo Espanol—El Pueblo Vasco*, July 8.

Sally Vallongo, "Columbus Exhibition Contrasts Top Architects," *Blade*, July 19.

Roberta Smith, "Frank Gehry: New Bentwood Furniture Designs," *New York Times*, Living Arts, July 24.

Alfonso Quinta, "Frank O. Gehry: 'No se Aprecia lo Suficiente a Gaudi' (Frank O. Gehry: 'Gaudi Is Not Appreciated Enough')," *El Mundo*, July 30.

Mario Antonio Arnaboldi, "The Walt Disney Concert Hall," *L'Arca*, July–August.

Peter Davey, "La historia en venta: Disney conquista Europa (History for Sale: Disney Conquers Europe)," *Arquitectura Viva*, July–August.

"Disney Hall Approved," *Los Angeles Architect*, July–August.

"Frank Gehry, Praemium Imperiale," *Arquitectura Viva*, July–August.

"Gehry Collection," *I.D.: Annual Design Review*, July–August.

Eileen Imber, "Pool Blues," *Metropolis*, July–August.

Martin Pawley, "A Full and Frank Talk," *Blueprint*, July–August.

Deyan Sudjic, "Barcelona: The Architects' Olympics: City in the Fast Lane," *Blueprint*, July–August.

Michael Webb, "Chiat/Day: A Gift to the Street," *Los Angeles Architect*, July–August.

B. J. Novitski, "Gehry Forges New Computer Links," *Architecture*, August.

"Olympic Village," *Architectural Record*, August.

Sally Vallongo, "Shock at First Sight," *Blade*, August 9.

Rone Tempest, "America's Designs on Europe," *Los Angeles Times*, August 25.

"Knoll Chairs," *Museum of Modern Art*, fall.

Henry Pillsbury, "Counting Down to American Center Opening," *Commerce in France*, fall.

Paola Antonelli, "Interview: Joel Stearns," *Abitare*, September.

"Frank O. Gehry's New Bentwood Chairs," *SD*, September.

Charles Gandee, "Mickey and His Architects," *House and Garden*, September.

Morris Newman, "Encouraging Eclecticism: California Vernacular," *Architectural Review*, September.

Kate Pocock, "Nota Bene: Gehry on Ice," *City & Country Home*, September.

Deyan Sudjic, "Frank Gehry Reinvents the Chair," *Blueprint*, September.

"Santa Monica Passion: Frank Gehry," *Sankei Shinbun*, September 9.

"Whistling While It Works," *New York Times*, September 13.

Elizabeth Ross, "A 'Gehry' Just for Children," *Washington Home*, September 17.

Steven Litt, "Exhibit Explores Master Architect's Visionary Works," *Cleveland Plain Dealer*, September 20.

Teresa Scalzo, "Frank Gehry: Architect for the Times," *Minnesota*, September–October.

"Architektur: Schöne Bauten für Kinder," *Ambiente*, October.

Alex Buck, "Blue Chip des Designs: Die Grossen Gewinner," *Ambiente*, October.

"Gehry's Kids," *Esquire*, October.

Juan Ignacio Vidarte, "Nueva York, Venecia, Bilbao: Museo Guggenheim (Guggenheim Museum: New York, Venice, Bilbao)," *La Ciudad y el Puerto*, October.

Jerry Adler and Marc Peyser, "A City Behind Walls," *Newsweek*, October 5.

"The Cultural Elite, the Newsweek 100, Who They Really Are," *Newsweek*, October 5.

Jay Thomson, "Tickets Going Fast for Architect's Talk," *UW Gazette*, October 7.

Sonia Nanclares, "Gehry Presentará en Junio el Proyecto de Ejecución del Museo Guggenheim (Gehry Will Present Plan for Guggenheim's Museum Project Execution in June)," *El Correo Español—El Pueblo Vasco*, October 10.

Eliot Nusbaum, "A Triumph of Architecture," *Des Moines Sunday Register*, October 11.

Rostislav Svacha, "Americky Architekt Frank Gehry v Praze," *Lid. Noviny*, October 13.

E. Portocarrero and A. Gorostola, "Thomas Krens: El Arte Tiene Impacto Político y Económico (Thomas Krens: Art Has Political and Economic Impact)," *El Correo Español—El Pueblo Vasco*, October 18.

M. Jose Carrero, "Arregi Anuncia que la Edificación del Museo Guggenheim Comenzará a Mediados de 1993 (Arregi Announces Construction of Guggenheim Museum to Begin Mid-1993)," *El Correo Español—El Pueblo Vasco*, October 22.

"Prince Takamatsumiya Memorial World Culture Award: Architecture," *Sankei Shinbun*, October 22.

"González Durana y Barañano forman parte del comité asesor del Museo Guggenheim (Gonzalez Durana and Baranano Are Part of Guggenheim Museum Advisory Committee)," *El Correo Español—El Pueblo Vasco*, October 23.

Lynda Coye, "Groups Back New Plans for Children's Museum," *Boston Herald*, October 30.

"Public by Design," *Boston Globe*, October 31.

Joseph Giovannini, "Revolution by Design," *Modern Maturity*, October–November.

"Mobilier en Bois Lamellé: La Gehry Collection," *Techniques & Architecture*, October–November.

"The City of Barcelona Public Art Program," *SD*, November.

"Claes Oldenburg/Coosje van Bruggen," *SD*, November.

Daniel P. Gregory, "Billboard Buildings," *Sunset*, November.

Enrico Morteo, "Frank O. Gehry: Il pesce al Villaggio Olimpico di Barcellona," *Domus*, November.

Adele Freedman, "Frank Gehry Shoots and Scores On and Off the Ice," *Globe and Mail*, November 10.

"Hagey Lecturer Discusses His Work," *UW Gazette*, November 11.

Linda J. Howe, "Local Gallery Is

Nearly Open," *UW Gazette,* November 11.

David Flynn, Alan Leung, and Eric Taker, "Great White Architect Gehry Sez: I Came, I Spoke, I Played," *Imprint,* November 13.

"Student Centre," *UW Gazette,* November 18.

"Apoyar otras iniciativas (Sponsoring Other Initiatives)," *El Correo Español—El Pueblo Vasco,* November 21.

Joseph Giovannini, "Wrapmaster Gehry and the New Culture Palace," *Los Angeles Times Magazine,* November 22.

Robert Johnson, "Art Museum Gets a Tannenbaum Topper," *Minnesota Daily,* November 25.

J. A. Gonzales Carrera, "El Museo Guggenheim se abrirá un año despues de lo previsto (Guggenheim Museum to Open One Year Later)," *El Correo Español—El Pueblo Vasco,* November 27.

Sally Vallongo, "New Design Era Dawns in Toledo," *Blade,* November 29.

"Guggenheim in Europe: Projects by Hans Hollein and Frank Gehry," *Guggenheim News,* winter.

"Guggenheim Museum Bilbao on Schedule," *Guggenheim News,* winter.

"The Products, People and Programs on Design: Exhibitions Explore Design," *Perspectives,* winter.

Sebastiano Brandolini, "Entertainment Center di Eurodisneyland a Marne-la-Vallée, Walt Disney Concert Hall a Los Angeles, di Frank Gehry," *Casabella,* December.

Joseph Giovannini, "Holy Toledo!," *Harper's Bazaar,* December.

John Rockwell, "For American Center in Paris, New Home and Bitter Dispute," *New York Times,* December 1.

Joy Hakanson Colby, "Vision and Innovation Combine to Give Toledo a Mighty Fortress for the Arts," *Detroit News,* December 5.

Marsha Miro, "Toledo Art School is a Work of Art in Itself," *Detroit Free Press,* December 6.

Steven Litt, "Inspired Creation at Toledo U.," *Cleveland Plain Dealer,*

December 6.

Holden Lewis, "New Building Both Startles and Inspires," *Blade,* December 7.

Holden Lewis, "Opening-Day Crowd Digs Zigs and Zags of UT's Arts Center," *Blade,* December 7.

Eric Levin, "What Is That New Fish on the Banks of the Maumee River? Frank O. Gehry," *Maverick,* December 8.

"Ground Broken for Disney Concert Hall," *Outlook,* December 11.

Herbert Muschamp, "Gehry's Disney Hall: A Matterhorn for Music," *New York Times,* December 13.

Sam Hall Kaplan, "A Concert Hall for Fantasyland," *Los Angeles Times,* December 21.

Frederick M. Nicholas, "In the Spirit of Our Times," *Los Angeles Times,* December 21.

Ernest Lluch, "Arquitectura y Costos (Architecture and Costs)," *Cinco Dias,* December 23.

"1992 AIA/LA Design Awards: Festival Disney," *Los Angeles Architect,* December–January.

"Disney Hall Commences," *Los Angeles Architect,* December–January.

1993

"Amerikanisches Kulturzentrum in Paris, Frankreich (American Cultural-Center in Paris, France)," *Architektur + Wettbewerbe* 154.

Daniel Burckhardt and Daniel Wittlin, "Vitra Design Museum und Möbelproduktionshalle," *Architekturführer Basel und Umgebung 1980–1993.*

Werner Dagefoer, "The Great Guggenheim," *BMW Magazine.*

Estrella de Diego, "La Histeria de la Historia: Sobre los Nuevos Museos Españoles (History's Hysteria: New Spanish Museums)," *A&V.*

"Frank Gehry and Philip Johnson: Lewis Residence," *Architectural Design Profile* 102: "Folding in Architecture."

"Frank O. Gehry," *GA Architect* 10.

"Frank O. Gehry: University of Toledo Art Building," *GA Document* 36.

"The Gehry Collection," *Internationaler Designpreis des Landes Baden-Wurttemberg.*

"Goldstein-Sued," *Wohn-Stadt: Die Zukunft des Stadtischen* (Campus Verlag).

David Hanks, "Frank Gehry: Bentwood Furniture," *Architectural Design Profile* 102: "Folding in Architecture."

Ich will Architektur Zeigen, wie sie Ist (exhibition catalog for Kunsthalle Bielefeld, Düsseldorf: Richter Verlag).

Philip Jodidio, *Contemporary American Architects* (Cologne: Benedikt Taschen).

John Richardson, "Museos de franquicia: La Saga de los Guggenheim (Tax Exempts Museums: The Guggenheim's Saga)," *A&V.*

"A Space for Music," *Los Angeles Philharmonic 75th Season Program.*

James Steele, *Los Angeles Architecture: The Contemporary Condition.*

James Steele, *Schnabel House: Frank Gehry* (London: Phaidon).

Vitra Design Musuem (Tokyo: GA Design Center).

Mirko Zardini, "Los Angeles as Context: Frank O. Gehry's Edgemar Development," *Lotus* 74.

"The 40th Annual P/A Awards: Architectural Design Award: Walt Disney Concert Hall," *Progressive Architecture,* January.

Sergio Butti and Maurizio Vogliazzo, "Il conte de Lautréamont no Ha Visto il Pop," *Progex,* January.

"Frank Gehry and Associates," *World Architecture Review,* January.

Michael Webb, "Bottom Line," *Peak,* January.

"Where to Go Next: 10 Reasons to Cheer in 1993: Americans in Paris," *Travel & Leisure,* January.

Michael Rotondi, Claes Oldenburg, Coosje van Bruggen, Allan M. Mannheim, Daniel N. Fox, and Robert Benson, "Letters to the Editor: Gehry's Disney Hall," *Los Angeles Magazine,* January 3.

"The Best Design of 1992: (1) The Work of Frank Gehry," *Time,* January 4.

Benjamin Forgey, "Holy Toledo!

A Smash Clash," *Washington Post,* January 9.

J. A. Gonzalez Carrera, "Thomas Krens Retoma los Contactos Directos con las Instituciones Vascas (Thomas Krens Reassumes Direct Contacts with Basque Institutions)," *El Correo Español—El Pueblo Vasco,* January 28.

Roberta Smith, "The New Guggenheim Starts to Show Its Face," *New York Times,* January 29.

Jorge Sainz, "Maquetas Digitales (Digital Models)," *Arquitectura Viva,* January–February.

Karen Fishburn, "Walt Disney Concert Hall Breaks Ground," *Design Journal,* February.

"Frank Gehry per Euro Disneyland," *L'Arca,* February.

"Prague: Rounding the Corners and Tilting the Angles, Gehry Style," *Architectural Record,* February.

Kristen Richards, "Harmonics by Gehry," *Interiors,* February.

"Walt Disney Concert Hall Breaks Ground," *Performing Arts,* February.

Joseph Giovannini, "Das Teleskop des Architekten," *Frankfurter Allgemeine Zeitung,* February 4.

Suzanne Muchnic, "State of the Art (Museums)," *Los Angeles Times,* February 14.

Leon Whiteson, "Los Angeles Architecture: Trashy Sophistication?," *Los Angeles Times,* February 14.

Sally Vallongo, "Gehry Gearing Up to Design Second Building Near Museum," *Blade,* February 15.

Blair Kamin, "Frank Gehry Designs an Ark for Los Angeles," *Chicago Tribune,* February 17.

"Lines, Angles and Patterns," *Star Tribune,* February 17.

"El Gobierno vasco preside por primera vez el Museo de Bilbao (Basque Government Presides Bilbao's Museum for the First Time)," *El Correo Español—El Pueblo Vasco,* February 19.

Francisco Chacon, "El Museo Guggenheim de Bilbao Reduce Un Tercio El Proyecto Original pero no su Presupuesto (Bilbao's Guggenheim Museum Reduces Original Project by One Third, but Budget Remains the Same)," *El Mundo,* February 26.

J. A. Gonzalez Carrera, "Frank Gehry Arquiteco: Bilbao tiene la estética de la realidad (Architect Frank Gehry: Bilbao Has Realistic Aesthetic)," *El Correo Español— El Pueblo Vasco*, February 26.

J. A. Gonzalez Carrera, "Guggenheim y las Instituciones Vascas Respaldan el Proyecto Ideado por Gehry (Guggenheim and the Basque Institutions Endorse Gehry's Design Project)," *El Correo Español—El Pueblo Vasco*, February 26.

Eva Larrauri, "Gehry se inspira en el perfil industrial de Bilbao para el Museo Guggenheim (Bilbao's Industrial Profile Inspires Gehry for Guggenheim Museum)," *El País*, February 26.

Nekane Lauzirika, "Frank O. Gehry: El Edificio Sigue Fiel al Contrato Estético que Suscribí con la Ciudad (Frank O. Gehry: The Building Faithfully Follows the Aesthetic Agreement I Made with the City)," *DEIA*, February 26.

Nekane Lauzirika, "El futuro Museo Marcará Criterios en la Revitalización de la Ciudad (Future Museum will Set Criteria for City's Revitalization)," *DEIA*, February 26.

Amaia Okariz, "Guggenheim acorta distancias con Bilbao (Guggenheim Lessens Distances with Bilbao)," *Egin*, February 26.

"Presentado el Diseño Básico del 'Guggenheim' (Guggenheim's Basic Designed Presented)," *DEIA*, February 26.

Anna Somers Cocks, "The Guggenheim Goes Global," *London Magazine*, spring.

Rostislav Svacha, "Jiraskove Square," *Architekt*, spring.

K. Michael Hays, "Frank Gehry and the Vitra Design Museum," *GSD News*, winter–spring.

Richard Feibusch, "Visible City," *Metropolis*, March.

"Frank O. Gehry: Architect on the Scene," *Kenchiku Bunka*, March.

Andrea Truppin, "Iowa Enlightenment," *Architecture*, March.

Tomas Smrcek, "Nová Pražská Architektonická Kvalita," *Z Domova*, March 5.

Frank-Michael Kiel-Steinkamp,

"Amerikas profiliertester Architekt Frank O. Gehry Beschreitet für das EMR in Bad Oeynhausen: Neue Wege zur Architektur der Energie," *Zwischen Weser und Rhein*, March 27.

Christian Althoff and Stefan Hörttrich, "Ein Haus, Das Man nie Kennenlernt," *Ostwestfalen-Lippe*, March 27–28.

"Una Factoria Ilustrada; Fabrica Para Vitra (Vitra's Factory: An Enlightened Plant)," *A&V*, March–April.

"Frank Gehry Awarded Patent for Furniture Collection," *Design Journal*, April.

Jorge Glusberg, "Entre o Obvio e o Subliminar," *Projeto*, April.

"Kobe, Fishdance Restaurant," *Lotus*, April.

David Leclerc, "Un Moment de Vérité (A Moment of Truth)," *L'Architecture d'Aujourd'hui*, April.

Gordon Lore, "Disney Conert Hall: Space Age Alliance of Computer Technology and Stone," *Dimensional Stone Magazine*, April.

Michael Webb, "A Civic Delight," *LA Architect*, April.

Wolfgang Jean Stock, "Ein Juwel Braucht eine Fassung," *Feuilleton*, April 12.

Gillian Darley, "A Brave Risk Taker of Formidable Nerve," *Observer*, May.

"Museo Guggenheim Bilbao (Bilbao's Guggenheim Museum)," *Architecturas para Bilbao*, May.

"Southland Architects Win Awards," *Los Angeles Times*, May 2.

Glen Justice, "SM Architect's Modern Designs Too Far-out for Some in Prague," *Outlook*, May 5.

Alberto G. Alonso, "Los Primeros Cuadros del Museo Guggenheim se Podrian Adquirir antes de Finalizar el Ano (First Paintings for Guggenheim Museum Could Be Acquired Before Year End)," *DEIA*, May 28.

Encarni Bao Aguirre, "Me Encanta trabajar en mi País (I Am Delighted to Work in My Country)," *El Correo Espanol— El Pueblo Vasco*, May 28.

F. de Orozko, "Arquitectos en la Bilbao envidiada del futuro (Architects of the Future Enviable Bilbao)," *DEIA*, May 28.

"El Lehendakari Anima a las Instituciones a 'Realizar Pronto' los Proyectos para Bilbao (Lehendakari Encourages the Institutions to 'Promptly Carry Out' Bilbao's Projects)," *El Correo Espanol—El Pueblo Vasco*, May 28.

Maite Redondo, "Santiago Calatrava: Autor del Proyecto de la Nueva Terminal de Sondika (Santiago Calatrava: Author of Sondika's New Terminal Project)," *DEIA*, May 28.

"Siete Prestigiosos Arquitectos Presentan sus Aportaciones a un Bilbao Innovador (Seven Prestigious Architects Present Their Contributions to an Innovative Bilbao)," *DEIA*, May 28.

"Los Arquitectos Vascos Piden a los Politicos un Mayor Interes por el Urbanismo Cotidiano (Basque Architects Ask Politicians for More Interest on Daily Planning)," *El Correo Espanol—El Pueblo Vasco*, May 29.

Encarni Bao Aguirre, "No Tengo Una Varita Magica: Michael Wilford, Arquitecto (Architect Michael Wilford: 'I Don't Have a Magic Wand')," *El Correo Espanol—El Pueblo Vasco*, May 29.

Concha Lago, "Frank O. Gehry: Arquitecto del Guggenheim (Frank O. Gehry: Guggenheim Architect)," *DEIA*, May 29.

Kurt Anderson, "Philip the Great," *Vanity Fair*, June.

Jean-Louis Cohen, "Main Street Blues: Frank O. Gehry's Festival Disney," *Lotus*, June.

"Frank O. Gehry, University of Toledo Art Building," *A+U*, June.

"Yale Psychiatric Institute and University of Iowa," *GB Progetti*, June.

Adele Freedman, "A Font of Innovation, Down to the Letter," *Globe and Mail*, June 5.

"Artful Work for a New Museum," *Minneapolis Star Tribune*, June 8.

John Gallagher, "Shocking Edge— Daring Projects Rise in Ohio— But No Detroit Area," *Detroit Free Press*, June 8.

Luis Alfonso Gamez, "Bilbao es una ciudad desafio (Bilbao a Defiant City)," *El Correo Espanol— El Pueblo Vasco*, June 8.

Kathleen McGuigan, "A Maverick

Master," *Newsweek*, June 17.

Larry Millett, "U's New Museum Is Art in Its Own Right," *St. Paul Pioneer Press*, June 20.

Burton Bollag, "Un Projet de l'Architecte Frank Gehry Divise Prague," *Nouveau Quotidien*, June 28.

Karen D. Stein, "Center for the Visual Arts, University of Toledo, Ohio," *Architectural Record*, July.

Burton Bollag, "A Puzzle for Elegant Prague: Will Gehry Fit In?," *New York Times*, July 6.

Burton Bollag, "Frank Gehry in Prague: Is City Ready for 'Fred and Ginger'?," *International Herald Tribune*, July 10–11.

"Der Spass, der aus den Wänden kommt," *Stadtblatt*, July 15.

"Die scheinbare Unordnung eines Meisters der Lichtregie," *Westfalen-Blatt*, July 16.

"Visionen Künftiger Entfaltung," *Westfalen-Blatt*, July 16.

"Architektonische Visionen, Museale Träume," *Die Glocke Oelde*, July 17.

"Keinen Einfall unterdrücken," *Neue Westfälische*, July 17.

"Zur Sache," *Neue Westfälische*, July 17.

"Gehry-Ausstellung in der Kunsthalle," *Neue Westfälische*, July 19.

"Ein hoffnungsvoller erster Schritt ist getan," *Westfalen-Blatt*, July 19.

Linda Mack, "Museum Grabs at First Sight," *Minneapolis Star Tribune*, July 19.

"Ein Architekt auf Spurensuche," *Neue Westfälische*, July 20.

John Morris Dixon, "The Vitra Campus," *Progressive Architecture*, August.

Marco Frascari, "Il Mostro Taumaturgico," *GB Progetti*, August.

Annette Le Cuyer, "Object Lesson," *Architectural Review*, August.

Mary Abbe, "A Bent for Wood, Chairs by Architect Frank Gehry Bring New Twist to Seating," *Minneapolis Star Tribune*, August 14.

Elaine Louie, "Cardboard Comeback," *New York Times*, August 26.

605

Lee Klancher, "New Art Museum Rocks the Campus," *Minnesota Explorer*, fall.

"Il Campus della Vitra," *Abitare*, September.

"How We Got from There to Here," *Blueprint*, September.

"Kunst und Klotz (Art and Blocks)," *Ultimo*, September.

"Vitra Museum: Frank Gehry," *Blueprint*, September.

Helene Laube, "Später Ruhm für den alten Ketzer," *Cash*, September 10.

Blair Kamin, "Disney Concert Hall in Los Angeles Will Be Ship-Shaped by Computer," *Philadelphia Inquirer*, September 19.

Pamela Lavigne, "Both Sides Now," *Minnesota*, September–October.

"8 Impressions of the Frederick R. Weisman Art Museum at the University of Minnesota," *Minnesota Monthly*, October.

Francesco Garafalo, "Frank O. Gehry: Advanced Technology Laboratories, Iowa City," *Domus*, October.

Mary Mussell, "Reynolds Wrap, a Tin Can, and a 3-Year-Old," *University Graffito*, October.

"Toledo and Walt Disney Concert Hall," *GB Progetti*, October.

Herbert Muschamp, "The Gehry House: A Brash Landmark Grows Up," *New York Times*, October 7.

Benjamin Forgey, "The Debonair American in Paris," *Washington Post*, October 9.

Olivia Snaije, "A Theme Park for Top Architects," *Christian Science Monitor*, October 14.

Burl Gilyard, "The Best 10 Reasons Life Is Worth Living in the Twin Cities: Reason #1, the Museum That Just Landed," *Twin Cities Reader*, October 20–26.

"Frank Gehry's Courage," *New York Times*, October 28.

"Adele Freedman on Great Buildings," *Toronto Life*, November.

"Faceted Stainless Steel Skin Provides Striking Appearance," *Building Design and Construction*, November.

Scott Gutterman, "Guggenheim Museum Bilbao 1997," *Guggenheim Magazine*, November.

Michael Webb, "Los Prismaticos de Venice (Venice Binoculars)," *Diseño Interior—Oficinas de Concepto Innovador*, November.

John Kalbfleisch, "McGill Students Race Clock to Build Perfect Float," *Montreal Gazette*, November 9.

"Los jueces Permiten que el Ayuntamiento de Bilbao Ocupe el Solar de Guggenheim (Judge Allows Bilbao City Council to Occupy Site of the Guggenheim)," *El Correo*, November 12.

Jonathan Saville, "Take a Load Off Your Feet . . . Artistically," *San Diego Reader*, November 24.

"Nuevo Milenio, Nuevo Bilbao (New millennium, new Bilbao)," *El Correo*, November 28.

Aaron Betsky, "Easy Edges Squiggles Back," *Metropolitan Home*, November–December.

"Gehry Designs a Museum Masterpiece," *Guggenheim News*, winter.

"Trustees and Top Officials Attend Ground-Breaking Ceremony in Bilbao," *Guggenheim News*, winter.

David Leclerc, "Le Walt Disney Concert Hall, un Projet et sa Méthode," *L'Architecture d'Aujourd'hui*, December.

Manfred Ragati, "Gehry's Headquarters for Communication and Technology," *Miteinander*, December.

Nasrine Seraji, "The American Center in Paris, Temporary Building," *Assemblage*, December.

"Czech Architecture: Dancing-Masters," *Economist*, December 11–17.

Herbert Muschamp, "Frank Gehry Lifts Creativity out of the Box," *New York Times*, December 12.

"Prag: Diskussion um Gehry," *Ambiente*, December 12.

Jorge Glusberg, "Gehry: La Arquitectura de Resonancia Escultorica (Gehry: Architecture of Sculptural Resonance)," *La Revista del Mundo*, December 13.

"1993/Hail to Minnesota Buildings, Movies: Mother Lode of Silver," *Minneapolis Star Tribune*, December 26.

Herbert Muschamp, "Architecture 1993: Hello to All That," *New York Times*, December 26.

"AIA/LA Design Awards: Iowa Advanced Technology Laboratories Building and ING Office Building," *Los Angeles Architect*, December–January.

1994

"Frank Gehry," *Design World* 29.

Frank O. Gehry: Biography (Officina Alessi).

"Interview with Frank O. Gehry," *Umriss-Gespräch*.

"It's So Obvious . . . It's Crazy," *Umriss-Gespräch*.

Krzysztof Kliche, "Amerykanin w Paryzu," *Architektura & Biznes* 12.

"Lewis Residence," *GA Houses* 4.

"Loyola Law School, Los Angeles, California, Frank Gehry," *La Escalera, Una Perspectiva del Siglo XX (The Stairway, A Twentieth Century Perspective)*.

Hillary Miller and Joycelyn Chi Fawaz, "Architecture & Art," *Traveler's Journal: Los Angeles Issue*.

"Weisman Art Museum, University of Minnesota, Minneapolis," *GA Document* 38.

Mirko Zardini, ed., "Frank O. Gehry: America as Context," *Lotus Documents*.

Rubin Carson, "The Fifty Most Interesting People (in Los Angeles)," *Los Angeles Magazine*, January.

Fulvio Irace, "Frank O. Gehry a Minneapolis: Frederick R. Weisman Art Museum," *Abitare*, January.

Pamela LaVigne, "WAM: Gift of the Weisman," *University of Minnesota Update*, January.

"The Best Design of 1993: Frank Gehry: Weisman Art Museum," *Time*, January 3.

Ursula Rellstab, "Architektonische Aufbruchstimmung in Prag," *Neue Bürcher Beitung*, January 7.

"Getting Bent," *Sun Journal*, January 9.

"Museum Evokes Strong Sentiment," *USA Today*, January 12.

"El Palacio Euskalduna Absorberá el 25% del Presupuesto Foral de Cultura; La Diputación Destina 1.100 Millones al Museo Guggenheim (Euskalduna Palace to Absorb 25% of Authorized Budget for Culture; Council Sets Aside 1,100 Million for Guggenheim Museum)," *El Correo*, January 12.

Vicente Verdu, "Nuestra Epoca Exige Edificios con Movimiento (Our Time Demands Buildings with Illusion of Motion)," *El País*, January 14.

Carol Vogel, "Guggenheim Receives Another Gift of $10 Million," *New York Times*, January 20.

Kurt W. Forster, "Berliner Balance," *Die Zeit*, January 21.

Fulvio Irace, "Frank Gehry at Minneapolis: An Explosion on Campus," *Il Sole*, January 30.

"The Talk of the Town," *New Yorker*, January 31.

Javier Cenicacelaya and Iñigo Saloña, "Piezas de Recambio, La Renovación de Bilbao (Bilbao's Renovation, Substitution of Parts)," *Arquitectura Viva*, January–February.

Robert Gerloff, "Postcard Perfect," *AM (Architecture Minnesota)*, January–February.

Roger K. Lewis, "No Brick Lump: Frank O. Gehry's Frederick R. Weisman Art Museum at the University of Minnesota," *Museum News*, January–February.

"Be Seated, Please. Setzen Sie sich, Bitte. Asseyez-vous, S'il vous plait . . . ," *Esquire*, February.

"Gehry Museum Shows Best Face to the Mississippi," *Progressive Architecture*, February.

Frank-Michael Kiel-Steinkamp, "What Will Your Grandsons Say to This?," *Progressive Architecture*, February.

"Star Architect in Europe: Topping up Party at the 'Zentrum für Kommunikation und Technologie,'" *Progressive Architecture*, February.

"La Exposición del Guggenheim Desborda Todas las Previsiones de Asistencia (Attendance to Guggenheim Exhibit Surpasses All Expectations)," *El Correo*, February 5.

Maria Arana, "Todos con Klee (Everyone with Klee)," *El Correo*, February 11.

Morgan Baker, "Museum Expansion Envelops Waterfront,"

Boston Business Journal, February 11–17.

Michelle Davidson, "Final Strokes Still Going on Art Building," *University of Toledo News*, February 17.

Carey Hoffman, "Celebrity Talent Helps Ensure Vision of Unfolding Campus Plan," *University of Cincinnati Currents*, February 18.

"Rebirth," *University of Cincinnati Currents*, February 18.

Mike Steele, "Several Steps for the Weisman," *Minneapolis Star Tribune*, February 20.

Vera Graaf, "Alien as a Spaceship," *Die Zeit*, February 25.

Vera Graaf, "Alien as a Spaceship," *Herford/Hannover Newspaper*, February 25.

Herbert Muschamp, "Architecture as Social Action, and Vice Versa," *New York Times*, February 27.

Michael Webb, "Power Gardens," *Garden Design*, February–March.

"The Opening Benefit Gala for the New Weisman Art Museum Was a Sellout," *WAM: Weisman Art Museum*, spring.

Diana Phillips Mahoney, "Avant-Garde Architects Look to CAD," *Computer Graphics World*, March.

"Studio News: Frederick R. Weisman Art Museum," *Design News*, March.

Michael Webb, "Vitra: Un Mecenas para el Diseño de Vanguardia (Vitra: A Benefactor for Avant-Garde Design)," *Diseño Interior*, March.

Encarni Bao Aguirre, "Bilbao-Ría 2000 Destaca el Interés de los Promotores por Edificar en Abandoibarra (Bilbao-Ria 2000 Underlines Promoters' Interest to Build in Abandoibarra)," *El Correo*, March 5.

Marta Fdez. Vallejo, "La Policía Libera Terrenos en el Depósito de Uribitarte por las Obras del Guggenheim (Police Vacates Land of Uribitarte Lot for Guggenheim Works)," *El Correo*, March 6.

Fernando Iturribarria, "El Museo Guggenheim se Presenta en París Ante la Sociedad Cultural Europea (Guggenheim Museum Presented to European Cultural Society in Paris)," *El Correo*, March 8.

Beatriz Iraburu, "El Guggenheim Neoyorkino Quiere 'Bautizar' el Museo con los Nombres de sus Mecenas (Guggenheim New York Wants to 'Baptize' Museum With Its Benefactors Names)," *El Correo*, March 13.

Fernando Redondo, "Museos Que Revitalizan Ciudades (Museums that Revitalize Cities)," *El Correo*, March 16.

Txema Izaguirre, "Arquitectos Vizcaínos Recomiendan Que se Limite la Altura de Los Edificios en Bilbao (Vizcayan Architects Recommend Height Limits for Guggenheim Buildings)," *El Correo*, March 22.

David W. Dunlap, "Former Gulf and Western Building to Be a Luxury Apartment Tower," *New York Times*, March 23.

Encarni Bao Aguirre, "AESA Recurre la Orden de Acelerar la Expropiacion de Solar de Euskalduna (AESA Appeals Order to Accelerate Expropriation of Euskalduna Grounds)," *El Correo*, March 24.

Gonzalez Carrera, "Las Instituciones Inician la Promoción Internacional del Museo Guggenheim en París (In Paris Institutions Initiate International Promotion of Guggenheim)," *El Correo*, March 29.

B. J. Archer, "Bus Fare: A Short Trip to Frank O. Gehry," *Busstops*, April.

Claire Downey, "American in Paris," *Architectural Record*, April.

"Standing Glass Fish," *Walker Art Center: Artwork of the Month*, April.

Deyan Sudjic, "Gehry's Blockbuster," *Blueprint*, April.

Enrique Porto Carrero, "Se Buscan Ideas (In Search of Ideas)," *El Correo*, April 3.

John Rockwell, "American Center in Paris Awakens," *New York Times*, April 5.

John Rockwell, "American Center in Paris Cuts Back," *New York Times*, April 5.

John Rockwell, "Paris American Center, with New Team, Plans June Opening," *International Herald Tribune*, April 6.

Diane Haithman, "When Disney's Done, What Then?," *Los Angeles Times*, April 10.

K. Banik, J. Gordon, "Wir Haben die Schönsten Haltestellen der Welt," *Hannover Bild*, April 11.

"Busstops Eroberten Hannover im Sturm," *Neue Presse*, April 11.

"Busstops fertig: 20,000 feierten," *Hannover Bild*, April 11.

Sybille Nobel-Sagolla, "Gut für's Image," *Neue Presse*, April 11.

"Strassenkunst zum Abfahren," *Hannoverische Allgemeine*, April 11.

Fernando Iturribarria, "Arregi Revela que Bilbao Podrá Disponer 75 Años Más de los Fondos Guggenheim (Bilbao May Dispose of Guggenheim Funds for Another 75 Years, Reveals Arregi)," *El Correo*, April 14.

Morris Newman, "Instant Classic?," *Downtown News*, April 25.

Claire Downey, "An American in Paris," *Architectural Record*, May.

"Frank O. Gehrys neuster Bau: Das Kunstmuseum in Minneapolis: Freches Schloss," *Die Zeit*, May.

Jean-Pierre Menard, "Frank O. Gehry à Paris: American Center," *Le Moniteur Architecture*, May.

"Wiederaufbau des Neuen Museums Berlin," *Wettbewerbe Aktuell*, May.

"L'American Center," *Formes et Structures*, May–August.

J. A. Gonzales Carrera, "Jorge Barandiaran: El prado podria tener un pie en Bilbao (Jorge Barandiaran: El Prado Could Have a Foot in Bilbao)," *El Correo*, May 2.

"El Consorcio Guggenheim Expondra en Bilbao 96 Dibujos de Grandes Maestros (Guggenheim Consortium Will Exhibit Sketches and Drawings of 96 Great Masters in Bilbao)," *El Correo*, May 4.

Francis Rambert, "L'American Center, un Bâtiment Tristement Sexy," *Le Figaro*, May 8.

Larry Gordon, "Los Angeles Builds up a Reputation Among Architects," *Los Angeles Times*, May 9.

Steven Litt, "Executive's Modern Home Stirs Buzz Even on Paper," *Le Figaro*, May 9.

Deyan Sudjic, "Frank Speaking," *Guardian*, May 10.

Joseph Giovannini, "Los Angeles Architects: They Did It Their Way," *Los Angeles Times Magazine*, May 15.

"Pedir perdon (Asking Forgiveness)," *El Correo*, May 15.

Simon Beeson, "Bathing in Reflected Glory," *Building Design*, May 20.

Paul Finch, "Skating on Thick Ice," *Building Design*, May 20.

Fernando Redondo, "El logotipo del Museo Guggenheim-Bilbao Refleja una Síntesis del Edificio de Gehry (Anagram of Bilbao's Guggenheim Museum Reflects a Synthesis of the Gehry Building)," *El Correo*, May 20.

Steve Harvey, "Only in Los Angeles," *Los Angeles Times*, May 26.

Naomi Stungo, "An American in Paris," *Independent on Sunday*, May 29.

"Frank Gehry: Wing and Wing," *ANY*, May–June.

"The Guggenheim Museum . . . ," *Guggenheim Magazine*, spring–summer.

Tom Balaban, Greg Dunn, and Terrance Galvin, "Frank O. Gehry," *Fifth Column*, summer.

"Frank O. Gehry," *Wind: World Interior Design* 27 (summer).

Hiroshi Watanabe, "Taken Out of Context, Western Architects in Japan," *Design Quarterly*, summer.

"Berliner Akropolis," *Architektur Innenarchitektur Technischer Ausbau*, June.

M. Lindsay Bierman, "Metallic Muse," *Architecture*, June.

"F. O. Gehry & Associates, Museo Guggenhcim de Bilbao (F. O. Gehry & Associates, Bilbao's Guggenheim Museum)," *Museos y Architectura; Nuevas Perspectivas* (Ministerio de Obras Publicas y Transporte), June.

Joseph Giovannini, "American Center Opens in Paris," *Architecture*, June.

Philip Jodidio, "La Ballerine de Gehry," *Connaissance des Arts*, June.

"Vitra Biersfelden Headquarters," *Architektur Innenarchitektur Technischer Ausbau*, June.

Thomas Vonier, "Good Neighbor Gehry," *Progressive Architecture*, June.

"Weisman Art Museum," *Nikkei Architecture*, June.

Joseph Giovannini, "Back-Lot Bravado," *Architecture*, July.

Joseph Giovannini, "Mighty Shed for Ducks," *Architecture*, July.

"New Commissions: Experience Music Project," *Architecture*, July.

Elena Velarde, "Ideas for Rescuing Disney Hall," *Los Angeles Times*, July 8.

Dean E. Murphy, "Fred and Ginger and Frank," *Los Angeles Times*, July 14.

Herbert Muschamp, "In the Public Interest," *New York Times Magazine*, July 21.

Bernard Holland, "A Phantom Hall Filled With Discord," *New York Times*, July 28.

Marisa Bartolucci, "Barcelona," *Metropolis*, July–August.

Marisa Bartolucci, "Bilbao," *Metropolis*, July–August.

Andrea Moed, "Mixed Media: The Program," *Metropolis*, July–August.

David D'Arcy, "Why Los Angeles Hates Frank Gehry," *Los Angeles Magazine*, August.

"Disney Ice," *GA Document*, August.

"Goldstein-Sud Housing Development," *GA Document*, August.

"Team Disney Administration Building," *GA Document*, August.

Benjamin Forgey, "Prague's Gingerfred House: A New Stone Waltz," *Washington Post*, August 4.

Diane Haithman, "Ace in the Hall," *Los Angeles Times*, August 4.

Paul Karon, "Built on the Process of Architecture," *Los Angeles Times*, August 12.

Richard Koshalek, "Walt Disney Concert Hall: A Conversation with Frank O. Gehry," *Contemporary*, fall.

Clemens F. Kusch, "Twice Guggenheim," *Deutsche Bauzeitschrift*, September.

Christian Troster, "Gehry in Goldstein," *Design Report*, October.

Mark Swed, "Conductor in a Candy Store," *Los Angeles Times: Calendar*, October 20.

Linda Keene, "Museum to Embody Hendrix Music," *Seattle Times*, October 24.

Linda Keene, "Design Embodies the Hendrix Spirit," *Seattle Times*, October 25.

Nicolai Ouroussoff, "Sound Vision," *Los Angeles Times*, October 29.

Russ Zabel, "Experience Music Project Unveiled," *Queen Anne News*, October 30.

Laurie Attias, "C'mon Let's Twist Again," *Art News*, November.

"Disney Ice Center at Anaheim, California," *Domus*, November.

"The Guggenheim Museum, Bilbao, Spain," *Structural Engineering International*, November.

Nicolai Ouroussoff, "West Coast Showdown," *Harper's Bazaar*, November.

"Team Disney Building at Anaheim, California," *Domus*, November.

"Saturday Letters: Battling Over the Architecture of L.A.," *Los Angeles Times*, November 2.

John Pastier, "Fender Bender," *Seattle Weekly*, November 6.

Steven Litt, "Top Architects Hired for 3 Jobs," *Cleveland Plain Dealer*, November 27.

Lee Burns, "St. Disney of Vibiana," *Art Issues*, November–December.

"Moneo contruira la catedral de Los Angeles," *Arquitectura Viva*, November–December.

Hraztan Zeitlian, "Walt Disney Concert Hall: A Celebration of Art & Architecture," *LA Architect*, November–December.

Ned Cramer, "On the Boards: Pariser Platz 3," *Architecture*, December.

"The Faces of Power," *Art & Auction*, December.

Frank O. Gehry, "Chess Game with Philip," *Turning Point: Philip Johnson*, December.

Joseph Giovannini, "Architects' Own Houses," *Architecture*, December.

"Guggenheim Museum," *L'Arca*, December.

"Guggenheim Museum, Bilbao," *Werk, Bauen + Wohnen*, December.

Mark L. Hinshaw, "Gehry to Rock Seattle with New Music Museum," *Architecture*, December.

Marta Rodriguez y Arino, "Frank O. Gehry: Escultor De Edificios," *Experimenta*, December.

Marta Rodriguez y Arino, "Mirando La Materia,"

Experimenta, December.

Manuel Serrano Marzo, "Guggenheim Bilbao," *Experimenta*, December.

Jack Skelley, "Highbrow Sales Job," *Los Angeles Downtown News*, December 9.

Gene Stout, "Experience This, Seattle," *Seattle Post-Intelligencer*, December 10.

Suzanne Muchnic, "Taking the First Step Toward Cozier Norton Simon Museum," *Los Angeles Times*, December 12.

Herbert Muschamp, "Architecture of Light and Remembrance," *New York Times*, December 15.

Diane Haithman, "Times Mirror Set to Pledge $5 Million for Disney Hall," *Los Angeles Times*, December 25.

Diane Haithman, "Disney Hall Seeks Funds as Deadlines Draw Closer," *Los Angeles Times*, December 26.

Mark Swed, "For L.A., History's Knocking," *Los Angeles Times*, December 26.

"Saturday Letters: How's This for a Hollywood Ending to Disney Hall Woes?," *Los Angeles Times*, December 28.

Mark Swed, "Classic Struggle," *Los Angeles Times*, December 29.

Michael Stremfel, "What's Hot, What's Not," *Los Angeles Business Journal*, December 30.

"Times Gives $5 Million to Disney Hall," *Los Angeles Downtown News*, December 30.

Francesco Garofalo, "The Church of the Year 2000," *Casabella*, December–January.

1997

David D'Arcy, "A Thing for Models," *Art & Auction*, January.

"Gehry Designs 'Far Out' Interactive Music Museum," *Architectural Record*, January.

Piers Gough, "The Building as Jujitsu," *Modern Painter*, January.

Parick Pacheo, "Museums Face the Millennium," *Art & Antiques*, January.

"Wohnsiedlung mit Gehry-Brosche," *Häuser*, January.

Cathleen McGuigan, "Basque-ing in Glory," *Newsweek*, January 13.

John Nunez, "Letters: Disney Donors," *Los Angeles Times*, January 19.

Dan Turner, "Chiat/Day Deal to Vacate Its 'Giant Binoculars' Building Is Off, for Now," *Los Angeles Business Journal*, January 27.

Aaron Betsky, "I.D. Forty: Frank Gehry," *I.D.*, January–February.

"Gehry Goes Grunge," *I.D.*, January–February.

"Ginger y Fred," *Arquitectura Viva*, January–February.

Joseph Giovannini, "Fred and Ginger Dance in Prague," *Architecture*, February.

Julie Moline, "Fund-Raisers Optimistic as Deadline Looms for Disney Concert Hall," *Architectural Record*, February.

"Office Building in Prague," *Domus*, February.

Blair Kamin, "Jumping the Gun," *Chicago Tribune*, February 2.

Terry Pristin, "Disney Hall: A Mirage Is Looking More Real," *New York Times*, February 18.

"Our Heritage From Artists in Exile," *Los Angeles Times*, February 20.

Diane Haithman, "Disney Hall Drive: Back on Track?," *Los Angeles Times*, February 21.

"Disney Hall Will Exceed Goal, Says Broad," *Los Angeles Downtown News*, February 24.

Jon Regardie and Jack Skelley, "2000: A Billion-Dollar Space Odyssey," *Los Angeles Downtown News*, February 24.

Jon Regardie and Jack Skelley, "Billion-Dollar Checklist," *Los Angeles Downtown News*, February 24.

Karin Heflmann, "A Strong Presence: Frank Was Here," *Architektur Aktuell*, March.

Diane Haithman, "Disney Hall Hangs Its Pitch on the Future of Downtown," *Los Angeles Times*, March 11.

Diane Haithman, "Arco to Make $10 Million Gift for Disney Hall," *Los Angeles Times*, March 12.

"Arco to Give $10 Million for L.A. Concert Hall," *San Francisco Chronicle*, March 13.

"Editorial: A Great Boost for

Disney Hall," *Los Angeles Times*, March 13.

Reed Johnson, "Alliance of Elites Tuned in to Aid Music Hall," *Daily News*, March 13.

Lisa Steen Proctor, "Arco Donation Puts Disney Concert Hall Funding Effort Back on Track," *Los Angeles Business Journal*, March 17.

Lisa Steen Proctor, "Disney Hall No Longer a Fantasy," *Los Angeles Business Journal*, March 31.

Lisa Steen Proctor, "Downtown Rebirth Hinges on Venue," *Los Angeles Business Journal*, March 31.

"Chiat/Day, Hampton Drive," *Arch +*, April.

"DG Bank am Pariser Platz," *Arch +*, April.

Deborah K. Dietsch, "Build Disney Hall," *Architecture*, April.

"Fred and Ginger: Two Views," *AIA Architect*, April.

Bradford McKee, "Disney Hall's Uncertain Fate," *Architecture*, April.

Michael Webb, "Musical Masterpiece," *Hotel Bel Air Magazine*, April.

Nicolai Ouroussoff, "Basic Instinct," *Los Angeles Times Magazine*, April 6.

Herbert Muschamp, "Heart of Whimsy in Times Square," *New York Times*, April 7.

Diane Haithman, "$15 Million Gift for Disney Hall Expected," *Los Angeles Times*, April 10.

Ron Russell, "Buddy, Can You Spare $150 Million?," *New Times Los Angeles*, April 10–16.

"A Hall with Many Names," *Los Angeles Times*, April 11.

Nicolai Ouroussoff, "Gehry Cranks It Up," *Los Angeles Times*, April 11.

Diane Haithman, "Disney Hall Is Dusted With Optimism," *Los Angeles Times*, April 12.

Rowan Moore, "Heroic, Chaotic, Fabulous," *Sunday Telegraph*, April 13.

Jon Regardie, "Phil 'er Up," *Los Angeles Downtown News*, April 14.

Lisa Steen Proctor, "Another $15 Million for Disney Hall," *Los Angeles Business Journal*, April 14–20.

Jill Stewart, "Billionaires on the

Titanic," *New Times Los Angeles*, April 17–23.

"Frank Gehry and Disney Hall Going Up," *Economist*, April 19.

Rochelle Dynes Mills, "Disney Concert Hall Becoming a Reality," *LA Architect*, April–May.

Claudine Mulard, "Le Disney Hall de Los Angeles conçu par Frank Gehry ouvrira en 2001," *Le Monde*, May 3.

William Fulton, "Disney Hall: Why Isn't Hollywood Giving to L.A.'s Cause?," *Los Angeles Times*, May 4.

Nicolai Ouroussoff, "Eli Broad: Building Disney Hall—and a New Downtown," *Los Angeles Times*, May 18.

Diane Haithman, "Bank of America to Give $5 Million for Disney Hall," *Los Angeles Times*, May 21.

David Galloway, "Frank O. Gehry," *Lufthansa Bordbuch*, May–June.

Ned Cramer, "Gehry's Montreal Museum," *Architecture*, June.

"Der Gigant von Bilbao," *Art, Das Kunstmagazin*, June.

Claudia Kugel, "Frankfurt Collage," *Architectural Review*, June.

Eric D. Kuritsky, "Letters: For Art's Sake," *Architecture*, June.

Pietro Valle, "Frank O. Gehry," *Juliet*, June.

Nicolai Ouroussoff, "Gehry's Guggenheim: An Instant Landmark," *Los Angeles Times*, June 2.

Diane Haithman and Larry Gordon, "Disney Hall Fund-Raisers, Designer Gehry in Conflict," *Los Angeles Times*, June 3.

"Architect May Drop Music Hall," *Santa Monica Outlook*, June 4.

George Rand, "No Clones, Please: Give Us the Original," *Los Angeles Times*, June 4.

Patricia Leigh Brown, "A Xanadu That Didn't," *New York Times*, June 5.

Diane Haithman, "Gehry, Fund-Raisers Face Showdown on Disney Hall," *Los Angeles Times*, June 5.

"Gehry, Disney Hall Leaders Meet to Discuss Differences," *Los Angeles Times*, June 6.

Bruce McCall, "Who Needs an Architect!," *Los Angeles

Times*, June 8.

Chris Reed, "Discord in Disney Concert Hall Fantasia," *Guardian*, June 9.

"Letters: Frank Gehry," *Los Angeles Times*, June 10.

Richard Seven, "Shape of Things to Come at Seattle Center," *Seattle Times*, June 13.

"Saturday Letters: Misunderstood Architect in Company With Greats," *Los Angeles Times*, June 14.

Patricia Leigh Brown, "The House that Gehry Never Built," *Globe and Mail*, June 21.

Christopher Reed, "Disney Concert Hall Mired in Disputes," *Globe and Mail*, June 21.

Nicolai Ouroussoff, "A Project in Need of Greater Harmony," *Los Angeles Times*, June 24.

Alan Riding, "The Basques Get Modern," *New York Times*, June 24.

"Disney Hall's Glass: More Than Half-Full," *Los Angeles Times*, June 30.

"Hufford Relinquishes Disney Hall Post," *Los Angeles Downtown News*, June 30.

Kim Bradley, "The Deal of the Century," *Art in America*, July.

Barbara A. Nadel, "Gehry and the Disney Concert Hall: 'Trying to Work It Out,'" *Architectural Record*, July.

Bonnie Churchill, "Laying the Cornerstone for a City's Dream," *Christian Science Monitor*, July 2.

"Disney Hall Gifts," *Los Angeles Times*, July 2.

"Disney Hall Beats County's Goal, but Not Broad's," *Los Angeles Downtown News*, July 7.

"More Donations for Disney Hall," *Los Angeles Business Journal*, July 7.

Calvin Tomkins, "The Maverick," *New Yorker*, July 7.

Nancy Rivera Brooks, "Models of Efficiency," *Los Angeles Times*, July 13.

Elizabeth Nash, "Never Mind the Art, Enjoy the Architecture," *Independent*, July 13.

"Virtual Disney," *Los Angeles Downtown News*, July 21.

Raymond Sokolov, "Vitra Furniture Co.: Architecture Mecca," *Wall Street Journal*, July 23.

Diane Haithman and Nicolai Ouroussoff, "Disney Family Acts to Keep Gehry on Project," *Los Angeles Times*, July 31.

Joseph Giovannini, "Disney Hall Saga Continues," *Architecture*, August.

Charles Jencks, "Gehry in Bilbao," *World of Interiors*, August.

"Chow Delux," *New York Post*, August 13.

Allan Schwartzman, "Masterwork," *Elle Decor*, August–September.

Peter O'Gorman, "The Dancing House," *Architectural Review Australia*, fall.

Ned Cramer, "On the Boards: Samsung Museum of Modern Art," *Architecture*, September.

Herbert Muschamp, "The Miracle in Bilbao," *New York Times Magazine*, September 7.

Roger Mahoney, "Where's the Vision for Downtown?," *Los Angeles Times*, September 12.

"It's the 'D'-Word Again for Disney Hall," *Los Angeles Times*, September 15.

Charles Gandee, "Spanish Conquest," *Vogue*, October.

David Rimanelli, "When Gehry Met Bilbao," *Elle*, October.

Diane Haithman, "Dutchman to Manage Philharmonic," *Los Angeles Times*, October 5.

Anthony Vidler, "L.A.'s Only Constant Is Change in Its Architecture," *Los Angeles Times*, October 5.

Marco R. Della Cava, "The 'Miracle' of Bilbao," *USA Today*, October 8.

Paul Goldberger, "The Politics of Building," *New Yorker*, October 13.

Illustration Credits

Frank O. Gehry and Associates has generously supplied the illustrations in this book. Particular thanks to:

Peter Aaron/Esto
Jay Ahrend
Morley Baer
Gabriele Basilico
Perry Andelin Blake
Olivier Boissière
Tom Bonner
Jens-Olaf Broksche
Donatella Brun
Richard Bryant
Giovanni Chiaramonte
G. Clements
Kevin Daly
J. Davis
Jon Drezner
Esto Photographics
Stephen Evans
Scott Frances
Y. Futagawa
Jeff Goldberg/Esto
Hedrick Blessing
George Heinrich
Timothy Hursley
Christophe Kicherer
T. Kitajima/Retoria
Erich A. Koyama
Waltraud Krase

Salvatore Licitra
Michael Maltzan
Peter Mauss
Ronald Moore
Michael Moran
Grant Mudford
David Pakshong
Douglas M. Parker
Eugeni Pons/Eidos Photography
Marvin Rand
Christian Richters
Otto Rothschild
Mark Schwartz
Walter Smalling Jr.
J. Scott Smith
Gordon Sommers
Squidds and Nunns
Randall Stout
Tim Street-Porter
Martin Tadder
William Taylor
Tomko
Dane Twichell
Greg Walsh
Michael Webb
Joshua M. White
Don F. Wong
Brian S. Yoo

Please notify the publisher if any photographs have been reproduced without the proper credit.